The
Lordship
of
Canterbury

AN ESSAY ON
MEDIEVAL SOCIETY

The
Lordship
of
Canterbury

AN ESSAY ON
MEDIEVAL SOCIETY

One of the five tenants of Wingham who did penance on Sunday, 10 April 1390, in Wingham churchyard for avoiding carrying-service due to the archbishop (drawing from the Register of Archbishop Courtenay in Lambeth Palace, fo. 337v.). (See p. 189)

The Lordship of Canterbury

AN ESSAY ON MEDIEVAL SOCIETY

F. R. H. Du Boulay

*Professor of Medieval History in the
University of London*

BARNES & NOBLE Inc.
NEW YORK
PUBLISHERS & BOOKSELLERS SINCE 1873

First published
in the United States
1966
BARNES & NOBLE, INC.
New York, N.Y. 10003

Printed in Great Britain by
Thomas Nelson (Printers) Ltd, London and Edinburgh

Contents

List of Maps

List of Tables

Acknowledgements

It is a pleasant duty to acknowledge my debts to others. First, to His Grace the Archbishop of Canterbury thanks are due for the freedom of Lambeth Palace Library, and also to the late Dr Irene J. Churchill, Deputy Librarian, who did so much to make work in the Library's collections pleasant, and to her successor, Dr E. G. W. Bill, who has kindly permitted me to continue working there. Thanks are likewise due to Dr W. G. Urry, Keeper of the Manuscripts of the Dean and Chapter of Canterbury Cathedral, to Dr Felix Hull, Kent County Archivist, to the officials of the Public Record Office, and to Mr Lawrence Tanner, c.v.o., Keeper of the Muniments at Westminster Abbey. The Viscount De L'Isle kindly gave me permission to see and quote from his family papers.

Advice on particular matters was generously given by Mr H. M. Colvin, c.b.e., f.b.a., Dr J. R. L. Highfield, Mr L. F. Salzman and Dr R. L. Storey. I owe special gratitude to Professor R. R. Darlington, f.b.a., who read a draft of Chapter 2 and has encouraged me, and to Dr Edmund Fryde, who read the proofs and made many valuable comments. Members of my graduate seminar at the Institute of Historical Research have my affectionate remembrance for so many helpful discussions.

The maps were drawn by Miss Cherry Goatman, research student in the Department of Geography of Bedford College. Miss Charlotte Grabner kindly typed much of the text.

Leave to use previously published work has been given by the Editors of the *English Historical Review*, the *Economic History Review*, *Archaeologia Cantiana* and the Faith Press.

My wife has borne the burden of living with this work: she knows what this means, and I know how much I owe her.

F.R.H. DU B.

1 August 1964

LIST OF PRINCIPAL UNPRINTED SOURCES

The following list is limited to showing the general nature and location of the sources. Detailed references are, of course, given in the footnotes.

LAMBETH PALACE LIBRARY

1. The large collection of court-rolls, ministers' accounts and rentals was listed in 1880 by S. A. Moore and R. E. Kirk. Their handlist, which is in Lambeth Palace Library, has been of the utmost value. It has recently been superseded by Miss Jane Sayers's short catalogue of *Estate Documents at Lambeth Palace Library* (University of Leicester Press, 1965). The rolls are numbered and classified; those chiefly used for the present work have been taken from the following series:
   Nos. 95–105, accounts of the archbishop's Liberty, fifteenth and sixteenth centuries.
   Nos. 133–1159, 1193–1342, account rolls (thirteenth to early sixteenth centuries) and court-rolls (fourteenth to early sixteenth centuries) of individual places, arranged in alphabetical order.
   Nos. 1343–77, receivers' accounts, fifteenth and sixteenth centuries.
   No. 1973, portion of household roll of Archbishop Bourgchier, October 1459.
   Nos. 1401–25, receiver-general's accounts, reign of Elizabeth; these deserve separate study.
   Some court-rolls belonging to the archbishopric, formerly held for the Ecclesiastical Commissioners in the Public Record Office, are now in Lambeth Palace Library and have been aggregated to the existing collection.
2. The 'Cartae Antiquae et Miscellaneae', formerly arranged in a number of bound volumes, are now preserved individually, though they retain their reference numbers according to volumes. Those in volume XIII have been especially useful. They are catalogued in cyclostyled format by Mrs Dorothy Owen, and copies of this catalogue are available in the library, in the Institute of Historical Research and elsewhere.
3. MS. 1212. Cartulary of the archbishopric, mainly thirteenth-century transcripts. The MS. is discussed at length in Chapter 1.
4. The unprinted registers of Archbishops Reynolds, Islip, Witlesey, Sudbury, Courtenay, Arundel, Stafford, Kemp, Morton, Deane, Warham and Cranmer.

THE PUBLIC RECORD OFFICE

1. Ministers' Accounts (Class S.C. 6, listed in *Lists and Indexes*, vols. V, XXXIV and XXXVII), nos. 1128/1 to 21; 1129/1 to 9; 1130/1 to 10; Henry VII, 331 to 337, 859; Henry VIII, 1685 to 1698, 1757 to 1761, 2105, 7153; Edward VI, 233, 237, 240.
2. Rentals and Surveys (Class S.C. 11, listed in *Lists and Indexes*, vol. XXV, pp. 136–7), Portfolio 18, No. 43, and Rolls 343, 844, 856.
3. Pipe Rolls (Class E 372), Nos. 58, 73, 76, 119, 124, 141, 159, 173, 180, 194, 196, 199 for accounts of the archbishopric during vacancies of the

see, thirteenth and earlier fourteenth centuries. See M. E. Howell, *Regalian Right in Medieval England* (Athlone Press, 1962), and *Kent Records*, vol. XVIII (1964), pp. 41–7.

4. Ancient Deeds. Individual and small collections of deeds relating to particular families of archbishopric tenants are to be found among the various series and are referred to in the notes.

5. De Lisle and Dudley MSS. These are housed in the Public Record Office in the care of the Historical Manuscripts Commission, and were consulted by leave of Viscount De L'Isle, V.C. Rolls 458, 459, 476, 478, 505 (court-rolls of fourteenth to sixteenth centuries) were of particular use.

THE BRITISH MUSEUM

1. Additional MS. 29794, general account roll of the manors of the see, 1273–4.
2. Additional charters. This collection furnished a few documents analogous to the Ancient Deeds noted above.

KENT ARCHIVE OFFICE, MAIDSTONE

1. There are some account rolls, court-rolls, rentals and surveys of various provenance among the 'unofficial' documents, notably:

U 47/3, M 19 and T 46, documents relating to Martin of Peckham, thirteenth and fourteenth centuries.

U 55, M 13–18, court-rolls of Wrotham, fifteenth and sixteenth centuries.

    M 59, rental and survey of Wrotham, 1494.

    M 63–72, account rolls of Wrotham, 1382–1527.

    M 373, rental of the *borgh* of Otford (part of Otford manor), c. 1440.

U 270, M 304–7, account rolls of Bishopsbourne, fourteenth and fifteenth centuries.

U 386, M 17 and U 409, M 3, account rolls of Maidstone, fifteenth century.

U 398, M 1a, survey of Gillingham, c. 1446.

U 498, M 1–23, court-rolls of Maidstone, fourteenth to sixteenth centuries.

2. Will registers of Rochester consistory court, from the mid fifteenth century.

CANTERBURY CATHEDRAL LIBRARY

Among the manuscripts of the Dean and Chapter of Canterbury, described in the Appendixes to the fifth, eighth and ninth Reports of the Historical Manuscripts Commission, the following have made major contributions:

1. MS. E 24, rental and survey of archbishopric manors, 1283–5 (a late medieval copy, not quite complete, but complemented by L.R. 2068, a near-contemporary excerption of the same survey).

2. Register T, monastic register of temporal business, especially leases and appointments of officials, including those relevant to the archbishopric, early sixteenth century.

PRINCIPAL PROBATE REGISTRY, SOMERSET HOUSE, LONDON W.C.2

Will registers from the Prerogative Court of Canterbury have proved invaluable. They belong administratively to the same series as the testaments found in the archbishops' registers at Lambeth, as, for example, in those of Arundel and Chichele, but the Somerset House registers are usually numbered by quires or gatherings instead of by pages or folios, and must often therefore be cited in this way.

LIST OF PRINCIPAL UNPRINTED SOURCES

WESTMINSTER ABBEY MUNIMENTS

Nos. 9222 and 9223 are portions of household rolls of 1341 and 1343, from the time of Archbishop Stratford.

OTHER COLLECTIONS

There are fragmentary collections of estate documents, not all of which have been examined, in certain local offices, viz.:

Barbican House, Lewes, Sussex, contains MSS. of the Gage family which also pertain to the South Malling properties.

East Sussex County Record Office, Pelham House, Lewes, houses Glynde MSS. referring to South Malling and the family of Waleys. Of these, MS. 954 is the list of knights of the archbishopric of the time of Henry II, and almost certainly of 1171, which is edited by H. M. Colvin and discussed in *Kent Records*, vol. XVIII; and MSS. 955 and 957–9 are rentals and custumals of South Malling, printed in *S.R.S.*, vol. 57.[1]

West Sussex County Record Office, County Hall, Chichester, has some fifteenth-century account rolls of Nyetimber (Ac. 600).

Essex Record Office, Chelmsford, possesses a rental, court-rolls and deeds belonging to Otford, numbered D/DL M48–51; D/DL T4/19–38, T5/1–10, T5/41–6, T7/1–37; and catalogued more fully in D/DL Z36.

---

[1] Since this was written a valuable catalogue has appeared: *The Glynde Place Archives* by R. C. Dell (Lewes, 1964).

LIST OF ABBREVIATIONS

A.C.: Archaeologia Cantiana.

Addit. ch.: Additional charter (British Museum).

Addit. MS.: Additional manuscript (British Museum).

Biog. Reg. Oxford: A Biographical Register of the University of Oxford to A.D. 1500, ed. A. B. Emden, 3 vols. (Oxford, 1957–9).

Arch. J.: Archaeological Journal.

C. Inq. Misc.: Calendar of Inquisitions, Miscellaneous (H.M.S.O.).

C.Ch.R.: Calendar of Charter Rolls (H.M.S.O.).

C.Cl.R.: Calendar of Close Rolls (H.M.S.O.).

C.P.L.: Calendar of Papal Registers: Letters (H.M.S.O.).

C.P.R.: Calendar of Patent Rolls (H.M.S.O.).

Cart. of St Gregory's Priory: Cartulary of the Priory of St Gregory, Canterbury, ed. Audrey M. Woodcock, Camden Third Series, vol. LXXXVIII (Royal Historical Society, 1956).

CS: Cartularium Saxonicum, ed. W. de Gray Birch, 3 vols. (1885–93).

D.B.: Domesday Book, vols. I and II (Record Commission, 1783).

D.N.B.: Dictionary of National Biography.

Dom. Mon.: The Domesday Monachorum of Christ Church, Canterbury, ed. D. C. Douglas (Royal Historical Society, 1944).

Ec.H.R.: Economic History Review.

E.H.R.: English Historical Review.

Eyre of Kent: The Eyre of Kent, ed. F. W. Maitland and others, 3 vols. (Selden Society, 1909–13).

F. of F.: Calendar of Kent Feet of Fines to the End of Henry III's Reign, ed. I. J. Churchill and others (*Kent Records*, vol. XV, 1956).

HMCR: Reports of the Historical Manuscripts Commission (H.M.S.O.).

H.M.S.O.: Her Majesty's Stationary Office.

IPM: Calendar of Inquisitions post mortem (H.M.S.O.).

KAO: Kent Archive Office (County Hall, Maidstone).

KCD: Codex Diplomaticus Aevi Saxonici, ed. J. M. Kemble, 6 vols. (London, 1839–48).

KPN: Kentish Place Names, J. K. Wallenberg (Uppsala, 1931).

K.R.: King's Remembrancer.

LCM: Cartae Antiquae et Miscellaneae (Lambeth Palace Library).

L. & P.: Calendar of Letters and Papers, Foreign and Domestic, Henry VIII, ed. J. S. Brewer, J. Gairdner, etc. (H.M.S.O.).

Lit. Cant.: Literae Cantuarienses, ed. J. Brigstocke Sheppard, 3 vols. (*Rolls Series* 85, 1887–9).

L.R.: Collection of account and court-rolls in Lambeth Palace Library.

L.T.R.: Lord Treasurer's Remembrancer.

Mins. Accts.: Ministers' Accounts (Public Record Office, Class S.C. 6).

PCC: Prerogative Court of Canterbury Will Registers (Somerset House).

PNK: Place Names of Kent, J. K. Wallenberg (Uppsala, 1934).

P.R.: Pipe Roll (Public Record Office, Class E 372).

P.R.: Pipe Roll (Publications of the Pipe Roll Society).

P.R.O.: Public Record Office.

Reg.: Unprinted archbishops' registers in Lambeth Palace Library.

Reg.: Registers of archbishops printed by the Canterbury and York Society.

Regesta: Regesta Regum Anglo-Normannorum, vol. I, ed. H. W. C. Davis (Oxford, 1913); vol. II, ed. Charles Johnson and H. A. Cronne (Oxford, 1956).

Rot. Chart.: Rotuli Chartarum in Turri Londonensi asservati, 1199–1216 (Record Commission, 1837).

Rot. Hundr.: Rotuli Hundredorum, ed. W. Illingworth and J. Caley, 2 vols. (Record Commission, 1812–18).

Rot. Litt. Pat.: Rotuli Litterarum Patentium in Turri Londinensi asservati, 1201–16, ed. T. D. Hardy (Record Commission, 1835).

R.S.: Rolls Series.

S.R.S.: Sussex Record Society.

TPN: Taxatio Ecclesiastica Angliae et Walliae auctoritate P. Nicholai IV, c. A.D. 1291, ed. S. Ayscough and J. Caley (Record Commission, 1802).

TRHS: Transactions of the Royal Historical Society.

Valor Ecclesiasticus: Valor Ecclesiasticus, temp. Henrici VIII, auctoritate regia institutus, ed. J. Caley and J. Hunter (Record Commission, 1810–34).

V.C.H.: Victoria County History.

CHAPTER 1

The archives of the archbishopric

Every historical book worthy of the name ought to include a chapter or, if one prefers, a series of paragraphs inserted at turning-points in the development, which might almost be entitled: 'How can I know what I am about to say?' I am persuaded that even the lay reader would experience an actual intellectual pleasure in examining these 'confessions'.[1]

It is twice necessary to regard this advice. In the first place, each of the many monographs on the life and development of a medieval group of estates has proved to be different from every other one by reason of the surviving evidence that has gone to its making, and students require to know what title their author has to discuss what he does, or to be silent where they would rather he spoke; and in the second place, the writer himself is by nature compelled to imprint his own mark upon his product by reason of the problems that have inexplicably aroused his interest, and it is only fair to confess this other kind of accident at the same time.

The present essay, it must be admitted, grew originally out of a dissatisfaction with an 'ecclesiastical history' which seemed absorbed in the formalities of church administration. Not far behind the *acta* and the registers of the archbishop could be discerned a multitude of documents insisting that the chancellors, registrars and so forth did not stand by themselves in giving account of their master's works, and that the 'lordship of Canterbury', ecclesiastical though it was, had a thoroughly secular being

1. Marc Bloch, *The Historian's Craft*, trans. Peter Putnam (Manchester, 1954), p. 71.

too. Needless to say, this dual character of the archbishopric was not a sort of Jekyll and Hyde morbidity but a common feature of medieval civilization which owed so much of its spiritual confidence and administrative expertise to an economic nourishment. This is a theme to be developed elsewhere. Here and now the intention is only to supplement the work of devoted scholars who have studied the government of the church of Canterbury by some observations on the archbishop as territorial magnate and on the communities whose lord he was. In particular, the task of the introductory chapter is to comment on the evidence and to describe how its character owes something to the historical accidents of loss or survival but much more to causes that cannot be called accidental, since there are good historical reasons why different kinds of documents were made at different periods of the Middle Ages.

But before reviewing these archives it may be allowed once and for all to refer to the imprint which the author has at least desired to place upon the material. Aspiration would be satisfied if the work were seen to bear even faintly the imprint of Marc Bloch, who died twenty years to the day before these lines were written. For Bloch always tried to vivify institutions, and reproached '*ces érudits pour qui le paysan d'autrefois ne semble avoir existé qu'afin de fournir l'occasion de plaisantes dissertations juridiques*'.[1] The ambition to resurrect the past as well as to analyse it is a dangerous one, for it requires, as well as a competence with texts and figures, a continuous series of imaginative acts in response to detailed and precise self-questioning. The risk is not only of error but of plying readers with local details, an offence to an age suspicious enough of medieval history in any case, let alone of regionalism and the minutiae of behaviour. Yet most people would be willing to allow the biologists their 'histology', for only by studying the minute structure of the tissue of organisms can the larger world itself be understood: so too with past societies.

The six hundred years from the conversion of England to the late twelfth century was the age of charters. It may seem strange that all this time was to pass before regular and orderly records were kept of the archbishops' spiritual acts, while title-deeds to

---

1. *Les Caractères originaux de l'histoire rurale française*, Supplement (ed. Robert Dauvergne, Paris, 1956), p. xxvii.

their landed property and secular rights began to be written on the morrow of the conversion and thereafter treasured with great care. But a moment's reflection provides both a general and a technical reason for this. It was of the nature of conversion to be tribal, and to leave little but what we may call political signs of the interior changes that such conversion was working. Kings and great men accepted Christianity, and their peoples followed suit. Rulers signified their acceptance of the kingdom of God by granting portions of their own lands to the representatives of the Saviour, and protecting what they had given with the strongest sanctions of law. As for the clergy, the elaborate land-books they received were a witness of their success, whether in the victory of Christ or, in unknowable proportion, in the aggrandizement of their own estate. But in an age when writing was too rare an art for routine administration, it would be useless to expect more detailed evidences of their victory. More narrowly, the archbishops' earliest muniments refer to temporal matters because not until about 1200 did institutions of government habitually keep copies of their out-letters and records of their routine administration. The charters of donation, even though written by churchmen, were in effect evidences bestowed on the church from without, solemn, rare and precious. Hence, the archbishop in his nature as a territorial magnate is a topic which suitably prefaces the history of English Christianity, not only because of a preoccupation with territory and lordship on the part of early churchmen, but because endowment was the instrument of conversion and the guarantee of its continuance, and the charter was its everlasting testimony.

Even so, the destruction of these titles by age, theft or fire was serious and provided an understandable and justifiable impetus to forgery. The character of this charter evidence will be briefly discussed in the next chapter. Here we may pass on to consider the efforts to repair these mishaps of loss by the Canterbury monks and the archbishops' clerks who at various times listed the contents of their treasury.

The stage of listing or calendaring the charters came relatively late in the day. Of two surviving cartularies and nine lists of Canterbury properties, it is possible that one was written in the first half of the twelfth century and that others are based upon lists of that time, but otherwise they date from the thirteenth century and later.[1] In the thirteenth century the activity became intense. Its principal monument is the collection of transcripts gathered together under the modern name of Lambeth Palace MS. 1212, which in the temporal sphere is the lordship of Canterbury's most important single archive. The scribes who wrote it littered their pages with remarks about what they were doing, so that a presentable picture can be pieced together of the state of the Canterbury archives when they wrote. The manuscript itself is, as a whole, the keystone of the documentary arch that connects the age of charters with the age of registers.

Lambeth MS. 1212 is a composite volume. Its several portions were written at different times in the thirteenth century, and were ultimately put together with little regard to sequence. In addition, the sections themselves are sometimes confused by disarrangement of the leaves, and by subsequent jottings and insertions.

The earliest portion is in a hand of c. 1240-50, and in this the latest document belongs to 1224-5.[2] With its neat arrangement and red and blue initials it is the most attractive of the book's gatherings, though not the most interesting. The charters contained in it belong to the period between William I and Henry III. The witness-lists are sometimes abbreviated, so that the section cannot have been the only exemplar of the later lists in the MS. which furnish fuller witness-lists.[3] Against most, but not all, of the documents the same hand that transcribed them has written *hec invenitur*, or, on one occasion, *hec deest*. It would therefore appear that the compiler was transcribing some existing register, and checking as he went whether or not the original was also in the church's archives. If he were copying the originals only, it is difficult to see why he should write against some, but not all, 'this is found', and against one 'this is missing'.

The same is true of the scribe who later on wrote the portions of

1. E. G. Box, 'Donations of Manors to Christ Church, Canterbury, and Appropriations of Churches', *A.C.* XLIV (1932), pp. 103-19. cf. G. R. C. Davis (ed.), *Medieval Cartularies of Great Britain* (1958), p. 20; W. Holtzmann, *Papsturkunden in England*, I (Göttingen, 1930), pp. 197-9.
2. Lambeth MS. 1212, pp. 186-225. This dating is based upon the work of Miss Major, *Acta Stephani Langton*, Canterbury and York Society, vol. 50 (1950), 158n.
3. e.g. charter of Roger of Crimsham, 1197. The transcript in the oldest section (p. 216) gives three witnesses; a transcript of the same charter on pp. 91-2 gives an additional nine. See likewise the charter of Thomas and John of Wodenhale, pp. 217 and 93.

the MS. that make up its greatest bulk.[1] These were said by Miss Major to be in a hand of *c.* 1260–70. One sequence of royal charters, however, is numbered consecutively up to 1277, with additions up to 1290.[2] Also, against numbers of papal bulls transcribed in the same hand, annotations suggest that the transcription was made after Gregory X's accession in 1272.[3] So work on this main portion of the MS. was going on after Edward I had become king.

This scribe, like his earlier brother, was working partly from charters which lay in the church's repository, and partly from one or more existing lists. A small section of pre-Conquest documents is headed with the statement that they are transcribed from codices anciently called 'landbooks': '*transcripta de codicellis primariis sive cartis terrarum antiquitus dictis "Landboc"* '.[4] Then there is a whole group of royal charters, and each one has a holograph Roman numeral against it in the margin. There is a series of four for William I, one for William II, eight for Henry I, and so on up to Edward I. The charters of each king are numbered separately starting at I. And these numerals correspond with those found in the same hand on the few original royal charters surviving among the 'Miscellaneous Charters' at Lambeth Palace.[5] When the compiler of Lambeth MS. 1212 was writing, the collection of these charters must have been very large. He frequently noted the existence of more than one copy of the charter he was transcribing: 'this is in duplicate', 'this is in triplicate', or even occasionally, 'this is in quadruplicate'. Some of the additional copies were often not in the custody of Canterbury, but were known by the scribes to be in the possession of an interested party: at St Augustine's, Dover Priory, Harbledown Hospital, South Malling College or St Paul's Cathedral.

But sometimes the originals were not in the archbishop's possession at all: '*non sunt in thesaurario archiepiscopi*'. In such a case the scribe was taking his text from an existing register. The main list of pre-Conquest charters was transcribed, he tells us, from an old book at Canterbury.[6] In his collection of more recent docu-

1. pp. 14–185, 234–85, 294–301, and probably 304–39.   2. pp. 62–74.
3. Numbers of the bulls transcribed on pp. 234–85 are annotated '*Hec est hic duplicata de novo de Regestro sub bulla Gregorii X*'.
4. p. 384.
5. This was pointed out by A. J. Collins, 'The Documents of the Great Charter, 1215', *Proceedings of the British Academy*, XXXIV (1948), pp. 237–9.
6. Lambeth MS. 1212, p. 304.

ments, he notes against one item: 'this is not in our possession as a sealed instrument, but is transcribed out of an old register from among the charters of King John. The original remains with the bishop of Rochester.'[1] This 'old book' was very likely, as Miss Major thought, the earliest portion of Lambeth MS. 1212, with the rubricated initials, not yet bound up in the present volume, of course, but existing as a little register in its own right, for the same document may be found in its place there.[2] Yet, as we have seen, this earliest portion of the manuscript cannot have been the only exemplar from which the later scribe was working, and we must imagine him to have had a number of earlier compilations at his elbow in which charters, precedents and acts concerning the temporalities were recorded. Reference in Lambeth MS. 1212 is also made to vanished records of the central estate administration, like 'the book of Roger of Northwood', who was steward of the archbishop's estates between 1258 and 1274.[3]

Occasionally the archbishop's scribe had neither the original nor a transcript in his possession. Of some charters concerning South Malling College it was noted that the dean and canons had them, and that they were not in the treasury of the archbishop.[4] Again, in an account of the composition with the see of London about jurisdiction *sede vacante*, a marginal note says, 'the archbishop does not find this, but he had this transcript from the chapter of London'.[5] In this way we must also suppose a good deal of administrative co-operation between the clerks in the service of these religious corporations, exchanging information and providing each other with the documents they wanted.

These thirteenth-century problems were the problems of the archbishop's scribes, not of the monks. The lists and registers they were copying, the new registers they were making, even the numbered originals at their disposal, belonged to the archbishopric. The priory's archives were within the monastery, stored in files, hampers, chests, desks and linen sacks.[6] The archbishop's own archives, as Miss Churchill showed some years ago, were by the thirteenth century no longer in Canterbury Cathedral but in the

1. ibid., p. 56.
2. ibid., p. 200; cf. *Acta Stephani Langton*, p. 159.
3. Lambeth MS. 1212, pp. 158, 159.
4. ibid., p. 107.
5. ibid., p. 162.
6. *HMCR*, IX, Appendix, pp. 74–5.

Augustinian priory of St Gregory's, Canterbury, where they were placed in receptacles called *vasa*.[1] A group of documents about the archbishop's manor of Wrotham was said in Lambeth MS. 1212 to be 'in a certain pyx in the treasury of St Gregory's at Canterbury'.[2] The main collection of temporal archives must have remained at Canterbury throughout the Middle Ages, because in the mid sixteenth century a man who was making extracts from the medieval court-rolls of Wimbledon, a Canterbury manor, wrote: 'here followeth the copye of the custumary and custums of the lordshipp of Wimbledon . . . taken out parte of the black boke of Canterbery and part of old Court Rolls and Custumary Rolls, the which resteth in the Archebishopes treasaurye hows att Canterbury of Record'.[3] But Canterbury was not the only repository for the archbishop's records. By the early fourteenth century at latest Lambeth was being used, particularly for documents concerned with episcopal elections, and probably also for many manorial rolls, like those which were destroyed in the Revolt of 1381.[4] In addition, muniments were carried about and left from time to time at various manor-houses. When Archbishop Reynolds died in 1327 he left nine chests filled with vestments and precious objects belonging to his Chapel. Five of the chests contained bulls, charters of liberties, muniments, rolls and memoranda.[5] That great contemporary, Prior Henry of Eastry, knew a good deal more about the archbishops' records than did some archbishops themselves, and soon after Reynolds's death he wrote to the new archbishop, Simon Meopham, telling him that a particular papal privilege he wanted had recently been seen 'in your archiepiscopal archives at Canterbury'. In the same letter he recalled that Reynolds had on one occasion collected together the charters of Henry I and II in a room at Maidstone so that they could be inspected by the prior and monks of Christ Church.[6]

The physical division of these archives of course means that the archbishop and the priory were now each manufacturing their own records, and had also come to some arrangement about the ancient

1. 'The Table of Canterbury Archbishopric Charters', *Camden Miscellany*, xv (1929), p. vii.
2. Lambeth MS. 1212, p. 124.
3. *Extracts from the Court Rolls of the Manor of Wimbledon 1461 to 1864*, preface by P. H. Laurence (privately printed 1866: available in Wimbledon Public Library), part III, p. 65.
4. *Lit. Cant.*, I, no. 61; and see below, pp, 188–9.
5. Mins. Accts 1128/7 and 8.   6. *Lit. Cant.*, I, no. 283.

body of records which had once been the church's undivided possession. Problems were solved by duplicating originals and copying registers. Against one document in Lambeth MS. 1212 which was of interest to archbishop and monks alike the words are written, 'this is in quadruplicate, of which the archbishop has three parts in his treasury and the chapter one'.[1] The same manuscript illustrates this decisive separation in another way. The clerk who was at work transcribing the Old English charters for the archbishop in the mid thirteenth century was doing so from an older transcript into which the word *monachi* had been interpolated in suitable places to give the impression that the original grants had been made to the monks, even though the grants had really been made at times when there were no monks, but only clerks, at Christ Church.[2] But our thirteenth-century scribe did not even recognize the abbreviation for *monachi*, and extended it as *modo*. The earlier lists he was using were monastic in character, and show how intermingled were the monastic and archiepiscopal archives up until the twelfth century. But the thirteenth-century archbishop's clerk was not at all interested in specifically monastic claims, and did not recognize them when he saw them.

The bulk of Lambeth MS. 1212 consists of copies of ancient or permanent documents witnessing to the transfer of lands and jurisdictional privileges. But the final section as it is now bound up is different in character, for it contains memoranda, mainly of financial affairs.[3] The gathering is actually referred to as 'the quaternion of memoranda' on an earlier page of the manuscript, and was obviously known as a dossier that was being kept concurrently and written up as occasion required. Most of the notes belong to the pontificates of Boniface of Savoy and Robert Kilwardby (1245–78). There is a remarkable series of extracts from the royal Pipe Rolls which bear upon the archbishop's fiscal liberties and had evidently been taken from some private rolls of the archbishopric, duplicating information that appears on the royal Pipe Rolls, but even then crumbling with age.[4] But this

---

1. Lambeth MS. 1212, p. 113. For the separation of the estates of archbishopric and priory, see below, Chapter 2, and references there given.
2. J. Armitage Robinson, 'The Early Community at Christ Church, Canterbury', *Journal of Theological Studies*, XXVII (1926), pp. 235 *n*.1, 236 *n*.1.
3. Lambeth MS. 1212, pp. 410–31.
4. cf. p. 413: '. . . *in quodam rotulo cuius titulus consumptus est vetustate*'. The roll in question corresponds with *P.R. 24 Hen. II*, p. 123. For a discussion of their subject-matter, see Chapter 7, p. 284 below.

quaternion of memoranda was also not kept up. Not only is nothing more found of it, but some haphazard financial jottings of the same nature from the reign of Edward II, which ought to have been entered in due course on its leaves, are found inserted on odd sheets throughout the whole manuscript.[1]

Bearing in mind all these characteristics of Lambeth MS. 1212, it seems clear enough that it represents a well-marked stage between the age of charters, which culminated in the twelfth century in the making of handlists, and the age of registers, which from 1279 at latest were answering a rather new purpose in the archbishop's administration. The clerks of Boniface of Savoy, of Robert Kilwardby, and to a declining extent of John Pecham, had an orderly intention in the making of MS. 1212, which was to transcribe and classify all the charters and chirographs relating to the archbishopric that they could find, whether originals, copies or notes. They knew that the separate quaternions they were writing, devoted respectively to the charters of kings, the charters of those other than kings, compositions between the archbishop and others, and papal bulls, were legal evidences which belonged together. There are cross-references between the quaternions. A grouping of them is upon occasion referred to as a *liber*.[2] The whole thing was a work of reference which might have to be kept up to date but would not have to be done again, at least for a long period.[3] The last quaternion of memoranda was, however, partly financial and concerned more directly with the administration of the estates. It was the sort of thing that might have become a quaternion of a register, dealing with current temporal business.

Yet Lambeth MS. 1212 slows down and stops at just the moment when the archbishops' registers were accelerating into their non-stop run. So far as the temporalities of the archbishopric are concerned, the registers are a sad disappointment, but the clerks of the registry did apparently intend at the beginning to set aside quaternions in which temporal items could be found. Pecham's register has a section headed '*Littere Temporalitatis*'. Nevertheless, the amount of information to be found there and in subsequent registers about the temporalities of the see is extremely limited. In

1. Lambeth MS. 1212, pp. 291–3, 330.
2. ibid., pp. 68, 427. The scribe also refers to a *liber conciliorum*, now lost (p. 113).
3. Lambeth MS. 1212 was copied in the late Middle Ages, some time before 1527 and possibly at Croydon, and this copy is now in the Bodleian Library at Oxford as Tanner MS. 223.

this respect we should have been better off if the Canterbury registers had been kept on the same lines as those of the northern archbishopric, for at York the archiepiscopal registers were used to record temporal transactions in detail. Archbishop Wickwane of York, for example, was roughly contemporary with Pecham of Canterbury, and his financial business was entered systematically in three similar sections of his register, devoted respectively to the archdeaconries of York, Nottingham and Richmond.[1] These sections were headed '*Extrinseca*', '*Intrinseca*', '*Obligationes et Liberationes*'. Such records, kept at York at least from 1266 to 1359, allow us deep insight into the wardrobe and household of the northern archbishops, and their financial operations. There is nothing like it to show Canterbury manipulating credit or buying and selling land. A companion section in the York registers is entitled *Ballive*, or 'the register of the bailiffs', and comprises the archbishops' correspondence with their secular officers, and business concerned with their franchises and feudal tenants.

Canterbury failed to establish a traditional arrangement like this, though in compensation there is a mass of ministers' accounts which York lacks. In Pecham's register the *Littere Temporalitatis* occupy only five folios, and other secular matters are scattered about on some dozen more. The amount of temporal business recorded in subsequent registers varies, and is sometimes to be found among the miscellaneous letters, but no regular group of quaternions was set aside to document the running of the vast estate.

It is natural that we should ask why the registers contain so little about the temporalities. The reason certainly does not lie in an apostolic indifference to the revenues and lordship of the Church. It is a question of specialization, and the form which that specialization took in the see of Canterbury.

In the earlier part of the thirteenth century when, as we have seen, the archbishop's own store of charters was beginning to be sorted out and transcribed, the keeping of his estate records was also being subjected to more careful systematization, and this system became ever more elaborate as time went on. Take the manufacture of rentals. The first large-scale one to cover the

1. *Register of William Wickwane (1279–85)*, ed. W. Brown, Surtees Society, CXIV (1907). See also E. F. Jacob, *The Medieval Registers of Canterbury and York* (St Anthony's Hall Publications, no. 4, 1953).

archbishopric manors appears to have been made by Stephen Langton's steward, Elias of Dereham, possibly between 1213 and 1220.[1] Rentals and surveys of individual properties were also being made in the middle of the thirteenth century. The tenants of Charing complained of Richard de Clifford's unjust 'extent' of their manor in the troubled days before Archbishop Kilwardby's accession.[2] In 1273–4 a clerk was paid 4s. for writing the customs of Wingham.[3] These chance examples were probably typical of what was happening everywhere. The largest and most elaborate general rental and custumal was made by Archbishop Pecham's officers in 1283–5. On every manor the information was supplied on oath by a jury of local tenants, often twelve in number, who told the presiding clerks the names, rents and services of tenants who were officially known to hold of the manor. The text of the new rental shows that the jurors had Elias of Dereham's rental and custumal, in roll form, before them. But their task was now considerably greater than before, as the population had increased and it was not always possible even for well-informed local men either to know the names of all the 'heirs' of holdings or to be sure who, on a given day, were the effective tenants. No full contemporary copy of this very large document has survived, and it is known in its virtual entirety only from a late medieval version;[4] but soon after the time of its manufacture an abbreviation of it was made, containing the description of the demesnes and summaries of rents owing, without names. This roll came into the hands of John Selden after the execution of Archbishop Laud in 1645, and after three centuries of mysterious disappearance was bought back by Lambeth Palace Library in 1963.[5] The survey of 1283–5 was very likely the last general one on the archbishopric estates. When the demesnes began to be leased out, the obligation to renew the

1. This prototype rental is several times referred to in the later thirteenth-century one (Dean and Chapter of Canterbury MS. E 24, e.g. fos. 39v., 52, 91).
2. *Rot. Hundr.*, I, p. 213.   3. Addit. MS. 29794 m.4d.
4. Dean and Chapter of Canterbury MS. E 24, which seems to be in a late-fifteenth-century hand.
5. It is now L.R. 2068. For the story of this MS., see D. M. Barratt, 'The Library of John Selden and Its Later History', *Bodleian Quarterly Record*, III (1950–1), p. 128 *et seq.*, and also *The Times*, 18 October 1963. After the Second World War the MS. was for a short time in the library of St Paul's Cathedral, and during this time a transcript was made of it by Mr Peter Partner. I am grateful to him, and to Mr A. R. B. Fuller, Keeper of the Manuscripts there, for permission to see this transcript. Later I was able to see the MS. itself at Sotheby's, and at Lambeth after its purchase.

rentals fell on the farmers. An instance of this practice occurs at Romney in 1364, when the archbishop required John Fraunceys, his farmer, to make a new rental and custumal for the use of the church and to deliver a copy within a year to serve as evidence in the future collection of rents.[1] The procedure was quite usual thereafter, and long-term lessees had to renew their rentals at stated intervals. In this way, the early general rentals were replaced by rentals of particular properties.

The same process of fragmentation occurred with the account rolls of the archbishopric. Two (incomplete) general account rolls of the archbishopric are known from the days before Archbishop Pecham. They are in the form of annual 'pipe-rolls', that is to say, accounts of every manor from Michaelmas to Michaelmas, set down separately, one after the other and without general statements or summaries, upon a bunch of large membranes fastened together at the top.[2] But under Pecham the manors were grouped into the six large bailiwicks which continued in being for the rest of the Middle Ages. The general pipe-roll disappears, and in its place come individual accounts for separate manors, kept by reeve or serjeant and engrossed separately after audit. The last known 'pipe-roll' dates from 1273–4; the first surviving individual account roll from 1279–80.[3] These individual accounts themselves subdivide and specialize in the course of the fourteenth and early fifteenth centuries. By 1400 the archbishop, like other large-scale landlords, was ceasing to cultivate most of his own demesnes, and the demesne fields, manorial buildings and sometimes even the rents of the tenantry were being leased out to farmers for terms of years. The archbishop generally kept his woods and parks, and intensified their exploitation by selling firewood and timber of many kinds to industrial users while enjoying the recreation and status that wide parklands filled with deer afforded. So, from about 1400 we get multiple series of farmers' accounts, woodwards', foresters' and parkers' accounts, drawn up annually (or occasionally biennially), written out roughly before the audit on paper, accompanied by sheaves of paper receipts and particulars of local

1. Reg. Islip, fo. 202v.
2. L.R. 1193 (probably 1236–7), and Addit. MS. 29794 (1273–4). The disappearance of all the rest of the series is most unfortunate. Needless to say, these archbishopric accounts must be distinguished from the royal accounts kept during vacancies of the see, to be found on the royal Pipe Rolls.
3. L.R. 234 (Bexley).

expenditure, and engrossed on parchment for the record. The archbishop's accounts were now of interest to his treasurers as sources of financial rather than agrarian information. The collection of rent was the prime administrative task of the temporal organization. At this point a new sort of official came into existence with his own annual roll. This was the receiver, who was placed over one or more bailiwicks, and whose accounts consolidate the cash receipts from the local ministers and give good information about the upkeep of the estates.[1] A further refinement at this time was the keeping of special annual rolls by the steward of the Liberty, whose task, again a basically financial one, was to claim at the Exchequer and in the localities the profits of the archbishop's franchises.[2]

In the later Middle Ages, then, specialization proceeded by the creation of new and parallel series of records: sometimes books, like the stewards' books we glimpsed in the thirteenth century, or the books of the household to which fleeting allusions are made in the fifteenth; but often rolls, made under the responsibility of many kinds of local ministers operating in different places.

These archives were very vulnerable. A first-class catastrophe like the revolt of 1381 obliterated masses of them. Croydon and Harrow were plundered and fired. Parchments burned in the streets of east Kent villages.[3] On 13 July 1381 Lambeth itself was burned, and royal letters patent a year later summarized the destruction:

Since all rentals, feodaries and other memoranda of the manors and lordships of the archbishopric, through which the farms, rents, services and other profits belonging to the archbishopric ought to be levied, were burnt and entirely destroyed by certain malefactors in their recent insurrection against us and our peace, we ... compel the tenants and inhabitants of these lordships to reconstitute these titles exactly, and give them to the archbishop.[4]

Alas for us, the order was beyond the capacity and will of the local inhabitants.

The catastrophe left an enormous chronological gap in the

1. See below, p. 271 ff.; also Ec.H.R., 2nd series, vol. XVI, no. 3 (April 1964), p.4 33.
2. See below, p. 288 ff.   3. A.C., III (1860), p. 94, and below, pp. 188–9.
4. Cited by A. Réville, Le Soulèvement des travailleurs d'Angleterre en 1381 (Paris, 1898), App. II, Series A, no. 6. cf. The Anonimalle Chronicle, ed. V. H. Galbraith, (1927), p. 140.

temporal records, for the fourteenth century is almost unrepresented in the ministers' accounts. But from the historian's viewpoint the loss of archives is even more severe through lack of custody. This was not altogether due to the failure to centralize the records. There must have been an impressive series of household rolls to record the purchase week by week of supplies and note the numbers in hall and the names of guests, for fragments of three such rolls survive, from 1341, 1343 and 1459.[1] Likewise, the books of the treasurer were made and used in the household, at the centre of affairs. To contemporaries they were of passing value, and they were discarded. Yet the erosion of the temporal archives did in fact take place largely because they were not all kept together in one central place. Rentals, as we have seen, were in the later Middle Ages made by the farmers, and must often have been retained by them. Ministers' accounts, too, not infrequently entered the private archives of stewards, surveyors and local men of substance, in whose hands (indeed, in whose interest) the estates were increasingly administered. One roll concerned with Maidstone, for instance, came to light not long ago among the papers of the Kentish family of Darell-Blunt, a forbear of which, Sir John Darell, was steward of the lands to the archbishop during 1428–32.[2] In the end, the collection of estate rolls which remained was split into two lots by the transference of the Otford records to the Crown in the sixteenth century. Otford manor was transferred in 1537. In 1574 Archbishop Parker's receiver, Peter Marsh, esquire, handed into the Exchequer a bundle of Otford court-rolls and accounts dating from the late fourteenth and fifteenth centuries with a covering note saying that they concerned the Queen's manor of Otford, and were to be put into the chest at Westminster.[3] Others doubtless went the same way. Today the surviving collection is distributed not unevenly between Lambeth Palace and the Public Record Office in Chancery Lane.

The history of the temporal records from the time of Archbishop

1. The household and its muniments are discussed in Chapter 6 below.
2. KAO U 409, M 3; cf. L.R.s 858, 860. Here is another instance: in 1488–9 there died one Richard Welbeck who held of the archbishop copyhold lands in Wimbledon, Putney and Hampton. The court-roll said, 'and there remained in his custody a rental of this lordship, and a book called a Terrory [Terrier], but in whose hands they are now the suitors do not know.' (*Extracts from the Court Rolls of . . . Wimbledon*, op.cit., p. 58).
3. State Papers Domestic (suppl.) (S.P. 45), no. 125, fo. 84. I owe this reference to the kindness of Professor S. T. Bindoff.

Pecham onwards, therefore, is punctuated with annihilating accidents, and these accidents were to some extent made possible by the fact that the financial and secular business of the see, specialized into parallel series of records and distributed by chance over the countryside, found little place in the monumental series of archbishops' registers. Not that the clerks of the archbishop's registry were totally uninterested in their lord's temporalities. If their interest was selective, or subject to momentary quickenings here and there, it bore not upon money, nor upon territory, but upon his lordship over men. Few of the temporal entries in the registers fall outside this scheme. The homage of feudal tenants, grants of office to men of importance, monitions protecting jurisdictions and liberties, and manumissions freeing bond tenants or, conversely, insisting on services, were all of greater consequence to the registry staff than sums of money or precise acreages.

The temporal archives of the see passed thus through their own historical development, from the age of solemn charters, through the age of handlists, catalogues, registers and general rentals, to the last stage in which demesne leasing and professional management fragmented the documentation and brought it more and more into the hands of private men and their families, the tenants and officers of the see, while the registrar contented himself with sporadic reminders of the archbishop's juridical lordship. It is scarcely surprising that for the last period of the medieval lordship our evidence has so often a private provenance, in the wills and deeds and family papers of those men and women whose power and influence was growing while that of great ecclesiastical landlords was under attack.

CHAPTER 2

The endowment of the see

Although the Domesday survey of 1086 would provide a convenient starting-point for this study, it stands at the end rather than at the beginning of a long series of historical events. The present book is about the landed possessions and rural communities which during the Middle Ages until the time of Cranmer were held 'of the archbishop in right of his church of Canterbury'. The Domesday survey and the related documents prepared shortly afterwards by the monks for their own use, and nowadays known as *Domesday Monachorum*, offer us descriptions of the estates in which the properties of archbishop and of monks are distinguished fairly completely from each other, and from then onwards the manors of the archbishopric formed a separate and identifiable mass of property. It would be simple to accept this exclusively as the subject-matter and to ignore the pre-Conquest age altogether. Yet to do so would cheat the natural curiosity which asks about origins. An excursion beyond Domesday is required in order to trace the course of the see's endowment and explain the form which that endowment took, even though most attention is to be concentrated on later medieval society.

There are three preliminary obstacles to a clear view of the pre-Norman estates.

In the first place, the ample charter evidence is often of doubtful authenticity. Some contemporary charters survive, but a general reliance must be placed upon copies of them in cartularies and upon lists of acquisitions, of which the fullest and most convenient are contained in Lambeth Palace MS. 1212. In this codex, discussed in the previous chapter, the documents are copies, or copies of copies, and have sometimes been interpolated, usually abbreviated, and on occasion obviously constructed for particular reasons at dates long after the original events. The 'original' charters themselves, which exist in the British Museum and elsewhere, are sometimes untrustworthy for similar reasons. It would be wrong to make too much of this difficulty. There was a limited number of reasons why monks or clerks invented what they wanted to be true. By ignoring obviously spurious elements and accepting what good authorities accept, a broadly credible story of the endowment emerges. Worse than this are the losses of early charters. The suspicion can never be allayed that the estates of the archbishopric are really much older than the evidence surveyed in this chapter allows.

The second difficulty is in identifying some of the places to which the charters refer. Although many properties given or sold to the church during the four centuries before the Conquest feature in the clearer light of Domesday, it often happens that some early acquisition never reappears or, conversely, that no certain origin for important Domesday possessions can be found. Yet, as Maitland saw, this lack of exact correspondence between Domesday and the charters is to the charters' credit.[1] Systematic manufacture of evidence would have been more lucid. We are persuaded to believe much of what the cartularies tell us, even though this is sometimes less and sometimes more than the truth. Certain discrepancies may also be explained by the rise and fall of place-names. Villages which gave their names to the Domesday manors seem in several instances to be appearing there for the first time, even when they stand with tolerable certainty for property granted earlier under different names. For example, there appears to be no explicit charter evidence for the greatest of all the archbishop's medieval manors, that of Aldington on the northern shores of Romney Marsh. But numerous charters can be collected which grant land round about, at Lydd, Lympne, Stowting and elsewhere, and some of these districts were members of the vast medieval manor of Aldington.[2] Again, there is no Petham in the early charters, but there is Swarling, and Swarling was in Petham.[3]

1. F. W. Maitland, *Domesday Book and Beyond* (1897), p. 466.
2. e.g. *CS*, 214.
3. *CS*, 341. Also Bocholt, etc., granted in 805 (*CS*, 322–3), which J. K. Wallenberg identified with Petham (*KPN*, pp. 105–6).

Gillingham, near Rochester, also appears for the first time in Domesday Book, but lands in that vicinity were granted in 798 and 811.[1] It will be suggested at the end of this chapter that the very nature of the Kentish 'manor' may have contributed to the instability of place-names.

The third difficulty is that the chronology of the endowment is confused by historical happenings as well as documentary inadequacy. Estates once granted were sometimes lost again, and might be recovered later. If the fact of loss were not recorded, the visible evidence would consist of two separate grants at different times, and it would then not be readily apparent whether one, both, or neither were credible. Or a grant may have been entirely abortive. Or at certain moments the history of the holdings may be obscured by exchanges and rearrangements the terms of which are hard to understand, like that between Archbishop Aethelheard and the Abbess Cynethryth in 798, whereby Canterbury received lastingly important property at Northfleet and Teynham in Kent in exchange for a monastery at Cookham in Berkshire, which thereafter passes out of history.[2]

When all this has been said, an attempt to sketch the known course of the endowment remains justifiable. Before making it, one further matter requires explanation, and this is the separation between the lands of the archbishop and those of the monks.

The distinction met in Domesday between the monastic and the archiepiscopal manors was not new then, but neither was it aboriginal. Monastic writers at Canterbury were themselves deceived about the facts: Eadmer supposed it the recent work of Lanfranc, Gervase remarked that it went back to Theodore.[3] In fact, the beginning of a small separate endowment for the community was traced back by Armitage Robinson to 799. In that year Archbishop Aethelheard persuaded King Cenwulf of the Mercians, then dominant in Kent, to restore to the church considerable lands at Charing and Chart which earlier had been granted to the *familia*

---

1. *CS*, 291, 335–6.
2. F. M. Stenton, *Latin Charters of the Anglo-Saxon Period* (1955), pp. 13–14; *CS*, 291.
3. The following paragraphs are indebted to three important papers: J. Armitage Robinson, 'The Early Community at Christ Church, Canterbury', *Journal of Theological Studies*, xxvii (1926); B. W. Kissan, 'Lanfranc's Alleged Division of Lands Between Archbishop and Community', *E.H.R.*, liv (1939); Eric John, 'The Division of the *Mensa* in Early English Monasteries', *Journal of Ecclesiastical History*, vi (1955).

but confiscated by King Offa. A new clause in 799 added the gift of four ploughlands at what is now Bishopsbourne 'to the congregation and *familia* of the church of Canterbury as their very own'.[1] The transaction was a complex one, spread over a number of years, and needs to be disentangled from complementary documents. The clause of 799 which gave Bishopsbourne in a special way to the *familia* took effect only in 805, shortly before Archbishop Aethelheard's death. In that year he parted with the property in favour of the brethren, whose table the income was intended to supply.[2] One of the witnesses was Wulfred the archdeacon, a man well endowed with his own land, who almost at once became archbishop. In a third charter, dated 811,[3] the whole story was told again and the properties of the archbishop and the community were elaborately rearranged. Archbishop Wulfred took the Bishopsbourne ploughlands for himself, but as a handsome exchange gave to 'his brothers, in perpetual inheritance' lands in the districts of Eastry, Lympne and probably Old Romney, where the church of Canterbury already possessed property. Remote though such manoeuvres may seem, they form a historical landmark by bringing into view a clearer relationship between the archbishop and the community. Archbishops like Wulfred, and his predecessor Jaenbehrt whose kinsman Aldhun had originally given Charing and Chart, were rich men, holding lands in hereditary right and belonging to a social class that provided the ecclesiastical as well as the secular rulers of the region. The property of these leading aristocrats was forming the embryo of the medieval archbishops' fee.

Apart from the property conferred especially upon the community and the lands which belonged especially to the archbishops, there were also estates of which it can only be said that they belonged to the church of Canterbury in an undifferentiated way. But the setting aside of a portion for the community makes the late eighth and early ninth centuries a noteworthy point in the history of the estates.

The development was connected with religious reform. Archbishop Wulfred was trying to re-establish at Canterbury the common life of dormitory and refectory, and in pursuing this aim

1. *CS*, 293 ('. . . *congregatione et familiae Dorovernensis ecclesiae in jus proprium*'). cf. F. M. Stenton, *Anglo-Saxon England* (1943), pp. 35–6, and *Latin Charters*, p. 28; and *KPN*, pp. 85–7.
2. *CS*, 319.   3. *CS*, 332; Stenton, *Latin Charters*, p. 28n.

2

he carried the separation of the estates a stage further. In 813 he secured to the *familia* in perpetuity 'the houses they have built by their own labour'.[1] In 824 he added part of his own landed inheritance at Shelford, between Eastry and Wingham, which the community was to enjoy after his death, and was not to alienate.[2] In succeeding years the practice of making special gifts and bequests to the communal *mensa* was continued, even though a properly monastic life was not yet successfully re-established. About 837, one Badanoth Beõtting directed in his will that an estate be given to 'the refectory of the community as a perpetual inheritance to be used as they think fit',[3] and a bequest made between 973 and 987 by Brihtric and his wife Aelfswith granted with the clearest distinction sixty mancuses to Christ Church, that is, thirty to the bishop and thirty to the community.[4]

In the tenth century, one of the probable intentions of the reformers was to guarantee monastic endowments and prevent them being lost into the hands of kings or rulers. One might expect that a reform which set such store by the true Benedictine spirit would prefer the estates of abbot and community, as father and family, to be reintegrated. But in fact the endowment of the revived Benedictine communities continued to be divided. At Canterbury, the evidence for the separate possessions of the archbishop (who was titular abbot) and the community is compelling. For example, Monks Eleigh in Suffolk was willed conditionally to the community between 946 and 951, and finally between 998 and 1002. Between those two periods the Canterbury clerks had been replaced by monks, yet the change clearly made no difference to the separation of estates as between the community and its head.

It is not easy to write with assurance about the continuance of separate community estates throughout the obscure century before the Norman Conquest. Copies of eleventh-century charters often enough record that properties acquired were intended to supply the needs and the food of the monks (*ad opus et victum monachorum*), but this is just the sort of interpolation that cannot be immediately believed, as monastic copyists had a vested interest in saying this sort of thing. Yet it is not at all unlikely that a separation of estates continued. Estates which the church of Canterbury

1. *CS*, 342, observed by W. H. Stevenson to be genuine (*E.H.R.*, xxix, pp. 689–703) 2. *CS*, 380.
3. Eric John, art. cit., from A. J. Robertson, *Anglo-Saxon Charters* (1939), p. 10.
4. Dorothy Whitelock, *Anglo-Saxon Wills* (1930), pp. 26–8.

apparently received during this period often appear in Domesday as in fact the possession of the monks, in company with other monastic estates, like Monks Eleigh, which without any doubt were originally granted especially to the community. For instance, the gift of Stisted in Essex 'for the food of the monks' by a certain Godwin in 975–9, which is noted in the Lambeth cartulary,[1] would at first sight be viewed with a certain scepticism. But property in the same place was certainly willed to the community in the eleventh century,[2] and much later we find Archbishop Anselm returning Stisted to the monks since 'it is known to belong to their substance'.[3]

If these remarks show in outline how the division of estates came about, it must still not be assumed that the division was complete in Old English times. The relationship between the community and its head, the archbishop, was not as distant as it later became. Despite its separate accounts of the lands of archbishop and monks, the Domesday survey indicates that the division of property was still less than total. The small borough of Seasalter was described in the Exchequer Domesday as belonging to the archbishop's kitchen, and in the *Domesday Monachorum*, a little later, as pertaining to 'the food of the monks'.[4] This may have signified a real change in the assignment of Seasalter, but perhaps more likely it refers to common living arrangements at Canterbury. In a roughly coeval document, eight prebends of the church of Newington-by-Sittingbourne were said to belong to the archbishop *and* to Christ Church.[5] Further, the text of Domesday shows the landed interests of archbishop and community much bound up together: monastic income could be derived from archiepiscopal manors like Maidstone and Lyminge,[6] and conversely the archbishop placed tenants upon monastic lands. Indeed, the archbishop is commonly described in Domesday as holding the lands which were assigned to the monks. Not until Anselm's time were the monks granted power to administer their own lands separately.[7]

1. Lambeth MS. 1212, p. 331 ('*ad victum monachorum*').
2. Whitelock, op. cit., pp. 84, 197–8.
3. Lambeth MS. 1212, p. 333 ('*ad res eorum pertinere et pertinuisse scitur*').
4. *Dom. Mon.*, p. 90.   5. Lambeth MS. 1212, pp. 335–6.   6. *D.B.*, I, pp. 2b, 3.
7. Eadmer, *Historia Novorum*, ed. M. Rule (*R.S.*, 1884), p. 219 ('*Nam res monachorum posuit [archiepiscopus] in dispositione eorum . . .*'). Even in 1127 well-informed men swore that the tolls and customs of Sandwich belonged to the archbishop *and* the monks of Christ Church (D. M. Stenton, *English Justice between the Norman Conquest and the Great Charter* (1965), p. 120).

It is therefore difficult to measure the degree of separation between the monastic and the archiepiscopal estates, although it is quite clear in a general way that such a separation continued, and that a considerable proportion of the church's property was earmarked to supply revenue in cash and kind for the community.

It is now timely to attempt a chronological sketch of the endowment up as far as the Domesday period, when most of the estates enjoyed by the medieval church of Canterbury had been acquired. This can best be done with the aid of the manuscript catalogues described in the first chapter, because they are reasonably complete and already arranged in a more or less chronological order. In Lambeth Palace MS. 1212 there are two lists of pre-Conquest acquisitions. The longer one[1] is a thirteenth-century transcript of a twelfth-century book of memoranda and contains ninety-one charters, three papal letters and the record of nine councils. The charters are in short form, without attestations, and their texts had already been modified in the twelfth-century exemplar. Nevertheless, the list is useful, for its contents range in supposed date from the seventh century to the early twelfth, and comprise copies, even if doctored ones, of almost all the known grants to Canterbury belonging to that era. Also the texts can sometimes be controlled from good, early copies. The second list in this manuscript consists of twenty-eight documents transcribed, so the heading tells us, 'from early charters of lands anciently called landbooks'.[2] Of these, twenty-three are charters and five are records of councils. These charters have attestations and sometimes the Saxon boundaries, and where an 'original' charter survives, the text from this section compares with it accurately. All its documents are also found, in their abbreviated and sometimes interpolated form, in the longer list already discussed. Thus the occasional possibility of comparing a contemporary document with its transcribed forms in the two sections of the Lambeth MS. strengthens the confidence with which, for the purposes of this chapter, the Lambeth transcripts may be

---

1. Lambeth MS. 1212, pp. 304–39, a section headed *'Transcripta de veteri libro Cantuar. Memoranda cartarum et conciliorum archiepiscoporum et ecclesie Cant'*. The intrusion into the texts of the word 'monks' probably goes back to the end of the eleventh century when stories about monks at Christ Church were inserted into the *Anglo-Saxon Chronicle* (Armitage Robinson, art. cit., esp. p. 235 and *n.*).
2. Lambeth MS. 1212, pp. 384–408, headed *'De codicellis primariis sive cartis terrarum antiquitus dictis "landboc"'*.

used.[1] After all, the most evident causes which stimulated forgery or faking were the claims to Canterbury's superiority over York, the need at certain junctures to prove a specifically monastic title to property, the claim to jurisdictional and fiscal immunities, and the need to replace evidences lost in disasters or perished with age.[2] It is not very often that the territorial substance of the cartularies seems at fault, even where the dating requires to be controlled and the names and styles of grantees received with scepticism.[3]

According to its attributed date, the earliest donation in the church of Canterbury's tradition was of Adisham, six miles southeast of Canterbury, made by King Eadbald in 616. Of this, Sir Frank Stenton wrote that it 'must collapse before the most elementary of diplomatic tests', yet he allowed that ancient memoranda, now lost, might lie behind it.[4] No other record of Adisham appears until the general confirmations of the eleventh century.[5] In Domesday it was among the established possessions, supplying the monks' table. In the twelfth-century lists it was treated as a prototype endowment, carrying clauses of exemption from services which, under the phrase *libere sicut Adesham*, provided the model for subsequent grants. It is likely that Adisham was the subject of an early grant, and that is all one can say.

Lands which formed especially early nuclei of the future Canterbury estates are those which were given in the seventh and eighth centuries to the minsters of Reculver and Lyminge, and which fell ultimately to Christ Church. In 679, King Hlothar of Kent granted land in Thanet, and at Sturry on the north-east outskirts of

1. Birch made use of both these portions of the Lambeth MS. in addition to the contemporary charters he examined in the Cottonian collection and elsewhere. Although the Lambeth cartularies have provided a useful framework in the preparation of this account, citations will be made from Birch's *Cartularium* wherever this is possible up to the tenth-century termination of that work, since it will be more convenient for scholars who wish to look up references.
2. cf. R. W. Southern, 'The Canterbury Forgeries', *E.H.R.*, LXXIII (1958).
3. Similar remarks are made about the charters of St Augustine's abbey, Canterbury, by G. J. Turner and H. E. Salter in *The Register of St Augustine's Abbey . . .* (British Academy Records of the Social and Economic History of England and Wales, vol. II), Introduction, p. xvii.
4. *CS*, 12; Stenton, *Latin Charters*, p. 31. A like probability that genuine substance lies behind spurious or constructive charters is acknowledged by Stenton in a discussion of Canterbury's possessions at Newington and Britwell in Oxfordshire (*KCD*, 896; *V.C.H. Oxfordshire*, I (1939), p. 377 and *n.*). Similarly with a grant of 784 to the minster of Reculver (*CS*, 243), mentioned below (Stenton, *Anglo-Saxon England* (1943), p. 206).
5. But see below, p. 32.

23

Canterbury, to Behrtwald, abbot of Reculver, who became arch-bishop in 692.[1] About 765, King Eardwulf of Kent gave Heabehrct, abbot of Reculver, and his *familia* there some land at Palmstead near Canterbury and at Higham near Rochester.[2] In 784, at a moment when the Mercian overlord Offa was in a weak position in Kent, King Ealhmund of Kent granted of his own volition to Abbot Hwitred and the minster of Reculver twelve ploughlands at Sheldwich, to the west of Canterbury and some three miles south of Faversham.[3] Reculver, on the exposed north coast of Kent, had thus by an early date acquired a rather scattered but considerable collection of properties. According to a charter which Stevenson said was not contemporary, Reculver was granted with its pos-sessions to Christ Church, Canterbury, in 949.[4] In Cnut's time the demesnes were evidently still thought of as belonging to the minster of Reculver,[5] but there is no doubt that the places once granted to Reculver came later to Christ Church, and their identity can some-times be proved in detail.[6]

In a sheltered position among the downlands north of Hythe lay the minster of Lyminge, one of the earliest centres of Kentish ecclesiastical life.[7] Arable lands in the vicinity, together with fisheries and grazings which we are told already existed on Romney Marsh, were granted to this minster by kings of Kent in the first half of the eighth century.[8] This nucleus was augmented. In 804 the minster, then ruled by the Abbess Selethrytha, recovered from the king some property in Canterbury itself, the original title-deeds of which were probably destroyed in the eighteenth-century fire at Canterbury.[9] Archbishops also acquired property at Lyminge, bordering on that already possessed by the minster.[10] The connexion

1. *CS*, 45. Stevenson and Stenton described this as one of our earliest genuine charters. A reduced photograph of it is printed in R. H. Hodgkin, *History of the Anglo-Saxons* (1935), II, p. 454.
2. *CS*, 199, also called 'contemporary' by Stevenson. For these place-names, see *KPN*, 51.
3. *CS*, 243.   4. *CS*, 880.   5. *KCD*, 754.
6. The Saxon boundaries in *CS*, 880 (in an eleventh-century hand), include *ceolulfing tune* which is to be identified with Chilmington (*KPN*, p. 282), and Chilmington in the thirteenth century was part of the archiepiscopal manor of Reculver (Dean and Chapter of Canterbury MS. E 24, fo. 19).
7. For Lyminge and other early Kentish churches, see *Dom. Mon.*, pp. 5–15, esp. pp. 9–11; also R. C. Jenkins, *Chartulary of the Monastery of Lyminge* (Folkestone, n.d.).
8. *CS*, 97–8 and 160, regarded by Stevenson as genuine; also *KCD*, 627. On the dating and relationship of *CS*, 97 and 98, see Gordon Ward, *A.C.*, XLVIII, pp. 11–28.
9. *CS*, 317.   10. *CS*, 419, 420; *KPN*, p. 180.

between Lyminge and Canterbury was close, like that between Canterbury and other ancient central churches of the see such as Reculver and Folkestone, but it is an obscure connexion, and one of the obscurer processes is the integration of its lands among the lands of Christ Church. Possibly the endowments of Lyminge were transferred to the archbishop in Dunstan's time. Certainly Lyminge, with its lands and customs, were recovered for the see under the Conqueror, and Lanfranc, in referring to 'our town of Lyminge', remarked that the remains of some of his predecessors, archbishops of Canterbury, had been buried there.[1] There is little doubt that the manor of Lyminge, property of the medieval lordship of Canterbury, included the territories originally bestowed by kings of Kent upon the minster.[2]

Leaving aside the possessions of Reculver and Lyminge, a number of important medieval manors of the see may be traced to the early years, before the pontificate of Wulfred. In the first place, there is the well-known charter, falsely dated 680 but quite possibly based upon a genuine prototype, in which King Caedwalla of Wessex was said to have granted to Bishop Wilfrith of the South Saxons the west Sussex lands of Pagham, Slindon, Shripney, Charlton, Bognor, Bersted, Crimsham and Mundham.[3] Although Stevenson dismissed this charter as spurious, the possibility was allowed that Wilfrith may in fact have handed over this great estate on his departure from Sussex in 686. At all events, these are the lands which the archbishopric possessed in west Sussex throughout the Middle Ages, this was the Canterbury explanation in the twelfth century of how the property had been acquired, and no other evidences of its original acquisition remain.

Of the other pre-Wulfredian grants, most seem to have been made by King Offa: five ploughlands at Higham near Rochester to Archbishop Jaenbehrt in 774;[4] three sulungs at Lydd the same

1. *Cart. of St Gregory's Priory*, p. 1.
2. No doubt, too, the monks viewed charters once made to Lyminge as their own: *CS*, 247, in a ninth-century hand, was from Offa to the Abbess Selethrytha; *CS*, 263 (from Lambeth MS. 1212), is almost identical, but is represented as from Offa to Christ Church. I owe this observation to Mr Nicholas Brooks.
3. *CS*, 50. cf. Stevenson, art. cit., pp. 695–6. The charter was apparently forged at Christ Church before the Conquest, and came from the same *scriptorium* that, about A.D. 1000, manufactured *CS*, 335, a forged copy of a *genuine* charter, and *CS*, 881, also a copy of a *genuine* charter. For the historical background, see Stenton, *Anglo-Saxon England*, pp. 138–9.
4. *CS*, 213, called by Stevenson 'contemporary' (art. cit., pp. 692n., 698n.).

year;[1] sixty *tributaria* of land in Hayes and Yedding, Middlesex, and thirty at Twickenham, Middlesex, in 790.[2] It will be noticed that the minster of Reculver had received land at Higham not long before, and that Lydd on Romney Marsh was in the district where the people belonged to Lyminge minster.[3] But the Middlesex grants were breaking new ground, and once made they remained to the see. There seems to be no interruption in the archbishopric's enjoyment of Hayes and its environs between the eighth century and the sixteenth.

The acquisition of the rich north Kentish properties of Northfleet and Teynham may confidently be traced to this period, but they were joined to the Canterbury estates as the result of a complicated plea and not by a direct grant.[4] In 798 at a synodal council at Clofesho Archbishop Aethelheard complained in a general way about the losses which churches had been suffering through the disappearance of their *cirographa*, and claimed in particular a monastery at Cookham in Berkshire, given to Christ Church by King Aethelbald more than forty years earlier. The title-deeds had been stolen, and had come into the hands of King Cynewulf of Wessex. The monastery itself was seized by King Offa of Mercia. Later, the charters returned to Christ Church, and in 798 it was decided that Christ Church should at last receive back the property to which these deeds related. But by this time the abbess of Cookham was Cynethryth, Offa's heiress, who desired to go on holding the Berkshire monastery. Christ Church was therefore given in exchange some wide estates on the south bank of the Thames estuary at Northfleet and Teynham, and in the Cray valley.[5]

The endowment of the Canterbury community with certain lands earmarked for itself belongs, as has been seen, to this point in time, and the property in question need not again be listed. But the special place of Archbishop Wulfred (805-33) in the chronology

1. *CS*, 214, also contemporary. cf. Stenton, op. cit., p. 206, and, for discussion of the boundaries, R. F. Jessupp in *A.C.*, LV, pp. 12-15.
2. *CS*, 265. In the twelfth century it was believed that this deed of grant had included also the great manor of Otford in Kent, for three manuscript copies of the original charter contain the words '*iste idem Offa dedit ecclesie Christi in Dorobernia villam nomine Otteford*' (cf. *A.C.*, XLIII, pp. 115-17). But it is probable that Otford was a ninth-century addition to the church's territories.
3. See *Dom. Mon.*, p. 10, citing the endorsement to *CS*, 98.
4. *CS*, 291. What follows is taken from Stenton, *Latin Charters*, pp. 12-14.
5. For identification of place-names, see *KPN*, pp. 83-4.

of the endowment requires notice. 'In all his works,' wrote Gervase, 'he considered the advantage and peace of the church of Canterbury which he ruled.'[1] His task was not easy, for he had to contend with Cenwulf, king of Mercia, then overlord of Kent and a man of ruthless behaviour. In the earlier years of his pontificate, Wulfred received a good many lands from the king, usually, if not always, in exchange for payment. In 805 he bought for thirty mancuses two ploughlands in what was later known as Petham.[2] The same year the king sold land at Swarling and elsewhere in the Petham district to a certain Uulfhard, priest of the late Archbishop Aethelheard.[3] From a charter dated 812 we learn that Uulfhard had resold this land to Archbishop Wulfred for a good price.[4] In 809 Wulfred bought seven ploughlands at Barham for £30.[5] A copy of this charter in the less reliable section of Lambeth MS. 1212 adds a grant of twenty-five yokes at Ibbinctun (Davington in Faversham?) to the monks. But this obvious example of forgery does not lessen the credibility of the original purchase by Wulfred. The series of charters shows a rich archbishop augmenting his church's possessions out of his own pocket.

The years 811–12 were important ones for the acquisition of possessions, partly but not entirely because the archbishop was building up the community's own endowments. Lands at Rainham and Faversham, both on the outskirts of settlements in the king's own lordship, passed to Wulfred, in perpetual inheritance, for large sums of money; so, too, land in Graveney (near Faversham) and plots in Canterbury with meadows by the river Stour.[6] Again in 811, in a charter which has been authoritatively accepted,[7] Wulfred made over lands to the community, getting in exchange the manor of Bishopsbourne, which was to remain in archiepiscopal hands. Other sales of lands in the wooded Faversham district by the king to the archbishop occupy these years.[8] Two further grants belong to the years before Wulfred's quarrel with the king. About the year 810, Osuulf, alderman of east Kent, and his wife Beornthryth, willed twenty sulungs at Stansted in Lympne, near Aldington, to

1. Gervase of Canterbury, *Opera* (*R.S.*, 1880), II, p. 348.
2. *CS*, 322–3. 3. *CS*, 321. 4. *CS*, 341.
5. *CS*, 328; cf. Lambeth MS. 1212, p. 315.
6. *CS*, 335–6, a contemporary and an interpolated version.
7. *CS*, 332; cf. Stenton, *Latin Charters*, p. 28n.
8. *CS*, p. 340 (Davington and Faversham); *CS*, 348 (Kingsland near Faversham, with woodland in the Blean); cf. Stenton, op. cit., p. 39 and *n.*; *KPN*, pp. 28, 106, 140; *CS*, 353 (Faversham district).

Christ Church, the bequest to take effect after the deaths of themselves, their son and daughter.[1] The grant was confirmed in 844, when Archbishop Ceolnoth finally adjudicated on the Osuulf inheritance.[2] Secondly, a splendid genuine charter records the grant of ten ploughlands at Bexley to the archbishop by King Cenwulf.[3]

The quarrel between king and archbishop which broke out in 817 probably concerned the king's claim to various possessions of the see, and in particular the archbishop's minsters in Thanet and Reculver.[4] Because of this quarrel, the archbishop was apparently superseded between 817 and 821, but the dispute was then ended by King Cenwulf's imposition of a settlement upon Wulfred. A condition of the settlement was that Wulfred should surrender an estate of 300 hides[5] and pay a fine of £120. The years of settlement after the quarrel produced documentary evidence telling us about it from Wulfred's point of view, but, as Sir Frank Stenton wrote, 'drafted so execrably that at crucial points the meaning becomes obscure'.[6]

In 821 Cenwulf was succeeded by his brother Ceolwulf, who the next year granted Archbishop Wulfred land at a place called Milton. This was almost certainly at Shoreham in Kent, and is the second certain acquisition of that territory round Otford which was to form so important a part of the see's medieval temporalities.[7] The enormous manors of the early Middle Ages were not all gained in one piece, but often seem to have been built up like jigsaw puzzles. This particular grant complemented one of the previous year, by which King Cenwulf, in the last moments of his reign, had bestowed land at Copton (later Westwood Court) and Greatness, in Otford, upon the archbishop.[8] By the two grants of 821-2 Wulfred's lordship was extended over most of the territories between Shoreham and Sevenoaks, the River Darent and Kemsing, designated later as the manor of Otford, but comprising members

1. *CS*, 330.
2. *CS*, 445-6; Haddan and Stubbs, *Concilia*, pp. 567, 628.
3. *CS*, 346; cf., for discussion of boundaries, *A.C.*, LIV; *KPN*, pp. 134-9; and Dorothy Whitelock, *English Historical Documents*, I (1955), p. 338. Also *Medieval Bexley* by the present writer (Bexley Corporation Public Libraries, 1961), pp. 1-3.
4. Stenton, *Anglo-Saxon England*, pp. 227-8.
5. *CS*, 384. The estate was 'at Iognes', but is unidentified. In *CS*, 385, the name is rendered 'Leogeneshamme'. Just possibly it might be Ickham (*PNK*, p. 521).
6. Stenton, *Latin Charters*, p. 41.
7. *CS*, 370, with a full exemption clause. Stevenson pronounced it contemporary. For the topography, see *A.C.*, XLIII, pp. 120-1.
8. *CS*, 367.

and settlements that were to generate an independent life and ultimately to split into separately accounting properties.

Before his departure, Ceolwulf added to the estates which his late brother had transferred to the church in and about Canterbury. In return for a vessel of choice gold and silver worth £5½, Wulfred received an area of 1,800 square feet in addition to what the church held there already, together with twenty-five yokes of arable and five yokes of meadow in the northern suburbs.[1] The piecemeal acquisition of tenements in Canterbury suggests that the archbishop was investing in house property.[2] Some of this would have come into the hands of the monks by the time of Domesday. Other portions of such gains were doubtless incorporated into the medieval archiepiscopal manor of Westgate, the origins of which are not clear, and the structure of which was very scattered.

Ceolwulf was deposed in 823 and succeeded by Beornwulf, who, if the charter may be believed, gave eight ploughlands at Godmersham to Christ Church,[3] and presided over the final settlement with Wulfred. According to this, Cenwulf's daughter Cwoenthrith, abbess of Minster-in-Thanet, was to retain there certain lands of which the archbishop had been deprived, but in return eventually allowed the archbishop to receive Easole in Nonington, near Wingham by Canterbury,[4] and considerable lands in Middlesex.[5] Easole had in fact already been granted to the archbishop by the Earl Aldberht and his sister, but the Middlesex property appears to have been a real *quid pro quo*. Twice within a generation the composition of the Canterbury estates had thus been markedly altered by the powerful wishes of a royal Mercian abbess. Whatever the losses or gains of the moment, however, each of these occasions had brought to the church of Canterbury some valuable property which was to be counted permanently among the archbishop's medieval estates. In 798 it was Northfleet and Teynham; in 823 it was Harrow, Wembley, and other Middlesex land which probably included a portion of Hayes.

It will be noticed how the Middlesex estates of the see, as well as the north Kentish ones, were being augmented during the first half of the ninth century. In addition to the properties just

1. *CS*, 373. Stevenson called it contemporary.
2. Dorothy Whitelock, *The Beginnings of English Society* (Pelican Books, 1952), p. 128.
3. *CS*, 372.
4. *CS*, 378; cf. Stenton, *Latin Charters*, p. 23; *KPN*, pp. 145–56.
5. *CS*, 384–5; Haddan and Stubbs, op. cit., pp. 596–601, 604.

recorded, a grant to Wulfred by King Wiglaf of the Mercians in 831, comprising five ploughlands at Botwell in Hayes, shows by its boundaries that the archbishop was already in possession of land there.[1] This may well have been from Offa's grant in 790.[2] Further, Werhard the priest, whose will is to be discussed immediately, added thirty-two hides of his own patrimony in Hayes, together with the vill of Twickenham, to the possessions of Christ Church.

Werhard was the nephew of Archbishop Wulfred, and a rich man. His will,[3] made in 832, tells us that when his uncle was on his death-bed he had executed a certain writing concerned with the division of his property, and enjoined upon his nephew that he should ultimately return to the church of Canterbury the lands which he had given him. Werhard's will specifies these lands, saying that Wulfred had bought and laboured for them for the use of the *familia*. They were as follows: 104 hides in Harrow, 100 hides in Otford, 32 hides in Graveney, 44 hides in Bishopsbourne, 10 hides in Easole, 36 hides in Barham (in exchange for which Werhard had immediately given Cliffe), some marshland east of Lyminge and some smaller properties round about Canterbury. Attached to the various estates here enumerated were prescribed duties of doing daily alms to fixed quotas of poor people. It would be too much to say that the will sums up the Canterbury estates of the time, for they were already of wider extent than those listed. But the property in Werhard's hands was very considerable and provokes speculation about the reason for his possession of it. The will exists only in a twelfth-century text into which the word *monachi* was interpolated.[4] Gervase, who was concerned to emphasize the monks' rights, was also at pains to say that Wulfred's gift was a 'restoration' to them.[5] What is more, the separate endowment of the convent which Wulfred finally arranged in 811 (the lands round Folkestone and Lyminge) does not seem to feature in Werhard's will. On the contrary, most of the lands which Werhard was given or lent proved ultimately to be especially the archbishop's property. It therefore seems likely that either Wulfred was giving to his nephew his own property, which he wished to be preserved

1. *CS*, 400, described by Stevenson as contemporary.
2. *CS*, 265, and see p. 26 above. This includes land at Hayes, Yedding and Twickenham, but does not mention the vill of Twickenham itself.
3. *CS*, 402; cf. *A.C.*, xliii, pp. 117–20; *KPN*, pp. 166–9.
4. Armitage Robinson, art. cit., p. 235.
5. Gervase, *Opera*, ii, p. 348.

to his church in afterdays (rather as a later landholder might enfeoff a strong and trusted third party to the use of himself or his assigns), or that Wulfred's gift was a straightforward piece of nepotism, designed to benefit his kinsman during his life and the archbishopric thereafter. The second supposition is perhaps the more likely. If Wulfred wanted protection for the church's lands over the period following his death, it is probable that he would have made a more wholesale grant to his nephew. But by granting Harrow, Otford, Bishopsbourne and the rest he was simply manipulating at his will and for his nephew's benefit estates which were not now especially earmarked for the community, though they were later to return to the see, enlarged by a further grant from Werhard's own patrimony. Possibly this was part of a bargain of which Wulfred had knowledge. Inconclusive though the document is, it at least brings into relief the division of the estates, their marked growth in the earlier ninth century, and the power of the archbishop over their disposal.

The long pontificate of Archbishop Ceolnoth (833–70) embraced a period when the rulership of Kent was in irresolute hands, and takes us to the eve of the most serious Danish onslaughts.[1] After the great Wulfredian days, the accumulation of Canterbury estates seems to slacken. Some east Kentish lands, including Ebony and Thanington, and swine pastures in the Tenterden district, may have been added about 833.[2] Archbishop Ceolnoth bestowed some of his own land at Langdon upon his *familia*,[3] and pious folk are said to have given food rent-charges on Mongeham and Challock to the *familia* in the same year.[4] Another rent-charge, from Derbyshire, is attributed to 835,[5] and the grant by Badenoth Beðtting in 837, already referred to,[6] indicates that it was particularly the community at Canterbury that was benefiting during these years. In 838 King Ethelwulf, with the consent of his father Egbert, king of the West Saxons, is said to have given more land to the archbishop at Lyminge.[7] But the most notable document of these years is a record of a council at Kingston in 839, under the presidency of the archbishop, at which Egbert and his son restored to the archbishop the lands at South Malling in Sussex, first given by King Baldred

1. Stenton, *Anglo-Saxon England*, p. 243.
2. *CS*, 407–8: late copies which Stevenson said were not necessarily spurious; cf. *KPN*, p. 172.
3. *CS*, 406.   4. *CS*, 405, 412.   5. *CS*, 414.   6. See above, p. 20
7. *CS*, 419–20, from a bad Middle English copy. See *KPN*, pp. 180–1.

of Kent some years earlier.[1] South Malling, set just north of Lewes, was a vast and permanent possession of the medieval see of Canterbury, with members extending northward into the wealden country.

A purchase of land at Chart near Canterbury by Archbishop Ceolnoth from a local dignitary in 839[2] brings to an end the known activity in estate building during his time, and after the 830s a silence settles until the reign of Alfred. Even when the tale is resumed, the lands specified are small and obscure: an exchange in 871 whereby Canterbury received Chartham from a nobleman in exchange for Croydon, Surrey,[3] leaves it unclear when Croydon had been acquired, or even whether this arrangement was ever effective, since Croydon appears from Domesday onwards as an important manor of the archbishops. A sale by the archbishop in 873 of land in Womenswold for twenty-five mancuses of gold is known from a charter,[4] called contemporary by Stevenson, but not registered in the Canterbury lists of donations. Until the mid tenth century, the lists are occupied with only a few further accessions: an acre at Rotherhithe,[5] marshland in Romney,[6] fields near Canterbury,[7] the lands of Folkestone nunnery, destroyed by the Danes,[8] lands in Meopham, and in Darenth,[9] ultimately to be exchanged with the neighbouring monks of Rochester for Lambeth.

At this point there occurs a spurious charter which may yet, as Birch surmised, be a constructive one belonging to some time after 955, declaring that Kings Edmund, Edred and Edwy had restored 'to the monks' clothing' a whole array of places which have already featured in this narrative:[10] Twickenham, Preston (in Faversham), Swarling, Wingham, Graveney, Bossington (in Adisham), Ulcombe and Tarring (in Sussex). It is worth noting that although Adisham itself is not referred to, Bossington, now Bossington Farm near Adisham, provides a tenuous link between the putative charter of the seventh century and the Domesday manor of Adisham. To this same period in the mid tenth century are attributed some

---

1. *CS*, 421; Haddan and Stubbs, op. cit., III, pp. 617, 624. Stenton, *Latin Charters*, p. 41, implies that this charter is practically contemporary.
2. *CS*, 427.   3. *CS*, 529–30.
4. *CS*, 536; *KPN*, pp. 221–2.   5. *CS*, 577–8.
6. *CS*, 638 (A.D. 914); cf. *CS*, 572.   7. *CS*, 637, 733.
8. *CS*, 660.   9. *CS*, 747; cf. *CS*, 741.
10. *CS*, 766; cf. *CS*, 811, and *KPN*, p. 252.

charters purporting to grant places already held by Christ Church: Twickenham, Reculver, Milton (in Otford) and Meopham.[1]

Though the earlier tenth century is comparatively barren in the history of the endowment, its second half was an age in which substantial estates accrued to Canterbury. Many of the charters have the common characteristic that they record grants of lands outside Kent, bestowed specifically upon the community. Just as at Ely and Ramsey[2] a great part of the endowment sprang from the tenth century, especially its latter half, so at Canterbury a large number of manors which in Domesday are listed as possessions of the monks (and particularly manors at a distance from the monastery) were granted by the kings of Wessex and their greater subjects in this age of religious revival. Such were Patching in Sussex;[3] Lawling, Vange, Bocking, Stisted and Coggeshall in Essex;[4] Monks, Eleigh and Hadleigh in Suffolk;[5] Risborough in Buckinghamshire;[6] and Newington and Britwell in Oxfordshire.[7] Sunbury in Middlesex and Send in Surrey were bought by the archbishop between 960 and 962,[8] but do not appear later either among the monastic or the archiepiscopal properties. In Kent, the manor of Hollingbourne, later a monastic manor, was also acquired at this time.[9]

A circumstantial account of how Eynsford was acquired by the see of Canterbury belongs to these years, and is given an added interest by the future importance of Eynsford as a 'barony' of the see.[10] It is told that Wouldham, a few miles south of Rochester, was given to the church of St Andrew, Rochester, by King Aethelbehrt (II), who committed it to the guardianship of Bishop Eardwulf (747–c.765). The gift was taken away again by kings and kept in their hands until the time of King Edmund (939–46), from whom it

1. CS, 860–1, 880–1, 1049, 1064–5. 1064 is reckoned genuine (F. E. Harmer, Select English Historical Documents of the Ninth and Tenth Centuries (1914), no. xxiii).
2. E. Miller, The Abbey and Bishopric of Ely (1951), ch. II; J. A. Raftis, The Estates of Ramsey Abbey (Toronto, 1957), ch. I.
3. CS, 823, but cf. CS, 1055.
4. CS, 1101–2; Lambeth MS. 1212, pp. 326, 331; Whitelock, Anglo-Saxon Wills, pp. 84, 197–8.
5. Lambeth MS. 1212, pp. 322, 326; Whitelock, op. cit., pp. 6, 38, 147.
6. Lambeth MS. 1212, p. 326; Whitelock, op. cit., pp. 52, 166; KCD, 689, 690.
7. Lambeth MS. 1212, p. 327; KCD, 697.
8. CS, 1063.
9. Lambeth MS. 1212, p. 326, but cf. Whitelock, op. cit., p. 98.
10. Printed by A. J. Robertson, Anglo-Saxon Charters (1939), no. XLI, and dated between 964 and 988.

was bought by a rich man called Aelfstan for 120 mancuses of gold and thirty pounds of silver. Most of this money was paid over by Aelfheah, the son of Aelfstan, on his father's behalf. When King Edmund died, his successor, King Edred, confirmed Wouldham in inheritance to Aelfstan, and Aelfstan's son Aelfheah duly succeeded his father in possession. It appears that Aelfheah received all the lands and money of his dead father, so that his brother Aelfric had none. But 'because they were brothers' Aelfheah relented and gave his brother a group of neighbouring properties, namely, Wouldham, Erith, Cray and Eynsford. The grant was for life only, and when Aelfric died his brother Aelfheah took them back. Aelfric, however, had left a son called Eadric, while Aelfheah had no son. Aelfheah therefore granted Erith, Cray and Wouldham to his nephew Eadric, still keeping back Eynsford for himself. Some time later Eadric too died, leaving a widow but no children, and without having made any arrangements about the disposal of his property. Once again Aelfheah took back the property, but allowed the widow to keep Cray, which Eadric had given her as a marriage-gift. Erith, Wouldham and Littlebrook remained on lease from Aelfheah. He collected his food-rent from Wouldham and intended to do the same from the other properties, but at this point he fell ill and urgently summoned Archbishop Dunstan to him. They met at Shelve near Lenham, a long way from the villages in question: either Aelfheah was visiting widely-dispersed estates to receive the supplies to which he was entitled, or he had simply gone part of the way to meet the archbishop. But here Aelfheah declared his will before the archbishop, appointing one copy to be sent after his death to Christ Church, another to St Andrew's and a third to be given to his widow. After this, the widow took as her second husband a man called Leofsunu, who broke the terms of the will, disdained the archbishop's testimony, and with his wife seized the lands. At once Dunstan counter-claimed, and a remarkable plea was held at Erith, to which there came as witnesses,

Aelfstan, bishop of London, and all the community and that at Christ Church, Aelfstan, bishop of Rochester, the sheriff, [that is] Wulfsige the priest, Brihtwold of Mereworth [near Wrotham], and all the men of East Kent and West Kent. . . . And it was known [the narrative continues] in Sussex and Wessex and Middlesex and Essex that the archbishop with his own oath had secured possession of the estates, which

Leofsunu had usurped, on behalf of God and St Andrew, with the title-deeds on the cross of Christ. And Wulfsige the sheriff, as the king's representative, accepted the oath when Leofsunu refused it. And there were in addition a good thousand men who gave the oath.

The story contains a number of points that bear upon our history of the Canterbury estates and the society that formed and dwelt upon them. The first is the apparent ease with which they could be lost in pre-Conquest times. Then there is the power that well-to-do Kentishmen possessed to do what they would with their own. In Aelfheah's acquisition of the whole of his father's inheritance there is no customary compulsion to partition the estate, yet he had qualms about his brother's failure to receive anything. Again, at the onset of his last illness, there is another example of that train of events so well known in contemporary Christendom: the sudden appeal to ecclesiastical authority and the massive generosity which helped to build up the great church estate. Finally, the archbishop's plea at Erith, backed by many men of influence and by the king's sheriff (himself a priest), sets him in the succession of archbishops who with oath and argument defended the church's property, from Wulfred negotiating in the ninth century against overbearing royalty, to Lanfranc in the eleventh century recovering two dozen manors from the grip of Norman opportunists. Eynsford remained to the archbishopric, and is discovered in Domesday enfeoffed to a knightly family whose first known member bore a Scandinavian name.[1]

The wave of grants, which in the later tenth century had brought to Canterbury many of its permanent possessions in the south-eastern counties, continued with slackening momentum into the eleventh century. By 1018 Warehorne and possibly Farningham in Kent, and Merstham and Cheam in Surrey, were in the possession of Christ Church.[2]

The reign of Cnut (1016–35) appropriately fastens attention upon the sea-coast. The port of Sandwich may have first come to the church of Canterbury earlier, but its grant in 1023 with an extraordinary set of customs and privileges is likely, on historical grounds, to be an authentic record.[3] During the same period

1. *Dom. Mon.*, pp. 44–7.   2. Lambeth MS. 1212, pp. 328–9.
3. *CS*, 1185 (A.D. 972–3); Lambeth MS. 1212, p. 326; Stenton, *Latin Charters*, p. 17, and references there. The witnesses in Domesday imply that King Edward gave the borough to the church (*D.B.*, I, p. 3).

Folkestone was re-granted, and Saltwood near Hythe bestowed by one of Cnut's magnates.[1]

A handful of doubtful charters are dated from the late Old English period. They refer to places that later appear as monastic possessions,[2] but although the documents themselves were concocted long after the events, the acquisitions had in reality been made earlier. An example of this type is a confirmation by King Ethelred in 1006 to Christ Church of 'the substance to the church of monks newly placed there',[3] and the estates thus confirmed, 'bestowed by kings and others from most ancient times', range over the east Kentish territories of Thanet, Eastry, Adisham, Appledore and so forth, to the distant monastic manors in Sussex, Surrey, Essex, Suffolk and Buckinghamshire. All are in the monastic list in Domesday. From the character of this document and by analogy with that now to be described the confirmation itself appears to belong to the early Norman age.

An even more comprehensive title-deed is the confirmation by 'King Edward' to Christ Church, Canterbury, and the monks there of all lands they held, whether given by king, archbishop or others.[4] The places lie in seven counties and form an almost duplicate list of the estates credited to the monks in the Domesday survey. Although the first part of the document is in a hand of the Confessor's time, the place-names seem to have been written in towards the end of the eleventh century. The very order of the places corresponds closely with that in the *Domesday Monachorum*. It looks as if the monks of the Norman age, faced with the problem of claiming and re-assembling estates lost in the confusion of the Conquest, took trouble to describe their property more systematically and to give it the appearance of having been authoritatively confirmed to them in the recent past.

The Norman age was in the history of the Canterbury estates one of serious loss followed by painstaking recovery. Though Lanfranc himself is not wholly free from the suspicion of acquiring lands

1. Lambeth MS. 1212, pp. 330, 407; *KCD*, 742.
2. Appledore, East Horsley (Surrey), Godmersham, West Thurrock (Essex), Mersham (Kent) and Walworth (Surrey), all in Lambeth MS. 1212, pp. 329–331.
3. Lambeth MS. 1212, pp. 327–8; *KCD*, 715.
4. Lambeth MS. 1212, p. 331; *KCD*, 896; cf. B. W. Kissan, art. cit., p. 287, and Stenton, *V.C.H. Oxfordshire*, I (1939), p. 377 and *n*.

which were not his before,[1] the credit for the restoration of seized lands to Canterbury and other Kentish churches is also chiefly his. The process of bringing order out of chaos must incidentally have helped to sharpen the already existing division between the lands of the monks and those of the archbishopric. The texts of Domesday and the *Domesday Monachorum* are proof enough of such a conscious effort.

When Lanfranc, who became archbishop in 1070, surveyed the losses which Kentish churches had sustained, it would have been plain that the principal culprit was Odo, bishop of Bayeux, the king's half-brother. Eadmer wrote of this man's dominating position and his large-scale invasion of church lands and liberties which none had been able to resist. To the Domesday scribes and the writers of the documents that will be discussed below, Odo was simply 'the bishop'. He also had a powerful following of vassals. Men like Herbert son of Ivo, Osbern Paisforer, Thorold of Rochester and Ralph of Courbépine had commandeered or been placed in possession of church lands during the years of the Conquest, especially where such lands had been in the possession of defeated English magnates. The problem was a general one in Kent and in England at large.[2]

The earliest formal record of the recovery of these estates tells us that the king ordered a meeting of the shire court, at which Frenchmen and Englishmen who knew about the ancient laws and customs were required to attend, in order that the possessions and liberties of Christ Church might be reclaimed. The present concern is with the lands rather than the liberties. The meeting took place in 1075 at the customary site on Penenden Heath, near Maidstone. During the three days of its session Lanfranc succeeded in establishing the claims of his own church to Detling and Preston,

1. At four places in Hertfordshire the survey describes Lanfranc as holding land which before the Conquest had been held by Aelfric, a man of Archbishop Stigand, partly from Stigand and partly from Westminster Abbey. Round pointed out that Lanfranc, when he secured the lands that Aelfric had held of Stigand, annexed also the lands belonging to Westminster Abbey because Aelfric was their tenant. 'This was the way in which religious houses frequently lost their lands at the time of the Norman Conquest.' (*V.C.H. Hertfordshire*, I (1902), pp. 275, 305.)
2. Gundulf was occupied in 1089 in coming to agreement about usurpations with Richard de Clare. For what follows here see the account printed in translation in *English Historical Documents 1042–1189*, ed. D. C. Douglas and G. W. Greenaway (1953), pp. 449–51, together with the bibliography of modern literature, to which should be added D. M. Stenton, *English Justice between the Norman Conquest and the Great Charter* (1965), p. 18.

and those of the church of Rochester to Stoke and Denton, near Rochester, all from Odo of Bayeux; also the claims of Canterbury to Ruckinge and Brook from Hugh de Montfort, and to 60s. worth of pasture in the Isle of Grain from Ralph de Courbépine.

Considering the elaborate preparations which had been made for the hearing, this seems a mediocre result. The church's liberties were conceded, but no further Canterbury estates, and no specifically archbishopric estates, if such there were, were recovered for the moment. But matters did not rest there, for the documents make it clear that the claim was pursued throughout the Conqueror's reign against the resistance of Odo and others, and was brought only slowly to its more or less successful end.

The next landmark is the memorandum of an inquiry held about 1078 or 1079, probably by a royal official who was investigating the still-disputed property.[1] Here is a translation:

Folkestone is the king's benefice. Richborough belongs to the archbishopric, and [Archbishop] Eadsige [1038–50] gave it to Godwin. Statenborough belongs to the archbishopric, and Christ Church was in possession of it when the king crossed the sea, and now the bishop of Bayeux has it. In Tilmanstone, when the king crossed the sea, Christ Church was in possession of 200 *jugera* of land; and in Finglesham of 100, and in Elme[2] of 25; and now Osbern Paisforer holds them from the archbishop. Aethelnoth [or Alnodchild] held Totesham of the monks when the king crossed the sea, and rendered them farm for it, and now the bishop [of Bayeux] has it. Torentun [Tottington in Aylesford?][3] has twenty-five *jugera*, and Christ Church had it when the king crossed the sea, and lately the bishop had it but leased it. Christ Church had Wittersham when the king crossed the sea, and now Osbern Paisforer has it from the bishop. When the king crossed the sea the church had *Auuentingesherst* and *Edrunesland*[4] and *Aduuoluuinden* [Adelwesden in Rolvenden],[5] and had the farm thereof, and now Robert of Romney has them from the bishop. Preston [east of Canterbury] was held by Aethelnoth when the king crossed the sea, and he rendered farm, and

1. Brit. Mus. Cottonian MS. Aug. II, 36. Fascimile, transcription and discussion in Douglas, art. cit. A transcript of the document not noted by Professor Douglas was also made into the Canterbury register, Lambeth MS. 1212, pp. 336–7.
2. Despite Wallenberg (*PNK*, p. 431), this was most probably *Aelmesland* in Lyminge, and not Elham. cf. *Dom. Mon.*, p. 84, and *KPN*, p. 25.
3. Held in *D.B.* of the king 'by the new gift of the bishop of Bayeux' (fo. 7), though there is no sign it had been held by Christ Church.
4. Unidentified, but it was, like the *Elme* above, in Lyminge, and some twenty miles from Rolvenden.
5. *PNK*, p. 350.

now Thorold has it from the bishop. Godric the dean gave to his brother a quarter-sulung that belonged to St Margaret-at-Cliffe, and now Robert William has it from the archbishop. Sundridge belongs to the archbishopric, and the archbishop gave it to Godwin, and now the bishop has it. Langport and Newenden belong to the archbishopric, and the archbishop gave them to Godwin, and the bishop acknowledged at once in the trial (*in placito*) that they belonged to the church. Saltwood belongs to the archbishopric, and the archbishop gave it Godwin, and now Hugh [de Montfort] has it as a gift from the king.

Archbishop Lanfranc made other claims against the bishop and against Hugh, but they are to be determined in the hundreds.

Pimpe [in East Farleigh] and *Chinton* [Kennington near Chart][1] and *Uuestaldingis* [Yalding near Maidstone][2] were held by Adalredus from the archbishop, and now Richard [fitzGilbert of Clare] has them. Penshurst belongs to the archbishopric, and the archbishop held it when the king crossed the sea, and had *census* and farm from it.

The archbishop before Eadsige [i.e. Aethelnoth, 1020–38] had the third penny of the county, but in Eadsige's time King Edward gave it to Godwin.

They have witnessed that all the lands which belong to the archbishopric and to St Augustine's abbey, and Earl Godwin's lands, are free of all royal custom except for the ancient roads which lead from city to city, market to market, and sea-port to sea-port.

In the matter of the claim which Bishop Odo made to the meadow-lands of the archbishop and St Augustine's, they all judge him unjust,[3] and say that the meadow-lands of either church ought, like the other lands, to be free.

The land given to Godwin[4] belongs to the church of St Augustine, and when the king crossed the sea the church had the service from that land, and now Hugh has it of the king's gift.

This full memorandum was once thought to be a statement of proceedings in the Penenden plea. But only a few of the places alluded to appear in any of the Penenden reports, and, on the other hand, most of the localities dealt with in the Penenden

1. ibid., p. 414.
2. ibid., p. 168; cf. *D.B.*, fo. 14, where Aldret is said to have held Yalding of King Edward.
3. Professor Douglas transcribed this passage '*iudicaverunt omnes quod in iusticia haberet et prata utriusque ecclesie sicut cetere terre libera esse deberent*'. But the sense requires *iniusticiam haberet*. This reading seems likely from *Domesday Monachorum* itself, and is confirmed by the transcript in Lambeth MS. 1212, p. 337.
4. Both MSS. have '*Terra Goduini dame*', possibly in error for *Goduino data* or *Goduini manu*.

documents are not referred to in this memorandum. It is much more likely to be an impartial statement, written possibly by a royal clerk at some moment between the Penenden trial and the Domesday survey, concerning the landed interests of the great local churches: St Augustine's, Canterbury, St Martin's, Dover, and Rochester Cathedral besides Christ Church. However much Lanfranc was a prime mover in the litigation, with his own church specially at heart, the present memorandum emphasizes that the whole plea was wide in scope and protracted in time. What had not been settled at Penenden or up to the time of writing was to be referred to the hundred courts. A multitude of local decisions were to be taken, the traces of which can be glimpsed occasionally in the Domesday documents.

Clearly, too, the alienations of land from church possession of which Eadmer writes so feelingly had not begun with the Norman invaders. A quarter of a century before, the powerful Godwin, earl of Wessex, had in some circumstances received from the archbishop Richborough, Sundridge, Langport, Newenden and Saltwood, as well as the 'third penny' of the county, and these had come into Norman hands. The great English landowner known as Alnod Cild, or Aethelnoth of Canterbury, had also established some sort of lordship, even if legal, over Canterbury property which, when he disappeared as hostage into Normandy in 1067, fell to the power of Odo or Odo's men.[1]

But in the years between Penenden and Domesday the most massive figure which stood between ecclesiastical property and its claimants was Odo, either himself or through the men he had favoured and enfeoffed. His grip was not broken until after the date of the survey, and *Domesday Monachorum* as well as the survey itself witnesses to his continuing territorial strength. Yet somehow, through the pertinacity of Lanfranc and the testimony of unknown countrymen, the process of recovery was well begun before that time. We need not credit the vision of Dunstan said to have been beheld by Lanfranc in order to marvel at the success of his manoeuvres. A few properties, especially in north Kent, had been won back at the original Penenden plea. Some time later, as the memorandum tells us, Odo had been brought to acknowledge the church of Canterbury's right to Newenden and Langport, and had been condemned by sworn men in his possession of unspecified

1. *V.C.H. Surrey*, I (1902), p. 282: introduction to Domesday text by J. H. Round.

meadow-lands. If we examine more closely the relationship between this memorandum (attributed by Professor Douglas to 1078-9) and the Domesday survey, we become aware of Lanfranc's continued if not unqualified success. By 1086 he had got back Statenborough from Odo and enfeoffed his own knight, William Folet, upon it. He had further enfeoffed Folet with land at Tilmanstone, Finglesham and Lyminge which Osbern Paisforer had previously held. (Paisforer had been somewhat committed to Odo and was never so substantial a Canterbury tenant as was Folet.) Lanfranc had recovered more land at Lyminge ('Edrunesland') from the lordship of Odo and enfeoffed his own man there. Similarly, he had recovered Sundridge in north Kent, which like Lydd in Romney Marsh, previously regained, was made to supply a knight for the archbishop.[1] By 1086 the lordship of Saltwood had been recovered from the king by Lanfranc 'to the profit of the church'.[2] Only in Tottington, Pimpe, Wittersham and the small denn of Adelwesden had the archbishop failed to shake off what were believed in the memorandum to be usurpations. Tottington was given by Odo to the king shortly before 1087. Pimpe passed from Odo to Richard of Clare, though most of East Farleigh remained to the monks. In Wittersham and Rolvenden (where Adelwesden lay), Odo remained chief lord. Sandlings in St Mary Cray had also fallen to Odo and was permanently lost to the monks who had originally held it.

The memorandum is a chance survival, illustrating rather than exhaustively describing a strenuous web of negotiations, but it is valuable none the less. A more general appraisal of Lanfranc's achievement in bringing back church property to church possession is to be had from later statements of Canterbury writers. Milo Crispin wrote that Lanfranc recovered twenty-five manors by ecclesiastical process.[3] This figure is nearly matched by the monk who wrote an obituary notice of William I in a twelfth-century Canterbury book, and noted twenty-seven properties which he said the king in his time had caused to be returned to their ecclesiastical lords. This obituary has also been printed

---

1. Stenton pointed out in the case of the under-endowed see of Lincoln that William's favour towards the acquisition of land by churches was given with an eye to the *servitium debitum* which the church in question was to provide (*Anglo-Saxon England*, p. 626). This may apply in some measure to the Canterbury recoveries.
2. Lambeth MS. 1212, pp. 15, 332.
3. Cited by A. J. Macdonald, *Lanfranc* (1926), p. 129.

before,[1] but may be given here in English since it offers a useful and comprehensive list of the recovered lands:

William king of the English died. He returned to the church of Christ almost all the lands taken away in ancient and recent times from the right of the church. The names of these lands are as follows: in Kent, Reculver, Sandwich, Richborough, Wootton,[2] the monastery of Lyminge with the lands and customs belonging to it, Saltwood with the borough of Hythe belonging to Saltwood, Langport, Newenden, Ruckinge, Detling, Preston not far from the river Medway [in Aylesford?],[3] Sundridge, Crayford, Orpington, Eynsford, Denton, Stoke, the four prebends of Newington, and besides all these many other little territories both on and off the islands in Kent.[4] Stoke and Denton Lanfranc returned to the church of St Andrew [Rochester] since they were anciently in the right of that church. In Surrey, Mortlake; in London, the monastery of St Mary [le Bow] with the lands and houses which Living the priest and his wife had in London; in Middlesex, Harrow and Hayes; in Buckinghamshire, Risborough and Halton; in Oxfordshire, Newington; in Suffolk, Freckenham; and this vill Lanfranc returned to the church of St Andrew to which it used of old to belong; in Essex, Stisted and Stambridge. He returned all these things for the sake of God and his soul's salvation, freely and without price.

The list of recovered properties is a general one, belonging to the whole period of William I's reign and not to a single episode. The obituary includes the half-dozen manors mentioned in the original Penenden accounts, as well as Langport and Newenden, disgorged by Odo in *c*. 1078–9, and about nineteen other estates which must have been regained between then and the time of the survey, when all the manors in the list had been returned to their rightful possessors.

To follow these documents is to become convinced that 'Domesday Book is not a record in isolation',[5] but the climax of a

---

1. Le Patourel, art. cit., in *Studies . . . presented to F. M. Powicke*, esp. pp. 18–19, 24–6. This obituary was also copied with minor alterations into Lambeth MS. 1212, p. 13.
2. Le Patourel suggested Wootton, Sussex. But this is a Kentish list of names. It is probably Wootton near Bishopsbourne, which had been granted along with Giddinge to Christ Church in 687 or 799 (*CS*, pp. 69, 296). See also *KPN*, p. 15, and *Cart. of St Gregory's Priory*, p. 2.
3. *PNK*, p. 146.
4. e.g. the 60*s*. worth of pasture in the Isle of Grain recovered from Ralph de Courbépine at Penenden.
5. Douglas, art. cit., p. 56.

series of judicial inquiries which had occupied the 1070s and 1080s.

If the work of recovery was not even then quite complete, it will none the less be useful to pass in review (in Table 1) the properties which at that moment were described as belonging to the church of Canterbury. This will provide a summary of the estates, and a natural term to the chronology of the endowment.

TABLE 1. *Properties of the see of Canterbury as arranged in Domesday Book*

Note: Assessments are given as they were in 1086, in sulungs (s.), hides (h.) or carucates (c.). Variations to these assessments in *Domesday Monachorum* are shown in the footnotes.

Properties known to have been recovered for the church by Lanfranc, in whole or in part, are prefixed with the letter R.

Manors assigned to the lists of the archbishopric and of the monks of which nevertheless some portion or member was held in fee by a knight of the see at this time are prefixed with the letter F.

KENT

Archbishopric[1]		Archbishop's Knights		Monks[2]	
Canterbury		Farningham	1s.	RF Orpington	2½s.
32 burgages[3]					
R Sandwich[4]		R Eynsford	6s.	East Peckham[5]	5¼s.
383 burgages					
Darenth	2s.	R Orpington	3¼s.	Hollingbourne	6s.
F Otford	8s.	Brasted	1½s.	Meopham	7s.
RF Sundridge	1½s.	Ulcombe	2s.	F East Farleigh[6]	6s.
Bexley	2s.	Boughton		Cliffe	3½s.
		Malherbe[7]	½s.		
R Erhede[8]	4s.	Leaveland	1s.	Monkton	18s.
East Malling	2s.	Graveney[9]	1s.	F Ickham	4s.
Northfleet	5s.	Lenham	2s.	Northgate[10] near	
				Canterbury	1s.
F Wrotham	8s.	Sheppey	½s.	Seasalter 'a small	
				borough'	

1. In *Dom. Mon.*, the following are also listed among the archbishop's manors: Teynham (5½s.), of which Godfrey of Malling held ½s. either in fee or in leasehold, and Newington near Sittingbourne (four prebends).
2. In *Dom. Mon.* the monks' list includes *Saendlinge* (St Mary Cray), but though claimed by the monks it was then, as in 1086, in the hands of Odo of Bayeux.
3. Held by 'the clerks of the vill for their gild'. It is apparent that in *Dom. Mon.* the canons of St Gregory's are meant.
4. Assigned in *D.B.* to the monks though it appears under the archbishop's heading. In *Dom. Mon.* it is also assigned to the monks and consisted of 383 *mansurae*.

Archbishopric		Archbishop's Knights		Monks	
RF Maidstone[1]	10s.	Buckland	¼s.	R Preston	1s.
F Gillingham	6s.	R Tilmanstone	1s.	Chartham	4s.
R Reculver	8s.	R Finglesham	½s.	Godmersham	8s.
F Northwood[2]	13s.	R Statenborough	½s.	Great Chart	3s.
F Petham[3]	7s.	R Saltwood[4]	3s.	F Little Chart	2½h.[5]
F Westgate[6]	7s.	Berwick in Lympne	½s.	Westwell	5s.
Bishopsbourne	6s.	R Langport[7]	1½s.	Eastry	7s.
Boughton-under-Blean	5½s.			R Giddinge in Wootton[8]	¾s.+ 5 acres
Charing[9]	8s.			F Adisham	17s.
Pluckley	1s.			Warehorne	1s.
F Wingham	35s.			Appledore	1s.
F Mersham[10]	3s.			R Brook[11]	½s.
F Aldington[12]	15s.			R Asmelant[13]	1s.
RF Lyminge[14]	7s.				
R Newenden[15]	1s.				

1. In *Dom. Mon.* ½s. at *Burricestune* in Maidstone was assigned to the monks.
2. Now in Whitstable.
3. In *Dom. Mon.* ½s. at Swarling in Petham was assigned to the monks.
4. Saltwood included 225 burgesses at Hythe. Assessed in *Dom. Mon.* at 5s.
5. In *Dom. Mon.* assessed at 2½s.
6. MS. *Estursete* (see p. 48). *Dom. Mon.* adds seven *mansurae* in Fordwich.
7. Langport included twenty-one burgesses in Romney.
8. *Dom. Mon.* says Giddinge belonged to Eastry, though '*in alia parte*'.
9. In *Dom. Mon.* assessed at 7½s.
10. In *Dom. Mon.* assigned to the monks.
11. In *Dom. Mon.* assessed at 1s.
12. Aldington included eighty-five burgesses in Romney. In *Dom. Mon.* it was assessed at 20s.
13. '*Elmesland*', in Romney Marsh.
14. Lyminge included six burgesses in Hythe.
15. In *Dom. Mon.* assigned to the monks and said to be subject to Saltwood. It was probably Newenden near Sandhurst.

---

5. Assessed at 6s. in *Dom. Mon.*
6. In *Dom. Mon.* 1s. at Loose and ½s. at *Huntindune* (Hunton) belonging to the parent manor of East Farleigh were also assigned to the monks.
7. Part of Hollingbourne.
8. Crayford, not Erith.
9. Part of Boughton-under-Blean. In *Dom. Mon.* 1s. in Graveney was listed under the monks' lands, since the feudal tenant rendered farm also to them.
10. MS. *Nordewude*.

SUSSEX[1]

Archbishopric		*Monks*	
F South Malling	75h.	Wootton	4½h.
F Pagham	34h.	Patching	3h. 3½ virgates
Tangmere	6h.	Tarring[2]	7h. 1 virgate
East Lavant	9½h.		
Stanmer[3]	20h.		

SURREY

F Croydon	16h. 1 virgate	Cheam	4h.
R Mortlake	25h.	F Walworth	?
		Merstham	?
		East Horsley	?

MIDDLESEX

RF Hayes	59h.
RF Harrow	100h.

OXFORDSHIRE

Oxford	7 dwellings (4 waste)
F Newington	15h.

HERTFORDSHIRE[4]

Datchworth	1h.
Watton	2½h.
Sheephall[5]	2h.
Libury	2 acres
Stuochampe [Sacomb?]	½ virgate

1. Outside Kent there is no separate list for the archbishop's knights, but manors in which there were knight's fees are marked F, as before.
2. Tarring subsequently belonged to the archbishopric, though it is noted in *D.B.* '*semper fuit in monasterio*'.
3. Stanmer was held until the Dissolution by the canons of South Malling College from the archbishop. Sixteen hides at Stanmer were supposedly given in 765 by King Aldwulf of the South Saxons to build a monastery (*CS*, 197; *Sussex Archaeological Collections*, LXXXVI (1947), pp. 85–90).
4. All the Hertfordshire properties were either totally enfeoffed or totally farmed.
5. Sheephall was held by Anschitil de Ros of the archbishop, but at the end of William I's reign the abbot of St Alban obtained restoration of these two hides (H. Chauncy, *History . . . of Hertfordshire*, II (1826), pp. 413–14).

BUCKINGHAMSHIRE[1]

Nidreham [Cuddington and Haddenham?]	40h.	R Halton	5h.
		R Risborough	30h.

ESSEX

Little Coggeshall	3 virgates
Bocking	4½h.
East Mersea[2]	2h.
R Stisted	½h.
Lawling	14h.
Latchingdon	2h.
West Newland	3h.
Milton Hall	2h.
Southchurch	4h.
RF Little Stambridge	1h.

SUFFOLK

Moulton	7c.
Hadleigh	5c.
Monks Eleigh	5c.
Topesfield[3]	½c.

This table, based upon the Exchequer Domesday, will show at a glance the possessions of the archbishop and of the monks, and the enfeoffments that had been made to the knights of the see. It will show, too, that the property of the archbishopric was in the aggregate much more extensive than that of the monks, particularly because of its huge possessions outside Kent, at South Malling in Sussex and at Harrow and Hayes in Middlesex. It is problematical why the Domesday scribes chose to record separately the 'Lands of the Knights' in Kent. Possibly they listed in this way the manors which could easily be regarded as *wholly* enfeoffed. They were certainly not comprehensive about this, for some manors

1. The Buckinghamshire manors are listed in *D.B.* as 'the land of Archbishop Lanfranc', but Halton and Risborough are known subsequently to have belonged to the monks.
2. Part of Bocking.
3. Topesfield was willed to Christ Church by a free woman called Leveva, but probably never transferred.

shown in demesne had none the less considerable portions in fee, while a small member of Hollingbourne like Boughton Malherbe was noted apart as an enfeoffment. This means that the picture of the Canterbury enfeoffments, to be discussed in the next chapter, will have to be composed with care after inspecting the complete Domesday text, and not merely taken from the list of *Terrae Militum*.

Another important point concerns the changes after Domesday. Between 1086 and the *Domesday Monachorum* some fourteen years intervene. When about 1100 the church of Canterbury produced this survey for its own purposes, both the substance and the arrangement of the resulting document differed somewhat from those of the survey itself. Not only had the 'Lands of the Knights' as a separate category disappeared, but some rearrangement of estates as between archbishops and monks had also taken place. These changes are shown in the notes and need not be rehearsed here, but it must be realized that the process of adjustment and recovery continued into the twelfth century. Henry I, for instance, returned to the church of Canterbury the village of Slindon in Sussex 'which had been violently alienated for some years and had come recently into the king's hand';[1] and Eadmer tells us that Anselm himself recovered lands from laymen who claimed them in inheritance.[2] The Canterbury cartulary records Anselm's return to the monks of Stisted in Essex 'which pertains and is known to pertain to their property'.[3] In the time of Archbishop William of Corbeil (1122–36), too, jurors appeared before him at Wrotham and gave evidence about the interests which the Clare family had in three Canterbury estates: Meopham with Cooling, East Peckham and East Farleigh,[4] and the exact boundaries between the archbishop's fee and the Tonbridge lowy were discussed.

But all in all these changes were marginal, and the *corpus* of the estates as they were during the course of the Middle Ages was substantially the same as described in Domesday Book. The present discussion may be ended by making a general review of

---

1. Lambeth MS. 1212, p. 25; *Regesta Regum Anglo-Normannorum*, ed. C. Johnson and H. Cronne, II (1956), no. 756. Though situated among the west Sussex manors, no early reference to Slindon has been found.
2. *Historia Novorum*, ed. M. Rule (*R.S.* 81, 1884), p. 219.
3. Lambeth MS. 1212, p. 333.
4. ibid., p. 340; cf. R. S. Hoyt, 'A Pre-Domesday Kentish Assessment List', in *A Medieval Miscellany for Doris Mary Stenton*, Pipe Roll Society n.s. 36 (1962), p. 196, who suggests the date of this inquest may be 1136.

them, and deciding what contact can be established between the survey and the past.

If we look backward from these Norman lists of manors, it is not easy to find clear and detailed continuity with Anglo-Saxon England. Many of the place-names occur in Domesday for the first time, and it is not often possible to prove convincingly that they correspond with places granted in Old English times. To confine attention to the archbishopric possessions: the names of Wrotham, Maidstone, Gillingham, Petham, *Estursete*, Boughton-under-Blean, Pluckley and Aldington, all of major importance, have not been found in pre-Conquest documents. As has been suggested,[1] Aldington, Petham and Gillingham may have been represented by other names, for Lydd, Lympne and Stowting were in Aldington, Swarling in Petham, and Rainham and *Appincglond* in the neighbourhood of Gillingham, and all these appear in Anglo-Saxon charters. *Estursete* (or *Stursaete* as the *Domesday Monachorum* has it) may with tolerable certainty be identified with the complex of archiepiscopal lands in Canterbury later forming the manor of Westgate. Grants of land in Canterbury and by the Stour are recorded from the ninth century at latest.[2] *Estursete* in 1086 included St Martin's, Canterbury, and as late as 1512 *Stoursete* was the name of a borgh in the manor of Westgate which embraced Tylerhill, two miles north of the city.[3] In other cases, one must conclude that pre-Conquest evidences for important medieval manors have perished.

Changes occurred in the names of Kentish manors because of the very nature of the countryside. Students of medieval history, who are almost too fond of using the word 'manor', may sometimes slip into the habit of visualizing a unit of more or less compact property which will bear the name of some lastingly important vill within its bounds. But the Kentish manor was more often a scattering of discrete parcels, of arable, pasture, marsh and relatively distant woodland which might itself undergo cultivation in the course of time and form new permanent settlements. We have examples of this in the woodland members of large manors like Aldington and Otford, which were called *Walda*, or Weald, and which by the thirteenth century had hived off into virtually independent manors rendering just the same kind of dues as came from

1. Above, pp. 17–18.   2. *CS*, 344, 373.
3. L.R. 1162. My attention was called to this by Dr William Urry.

48

any other Kentish manor. Even in Domesday Book, the scattered nature of manors is often readily seen: portions of Aldington were said to lie in Romney, Lympne and Stowting. Discrete manors like this were naturally intermixed with the parcels of other manors to form a tenurial patchwork of great complexity. William I's obituary referred to 'the many other little territories both on and off the islands of Kent'.[1] Inspection of the pre-Domesday charters likewise suggests a bewildering variety in the physical reality of church property, whether it was the rectangular *jugera* at Rotherhithe in 898,[2] the messuages in Canterbury and its suburbs, the distant wood-pastures appurtenant to the settlements,[3] the scattered meadows, or the ploughlands, yokes and fields themselves which, when they are designated, were obviously sprinkled over the land-scape.[4] Small wonder that a property sometimes changed its name.

Hence, because of the partial disappearance of evidences, because of the chequered history of the estates, and because of their physical character, it is not reasonable to expect that a very close correspondence can be worked out between the original deeds of endowment and the Domesday form of the temporalities.

What of the general geographical character of the archbishops' temporalities? The third map[5] shows demesne manors of both archbishopric and priory thickly spread and intermingled in east Kent. In Canterbury the archbishop had property, his palace, and in Norman times his monastic home, and the largest of his Kentish estates was at Wingham, five miles to the east, on the road to the port of Sandwich. Wingham was an immense manor composed of many villages as well as of demesne, and interspersed with portions belonging to other lordships. He had other large and profitable manors in east Kent: Northwood (now in Whitstable), Reculver, and large tracts of woodland which still extend to the west and north of the cathedral city. South of Canterbury, on the downland and about Romney Marsh, lay the second major complex of his property, centred in Aldington, which was later to be the richest bailiwick of all. On the coast he had property, burgesses and juris-diction in the ports of Hythe and Romney. Domesday describes

1. See above, p. 42. The nature of Kentish settlement was, of course, analysed in brilliant fashion by the late J. E. A. Jolliffe in *Pre-Feudal England: the Jutes* (1933). It is right that the work of this undervalued thinker should be especially acknowledged.
2. *CS*, 578.
3. e.g. *CS*, 322–3.
4. e.g. *CS*, 373–4, 637.
5. See p. 195.

these burgesses as belonging to manors outside the ports them-selves, namely, to Aldington, Langport, Saltwood and Lyminge. Although the archbishop during the Middle Ages held jurisdiction and the right to nominate the bailiffs of Hythe and Romney, his lordship was here less direct than that which he enjoyed over his demesne manors, for they belonged to the privileged federation of the Cinque Ports.[1] A third and more scattered group of manors lay across mid Kent, and included Boughton-under-Blean, Charing, Teynham, Gillingham and Maidstone. These would later form the bailiwick of Maidstone. In north Kent a well-defined group looked to Otford and included, reading from the Thames southwards, Northfleet, Crayford, Bexley, Darenth, Wrotham and Sundridge.

The finger which traces the routes from the Channel north-westwards along the ancient arable lowlands on either side of the North Downs and thus to London will never stray far from archiepiscopal property. It can hardly be accidental that the pattern emerged thus, or that the chain of his lordships from Canterbury to London was completed by the Surrey manors of Croydon and Mortlake, giving access to the world of Westminster, and aug-mented in the late twelfth century by the central and riverside manor of Lambeth, taken in exchange for Darenth.

After Kent, the county richest in the archbishops' manors was Sussex. Here they lay in two groupings. In the eastern part of the county the great manor of South Malling ramified itself north-wards into the Weald, flourished and put forth new members in the Middle Ages. Away in the west by Chichester and Bognor, the manor of Pagham also presided over an ancient collection of properties and gave its name eventually to another of the medieval bailiwicks.

North of the Thames, the archbishop possessed in demesne the very large manors of Hayes and Harrow in Middlesex, but other-wise the more northerly possessions of the see were less important. The Hertfordshire manors were infeudated and never came into demesne. Those in Oxfordshire, Buckinghamshire, Suffolk and Essex, not numerous in any case, belonged mostly to the monks. It may, however, be recalled that in all these areas which lay outside the ecclesiastical diocese of Canterbury but where the archbishops had from ancient times been territorial lords, the

1. cf. K. M. E. Murray, *The Constitutional History of the Cinque Ports* (Manchester, 1935), chs. I and II.

churches remained subject to his special jurisdiction and patronage, outside the scope of the archdeacon of Canterbury, and often organized under a special Dean into a jurisdictional 'peculiar'.

Such were the Domesday nuclei of the archbishopric's lands. The largest of them were indeed vast. Wingham, Aldington and Otford, South Malling and Pagham, Croydon, Hayes and Harrow are outstanding examples of huge Old English estates, once transferred from royal to church lordship, and each covering many square miles with their constituent villages and fields. In time they were destined to break up. As populations increased and cultivation extended, the map of the same estates will come to look more complex. But in essence the Canterbury endowment was complete by the Conqueror's day, great even by comparison with Continental church lordships.

CHAPTER 3

The knights of the archbishopric

THE ARCHBISHOP'S ENFEOFFMENTS

According to Matthew Paris it was in 1070 that the Conqueror obliged his tenants-in-chief to supply him with the service of certain quotas of knights. It was in this year, too, that Lanfranc became archbishop of Canterbury, and so was brought suddenly to face the new requirement of finding sixty knights for the king. Although there was no strict need to supply these knights with their own estates in respect of their feudal duties, Lanfranc obviously acted rapidly and completely in enfeoffing them, and when he died in 1089 a good many more knights' fees had already been created out of the Canterbury estates than the sixty which would have been enough to endow his obligation. No texts of this age can give a wholly satisfying picture of feudal arrangements, but the see of Canterbury is fortunate in possessing not only a careful account of the knights' lands as they were in 1086, from the pen of a royal clerk, but also its own, nearly contemporary, version of the great survey (in which some names of tenants otherwise unknown were incorporated), and in addition a list of the archbishop's knights dating from 1093–6, which may be collated backwards in time with Domesday itself and forwards with another fine list, made in 1171. Accordingly, the historian has an unrivalled opportunity to look at a great honour, both in the men who composed it, the property they held and, in a slighter degree, the services and actions of their public lives.

The bare facts of Domesday and *Domesday Monachorum* tell

nothing of the archbishop's own attitude in the years after his arrival in England. Monks and clergy of Norman England who saw church lands falling into the hands of adventurers often wrote in disapproving or even bitter terms, complaining of the favour shown by their prelates to kinsmen or friends at their churches' expense. In a mood to excuse, they might argue that such grants could not be helped, or even that to enfeoff the necessary knights with church lands was better than to endure their presence in the precincts.[1] What was true of one part of the country was not necessarily true of another, but obviously the circumstances of the enfeoffment depended upon the motives of three parties: the king, the tenant-in-chief, and the feudatories themselves. Although their minds can never certainly be known, the situation of each must at least be considered. The king himself, there is reason to think, maintained the idea that church lands ought in some measure to support knights directly. At Lincoln he granted Bishop Remigius numerous new manors, which were then rapidly enfeoffed.[2] At Canterbury, where the favour he showed for the large-scale recovery of possessions to the church's dominion earned him the gratitude of religious men, the restored lands themselves were in many instances soon enfeoffed, and some appear to have passed straight from unlawful tenure to licit infeudation without first returning to the immediate control of the church. As for the mind of the archbishop, Lanfranc's students have now softened the image of the '*harter, strenger Mönch*' and vindicated for him that remarkable, combined temperament of the scholar-monk, free from the more obvious and violent of the world's ambitions, and the man of affairs who could negotiate and command.[3] It was well within his scope to distinguish between a *loricatus* and *ballistarius*,[4] but the eager feudal nepotism of some Norman ecclesiastics seems for him an unlikely characteristic. In 1070 he was in a strange land, *incognitae linguae gentiumque barbararum*, kinless and oppressed with unlooked-for burdens. 'What weariness I bear,' he wrote in

---

1. See the instances collected by J. H. Round, *Feudal England* (1895), pp. 298–303; and the interesting and more detailed reflections in J. A. Raftis, *The Estates of Ramsey Abbey* (Toronto, 1957), pp. 27–30.
2. F. M. Stenton, *Anglo-Saxon England* (1943), p. 626.
3. Notably R. W. Southern, 'Lanfranc of Bec and Berengar of Tours', in *Studies in Medieval History Presented to F. M. Powicke* (1948), esp. p. 31; cf. 'The Canterbury Forgeries' in *E.H.R.*, LXXIII (1958), pp. 193–226.
4. *Lanfranci . . . opera omnia* (Venice, 1745), Epistola xxxv; *Patrologia Latina* (ed. J. P. Migne), vol. 150, col. 534.

an unsuccessful plea for release, 'such disturbances, trials, damage, harshness, greed and filthy insults. . . .'[1] Among these problems obtruded that of his new church's losses: the alienation of a countryside to the lordship of Odo of Bayeux, and those who followed him and remained even after their master's final forfeiture an aristocracy of power in Kent and the kingdom at large. In fact, about a quarter of the men who shortly appear as knights of the see either were or had been also the men of Odo, and they were frequently the best endowed of Lanfranc's knights as well as the possessors of ample estates elsewhere.[2] At the same time, the enfeoffments at Canterbury cannot have been merely an unwilling recognition of facts. Lanfranc's grants include one to the butler of his own household, and a generous one to the brother of his close friend Gundulf, bishop of Rochester. In his foundation charter for St Gregory's Priory at Canterbury, too, he refers to enfeoffments he had deliberately made, using words various and particular enough to persuade us that these acts were gladly willed:[3]

. . . also we have given to the same church the tithes of the lordships [de dominiis] of our knights whom we have enfeoffed [feodavimus] in Kent: all the tithes, that is, of the lordship of Thanington, the vill we have conferred [contulimus] on Godfrey; and of the lordship of Goss Hall and of Goldstone [both in Wingham], little vills [villulas] which we have given [dedimus] to Arnold; and of the lordship of Fleet, the fee we have given to Osbern; and of the lordship of Barham, the little vill we have given to Roger; and of the lordship of Wootton we have given to Ralph; and of the lordship of Whiteacre and of Wadden Hall and of Little London and of Denstead which as one whole fee we have conferred upon the two knights Nigel and Robert; and all the tithes of the lordship of Lenham which we have given [donavimus] to Godfrey; and of the lordship of Leaveland and of Godinton, little vills we have conferred upon Richard and Robert; and of the lordship of Pluckley which we have given to William, and of the lordship of Eynsford, a vill we have given to the other William. . . .

1. *Lanfranci . . . opera omnia*, Epistola I.
2. Anschitil de Ros, the Count of Eu, Gilbert fitzRichard of Clare, Geoffrey de Ros, Haimo the sheriff, Hugh de Montfort, Hugh de Port, Malger, Osbern (or Osbert) Pasforir, Richard de Mares, Vitalis, Wibert. Also, the wife of Buselin de Dives was a tenant of Odo, and so were Robert, the predecessor of Lambert of Romney, and William of Arques, the predecessor of Niel de Monville.
3. *Cart. of St Gregory's Priory*, p. 2. For details of these enfeoffments, see Appendix A.

Behind all these events it is realistic to suppose the meeting and compromise of many intentions: the approval of the king for the integrity and the secular service alike of the church, the acceptance by Lanfranc of men who had first arrived without his invitation as well as of some he chose himself, and the demands which may be presumed from men of power to possess without continued contradiction the territories they held.

Information about the Canterbury fees themselves is unusually copious and specific. In many cases it is possible not only to identify those held by particular men in the Norman age, but to trace their descent into the twelfth and thirteenth centuries, and even beyond. More generally, it is possible to reckon what proportion of the church's endowment was infeudated and to sketch out a fairly clear feudal geography of the estates, and it will be best to look at these matters before passing on to later developments.[1]

In 1086 the lands of the Canterbury knights were described partly in a special column headed *Terrae Militum*, and partly by sentences and paragraphs in the columns devoted to the archbishop and to the monks which tell how portions of their demesne manors were held by the archbishop's men. There is no obvious reason why certain knightly estates were isolated for special description. Most of the so-called *terrae militum* were not noticeably larger than the others (the Eynsford estate is an exception) and they were not in the hands of a special category of tenants.[2] Three of them, Boughton Malherbe, Graveney and Orpington, were even regarded as attached to manors which remained in demesne.[3] The separate category of *terrae militum* may well owe its existence to nothing other than a certain topographical isolation, evident to the local jurors who supplied the information. There was a great deal of knightly land at Wingham, for example, but so intermixed with

1. What follows is illustrated by the maps opposite page 56 and on page 58. General reference here to Appendix A will make it possible to dispense with many notes to the text of this chapter.
2. They were: Farningham, Eynsford, Orpington, Brasted, Ulcombe, Boughton [Malherbe], Leaveland, Graveney, Lenham, Sheppey, Buckland, Tilmanstone, Finglesham, Statenborough, Saltwood, Berwick-in-Lympne and Langport in Romney Marsh. See Table 1 above, pp. 43–4.
3. It is possible that *terrae militum* which, though separate, were noted as attached in some way to demesne manors may have been free lands before the Conquest on the analogy of the half-sulung of East Peckham held in 1086 by a man of the archbishop, which TRE gelded with the six sulungs of the manor, 'but did not belong to it as the land was free' (see Appendix A, under EAST PECKHAM).

Map 1. KNIGHTS' FEES ON THE ARCHBISHOP'S ESTATES

Key

Principal demesne manors of the see	▲ Reculver
Enfeoffments made by the archbishop in the Norman period	● Buckland
Enfeoffments made by the archbishop after the Norman period	● *Evegate*
Enfeoffments held of the bishop of Rochester	■ Fawkham

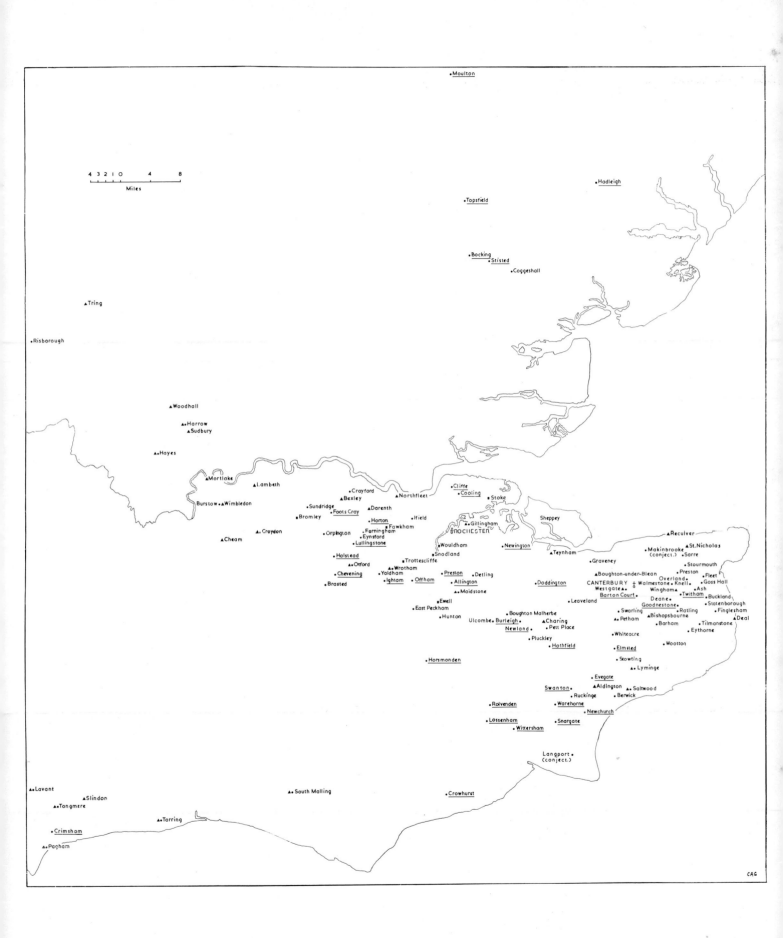

•Moulton

4 3 2 1 O   4   8
Miles

•Hadleigh

•Topsfield

Bocking•
•Stisted
•Coggeshall

▲Tring

•Risborough

▲Woodhall

▲•Harrow
▲Sudbury

▲•Hayes

▲Mortlake
•Lambeth   •Crayford
Burstow•▲Wimbledon   ▲Bexley   ▲Northfleet   •Cliffe
                •Sundridge •Foots Cray •Darenth   •Cooling
                •Bromley   •Horton   •Stoke
                •Croydon   •Orpington •Farningham •Ifield   •Gillingham   Sheppey
▲Cheam   •Eynsford   ┬ROCHESTER
                            •Lullingstone   •Wouldham   •Newington   •Teynham   ▲Reculver
                •Halstead   •Snodland   •Makinbrooke   •St.Nicholas
                •Otford   •Trottescliffe   (conject.)   •Sarre
                •Chevening ▲Wrotham   •Graveney   •Stourmouth
                •Brasted   •Yaldham   •Preston •Detling   •Preston   •Fleet
                            •Ightam •Offham •Allington   ▲Boughton-under-Blean   Overland   •Goss Hall
                                        •Maidstone   •Doddington   CANTERBURY ┼Walmestone•Knell•
                                                                                   Westgate▲▲   •Ash
                            •Ewell   Barton Court•   Wingham• •Twitham •Buckland
                            •East Peckham   •Leaveland   Deane•   Goodnestone•   •Statenborough
                            •Hunton   •Swarling •Bishopsbourne •Ratling •Finglesham
                                        •Boughton Malherbe   Ulcombe• •Burleigh •Charing   ▲•Petham •Barham   ▲Deal
                                                  Newland•   ▲Pett Place   •Whiteacre   •Tilmanstone
                                                  •Pluckley   •Eythorne
                                                  •Hothfield   •Elmsted •Wootton
                                                                                      •Stowting
                            •Horsmonden   ▲•Lyminge
                                                                            •Evegate
                                                                            ▲Aldington
                                                  •Swanton   ▲•Saltwood
                                        •Rolvenden   •Ruckinge   •Berwick
                                                  •Warehorne
                                        •Lossenham   •Newchurch
                                                  •Snargate
                                            •Wittersham

                                        Langport •
                                        (conject.)

▲•Lavant
    ▲Slindon   ▲•South Malling   •Crowhurst
▲•Tangmere

    ▲•Tarring

•Crimsham

▲•Pagham

CAG

demesne hamlets that a separate description was not required there as it was for an infeudated settlement physically remote from the demesne, like Boughton Malherbe. The distinction, however, was quite eliminated by the monks themselves in the survey made for their own use, for in the *Domesday Monachorum* the 'lands of the knights' have disappeared as a separate category and must be sought among those assigned to the archbishop and, to some extent, those of the monks themselves.

Wherever they are found, the lands belonging to the knights are described according to their assessment in sulungs (or hides outside Kent) and according to their value, just as are the demesne manors. Apart from the *terrae militum*, the usual method is to give the whole assessment of a manor, and then to say that such-and-such a proportion of this has been granted to a man or men of the archbishop. Since the assessments do not necessarily represent exact amounts of land, and the values themselves were subject to certain qualifications which will appear in due course,[1] any calculations based upon them are bound to be approximate only. Yet it will be helpful, in gaining an idea of the extent of the knights' possessions in relation to the demesne, to work out the proportions, one of the other, in terms of assessed areas and of money values. These two calculations produce, in fact, nearly the same result, and the discrepancy between them cannot be allowed much significance, since the original figures themselves are inexact. The knightly lands in 1086 comprise 16·8 per cent of all the Canterbury lands (archbishop's and monks' together) according to assessed area, and 15·4 per cent according to value: in general, that is, between one sixth and one seventh of the endowment had by 1086 passed into military tenure.[2] Since at this date the bulk of the

---

1. See p. 95, below.
2. The Kentish sulung has for the purposes of calculation over several counties been reduced to hides on the basis of 2 hides = 1 sulung (cf. P. Vinogradoff, 'Sulung and Hide', *E.H.R.*, xix (1904), pp. 282–6). Thus:

(i) Hideage of archiepiscopal manors (to nearest whole number, and including enfeoffed portions)	721
Hideage of monastic manors (as before)	335
Hideage of *terrae militum*	47
Total hideage of Canterbury estates	1,103
Hideage of knights' lands (enfeoffed portions + *terrae militum*)	186

Knights' lands comprised therefore 16·8 per cent of the total.

enfeoffments had already been carried out, the proportion has a permanent validity.

The properties thus granted out did not lie in some special corner of the Home Counties. A glance at the map[1] will show that the

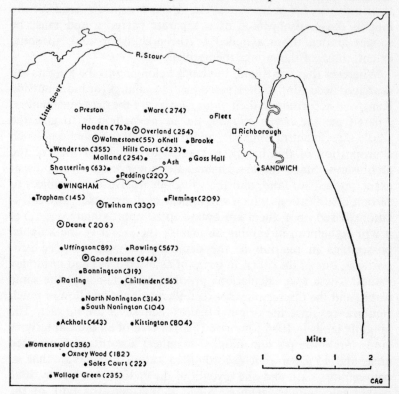

Map 2. THE SETTLEMENT OF KNIGHTS AND TENANTS IN WINGHAM, KENT, 1086–1285

1. Map 1, opposite p. 56. The excellence of the knightly estates will be suggested by the numerous cases in which they became the country seats of gentlemen in later days.

(ii) Value of archiepiscopal manors, as above	£1,486
Value of monastic manors, as above	£600
Value of *terrae militum*	£148
	£2,234
Value of knights' land only	£ 344

Knights' lands were therefore worth 15·4 per cent of the total.

knights' fees marched with the demesnes, occupying lands that perhaps were less likely to have been carefully allocated by Lanfranc than requested, with varying degrees of insistence, by the recipient according to his choice and discernment. Boys's map of the soils of Kent, which he made in 1796,[1] indicates particularly rich lands, and it is remarkable how many of the knights' fees were in those regions: not that maps were needed by the invaders, to whom the best existing demesnes would have been obvious, and who were also guided by strategic considerations.

An overall view of the feudal geography comes more instantly from the map than from words, but the settlement may be studied in greater depth through the local example of Wingham, where the archbishop had one of his largest demesnes, and where at the same time knights' tenures clustered thickly.[2] Wingham lies half-way along the road which runs from Canterbury eastwards to Sandwich, and was therefore on the route to a port of consequence throughout the Middle Ages.[3] The road was straight and the country on either side flat and fertile, becoming marshy as one approached the Stour to the north, but subject to progressive reclamation.[4] The manorial centre of Wingham lay on the road, surrounded by its demesne fields, but the whole manorial area occupied a wedge-shaped territory of some twenty square miles. The area was covered with hamlet settlements, of which some were in the hands of the archbishop's own demesne tenants, some belonged to his knights and their tenants, and others where the tenures were mixed. Although the demesne of the archbishop himself was large in comparison with most of his other demesnes, its 1,200 acres seem few compared with the tenants' lands, amounting to about 8,500 acres scattered through thirty-four hamlets. The knightly tenants were seated in nine villages, and in perhaps two more by the thirteenth century. Of these villages in military tenure, Fleet is particularly

---

1. Printed, with the manors of Canterbury Cathedral Priory superimposed, by F. W. Jessup in *A History of Kent* (1958), p. 69.
2. See Map 2 on p. 58.
3. Sandwich was receiving heavy consignments of Caen stone for the building of Bell Harry at Canterbury in 1497–8 (L.R. 1360). It was also an entrepôt for the Mediterranean trade, and a centre of political importance to the Yorkists in the 1450s and 1460s (E. F. Jacob, *The Fifteenth Century* (1961), pp. 353, 517–18, 555).
4. By the thirteenth century the *mariscus Flemingorum* here was being cultivated (Dean and Chapter of Canterbury MS. E 24, fo. 5v.). In the late sixteenth century, market gardening was intensified by Walloons (Jessup, op. cit., p. 100).

interesting. It had been taken over by William of Arques who held of Odo, and was passed on afterwards to William's son-in-law, Nigel of Monville, and then to Nigel's son-in-law, Rualon d'Avranches, sheriff of Kent.[1] A fine of 1197 describes in minute detail the fields of this fee, some of which lay within and about the massive Roman walls of Richborough Castle.[2] Another half-fee in Fleet belonged to the archbishop's butlers, who can be traced from Lanfranc's own enfeoffment of Osbern through generations of *pincerne* in the settlement later known as Butlers' Fleet. Norman knightly tenants were thus leaving their lasting imprints in the heart of the archbishop's best demesne manors. Walmestone, another of the Wingham hamlets, was in the possession of Vitalis, or Viel, immortalized in the Bayeux Tapestry as the man who announced the approach of Harold's army to Duke William.[3] Like Walmestone, so also Ratling, Knell Farm, Goss Hall, Overland, Preston, Ash and Deane can be traced after a century, village by village, in the hands of the knightly successors of the Norman tenants. Their estates were sometimes contiguous with those which belonged to the archbishop's lesser tenants; but non-knightly tenants might occasionally flourish so much in the amassing of acres—as did the families of Twitham and Goodnestone—as to become numbered among the tenants by military service.

The mixture of tenures thus formed was not an altogether stable pattern, like that of a patchwork quilt, but to some extent kaleidoscopic, given motion by individual histories of enterprise or misfortune, which raised families such as the Twithams and Goodnestones to the ranks of tenants in fee, or broke the knightly holdings in Deane into tiny fragments, or permitted the French Herengods of Domesday Overland to merge into the gavelkinders of Rowling and Ware near by while the family's leaders moved elsewhere.

The elaborate example of Wingham not only illustrates how the enfeoffments might appear on the ground, but introduces the question of the descent and heritability of the fees. Instances have been pointed out from Norman England, where the right of

1. References for this paragraph will be found in Appendix A, under WINGHAM and WHITSTABLE.
2. 'Calendar of Kent Feet of Fines', ed. I. J. Churchill and others, *Kent Records*, vol. xv (1956), pp. 5–7.
3. See also W. G. Urry, 'The Normans in Canterbury', *Annales de Normandie*, no. 2 (1958), pp. 131–2.

inheritance in military lands was not taken for granted,[1] but heritability appears as a matter of course as we trace fees from Domesday to the *Domesday Monachorum* and thence through the list of knights of 1093–6 to that of Henry II's time. In the Norman age itself, Professor Douglas has shown the family descents of Clare, Haimo, Romney, Arques, Leaveland and Eynsford, to name no more.[2] Mr Colvin has carried the demonstration on by pointing out at least a dozen instances where the tenant under Henry II is the descendant of one named in the Domesday texts: Montfort at Saltwood, Clare at Tonbridge, Eynsford at Ightham, the count of Eu at Ulcombe, Jarpenville at Langport, William son of Haimo and grandson of Vitalis in various Stourmouth properties, Folet at Pluckley, de Ros in Maidstone, d'Avranches and the Butlers (*Pincerna*) at Fleet, de Mayenne in Preston and de Port at Crayford.[3] In general, the first descendants of the Canterbury knights must have entered upon their inheritances with the same assured satisfaction as that shown by Robert de Ferrers I about 1110, *'nutu divino succedens in hereditatem'*.[4]

The passage of villages and fields from the church's endowment to the archbishop's knights, and thence to their heirs, raises a further question. Was this property lost for ever to the church's demesne? Or do the enfeoffed manors ever appear again to be exploited in the archbishop's hands? Broadly speaking, it is true that land once infeudated rarely returned permanently to the demesne. There were instances, of course, where lands were forcibly alienated from the archbishopric altogether, enfeoffed to powerful men, and later returned to the lordship of Canterbury. Saltwood is a case in point. But 'dis-infeudation' by the archbishop is a different matter. The only documented forfeiture for unsatisfactory conduct

1. F. M. Stenton, *The First Century of English Feudalism* (1932), p. 154. J. H. Round thought the normal tenure of a fee held of the church at the time of Domesday was still by the limited grant of three lives (*V.C.H. Hampshire*, I, p. 436). For reference to grants in hereditary right by William II, see *Historia Novorum*, ed. M. Rule (*R.S.*, 1884), p. 40. The king's request to Anselm to pardon him for having made grants of land in inheritance during the vacancy of the see does not to me imply that inheritance was abnormal but only that King William had been exceeding his rights in making enfeoffments at all (cf. Marjory Hollings, 'The Survival of the Five-Hide Unit in the Western Midlands', *E.H.R.*, LXIII (1948), p. 483).
2. *Dom. Mon.*, pp. 39, 55, 41, 42, 44.
3. See H. M. Colvin, 'A List of the Archbishop of Canterbury's Tenants by Knight-Service in the Reign of Henry II', in *Kent Records*, vol. XVIII. Of these examples, Jarpenville and Avranches were descents through the female line by reason of failure of sons.
4. *The Cartulary of Tutbury Priory*, ed. A. Saltman (H.M.S.O., 1962), p. 103.

by a knightly tenant dates from the thirteenth century and concerned land held in fee-farm.[1] Yet at moments it appears, if mutilated or ambiguous documents are understood aright, that not quite all the property once enfeoffed remained so. Appledore and Brook, monastic manors, may once have been granted out in fee,[2] and Tangmere in Sussex, probably enfeoffed in Norman times to William of Pagham, was in Henry II's time again in the archbishop's demesne control. A protracted and obscure dispute took place between the Pagham family and the archbishop, for in 1218 Richard of Pagham was suing for nine hides, and in 1221 he made over nine hides to Stephen Langton, receiving back one hide of sixty acres to hold as one ninth of a knight's fee. In 1284 a William of Pagham was holding two hides as quarter-fee, but then and later Tangmere itself remained a demesne manor.[3]

In the course of time the pattern in the feudal kaleidoscope changed. A small number of the knight's fees which appear in the Domesday age vanish, as has just been seen. Some more were reduced or changed in feudal value. Some, though not a great many by comparison with the first enfeoffments, were added. More important, for one reason or another, very many fees were split up into fractions.

Changes in the history of individual fees can often be traced in cartularies and private documents and, from the thirteenth century onwards, in the royal inquisitions *post mortem* at moments when the see was vacant and the archbishop's rights recorded in the royal archives. But more general views of the feudal tenures after Domesday are available from the reign of Henry II, from 1210–12 and from 1253–4. The first of these general views derives from a list of knights discovered by Mr H. M. Colvin, which was pretty certainly drawn up in 1171 and which notably fills the notorious gap left in our knowledge by the absence of a Canterbury return to the questionnaire of 1166.[4] The next general list is that of 1210–12, printed in the *Red Book of the Exchequer*, and was made as a result of John's feudal inquiries after the Interdict of 1208, when he proposed to administer the estates of the dispossessed clergy.[5] The third is a list of knights' fees in 1253–4, evidently made by the Exchequer

1. For the Waleys' loss of Tarring, see below, pp. 100–3.
2. Colvin, op. cit., p. 15.
3 See Appendix A, under TANGMERE.
4. See p. 61, *n*.3 above. For the dating, see *Kent Records*, vol. XVIII, p. 2.
5. *Red Book of the Exchequer,* ed. Hubert Hall (*R.S.*, 1896), pp. 469–73; cf. pp. 724–7.

in connexion with the knighting of the king's eldest son. The government's list was still thought important enough in the early fourteenth century to be copied into Henry of Eastry's memorandum book;[1] it contains, however, only a list of the fees in Kent, and omits the considerable number which the see held in other counties. Hence, the Canterbury feudal tenures can be traced in great detail from one list to the other through the twelfth and thirteenth centuries. A remarkable observation by Mr Colvin was that the order of the 1171 list corresponds closely with that of the list of knights from 1093–6 printed in *Domesday Monachorum*. It is as though the clerk in 1171 were bringing his information up to date, fee by fee, with the earlier list at his side, until, towards the end of the list the correspondences began to fail because of enfeoffments which had been made in more recent days. This correspondence of order allows a good many fees in 1093–6 and in 1171 to be identified, the one from the other, but it is not exact. If the number of fees in both lists is added up it will be found that the total number actually declined during the first century of Canterbury feudalism from ninety-eight to just over ninety-two. This is partly because of the elimination of a few fees from the archbishop's honour, and partly because of a few reductions in the amount of service owed. For example, the fief of William Peverel, formerly held for two knights, had escheated to the crown, and the fees of certain of the Norman knights cannot, for reasons unknown, be found in the 1171 list at all. Also, the feudal value of Robert fitzWazo's fief had been reduced from six to three knights. This is a feature which is frequently to be noticed in the honour's history: especially after 1200, but also before, the knight-service owing from a given property was liable to reduction, sometimes, no doubt, because of an unnoticed subinfeudation, later on perhaps because the quantity of knight-service affixed to an estate was not of much significance anyhow and might be casually and wrongly stated, but sometimes again because of bargains struck between the lord and his tenants.[2]

1. Printed by James Greenstreet in *A.C.*, XII (1878), pp. 197–237, from P.R.O˙ Treasury of Receipt Books, vol. 70. Prior Henry of Eastry's list, virtually identical, is in Brit. Mus. Cottonian MS. Galba E IV, fos. 37–44.
2. An example of the complex changes in feudal values may be found in the village of Sibton, in Lyminge, Kent. This was once held by Robert son of Wazo as part of his fief held for six knights. The total service had been reduced to three knights by 1171. By 1210–12 Eythorne, Sibton, Eastleigh in Lyminge and Sundridge were being held for two knights. In 1279 the same family held Sibton and New Romney for three fees (references in Appendix). In 1306 the same family of fitzBernard

On the other hand, augmentations could take place. There are some places enfeoffed in 1171 which, so far as can be seen, had not been enfeoffed in *Domesday Monachorum*. Of course, care has to be taken in deciding which were truly new enfeoffments, for places were liable to change their names. To take one instance, it is altogether likely that Westenhanger, enfeoffed in 1171 to William de Auberville as one fee, was the same as Berwick-in-Lympne, which happens to adjoin it, and which was also held of the Auberville family: their predecessor, William of Adisham, had held a half-sulung and answered for one fee in Berwick at the time of Domesday. The need to know something of local topography is also shown by the example of Croydon in Surrey, where a Domesday knight was evidently enfeoffed, though the location only appears as Bensham, a district of Croydon, in the thirteenth century. But even after due care has been taken about identifications, it remains clear that some new feudal tenures came to be held of the archbishopric in the course of the twelfth century. Some seem to have been once in the hands of Odo of Bayeux and later either returned or newly given to the lordship of Canterbury. Such were Cooling near Maidstone, Lullingstone, Wittersham, Benstead and part of Deane in Wingham. Some had been knightly tenures held of lords other than the archbishop: Evegate in Smeeth had been held by Hugh de Montfort, and Hothfield by the Chilham lords of Dover, though the circumstances in which they came to the archbishop's lordship are obscure. There were also fresh enfeoffments of archbishopric lands, not many and not large, but enough to show that the process had not been finished once and for all: such may be found in the Kentish demesne manors of Teynham and Wrotham, at Elmsted in Aldington, in the weald at Horsmonden and possibly at Wimbledon in Surrey. Further details may be sought in the Appendix and on the map (opposite p. 56), and there will be more to say of the creation of knightly land in a moment. But the main truth is clear: most of the knights' fees had been created in the Norman age. They were scattered in the same regions as the demesne manors, but they were smaller than the demesne manors. The portions of knightly land added to the

---

held the manor of Sibton for one fee (together with some gavelkind land there), and in the course of the fourteenth century the manor of Sibton is recorded as held for the service of a quarter-fee, two fees and no fees (*IPM*, IV, 387; VII, 606; VIII, 142, 185; IX, 16; X, 419, 519, 523; XIII, 212; *C.Cl.R. 1354–60*, p. 605).

archbishop's honour after the Norman period were smaller still, and not numerous.

The relatively small size of the knights' fees is not by any means an index of their historical interest and importance. What matters is their fragmentation, and their relationship to the countryside at large.

The breaking up of fees into fractions is a development very familiar to medieval historians, but its implications are worth the reflection for which a special study affords the opportunity. The mechanics are fairly simple. Fractions of knights' fees might appear in the countryside for any one of several reasons: (a) either a certain amount of land was from the beginning granted out by the archbishop as the fraction of a fee; (b) a collection of lands had originally been granted as a whole fee, but to more than one man jointly, so that partition among heirs appeared normally in the course of time; or (c) a tenant of the archbishop in knight-service subinfeudated a portion of his holding, which in everyday language means he sold some of his fields and rights to someone else who would receive with them an agreed burden of feudal service; or (d) the tenant had died leaving daughters and no son, so that the estate would be partitioned according to feudal custom between the women and pass thus to their husbands. The permutations brought about by individual family histories, such as subsequent marriages, are numerous, not to say the power a chief lord might possess to solve doubtful cases or force through unusual decisions,[1] and the possible malice or trickery of anyone involved. There is also a fifth possibility, that knight's fee might be created *de novo*, not by normal enfeoffment of the archbishop's demesne as in (a) above, but by the conversion of socage (gavelkind) lands in the hands of his tenants, and this raises the question of the relationship between knight's fee and gavelkind tenure, which must be considered in due course.

It is not difficult to illustrate these various processes, though harder to be sure which were the most important in changing the tenurial pattern of the countryside. (a) The original creation of fractions of fees in the Norman age is commoner than sometimes imagined. In the list of 1093–6 there are no fewer than fourteen

---

1. e.g. Hubert Walter's attempt, related below (p. 100), to grant lands in South Malling and elsewhere to Ralph Arderne, stepfather of Godfrey Waleys, the natural heir.

half-fees and nine quarters, matched on the ground by proportionately modest amounts of land. Later creations of fractions of fees out of the archbishop's own demesne appear to be much fewer, but from time to time newly assarted pieces of land were granted in knightly tenure.[1] (b) Several interesting joint enfeoffments are found in *Domesday Monachorum*: Ulf and Herbert shared a fee at Risborough in Buckinghamshire; Ralph de Ferno and William Pollex held a fee which the list of 1171 shows to have been at West Lavant in Sussex; in Henry II's reign both these were still shared by male *socii* but later became split. Wibert and Arnold held three sulungs in Wingham (probably at Knell), though by 1093–6 they answered for one fee each and the holdings were probably separated very early. (c) Subinfeudations by the archbishop's own knightly tenants which resulted in the division of their fees are quite usual in the twelfth and thirteenth centuries, and may be traced in Appendix A. An example of the division of existing knightly land in this way may be found in the subinfeudation of Chevening near Sevenoaks, now the seat of the lords Stanhope, to Adam of Chevening by the family of Crevequer. More rarely, a knight of the archbishop might himself create knightly land out of former waste: in the early thirteenth century William of Eynsford had granted some pieces in Wrotham called *Spytillbond*, *Nocmeden* and *Bruera* by his charter to Hamo of Bearsted, who was to hold it of him for one fortieth of a fee.[2] But only occasionally can an early feudal transaction be seen in terms of actual fields, as in 1197 when the half-fee in Fleet near Sandwich was divided between Elias de Beauchamp and Rualon d'Avranches so that Elias and his wife got the capital messuage, the land within the Roman walls of Richborough, and precisely defined portions of named and located fields, together with their share of marshes and salt-pits and the fee's complement of named tenants and their services.[3] (d) The partition of fees between daughters may be illustrated from Langport, now a lost village near Old Romney. In 1086 it was held by Robert of Romney. By 1093–6 he had been succeeded by Lambert of Romney, who was listed as owing the

---

1. By 1285 thirty acres of 'new land' in Stansted, Wrotham, were thus held of him, doing scutage, when it occurred, for 2d. (Dean and Chapter of Canterbury MS. E 24, fo. 79v.).
2. ibid., fo. 78v.
3. *F. of F.*, pp. 5–7.

archbishop the service of three fees. David of Romney was holding it in 1159, but he and Robert of St Leger had the misfortune to be drowned in the marsh about 1167,[1] and David's successor, probably his daughter, called Aubrée, carried it to her husband, William de Jarpenville. Yet in 1171 William owed only one and a half knights, and the other one and a half knights were owed by Peter of Langport. The original estate had evidently been split into two and since both halves were held directly of the archbishop it is likely that Aubrée had had a sister and co-heiress whom Peter had married.

Anyone who watches the appearance of new enfeoffments and the division of old ones, and who is familiar with the countrysides where these legal events occurred, is bound to wonder whether particular fields and villages were recognized by the local people as held in knightly tenure and could easily be discerned from other fields not held in that tenure. To carry the same questioning further, it may be asked whether the amount of land held in this tenure by knight-service increased in the course of time, or whether the converse is true and military tenure sometimes lapsed into the ordinary socage tenure of gavelkind, either by formal act, tacit intention or simple inadvertence. Though obscure, the question is not wholly speculative, and needless to say it is of great importance for understanding medieval Kentish society.

The easy compatibility of holding by knight service with holding by the tenure of gavelkind is apparent on all hands and from an early time.[2] This was so both for social and topographical reasons. Gavelkind itself was not a servile tenure (although this remark will have to be qualified in the next chapter) and the vigorous market in gavelkind land was later recognized by the 'Custom of Kent' and may indeed have been a reason for that Custom's sanctity.[3] Further, if an ownership map of medieval Kent could be drawn, it would be quite plain that the possessions of different kinds of men adjoined each other in a manner so complex as to defy generalized description. This may be guessed from our map of Wingham even without more detailed knowledge of field boundaries. The 1284 rental occasionally alludes to tenements of

---

1. *P.R. 14 Henry II*, p. 154.
2. The following matter is based upon a paper by the present writer in *E.H.R.*, LXXVII (1962), pp. 504-11, by the Editor's kind permission.
3. See Chapter 4 below.

different tenures juxtaposed with each other,[1] but the intermixture of the two tenures must have obtained even in the Norman period before the economic changes of the next hundred and fifty years had obliterated many of such social and tenurial landmarks as there were. It is hard to believe there was ever any stigma in holding gavelkind land. Odo himself held half a sulung of Hollingbourne per *gabulum*.[2] Knightly families whose names occur in Domesday can be traced as gavelkind tenants, and not always major ones, in the rental of 1284 and in the places where their forbears held feudal land and sometimes their senior contemporaries continued to do so. Such were Herengod in Wingham, Pasforir (Peyforer) in Lyminge and round Faversham, and Fareman in Wrotham. In short, the family acquired land where it settled: and the 'family' might mean the matrimonial family of the knightly tenant himself, or that of his progeny or collaterals. The head of the family might move away. The important knightly Herengods of the thirteenth century were centred at Stowting and their original fee at Overland in Wingham passed to the Bendings and then to the Valognes; but lesser descendants remained. If the family stayed put, the eldest branch with its natural advantages was even more likely to flourish and augment its property than the younger ones. This doubtless happened with the Brutins of Gillingham. They were knightly people in the Norman age, for not only did Robert owe the archbishop the service of half a knight and receive a little estate there, but shortly a Ralph Brutin appears as a knight of the bishop of Rochester, and another Brutin became a monk at Rochester. Yet their gavelkind lands came to equal and then to overtake their feudal tenement in extent and value, perpetuating their memory in the 'yoke of Brutin', *iugum Brutini*, now 'Britton Street' within the township of Gillingham. Through the same compatibility of tenures and the growing likeness between landholders who flourished irrespective of their tenures, it was possible for the family which does not feature in Domesday or the feudal sources of early Angevin times to rise into the ranks of knightly tenants by virtue of local self-aggrandizement. Thomas

---

1. *Johannes de Bonynton et Willelmus de Uffyntone receperunt de m. Petro de Soleriis senescallo domini Bonifacii archiepiscopi anno ejusdem xxvij unum campum ad feodum firmam . . . et jacet campus subtus Uffyntone inter liberum feodum de Retlinge et tenementa tenencium de Uffintone extend' super terram Thome de Godwinestone et regiam stratam, et continet xlviij acras* (MS. E 24, fo. 11v.).
2. *Dom. Mon.*, p. 91.

of Goodnestone held hundreds of acres in the Wingham hamlet of
that name by 1285, and so did his neighbour, Alan of Twitham.
Each had done homage in 1279 for a quarter-fee, and the Twithams
were litigating over land in the fourteenth century in the best
tradition of medieval gentlemen.[1] Social mobility may be inferred
in many ways and places. The estate once infeudated at Whiteacre
in Petham by Lanfranc himself could be found in 1253 in the hands
of one whose name suggests that he or his forbear was a cheese-
maker.[2]

It has been necessary to anticipate some of the next chapter's
themes precisely because gavelkind tenure was so prominent in
medieval Kent that it cannot be kept away from a discussion of
knights, in a conceptual compartment. This truth provides the
background to the charter which Archbishop Hubert Walter
obtained in 1201 from King John, allowing him and future archbishops at their will to convert lands held of them in gavelkind into
knight's fee, so that the tenants and their heirs should possess the
same liberty that other knights of the church of Canterbury had,
and in such a way that their customs and services should be converted into money rents. A charter granted the same day allowed
the archbishop to hold the grand assize of gavelkind lands in his
court.[3] Maitland offered two tentative explanations of this charter.[4]
He thought that the archbishop may have wished to increase his
financial income from the converted rents and the scutages he
would get in place of the former services and rents in cash and kind
owing from tenants in gavelkind; and he linked John's charter
with the preamble to the charter of 1276, in which Edward I,
disgavelling the lands of John of Cobham, declared that 'it often
happens that tenements held in gavelkind, which so long as they
remained whole were sufficient for the maintenance of the realm
and provided a livelihood for many, are divided among co-heirs
into so many parts and fragments that each one's part will hardly
support him'. But his grant that Cobhhm's gavelkind lands were
to descend for ever, as though they were held by knight's service,

---

1. cf. *Literae Cantuarienses*, II ed. J. Brigstocke Sheppard (*R.S.*, 1888), nos. 748, 749.
2. Furmentinus de Whetacre. See P. H. Reaney, *A Dictionary of British Surnames* (1958), p. 120; also Appendix A under PETHAM.
3. Lambeth MS. 1212, pp. 48, 224–5; LCM, XI, p. 10.
4. F. Pollock and F. W. Maitland, *History of English Law to the Time of Edward I* (2nd ed., 1911), II, pp. 272–3.

was a special favour which does not appear to have been much if at all repeated,[1] and it cannot be said that Maitland's explanations are satisfying. As to the question of rent income: gavelkind services and renders in kind already could be, and often were, commuted by the lord for money if he were so minded. The additional rent from military land was not likely to be very much, and the profit of scutages, as will be shown in the next section, has been much overrated by historians. The bad effects of partible inheritance certainly provide a motive worth serious consideration. But if what Edward I said was the truth, the real sufferers would have been those who in fact held in gavelkind. There was no question of lords losing profits from socage lands as they did when subinfeudation became extreme, because gavelkind heirs and their lands remained in the custody of their own families. And if important tenants in gavelkind, of whom there were many, were suffering in this way, it is necessary to explain why the power of the king and of the archbishop to disgavel their holdings was not more called upon. For it is not easy to find instances where the archbishop took advantage of his power to make this conversion. There is an explicit one where Archbishop Edmund (1233–40) created one twentieth of a fee out of some small holdings in Rolvenden for William of Kensham.[2] Archbishop Boniface (1245–70) freed a yoke of gavelkind land in Teynham for John de Burne, knight, or his predecessor. Some of the fractions of fees which first appear in the thirteenth century or even later may owe their existence to the same process, though it is impossible to be sure.[3] But the instances are few, and this must surely be because the tenantry of Kent did not wish their gavelkind lands to be thus converted to knight's fee. The archbishop's charter was doubtless requested and obtained by him for his own purposes, not out of benevolence towards his tenants. Hubert Walter was a great administrator who knew what he was about, and he lived at a critical time when the value of money was falling quickly and the apparatus of government was becoming more elaborate and needed men of knightly status to work it. To a feudal lord, the most profitable incident of tenure was the custody of wards and their

1. Cobham was not, incidentally, a tenant of the archbishop.
2. See Appendix A; cf. Sir Maurice Powicke, *King Henry III and the Lord Edward* (1947), I, pp. 9–10.
3. Reference to this and other possible instances will also be found in Appendix A under BURLEIGH, MAIDSTONE (Detling), TEYNHAM and WROTHAM (Stansted).

lands, both in itself and because the income thus derived kept pace with the rise of prices. To one who cared for government, an increase in the number of men qualified for knighthood would be nothing but good. It is therefore likely that the motives of Archbishop Walter's charter were connected with feudal wardships and the need for men of knightly status. His men might want to treat knightly land as though it were gavelkind, but the reverse was also true, that the archbishop wished to handle gavelkind like knightly tenures.[1]

Whatever the archbishop's intentions, events did not favour his efforts, for the interests of his tenants were in powerful conflict with his own. If they found it a hardship that their estates were by custom partible among male heirs, they had a remedy to hand in another attribute of the same tenure, namely, that gavelkinders might freely buy, sell or lease such lands, thus by private arrangement counteracting the fragmentation towards which unmodified custom tended, and it will be shown in due course that Kentishmen of affluence and prudence took these steps. But they did not like knightly tenure. What Kentishman without some special reason would choose a feudal holding, bearing in mind the arrival of his lord's officers during the days after his own death, rather than a socage tenure that would leave the way free for the domestic fulfilment of plans the family would have already made? For the guardian of minors and their lands in gavelkind was the *procheyn ami*, often the mother or an uncle, and it is hard to believe that most families would readily tolerate a feudal custody, which might be granted to an archbishop's cook[2], to their own arrangements. Besides, in gavelkind the decision how to deal with the estate was the father's, and if land were to be converted into knight's fee the father could scarcely go unconsulted. Indeed, the effective choice must have been his, for no evidence suggests an archbishop ever

1. In 1313 the demand was still being made in Kent that young men who held a whole fee should be knighted when they came to their majority (*Eyre of Kent*, I, pp. 31, 93). Further, the archbishop, like other Kentish lords, was trying to make those who claimed the custody of their heirs in gavelkind pay for the right to do so, and the Hundred Rolls are full of protests that in Kent '*non est warda*' (see below, Chapter 4, and also P.R. 141 m.28d. (Wingham) for evidence that this was still happening in 1292–5 during the vacancy of the see. Perhaps the presentation of the 'Custumal of Kent' to the royal judges in 1293 was a crystallization of these complaints).
2. e.g. custody of knightly tenements in Shoreham and the wardship and marriage of the heir of Henry of Okebourne granted in 1356 to master John Cayly, archbishop's cook (Reg. Islip, fo. 130v.).

altered the tenure against the tenant's will. Kentish landed society was not easily subject to such pressures.

The argument of these pages leads to the view that the land which was created knight's fee by acts of enfeoffment was mostly in existence by the end of the Norman age, but that a few enfeoffments did thereafter occur, either out of the demesne land of the archbishop or one of his mesne tenants, or very occasionally by converting the gavelkind land of a tenant into fee. At the same time, we have to reckon with a mere decay of strict terminology. When military service declined, when fees became morcellated, when land transactions multiplied and, above all, the distinction between fee simple and fee tail became of importance,[1] then references to a quantity of knight-service attaching to a piece of land when it was bought, sold or leased was probably little more than a conservative gesture, and any freely negotiated land might have imposed upon it the name of fee simple.[2] In inquests and extents from the thirteenth century onwards the amount of knight-service or of scutage attaching to small estates is often quite capriciously rendered or omitted altogether if the local jury did not bother to record it.[3] The other face of this problem now appears: whether land which once was knightly ever came to be treated as though it were not so. The answer cannot be more than conjectural, but the general Kentish setting and certain particular facts both make it seem likely that land once knight's fee may occasionally, either through ignorance or by intent, have been treated like gavelkind land and divided between male heirs. The setting has already been outlined: the topographical confusion between fields held in fee and fields held in gavelkind; the likelihood that either might be held by a man of some status; the reasonable preference of such a man for holding in gavelkind, where the slight services he might owe would neither incommode nor degrade him, and where he retained freedom to alienate duringhis life and his family its income afterwards. The particular facts are the cases where knightly holdings appear to be morcellated among male parceners, not all of which can be explained by original joint enfeoffments or the marriage of co-heiresses. If we look at the list of 1171 we find

1. F. Pollock and F. W. Maitland, op. cit., II, p. 19.
2. For instance, the eleven acres in Wingham first heard of in 1364 as held for a quarter-fee. See Appendix A, under WINGHAM (under 'Other fees in Wingham').
3. See, for example, Sibton, p. 64 n.1 above.

the phrase, 'the sons of William of Deane owe half a knight, but they acknowledge only an eighth'. These may, according to Mr Colvin's collation, be the successors of Robert Livegit, who owed half a fee in 1093-6, but there is no escape from the fact that in 1171 the obligation was in the plural, and upon the sons of one man.[1] If, as also seems possible, they were the brothers Thomas and Harlewin of Deane, who were exchanging lands in the Wingham area with Thomas of Goodnestone in 1196, they were also gavelkind tenants of some local substance. The list of 1210-12 also yields examples where military land appears held by more than one male heir, though not by subinfeudation. Among the knightly tenants of the bishop of Rochester were Roger and John, heirs of Eustachius, and tenants of a quarter-fee in Borstal, and also Henry of Pevensey and Robert his nephew, tenants of another quarter.[2] In the Kentish list of 1253-4 there are still more: half a fee in Wootton was held by John and William de Gestlinges; a fee in Stourmouth was said to be held by the tenants of the land which used to belong to William of Shofford; half a fee in Ash by Sandwich was held by the tenants of the land of Richard Musard; and Robert de Raleghe held half a fee in the hundred of Milton at farm from the heirs of William Malet, who held it of the archbishop. This is to omit several instances here and in the other lists where tenure by unnamed *heredes* occurs, for that proves nothing but the clerk's ignorance of the current tenant's name, though it may indicate that the official mind thought in the plural when dealing with the descent of fees. Reference to the farming of military tenure in the above examples, and the fact that the half-fee in Ash, alluded to above, had earlier been sold for forty-three marks by a William Musard to one Richard the chamberlain,[3] remind us that knight's fee, like gavelkind, was more and more the subject of commercial transaction,[4] and it would hardly be surprising if in family settlements the distinction between the two sometimes became blurred in practice, especially among men whose instinctive sympathies were with the arrangements to which their countryside was anciently accustomed. If we look for a moment outside the honour of the archbishop, some corroboration

1. See Appendix A, under WINGHAM (Deane).
2. *Red Book of the Exchequer*, II, p. 474.
3. *F. of F.*, p. 130.
4. T. F. T. Plucknett, *Concise History of the Common Law* (1948), p. 527.

of this development may be found, in 1255, where the gavelkind rule of inheritance appears to have been applied to a military tenure in Linstead.[1] Within the archbishop's fief, the partition of fees becomes more pronounced with the passage of time, through failure of male heirs, certainly, and through sales, but also, it is hard to deny, through the habit of mind which accepted the sharing of property. By 1346 the original half-fee at Whiteacre in Petham once bestowed by Lanfranc on Nigel and Robert (though it fell to Robert) was being reckoned in eightieths, shares of which were being held by the heirs of named former tenants. The most elaborate fraction here was the nine eightieths held by the heirs of William of Cranbrook, Alice his sister, and their tenants. The same thing is observable at Sarre and at Westgate, while in the same year (1346) even the half-fee in Gillingham, whose feudal descent since Domesday is so respectably vouched for, was being held by Thomas of Gillingham *et parcenarii sui*.[2]

It is probably unnecessary to offer any reason more deliberate than confusion amid the welter of transactions for the occasional treatment of knightly land as partible among males. It was a confusion which became ever more possible as the thirteenth century advanced and the knowledge of local inhabitants was taxed to keep up with the latest developments in land-tenure in their vicinity. Even in the early thirteenth century some deliberation was required. In 1206 a jury was asked to determine whether Haimo the son of Vitalis had given, more than a century before, a certain ploughland as a marriage portion for his sister to one William Cauvel, and they said

that Haimo gave all that land as marriage-portion with Maud to be held as the eighth part of a knight's fee; and William had many sons, the eldest of whom was called Ralph, who held it all his life without a claim from any of his brothers, and therefore they say it was not divided nor is it partible.[3]

Here the recognized fact of undivided tenure proved the tenure's feudal quality, but it was a point that needed proving in this way,

1. *F. of F.*, pp. lxiv, 273–4. Investigation of other Kentish honours would doubtless reveal more joint family tenures: e.g. *The Black Book of St Augustine*, I, ed. G. J. Turner and H. E. Salter (British Academy, 1915), pp. 9, 11, 64, etc., for tenure of feudal land by brothers, heirs and parceners.
2. *Feudal Aids*, III, p. 46.
3. W. G. Urry, op. cit., p. 134.

and had some earlier claim by a brother forced its way through, the later verdict might have been different. The detailed knowledge continually required of juries is again well illustrated in an inquisition of 1349 which found that a messuage and 100 acres of arable in Sandhurst were held for an eighth of a fee, and another messuage and 120 acres in the same place were held of the archbishopric in gavelkind for the service of 6s. 8d. a year.[1] But there was a limit to the clarity possible, and it was not unknown for the same property to be described as fee and gavelkind at one and the same time.[2]

The confusion of tenures which has occupied so much space was never by any means complete, as the later medieval inquisitions *post mortem* and the archbishop's own modest but continued profit from his wardships immediately prove. But it seems at the moment historically appropriate to minimize the difference between knightly and non-knightly tenure and thus to try and correct the exaggerations of an English scholarly tradition which has regarded feudal society as military and aristocratic without giving due place to the land itself and those family transactions which cut across merely feudal interests.

THE SERVICE OF THE FEES

The amount of knight-service owed by the archbishop to the king is better known in terms of the figures recorded in the Exchequer than in its military meaning. Twelfth-century kings, as is common knowledge, required service from their tenants-in-chief according to the amount fixed upon each, and if the physical service were not required, then scutage was payable for that number of fees which supplied no service. Originally, the number of knights the tenant-in-chief enfeoffed with lands of their own did not affect the king's demands, but Henry II after 1166 tried to charge according to the number of knights they had enfeoffed since 1135 wherever, as often

1. *IPM*, IX, 335; *C.Cl.R. 1349–54*, p. 122.
2. *IPM*, XIV, 141: in 1375 Thomas de Graunson, kt, died holding, *inter alia*, the manor of East Hall, Orpington, immediately of the prior of Christ Church by knight-service, as of gavelkind tenure. Also *IPM*, XII, 9: a tenure in Boughton Malherbe, 1365.

happened, that number was greater than the original quota. These developments took place on the Canterbury estates as well as elsewhere, though they have been rather obscured by the fact that Becket was in exile and the see's property in royal hands during much of the 1160s, and by the concurrent fact that Canterbury did not make reply in 1166 to the general inquiry about the enfeoffment of knights.

The see of Canterbury paid no scutage in 1156 and 1159, when other church fiefs did, but when it fell into crown hands after Theobald's death in 1161 it paid to the scutage of that year on its *servitium debitum* of sixty knights.[1] In 1165, during Becket's exile, it paid scutage again, but this time on $84\frac{3}{4}$ knights' fees.[2] In 1168 it contributed on the same number to the aid, but after 1174, when the see was again occupied, it began to claim that the proper *servitium* was sixty fees. A quarter of a century later, when the *Red Book of the Exchequer* was compiled, the fees held of the archbishopric numbered eighty-six, all but a fraction, but in the scutage of Scotland (1209) and Wales (1211) it was again charged on $84\frac{3}{4}$.

It has been seen that almost from the beginning the archbishop had, like most other tenants-in-chief, created more fees on his estate than were necessary to meet the *servitium debitum*. Attention to the details of the infeudations also makes it clear that the number of fees actually in existence was likely to fluctuate all the time, through reductions in the feudal value of sub-tenants' fiefs, through fresh enfeoffments, and so on. The list of archbishop's knights made in 1171 shows that argument about the number of fees owing was not confined to a dialogue between the tenant-in-chief and the Exchequer, for no fewer than seven of the see's tenants were claiming that they owed it less than they were charged with, and their claims to remission amounted altogether to $16\frac{1}{8}$ fees. The *Red Book* and subsequent documents prove that most of them succeeded in obtaining their reductions. So from the purely notional basis of sixty fees, which was the original assessment on the archbishopric, there were various divergences in the course of time in the real number of fees: about ninety-eight in 1093–6, $84\frac{3}{4}$

1. *Red Book of the Exchequer*, p. 22: at the scutage of 1160–1, '*archiepiscopus £80 per Willelmum filium Aldelini—60 milites*'. The foundation of the present subject, apart from the work of Round and Stenton, is in H. M. Chew, *Ecclesiastical Tenants in Chief and Knight Service* (1932).
2. *P.R. 11 Henry II*, p. 109.

in 1165, seventy-nine in 1171 according to the *Red Book*,[1] but slightly more than ninety-two in the archbishopric list of knights made that year,[2] nearly eighty-six in 1210–12. The Exchequer may well have decided in 1165 that $84\frac{3}{4}$ should be the official number, and that it could not keep pace with every change in the local situation, but under Henry III the see is found paying scutage on lower numbers which appear genuine ones: $67\frac{3}{8}$ fees in 1228–9,[3] and $64\frac{1}{10}$ fees in 1231.[4]

The military service which lay at the basis of all these calculations is still the subject of acute debate upon slight and elusive evidence. Apart from the payment of scutage, which is attested through the Pipe Rolls on various occasions up to the thirteenth century, and of certain other sums, the service of knights themselves was also provided from time to time, though the records are rather scarce. In a celebrated passage Eadmer tells how William II wrote to Anselm after the Welsh campaign of 1097, saying that he returned the archbishop no thanks for the knights he had sent on the expedition, as taey were not properly trained nor suitable for the fighting that was required of them, and the archbishop was to hold himself responsible for their deficiencies.[5] The passage has enjoyed a rarity value, but it is doubtful whether it can be made to support any assertion about the see's capacity to provide military service other than that on one particular occasion the archbishop had sent a contingent which was considered by the king unfit for the task in hand, and that the king chose to blame the archbishop. More concretely, the Pipe Roll of 1165 notes nineteen archbishopric knights going in the army.[6] In 1201, 1202, 1203 and 1204 the archbishop was marked in the Pipe Rolls as quit by the king's writ, presumably for service rendered in the Norman campaigns.[7] In

1. *Red Book*, p. 49: '*archiepiscopus Cant' £60 . . . de militibus quos recognoscit se debere regi, et £19 de militibus quos non recognoscit praeter superius 60, quia archiepiscopatus est in manu regis . . .*'.
2. The list supplies the compiler's addition of $80+\frac{1}{2}+\frac{1}{3}+\frac{1}{8}$, but this does not tally with the real sum of the fees in the list.
3. P.R. 73 m. 1.
4. P.R. 76 m. 5d.
5. '. . . *turbatorias litteras rex a Gualis reversus archiepiscopo destinat, mandans in illis se pro militibus quos in expeditionem suam miserat nullas ei nisi malas gratias habere, eo quod nec convenienter, sicut aiebat, instructi, nec ad bella fuerant pro negotii qualitate idonei. Praecepitque ut paratus esset de his juxta judicium curiae suae sibimet rectitudinem facere, quandocumque sibi placeret inde eum appellare . . .*' (*Hist. Novorum.*, p. 78), ed. M. Rule (*R.S.*, 1884).
6. *P.R. 11 Henry II*, p. 109.
7. Chew, op. cit., p. 43.

1211 an unstated number of knights was sent to Scotland, but the service must have been considerable as no scutage was paid and the roll says 'all the knights were in the army of Scotland'.[1] In 1218 the archbishop led fifteen knights to the siege of Newark,[2] and in 1223, the last time the archbishop served, he had knights with him on the Welsh expedition.[3] But in 1254 Archbishop Boniface, like some other bishops, said he was ready to go with the king, accompanied by knights, if the king of Castile should attack.[4]

It was at this time that the contribution of the archbishop to the king's service began for some reason not yet explained to peter out, even though other bishoprics were being called upon to increase their feudal services.[5] The archbishop was not notified as quit for service after 1223, and after 1232, according to Miss Chew, there is for Canterbury no record either of service or of commutation. There are, however, later instances of scutage being received by the Exchequer from the archbishop,[6] and the question of military service continued to agitate the bishop of Rochester. In 1229 the bishop was in the muster roll,[7] in 1244 he begged the archbishop to indemnify him for the knights he had sent in the expedition against the Scots,[8] and in 1259 the whole system by which the archbishop was responsible for Rochester's service was, as we shall see, regulated and confirmed by Archbishop Boniface.

The bare facts of the archbishop's military service give little idea about the military character or otherwise of the knights of the see. The fact that knights were from time to time sent on expeditions does not entitle us to assume that they were the same men whose names occur in the lists of the eleventh, twelfth and thirteenth centuries. Their places, or some of them, may for all we know have been taken by unknown stipendiary knights or a proportionate number of less expensive soldiers. It is possible that the fractional holders in 1093–6 combined in some way to render service, and

1. *P.R. 13 John*, pp. 93, 243.
2. I. J. Sanders, *Feudal Military Service in England* (1956), p. 113.
3. Chew, op. cit., pp. 32*n*., 52.
4. Matthew Paris, *Chronica Majora*, v, pp. 423–4; vi, pp. 282–4; cited by S. K. Mitchell, *Taxation in Medieval England* (1951), p. 214
5. Chew, op. cit., pp. 32, 52, 77 and *nn*.
6. e.g. 29*s*. 4*d*. scutage received from the archbishop in 1235–6 (*Book of Fees*, i, p. 481).
7. Sanders, op. cit., p. 128.
8. Lambeth MS. 1212, p. 143.

even more probable that this was happening by 1171. Domesday itself hints at knights by service rather than by tenure: there was the knight whom William of Arques had put by 1086 with a plough upon his demesne in Fleet,[1] and the knight supplied for the archbishop's service from the fee-farm of Sundridge, probably held by Robert fitzWazo.[2] An interesting charter of 1143, though it comes from a Rochester source, is addressed to the bishop, to Ralph the castellan and to the citizens of Rochester by Arnulf of Chelsfield, and says that he, his wife Agnes, Simon his eldest son and heir, Elias the clerk and Hugh a (or the) *knight of his son* had confirmed a certain grant of land to the monks of Rochester; and the witnesses include among relatives and household officers another knight called Adalulf.[3] If more private charters of Canterbury knights had survived, doubtless more *milites* than the enfeoffed ones would appear to have been available.

The tradition current in the cathedral priory in the late twelfth century that Lanfranc had made knights out of the archbishopric's pre-Conquest 'threngs' may be a remote reference to the existence of Englishmen among the first company of archbishopric knights.[4] That such men were the social equals of the newcomers is easy to believe, but their technical military prowess (or, for that matter, of the French individuals named among the *milites archiepiscopi*) is little more than a matter of conjecture, the more so in view of the growing scepticism hmong scholars about the military value of the twelfth-century feudal quotas as such.[5] But if it is impossible to believe firmly in the regular and professional military character of the archbishop's knights, it would be equally unwise to reject altogether the idea that they could at need perform military duties in return for their fees in the twelfth century and beyond. The Pipe Roll of 1211 says, after all, that from the archbishopric '*omnes*

1. *Dom. Mon.*, p. 83.
2. *Dom. Mon.*, p. 87. It is also worth noting the three knights on St Augustine's manor in Minster in Thanet, who had three ploughs and whose land was worth more in peace than in war (*D.B.*, I, fo. 2: *V.C.H. Kent*, III, p. 243b.). Professor Hoyt tells me (March 1961) that he has counted about a hundred like instances in Domesday Book.
3. *Textus Roffensis*, ed. T. Hearne (1720), p. 236.
4. Stenton, op. cit., pp. 145–6.
5. e.g. J. O. Prestwich, 'War and Finance in the Anglo-Norman State' in *Transactions of the Royal Historical Society*, 5th series, vol. IV (1954), pp. 19–43. I cannot agree with C. Warren Hollister that the lesser men in the *Domesday Monachorum* list of *milites* were not knights ('The Knights of Peterborough and the Anglo-Norman Fyrd', *E.H.R.*, LXXVII, esp. p. 430). Whatever the nature of their services, they were called knights and their tenures were military.

milites fuerunt in exercitu Scotie',[1] and the phrase must apply to at least some of those who appear in the *Red Book*'s list. We know that Robert de Septvans appeared in a muster in 1213–14.[2] Much later, in 1284–5, the archbishopric rental described the service which Walter of Bensham owed for the free tenement which he held in Croydon for the service of one twentieth of a knight's fee, and although the text does not say he was equipped for war in any specific manner, it required that his riding horse and harness, sword and arms, *if he had them*, should go to the archbishop after his death.[3] The same document records that certain of the archbishop's tenants in Sussex held 'by the free service of their arms': the lord of Edburton and the lord of Isfield one fee each, the lord of Horsted a quarter-fee and the lord of Courthope half a fee.[4] Nicholas de Criol, a knight of the archbishopric, was from time to time summoned by Edward I for military service, and in 1294 set out for Gascony in the retinue of Edmund, the king's brother.[5] More individual examples could doubtless be found.

The service of castle-guard was equally one which the knightly tenant was bound in theory to perform,[6] and one which was in fact performed under the command of twelfth-century archbishops. In 1127 Henry I granted Archbishop William of Corbeil and his successors the keepership and constabulary of Rochester Castle with the right to fortify it as they wished, allowing that the knights (*milites*) who were assigned to the garrison duty should continue as before to take it in turns to man and depart from the castle.[7] A writ, also from Henry I, tells the men of the archbishop that those of them shall perform ward-duties in Rochester Castle whom the archbishop shall choose, and that the archbishop shall also control other men, who are not his, and they too shall perform the ward-duties, which they had been accustomed to do, in their turn.[8]

1. *P.R. 13 John*, p. 93.   2. I. J. Sanders, *English Baronies* (1960), p. 1.
3. Dean and Chapter of Canterbury MS. E 24, fo. 152.
4. Printed from the same MS. in *S.R.S.*, vol. 57, p. 117. The lord of Isfield was Sir John de la Ware who had 600 acres locally (ibid., p. 83); the lord of Courthope was probably Sir Peter Scotney (ibid., p. 110).
5. *The Complete Peerage*, III (1913), p. 542 and *n*.(f).
6. Stenton, *First Century*, ch. VI.
7. ibid., p. 207, citing John of Worcester; but a copy of Henry's charter is in Lambeth MS. 1212, pp. 18, 23, and is calendared in Regesta II, no. 1475.
8. Lambeth MS. 1212, p. 23. For the castle-guard of Rochester, assigned to sixty fees belonging to certain Kentish baronies, see J. H. Round, 'Castle Guard', *Archaeological Journal*, LIX (1902), pp. 158–9. There is an unprinted roll of these fees as they were in 1248–9 in P.R.O. Exch. L.T.R. Misc. Rolls (E 370) 5/34 m.1. I owe this reference to Miss M. M. Barry.

The archbishop's continued responsibility for castle-guard appears from the will of Baldwin (November 1190), whose executors distributed certain sums of money among the garrisons of castles, namely, twenty knights and fifty serjeants, as the archbishop had ordered, so that their stipends might be paid for a proper period after his death.[1] Archbishop Langton continued to hold Rochester Castle. His refusal to surrender it to John in August 1215 made him a barefaced traitor in the king's eyes.[2]

The archbishop was responsible to the king for service not only in respect of his own archbishopric, but on behalf both of the cathedral priory and the bishopric of Rochester. In addition, he was in a special feudal relationship with the earls of Gloucester, lords of Tonbridge. Each of these relationships requires consideration.

The feudal service due from the church of Canterbury was from the earliest time rendered by the archbishop and not by the monks whose titular abbot he was, and they always claimed to be exonerated from this secular burden. The most explicit statement of this arrangement comes from the letter of the sub-prior Geoffrey to Henry II in the 1180s, in which he said that the monks had not created knights in the Conqueror's time but had given from their portion of the Canterbury lands 200 *libratae* to the archbishop so that he should answer for them by his knights and also conduct their business at the Roman *curia* at his own expense. Geoffrey added that there was still no knight on the monks' lands but only on the land of the archbishop.[3] There is no record of the transaction the sub-prior was referring to, but the tradition he was expressing certainly had some historical reality, though not necessarily in his terms. For in the Domesday records the manors described as belonging to the monks were sometimes already partly allocated to knights. Where this happened, the knights were said to hold of the archbishop in fee, even though the manor from which the knightly portion was taken was a monastic one.[4] No fewer than two dozen monastic manors had thus contributed by the time of *Domesday Monachorum* to the support of knights.[5] On the same

---

1. *Historical Works of Ralph de Diceto*, ed. W. Stubbs, (*R.S.*, 1876), p. 88.
2. J. C. Holt, *Magna Carta* (1965), pp. 255–6.
3. Stenton, op. cit., p. 145.
4. The wording is especially explicit at East Farleigh, Graveney, Leaveland and Lenham.
5. The whole tale is: Adisham, Berwick-in-Lympne, Boughton [Malherbe], Buckland, East Farleigh, East Peckham, Farningham, Finglesham, Graveney, Langport, Leaveland, Lenham, Little Chart, the sulung called *Aelmesland* or *Asmelant* in

basis of reckoning as was used in the previous section, it would appear that the monastic contribution to the enfeoffed lands was some twenty-eight sulungs' worth in 1086, rather more than £150. There is, therefore, a rough correlation between the amount of monastic land which had passed to knightly hands before 1100 and the amount said nearly a hundred years later to have been given to the archbishop for tsis purpose. Several of the portions thus granted over to the archbishop's men were noted in the Domesday texts as continuing to owe an annual farm to the monks, and it is interesting to see that a number of thirteenth-century agreements between the priory and the then holders forgave arrears of these sums but stipulated that in future they should continue to be paid at the monastic treasury as they had in the past. The amounts of the farms when they are mentioned in the thirteenth century had not varied from those expressed in Domesday. In Domesday they ranged from the £6 a year out of the £9 which was the annual value of the half-sulung possessed at East Farleigh by Godfrey of Malling, down to the 2s. 1d. payable from the half-sulung at Little Chart to the altar of the cathedral.[1] It is not impossible that in a few of these cases the tenure of monastic land by a knight of the archbishop was itself a farm rather than an enfeoffment. Godfrey of Malling, for example, was a great farmer of Canterbury lands, though he held in knight's fee as well. But that the monks' territory was in fact used to support knight-service itself is attested by the case of Ruckinge, which the Eynsford family, great knightly tenants of the see, gave back to the monastery, but from which Archbishop Theobald retained the service of the knight which the land owed.[2] In after days, when the taxation

---

1. Farms were due as follows: from East Farleigh £6 out of £9 value; from Farningham £4 for the monks' clothing out of £11; from Graveney £1 for the monks' clothing out of £6; from Lenham £12 10s. despite the total stated value of £8; from Little Chart 25d. out of £2; from *Aelmesland* in Lyminge 53s., payable to the sacrist by order of the prior; from Swarling 8s. for the monks' clothing; from Nackington 12s. out of £2. For references to the agreements in the *Feet of Fines*, see Appendix A.
2. A. Saltman, *Theobald* (1956), no. 42.

Lyminge, Mersham (held of Hugh de Montfort and possibly not of the archbishop), Newington in Oxfordshire, Orpington, Swarling in Petham, Ruckinge (part of Ickham), Saltwood, Little Stambridge in Essex, Statenborough, Tilmanstone, Walworth in Surrey, Nackington and Wick (portions of Westgate). Originally Appledore and Brook, in *Domesday Monachorum* held at farm by Robert of Ruxley from the monks for their food, seem to have been charged with knight-service, but later to have been exonerated (Colvin, op. cit.).

of the clergy rose to new heights, the prior always claimed, correctly, that while bishops should help to contribute forces for the defence of the realm, he himself held only in free alms and had no tenant who did for him any military service, and the archbishop said in support that the church of Canterbury was not bound to bear secular burdens.[1]

The bishopric of Rochester was in a category of its own. The arrangement by which Rochester owed military service to the archbishop, who included the Rochester quota among his own knights due to the king, was probably worked out between Lanfranc and his friend Gundulf.[2] Gundulf lived at Canterbury with Lanfranc from 1070 till 1076, bearing the burden, we are told, of the archbishopric's temporal administration, and hence, no doubt, concerned with feudal service during those formative years. In 1076 Lanfranc appointed him bishop of Rochester, sent him abroad for royal confirmation, and when this had been granted consecrated the new bishop of Rochester in Canterbury, himself investing him with the episcopal insignia. Till his death in 1108 Gundulf continued in this dependent relationship to the archbishops, in feudal arrangements as well as in the ecclesiastical sphere. The list of knights of the archbishopric of 1093–6 is headed by the bishop of Rochester and a note of his quota of ten knights. The bishop had enfeoffed knights by the time of Henry I,[3] like the archbishop creating more fees in his own estate than were necessary, arithmetically, to meet his obligations. Twenty-six people are listed, answering in sum for $12\frac{7}{8}$ fees. But few whole fees were probably ever created, and by the early twelfth century there were already signs of morcellation through the action of inheritance: a woman called Margaret answered for half a fee, William of Maidstone and Hugh his brother for half each, Gerald son of

1. *HMCR*, IX, Appendix, pp. 95–6 (*s.a.* 1326, 1327). In 1327 the bailiffs of Canterbury, who were trying to get a contribution from Prior Eastry towards the cost of fitting out troops for the Scottish war, claimed the convent held rents to the amount of *200 livres* as well as 500 acres within the city, and upon that property they were liable to be assessed to the same rate as other estate owners. The archbishop wrote that his council had collected evidence to prove that the church was exempt from taxation of this kind, but if the bailiffs could not agree after inspecting it, he would advise the prior to contribute a reasonable amount (ibid., p. 96; cf. *Lit. Cant.*, II, nos. 702–3). The reference to 200 livres is interesting though inconclusive.
2. For Gundulf, see R. A. L. Smith, *Collected Papers* (1947), pp. 83–102, reprinted from *E.H.R.*, LVIII (1943).
3. *Textus Roffensis*, ed. T. Hearne (1720), p. 223; cf. J. H. Round, *Feudal England*, p. 250.

4

Seran of Lambeth for half, William de Bunenesca and Robert his nephew for a quarter-fee, William himself holding three quarters of the quarter and the nephew the remainder. The Rochester knights were mostly local men, but the presence of Ralph Brutin among their number, an evident kinsman of the archbishop's knightly tenant, Robert Brutin, at Gillingham near Rochester, recalls how interwoven the tenures were. Gundulf's own brother William had already been made a knight of the archbishop and generously enfeoffed at Detling near Maidstone.

The accord between the archbishop and his subordinate of Rochester over the provision of knight-service was soon broken, and the ecclesiastical disputes between them had their counterpart in a skilful if disingenuous attempt on the bishop's part to deny a feudal obligation to his archbishop. In Henry II's reign, still charged in the archbishop's list with the service of ten knights, Rochester claimed he owed only one. In 1210–12 the Exchequer recorded that the bishop of Rochester held seven fees as of the archbishop's manor of Otford; but a separate list notes thirty-four knight sholding an aggregate of nearly thirteen fees of the bishop of Rochester.[1] In 1214 King John granted Archbishop Langton the patronage or advowson of the bishopric of Rochester, setting a seal on its dependence.[2] The bishops of Rochester were obliged in this way to do the services belonging to the temporalities of their see to the archbishop of Canterbury as their 'lords and patrons', and the archbishops were in turn supposed to perform those services to the king. The list of Kentish fees of 1253–4 gives the names and holdings of Rochester knights, which had by then become reduced from the early twelfth-century figure to $6\frac{1}{10}$ fees, without, however, noting his dependence on the archbishop, and during the next six years the bihsop of Rochester denied the archbishop's right to collect the aid due from the Rochester fees, and alleged that he acknowledged no overlord but the king.[3] When he was shown the charter of King John which had granted Langton the patronage of the church and bishopric of Rochester in 1214, he claimed that the lands of his see had always been held in free alms and free of secular services, so that the king could hardly transfer to Canter-

1. *Red Book*, pp. 471, 726; cf. pp. 473–4.
2. *Rot. Litt. Pat. 1201–16*, 124a (22 November 1214); cf. H. Wharton, *Anglia Sacra*, I, pp. 386–7; both cited by M. Howell, *Regalian Right in Medieval England*, pp. 201–3, cf. 62 *n*.1.
3. Chew, op. cit., pp. 184–5.

bury what he did not possess. Some unknown friend advised the bishop to appeal to the Exchequer rolls, which everybody accepted as the unanswerable record of military obligations, and sure enough the barons of the Exchequer could find nothing about Rochester's service to the king. Naturally, this was to beg the question, since Rochester owed this service to the archbishop and not directly to the king, and the bishop must have known this quite well, for a Rochester charter of 1244 to the archbishop acknowledged as much.[1] The dispute, however, was composed in 1259 as part of a larger agreement between the bishop of Rochester and Archbishop Boniface. The bishop was allowed in the form of words to go on maintaining he owed no military service, but agreed that if military service were to be demanded of him by the king, then he should put forward the archbishop in respect of this demand, and the archbishop would fulfil the obligations of service or make fine. For this, the bishop of Rochester gave the archbishop a pension of twelve marks a year, payable partly at the archbishop's manor of Hayes in Middlesex and partly at Gillingham in Kent, the whole being secured upon the Rochester manor of Trottescliffe.[2]

The pontificate of Boniface of Savoy was a vintage time for the making of compositions between the see of Canterbury and parties with whom it had been involved in dispute. Another agreement of 1259 was with Richard de Clare, earl of Gloucester and Hertford and lord of Tonbridge, and concerned among other things the feudal service owed by him to the archbishop.[3] Feudal relations between the two were naturally different in character from those between the archbishop and religious corporations which might have some claim, real or pretended, to be exempt from the provision of knights. But the earl's lowy of Tonbridge also stands apart from the fiefs of other military tenants of the see in being a complex liberty with lands and rents owing to it from portions of manors belonging to the archbishop and others.[4] In 1086 Tonbridge Castle was the principal possession of Richard fitzGilbert in south-east England. It lay at a point where the River Medway divided into five streams, and was the head of a privileged area called a lowy

1. Lambeth MS. 1212, p. 143.   2. ibid., pp. 146–7.   3. ibid., pp. 148–59.
4. *Dom. Mon.*, pp. 39–41. The castle itself is mentioned in the text only under Darenth (ibid., p. 88). For a careful study of the lowy, with maps, see W. V. Dumbreck, 'The Lowy of Tonbridge', in *A.C.*, LXXII (1955), pp. 138–47. A copy of the 1258 perambulation was also entered into Lambeth MS. 1212, pp. 157–9.

which included not only the wooded region of the neighbourhood but scattered areas farther afield. From the archbishop he held property in Northfleet, Otford, Wrotham, Darenth and, as a sub-tenant of Ralph son of Unspac, in Eynsford. From the monks of Canterbury he held in East Farleigh, East Peckham, Meopham and Farningham; from the bishop of Rochester in Frindsbury, Halling, Southfleet and Stone; from the bishop of Bayeux in Hadlow, Tudeley, Swanscombe, Ridley, Hoo, Ash, Seal, Leybourne, Eccles, Milton, Luddesdown, Offham, Cooling and Little Wrotham; from the king in chief in Yalding and Barming near Maidstone.

The services claimed from the earl by the archbishop had a twofold origin. The first was in respect of the lowy of Tonbridge. In the list of 1093–6 its lord, Gilbert fitzRichard, appears as having already taken over from his father, the Domesday tenant, who had become a monk. He was charged with the service of four knights. In 1171 the earl of Clare, then Richard III, earl of Gloucester and Hertford and lord of Tonbridge, was again charged with four knights by the archbishop, but was acknowledging two only, and the *Red Book* describes the same early in 1210–12 as holding two fees of the archbishop, though the location of these is not given. The second origin of Gloucester's obligation to the archbishop lies in the fact that the earls became through marriage part-heirs to the fief which had belonged to Haimo the sheriff when Haimo II died in 1129–30.[1] Haimo had owed the archbishop the service of six fees in 1093–6. After 1130 his inheritance was divided between Robert, earl of Gloucester, and Robert de Crevequer, and by 1171 Haimo's former responsibility to the archbishop was being shared between William, then earl of Gloucester, as to three knights, and Daniel de Crevequer also as to three. The manors to which Gloucester's part of the service was attached were Milton (in Westgate, Canterbury), Filston in Shoreham, near Otford, Pett in Charing, Brasted and Horsmonden, all in Kent but widely scattered. In 1210–12 the countess of Clare was holding one fee in Filston and another in Otford, but Horsmonden and Pett appear in the immediate tenure of others.

The agreement of 1259 with the then earl of Gloucester took account of the claims made by the archbishop upon his services for both of these historical reasons, and settled matters which con-

1. H. M. Colvin, op. cit.

cerned their franchises as well as the more strictly feudal demands.[1] Questions of franchise must be left to a later page.[2] But in respect of feudal service, the composition seems to have resulted, as at Rochester, simply in its tacit abolition. The archbishop had required homage and the service of four fees in respect of the lowy, and the same in respect of the manors of Filston, Hormonden, Milton and Pett, with homage alone for the manor of Brasted. In the upshot the earl claimed, and the archbishop apparently agreed, that the lowy should bear only Gloucester's services as chief steward at the archbishop's enthronement banquets, and the other manors the service of chief butler on the same occasions. The earl already performed these honourable and profitable functions, so that the effect of the agreement was not a substitution of one kind of service for another, but the quiet dropping of a knight-service which had in any case become more or less obsolete in form.[3] The real substance of feudal tenure remained in the right of the lord archbishop to custody during the heirs' minorities, 'without waste, sale and destruction as the law and custom of the kingdom demands, for the avoidance of damage and the praiseworthy example to posterity'.[4]

By the middle of the thirteenth century the knight-service received by the crown from the archbishop was devoid of what military meaning it had ever had. It remains to consider briefly the fiscal importance of the knights' fees to the crown and to the archbishop himself.

The sums taken by the crown from the see of Canterbury as scutage in lieu of knight-service may be traced upon the Pipe Rolls. In comparison with the revenues which lands in military tenure might yield in other ways they were very small. In 1160–1, for example, the treasury received £80 for the full scutage of 30s. based

1. One portion of the chirograph, lodged in the cathedral archives, is now Dean and Chapter of Canterbury MS., Chartae Antiquae A 28, from which it was printed with some errors and omissions in *HMCR*, v, App. 458b. Another portion is in the P.R.O., Chancery Miscellanea (C47) 9/59; for this reference I am indebted to Mr J. S. Moore. The documents were also copied into Lambeth MS. 1212, p. 148 *et seq.*
2. See below, pp. 295–6.
3. It should, however, be noted that four fees from the lowy of Tonbridge appear in the list copied into Archbishop Islip's register (1349–60), fos. 96–9, though the roll from which the list is derived may belong to a period before 1259. See p. 91 below. But there is no mention of knight-service in the inquisition of 1348 after the death of Hugh d'Audley, earl of Gloucester (*IPM*, IX, 57).
4. Lambeth MS. 1212, p. 153.

upon sixty fees, and in 1165–6 £113 were taken for two scutages of a mark each, based upon 84¾ fees. In 1168 the king took an aid on knights' fees at a uniform rate of one mark per fee. Though he tried to levy this on the new enfeoffments, it was only when bishoprics were in his own hand that he could do this successfully,[1] and although the see of Canterbury was in fact in Henry's possession and was charged on seventy-nine fees, the amount received from the knights' fees that year was only £44 18s. 6d.[2] The non-knightly inhabitants of the archbishop's manors who were tallaged at the same time, and paid almost in full, raised £220 16s. 6d. Forty-three years later, when another full scutage at two marks on the fee was taken for the expedition to Wales, and the archbishopric was charged on 84¾ fees, the treasury succeeded in gathering £74 16s. 2½d. out of a possible £133.[3]

The effect of these figures is to show up the insignificance of scutage, and more especially so when its proceeds are compared with the sums, running at £1,000 to £2,000 per annum, which were received by the crown on those fairly frequent occasions when the whole see was in its hands. For the enjoyment of custody during vacancy or sequestration was, no less than scutage, an incident of feudal law and custom, and the point of calling attention to what is well enough known in itself is to apply these facts not only to the king but, on a lower plane and smaller scale, to the archbishop himself, in his relations with his own knightly tenants. Possessed of parallel rights, he might both recoup himself for scutages taken, and receive under the safeguard of acceptable behaviour the profits of his knights' fees during the nonage of their heirs. It used to be argued that the creation by tenants of fees in excess of the *servitium debitum* might result in 'enormous profits'[4] for them when the king took a scutage based upon the old enfeoffment and the tenant-in-chief recouped himself on his own higher enfeoffment. Yet even in extreme cases—if the bishop of Lincoln could indeed for the service of five knights purchase the right to collect scutage from about a hundred fees—the total sums at stake were quite insignificant beside the profits available from wardships. In fact, it is doubtful how much profit a tenant-in-chief could make from such fees, even

1. S. K. Mitchell, *Taxation in Medieval England* (1951), pp. 165–8; cf E. Miller, *The Abbey and Bishopric of Ely* (1951), p. 162.
2. *P.R. 14 Henry II*, pp. 153–6.
3. *P.R. 13 John*, p. 244. 4. Chew, op. cit., p. 138.

when he operated scutage as a manorial tax.[1] In the see of Canterbury, the fiscal value of the knights can only be glimpsed through fragmentary records. Scutages taken by the archbishop cannot be estimated, but thirteenth-century Feet of Fines fairly often specify the performance of scutage 'when it shall happen' from the portions of knights' fees in question, and the sums referred to were shillings or pence rather than pounds.[2] At Lavant in Sussex, a demesne manor with a half-fee in the next village, it had by the thirteenth century become a work laid upon customary tenants to bring scutage when it occurred to Petworth at the lord's expense,[3] but such sums appear upon no surviving account rolls. The record of feudal custodies, though rarely found, are, on the contrary, more impressive when they do survive, not only because the archbishop may be seen enjoying the profits of a whole estate, even though for a limited time, but because the values involved naturally increased with the contemporary rise in prices, while scutage was customary, fixed and obsolete. An example from a royal account during the vacancy of 1270–2 is the sum of £40 paid by a John de Estwode to the king for having the wardship and marriage of Walter le Botiller who held of the archbishopric in chief.[4] This was not a bad profit from the half-fee in Fleet. Another instance, this time from the archbishop's own accounts, is an unusually full financial statement of the half-fee in Gillingham which fell to his custody after the death of Hugh of Gillingham some time before 1273.[5] The sale of corn alone from its 200 acres realized about £60. The pure profit cannot be calculated, and a good deal was spent on the manor, but the increase in value since the time of Domesday, where the half-fee's value was noted as 40s., is impressive.

The archbishop's custodies and wardships might include not only the lands and persons of his own knights, but also those he bought or was specially granted from time to time. Such a source of income was enhanced for the archbishop by the privilege of 'prerogative wardship' which he won during the course of the thirteenth century. This allowed him to enjoy the custody of knightly lands

1. For reasoning to the same effect, see J. A. Raftis, op. cit., pp. 29–30: '. . . in short, there would appear to be little economic rationale in the enfeoffment of knights. . .'.
2. *F. of F.*, lix, lx, xciv, xc.
3. *S.R.S.*, vol. 57, p. 19 (MS. E 24, fo. 110).
4. P.R. 119, m. 41d.
5. Addit. MS. 29794, m.8; see also *E.H.R.*, LXXVII (1962), p. 507.

I

held of him during the heir's minority even when that heir held also of the king in chief.[1] An interesting case in point is provided by the large fief held in Yorkshire by Robert Meinill of William Paynel. Between 1196 and 1198 Archbishop Hubert Walter bought it from William Paynel for fifty marks and a palfrey, and the transaction was confirmed to Stephen Langton by the king in 1214.[2] During the civil war the archbishop found it difficult to gain possession of his rights, but he held them from 1219 until 1299, when on the death of Nicholas Meinill a dispute arose between Archbishop Winchelsey and the royal escheator who had claimed them in the king's name.[3] The ensuing inquiry was honestly conducted, and by May 1299 Edward I was admitting the privilege of the archbishop (shared only by the bishops of Durham between Tyne and Tees and the earls and barons of the March) of having custody of the lands of his dead military tenants who were also tenants-in-chief of the king.[4] The lands in question amounted to sixty carucates in the Yorkshire villages of Swainby in Whorlton, Seamer and Braithwaite, Eston in Ormsby, Aldwark, Boynton, Fridaythorpe, Lowthorpe, Wauzs and Potto.[5] The land descended with the Meinill property to the family of Darcy. It was the most distant of all the Canterbury possessions, and needed to be administered by an especially remote control. In 1343 John Darcy agreed to build a stone house as a prison and court-house for the archbishop's franchise there, and a dwelling-house for his local steward and bailiff, in return for which the archbishop was to allow Darcy the profits of the franchise for three years.[6] The property was obviously best leased out altogether to local men who could look after it, and by 1419 the custody of the Darcy wards, valued at £73 6s. 8d. per annum, was assigned to Lord Henry fitzHugh and the money paid over to him by Christopher Boynton, fitzHugh's receiver, who in 1428 was evidently farming the lands himself.[7]

1. The prerogative wardship had evidently not been clearly defined by 1258 when the archbishop's rights were overridden by Henry III in favour of William de Valence (*C.Cl.R. 1256–9*, p. 276; ibid. *1227–31*, p. 85).
2. Lambeth MS. 1212, pp. 75, 204; 22, 49, 203.
3. *Complete Peerage*, VIII, pp. 619–35 for the Meinills.
4. *Register of Archbishop Winchelsey*, ed. R. Graham (Canterbury and York Society, vol. LII), pp. 878–80.
5. ibid., vol. LI, pp. 339–40; the descent of these Yorkshire lands may be traced in *IPM*, VI, 306; VIII, 118, 344; X, 36, 310; XII, 240.
6. LCM, VI, 80.
7. L.R. 95. By the fifteenth century wardships had generally resolved into fixed values.

I

The archbishop's right of prerogative wardship occasionally needed to be asserted during the later Middle Ages, but was always allowed,[1] and must have brought in a fair income. More would be known about his feudal custodies had more rolls survived from the office of Steward of the Liberty, for information about feudal income was transferred some time after 1274 from the general pipe roll of the see to a specialized series of 'liberty' rolls. Set beside the profits of demesne manors, the revenues derived from the feudal tenants often appear modest, but it was in their nature to fluctuate from year to year according to the domestic histories of the families which held in military tenure. What the escheators did for the king the stewards and bailiffs of his Liberty did for the archbishop,[2] and it was partly to keep a check on his knights' fees that Archbishop Islip (1349–66) had a list of hundreds and borghs in Kent which belonged to his liberty, enumerating (though not naming) the fees within each, copied into his register. The list was taken from an earlier roll, now lost, and the transcription was not completed, but slightly more than fifty-one morcellated fees scattered through twenty-nine hundreds of Kent are noted.[3]

The fiscal value of the archbishop's wardships, and to a smaller extent his feudal reliefs, endured to the end of the Middle Ages, although he must have lost much of the potential revenue through the device of enfeoffments to use, which by the fifteenth century was practised extremely widely. Five surviving rolls from the office of steward of the Liberty allow this source of income to be precisely illustrated though, in default of a good series, not analysed. The accounts are, however, well spread out over the century, for they come from 1419, 1427, 1479, 1489 and 1491.[4] The profits from wardships during these years were, respectively, £122 14s. 4¾d., £11 13s. 4d., nil, £11 13s. 4d. and £11 4s. 2½d. Despite the similarity of three of the figures, each year's profit was quite differently made up, and the similarity is a coincidence. The profitability of the feudal tenures was also potentially higher than these sums suggest, since the archbishop not only assigned dower, as, of course, he was

1. e.g. the two fees of Crayford in 1329 (*C.Cl.R. 1327–30*, p. 462).
2. For the fullest information on these royal rights during Canterbury vacancies, see M. Howell, 'The King's Government and Episcopal Vacancies in England from the Eleventh to the Fourteenth Centuries' (London Ph.D. thesis, 1955), pp. 377–9.
3. Reg. Islip, fos. 96–9.
4. These dates represent the Michaelmases ending the accounts (L.R. 95–9).

bound to do, but sometimes graciously assigned money to the heir before he was entitled to it. On occasion, too, unpaid arrears are noted.[1] By the fifteenth century the various fees and fractions held of the archbishop evidently each had a recognized annual value, and what was due to him was exactly calculated according to the number of days the estate had been in custody. Sometimes the whole custody was farmed out to a local man on the spot, like Christopher Boynton, to whom the Meinhill-Darcy fee was assigned in 1418–19 and 1427–8, or to an interested kinsman like Richard Nanseglos, the widow's second husband, who was part-lessee of Evegate in 1478–9 while the heir, his stepson, was still a minor.

THE KNIGHTS AND THEIR LANDS

To turn from the feudal tenures of the archbishop to the tenants themselves is to leave a problem which, though often complex, concerns only one particular kind of relationship, and to consider a large number of people who not only differ from each other according to the period at which they lived, but were also unlike each other at any single time, sharing only the characteristic that they could be called tenants of the see by military service.

The first list of *milites archiepiscopi*,[2] from the reign of William II, is of a miscellaneous collection of men. It contains the names of those who were among the greatest in the realm. Haimo the sheriff, Hugh de Montfort, Gilbert fitzRichard of Clare and Tonbridge and the Count of Eu all held more than four fees of the archbishop as well as much land elsewhere. Other men who held relatively little of the archbishop were scarcely less great. William de Braose was a prominent landowner in the Conqueror's England, though he answered the archbishop for a single fee. Hugh de Port owed the archbishop two knights, but held more than sixty manors in Hampshire, where he was sheriff, as well as other property in Cambridgeshire, Surrey and Kent. Like so many of his con-

---

1. Details will be found in Appendix A, under the relevant dates, for Crimsham, Evegate, Glynde, Harrow, Hothfield, Isfield, Lullingstone, Sarre, Wimbledon (Burstow), Wingham (Ash and Fleet), Wittersham (Palstre, etc.). All these concern wardships. There is evidence of feudal reliefs for Fleet (in Wingham), Hothfield and Sarre.
2. *Dom. Mon.*, p. 105.

temporaries he ultimately became a monk, and the little family church at Barfrestone, set in a fold of Kentish countryside and surviving today in its Romanesque perfection, recalls the close proximity of ambitions in the hearts of such men: armed conquest, competition for rights and revenues, and the service of God.

The Norman *milites archiepiscopi* seem almost an accidental grouping of individuals who at one end of the scale were of so extended a power that they can scarcely be called 'Canterbury' knights, together, at the other extreme, with some whose endowment was modest enough to make their social difference from substantial peasants doubtful. The origins of some have been traced in Professor David Douglas's learned essay.[1] They had been drawn together from various backgrounds on both sides of the Channel, and not least important of these was London, whence a native citizen like Deorman could become a tenant-in-chief of the Conqueror, connected by ties of tenure and marriage itself with the great Norman family of Clare.[2] The assimilation which thus was possible between leading families of Normandy and England has been established. Less attention has been paid to the knights of lower eminence, and to the assimilation which took place between their families and the occupants of the age-old countryside, and in its nature the evidence for this is slight and indirect. But some has been assembled for the estates of Ramsey Abbey by Father Raftis,[3] and the remarks in the first section of this chapter about the Peyforers, Herengods, Farmans and Brutins show the same processes at work in the south-east of England.[4]

What was the value and character of a knight's fee? The question has often been put, and some answers may be supplied, provided that their limitations are recognized. The first proviso is that, although the extent of knightly holdings in the Norman period can sometimes be inferred, these do not necessarily represent all that the knight possessed in a land where ample opportunity existed to increase his property by assart, purchase and lease. The second limitation, relevant to the twelfth century and later, when rentals were made, is that even a full and orderly rental which itemizes certain holdings of a man known to be a knight does not necessarily

1. ibid., pp. 39–73.
2. ibid., pp. 62–3.
3. *The Estates of Ramsey Abbey*, ch. II.
4. See above, p. 68.

tell the whole truth, since transactions in land took time to get into manorial records and sometimes did not get there at all.[1] A knight, in other words, may often have possessed more than the official documents ascribed to him.

This said, the size and value of the fees is well worth examining. The differences between the thirteenth century and the earlier period are most important. In the thirteenth century men were much more interested in the question, 'What *ought* a knight's fee to be worth?' for when it became necessary to persuade men of flourishing condition to accept the status and obligations of formal knighthood, then it was necessary to decide how flourishing that condition ought to be before exercising compulsion.[2] Distraint of knighthood was often applied by reckoning men's wealth, not by adding up the fractions of fees they may have held, and everybody saw that annual value was all that really mattered in an age when values had risen and fees fragmented. But there were occasions when tidy- or antiquarian-minded clerks thought of the fee as being equivalent to so much land. The Canterbury scribe who in the mid thirteenth century was making transcripts of *Domesday Monachorum* and allied documents, headed his work with the words

Sulungs of the manor of the archbishopric of Canterbury in Kent; also the sulungs of all Kent, as it seems; and it is to be known that two sulungs make one knight's fee.[3]

Another Canterbury clerk offered an opinion, this time in 1299 when he was writing up the dispute about the Meinill lands in Yorkshire for Winchelsey's register. The lands amounted to sixty (scattered) carucates, and ten carucates, he wrote, make a knight's fee.[4] Each of these statements has the character of an *obiter dictum* and neither is at all accurate, so far as can be seen, for any age. If taken literally, they would mean that a fee corresponded either to about 400 or 1,000 acres. They relate, of course, to widely different

1. See, for the general limitation of rentals and character of the village landmarket, M. M. Postan, *Carte Nativorum*, xx (Northamptonshire Record Society, 1960), pp. xxviii–lx.
2. On distraint of knighthood, see F. M. Powicke, *The Thirteenth Century*, pp. 546–8, 552–3; cf. F. M. Stenton, *First Century*, p. 157: '. . . the *feudum unius militis* is a concept which gradually developed as the process of subinfeudation went on . . .'.
3. Lambeth MS. 1212, p. 340.   4. *Reg. Winchelsey*, p. 339.

parts of the country and to different circumstances, but neither has any relationship to general contemporary or past realities.

Domesday Monachorum and the list of 1171 offer something more concrete than this, namely, a chance to observe what in fact, and not in theory, the Canterbury knight's fee might amount to during the first century of its existence. For by comparing the two documents it is possible to identify more of the estates possessed by particular knights in the 1093–6 list than can be done by using the *Domesday Monachorum* alone.[1] Further, by choosing the lesser knights and the simplest cases, it is more certain that these estates were in fact bestowed for the service they are known to have owed: it is unsafe to argue the value of a fee held by a major tenant, since his obligation may have been reckoned on the lands he held altogether, not each fee upon a particular estate. By selecting the cases, then, where estates and the service for which they were held in Domesday can with reasonable safety be isolated, Table 2 (p. 96) can be constructed. These knights were not men of the first rank in the archbishop's honour, and their fees, scattered over Kent and Sussex, form a representative selection of middling knightly estates. Their values are modest. Only William of Detling, brother of Lanfranc's close friend Gundulf, possessed an estate worth as much as £10 (and with a disproportionately small obligation of service). Of the rest, whether they held whole fees or fractions, the value of the estates ranges between £1 and £7. The average value of the fee in the sample is about £5. As for the archbishop's greater vassals, the value of their fees cannot be determined so certainly, but the impression with them too is that £6 or £7 per fee was a common scale of value.[2]

The Domesday jurors often said how many ploughs and peasants there were on the knight's fees as well as on the archbishop's demesnes, and it is possible to arrange these also in a table (Table 3, p. 37). The number of available instances here is much larger because the value of the fees does not have to be worked out. It is simply a matter of how the knightly estates were composed.

The Eynsford estate here as elsewhere stands out as the greatest among those of the archbishop's vassals. Leaving this aside, the

1. The following paragraphs are based upon work done independently by Mr H. M. Colvin and the present writer, who is as usual most grateful to Mr Colvin for sharing his information and ideas. The details of his working differ slightly in the present context from those of Mr Colvin.
2. H. M. Colvin, op. cit., pp. 4–6.

Table 2. The value of some Canterbury knights' fees, c. 1090

Knight	Fees owed	Estate	Assessment in sulungs[1]	Valuation	Value per fee
Robert Brutin	½	Gillingham	(land for 1 plough)	£2	£4
Ralph Ferno and William Pollex	1	Lavant, Sussex	1½	£3	£3
Wimund of Leaveland	1	Leaveland	1	£1	£1
William of Detling	½	Maidstone (Detling)	2	£10	£20
Malger	¼	Orpington	¾	£2 10s.	£10
Nigel of Whiteacre	½	Petham (Whiteacre)	1¼	£2	£4
William of Adisham	1	Ruckinge	1	£7	£7
William of Pagham	1	Tangmere, Sussex	3	£6 (but £1 to reeve)	£5
Albold	¼	Westgate of Canterbury (Wick)	¼	£1 10s.	£6
Wilbert Arnold	2	Wingham (Knell in Ash?)	3	£12	£6
Herengod	1	Wingham (Overland)	1 less 10 acres	£2	£2
Godfrey (*archibalistarius*)	1	Wingham (Ratling)	1½	£5	£5
William (*dispenator*) of Wrotham	½	Wrotham (Yaldham)	1	£3	£6

sixty knights' estates for which figures can be taken from Domesday possessed on average about one and a half demesne ploughs and two tenant ploughs each. Almost every knight had one or slightly more plough-teams working on his demesne, and most had their own tenants. To try and link the demesne ploughs up with the serfs or bordars among the tenants is a game hardly worth the attraction it has, since occasional correspondences (Saltwood, Whitstable, Wingham) are contradicted by far more instances. Besides, experience suggests that conditions on the day of a census are often untypical. It is more reasonable to connect the tenants' ploughs with the *villani* and probably the bordars, because the oft-repeated Domesday formula 'so many *villani* and so many bordars have so

1. Conversion from hides on the Sussex estates has been made as before, p. 58 *n*.2. Yokes have been rendered as quarter-sulungs.

Table 3. The properties of the knightly estates in Domesday

Estate	Demesne ploughs	Villani	Bordars	Cotters	Serfs	Tenant ploughs
Adisham (2 knights)	4	18	5	0	0	1
Berwick (1 knight)	2	9	9	0	0	1½
Boughton Malherbe (1 knight)	1	3	2	0	0	1
Brasted (1 knight)	2	24	16	0	15	12
Buckland (1 knight)	1	0	0	0	0	0
Crayford (1 knight)	2	27	2	0	0	8
E. Farleigh (1 knight)	2	7	10	0	4	3
Eynsford (1 knight)	5	29	9	0	9	15
Farningham (1 knight)	2	13	5	0	0	3½
Finglesham (1 knight)	0	6	0	0	0	1½
Gillingham (1 knight)	1?	0	2	0	0	0
Graveney (1 knight)	1	8	10	0	5	2
Langport (1 knight)	2	29	9	0	0	9
Lavant, Sx (1 knight)	0	1	3	0	0	1
Leaveland (1 knight)	1	2	1	0	0	1
Lenham (1 knight)	2	15	2	0	4	4
Lyminge (3 knights)	5½	0	0	0	1	0
Maidstone (3 knights)	3½	32	4	0	10	6
Orpington (1 knight)	1	4	1	0	4	½
Otford (3 knights)	3	16	11	0	5	4
Pagham, Sx (1 knight)	0	0	2	0	0	0
Petham (2 knights)	4	4	8	0	0	3
Pett (1 knight)	1	0	0	0	4	0
Pluckley (1 knight)	2½	16	7	0	8	11
Saltwood (1 knight)	2	33	12	0	2	9½
Sheppey (1 knight)	1	0	2	0	4	0
S. Malling, Sx (1 knight)	2	14	2	0	0	2
do. (1 knight)	1	11	2	0	0	3
do. (1 knight)	2	2	3	0	0	0
do. (1 knight)	2	1	1	0	0	1
Statenborough (1 knight)	0	12	0	0	0	1½
Stowting (1 knight)	2	27	13	0	8	7
Tangmere, Sx (1 knight)	2	15	15	0	0	4
Tarring, Sx (1 knight)	1	4	5	0	0	1½
Tilmanstone (1 knight)	2	0	5	0	0	0
Ulcombe (1 knight)	2	23	8	0	0	7
Westgate (5 knights)	5½	8	26	0	0	2
do. (1 knight)	2	0	5	0	1	0
do. (1 knight)	2	5	3	0	0	2½
Whitstable (1 knight)	5	0	29	0	5	0
Wingham (1 knight)	1	4 and 1 knight (*miles*)			0	1
do. (5 knights)	8	0	22	0	8	0
Wrotham (1 knight)	1	2	0	0	0	½
do. (1 knight)	1	6	1	0	0	2
do. (1 knight)	3	6	0	12	10	2

many ploughs' itself does so. Remembering, then, that perhaps four knights had no demesne at all but only tenants, and seventeen had demesnes only and no tenant-lands, it is possible for the sake of a general concept to work out the 'average' Canterbury knight as the possessor of one or two plough-teams and the lord of eight fairly substantial village families, and of four or five cottagers, who between them could also raise a couple of plough-teams. If he lived in north or north-west Kent he was likely to have a small group of serfs, but not if he lived in east Kent or Sussex. Whether he lived in west or east Kent, he may also have known by name—as we do not—a knight who himself dwelt on an estate with a plough as the tenant of one greater than he.[1]

Here and there the thirteenth century offers a more detailed view of a knightly estate. Though the leap forward in time begs many questions, it is useful to compare the property held in Gillingham by Hugh of Gillingham who died before 1273 with that of his forbear Robert Brutin, for it had continued through all the intervening years to owe the service of half a knight, and the existence there in the thirteenth century of one full-time plough suggests that the estate was not so very different from that which in 1086 had also been described as containing land for one plough. Outside the original estate the family had prospered moderately, acquiring land in Lincolnshire and a good deal more locally. But in 1273–4 the half-fee meant in agrarian terms $178\frac{1}{2}$ acres severally under wheat, oats, barleys, peas and vetches, with numerous marsh-pastures, some meadow and a garden. The estate's centre was a thatched manor-house, and its staff consisted almost entirely of hired labour, mostly full-time, working under a serjeant. A second plough was used in winter and another ploughman taken on, but the tenants who came along and paid some 30s. at Easter and again at Michaelmas did little else for the Gillingham lord except mow a few acres of meadow-land. This is not very surprising. The Domesday tenantry consisted of precisely two bordars, so the obviously much larger tenantry of the thirteenth century had come into existence at a more recent time, when new services were not imposed.[2]

1 cf. p. 79, above.
2. Addit. ms. 29794, m. 8. Such tenants would be justiciable to their immediate lord only in minor manorial matters, rarely for more, as in Domesday Romney; otherwise they would owe suit to the archbishop's court.

98

Knights did not only gain their livelihood by exploiting the estates which they had received in military tenure. Even in the time of Lanfranc they sometimes took leases of landed property or, conversely, might lease out their feudal land to a third party. The line between the knight and the farmer is a fine one.[1] On one side of this line was a man like Robert Latin or Latim(i)er, apparently not a knight, and certainly not in the archbishop's list, but the lessee of Kentish property, including some near Rochester from the archbishop, at an annual value of well over £100. He has been identified as Robert the interpreter, who held also of the archbishop in Otford, alongside Geoffrey de Ros and sharing with him from the pen of a Norman clerk the name of 'thegn'.[2] If the identification is correct, he was another of those distinguished Englishmen who collaborated in the government of Norman Kent: the son of an English priest, brother of a reeve of Chatham, and able, if his nickname is significant, to talk to ruler and ruled alike. On the other side of the line were those who though knights were also farmers. Robert fitzWazo was one, a great knight, owing for six fees, but also tenant of the fee-farm of Sundridge, for which he rendered £23 and one knight.[3] The knights who held Farningham, Graveney, Lenham, Hunton, Swarling and Pett did so in fee of the archbishop, but also on condition of rendering annual farm to the monastic treasury at Canterbury.[4] The farm might be only a few shillings, but it might in some cases be more than the published value of the fee. Later instances also show how a farm might shade into a tenure by knight-service. At Saltwood in the late twelfth century, Ingram de Praers was Hugh de Montfort's fee-farmer at £5 per annum, but when the estate was returned by de Montfort to the archbishop's lordship, the fee-farmer, kept on as a condition of the return, was additionally charged with the service of two knight's fees.[5]

By far the greatest of the knightly farmers of Canterbury was

1. cf. Reginald Lennard, *Rural England 1086–1135* (1959), esp. ch. VI.
2. ibid., p. 151*n*.
3. Sundridge was held in 1171 by Thomas son of Thomas fitzBernard, evidently fitzWazo's successor (Colvin, op. cit.). Sundridge continued throughout the Middle Ages to be held in fee-farm for approximately the same amount, though the render of a knight is not heard of again. FitzWazo is an instance of the knight who rented feudal land to another: his two sulungs at Eythorne in Adisham were said to be worth £7, though he who held them rendered £8 ('*ex iis sullinc habet Rodbertus . . . et tamen qui tenet reddit . . .*').
4. See above, pp. 81–2.
5. Lambeth MS. 1212, p. 76; *Curia Regis Rolls*, XII, nos. 1466, 2455.

Godfrey of [South] Malling. He and his descendants deserve special attention because they can be traced with a high degree of probability and illustrate in their story both the conjunction of knights and farmers and the life and preoccupations of their kind.

Godfrey of Malling owed the archbishop the service of taree knights in the time of William II. He held one hide of South Malling, Sussex (probably Glynde),[1] also some land in Thanington and Newenden, Kent, in fee, and Lenham and Hunton in Kent, for which he paid farm to the monks. The sums he paid for these, however, are dwarfed by the £90 he owed as annual rent for the entire manor of South Malling, which stretched northward from Lewes into the weald and comprised numerous villages and woodland settlements. In the reign of Henry II the Canterbury knight who owed the service of three fees for Glynde, Thanington, Lossenham (near Newenden) and Buxted (in South Malling) was Richard Waleys, who had married a certain Denise and by her had had a son called Godfrey. It is likely that Denise was the descendant of Godfrey of Malling and transmitted to her son both the name of her ancestor and the lands he had held of the archbishop in Sussex and Kent. When Richard died, Denise married again, and Godfrey had to sue his stepfather, Ralph de Arderne, for the lands which he, Godfrey, regarded as his inheritance, but which Archbishop Walter had granted to Ralph. The case was extremely expensive for Godfrey, but it secured his inheritance and enlarges our own knowledge of the family's history.[2] In 1210–12 Godfrey Waleys was holding Glynde and Tarring in Sussex, and Thanington in Kent by the service of $2\frac{1}{4}$ knights[3] to the archbishop, but the disagreements between his family and its lord were not yet at an end. Under Archbishop Edmund (1233–40) his Sussex manor of Tarring, held in 1210–12 for a quarter-fee, was being held by Godfrey (possibly the same one) at farm for the service of £18 a year or its value in provisions for the archbishop's household when he came to stay. Tarring lies to the west of South Malling, near Worthing, and may well have appeared a suitable staging-point for

1. See Colvin, op. cit., p. 19, and refs. there for this paragraph.
2. *Curia Regis Rolls*, vi, pp. 11–12; *F. of F.*, pp. 55–6.
3. The missing quarter may be accounted for either by the loss of Lossenham which does not appear in the *Red Book* among his estates and may have been fee-farmed with Newenden (see L.R. 1207 and pp. 104–5 below), or by a change of Tarring to fee-farm. But the Waleys' *servitium* appears again as three fees in 1285 (see Appendix A).

the archbishop's entourage on their way to or from the westerly manor of Pagham. At all events, the archbishop had agreed with Waleys that if he gave forty days' notice he might come once a year or, alternatively, four times a year, and find ready for him household supplies to the value of the farm, priced according to an exactly specified scale, together with all the equipment for dining, billeting and stabling.[1] When the archbishop was not there, Godfrey was bound to treat the men of the manor fairly, according to their tenures, without vexation hnd exaction, and just as the archbishop treated the men of his other manors. If he broke any of these conditions the archbishop might enter the manor and keep it at his will. Unfortunately, Godfrey did offend, was deprived of the manor and surrendered up the keys of the houses to master Richard de Wich, the archbishop's chancellor. The archbishop resumed seisin of the manor and took the fealties of the tenants. But Godfrey was persuasive, or the archbishop soft-hearted, and a new lease was sealed on 10 June 1237. The manor was granted to Godfrey on the same terms, though not to his heirs after him. Further, Godfrey promised to pay £80 by quarterly instalments over the next four years in compensation for his defaults, with an additional £10 every time he missed a quarterly payment. In return, the archbishop gave £80 as a marriage-portion to be divided between Godfrey's four daughters, and their portions were to be banked in the priory of St Pancras at Lewes until 'with the consent of their friends' the girls were provided for in marriage. The holding of the hundred court at Tarring by the archbishop's bailiffs had also been called in question, and this matter was to go to the arbitration of William de Ralegh and William of York, judges and future bishops. In due course Godfrey died and Archbishop Edmund entered upon the manor as was his right,[2] but once more, 'overcome by the insistence' of Godfrey, the son and heir, he relinquished it, this time making no mention of heirs one way or the other, on condition the farm was paid as before and the men treated properly. Things remained thus under Boniface of Savoy who became archbishop in 1245, and when Godfrey the younger died Boniface took the manor into his hand as a feudal custody,

1. For all this see below, p. 202.
2. The archbishops may, of course, have been influenced in trying to get the manor back by the greater contemporary attractions of demesne exploitation. See D. Sutcliffe, 'The Financial Condition of the See of Canterbury' in *Speculum* (1935), p. 61 *et seq.*; also pp. 204–5 below.

assigned Joan, the widow, a third part of it in dower, and kept the two thirds until the heir, Richard, reached his majority. Richard then did homage for the two thirds in the normal way, and held the property from Boniface and, after him, from Archbishop Kilwardby. But it was not long before the dispute broke out again, and was brought to a final settlement by a plea before the king. At some time before 1276 Kilwardby sent four of his agents (among whom was a certain John of Ardene) to take the two thirds of the manor of Tarring (less, for some reason, twenty-eight acres) in to his own hand on the grounds that Richard Waleys, knight, had broken the conditions of service by which he, like his ancestors, was bound. The case came to a first hearing in the archbishop's court in Sussex. Each side asked for judgment: Richard on the rather weak plea that—although he acknowledged that he owed £18 a year—his father and grandfather had not bound their heirs to the services in question, and that when the archbishop had come to Tarring he had come simply as a guest and had not received the keys. The arch-bishop through his bailiff argued that Richard could not be in better case than his father and grandfather if they were alive. The bailiff was asked if Richard had done homage, and replied shrewdly that Richard held other tenements for which his homage had been taken, and if he, the bailiff, took homage for this one he did so under conditions contained in the deeds of acknowledgement executed by Godfrey the elder and Godfrey the younger. These former written acknowledgements were exhibited, and copied into the proceedings with the result that this story can be reconstructed.

Issue was joined, but it was more difficult to secure a verdict. The first day assigned was Saturday, 18 July 1276, at East Grinstead, but Joan the widow, who seems to have been involved in the case on the side of her son, refused to proceed on the ground that the jurors were all drawn from places within the archbishop's liberty. Jurors from elsewhere could not be found on the spot, and the court was adjourned till a fortnight after Michaelmas. In the meantime the king's council was to be consulted. A month after Michaelmas the parties came before the king and agreed that he should hold an inquest by knights and others of the neighbourhood of Tarring agreeable to either side, to find out what services had been imposed upon Richard's ancestors when they first entered or held the manor. Until the case was settled the manor was to be taken into the king's hand. The formation of the jury was attempted on 20 November, but without success, partly for lack of knights, and partly because the free tenants who came were nearly all challenged by one side or the other. Another attempt was fixed for 30 November at Bletchingley, Surrey, and the sheriffs of Surrey and Kent were ordered to distrain enough men to get together a satisfactory jury.[1] But again on the day the knights and free tenants of Sussex were challenged away by the two sides, and Richard objected to any juror from Kent or Surrey, presumably because he regarded the archbishop as too powerful there. The third attempt was lucky. On 3 February 1277 the parties appeared at Westminster, a jury was chosen with the consent of all,[2] and it proceeded to declare as follows: that the manor of Tarring was *ius et membrum* of the church of Canterbury, that it had been handed over to Richard's ancestor on the conditions already described, but that Richard himself had treated the men of the manor otherwise than the archbishop treated the men in his other manors in that he had compelled them to thresh corn or else pay money regularly, and not only in preparation for the archbishop's arrival.[3] Richard's case collapsed, and he acknowledged the manor to be forfeit. Edward I's letters patent embodying the judgment soon followed and were placed in the archbishop's treasury among his charters, and a memorandum of the whole business was transcribed into his notebook of proofs and precedents.[4]

The central issue of Tarring was of sufficient importance to come before the king and bear the costs of his judgment, and it is instructive for us on a number of scores. But there was also a whole series of lesser matters at issue between Richard Waleys and the archbishop which were heard at South Malling and resolved at about the same time. One of these was Richard Waleys' claim to have a free chace at South Malling. His petition illustrates an

1. This was doubtless in addition to the provision of men from Sussex which was already being arranged.
2. Denis de Croft, Henry de Lyons, Robert de Sancto Claro, Simon de Sangelton, Thomas de Offinton, William de Henton, Aunfrey de Gatewik, William de la Rede, Adam le Justur, Robert Troytemenen, William de le Legh and John de Wyntreshull.
3. The custumal of 1284–5 recalls that Richard had spent the 'Bishop's Threshing' works in regular threshing and also hoeing and breaking clods (*S.R.S.*, vol. 57, p. 26).
4. Joan, the widow, was still holding her third during the vacancy of 1278–9; the royal keepers in accounting for the issues of the two thirds which were then in the archbishop's demesne noted that the remainder would return at Joan's death (P.R. 124, m. 23d.).

occupation of knightly men in detail so sharp and curious that it is worth translating aere from the excellent French in waica it was couched:[1]

Because it has pleased my lord archbishop that I, Richard Waleys, should inform him in writing under my seal before the feast of All Saints about the character of my chace which belongs to my free holding in the manor of South Malling, this is to make known that I claim it as my right, and as the seisin of my ancestors and of myself, to chase and course between *Wyburgstak*, Bolebrook [in Withyham] and Courthope [in Ticehurst] the hare, fox, wildcat, badger, otter, squirrel and rabbit, provided that the animal does not go to earth on the demesnes of my lord the archbishop; and to go after pheasant and partridge without using trap and cage on his demesne; and after larger beasts outside the park and chace of my lord archbishop. And if one of these larger beasts enter the park or free chace after being shot, I can follow it with my hound into the place and take it without danger of being accused. And if the hound lose the scent I must retire and abandon the chace. And if the beast while pursued but not struck by an arrow enter the park or chace and is caught therein, provided I can reach it with my couple on their leashes stretched out from the hedge of the park or boundary of the chace, then, giving a blast on the horn, the beast is mine. If it is captured further in, the huntsman shall blow three times, with a reasonable space between each blast, for the parker or forester, and shall deliver to him the four limbs if he comes. If he does not come, then I shall send them to the house of the parker or forester. But if the beast escape, I must recall my hounds with the horn and withdraw to the boundary. And from a river called Lymene [in south-west Kent] up to Bolebrook, Courthope and Croil [Ashburnham, in east Sussex] everywhere . . . [the MS. here breaks off].

The story of the Waleys may be brought to an end here, for it has served the purpose of illustrating the relationship of the archbishop with one of his knightly families. But a chance reference in an account roll of 1517 suggests that even after three hundred years the family still retained its hold on some ancestral land, and still was liable to misbehave itself, for the farmer of Newenden in Kent that year rendered £5 for the fee-farm of the manor, lately held by

1. Lambeth MS. 1212, p. 103. I am grateful for help with the translation to Dr M. F. Lyons, my colleague, and to Dr Evans of Queen Mary College; also to Mr J. S. Moore for some help with place-identification. For the rest of the process, ibid., pp. 103–6. The Waleys continued in South Malling till the fifteenth century. See Appendix A.

John Waleys, who had been outlawed, and now re-let to William Raynold.[1]

These incidents and conditions of knightly life raise a question of the widest importance which has not yet been considered. How far were the *milites archiepiscopi* the members of a social class that can be distinguished from other social classes? Obviously, no single answer could apply to the entire medieval period, during which the knight changed his character no less than other members of the community. But even within a short period an answer is not simply given. The question of military technique must be left aside, since it is impossible at present to decide how far the knight as such was the active and irreplaceable warrior of the first century of English feudalism. As a rural landowner, enough has already been said to show him even in the earliest period as one among others dwelling in a countryside of expanding population and wealth, acquiring fields and rents, marsh pastures and assarts, by the means that were available to all with money to spend, whether they were knights, knights' kin, or men of lesser ancestry. Yet to be a knight was not unimportant. Among the archbishop's men the tradition of knighthood passing from father to son is discernible in the feudal records that have been considered, and in the names of those *milites ecclesie* which recur, not seldom followed by the names of their sons, as witnesses to the acts of archbishops.[2] Of the making of the knights itself almost nothing is known. The joy with which Malcolm IV of Scotland in 1159 received the belt of knighthood from Henry II in a remote French meadow was possibly singular in its telling and in the dignity of the actors rather than in its essence.[3] Through all dilutions and disadvantages, rank has never counted for nothing, and we may note as a small and local illustration of this point that as late as 1335 Prior Robert Oxenden advertised the emoluments payable to a steward of the manors to be lower for those who were not knights than for those who were.[4]

1. L.R. 1207. Lossenham was in Newenden. Richard Waleys was farming Newenden in 1292–4 for £9 per annum (P.R. 141m. 28d.), and Godfrey Waleys likewise in 1313–14 (Mins. Accts 1128/4).
2. e.g. William of Eynsford, the father, and William, his son; William of Pagham and Giffard his son, who among the knights witness acts of Archbishop William (*Archaeologia Cantiana*, LXXII (1958), pp. 50–1).
3. G. W. S. Barrow, 'The Beginning of Feudalism in Scotland', *Bulletin of the Institute of Historical Research*, XXIX (1956), p. 6.
4. *Literae Cantuarienses*, II, ed. J. Brigstocke Sheppard (*R.S.*, 1888), no. 587.

Though related to property, knighthood was not merely a matter of wealth, but to be a *knight of the archbishop* was something which greatly changed in meaning during the Middle Ages; or rather, should we say, it is a concept which faded out somewhere in the thirteenth century when all over the feudal world new, professional organizations were coming into being. In the twelfth century, the *milites* or *milicia archiepiscopi* was a term of art to be found in documents.[1] It applied to a certain group of men who could be named, however much they might differ from each other in wealth, status or accomplishment. Aside from their obligations to arms, they might regularly or occasionally serve the archbishop by giving counsel in his ear, decisions in his courts or testimony to his acts, and they did so by virtue of their tenurial connexion with him. Up till the thirteenth century and the explosive fragmentation of tenures, these men and their families can be traced often and easily through the records of those tenures, and in them we can discern the regional aristocracy with its roots in the Norman revolution. It was not, of course, a caste, but it was sufficiently linked together by marriage and inheritance to form a society of landlords which stood between the archbishops and their communities of rural tenants. They were there because of their family histories, not as passing newcomers investing in local property, and they, together with local monks and the archbishop's household clerks, carried the burden of the estates' government. More light may be shed upon the rooted, local nature of the *milites archiepiscopi* by glancing at the inter-connexion between them and certain other lordships, and then by looking at the family of Eynsford.

Many of those who in the twelfth century held of the archbishop, or came to hold of him, in knight service, belonged also to other lordships. Notably, there were inter-connexions between the archbishop's barony and those of Aldington, Chatham, Chilham, Clare, Folkestone, de Ros, Little Dunmow and Swanscombe complex enough to make the 'tenurial heterogeneity' of Maitland's town seem as simple as the division of a modern school into houses.[2] It is interesting that the lands of many of those baronies can be traced back to the possession of Odo of Bayeux, whose constant obtrusion in these pages suggests him as perhaps the greatest single figure in

1. *Dom. Mon.*, p. 105; Colvin, op. cit., p. 6.
2. For these baronies, see I. J. Sanders, *English Baronies* (1960), and Appendix A, below.

Kentish history. Aldington, where the archbishop's own largest demesne manor also lay, became the head of a barony in the hands of a family descended from Helto, probably Odo's steward. In 1180 it was divided among three co-heiresses, one third passing to William of Cheriton, who also owed the archbishop a knight for Farningham, and thence to the Criols or Kyriels, probably through the Albevilles. Both these families were also tenants of the arch- bishopric. Another third descended to the Septvans, who became tenants of the see in the area of Canterbury.[1] Chatham had been held of Odo by Robert the Latin, but came in the time of William II to the Crevequers, who also became major tenants of the see. The probable barony of Chilham sprang from Fulbert I of Dover, another tenant of Odo, whose descendants brought Hothfield to the archbishop's lordship. The connexion between Canterbury and Clare has already been discussed.[2] Folkestone was held of Odo by William of Arques, who also held of the archbishop in Fleet, near Sandwich. On three occasions in its history the barony descended through women, the husbands or sons of whom were knights of the archbishopric, until in 1263 it was parted among four co-heiresses, two of whom passed on their shares to knightly tenants of the archbishopric. In 1253 the fee in Fleet was described as held by 'the heir of Folkestone', and by him of the archbishop. As for the probable barony of Ros, Geoffrey de Ros was tenant both of Odo and of the archbishop. William (I) de Ros died in 1190, and his heir, William (II), came of age about 1211. In the meantime, King John in 1202 granted to Archbishop Walter the whole fee of William de Ros 'over which there was contention between former kings and archbishops'.[3] When the estate was ultimately divided between Maud and Lora, half went to Maud's husband, Geoffrey de Percy, and in 1273-4 after Maud's death the archbishop received £33 6s. 8d. relief.[4] Little Dunmow was the centre of the Domesday lordship held by Ralph Baynard, who also

1. An extent of the barony of Aldington, in the hands of the Septvans, is to be found in *IPM*, IV, 349.
2. See above, pp. 85-6.
3. LCM, XI, p. 12; cf. Lambeth MS. 1212, pp. 47, 197-8. The archbishop granted custody of the heirs to Peter de Stokes (LCM, XI, p. 16; Lambeth MS. 1212, p. 91).
4. Addit. MS. 29, 794, m. 7. In 1246 Henry III declared that the marriage he had arranged between Maud, sister of Richard de Ros, deceased, and Geoffrey de Percy, his own tenant, was not to be regarded as prejudicial to the archbishop, as the king had no right therein but by the archbishop's favour (Lambeth MS. 1212, p. 59).

owed the archbishop the service of two fees. By 1171 a successor of this man was holding two fees of the archbishop in Graveney, but 'of the honour of Baynard'.[1] Finally, the lordship of Swanscombe, also once held of Odo of Bayeux, came eventually, it seems, to Geoffrey Talbot, whose son, another Geoffrey, died in 1140 leaving two daughters, one of whom married Walter de Mayenne, the archbishop's tenant of Preston near Aylesford, for which he owed one knight 'of the honour of Talbot'.[2]

These abbreviated accounts illustrate the feudal mosaic over two centuries and the growing complexity of its pattern as the secular lordships split and re-formed. But the names of the heirs, or the husbands of the heiresses, are frequently encountered in the records of the archbishopric itself, bearing as knightly tenants a part in the life of the estates more pronounced than that of their descendants in the later medieval generations.

The intricate scene can be illuminated from another angle by a single event. In 1261 an inquisition assembled at Otford in the presence of senior members of the archbishop's estate council to decide whether Nicholas de Criol and William Herengod were the true heirs of William of Eynsford, seventh and last of that name, lately dead, or whether Alan de la Lese might enjoy his claim through Agnes his wife.[3] The occasion was an important one, for us who see the end of a great and ancient local dynasty witnessed by the archbishop's feudal court meeting in the days of its decline, and in the presence of the estate council in the days of its youth, and for the actors by reason of the dignity of the estate now come to its partition. Though held of the archbishop as its chief lord, records styled the Eynsford estate a 'barony', and its head had once been sheriff of London and farmer of the counties of Essex and Hertfordshire.[4] Those who gathered now to give their testimony were Geoffrey de Percy, Henry de Aperfield and Richard de Pontefract, knights, and nine of the better suitors of the archbishop's court at Otford. In virtue of their fealty to the archbishop they declared as follows:

1. Colvin, op. cit., pp. 7, 20–1.   2. ibid., pp. 7, 29–30.
3. For what follows, see Lambeth MS. 1212, p. 417. The earlier pedigree of the Eynsfords was worked out by Professor Douglas in *Dom Mon.*, pp. 44–7. The document under discussion enlarges this and modifies it slightly. Herengod was the name of a *miles archiepiscopi* in Domesday.
4. J. H. Round, *Geoffrey de Mandeville* (1892), pp. 298, 360. In the thirteenth century the tenants had the hundred-court of Wrotham, and the right to hang men convicted by the royal justices (*C.Cl.R. 1273–9*, p. 23).

... that William the second lord, son of William Goram, begot in lawful wedlock four sons, namely, John, the eldest, William, Bartholomew and Ralph; that John in the lifetime of his father took a wife but never had seisin of the lands since he also died in his father's day. He begot upon his wife a certain William de Acrise, and this William begot upon his wife Robert de la Lese; and Robert begot Agnes, wife of Alan de la Lese who now claims the inheritance in the name of Agnes his wife. But neither John nor any descendants of his ever had seisin of the inheritance. And they know nothing more in favour of the right of Alan and Agnes his wife. But William, the third lord, brother of John and son of William the second, after his father's death entered upon the inheritance and kept it. And he begot William, the fourth lord of Eynsford, who begot William 'Rufus', the fifth lord, and two daughters, Joan, the elder, and Beatrice. William 'Rufus' himself begot a daughter called Beatrice, who married Henry the son of Robert of Ruxley. Upon her Henry begot William who was father of William the seventh lord now dead in the archbishop's wardship and without heir.

And thus the inheritance of Eynsford ought to revert to the heirs of Joan and Beatrice, sisters of William 'Rufus'. Now Joan married Hugh de Albeville who begot William de Albeville, the father of Joan de Albeville, wife of Nicholas de Criol who now claims the inheritance. And Beatrice married Stephen Herengod who begot William Herengod, who now claims the inheritance which concerns him through his father.

And so they say that Nicholas and Joan his wife, and William Herengod, are the next heirs of William of Eynsford the seventh, deceased.

The jury went on to declare that service of 4¾ fees was owed for the manor of Eynsford with its members at Toppesfield (Essex), Ightham and Ruckinge, and that tenure of Wrotham manor was in fee-farm for £32 per annum, payable in supplies, £4 12s. gafol at mid Lent, and 15s. to the archbishop's alms. Their ordered verdict hardly needs embroidering to show how the family had been woven into the countryside and the society of the archbishop's estates, though it may in addition be pointed out that Robert of Ruxley, probably the successor at Orpington of the Domesday Malger, was a steward of the archbishop, Stephen Langton, and a knight of some importance.[1] The Albevilles, as has been seen previously, held Westenhanger of the archbishop, until they were succeeded there by the Criols, and the Herengods had held Stowting manor and hundred, and are traceable back to Domesday Wingham.

1. K. Major, 'The *Familia* of Archbishop Stephen Langton', *E.H.R.*, XLVIII, pp. 545–7; Lambeth MS. 1212, p. 77.

Table 4. The descent of the Eynsford family[1]

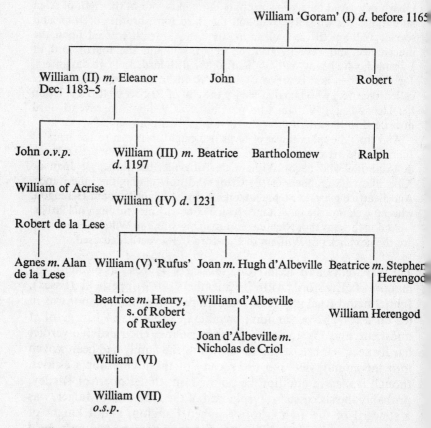

Ralph s. of Ospac, tenant of Eynsford in 1086.

William s. of Ralph of Eynsford, *m.* 'H'.
Prob. sheriff of London, and of
Essex in 1128. Became a monk
of Christ Church *c.* 1135.

William 'Goram' (I) *d.* before 116⁵

William (II) *m.* Eleanor   John   Robert
Dec. 1183–5

John *o.v.p.*   William (III) *m.* Beatrice   Bartholomew   Ralph
                 d. 1197

William of Acrise

William (IV) *d.* 1231

Robert de la Lese

Agnes *m.* Alan   William (V) 'Rufus'   Joan *m.* Hugh d'Albeville   Beatrice *m.* Stepher
de la Lese   Herengod

Beatrice *m.* Henry,   William d'Albeville
s. of Robert
of Ruxley   William Herengod

Joan d'Albeville *m.*
Nicholas de Criol

William (VI)

William (VII)
o.s.p.

The descent of knightly tenures can often be traced through the
thirteenth century and beyond, but a society based upon them was
becoming a thing of the past. The total area of land held in
military tenure was not capable of much expansion, and the fees

1. For a discussion of the earlier part of this descent, see *Dom Mon.*, pp. 44–7, where,
however, William 'Goram' is numbered II, and so on.

which composed it were constantly subject to fraction. Its heirs were reliant upon landed wealth other than this for their substance and position. The famous charter, already quoted,[1] wherein Edward I in 1276 disgavelled the lands of John de Cobham because partible inheritance supposedly led to poverty, said nothing about the diminution of fees themselves, nor the economic remedies which were the only real ones; but it expressed in its way the strains of transition, and reminds us that the Kentish knight by tenure might be in a poor way while his gavelkind neighbour throve. In that same year of 1276, the memorandum of the Tarring plea alludes to the lack of knights for the holding of inquisitions.[2] In 1313 a sheriff of Kent noted the small number in the county who held in knight's fee, and their poverty, whereas most who came to the county court held in gavelkind.[3] This situation may even have been in Hubert Walter's thoughts a hundred years earlier when he acquired the rights to convert gavelkind to fee and to hold grand assizes of gavelkind lands in his own courts.[4] Certainly the great gavelkind landowners like Thomas of Goodnestone and Alan of Twitham who appear as knights in the thirteenth century were explicitly charged with the customs of 'shirelands' and required to join juries when summoned to give judgments on the king's writ.[5]

The fading importance of knightly tenure was not the only or even the root cause of the changes which obliterated *milites archiepiscopi* as a term of art. The economic boom of the late twelfth and the thirteenth centuries touched everybody in one way or another. The demesnes which now offered such chances of profit called into being new skills of management to match the growing professionalism of purely ecclesiastical administration. While the officials and commissaries were developing their courts and displacing the older and more primitive gatherings of clerks and knights about their bishop, estate councils were also being elaborated, and officers allocated to newly particularized functions or districts: organization of Liberty was being distinguished from

1. See above, p. 70, and references there. 2. See above, p. 103.
3. *Eyre of Kent*, I, ed. F. W. Maitland and others (Selden Society, vol. 24, 1909), p. xx.
4. Lambeth MS. 1212, pp. 47–8; and see also above, pp. 69–71.
5. Dean and Chapter of Canterbury MS. E 24, fos. 2, 7, 8v; cf., among other instances of the same date (1284–5), William of Pagham, who held a quarter-fee of the archbishop in Tangmere, probably by a recent arrangement: 'and if on the king's writ some judgment in court shall lie in respite for lack of peers, then he must come to court' (ibid., printed in *S.R.S.*, vol. 57, p. 11).

organization of lands, and lands themselves divided into baili-wicks.[1] In either case, new expertise was required of men in authority such as knowledge of the law, of the management of property, and of methods and events beyond the locality. All these things came ultimately, of course, through the possession of land and thus of wealth and power, but they were not guaran-teed by it in any particular individual, least of all by the mere tenure of some archiepiscopal fee or its fraction. Hence, in the history of the Canterbury knights, there is a very rough parallel with that of the barons of the realm itself. Once identified by their tenures, which qualified them for their status and, indeed, served to describe them, they come in the end to owe their position (based upon wealth of some sort) to the deliberate choice of the chief lord who required their services, mindful of what they had to offer now or in the future rather than of their ancient obligations. It is no accident that during the fourteenth century the records of homages performed to the archbishops by their knights for their lands in military tenure disappear from the registers, while their place is taken up more and more with memoranda of appointment to secular offices on the estates: of stewards, bailiffs, auditors and the rest. The men to whom these appointments went, unless they were simply professional lawyers or accountants, were of high status and social influence, but not necessarily knights of the archbishop in the old sense of holding of him in military tenure. In one sense 'knights of the archbishop' might continue to mean those tenants whose split-up fees can be hunted through inquisitions *post mortem* or private feudal records. In a stronger sense, they were those laymen of high degree, to be met more appropriately in a later chapter,[2] who sometimes formed part of his entourage, sometimes presided as bailiffs over his local courts or business, sometimes drew handsome fees as his master of chaces or constable of Saltwood Castle, and so on. There were plenty of archbishop's kinsmen in such positions as the Middle Ages drew to an end: Chicheles, Bourgchiers and the proliferating race of Warhams. But they might also be men with little connexion with the arch-bishopric, engaged and well rewarded for their influence in the

1. For the growth of estate councils, see the pioneering essay on 'Baronial Councils and their Relation to Manorial Courts' in Miss A. E. Levett's *Studies in Manorial History* (1938).
2. See below in Chapter 6.

dangerous world of political power. Such was William Catesby, counsellor and squire of the body of Richard III, 'the Cat' who was executed after Bosworth, and whom a year earlier Cardinal Bourgchier had appointed bailiff of Pagham.[1] Another example is John Alpheigh, Bourgchier's bailiff of Otford, and one of the 'great extortioners of Kent' of the 1450s.[2] His will of 1489 reveals some but not all of the multifarious lands he had held, in villages once listed among the *terrae militum* of Domesday and elsewhere: Brasted, Sundridge, Chevening, Hever, Chiddingstone, Penshurst, Seal and Sevenoaks. His son-in-law in his time also gave counsel to the archbishop and was in 1485 granted right of succession to his father-in-law in the bailiwick of Otford. This was none other than 'the good Sir Robert Rede', Chief Justice of the King's Bench, who endowed the Rede Lecture at Cambridge University,[3] and to whom Alpheigh passed property by enfeoffments to use, means their forbears would have found subtle if not shocking, but in a tenure which lawyers, who will misdescribe anything to make it appear ancient, called 'fee simple'.

1. *Registrum Thome Bourgchier* (Canterbury and York Society, vol. LIV, 1957), p. 65.
2. ibid., p. 68; for Alpheigh's will, PCC Milles, fos. 147v. *et seq.*; cf. *IPM Hen. VII*, I, 530.
3. F. W. Maitland, *English Law and the Renaissance* (Rede Lecture for 1901, Cambridge University Press), pp. 1–5.

CHAPTER 4

Rural society

THE LAND AND ITS DIVISIONS

Scale is no less important to the historian than to the geographer, and each owes his readers some immediate sign of his subject's extension. The area which forms the subject of the present study belongs in an atlas rather than a guide-book, for although historians have sometimes set aside the south-east of England as wholly peculiar, it was neither small, unimportant nor exempt from the influences which transformed the rest of the country between the days of Lanfranc and those of Cranmer. On the one hand, therefore, no attempt is being made to pass off the history of a village as the truth about a region, nor on the other to generalize some readable selections into a rigid panorama of 'life on the English manor'. The essay is more than the one and less than the other, but in intention general rather than local. Kent was a large county, anciently settled and breeding articulate men, and the archbishop was for nearly a millennium its largest landowner. He traversed his manors constantly, and this took him in the normal course well beyond Kent itself as far as Bognor in the south-west and Harrow in the north-west. Wherever he went within the triangle formed by these places with Thanet at the tip of Kent, he was, save within the weald, within an hour or two's ride of his tenants. A small-scale manorial map would be misleading. The archbishop's manors were not solid little enclaves separated by long hours in the saddle, for most of them comprised hamlets, outriders and settlements scattered enough to make even the

114

internal manorial duties of his tenants as much a matter of serving communications as any other form of labour. Nor was the progress of a horseman as painfully slow as motorists might think, much less if the rider were anxious to be gone. Terrified by the violence of October 1326 in which Bishop Stapledon was murdered, Archbishop Reynolds took his party some twenty miles in an evening and farther next day. 'We were so stunned at the terrible deed,' he wrote to Prior Eastry, 'that we left Lambeth and went to Croydon and even as far as Otford that same night, and the next day to Maidstone, where we are remaining.'[1] It was not only the archbishop and his *familia* which moved about, bringing to village after village experiences and precepts from the outside world, for every manor itself owed external services of carrying, droving and court-going which were already defined and old by the thirteenth century, and which took a fair proportion of the inhabitants far afield on frequent occasions. So to draw lines linking the manors which were connected by customary routes is to produce a mesh over the south-east foreshadowing many first- and second-class roads of today. Over these men moved, sometimes slowly, driving swine to the depths of the weald and collecting the weary stragglers,[2] and sometimes fast, mounted and with sacks, bound for the markets, London or the coast on the archbishop's business. Therefore, whether it was a matter of carrying the steward's letters from London to Wrotham,[3] or seed-corn twelve leagues from Charing in any direction,[4] or provisions from Pagham to Winchester, Guildford or round by sea to Seaford, Winchelsea and Dover,[5] any picture of inertia and localism must be quite falsified. Little wonder that the power of the archbishop spread easily throughout a great area,[6] or that men of Kent had reason to fear the lightning descents of the French,[7] or that rumour, news, alarm and hope spread as

---

1. Dean and Chapter of Canterbury, Eastry Correspondence, Group I, p. 47. I owe this reference to Mrs Ian McFie.
2. Dean and Chapter of Canterbury MS. E 24, fo. 12v.: '... and they shall drive the pigs to pannage, and the lord shall find them a horse to carry their food and the pigs when they fail by the way'. See also the present writer's 'Denns, Droving and Danger' in *A.C.*, LXXVI (1961), pp. 75–87.
3. E 24, fo. 83 and L.R. 2068.
4. ibid., fo. 47v.
5. ibid., fo. 93.
6. See above, p. 103 (Waleys case, Chapter 3).
7. *Lit. Cant.*, I, no. 132: the people of the Canterbury district easily alarmed in 1324 by the *commune crie* and the sounds of trumpet and horn, warning of enemy approach from the sea.

rapidly as they did. There is nothing so strange about the Revolt of 1381 as the surprise of historians at the quick movements of the rebels' intelligence, and not long after the events themselves Gower, a Kentish man, described impressionistically the hasty rallying of countrymen with their abrupt cries:

> Watte vocat, cui Thomme venit, neque Symme retardat,
> Betteque, Gibbe simul, Hykke venire jubent. . . .[1]

The lives of villagers, like that of their lord, were designed for contact.

The societies of the manors were not isolated from each other, but neither were they exactly similar, nor simple and unitary within themselves. The south-east of England contained arable which at the time of the Conquest had already been cultivated for centuries: the rich flat lands of east Kent; the north Kentish lands which lay athwart the roads to London; the coastal plain about Bognor, Pagham and Chichester; Harrow and Hayes in Middlesex. The nucleus of almost every archiepiscopal manor was centred, naturally enough, upon this ancient arable. But the countryside was also a heavily wooded one, both in the wealden interior and in the blocks of uncleared forest like the Blean within the ambit of the older settled lands. The great manor of South Malling in east Sussex, indeed, consisted of a series of hamlets strung out northwards, some falling 'within the wood' and others subject to the older, arable regimen 'without the wood'. Besides the wood there were the marshlands which bordered the Thames estuary along the coastline west and east of Sheppey and again to the south in the expanse of Romney Marsh. Woodland and marsh alike were undergoing a progressive reclamation, centuries-long, and every manor had some share in the one work or the other, and often in both. Hence, the archbishops' estates contained remarkable contrasts of topograhpy and productive effort: the open arable of Wingham by Canterbury; the scarp slope of Wrotham, patchy with scrub, small fields and copse; the oak-denns of Aldington where communities of woodland settlers flourished, individualistic and unbiddable; the same manor's marsh pastures which became the homelands of larger-scale pioneers—farmers and yeomen— able to enclose and maintain many acres from the sea and receive favourable terms for doing so.

1. *Vox Clamantis*, ed. G. C. Macaulay, Lib. I, cap. xi (Oxford, 1902).

More must be said later about these major topographical types
and the tenant societies whose existence they influenced, but there
were other divisions of the land of which contemporaries were
perhaps more immediately aware and which need prior consideration. Today it is reckoned a simple matter for a family to belong to
several groupings at one and the same time: a hamlet, say, where
its members get their living, a rural district for the purposes of
rating, a postal village, and a parish. It is equally clear that the
medieval family on the archbishop's estates belonged to various
units, yet by no means so simple at this remove to distinguish their
purposes, relative importance or even exact nature. In Domesday
and the medieval rentals the most prominent units of measurement
are the sulung and the yoke in Kent, the hide and virgate in
the other manors, and according to them every manor was assessed.
But these divisions did not endure equally on all manors, and by
the thirteenth century other units had acquired new importance,
or at least can be newly seen to possess importance. These are the
borgh and the parish, and underlying these were the hamlets
themselves and their fields. Something must be said about each of
these divisions in turn.

In 1086 every Kentish manor of the archbishop was assessed in
terms of the sulung and sometimes also of its quarter-fraction, the
yoke. The yoke had an identity on the ground, and might even be
a place defined and separate from the other yokes composing a
particular sulung, like Orgarswick and Castweazel, two of the four
scattered yokes making up the monks' sulung of *Aelmesland* which
belonged in some way to Lyminge.[1] The Domesday texts also tell
the inquirer that sulung and yoke were made up of acres, though
not necessarily of the same number everywhere, but to know
precisely the sizes of sulungs and yokes it is necessary to wait for
the later rentals. Domesday supplies only hints and incomplete
equations. In Wingham, for example, Herengod had one sulung
less ten acres.[2] Whatever the origin of these units, the 'jugation'
which appears in Domesday was already old, had long been applied
to the cultivated settlements,[3] yet continued to be used and even

---

1. *Dom. Mon.*, p. 84.   2. ibid., p. 83.
3. In 1285 in Charing 'forland' was differentiated from *terra antiquitus iugata*
   (MS. E 24, fo. 47). The *iugum* was a theoretical unit invented at the end of the
   third century by Roman administrators to enable tax contributions to be
   assessed rapidly from parts of a large land area (F. Lot, 'Le Iugum, le manse et
   les exploitations agricoles de la France moderne', in *Mélanges d'histoire offerts à*

extended in many places while disappearing elsewhere for reasons which do not immediately appear.

Despite the ubiquity of the sulung in Domesday, it appears with completeness on only two of the archbishop's manors, Reculver and Thanet, in the thirteenth-century rental.[1] In either case the Domesday assessment is not very different from the later medieval sulungation. If the thirteenth-century Thanet was in fact the Domesday 'Northewode' or 'Nortone', as seems possible, then there were some nine and a half sulungs in demesne there in the late eleventh century, and rather more than eight sulungs two hundred years later. At nearby Reculver there were about eight sulungs at each period. The medieval rental gives the sulungs of Reculver names and exact areas. Each whole sulung was slightly more than 200 acres: the series ranges from 201 acres half a virgate to 213 acres. They were called the sulungs of Thomas at Brok, of Adam of Upedune, of Clement Potyn, of Salomon de Campo, of Hugh le Nene, of Adam de Aula, 'the sulung of Northwood of which Gervase the bedel was *Sulman*', and 'the sulung of Northwood of which John Austyn was *Sulyngman*'. It is clear enough that these names are not those of the owners or tenants of the sulungs as such, but of the men who were in some way responsible for the obligations which the sulungs existed to regulate. The names are recent ones, and the office of 'sulingman' is explicitly mentioned. On other manors where named yokes but not sulungs survive in the Middle Ages, though increasingly fragmented among tenants, it may be suggested by the same token that the man who gave the yoke its name was not necessarily the original tenant of the yoke itself, but rather the individual upon whose shoulders lay a one-time responsibility for the yoke's service. For to equate the yoke with the real holding of a family is to make an assumption which may or may not have once been true, but which is not true by the time fines and deeds allow us to see behind the rentals'

---

1. E 24, fo. 19ff.; L.R. 2068. Gray noted the persistence of the complete sulung as the rent-paying unit in east Kent (op. cit., pp. 299–300).

H. Pirenne (1926), pp. 307–26). The attempt has been made to trace the Kentish yoke to this (Gordon Ward in *A.C.*, XLII (1930), pp. 147–56), and also to link the compact, rectangular yoke to Roman centuriation, as at Gillingham (H. L. Gray, *English Field Systems* (1915), p. 415; M. Nightingale in *A.C.*, LXV (1952), pp. 150–9). But the evidence is insufficient, and even the rectangularity of the Kentish yoke is far from certain. See also D. Margary, 'Roman Centuriation at Ripe', *Sussex Archaeological Collections*, LXXXI (1940), pp. 31–41.

façade. Sulungs and yokes were artifacts, created at a time unknown, and continued into the Middle Ages, for the purpose of fixing the burdens of service and impost. They were real enough in the sense that they were of precise acreage and extended over the ground so that all the older fields lay within some sulung or other, and local men knew well enough in which sulung or yoke their possessions lay. But the sulungs and yokes were not themselves a field system, and possibly not even vestiges of one. Their fragmentation appears in the rentals among great numbers of tenants, but even a brief glance will show that it is a fragmentation (however intense) of an incredible regularity; and in fact it must have been a deliberately artificial device for apportioning burdens or their money equivalent, while the real partition of land went on in a parallel and far more complex and irregular way which can be illustrated from private deeds but never now comprehended as a whole.

It is remarkable that the sulung was not found useful on the archbishop's estates after Domesday save in those two instances of Thanet and Reculver. The name did not vanish entirely. There is a transitional case at Northfleet where four out of the forty-two yokes are grouped together and called *gedersuolinges* for the purpose of a certain service.[1] But generally the services were based upon yokes. And here again the assessments of Domesday, multiplying the sulungs by four to reduce them to yokes, are close to those of the thirteenth century. True, an exact correspondence never appears, but many hazards and unknown changes intervene between the two dates. For instance, the yokes on a given manor were capable of being re-formed, and sometimes new land was grouped into new yokes. A striking example of this is in the woodland denns of Haythurst and Finchurst which belonged to Gillingham, where the rental's scribe noted that 'the tenants of these denns shall associate together as two yokes when some *collectio* happens to be made for Rochester Bridge or for a taxation of the yokes'.[2] The Bexley yokes too show signs of regrouping at the hands of the lord's agent. By 1284 the fifth yoke had become 'the fifth yoke and a quarter, of fifty acres'. Of the seventh yoke, one acre was said to be now in the archbishop's park. Of the

1. MS. E 24, fo. 87v: '... *42 iuga in Northflete ... quorum 4 iuga sunt honyland et 4 gedersuolunge [sic] que non debent ... averare, sed 4 iuga de geder portabunt exennia Cantuar' Lamhith' vel alibi ad maneria archiepiscopi in Cantia'*.
2. ibid., fo. 32v.

twelfth, 'five acres are now wanting because they have fallen into
the lord's hand for lack of a tenant', and at the fourteenth the text
reads: 'it should be remembered that there are not many yokes
whole by themselves, but from two half-yokes joined together is
made one yoke, and thus there is made a fourteenth whole yoke of
forty acres'.[1] The rental often says how many acres the local yoke
was worth, but the acreage varied from manor to manor, and a
single manor might even possess yokes of different size, according
to the quality of the soil. In general, the better the soil, the higher
the value of the land and the smaller the yoke. At Maidstone and
Lyminge the yoke was fifty-two acres, at Petham fifty acres, at
Charing forty acres. Bexley had some yokes of forty acres and
others of thirty. The yokes of Gillingham, though usually about
twenty-five acres, varied between the twelve acres of yoke 'Hardyng'
to the fifty acres of the half-yoke 'Memeland'. The yokes were used
for the assessment of the rents and services, and despite the fact
that they were sometimes re-formed and always much morcellated
amongst co-heirs and parceners during the course of the Middle
Ages, they display in their names a great stability and power of
survival. It is sometimes tempting to think of them as fields which
owed their continuing identity to their physical separateness. A
certain Domesday yoke was said to consist of only two acres of
meadow.[2] Again, when Stephen Langton in 1219 exchanged some
land with Adam of Bending, he granted him *inter alia* half a yoke
and quarter of a virgate in Bechinghope, in the marshland near
Aldington, though the rest of the grant was measured in acres.[3]
Other instances of yokes which were not only physically identifiable by natural boundaries, but also by their tenure in the hands
of a man or family, might be found, yet this would not alter the fact
that at any rate by the thirteenth century they are the exception.
Although the yokes extended over precise fields and tenements,
they were not co-extensive with them, boundary for boundary, but
were rather a sort of notional grid superimposed upon real fields
whose own boundaries led a separate and parallel existence. This
is seen most clearly in the manor of Gillingham, which became
well known when H. L. Gray made it a prototype of the 'Kentish
field system'.[1] Gillingham lies at the mouth of the Medway on the

1. ibid., fo. 98v; cf. *Medieval Bexley*, p. 19.
2. *D.B.*, I, fo. 7.
3. Lambeth MS. 1212, p. 95.

right bank where the coastline runs from north-west to south-east
and the arable fields once sloped down towards the water. Over
the river to the north lay the 'Isle of Grain', which belonged in part
to the manor of Gillingham. On the mainland the manorial area
ran from the neighbourhood of Rochester along the Sittingbourne
road as far as Rainham, and in this direction the walker would
traverse numerous roads and ways running from the southern
slopes to terminate at the water's edge in hythes and landing-places.
The link with the Domesday information is very slight. Gillingham
was then assessed at six sulungs, and in the thirteenth-century
rental there is allusion to the tenants of 'the twenty-four yokes'.[3]
But by then there were more yokes than this, each identified by
the name of a man or, occasionally, of a place, and there were
already in addition numerous other units of smaller size, similarly
identified by proper names: *logi*, *campi*, *-ferthings* or *-ferlings*,
-crofts, *-hooks*, *-medes* and *-lands*. The Gillingham rental of
1447[3] shows that after nearly two hundred years these divisions
still remained. There are some marginal changes, but the correspondence, yoke for yoke, logus for logus, field for field, is
extremely close. The later rental also gives the topographical
boundaries of these divisions, and it was from them that Gray
painted his picture of rectangular yokes in their serried rows. But
it is not easy to plot the yokes from their literary description, and
even their exact physical correspondence over the centuries is not
certain. In the earlier rental their boundaries are not given, though
in the later rental they are. The order in which they are described
in the two rentals is entirely different and cannot be explained on
the assumption that the same thing was being described west to
east on one occasion and east to west on the other, or according
to some similar scheme. The acreages also were given only in 1447,
not in 1285, and they are very irregular, for the yokes ranged, as
has been said, from twelve acres to more than fifty, the logi from
five acres to 115, the fields and crofts being smaller but varying
greatly between one acre and forty-five. Since the units were fiscal
ones, determining services which as between yokes or logi were
equal, the sizes must have related in some way to land value, and
there can be no guarantee that the areas allocated to the fiscal

1. Gray, op. cit., pp. 282–6. 2. MS. E 24, fo. 33.
3. KAO U 398, M1a. Gray knew only the later rental, and used the inferior copy of
   it in the British Museum (Addit. MS. 33902).

divisions would remain stable even though their names endured. Further, in the deeds of land transaction which survive from medieval Gillingham, these fiscal divisions were only rarely used to describe the location of the parcels which were being sold or leased, and even then the description makes clear that the fiscal division was no more than a notional area within which the hedges and fences followed the laws of their own being.[1] In fact, a clear-headed reading of the 1447 rental enforces this impression throughout: its compiler described every fiscal division according to real landmarks, a lane, a certain man's croft, a boundary stone standing in the midst of a man's field.[2] Here was a terrain of very numerous fields, mostly small, mostly and increasingly enclosed by their tenants,[3] where the perfectly surviving jugation was little but a landlord's system for the imposition of rents and services, and was used as such till the end of the Middle Ages.[4] Yet the fiscal unit-names of Gillingham are interesting as a kind of verbal archaeology showing the stages of the clearance, settlement and new assessment of the land. For after the yokes come the 'log(h)i', probably 'lodges' in cleared woodland,[5] bearing family names and owing services similar among themselves but different from those of the yokes. The logi may even have been associated with the yokes through the enterprise of yokeland tenants in moving out and making fresh clearances and settlements. There is, for example, a *Mellesyok* in Gillingham, and also a *Melleslogh* of eight acres, with some tenants common to both.[6] The logi in turn were followed by multiform smaller areas from which rents but no services were due and which very frequently in the rental bore the names of their present tenants, like 'Baronesfeld' held by Henry Baron.[7] All this had been practically completed by 1285. In 1447 *campus Baron* was still

1. e.g. a garden and a virgate *in logo Westhelle* (P.R.O. Ancient Deeds, D3970).
2. e.g. KAO U 398, M1a, p. 27: '*Coppyng incipit ad Westsixacre et . . . ad lapidem stantem in terra Johanne Mille . . .*' I have benefited by some conversation about the Gillingham system with Mr A. R. H. Baker, of University College, London, who has since made a valuable study of Gillingham from the historical geographer's viewpoint in 'Open Fields and Partible Inheritance on a Kent Manor', *Ec.H.R.*, 2nd series, vol. xvii, no. 1 (1964), pp. 1–23.
3. That enclosure was not complete is suggested by the above extract, and by a lease like the one of 1352 to a local tenant requiring that *sepes prosternet seysonabiliter sine vasto* (Addit. ch. 46954).
4. It was used to check rents received in 1487 (KAO U 398, M1a, p. 84: '*summa totalis rec*' *in die Concepcionis beate Marie anno secundo Henrici vij . . .*').
5. The suggestion of Dr P. H. Reaney; cf. also a tenement of arable with a messuage in Wimbledon called 'le Logge' held for rent in 1343 (*IPM*, viii, 435).
6. MS. E 24, fos. 30v., 31v. 7. ibid., fo. 31v.

there, but shared among men with different names.[1] In this way it seems fairly clear that the lord had used the new areas as they were settled for his own arrangements, but that after the thirteenth century even these divisions had often ossified. Whether this was an area of Roman centuriation cannot be determined,[2] but the exceptionally clear nature of the Gillingham yokes doubtless springs from the peculiar topography of the manorial area. Elsewhere, too, on the archbishop's estates the system of yokes survived. The fifteenth-century yokes of Otford were almost the same as those of the thirteenth,[3] varying among themselves between about a hundred and two hundred acres, for the area contained a good deal of woodland to reduce its assessed value. The yokes of the scattered manor of Westgate in Canterbury also lasted on into the fifteenth century under the same names.[4] At Charing, Boughton-under-Blean and Saltwood the yokes had by the thirteenth century, and probably earlier, become more split up than in the manors already discussed, and their divisions often stabilized into virgates, or quarter-yokes, bearing personal or place-names, just as the yokes themselves did at Gillingham and Otford. If fifteenth-century rentals had survived for these places, it would probably be found that the older fiscal pattern survived there too. The form this pattern took in each manor seems to have become set by the thirteenth century, and a survey of the whole archbishopric estate shows a kind of descending series of fiscal morcellation, ranging from a slight degree in the Thanet area, where the sulungs are plain and clear, through the bold survival of yokes in Gillingham and Otford in north-west Kent, to places which had been affected by a much severer fragmentation, possibly because the local population had expanded early in a marked way, but more likely because the ground's configuration demanded a different scheme of assessment. There are two manors in Kent where the jugation survived little or not at all. They are far apart and quite unlike each other, except that each was large and rambling. One was Wrotham where in 1086 there were four and a half sulungs

1. KAO U 398, M1a, p. 62: *campus Baron*, of 8 acres 9 dayworks, shared in given proportions between Ralph Stephene, John Broun, Thomas Felder and Thomas Pyrrye.
2. cf. *Norfolk and Norwich Archaeological Society*, xxv, p. 373; but see also *Archaeological Journal*, ciii, pp. 61, 66 and refs. above, p. 117, *n*.3.
3. ms. E 24, fos. 71v.–72; cf. Gordon Ward, 'The Yokes of Otford', in *A.C.*, xlii (1930), pp. 147–56.
4. ms. E 24, fos. 22v.–24, and L.R. 1105.

(or eighteen yokes) remaining as tenant land of the archbishop's demesne. In the rental of 1284–5 there is an allusion to sixteen gavelkind yokes but only a few glimpses of some yoke or its fraction among the morcellated tenures. The other manor was Wingham, where in the thirteenth-century rental there is no sign at all of sulung or yoke, though in Domesday the tenant lands had been assessed at about thirty sulungs. The obliteration of the older fiscal units on this pair of manors is interesting, the more so for the topographical differences between them: the one close and sloping country, the other a land of long horizons. But each was huge and composed of scattered hamlets. In Wingham, as was seen earlier, there were over thirty such little villages. In Wrotham the walker may today turn either north or south from the main road and pursue the winding lanes up and down for three or four miles in either direction, to Stansted and Hodsell, or to Plaxtol, Old Soar, Roughway and back to Nepicar, and still remain within the former manor's environs. Doubtless on each of these manors the lord relied not upon sulung or yoke to locate and apportion his rights, but upon the hamlets, the names of which were written in his rental's margins. More than this, the hamlets are often found to be co-extensive with another of our distinct units of land division, the *borgh*. The borgh was a territorial tithing, and is found in Kent and east Sussex. Here, every hundred was composed of a number of borghs, and all the land was in one borgh or another except for certain townships like Seasalter, Newenden, Ospringe, Malling, Dartford, Lessness and Brasted. In many borghs the archbishop had jurisdictional rights over the tenants, sometimes even when the borgh itself did not lie within one of his demesne manors.[1] It has been argued that the pre-Conquest borghs kept their vitality from the requirements of the Assize of Clarendon in 1166 for village juries of four men, and that they were later used for the collection of Fifteenths.[2] Certainly the system was concerned with local justice and administration and must be discussed in that context upon a later page, but it is also plain that the borghs had their manorial uses, especially where the manor consisted of many

1. See Chapter 7 below.
2. By W. H. Hudson, 'The Three Earliest Subsidies for Sussex', in *S.R.S.*, vol. x (1910). A twelfth-century tract seeking to explain Old English law contains a long passage on the tithing which, it says, '*alicubi dicitur borch*' (*Consiliatio Cnuti*, ed. F. Liebermann, and later printed in *Die Gesetze der Angelsachsen* (Halle, 1903), pp. 618–19). Review by Maitland in *E.H.R.*, vol. ix (1894), pp. 137–8.

separate and scattered groups of homesteads. A small and compact manor had few. At Bexley, despite half a dozen manorial hamlets grouped fairly closely together, there were only two borghs, called simply East borgh and West borgh. Here the yokes could do the duty of locating and assessing the holdings. At Maidstone, a larger manor, the borghs were noted in the rental, but the land within them was still reckoned in yokes.[1] But at Wingham the great manorial area was dotted with hamlets which were also borghs, and upon which many of the services were based: Chilton, Overland, Wenderton, Twitham, Rowling, Goodnestone, Womenswold, Deane. At Wrotham, too, the borghs remained clear and their names were written boldly in the margins of the rental: Stansted, Nepicar, Winfield, Hale, Wrotham, and so on. After the piecemeal recital of holdings and the services attached to them, apportioned with minute care, they are summed up hamlet by hamlet: 'the tenants of this borgh shall plough so much, reap so much', performing an aggregated amount of service which could be checked on this local basis. Leaving Kent for a moment, the same organization is to be seen in an even more impressive form in the great Sussex manor of South Malling, strung out northwards from Lewes into the Weald. It was divided into two groups of borghs: Wadhurst, Mayfield, Greenhurst, Framfield and Uckfield being designated 'within the wood', and Wellingham, Gote and Middleham, Norlington, Aston, Southeram, South Malling and Stonham being 'without the wood'. The borghs of the first group were sub-divided into hamlets and the land of each of these was usually assessed at one virgate, though the virgate might be a very large one of eighty or one hundred acres; the borghs of the second group were subdivided simply into virgates of thirty acres each or less.[2]

Since all these land divisions were in one way or another the devices of superior administration, it is easy enough for the student, busy with his institutional themes, to overlook the meaning they sometimes had for the local inhabitants, and to forget the affection bred by familiar names and places. To men of the time the borgh could be more than a juridical category. It contained individual houses, and a man belonged to a borgh as he did to a parish. John Goodwin, parishioner of Wrotham, died in 1495 holding fourteen parcels of land in the borgh of Nepicar. These he knew as his

1. MS. E 24, fo. 26v.
2. ibid., fo. 79v.

'Nepicar tenement' and assigned to his second son, while the elder took the property in neighbouring hamlets.[1] William Hampton, pouchmaker of London and landowner in Wrotham, left money in 1492 to repair 'foul highways' in the borgh of Roughway there.[2] Or again, there was Thomas Magrigge who recalled that in 1354 he was chosen for the first time as *borsholder* ('tithing-man') of Guston by Dover and, exercising his office, entered one of the houses in his district and there saw a mother with a new-born baby, who told him she had no milk to nourish her child and asked him to find her a wet-nurse.[3]

Thus men might think of their homes and holdings sometimes in relation to a sulung or a yoke, sometimes to a borgh or a hamlet. But in another way everyone belonged to a local church. The formation of the south-eastern parishes was a slow business. *Domesday Monachorum* preserves the names[4] of certain central churches, of which Lyminge, Teynham, Wingham, Maidstone and Charing lay in the lands of the archbishop, and which may, like Reculver at an even earlier time, before the Danish invasions, have been collegiate institutions of some kind, connected with the archbishop and working at the conversion of the countryside. By 1086 the building of churches for the 'manorial' estates had progressed some way. There were still several priests at Lyminge, but the text shows churches on the manors of Westgate, Bishopsbourne, Aldington, Northwood, Gillingham, Northfleet, Bexley, Wrotham and Malling, besides Reculver and Maidstone, and two churches at Petham. In Sussex there was a church at Tangmere and two at Tarring; the manor of Pagham had both its local church and the church of All Saints in the Pallant in Chichester, and the manor of South Malling had its college of priests. In Surrey, Croydon, Cheam and Mortlake had their churches, as did Lambeth, which did not yet belong to the archbishopric. The Domesday description gives a notoriously incomplete account of churches and chapels, but shows adequately that the process was already well started by which a hamlet country, once served from a few centres, was provided with more and more local churches and dependent chapels as men built their separate homesteads on new lands. In a small manor a single church might suffice through-

1. Somerset House, PCC 29 and 34 Vox.
2. *IPM*, xiv, 300.
3. PCC Dogett, fo. 104.   4. *Dom. Mon.*, p. 8 *et seq.*

out the Middle Ages even for the tenants on its outskirts. The Saxon boundaries of Bexley compare precisely with those of the parish which for a thousand years was served by St Mary's, Bexley, alone.[1] But a single church did not always suffice, and sometimes dependent chapels sprang up, like that belonging to the manor-house of Otford, dependent upon the parish church of Shoreham, another village of the same manor, or that of Wimbledon, at first dependent upon Mortlake. The multiplication of churches is clearly seen at Wingham and Reculver. Domesday says nothing about the churches in the great area of Wingham manor, but when in 1286 Archbishop Pecham founded his college there, his schemes for assigning revenues to the prebends show that Wingham *cum omnibus hamelettis suis seu villulis* was served by six churches as well as that of Wingham itself: Ash, Overland, Fleet, Goodnestone, Nonington and Womenswold.[2] Their appearance cannot be traced in any detail, but we may be sure that the expansion of Christianity during the twelfth and thirteenth centuries owed much to a vigorous country laity. Overland was said to have been founded almost entirely out of alms.[3] At the visitation of 1294 small groups of the more important parishioners are seen helping to conduct the inquiries—which were not occasional affairs, for there had been one the year before. Their records have been used to paint a black picture,[4] but such a view seems unbalanced. Defects there were, especially where relations between parishioners and their chaplain were bad. At Nonington the parishioners complained of an over-managing chaplain who had much land and busied himself in secular affairs to the detriment of his spiritual work, but at Ash the parishioners had made good the defects noted the previous year and had just given a missal to the church.[5] The most usual charge was the farming out of tithes and offerings by the parish priest and

1. *Medieval Bexley* by the present author (Bexley Corporation Public Libraries, 1961), pp. 2, 5 and map.
2. *Register of J. Pecham* (Canterbury and York Society, part xiv, 1908), pp. 55–67.
3. *A.C.*, xxxii (1917), pp. 166–71.
4. See J. R. H. Moorman, *Church Life in England in the Thirteenth Century* (1946), pp. 210–12.
5. At the end of the Middle Ages the 'farmers' of the archbishop's demesnes in east Kent were also taking a lively interest in the upkeep of the local churches. There was, for example, Richard Knatchbull of Mersham, who in 1522 contributed to the new *stepull* of Aldington, to a new chalice at Mersham, and gave printed missals to Mersham, Sellindge and Barham, besides routine bequests to the high altars of parishes where he had landed interests—Mersham, Newington, Aldington, Bonnington, Eastbridge, Burmash, Sellindge and Hurst (P.C.C. 12 Maynwaryng).

his failure to give alms to the local poor. The parishioners' role appears a vital, even aggressive one, and parish life full of pride and activity. The fission of churches and the formation of ecclesiastical areas in a newly peopled countryside appears more dramatically at Reculver, itself an ancient centre with a church which the archbishops had possessed for a century before the Conquest.[1] By the late thirteenth century it was the mother church of four dependent chapels: Hoath, St Nicholas in Thanet, All Saints in Thanet (which was near Birchington and has now disappeared) and Herne. Reculver was rich, for the rectory and vicarage together were worth at least £130 a year, and Archbishop Kilwardby in 1276 had proposed to lighten an ancient burden on his own treasury by endowing the Canterbury hospitals of Harbledown and Northgate, which cost him about the same amount, with some of Reculver's revenues. The vicar of Reculver was in future to maintain chaplains for the dependent chapels, and contribute to their repair, but the parishioners of Reculver were to be responsible for the whole of their church, chancel as well as nave. The resentment of the parishioners is understandable, but of greater interest is the vigour of the local community which appears through Winchelsey's visitation and settlement of the business in 1310. As elsewhere, the parishioners had established their own chest and fabric-fund,[2] had witheld tithes and gained considerable voice in the management of parochial monies. The sins for which they were presented included usury as well as those of the flesh. When Winchelsey ordained three perpetual vicarages in the hitherto dependent chapels, he agreed that a single local vicar could not minister to the parishioners who under Pecham, his predecessor, had numbered over a thousand and who were, according to him, continually increasing. The matter was composed amicably and the headship of Reculver continued to be signified by an annual procession thither in September from the chapels, but it illustrates in many ways the character of this rural society: its wealth, the independence of its members, their secondary colonization of the land,

1. Above, p. 24, and see also for this paragraph Rose Graham, 'Sidelights on the Rectors and Vicars of Reculver from the Register of Archbishop Winchelsey', *A.C.*, LVII (1944), pp. 1–44. Hoath was licensed in 1398 to have a cemetery as well as a font, since the road to Reculver was said to get too muddy for the conveyance of corpses (*Cal. of Papal Letters*, v, p. 94).
2. cf. Charles Drew, *Early Parochial Organisation in England: the Origins of the Office of Churchwarden* (St Anthony's Hall Publications No. 7, Borthwick Institute of Historical Research, 1954).

their maintenance of old ties in spite of all. St Nicholas grew to be a thriving independent parish, but the connexion was maintained. The religious procession is a communal act, and Reculver was not the only place where it was an institution. At Wandsworth in Surrey, another possession of the archbishop, a procession-way was a jealously guarded local easement.[1] Walking to church has not over the generations ceased to be a family act, and the length of that walk is one of the indexes of human settlement. Even in 1557 Archdeacon Harpsfield on his visitation unconsciously commented on the hamlet structure of his district when he noted that

there is a village called Loddington belonging to Maidston and three myles distaunt from the towne, whiche village being xiiij howseholdes have neither Churche nor curate but were allwaies accustomed to goo to Linton to churche savinge apon the principall feastes, and then they came to Maideston and bare contribution bothe to Linton and Maideston. There is also an other village of fower howseholdes called Harberland, distaunte from the towne a mile, whiche com to Maideston to churche. There is also an other village of three howseholdes called Half Yoke, being a mile [off], whiche com to Maideston to churche ... also an other village belonginge to Maideston called Willington and Shouffotte [Shofford] of xxvij[ti] howseholdes, beinge distaunte from the towne a mile, and they com to Maideston to church. Memorandum that the hole parishe is tenne miles in compasse.[2]

The sulungs, yokes, borghs and parishes which have been reviewed in the preceding pages were all the creations in one way or another of lordship or government. When they are stripped away, villages and fields remain, but these are much more difficult for the historian to see, for the accommodation of men to their landscape not only varied from place to place but was rarely the subject of schemes expressed in writing. For example, even if sulungs and yokes had once, as Mr Jolliffe thought, been the homesteads and physical allotments of the families who, in a

1. In 1479 the parishioners of Wandsworth were thought to have encroached with their 'Procession Way' upon ground belonging to freeholders of Wimbledon, and the archbishop's council was consulted (*Extracts from Court Rolls of the Manor of Wimbledon* (privately printed 1869, available in Wimbledon Borough Library), part III, p. 44). For the processions from new churches to the mother church, see also G. C. Homans, *English Villagers of the Thirteenth Century* (1941, reprinted 1960), pp. 372–3; cf. pp. 363–4.
2. *Archdeacon Harpsfield's Visitation, 1557*, ed. L. E. Whatmore (Catholic Record Society, 1951), II, p. 214.

hamlet country, tended to keep themselves to themselves, this would still give little idea of the complex reality of settlements in actual localities. At some point, therefore, the countryside must be asked to speak for itself, however faintly or obscurely, through the general observation of present-day landscapes coupled with acts of imagination made from the surviving deeds and custumals. The first question, and the most difficult, is the nature of the villagers' fields. The south-east is well known as a land of early enclosure and several cultivation where, during the Middle Ages, a man's holdings were likely to lie scattered and hedged about, a field here, a piece of pasture there, a copse and an embanked tract of marshland beyond. But the country is large and various, and there is the evidence of one's eyes, let alone of the documents, that large and open fields existed too.[1] No one can doubt the close and always several nature of, say, the heights of Wrotham or the once-wooded slopes of Gillingham. But the walker who stands by Manston airfield and gazes southwards over the country to the east of Canterbury will see a flatness little broken by tree or hillock. Variety might exist, of course, on a single estate. At Wrotham the big fields below the slope were cultivated in long strips which belonged to more than one man, if a seventeenth-century map is correct.[2] But large fields which in the later Middle Ages were divided into individual properties present no less the problem of why and how they became so, and any answer which is given has to take account not only of what the fields looked like, but what kind of men they were who possessed and worked them. So in the rest of this section an attempt will be made, as far as the evidence will allow, to consider the topography of the fields and the social reasons for the way they were treated.

In looking for common fields on the archbishopric estates, the starting-point must be the thirteenth-century rental and custumal which provides the only overall view. This is naturally more con-

---

1. For a summary of the evidence, see W. E. Tate, *A Handlist of English Enclosure Acts and Awards*: part 17, 'Open Fields, Commons and Enclosures in Kent', *A.C.*, LVI (1943), pp. 54–66.
2. The Twysden map in KAO. It should also be noted that in 1285 cotmen residing at Wrotham within the bounds (*marcas*) of East Field and West Field had to co-plough on the demesne *cum omnibus suis* if they had plough-beasts, but outside those bounds the purchase of unburdened cotlands and forlands was envisaged (MS. E 24, fo. 83). There was a Middle Field in thirteenth-century Wrotham which seems to have been a large one with demesne and tenant parcels somehow intermixed (Lambeth MS. 1212, p. 124).

cerned with demesne fields, which it enumerates, than with the tenants' fields, which it does not, but it is not altogether useless, for the lie of the demesnes sometimes gives a little information about the nature of the arable in general. Every Kentish demesne lay in a great many places and consisted of portions, sometimes small, sometimes very large, which are described as lying *within* some large field. At Wingham,[1] for instance, there were twenty-nine acres *in Siredland*, 43¾ acres *in Torbestegh*, 102½ acres *in Blakeney*, and so on. The preposition has significance, the more because it is not always the same. There were in the Wingham paragraph also 34½ acres *apud la Med*, which suggests a piece on its own, not arranged within a larger field. It is also clear that on some demesnes the lord's crop was fenced, but that the enclosures were taken down after the harvest, 'in the open time' (*tempore aperto*), so that the beasts of the lord might graze there, together with the beasts of those tenants who had helped him to plough and of any others who had arranged terms with him by which their animals should feed upon his stubble. This is true on a large number of the archbishop's manors: Lyminge, where the open time is defined as from the end of August until the beasts were put into stall,[2] Reculver,[3] Boughton-under-Blean,[4] Aldington,[5] Saltwood,[6] Petham,[7] Bishopsbourne,[8] all of them in the eastern part of the county. The clearest instance of tenant arable lying unseparated from the demesne is at Wingham, where the first introduction of the ploughing-service of *graserth* was explained by saying that 'the tenants situated next the demesne could not avoid the demesne during the open time', so that their draught-beasts going to the plough fed upon it, and consequently the lord's bailiffs demanded a general service for this unavoidable perquisite received by the tenants.[9] Admittedly, this explanation of *graserth* is found in widely separate parts of England, and the phrases with their similarity to those of other custumals,[10] and the archaism of speaking only of oxen and not of horses, may be an old common form rather than a particular account, but it is inherently likely to be true in east Kent, and at Bishopsbourne the beasts' droveway certainly went over the demesne in summer.[11] On

1. MS. E 24, fo. 1.
2. ibid., fo. 64v. and L.R. 2068: '*quousque ponuntur "upestal"* '.
3. MS. E 24, fo. 18v.   4. ibid., fo. 46v.
5. ibid., fo. 54v.   6. ibid., fo. 64.
7. L.R. 2068.   8. MS. E 24, fo. 68v.
9. ibid., fo. 11v.   10. See below, pp. 170-1.   11. MS. E 24, fo. 68v.

some manors the archbishop had special enclosed pastures and meadows upon which the tenants' beasts were not allowed to go.[1] Altogether the custumal ought to be believed when it says there were common pastures on some demesne fields, and perhaps it might be treated as circumstantial evidence that common of pasture was very usual, at least in east Kent. Yet even if this is agreed, it does not tell very much. To speak of portions of demesne unseparated from tenants' lands is much less specific than describing strips of lord's and tenants' lands lying intermingled in large fields which practise common cropping courses, as in the so-called common field system, and there are many indications that even in the most open areas of the archbishopric estates this was not done. The nearest approach to this method appears to have been not on the Kentish but on the Sussex estates. As late as 1473 the tenants of Tangmere had to repair the hedges about the common fields (*communes campos*), both sown and unsown.[2] But even in thirteenth-century Sussex the separateness of the demesnes seems clear. At Pagham it was in 'butts', temporarily hedged. At South Malling the holdings of the lord's oxherds lay 'in the midst of the demesnes'.[3] In Kent the demesnes were even more obviously set on their own. Harvest-workers at Saltwood 'entered the lord's corn and hay' with their carts.[4] At Petham and elsewhere it was a customary work to *enclose round* the lord's corn, and to take straw from the *lord's fields* to roof his buildings.[5] Thirteenth-century accounts, too, show that the practice was for large demesne fields, however they might be hedged, to be treated as entities and sown with blocks of crops, or left fallow, on their own.[6] In Kent and other parts of the south-east the turn-wrest plough was often used, which by a movable mould-board allowed the ploughman to work along adjacent furrows and to cultivate squarish plots which easily fitted into large fields. Plots like this could quickly become consolidated and associated with

1. e.g. at Reculver, Boughton and Saltwood where a special cleared woodland pasture (a 'frith') was assigned to the lord's oxen (ibid., fos. 18v., 46v., 64). But at Wrotham and at Tangmere in Sussex common pasture for sheep as well as oxen was specified (L.R. 2068 and *S.R.S.*, vol. 57, p. 13).
2. L.R. 999.
3. MS. E 24, fos. 92–102; *S.R.S.*, vol. 57, p. 118.
4. MS. E 24, fo. 62.
5. ibid., fos. 68, 68v.
6. cf. 'Late-Continued Demesne Farming at Otford', *A.C.*, LXXIII (1959), esp. pp. 119–21.

enclosures.[1] Certainly, by the end of the Middle Ages the portions of Wingham demesne were independent fields, and called such.[2]

What is true of the demesnes is probably true of the tenants' lands also: not regularly intermingled strips, but blocks and patches of crops within larger fields, with pasture available elsewhere for the tenants' beasts. Under such a scheme there was a place both for better-off tenants who had whole plough-teams to themselves and for co-operation between men who contributed to a joint team. It is clear enough from Domesday that there were by no means enough plough-teams to go round the existing families of *villani* and *bordarii*, though not a hint is given how the ploughs were distributed or shared. But by the thirteenth century some tenants were expected to have a full team, others a beast or two, others none, and the rental admits that the situation was always fluctuating. At Wingham, Teynham, Boughton and Lyminge, ploughing service was owed by those who had a fully yoked plough, and proportionately less by those with less, and if a tenant joined his beasts with those of one who was not a tenant of the archbishop to make up a team for the tilling of his own soil, then he was obliged to plough for the lord with the number of beasts he himself had at the plough.[3] This he had to do even if he used a joint plough for as little as two days in the year.[4] At Wingham in the thirteenth century the lord's bedel took charge and made up composite teams for the day's work on the demesne from the various tenants' horses, and any odd horse over he could put to a harrow. The custumal speaks of the tenants' own teams as worked by *famuli* under a *dominus caruce*, three, four or five of whom might have a customary right to a meal when they worked for the archbishop. There is every reason to suppose that some tenants might hire their own *famuli*. At the same time, the *dominus caruce* might be quite an important man. Some Domesday knights in Kent were concerned with ploughing,[5] and in 1382 there was

1. M. Nightingale, 'Ploughing and Field Shape', *Antiquity*, XXVII (1953), pp. 20–6. For illustrations and comments on the turn-wrest plough, see A. D. Hall and E. J. Russell, *A Report on the Agriculture and Soils of Kent, Surrey and Sussex* (Board of Agriculture and Fisheries, H.M.S.O., 1911), p. 11.
2. Dean and Chapter of Canterbury MS. Reg. T, fo. 286v.
3. MS. E 24, fos. 11v., 12. cf. Teynham (fos. 36v., 40), Boughton (fo. 42), Lyminge: '*si aliquis huius [dominice] tenencium mergat carucam cum aliquo alio forinseco, arabit pro portione*' (fo. 64v.).
4. Isle of Grain: '*et licet caruca jungitur per ij dies tantum, debetur domino aruram dimidie acre*' (fo. 33).
5. See above, p. 79.

certainly a case in Oxford of a coroner dying suddenly while he walked behind his own plough.[1] Our ploughmen cannot be pursued on to their own land to see how they passed from the soil of one to that of another during their year's labour, but the strong impression is of severalty working, of a movement from patch to patch, croft to croft, field to field, and not of long hours in great communal expanses. The whole sense and atmosphere is of individualism and private enterprise, the clues to which are given in the custumal itself, and which evidence of social organization will strengthen. When, for example, the custumal is discussing the payment of hen-rents, it refers to their increase whenever 'an inheritance is divided into two or three portions among heirs, and each makes his messuage upon his own portion'.[2] In Thanet tenants bore individual responsibility for the defence of their individual holdings against the sea.[3] These fragments of information come from east Kent where, if anywhere, the excellent flat arable and the proximity of monastic Canterbury might have encouraged communal organization in the service of the fields. But this is to look at matters with only seigneurial interests in mind and to forget what was happening to the rural population. First and foremost, the population had been increasing vigorously in the twelfth and thirteenth centuries. This is obvious in general from the way in which the fiscal tenements had become partitioned by 1285, though it can be demonstrated more exactly at Bexley, where the form of the rental shows the jurors remaking it from Elias of Dereham's roll of two generations earlier. In yoke after yoke the single tenant or few tenants of former days has given place to a multitude of parceners.[4] At Lyminge it is assumed that *per capita* rents will increase,[5] and Winchelsey's remarks on the inhabitants of Reculver[6] only put into words what is implicit in every manorial rental. Now this growth of population was taking place in a region where the land belonging to the mass of the tenantry was both partible among heirs and freely alienable during the life of the tenant himself. It is not hard to appreciate the consequence of this,

1. R. F. Hunnisett, *The Medieval Coroner* (1961), p. 142.
2. MS. E 24, fo. 15.
3. L.R. 2068: 'And from la Wade to Sarre each shall defend his own against the sea. . . .'
4. MS. E 24, fos. 88v.–89v.; cf. *Medieval Bexley*, pp. 18–21.
5. ME. E 24, fo. 67: 'and thus the hens and eggs . . . increase in number according to the number of tenants'.
6. Above, p. 128.

the more so as the peasant of eastern England at the time of Domesday was often not very well endowed with landed property.[1] A growing population meant an increased demand for food, a better price for agricultural produce and hence a demand for land. Partibility made for subdivided holdings in the hands of men who were often too poor to possess a plough-team or even a beast. Of course, it was a possible alternative for heirs and others to practise joint-working of holdings, but reasons will be given for believing that this was rarely more than a temporary expedient.[2] A way out of the process of continual land division lay in the freedom which men enjoyed to buy and sell or lease their portions, so that consolidation also could take place and, in the simplest terms, the richer could buy and the poorer could sell. In fact, the documents illustrate this movement quite well. Even the rental, so strong in its *prima facie* evidence for morcellation, alludes to the busy market in humble holdings.[3] But private deeds and charters are a much better source of information, partly because they are concerned with the real things that were bought and sold rather than notional tenements which owed services, and partly because they are the relics of private people and families and were written to describe their doings. A single series of private deeds may be taken as an instance from the area of Wingham, and happily so because it is there that the countryside was most open and community methods most likely to be practised if they were practised on the archbishop's estates at all. Yet here, in the parish of Preston near Wingham in the reigns of Edward I and II, are to be found many half-acres and quarter-acres set within larger fields, changing hands often and at high prices: half an acre 'in the field of *Sowyntone* next the land of John de Doune, entry-fine £2'[4]; a quarter of an acre next the land of the heirs of Sampson de Nelme [Knell] and his parceners rented for eight years;[5] another three eighths of an acre sold for £3;[6] a piece of arable in *Atteneves* field next the land of

1. Reginald Lennard, 'The Economic Position of the Domesday Villani', *Economic Journal*, LVI (1946).
2. Below, pp. 147-8.
3. At Wrotham, 'if anyone residing outside these bounds shall buy forland or cotland within them . . .' (MS. E 24, fo. 83). At South Malling there are very numerous instances of the purchase of neif land by freemen and vice versa (*S.R.S.*, vol. 57, pp. 40ff., etc.). Similarly a charter of *c.* 1255 important enough to have been kept among the archbishop's muniments shows a substantial free man eager to take on customary land there (Lambeth MS. 1212, p. 85, no. xix).
4. P.R.O. Ancient Deeds, A 11727.
5. ibid., A 11729.   6. ibid., A 11731.

Maud Attenelme and the demesne land called 'Lenedy Doune', with a pasture called 'Averbroke' next to the marshes of Bartholomew Stake and William Brithred;[1] more telling still, a lot consisting of three quarters of an acre in one field, a half-acre in another and a quarter-acre in another, with a house built on one of them, exchanged in 1325 by private charter.[2]

The effect on the landscape of this kind of private enterprise when continued over the years may be imagined. An early and obvious one was the building of dwelling-houses and private barns in the fields and lanes, some no doubt ephemeral shacks like the one knocked down by Henry Herbert in 1291 on his brother's land in Bexley,[3] others substantial, like the Culpeper's house of Kentish ragstone, built at almost the same moment at Old Soar near Wrotham.[4] New houses under such circumstances would not appear so often in some central village street as scattered among the properties of parceners and purchasers, or helping to swell small nuclei of kinsmen and neighbours which already existed.

The changes of ownership on the anciently cultivated land, with the consequent rearrangement and appearance of closes and buildings within existing fields, is certainly a feature which appears very marked in deeds and custumals from the thirteenth century onwards, yet it would be wrong to regard this as the most startling characteristic of the really crucial period, the thirteenth century, when the effects of the growing population were becoming apparent on every hand. At this time attention should be turned to the ceaseless activity (concurrent with the re-forming of the ancient holdings) in clearing and reclaiming new land. On every manor of the archbishop the rental of 1284–5 is burdened with its tale of assarts. In Boughton there were 'new assarts' let out by Archbishop Walter (1193–1205);[5] at Wrotham, new land *super montem*;[6] in South Malling 'old assart' often held at 2*d*. an acre appears to date from the time of Stephen Langton (1207–28), and 'new assart' from the time of Archbishop Boniface (1245–70) was let out at twice

1. ibid., A 11741, s.d. 1135.
2. ibid., A 11765. These examples could be augmented from many sources. Another east Kentish manor, Aldington, shows enclosed blocks of arable within a larger field in the fourteenth century (Reg. Islip, fo. 212), and the same completely enclosed a hundred years later (Mins. Accts 1129/2, m. 2).
3. *Medieval Bexley*, p. 24, from L.R. 236 m. 3.
4. *National Trust Guide: Buildings* by James Lees-Milne (1948), pp. 64–5.
5. MS. E 24, fos. 46, 46v.
6. ibid., fo. 81v., etc.

that rate.[1] Activity had been particularly intense on this great woodland manor. Land was eagerly sought after for purchase and lease, and men might come thither from the next county.[2] Many cotlands were developed as 'messuages with curtilages', and owed hen-rents if they were occupied with smoke issuing from the chimney.[3] Sometimes the occupier was forgiven this rent on the ground of poverty, whether he were free man or neif.[4] Indeed, it was the neif who was sometimes the rich one, amassing property, like John de Iardhurst who leased out over two hundred acres in lots of twenty to thirty acres to free and unfree alike, passing on the obligations for physical service even to his free tenants.[5] In the borgh of Uckfield in the thirteenth century individual prosperity is betokened in another way by the sight of fulling-mills at rent, and men with the cognomen 'Fuller'. The same happened in Wadhurst, another woodland borgh.[6] In Kent the attack on the woodlands was also vigorous, and occurred in two ways: the clearing of wood round and about the manors themselves, and the lodgment and increase of settled colonies within the denns, the swine pastures in the weald, far away from their parent manors. Every manor without exception had its woodland in the neighbourhood, where tenants as well as lord had immemorial rights not only in the feeding of pigs but in taking materials to make and mend houses and ploughs and the hedges and enclosures which needed to be kept so constantly in repair. But these uses, no less than the lord's inclination to fence off bits for himself, thinned the woods. At Bexley the thirteenth-century tenants were complaining that they used of old to feed their pigs in West Wood, summer and winter, but 'now that the woods are in part destroyed and in part lie in the park they have none of these things'.[7] In the denns the efforts of the tenants were of greater consequence than those of the lord in fashioning an individualistic landscape. By the thirteenth century substantial, permanent colonies are visible in the wooded interior of Kent and Sussex, which in the rentals are given separate paragraphs headed *'tenentes de waldis'*.[8] The earlier colonists were

1. *S.R.S.*, vol. 57, pp. 31, 86, 103. 2. ibid., p. 47.
3. ibid., pp. 59, 81. 4. ibid., pp. 80–1.
5. ibid., p. 57. The acquisition of under-tenants by *custumarii* is also noted at Harrow in Middlesex (L.R. 2068).
6. ibid., pp. 32, 75, 80, 82. 7. MS. E 24, fo. 91v.
8. MS. E 24, fo. 28v. (Maidstone); fo. 32v. (Gillingham); fo. 40 (Teynham); fo. 50 (Charing); fo. 59 (Aldington); fos. 66v. (Lyminge). For the subject, see the present writer's 'Denns, Droving and Danger', *A.C.*, LXXVI (1961), pp. 75–87.

already assessed for rents and services and even grouped for some purposes into yokes on the model of the older jugated lands. Such arrangements were already well established in the time of Stephen Langton, and are especially striking in the denns belonging to Aldington and Lyminge. But the woodland colonization was ceaseless. New denns were made and old ones divided. Tenants cleared wood and ploughed, and in the fourteenth century the archbishop realized he could not prevent outsiders as well as tenants from felling and taking away the timber and so, by leasing the whole denn to the tenants, he parted with all his rights there save purely fiscal ones. But the denns of Aldington and Lyminge still existed in 1703 as two large entities of property, composed of the thirty-two denns of Aldington and the twelve denns (originally) of Lyminge, though now fragmented into many individual parcels of arable and pasture as well as wood, and developed by their holders with barns, stables and houses. In the account rolls the same process may be noticed in west Kent as in east, for just as Aldington had its separately accounting 'Weald' by the mid thirteenth century, so Sevenoaks Weald soon became a district of Otford manor.[1]

It is perhaps unreal to make too sharp a division between the work of lord and of tenantry in discussing the development of the countryside. The requirements of each played their parts. Faced with the long and uncertain journeys between his Sussex and Kentish manors, the archbishop felt no less than his men the impulse to colonize. In 1260 the pope agreed to appropriate to him the church of Mayfield, and shortly the same thing happened at Cranbrook, which, so the papal licence ran, 'is situated in a wooded and desert part of the diocese through which the arch-bishop has to pass, and where no lodging can be found during a long day's journey'.[2] Unruly though wealden tenants proved, they provided the archbishop with rents, escorts and guides, and he was

---

1. Addit. MS. 29794, m. 5; Mins. Accts 1129/1 (1450–1) where the assessed rents of Sevenoaks Weald often appear ancient. An interesting development rather outside the scope of this chapter is the formation of the Seven Hundreds of the Weald round Marden, and connected in some way with Newington-by-Sittingbourne, in both of which the archbishop had long-standing rights. (See Lambeth MS. 1212, pp. 335–6; R. Furley, *History of the Weald of Kent*, I (1871), ch. XXVII; B. H. Putnam, 'Kent Keepers of the Peace, 1316–17', *Kent Records*, vol. XIII, pp. xliii, lii–liv.)
2. *Cal. of Papal Letters*, I, p. 370 (*s.a.* 1260); II, p. 198 (*s.a.* 1320).

the lord under whose general protection they felled and ploughed and flourished.

The same mutual dependence is to be seen in that other virgin territory, the marshland. There was a long tradition of reclamation under the archbishops. In the thirteenth century at Newchurch in Aldington there were inned lands called '*sidlandis*' which owed nothing but suit of court and relief. They were held by individual tenants who had worked on them, but the rental looks back to their earlier enclosure under St Thomas, Baldwin, Boniface and Pecham.[1] By 1292 the former grass pastures of Newchurch were said to be under the plough on account of the drying-up of the marsh, and this had the unlooked-for effect of increasing the rector's income (corn) at the expense of the vicar's (hay).[2] There were *sidlandis* also on the northern coast of the county, belonging to Boughton-under-Blean (where Becket had also enclosed land),[3] owing rents and already firmly in the hands of substantial tenants like the Beaufitz, whose names we connect with later success and enterprise.[4] Other manors too possessed reclaimed lands, rented from the archbishop by tenants though directed from above according to the accepted custom of the Marsh.[5] The initiative of both archbishop and tenants may be illustrated from the year 1325. Archbishop Reynolds granted to William and Juliana Pesendene 150 acres of salt-marsh 'and more if more could be found' within the wall, when it should be made, in the parish of Stone in Oxney. This couple were to do suit to the court of Lyminge and to pay 12*d.* an acre, and they might also have the land on which the wall was to be built and twenty-four feet of foreland outside the wall, next to the sea, at 2*d.* the acre, but this was to become 10*d.* an acre if it were enclosed in its turn.[6] The same year the prior of Canterbury wrote to the archbishop as spokesman for the tenants of Seasalter who, he said, wished to embank the marshland of their manor. The principal tenant, Thomas of Faversham, said that the archbishop had demesne land in the

1. MS. E 24, fo. 59.   2. *A.C.*, XXXII, p. 158.
3. cf. *Kent Records*, vol. XVIII, pp. 39–40.   4. MS. E 24, fo. 44.
5. MS. E 24, fo. 21v. (Reculver), and fos. 66v.–67 (Lyminge, which already had a *collecta*, or rent-district, of the Marsh). For Thanet, L.R. 2068, and for Pagham, Lindsay Fleming, *History of Pagham*, I (1949), p. xxxix. For an excellent treatment of the custom of the Marsh, see R. A. L. Smith, *Canterbury Cathedral Priory* (1943), ch. XI, where the role of tenants seems to have been less than it was on the archbishop's land.
6. Lambeth MS. 1212, p. 126.

neighbourhood and tenants in Boughton, Hernhill, Graveney and Seasalter who also wanted to reclaim over seven hundred acres of saltmarsh there. The prior hoped the archbishop would pay his rate with the others, and Thomas said he would enclose the archbishop's portion at his own cost and pay him an average income for it if he might hold it of the archbishop by service of watch and ward.[1]

All this was profitable business for the leading tenants whose mark was imprinted more and more obviously upon the landscape during the later Middle Ages. In the fourteenth century there was a fall in the population, without notable recovery in the fifteenth. The scarcity of labour meant relatively higher wages could be earned by workmen than in the thirteenth century and these could be spent to a greater extent upon things other than food—upon, for example, small houses and their furnishings and utensils. It is not surprising that the land-market continued active, partly because small properties were within the reach of many people, but probably more still because spendable wages brought a modest prosperity to merchants and entrepreneurs who dealt in goods that numerous unassuming people could buy. The contraction of the total area under cultivation did not itself mean poverty for any section of the community as such, but it was accompanied by a natural willingness on the part of the lord to let land, and by estate building in a substantial way by a proportion of tenants, who were free to select their properties on the market and deal with them as the moment dictated. On the archbishop's estates the rentals and deeds show more consolidation than in the thirteenth century and not seldom the emergence of 'manors within manors', complexes of private property amassed by business methods. This was certainly a process already possible and familiar in the Kent of the thirteenth and even the twelfth century, but now exaggerated through the opportunities which the changing distribution of wealth and availability of land brought. In the Gillingham rental of 1447[2] the manorial area was intersected with innumerable lanes —*venellae*, *viae*, *stratae*, *semitae*—and dotted with the stables, houses and granges of individuals standing within crofts and messuages. Even the crofts were often divided. On the other hand, the larger tenants like John Pirrie, a butcher, or Richard Beaufitz,

---

1. *Lit. Cant.*, I, nos. 148, 149.   2. KAO U 398, M1a.

esquire (a great lessor himself), possessed many adjacent parcels. At Wrotham in 1495[1] there was also a multiplicity of paths, crofts, haughs, hedges, private scraps of woodland and meadow, both *super montem* and *in le playne*, yet the parcels were not all held *divisim* in bewildering severalty, but were often now being brought into consolidation and lay, or were placed, *sub una clausura*. It is a feature of the archbishop's manors—as of others in the same countryside—that within their great and scattered areas they contained the estates of certain tenants which even in early days were of consequence and which themselves developed into *soi-disant* manors. Such was '*la Reye*' in Wrotham, to be encountered in the next section,[2] or Stansted, also in Wrotham,[3] or Twedall in Gillingham.[4] Given the conditions which have been outlined, it is only to be expected that a great and ancient manor like that of Wingham, almost a lordship in itself, should break up into independent country properties, which it did,[5] and that the tenurial jig-saw should be as complex as the physical. The archbishop's tenants created a kaleidoscope of transactions among themselves, but the territories under his lordship were also islanded and fragmented among the lordships of others. An admirable example is Old Soar in Wrotham, which belonged to the Culpepers. A late medieval rental shows that it lay mixed almost beyond distinction with the archbishop's manor of Wrotham, so that the tenants of the one were often tenants of the other too, and a single field might be divided between the two lordships.[6]

The budding and blossoming of new communities within the areas of the archbishop's lordship was never only the work of a few favoured families. It might spring from numerous small enterprises like the settlement of the denns. Or it might issue in a privileged community, like Lydd, a member of the Cinque Ports. Although already a chartered community the inhabitants of which

1. KAO U 55, M59.
2. See below, p. 153.
3. MS. E 24, fo. 79v.: '*borgha* of Stansted: the lady of Ightham holds the manor of Stansted freely'. But the manor was held in gavelkind of the archbishop (*IPM*, IV, p. 91; VI, p. 328).
4. KAO U 398, M1a, p. 3; and see F. R. H. Du Boulay, 'Gavelkind and Knight's Fee in Medieval Kent', *E.H.R.*, LXXVII (1962), p. 510.
5. cf. the 'manor of Ratling', sold in 1453 by John Fyneux, esquire (Addit. ch. 36798).
6. Addit. ch. 37749 (*s.a.* 1520): 'William Dyne of Darenth holds one parcel called Lowyns containing 3 acres, of which 2 are held of the manor of Wrotham and the residue of the manor of Soar.'

enjoyed freedom from tolls,[1] Lydd appears in the thirteenth-century rental as a *collecta* of the demesne manor of Aldington, composed of two yokes morcellated among nearly a hundred tenants, a quarter-yoke, or virgate, held by the widow of Stephen Gerard, and a marsh once taken on lease from Archbishop Edmund and then held by two men pledged to keep the sea out.[2] Looking back from the reign of Elizabeth, the corporation of Lydd recalled that the archbishop had always been their chief lord, and that their Liberty contained the three borghs of Dengemarsh (Dungeness), Orwellstone and Lydd itself. The borgh of Lydd was, they noted, a circuit lying wholly within the area of the court of Aldington and known as the *collecta* or *cullet* of Lydd, divided into two yokes and one verge, where in the reign of Henry VI the services had been commuted by the archbishop so that the 'Baylif, Jurats and Commons', freeholders of Lydd, became 'lords in meane' of the borough, holding of the manor of Aldington for £7 8*s*. 3*d*. a year together with 30*s*. common fine and the profits of the court.[3] Here the history of two and a quarter yokes over three centuries can be seen in a single instant, and with it the transformation of a borgh into a remarkable little borough.

PEOPLE AND FAMILIES

Most of the tenants on the archbishop's Kentish estates were gavelkinders. The thirteenth-century rental often calls them 'gavelmen', though sometimes, when it is concerned with their services, the terms '*avermen*' or even '*werkmanni*' were used.[4] In contrast with these the rental names others who held different kinds of land. Some are said to hold freely. In the Kentish rental these were people who held in military tenure,[5] even though the gavelkinders were themselves reckoned free. In the Sussex rental, on the other hand, there are many free tenants who are contrasted with those in knight-service as well as with the unfree.[6] There were

---

1. For Lydd, see K. M. E. Murray, *Constitutional History of the Cinque Ports* (1935), esp. pp. 233 (for the royal charter of 1156, witnessed *inter alios* by Archbishop Theobald), and 46.
2. MS. E 24, fo. 60.   3. *H.M.C.R.*, v, Appendix, p. 531.
4. MS. E 24, fo. 12 (Wingham), fos. 34, 38 (Teynham); L.R. 2068 (Northfleet).
5. MS. E 24, fos. 78v., 79v.
6. *S.R.S.*, vol. 57, pp. 16, 30, 47, 60, 66, 74, 85, 92 (*coteria liberorum*), 95, 99, 102, 106, 111.

also inlanders and *formanni* in Kent, and cotmen everywhere. An obvious question is whether these words describe different classes or are simply terms useful in the narrow context of a rental to refer to the obligations which the lord required from those who held particular pieces of land. The answers can be provided by analysing the rental, and thus showing that most men held various kinds of land at the same time. True, there were a few smallholders who happened to possess nothing but their cots or inlands, but, whatever had been the state of affairs in former times, there were by the thirteenth century no classes that were distinct just because they were the tenants of yoke-lands or cotlands or even, for that matter, of free land. It was perfectly possible for any man to hold any kind of land if he could afford it, and the inequalities between man and man, though expressed in official texts in terms of custom and status, sprang rather from qualities conveniently called economic and apparent in men's varying endowments of land, money, intelligence, industry and luck. In one sense this must always have been so, for even descent from the gods can suggest itself to men only through external signs of superiority; at the same time there is in long-established societies a distinction and indeed a tension between wealth and status, and it is one of the most delicate tasks of the social historian to trace out their changing relationships. In the south-east of medieval England no more than the scaffolding of such a study yet exists. But it was clearly a region where original custom and economic situation permitted quite easily a rather free and individualistic economic activity. Whatever the continental origin of the south-eastern inhabitants, their position on the main route between England and the rest of the world must have stimulated the circulation of money and hence the mobility of their society itself. The laws of the early Kentish kings already show a mixture of social inequality and economic freedom. There were noblemen and free men of substance and dignity, who were distinguished by wearing their hair long,[1] and who possessed dependants apart from slaves; of the lower classes there seem to have been three grades, called *laets*. Marriage-law had a strong commercial element and in some respects foreshadowed the later 'custom of Kent'. Wives could be bought, and it was possible for a free man to marry an unfree woman.[2] The widows enjoyed half the

1. F. L. Attenborough, *The Laws of the Earliest English Kings* (1922): Aethelbehrt, nos. 13, 73 (cf. Jolliffe, op. cit., pp. 19–39).   2. ibid., nos. 77, 82, 83.

property of their dead husbands if a living child had been born, and the fatherless child stayed with his mother but fell under the guardianship of one of his father's relatives until he was ten years old.[1]

Only after the immense gap of half a millennium does a new statement of Kentish custom become available, and then in documents the history of which is still obscure. But it will be helpful to summarize what they say, and what they imply. Several copies exist in fourteenth- and fifteenth-century manuscripts of a statement about the usages and customs claimed by the community of Kent for those who held in the tenure of gavelkind. With one exception they are written in Anglo-French, and they differ in wording from each other, though there seem to be two principal versions, one on the lines of a Canterbury Cathedral copy, followed by Lambarde, the other of an earlier but also corrupt copy from Queenborough in Sheppey.[2] The first version tells us the customs were allowed in 1293 before John de Berewick and his fellow-justices on eyre in Kent, and that a royal charter embodying them was in the custody of Sir John de Northwood in Canterbury on 19 April 1293. There is also a Latin document, shorter than these and entitled *de consuetudinibus comitatus Kancie*, which embodies some principal points of the Kentish liberties, and complains in addition that the hundreds and liberties of Kent have been compelled to present Englishry and have been amerced for *murdrum*; the compiler regarded these penalties as contrary to ancient custom (though he was wrong here), and unnecessary anyway since, as he remarked, there was no longer any distinction between Normans and Englishmen.[3] The Latin text must be dated before the Kentish eyres of the justices R. de Seton and H. de Bacon, who are mentioned in it. If this, as seems likely, is Roger de Seyton, it must be earlier than 1278, when Seyton died.[4] Whatever the relationship between the texts of the Custom of Kent, it is evident that early in Edward I's reign a Kentish claim to certain regional privileges was being prosecuted with vigour enough to secure their formal admission by the king's justices. It is not unlikely the formal claim

1. ibid., nos. 75, 78; Hlothere and Eadric, no. 6.
2. cf. F. Hull, 'The Custumal of Kent', *A.C.*, LXXII (1958), pp. 148–59, for a preliminary discussion. On the legal aspects, see N. Neilson, 'Custom and the Common Law of Kent', *Harvard Law Review*, vol. XXXVIII, pp. 482–98.
3. L.R. 2068. The Latin document was undiscovered when Dr Hull wrote.
4. Edward Foss, *The Judges of England*, III (1851), pp. 152–3.

was stimulated by the series of seignorial aggressions against Kentish landholders which appear in the Hundred Rolls, and in particular the extortion of money by the archbishop and others from gavelkinders in return for allowing them the wardship of their kinsmen. In many different parts of Kent these lords were accused of taking or selling marriages and wardships of gavelkind families, and to the local people this was 'against the custom of the kingdom',[1] 'against the custom of the countryside and the royal dignity',[2] or 'against common justice and the manner and custom of all Kent',[3] for in Kent *non est warda*.[4] Possibly the wish to lay hands upon these valuable wardships lay behind Hubert Walter's charter from King John, already discussed, allowing him to convert gavelkind into knight's fee.[5] It was the same kind of profits that were being pursued in Henry III's reign, and the Custom of Kent was essentially a defensive statement of rights by middling landholders. To these the claim to personal freedom may have been a buttressing argument and seems not to have been canvassed earlier.[6] The economic provisions were more fundamental. The main terms of the custumal of Kent were briefly as follows. The tenant in gavelkind may freely give or sell his lands to whom he wishes during his lifetime, and after his death his lands shall be equally divided between his male heirs. His widow shall receive one half of her former husband's holding as dower as long as she remains a widow.[7] The heirs shall be in the guardianship of the *procheyn ami*—the nearest relative who could not inherit—and shall attain their majority for the purpose of controlling the inheritance at the age of fifteen. The execution of a man for felony shall not disinherit the heirs; and gavelkind lands for which the rent is in arrears shall only become forfeit to the lord after a long period during which there was opportunity for the defaulting tenant to make amends.

1. *Rot. Hundr.*, I, p. 204. 2. ibid., p. 207. 3. ibid., p. 209.
4. ibid., p. 202. 5. Above, p. 69.
6. cf. B. H. Putnam, *Kent Records*, XIII (1933), p. xiii and *n*.
7. It is interesting to note that the archbishop's rental of 1284–5 notes under Harrow, Middlesex, that the old custom was for wives of customary tenants to keep the whole tenement during widowhood, thus excluding the heir from the inheritance as long as his mother lived a single life, but that Archbishop Pecham's steward, master Henry Lovel, with the free and customary tenants of the court there, ordered that in future widows with heirs under age should keep the whole tenement only until the heir was twenty-two, and that then the heir should enter, having first dowered his mother with a third of the inheritance (L.R. 2068).

For present purposes, the two most important of these provisions are the partible inheritance and the freedom to alienate land, even though to a medieval lawyer others, like the right of inheritance from a felon, might have sounded more startling. The influence which these customs could have in Kentish families in helping to blur distinctions between the knightly and the non-knightly was seen in the previous chapter, but the generality of gavelkinders ought now to be considered. About partibility there is nothing that is particularly base, and much that is old.[1] There are numerous instances in the Domesday text for Kent (as well as elsewhere) in which men, often brothers, held in parage or separately in a joint tenement. Sifflington had been held by Lewin and Ulwin *in paragio* and they could go with their land to what lord they wished.[2] Teston had been held by three brothers as three manors;[3] Little Wrotham as two by Godwin and Edwin;[4] Cliffe by Aluric and Ordric, brothers;[5] Dean Court in Westwell by Ulnod, Wava, Alward and Ulveron, and *erat dispertita in tribus locis*;[6] Acrise by two brothers, each of whom had a hall.[7] But although the men named by the Domesday scribe were doubtless relatively rich and important, the tenure under which they lived was widespread and must have affected most of the county's inhabitants. Gavelkind rules applied not only to the anciently settled arable, but to assarts, marsh, woodland and burgages, so that by the thirteenth century the legal presumption was that land in Kent was in gavelkind unless the contrary could be proved. Had the extension of settled land kept pace with the rise in population, the equal sharing of a father's property between his sons might have appeared a simple and natural expedient by which the country could be brought into cultivation. But this did not happen. The twelfth and thirteenth centuries witnessed a great increase in population, an increase in total wealth, and a complex struggle of middling landholders to preserve their position against their lords and against the built-in weaknesses of their own inheritance custom. The increase in population led to the fairly rapid fragmentation of land among co-heirs so that the individual's portion sometimes became insufficient to

---

1. Mr T. H. Aston called attention to the pre-Conquest ubiquity of partible inheritance (*TRHS*, 5th series, vol. 8 (1958), p. 78).
2. *D.B.*, I, p. 7.   3. ibid., p. 8b.
4. ibid.   5. ibid., p. 9.
6. ibid., p. 10b.   7. ibid., p. 11b.

support him.[1] If the society in which these events occurred had been communal rather than individualistic in habit, and little affected by the growth of individual wealth, then no doubt the joint tenure of family holdings could have been carried further than it was, with brothers and even remoter kinsmen sharing a common dwelling for long periods as a matter of course, some of them perhaps forgoing marriage and giving their whole energies to the wider family. But physical partition was the means by which the custom was normally applied when in this expansive age a sharing took place. There is no doubt, it may be admitted, that joint tenure between heirs sometimes in fact occurred, but it is very unlikely that this is implied in the common phrase of the rentals which purports to say that particular tenements were held by groups of *heredes* or *pares*. The rentals existed to apportion burdens as best they could. When brought up to date they are filled with evidence that morcellation had occurred since the previous rental; but the local men who supplied the information were not always able to say who were the current tenants, especially in a society where leases as well as sales were of frequent occurrence, and *heredes* was in any case a convenient formula for those who owed the lord some service, and tells nothing of the individuals' mode of life. Nor can later legal devices like the writ of partition (1539–40) to enable one co-parcener to secure his portion against the wishes of the others be adduced, as Mr Jolliffe thought,[2] to show the existence of frequent, long-standing joint tenures. On the contrary, the whole appearance of the Kentish countryside from private charters as well as from rentals is one of intense severalty from the thirteenth century at latest and onwards. As to joint tenure, its commonest occasion was naturally that short period after a man's death when his estate was awaiting its disposal among his heirs, and those heirs, perhaps children, had not yet been able to make up their minds about the character of the division to be made. A *locus classicus* for those who believe in the practice of joint tenure in Kent comes from Bracton's *Note Book*, where a group of five brothers at Oare were said to live in common (*uixerunt de communi*

---

1. This is well known through the charter of Edward I disgavelling the lands of John of Cobham, quoted by Maitland (op. cit., II, p. 273) from Robinson. A MS. copy of the charter exists in the Cobham Cartulary (Marquess of Salisbury, Hatfield MS. 306), fo. 29v. I am indebted to Miss T. M. W. Szanser for this reference.
2. op. cit., p. 24 *et seq.*

in eadem curia) for an unspecified time upon the gavelkind land left them by their father. But it was not a very long time. One brother by agreement with the others let his portion to farm for three years to a certain Aaron on condition that the portion should at term revert to the common estate in order to be divided up so that each might have his part.[1] The common dwelling was explicitly temporary, and the conditions of the lease suggest that partition sooner or later was usual. Parallel cases are not hard to find. Archbishop Boniface of Savoy bought fifteen acres which lay at the entrance to his park at Lyminge from the five sons of Roger of Acsted, and since these sons do not feature, singly or collectively, among the tenants of Lyminge in 1285 it may be reasonably imagined that they took their cash and departed from the local scene.[2] A case from 1361 illustrates more vividly the problems of young brothers who found themselves co-heirs. John Aleyn gave all his lands in and about Dartford to three men by a charter of feoffment. This was one way at that date in which the customary partition among heirs could be carried out, and when John died his feoffees enfeoffed John's sons, who were called John, Thomas, William and Edmund. William, a minor, soon afterwards died, but before the land had been divided among the survivors John the younger leased his share to a London citizen, John Costantyn, for a term of years. Thomas also, while still under the age of fifteen, had enfeoffed Costantyn in his share, although no division of the land had been made, on condition that Costantyn should pay him ten marks and a gown annually for life and make him his apprentice draper in London.[3] In the event Costantyn defaulted on his obligation and the case got into the records, but the present point is to show the kind of circumstances which might surround a joint inheritance: the initiative open to boys even of tender age, though doubtless with advice; the negotiations which went on between them and others before the estate was divided; the normality of its eventual division, and the way in which some of the co-parceners might want to go off to another kind of life taking with them the proceeds of a bargain and leaving their father's lands again in a single pair of hands. The story shows too how a Londoner was on the look-out to acquire landed interests, especially in north-west Kent, which during the later Middle Ages was a fashionable area for well-to-do

1. *Bracton's Notebook*, ed. F. W. Maitland (1887), no. 1770.
2. Lambeth MS. 1212, p. 97.　　　　　　　　　3. *IPM*, XI, 8.

men.[1] Partibility itself stimulated the market in small pieces of land. As time went on, it was not only local men who aggregated parcels while their brothers sold out, but outsiders, from London and elsewhere, who brought investment and perhaps their persons into the local communities. In this way the practice of joint ploughing which was referred to in the thirteenth-century rental and described in the previous section appears much more likely as a simple and up-to-date convenience than as a sign of some mysterious kindred solidarity among a tribally minded people. On the contrary, the villagers of the south-east were highly individualistic and knew the value of money, and the rental itself alludes more than once to joint ploughing between the archbishop's tenants and those who have come to settle on the spot from outside.[2] The point might be pressed, were it necessary, by adding instances where property held of the archbishop was transacted with outsiders by means of increasingly subtle legal instruments, but it may suffice to quote only an indenture of 1377 whereby William Newport, Fishmonger of London, made a five-year lease *to* a local man of the 'manors' he had acquired as investments in Otford, called Upsepham and La Reye, in return for £10 a year to be delivered to his mansion-house in London, imposing upon his lessee the obligations, by then usual, to manure the land and to do all repairs save those made necessary through 'fire, storm and tempest'.[3]

Enough has been said to indicate the practical consequences of gavelkind tenure. The free economy of which the 'Custom of Kent' was an expression was carrying local society beyond that Custom's own archaic terms by the time it was formulated. Reading it, historians are easily tempted to think only of partibility and of personal freedom, and to connect these free conditions with the disturbances in later medieval Kent by imagining a world dominated by restless smallholders. But the truth is more complex, for Kent was a land of economic diversity and inequality. Freedom to

1. The attractiveness of north-west Kent appears in will after will. If the principal residences of those whose wills were proved by Prerogative Probate in the fifteenth century are mapped, then a heavy concentration is seen along the south bank of the Thames estuary and inland. Geoffrey Chaucer, it will be recalled, bought a house in Greenwich when he was doing well. Successful men lived on the archbishop's own manors in the area: e.g. Northfleet (William Wangford, serjeant-at-law, Rochester Will Book 5/387); Otford (George Multon, father-in-law of Lambarde, PCC Thower 20, and Westminster Abbey Muniments 14303), etc.
2. MS. E 24, fos. 11v., 64.   3. P.R.O. Ancient Deeds, B 5121.

deal in land was every whit as important as the basic idea of partibility, and there were echelons of prosperous tenants as well as poor ones, who resented seignorial attacks upon a custom to which they were habituated and which permitted them to organize their continued family prosperity.

The greatest difficulty, of course, is to get a sight of the inequalities in the time before the deeds and the rentals. Domesday is reticent about them. On the archbishop's estates it recognized in general only two classes of tenant, the *villanus* and the bordar, and these vary a great deal in numerical proportion one to the other from place to place. By and large there were twice as many *villani* as bordars, counting among the latter the cotters who were enumerated instead of bordars at Darenth,[1] Cheam and Harrow. But there were also serfs in small numbers at Petham, Aldington, Lyminge, Charing, Gillingham, Maidstone, Northfleet, Otford, Wrotham and Darenth in Kent, at Hayes and Harrow in Middlesex, and at Cheam, Mortlake and Lambeth in Surrey. Only on the Middlesex manors is there some sign of what must have been true elsewhere, that tenants simply called *villani* possessed quite unequal holdings; for at Hayes two *villani* had a hide each, twelve had half a hide each and sixteen bordars had two hides between them; and at Harrow thirteen *villani* had half a hide each, twenty-eight had a quarter each, thirteen more shared four hides between them, and forty-eight had half a virgate (or one eighth of a hide) each, the two cotters sharing thirteen acres, and the two *servi* holding presumably nothing. After Domesday there is a long period of darkness over the rural society of the archbishop's estates, lightened only by occasional and oblique reminders of the unequal struggle for a living. An act of Archbishop Theobald (1150–61) refers to thirteen tithe-payers of Woodnesborough who held amounts of land varying from one to fifty acres each. Their names were English, and they included Alfwin the priest with one acre, Wolfwin the smith with seven and Alfwin the fuller also with one only.[2]

In the thirteenth century much more detailed information is forthcoming about landholding in this society. In the light of private documents as well as of the official ones like the archbishop's rental of 1284–5, a populous landscape becomes visible

1. Darenth at that time was, of course, an archiepiscopal possession.
2. A. Saltman, *Theobald*, no. 49.

in which the ceaseless activity of at least the better-off members of the community may be observed, and some of the qualities of their family life illustrated. More and more, private enterprise in buying, selling and leasing, and soon in arranging the real succession of chosen heirs through enfeoffments to use, took the centre of the stage, and this made society very different from what it would have been had the common law of the countryside merely taken its course in the local courts, with nothing to stop the progressive partitioning. This is not to say that custom was abolished or that the manorial courts stood idle. The lord continued to try and keep abreast of his changing tenures, to collect his dues from the changes and his rents from the lands, and to regulate the problems of succession when they arose. When a tenant in gavelkind bought land he was supposed to do fealty for it and to pay the lord, not an entry-fine, but a 'relief'. These were the *minuta relevia* of the account rolls, usually worth only about a quarter of the annual rent and distinct, of course, from the relief of £5 per fee on knightly land. It was hard to keep track of private sales, and the existing court-rolls are full of entries which show men and women called upon to declare how they have entered upon lands acquired from someone else, and to pay the relief. The courts' demands might continue for months without result, and some people no doubt escaped altogether. The mere number of the transactions were not the only difficulty, because villagers who wanted to buy and sell land did so between themselves without prior reference to the court. For example, in 1290 Achard of Yaldham granted his son-in-law about nine acres in scattered parcels, and his deed witnessing to this was read out in Wrotham churchyard on a May Sunday in the presence of the donor.[1] Only when such private arrangements had been made did they come before the manorial courts. Thus at Bexley in 1504 Stephen Hall came and did fealty and was admitted as tenant of two crofts which had been sold him by Richard Erliche, *as is shown more fully* by the charter preferred in the court.[2] When a tenant died, other tenants present in court would be asked what lands he had held at the time of his death,

---

1. Addit. ch. 16507: '*et memorandum quod carta sigillata cuius istud est transcriptum lecta fuit anno regni regis E.xviij in cimiterio de Wroteham die dominica post festum invencionis sancte crucis per Henricum Fareman coram Achardo de Audeham*'.
2. Delisle and Dudley MSS., Roll 458. I am indebted to Viscount Delisle, V.C., for permission to quote from his family papers.

what rents the land owed, and who were the heirs. If the dead tenant had taken care to enfeoff others with a view to having his heirs put in possession after his death, there was nothing for the court to do, and this procedure will be discussed presently. But there were always cases where the succession fell to be regulated by the lord's court, sometimes where important men had not tied up all their property in advance, and usually where small people were involved who did not want or could not afford the charters, wills and rewards to executors which the well-to-do found it worth while to pay. In a straightforward case the heir came, paid the heriot in the form of a good animal if he had one or money if he had not, and in due course swore fealty, paid his relief, and entered his estate. If he were a minor, his *procheyn ami* had to be declared to the court and charged to undertake the wardship. A slightly more complex example from Penshurst in 1405 shows co-heirs entering as they reached their majority. Agnes, widow of William George, a tenant of the archbishop, died in possession of a messuage and half the yoke of Shipbourne belonging to the manor of Otford. John, one heir, was described in court as of full age and was required to pay his relief. Edwin, her other son and heir, was only three, 'so there came William, uncle of Edwin, and took charge of him (*cepit nutrituram ipsius Edwini*) until he attained legitimate age in gavelkind.[1] But on other occasions there were delays in getting the heirs to come along, and sometimes serious doubts about who the heirs were. Intermarriage between already connected families, the marriage or death of children during the parents' lifetimes, or the subsequent remarriage of a surviving parent might make it hard to say who should succeed, in what proportions, and what holdings there were to be divided. From the lord's point of view, the knowledge of neighbours was the only record, and his interest was in trying to keep track of the partitioning of the fiscal units in order to levy rents and services, as well as in trying to collect heriots and reliefs. Every now and then the manorial court empanelled a jury to find out the tenants of a particular yoke or, as the court-rolls put it, 'to proportion such-and-such a yoke'. This was a slow business. The jury would be set up at one court but might not be got together for months, nor present their report for longer still. They had to be men who had

1. L.R. 807.

no personal interest in the property involved,[1] and when they finally gave their verdict it would be written down on the roll in terms like the following, which comes from Otford in 1389:

They say that John Perys holds 4 acres of the yoke in Ysebournemede, John Chepstede holds one piece called Seneyard, Thomas Houte one meadow containing 2½ acres, Walter Stymere 3 acres of land and meadow, William Chepstede one croft containing 3 acres, Henry Birchet one croft called Ysbournesplayn, and the archbishop holds 3 roods called Schidyard.[2]

All these instances show that the lord's manorial affairs and the business lives of the tenants tended to run on parallel lines, and that contact between the two was often uncertain. There is nothing surprising about this, for their interests were quite different, but it makes it more relevant here to look at the activity of the tenants themselves, known to us through documents of their own making.

In the large manor of Otford in north-western Kent, one of the gavelkind yokes bore the name of 'Reye', which meant an island of land amidst wet ground, and which has now turned into the not uncommon place-name of Rye House.[3] In 1285 this yoke was being shared, as to services, by members of the families of Sepham and de la Reye. A series of deeds which begins at the same time shows the aggrandizement of the de la Reye estate. The earliest member to appear is Clement de la Reye who went on pilgrimage to St James of Compostella, having sold some property, perhaps in order to do so.[4] Before 1285 his son Godfrey had bought back this tenement and added six other fairly small portions of enclosed arable and meadow to his estate by purchase.[5] A family like this, already somewhat outstanding in the locality, was not, however, a race apart and it had its poorer members who may be seen in possession of small portions of land and paying to the archbishop insignificant sums for the right to pannage their pigs in the woods there.[6] But the main branch prospered and acquired more acres and rents during the reign of Edward II.[7] After this there is silence

1. L.R. 805, m. 3 (Otford, 1403–4): inquisition to proportion the yoke of Malevile in Otford. After the recital of names are added the words, 'And it is ordered to add six others none of whom have lands in that yoke.'
2. L.R. 804, m. 3. 3. *PNK*, p. 55.
4. P.R.O. Ancient Deeds, D 2116.
5. Ancient Deeds D 3097, 3099, 3546, 4636, 4637, 4638.
6. MS. E 24, fo. 71v.; L.R. 831. 7. Ancient Deeds D 5377, 8644, 8886.

until the later years of the fourteenth century, when other men acquired control.[1] By the early fifteenth century the complex of lands was known as 'the lordship of la Reye' and came into the hands of the affluent family of Palmer,[2] where it doubtless remained until the title-deeds came to the Crown. The dossier illustrates in part but in detail the development of a gentlemanly estate from a gavelkind embryo.

Estate building on a rather larger scale than this can be seen through the family of Peckham in the neighbourhood of Wrotham, where during the reign of Edward I Martin was busily collecting lands. The greater purchases and leases were from men of knightly rank, but he was also active in acquiring property from lesser customary tenants. To give an instance, in 1275–6 William the carter sold him

one piece . . . which lies in a field of [Wrotham] called West Field, and of this piece the western side adjoins land belonging to the same Martin, the eastern side land of the heirs of Ralph Wulnord, the southern side land of the heirs of William Fareman, and the northern side adjoins the royal way, called *Dunstrete*.[3]

Subsequent purchases were from John the carter, son of this William, and also, among others, from Geoffrey Morin, who was one of a number of brothers and possibly related to the Morins or Moraunts, who were also leading tenants in Wrotham.[4] Many of the pieces in question were described as adjoining land which Martin of Peckham held already. But the interest of the Peckham deeds is not only as an example of land accumulation. They contain memorials of his marriage and death which themselves were naturally events of economic consequence. In 1282 Martin drew up a contract in the form of a bipartite indenture for his marriage to Margery, daughter of a local notability called Henry of Shorne.[5] Henry came over to Martin's house at Yaldham

1. e.g. the London fishmonger noted above, p. 149; cf. Ancient Deeds D 7806, 9395.
2. Ancient Deeds A 5369, D 10817.
3. KAO U 47/3, T 46, no. 7.
4. Addit. chs. 16498, 16499, 16500, 16501, 16502, 16504, 16506. For the Morins, see Appendix A, *s.v.* WROTHAM. Martin of Peckham himself was one of a group of witnesses, some of them knights, to the deed under which Nicholas de Criol sold back to Archbishop Pecham half the fee-farm of Wrotham (Lambeth MS. 1212, p. 121). He may also have been the benefactor of the nuns of Fontevrault in Leighton Buzzard (*C.P.R., 1272–81*, p. 437).
5. Addit. ch. 16503 (Shorne was a village near Rochester).

(which he had bought seven years before)[1] and pledged himself under oath to pay to Martin *causa matrimonii* the sum of £53 6*s*. 8*d*. over four years in six-monthly instalments, that is, ten marks every November and June, promising to pay a penalty-sum of £2 every time he fell into arrears, and further obliging himself before Roger of Northwood and John of Cobham, knights, and other barons of the Exchequer, that they should distrain him if he failed to pay, and if necessary that the archbishop should use canonical coercion. The marriage took place, and in due course Margery bore her husband John, William, Henry, Alexander, Alice and Isabel. In 1307, after quarter of a century of married life, Martin died, and it fell to his executors to render account to the Dean of Shoreham, whose right it was to prove the wills of those who died in the neighbourhood, the archbishop's 'peculiar juris-diction' of Shoreham. Though all the records of the peculiar have disappeared, the dean's discharge of these executors happily sur-vives.[2] Martin's movable assets, including good debts owing to him, amounted to £134 12*s*. 6½*d*. For the funeral expenses (ten marks) and other immediate settlements the executors paid out £13 10*s*. 2½*d*., leaving £121 2*s*. 4*d*. to be divided between the widow and the children and good works for the testator's soul. A third of this, *portio defuncti*, was rightfully used by the executors for anniversary obits and money bequests for pious uses, but they overshot the mark to the extent of £11 8*s*. 0½*d*., so that there was only about £60 to go to the survivors. But there was an almost equal amount in debts which had not been successfully collected, but for which the widow (who was the guardian of the younger children) might sue. A rental made soon after Martin's death gives some idea of the landed property which came to the heirs, and gives in full the rents and customs owed by John, William and Alexander (Henry had probably died) to the manors of Kemsing and Wrotham for what was held there. It runs to two closely written membranes.[3] For the very numerous pieces of land and the commuted services due for them the annual total of debts amount to little more than 20*s*., but these were customary quit-rents and give no idea of the real value of the land or what had been paid for it. The Peckhams were clearly a substantial family, but it is their

1. Addit. chs. 16183–4; cf. KAO U 47/3, T 46, no. 3.
2. KAO U 47/3, T 46, no. 2. The Dean was Peter, vicar of Bexley and Wrotham [*sic*].
3. KAO U 47/3, M 19.

continuity in substance which is impressive. A hundred years later
they were even greater local notabilities, as the will of James de
Pekham in 1400 shows, with his bequests of money to the churches
of Wrotham, Kemsing and Ightham, of fine furnishings to numerous kinsfolk, and the remembrance of the outdoor servants.[1] In
spite of all the gold rings and green tapestries powdered with
popinjays, James de Pekham was a farmer who left to one son ten
oxen, 200 sheep and a fully equipped plough from the single
property at Chevening, though in the next breath he disposed of
'all my books in French to those who know how to read them'.
A hundred years later again the Peckhams were still the leading
gentry at Wrotham, rich, well connected and philoprogenitive.[2]
Indeed, there was about one of them a family sense so developed
that it amounted to eccentricity. This was Reynold Peckham who
died in 1523. The most careful study of his will shows not the
slightest hint that he had, or ever had had, a wife or children, and
he left everything to collaterals, yet he wrote:

also I will that myn executours shall provide a faire stone with the
pictures of a man and of a woman and of children therein sett of latyn
[latten], and hyt to be laide over and upon my grave within the space of
6 weeks next immediately after my decesse. . . .

The phrasing is conclusive that what he desired was this kind of
tomb, not a memorial to a family he had once had. Whether this
is an isolated case of pathetic disappointment or a sign of the high
value set upon children at that time and place, it may be a warning
against firm reliance upon brasses for genealogical purposes.

The de la Reyes and the Peckhams provide early examples of
private enterprise which in the later Middle Ages is seen everywhere, and came to distinguish the families of yeoman and gentleman from those of little or no estate who rarely enter the records
by name save as malefactors. The welfare of the better-off was
improved by the devices which they invented for themselves to pass
their lands as well as their chattels to the heirs of their choice.
Instead of submitting to the course of the common law under

1. Register of Archbishop Arundel (Lambeth Palace), fo. 176v.
2. For the early sixteenth-century Peckhams, see the PCC Registers: Thomas, 1515,
6 Holden; Reynold the elder, 1523, 31 Bodfelde; James, 1532, 23 Thower. The
family was still there in the seventeenth century, see the will of Reynold the elder,
1675 (Deanery of Shoreham Register I, Lambeth Palace, fos. 291v.–293v.).

which their houses, fields, shops and pastures would after their deaths go automatically to the eldest son in the case of knightly tenure or, if in Kent, to the sons equally under gavelkind tenure, men began in the fourteenth century to enfeoff groups of others whom they trusted with their landed property and to leave instructions to those feoffees how to dispose of the property when they themselves were dead. When the king's escheator arrived to ask a jury what lands a dead tenant of the king had held in his day, it became common to say that the tenant 'long before his death had divested himself of his manors',[1] enfeoffing others yet continuing, as we well know, to enjoy the estate which was now equitable rather than legal, but as real to his daily inspection as ever it had been.[2] And when they came to draw up their testaments, men of property added with increasing frequency their last wills—*ultimae voluntates* —prescribing in the English they spoke the manner in which their feoffees should deal with the lands, preferring one son, perhaps, above all others, or alternatively sharing things more equally, as each saw fit, designating the widow's dower house, chiding an obstinate boy, and trusting that eloquence, faith or at least the power of a friendly lord would keep their wills safe from the rocks of litigation and the currents of avarice. Such intentions cannot have been merely or even primarily to deprive feudal lords of the incidents of custody or relief, for non-feudal lands were treated in just the same way and must have been of equal or greater extent. The procedure was simply the convenient one, and fulfilled the wishes of men who knew what they wanted.

The men and women who made wills and created trusts in this way were also continually buying, selling and leasing lands, houses and other properties during their own lives. It is impossible to read many of their wills without realizing how active the market in land must have been, and how fluid the estate of any particular family, notwithstanding men's desire to guide and guard their inheritances. This was partly a result of the wish to invest in land or enlarge one's rent-roll on the one hand, partly a result of the need to endow daughters given in marriage on the other, for even if marriage gifts

1. e.g. Sir Arnold Savage of Bobbing, d. 1375 (*IPM*, XIV, 202).
2. Feoffors to use often behaved as though they continued to have legal estate, cf. *IPM*, XIV, 227. The equitable protection which Chancery afforded them is, of course, well known. See, especially for Kent and Essex, the unprinted London M.A. thesis (1958) of my former pupil, Miss Margaret Avery, *Proceedings in the Court of Chancery up to c. 1460.*

of fathers were usually in money, land might have to be sold to provide it. But above all the wish of almost every testator to provide masses and prayers for himself, his kinsmen and benefactors led him to order the sale of some property 'at the best price the executors can obtain', in order to raise the needed funds. Ownership of property in this part of the world therefore changed hands rapidly if it were not in direct church possession. Though we know nothing of them, it would be surprising if local estate agents had not come into existence by the fifteenth century. Certainly, the purchase of land was in Kent a matter of sufficiently common occurrence to make hand-guides for purchasers useful, like this rhyme bound up in a memorandum book from Canterbury, listing the leading points to remember:[1]

> Who will be ware in purchesyng
> Consider the poynts that be followyng:
> First se that the lond be there
> In title of the seller;
> Se that he not in prison be
> And that he be in myende and memore,
> And that it stande in no daunger
> Off no womannys dower;
> Se that the seller be of age
> And that it be in no morgage;
> Se wher a tayle therof may be founde,
> And whether it stande in statute bounde;
> Consider what since longeth therto,[2]
> And what quyte rent therout must go;
> And yf it meve [come from] a wedded woman
> Thynk on *covert de baron*;—
> And thou maist in any wise
> Make a chart with warantise[3]
> To thyne heyres and assigneis also,
> For this a wise purchaser will do.
> In xv yer if thou wise be
> Thou shalt ageyn thy money se.
> Se whether the tenure be bonde or fre,
> And se a release of every feoffe.

1. Dean and Chapter of Canterbury MS. B 2 (formerly Y.10.16): an account book from St Augustine's Abbey, Canterbury, of about 1519.
2. The line is obscure, and may mean: 'Consider what has come to belong to the property since your negotiations about it were opened.'
3. i.e. 'make a charter with warranties'.

Frequent land buying and selling should therefore be taken for granted. Yet it is still true that society remained a 'dynastic' one in the sense that men of any landed property were anxious to keep and augment it and to hand it on to their heirs. It would also seem that the richer and higher in social status they were, the more careful they tended to be in preserving the bulk of their property in the hands of one son. But to substantiate this it is necessary to look at some specific examples.

If Kentish custom, long-standing and still valid, ordained the partition of inheritances among heirs, how strong, one might well ask, was this idea of partibility in the minds of those who had created the power to please themselves? The question might be extended from men's intentions to harder facts by wondering how many children there were to share what fathers left. The rarity and danger of medieval statistics is well enough known, but the question is perhaps not wholly unanswerable, for the very self-assertion of well-to-do men provides in the end at least a rough means of assessment. For this purpose it has therefore been worth collecting some last wills—they number forty-six—of lay land-holders who possessed property on or close to the archbishop's Kentish estates during the fifteenth and early sixteenth centuries and which can be found in the registers either of the archbishop's prerogative probate at Somerset House or in those of the bishop of Rochester.[1] These, it will be noted, are records of society's more affluent section. Though few in number, they were made at solemn moments and with appropriate care. In most instances it is probable that all the surviving children were remembered; married daughters were certainly named, and rebellious sons, too, even if only as the target for reproaches. It is therefore of interest to find that of the forty-six testators fourteen had no surviving sons, twelve had only one and twenty had more than one. Nine indeed had no children at all, and three had one daughter only. Hence, in fifteen out of the forty-six cases there was an only child, and the question of partition was in the course of nature unlikely to arise;

1. The experiment could be extended by searching the MS. registers of the archdeacon and commissary-general of Canterbury which are, like the Rochester books, at Maidstone; also the archiepiscopal registers at Lambeth Palace contain wills which could be analysed in the same way. One of these (James Pekham) has got included in the present series. But the medieval archives of the Dean of Shoreham, which would have been valuable for the north-west Kent manors of the archbishopric, have vanished. The wills used here are listed at the end of the chapter.

and, in fact, the property was passed to the single heir in fourteen of the cases, and in the remaining one was shared, for no clear reason, between three grandsons. Even had property been partitioned in all the other instances, the figures are enough to blunt the image of numerous progeny eagerly awaiting their equal shares in later medieval Kent. Expressing the facts in a different way, the average number of legitimate and surviving sons in these families was 1·37, of daughters 1·15, making an average of 2·52 legitimate children surviving and recorded at the time when the father made his will. Observing the contemporary scene in Europe, some scholars have agreed to call this 'the age of bastards'[1] and illegitimacy must be reckoned with in England too. But it is very difficult to decide how important it was statistically, and it seems scarcely to have affected the inheritance pattern which is our immediate topic. Only two bastards are mentioned in the wills under consideration. Neither was made an heir, but each was left money.[2] As to the passage of estates to legitimate children, we shall find a greater emphasis upon inheritance by one son than might have been suspected in Kent, though the practice of partition was by no means uncommon. The cases where there was an only child have been dealt with, and present no difficulties. The nine childless testators tended to distribute the bulk of their estates to friends, brothers and charitable purposes. Leaving aside the few cases where there were daughters only, who became co-parceners, we may turn to the twenty instances where there was more than one boy. In one of these the succession is not clear from the document, but in thirteen the whole or the bulk of the real property was directed to the eldest son,[3] and only in six was the landed inheritance partitioned in a more equal way.[4] Primogeniture appears to have been commoner at the higher end of the social scale. Two of those who partitioned their estates were, it is true, gentlemen, but the others were yeomen, while almost all those in the larger group were of gentle status. Not only, therefore, were the words of the 'Custom of Kent' of no account in this matter, even though much

1. R. Aubenas in *Histoire de l'église* (A. Fliche et V. Martin), t. 15, pp. 327–8, and references there.
2. James de Pekham of Wrotham in 1400 left 40s. to John *filio meo bastardo vocato Wrotham*; Richard Bamme in 1452 left £20 to his bastard son to promote him to any useful art to which he might have an inclination.
3. Bamme, Goodwin, Wm Hall, Hampton, Kene, Multon, James Pekham, Thos Pekham, James Pekham (1532), Shelley, Surrenden, Tottisherst, Wombwell.
4. Boone, Judde, Kelom, Ketyll, Roger, Swetesyre.

of the land was in gavelkind, but the age at which the children
were to attain their majority, often laid down in the wills, was
usually in the twenties rather than at fifteen. The provisions of
these wills show exact care for all the eventualities, leaving nothing
to habit and frequently imagining the worst. Provision was made
for the life of the widow; younger sons and sometimes daughters
were frequently left small amounts of land as well as money, and
the accidents of nature were faced with elaborate cross-remainders.
Fathers not only prescribed the destination of those lands which
they had been busy acquiring during their lives, but sometimes
referred in their wills to estates which their wives may have brought
to the marriage, and to entails which they themselves had inherited.
Affairs were often complex, and some rearrangement by the
testator necessary, so that his various children got what he thought
right in particular cases: the mother's inheritance, for instance,
could be passed to a younger son,[1] or the elder son might at least
be asked to relinquish his share in it.[2] Even where the division was
quite unequal, a sense of family solidarity remains, brothers having
first refusal, perhaps, in any sale of the inheritance,[3] or being
provided by a father who knew the ways of the world with a
collective compensatory fund for any one of them who might fail
to substantiate at law his claim to some part of a scattered
birthright.[4]

Behind the immediate humanity of the wills emerges the changing pattern of land-tenure. The contracted population, which may
be dimly reflected in the modest number of children mentioned in
the wills, is evident on a wider view of the rentals. For Gillingham,
Wrotham and part of Otford there are fifteenth-century rentals
which may be compared with their counterparts in that of 1284–5,
and in every case the tenant-population had very markedly
declined.[5] Although what these documents prove is a smaller
number of tenants rather than an absolutely smaller population,
it cannot be doubted that the population was, in fact, smaller, and

1. Judde, Surrenden, Wombwell. 2. James Pekham (1400).
3. Ketyll. 4. Roger.
5. The fifteenth-century rentals, with the numbers of tenants they show, followed by
   the tenant-numbers in 1284–5 in brackets, are as follows: Gillingham, 1447
   (KAO U 398, M1a): 106 (316); Wrotham, 1498 (KAO U 55, M 59): 148 (409);
   borgh of Otford, c. 1440 (KAO U 55, M 373): 72 (99). The general decline of later
   medieval population in England has been skilfully argued from the indirect
   evidence of wages and prices by Professor Postan in Ec.H.R., 2nd series, II, no. 3
   (1950), pp. 221–46.

also that fewer tenants held more land than before. On the other hand, there existed a more clearly differentiated class of small-holders, about whose financial status it is hard to be sure. This may be seen from the Gillingham rentals. It will be recalled that Gillingham was divided into yokes, logi, campi, and so on, which were much the same in 1447 as in 1285. At the first date three quarters of the tenants had land which lay in only one of these divisions, and almost all the tenants had their land in less than five. But by 1447 only one third of the tenants were confined to one division, and a quarter of them had their possessions scattered in more than five. Of all the 1447 holdings, a quarter were extremely small, of two acres or less, but on the other hand fifteen per cent of the tenants possessed over fifty acres each, and many of these held property elsewhere as well.[1] It is true that rentals do not give an entirely accurate picture since they did not record what the lord did not officially know, but the broad comparison over the centuries is compelling enough. It was the same at Wrotham, where by the fifteenth century a smaller number of people held more land than in the thirteenth, and where an individual's land, though possibly scattered more widely than before in its totality, showed at the same time a tendency to become consolidated where numbers of fields or closes fell into his hands in one part of the manor.

Rentals, deeds and wills of the late Middle Ages portray a society where economic distinctions were more clearly referred to than formerly, and behind these distinctions are visible increasingly strong feelings about social status. In the reign of Henry V the law began to require the exact description of a man's condition and habitation in order to validate the writs for certain kinds of action,[2] and it is from this time that in the south-east, as elsewhere, the English terms 'gentleman', 'yeoman' and 'husbandman' came into more and more frequent use to describe men of the more affluent sections of the community. Between yeoman and husbandman there was little if any difference in south-east England and the same man might be called either.[3] But the gentleman had leaped

1. I am grateful to Mr Alan Baker for showing me his analysis of the figures, with which my own closely agreed.
2. 1 Hen. V, c.5 (Statute of Additions).
3. e.g. Edward Weston of Tarring, Sussex, called yeoman in 1517 and husbandman in 1527 (Dean and Chapter of Canterbury MS. Reg. T, fos. 148v., 293v.). 'Husbandman' seems a little commoner in Sussex, 'yeoman' in Kent, but there are no clear distinctions.

a social gulf. Books of etiquette multiplied on the market to set the gentlemanly standards for an uncertain and fluid society. Sumptuary laws were enacted in the ever-fruitless attempt to keep *nouveaux riches* in their place.[1] The possession of land was a touchstone, and already 'every gentleman flyeth unto the country'. Our rentals of fifteenth-century Gillingham and Wrotham are rich in the names of tenants who were also masons, carpenters, shinglers, glaziers, tanners and poulterers, and one of the biggest landholders of Gillingham in 1447 was John Pirrie, butcher. John Kelom, gentleman of Lessness near Bexley, who died in 1466, bore the alias Draper.[2] Tradesmen were passing into the ranks of the gentry. It is obvious enough that land was not everything in the lives of prosperous people, and there must have been many who possessed little or no land and suffered neither poverty nor sense of failure. This point could probably be made from among the clothiers of the Cranbrook-Goudhurst area if records were forthcoming, but it can be made here in a different way by referring to women. Few women feature in the archbishop's rentals,[3] for it was not usual to leave daughters substantial holdings. Yet wills and leases often show well-to-do women running enterprises of their own where the skills of management or technique rather than of muscle were needed. Such was Joan Langton, Silkwoman of London, who died in 1474 with property in Bexley and elsewhere in Kent as well as in Lincoln and London;[4] or the lessees of the archbishop's mills: Helen Redmayne, part-holder of Maidstone water-mill in 1515 at £7 6s. 8d. a year,[5] Joan Barton, who took on her late husband's lease of Otford mills in 1526 for fifteen years at £6 a year,[6] or Joan Lowman, who with her husband became lessee and manager of a sizeable brewery near Sevenoaks in 1526.[7] Beneath the landholders who can be counted or identified, the wills of the well-to-do are sufficient to show us a whole unknown world of servants, indoor and outdoor, who not only cooked and cleaned and carried but were the hired labourers through whom farmers lived in comfort upon the profits of their fields. The merest husbandman might have several of these, and the gentleman many. Such servants might also, if it came to the

1. e.g. 35 Edw. III, c. xxii.   2. Rochester Will Book, IV, fo. 221b. (KAO).
3. e.g. at Wrotham in the rental of *c.* 1285, out of 409 named tenants twenty-three were women; in 1498 six out of 148, not counting the Prioress of Dartford.
4. P.C.C. 18 Wattys.   5. Reg. T, fo. 131.
6. ibid., fo. 268.   7. ibid., fo. 309v.

pass, turn themselves into the tough gangs who made their masters' presence felt with swords, daggers and staves, and who, less amenable to the common law than to the power of the Chancellor or the Council, force an entry into history through the Early Chancery Proceedings.[1] It is an interesting speculation whether a sense of oppression weighed more heavily upon the lesser members of the community during the thirteenth century when wages were less and the rights of lordship less questioned, or in the late fourteenth and fifteenth centuries when a man's labour was at a premium, the meek could be exalted, yet the mighty would not be put down from their seat. Here we may try to look at the exact conditions to which men were bound.

OBLIGATIONS

The physical work, payments and forms of obedience required of the archbishop's tenants are known chiefly through the custumal of 1284–5 and partly through the account rolls of the thirteenth and early fourteenth centuries. These sources are not wholly satisfying because they leave earlier ages unknown, and because, full and even garrulous though they are, they cannot by themselves tell the reader whether the impact of the archbishop's lordship upon his tenants was felt to be severe or light, or different at different times and places. For a medieval historian to ask questions like this is always, of course, to ask too much, for even with perfect statistics he cannot measure suffering or contentment, but he can at least assess burdens, and the more comparatively this can be done the better. The evidence available for the present task is reasonably adequate. In the matter of chronology, the custumal was amplified from a similar document of the early thirteenth century, and retains traces of even more archaic matter as well as of minor changes during the course of the thirteenth, fourteenth and fifteenth centuries. The account rolls for their part record the works taken by the lord, in a very fragmentary manner, it is true, but over a long span, so that it is possible to see in outline the coming of commutation. As to geographical

1. cf. Margaret Avery, unpublished London M.A. thesis cit.

extent, the custumal has survived fully for Kent and Sussex, which makes an interesting comparison between the two possible, but only a summary view can be taken of the manors in Surrey and Middlesex.

It will be best to consider first the main forms of labour service, and then the rents, in kind and money, paid by the tenants for their holdings, recalling first that whatever the difference in men's conditions from place to place their obligations all served a lord whose fundamental nature, on the economic view, was to travel with a large household f. om manor to manor. The archbishop's mobility distinguishes the custom of his rural communities from that of manors which belonged to a great monastic house like the cathedral priory. For the monks, food and money were wanted at an unmoving centre; for the archbishop supplies had to be made ready now here, now there. There are signs that his manors had anciently been charged to support him for set periods of one, two or four weeks each year,[1] and many of the services were organized for those occasions, when provisions had to be got in, guides and bearers alerted and fires lit in the halls.

Every manor had a minority of free-holding tenants who generally owed rent and suit of court only (in respect of their free tenements), and a majority of customary tenants, who in Kent were often called *gavelmen* and, though personally free, owed various services as well as rents. In addition there were numbers of smallholders, like the ubiquitous cotmen, the inlanders who are sometimes similar and sometimes distinct from the cotmen, the 'forlanders' who held small amounts of newly cultivated land, and the specialist servants like the smiths and the lord's oxherds. This is an ordered classification from the viewpoint of the lord's custumal, though by now it will be clear how artificial the scheme had really become by the later thirteenth century. For by then the land market had everywhere put customary land into the hands of free men, and vice versa, making the distinction between man and man much more a matter of how much land he held than the kinds of tenure in which he held it. At Harrow the customary tenants were noted as having *subsedentes* under them, some of whom were very poor. At South Malling there were free men who held of rich villeins as well as villeins who held of villeins. It is common sense

1. MS. E 24, fos. 54v. (Aldington); 91 (Bexley); Lambeth MS. 1212, pp. 421–2, 212 (Wrotham and Charing).

to think of the lord's services being done, when required, not by free or customary tenants as such, but in respect of precise pieces of land or of actually existing ploughs upon which defined burdens were laid. By a multitude of private arrangements the richer men found hands to discharge their obligations for them,[1] the smaller men were able to earn food and money when the call for services came.

The services themselves may be grouped into two main types: the supply, carriage and storage of provisions against the arch-bishop's periodic visits with his household to the neighbourhood; and the work which everywhere and always is necessary to keep the rural economy going. In the first group, the characteristic service was *averagium*, which meant carrying-service performed by a tenant with a draught-animal. *Averagia* were assessed in exact numbers of works upon each yoke or virgate. The *averman*'s special duties began as his lord's arrival was announced. At Aldington this was from the moment the cross-bearer entered the gate of the precincts.[2] The duties were then continued without special summons as long as the lord stayed, provided he did not exceed his custo-mary sojourn. If he departed early and the full quota of services had not been performed, the rest were cancelled and neither side had any further claim in respect of that occasion.[3] At Newchurch in Romney Marsh each yoke owed one *averagium* daily and had to provide a mounted man with a sack who need carry only what could be put into the sack and weighed less than four bushels of wheat. If he went from there to Lyminge, Saltwood, Lydd or Charing, it counted as one service, but if to Canterbury, then as two.[4] *Mutatis mutandis* this was the arrangement elsewhere. At Wingham the serjeant summoned as many *avermen* as were wanted that day. They were expected to come *ad horam primam ad ultimam* and to take their turns in order. Undoubtedly there were substitutes to do the work if a landholder who was liable wished to arrange it thus, but to default altogether made the tenant liable to pay an

---

1. It was common for ploughmen to hire their services to their neighbours, and at Chelmsford, Essex, in 1352 some were indicted for asking 18*d*. to 20*d*. an acre instead of 10*d*. or less which had been the previous price (B. H. Putnam, *Enforcement of the Statute of Labourers* (New York, 1908), p. 405).
2. MS. E 24, fo. 54v.
3. ibid., fo. 40. But of course the lord could make a general commutation of *averagia*. The 129½ such works due at Aldington in fourteen days were commuted for £10 15*s*. 9*d*. (ibid., fo. 61).
4. ibid., fo. 58v.

amercement as well as money for the extra work which the lord's employees had to do as a consequence.[1] Sometimes, as on the Sussex manors of South Malling and Pagham, carrying-services took the rider farther afield, to Winchester, to Guildford or to London, and for this he got credit in the number of works allowed. The horsemen with their sacks had not only to bring food and litter into the local manor for the household, but to escort the cavalcade towards the next halting-place, sometimes along paths known only to local men, or to travel across several counties with delicacies for the table of the lord or his friends. Carrying-services of the same kind are found on the Surrey and Middlesex manors of the archbishopric. At Croydon, Cheam and Mortlake they were owed from the *rodlands*, at Harrow and Hayes they were due from the *hydmanni*. As in Kent, a roster system is discernable, and since they were owed only when there was actual need of them the custumal noted of them 'there is no certainty'.[2] Other carrying-services were done by cotmen, but generally on foot and designated by the rental's hybrid term *fotaveragia*, occasionally assimilated to Kentish dialect as *votaveragia*. These might be special to the visit of the lord or his steward, when an intensive messenger-service was called for to take letters about the country, or they might be wanted to carry to Canterbury the ancient Christmas and Easter presents (*exennia*) of hens and eggs, once a monastic privilege but partly appropriated by the archbishop. Apart from the carrying, other preparations were needed for the archbishop's arrival and were charged upon the local tenants, often according to some systematic roster. At Boughton the provision of litter, forage and some stabling were assigned to particular yokes, each of which looked after one of the *familiares* who accompanied the lord: those named were the almoner, the *summus clericus de familia*, the *hostiarius*, a knight, *nuntii*, the cross-bearer, a monk, a carter, washerwomen, purveyor, a janitor, a baker and the chief steward, and their horses numbered over fifty.[3] Tenants were always on their guard against performing these services for more than the agreed number, or for others than 'the quality'. At Boughton firewood would be provided in hall for the *libera familia*; at Wingham hay and litter were

1. ibid., fo. 12. For an instance of default, see below, p. 189. For a similar sort of carrying-service, with horse, sack and skewer, performed for forty days for the king in his army in Wales by a Kentish tenant, see *IPM*, IV, 144.
2. L.R. 2068.
3. MS. E 24, fo. 46v. (2nd enumeration). See also below, Chapter 7.

specifically said to be for the *specialis familia* only;[1] at Bexley hospitality was grudgingly agreed for the clerks, knights and servants of the archbishop or his chief steward, but not for other guests.[2] Services like this were required by every medieval archbishop, whether his manors were being held in demesne or not. But in either case the tenants had the strength to protect themselves against arbitrary additions to these agreed burdens. Nor could a farmer at his will convert to his own use the services which tenants performed in preparation for the archbishop's arrival, and it was for just this kind of high-handedness that the Waleys lost their fee-farm at Tarring in Sussex, even though it was in a relatively more servile area than Kent.[3]

The servicing of communications formed a large part of tenurial works in medieval Kent, and this will cause no surprise to those who have in modern times experienced the difficulty of moving across country there. Although it was characteristic of the Middle Ages to supply public works through private liberties, these communications were not always a strictly intra-manorial matter. Rochester Bridge is a case in point. The liability of certain Kentish estates for the bridge's upkeep probably dates from the tenth century in a form which made the archbishop responsible for the fifth and the ninth piers, but the estates attached to these were not all the archbishop's, whereas Gillingham, which did belong to him, was assigned to work on the second pier.[4] In the thirteenth century the archbishop's custumal for Wrotham noted the local obligations for the fifth pier, and allocated the payment of Wrotham's 'scot' upon six sulungs; but other estates also had to contribute to this pier: seven sulungs from Maidstone, four from Wateringbury, two from Nettlestead, two from East Peckham, one and a half from West Peckham, two from Mereworth, one and a half from Leybourne, a half from Offham, one from Ditton and four from Westerham.[5] The wooden bridge was burned in 1264 and severely damaged by flood in 1281. By 1340 the fifth pier was neglected and it took a royal inquisition to compel the men of these places, especially the recalcitrant people of Westerham, to acknowledge

1. ibid., fo. 12.   2. ibid., fo. 91.   3. See above, p. 103.
4. *CS*, 1321–2; A. J. Robertson, *Anglo-Saxon Charters* (Cambridge, 1939), pp. 106–9; cf. *A.C.*, VI, pp. 45, 117; X, pp. 212–40; also Gordon Ward, 'The Lathe of Aylesford in 975', *A.C.*, XLVI; E. Hasted, *History of Kent* (edition 1797), IV, p. 74 *et seq.*
5. MS. E 24, fo. 83.

their duty.[1] In 1387 the wooden structure was replaced by a stone one, not long after Archbishop Courtenay had granted indulgences for contributions to the work.[2] The older arrangements had proved inefficient.

Labour-services on the archbishop's manors which were directed to the maintenance of agriculture were generally light, with the partial exception of Sussex. Tasks so highly varied naturally occupy a good deal of space in their telling but analysis shows that they cannot have been in themselves very burdensome. They may be classified as 'gavel' services, 'graserth', boon services and the specialized services of certain smallholders.

The custumal shows that the gavelkind lands of Kent owed from every yoke a small amount of ploughing, sowing and harrowing (*gavelerth*) and of reaping (*gavelrip*). *Gavelerth* was of the order of half an acre or one acre from every yoke, *gavelrip* was double that amount. A simple calculation proves the insignificance of the result. At Wingham, where some 5,500 acre sowed labour services, the whole *gavel* ploughing only amounted to some thirty acres, and that for a demesne arable of about 1,200 acres. Wingham was the largest demesne and possessed the largest extent of tenant-land too, but elsewhere the contribution of *gavelerth* to demesne cultivation was also a minor one. It was suggested by Mr Jolliffe that Kentish tenants originally owed money rents only, and that *gavelerth* and similarly named works represented former rents exchanged 'for help with the rising industry of demesne farming'.[3] It is not possible to say how old was the practice by which the archbishop required work as well as rent from his Kentish tenants, but it seem unlikely that the amount of *gavelerth* he received can have been very much help with any 'rising industry' of demesne farming, whenever this may have been. When demesne activity was undergoing the greatest expansion of which there is record, in the late twelfth and thirteenth centuries, the ancient *gabulum* was being paid *in addition* to the performance of gavel services. Probably both the work and the rent were ancient, and each could be described by the word 'gavel'. But in the thirteenth century itself the tendency was certainly to commute these customs into money rather than

1. 'Public Works in Medieval Law', ed. C. T. Flower (*Selden Society*, vol. XXXII 1915, pp. 203–9).
2. Reg. Courtenay, fo. 38v.
3. Jolliffe, *Pre-feudal Society: the Jutes* (1933), p. 35.

vice versa. At Charing it was said that the yokes were at one time obliged to carry wood for the lord (*gavelwode*), but that this had been brought to a money payment called *wodegavel*.[1] Altogether, the old, regular services described as compound words with 'gavel' do not appear to have been economically very important by the thirteenth century, even if they once had been. Only *gavelrip*, the reaping service of a fixed number of acres from each yoke, seems to have been a partial exception to this rule. The amount required, in terms of acres, was rather greater than in the case of ploughing, and on a manor with a small demesne and substantial tenant-lands the tenants' customary reaping was worth while. At Northfleet there was a demesne of 383 acres of which some 200 were sown each year during most of the fourteenth century, and about half the reaping of these was performed by customary service.[2] As a reaping service, however, *gavelrip* might be classified with the boon works which were clearly the most lastingly important ones on the archbishop's estates.

Another ploughing service, which was more important as a sign of seignorial dominance than as an economic asset, was *graserthe*, often written in the Canterbury records as '*gerserthe*'. The custumal explains this in some detail. It was the ploughing of one acre of demesne from every full plough-team in the tenants' possession. The tenant who owned only one or two animals owed proportionately less, even though he joined up with others to plough his own land. As tenants sometimes joined with those who were not archbishop's tenants (though they lived in the same community) to form composite plough-teams, when it came to doing *gerserthe* the lord's officer (at Wingham it was the bedel) had to organize complete teams from the several beasts of lesser tenants.[3] It is the Wingham custumal that gives the best account of the custom's origin, when it says that the tenants whose lands lay next the demesne could not in former times avoid the demesne in the 'open time', so they were given permission for their draught-beasts to feed upon the demesne provided they performed this service in return; but 'later it was levied throughout the whole hundred by compulsion of the bailiffs'. The remarkable feature of this account is that it is found in virtually the same form as the explanation of

1. MS. E 24, fo. 47v
2. L.R. 777–84·
3. MS. E 24, fo. 11.

graserthe in widely scattered religious estates in England. At Bury St Edmunds and at Glastonbury a similar explanation was given,[1] and the service is found on most of the archbishop's manors in Kent, Sussex, Surrey and Middlesex, however much their topography differed. Taking together its universal character and the role assigned in the Wingham account to the bailiffs and the hundreds, it looks as if *graserthe* was not so much the result of a local economic need than an exercise of seignorial jurisdiction which had perhaps been talked over at some time among ecclesiastics and rulers and based upon *a priori* ideas of what was rightfully due. One is often reminded of this aspect of labour-services on the archbishop's estates.

More enduring and indeed more energetic than any of the other services were the boon works, for they were needed by the demesnes at urgent moments in the yearly round. Boon ploughing, called *benerth* or ploughing *ad precem*, is found everywhere and carried a good food allowance. At Northfleet in the thirteenth century this was worth 4*d.* for each plough, at Wingham 3*d.*, at Slindon in Sussex 2*d.* with food.[2] Besides the usual boon ploughing required from every customary plough there was the 'great boon' which could be asked if the lord got into serious arrears with ploughing. But important though they were, these services were likely enough to be performed by hired men, as the text shows when it expects the tenants' teams coming to dinner to be made up of the *domini caruce* each with his three, four or five *famuli* or *garciones*. For the real work needed on the demesnes plenty of labour was available in the thirteenth century, hired in contractual terms, however much they were couched in the language of obligation. With boon reaping the pressure of the lord's demands was greater still because of the sheer urgency of the task and because, sickles being cheaper than ploughs, more men, and humbler and more easily coercible men, could be got. The *bedrip* was sometimes demanded of whole households, and not from the yokes or virgates.[3] Even free tenants had to find several men,[4] and

---

1. N. Neilson, *Customary Rents* (Oxford Studies in Social and Legal History, II, 1910), pp. 69–70.
2. MS. E 24, fo. 12; *S.R.S.*, vol. 57, p. 1; L.R. 2068.
3. *S.R.S.*, vol. 57, p. 1.
4. ibid., pp. 17, 21. At Laughton in Sussex in the fourteenth century both freemen and customary tenants had to reap at harvest on the demesne 'with all their household except wives and shepherds' (*S.R.S.*, vol. 60 (1961), p. 81).

smallholders in Sussex and Surrey might be routed out of their households in large numbers.[1]

On every manor cotlands or small-holdings provided men who were jacks of all trades and sometimes specialists and full-time workers for the lord. A good example is Wrotham, where the cotlands, of nine acres each, supplied *cotmanni* to work every day of the year at threshing, weeding, reaping, stooking, wattle-making, brewing and carrying letters to London, Canterbury, Gillingham or Maidstone. The Wrotham cotter was also allowed an acre upon which he might keep his dog.[2] The cotter's position was similar elsewhere, and slid easily into that of the scarcely free, full-time *famulus* who did for payment what he was bidden day by day.[3] At Petham, where the cotland was five acres, the cotter acted in addition as drover, even to distant manors, lay out at night to guard the lord's corn, roofed buildings, sheared sheep, and if there were not enough *servientes* for the lord's ploughs, acted in their stead.[4] His service as ploughman, indeed, might last the whole year.[5] Those who were called up for full-time demesne ploughing had the right to use the lord's plough on their own pieces every second or third Saturday. On the Sussex manor of Pagham the full-time ploughmen were called *bovarii* or *akermanni* and were expected to work a five-day week for the lord, having the lord's plough for themselves, or else $\frac{1}{2}d.$, on alternate Saturdays. Their tendency to slacken off at the end of the week is made clear by the threat that absence from work on Friday meant losing the Saturday benefit.[6] Smallholders like this, personally subject to the lord's authority, were the sort of people to supply the force with which authority is upheld. At Petham the cotters got ready the wood for the fire when the lord or the farmer held one of the compulsory subscription drinking-parties called 'scotales';[7] in many places they had to guard prisoners suspected of crimes, in the manor-house or in the mill, and at South Malling they hanged the thieves whom the royal justices had sentenced.[8]

1. Boon works are prominent on the Surrey manors. From Croydon 101 reapers had to come 'from the hamlets' for three separate boons, but, as usual, they got food and drink.
2. MS. E 24, fo. 83v.: '*et habuit 1 acram vocatam Hundesland ad pascendum canem suum*'.
3. ibid., fo. 83: '*et debent qualibet die in septimana a festo sancti Michaelis usque ad festum sancte Trinitatis facere quod sibi preceptum fuisset . . .*' (Wrotham).
4. ibid., fo. 68.   5. ibid., fo. 71.   6. ibid., fo. 97.
7. ibid., fo. 68, and see below, 182, *n.* 6.   8. *S.R.S.*, vol. 57, p. 118.

Whether they were lifelong *famuli* of the lord or not, the cottagers usually worked harder for him than did the other tenants, but there is an exception to this state of affairs in Sussex, where tenants of major holdings were liable to render the typically servile week-work. The archbishop's Sussex manors fell into two main groups, those round Pagham in the west, and those round South Malling in the east. Servility is found in the west, and in those parts of the eastern manors which lay outside the weald. At Slindon, in west Sussex, some virgates on the *terra operabilis* owed the first four days in every week throughout the year, and sometimes Friday too, to work at the lord's will. Also at Tangmere, Lavant, Tarring and Pagham and its bartons, all in the west of the county, a virgater could expect to owe every day's work till mid afternoon. There was provision for a month's sick-leave, and since the demand was from the virgate, or occasionally the hide, rather than from any named individual, the tenant could doubtless send someone else from his family; but the fact remains that this was week-work, which did not exist in Kent nor, apparently, on the archbishop's Surrey and Middlesex manors. On the east Sussex manors there was a marked distinction between the borghs within the woodland area where the unfree virgates owed hedging, fencing, works of building and repairing with wood, the carriage of wood, the manufacture of casks, troughs and other wooden objects under the bailiff's direction, the finding of honey and hawk's nests, and help with the lord's hunting, and the borghs outside the woodland where the more familiar and heavy works of ploughing, manuring, threshing and so on were owed weekly by the virgaters of neif land. Here too there was provision for sick leave, but here too the conditions were more arduous and servile than anything that can be found on other parts of the archbishop's estates.

Details of rural life by themselves lack significance unless we ask about their total importance in the lives of tenants and lord. What proportion of the tenants' time did the labour-services take if they were all performed in full? What proportion of the lord's demesne needs did they supply? And how far were they in fact exacted? The first two of these questions are the easiest to face. The Kentish gavelkinder cannot have given much time to the lord in the normal course of events. If the customs as we know of them after 1200 existed in 1100, then there would of course have been fewer men to perform them and their incidence upon each would have been heavier. Lack of twelfth-century evidence makes this a matter of surmise. But by the thirteenth century the total quantity of service owed was, as exemplified above with Wingham, very small. At the same time, it is certain that the archbishop always employed considerable numbers of full-time *famuli* as long as he held his manors in demesne. Customary services can therefore have given no more than marginal help in the routine tasks of ploughing, sowing and harrowing, and when accounts become available, in the later thirteenth century, it is apparent that other tasks too, like threshing and mowing, were done or partially done by hired piece-workers.[1]

As for the commutation of labour-services, the evidence from the archbishopric estates is only fragmentary, but it is enough to suggest that it was not in any way a simple or coherent change. Even during the best period of seignorial agriculture, in the thirteenth century, there was some commutation of services, yet services were here and there demanded in the middle or even later fifteenth century. This may be seen from what follows. Demesne production was clearly in full swing by 1205,[2] yet in 1211–12 some works were being placed *ad firmam denariorum*[3] and in 1231–2 more still.[4] In this year a good deal of money was spent in paying full-time workers like the fourteen *servientes* and fourteen ploughmen at Harrow alone, who worked at 5*d.* a day each. It was, of course, the business of the custumal of 1284–5 to itemize the services which could be asked, but the document refers in places to the action of past archbishops in relation to particular services. Stephen Langton had commuted the cotters' work at Aldington and had taken 20*s.* per annum in place of their letter-carrying, collecting of hens and eggs and levying of distress.[5] On the other hand Langton's steward, Elias of Dereham, was a strict character, paring away food payments for the Wingham carrying services and insisting on threshing duties at Bexley.[6] By contrast, Archbishop Edmund seems to have been made of softer stuff, acquiescing when the Maidstone tenants ceased to make malt, though doubtless the tenants of Tarring suffered when he gave in to the Waleys.[7] There was further commutation at Aldington under Archbishop Boniface,

---

1. e.g. in the custumal of 1284–5 references are made to the hired threshers—*trituratores locati.*
2. *P.R. 8 John*, pp. 54–5. (This and the following are vacancy accounts.)
3. P.R. 58 m. 5 (customs and works farmed realized £6 16*s.* 5½*d.*).
4. P.R. 76 m. 5d (customs and works sold realized £33 1*s.* 0*d.*).
5. MS. E 24, fo. 55.   6. ibid., fos. 12, 91v.   7. See above, p. 101.

though he insisted on full boon-works at Saltwood.[1] This custumal shows at every turn the influence of mutual bargaining and adjustment.[2] In the fourteenth and fifteenth centuries the bargaining was still going on, but by then the tenants seem to have been getting the upper hand. In 1356 Archbishop Islip granted his men of Otford relief from the carrying of wood as long as they behaved well towards him, paying their rents and doing their customs well and loyally;[3] but Otford was a trouble-spot where the tenants refused the service of reaping and mowing in 1381 and where they often refused rents in the fifteenth century.[4] By the middle of that century most *gavelerths* and *gavelrips* seem to have been redeemed for 10*d*. an acre and haymaking and wood-carting sold *pro rata*.[5] At Northfleet the *gavel* services were exacted throughout the fourteenth century. In 1317–18, of 204 acres of demesne wheat and barley, all but forty were reaped by *gavelrip*.[6] That they were still enforced in 1366–7 is shown by the exaction of 102 acres of *gavelrip* and the remark that eighteen and a half acres of reaping had been sold because they were owed by parcels of tenant-land *circa quod non potuit compellere*.[7] But here too the services grew increasingly difficult to exact. Refusal of service was widespread during the late fourteenth and fifteenth centuries. It is apparent at Sevenoaks in 1461,[8] Northfleet in the 1450s and 1478.[9] Wingham in 1390.[10] But light though the services were, the lord continued to try and exact them and in the late fifteenth century may still be found coming to terms with the tenantry.[11] Leases of the demesnes to farmers sometimes made over the *opera tenentium* with the fields, and a few works were being performed by tenants for their lord's lessees at the end of the Middle Ages.[12] In general, boon

---

1. MS. E 24, fo. 54 (carrying-services and the making of enclosures), and fo. 64.
2. ibid., fos. 63v., 64 (bis) (Saltwood), 88v. (Bexley).
3. Register of Archbishop Islip, fo. 128v.
4. A. Réville, *Le Soulèvement des travailleurs* (Paris, 1898), Appendix no. 76; cf. L.R. 1243 (A.D. 1460–1).
5. MS. E 24, fo. 74v.
6. L.R. 778.
7. L.R. 782.
8. L.R. 1263.
9. Mins. Accts 1129/2, 1130/7.
10. Reg. Courtenay, fo. 337v.
11. Mins. Accts 1130/10: payment of 13*s*. 4*d*. to John Alfey '*pro eius labore . . . pro domino apud Wrotham circa levacionem operum custumariorum ibidem hoc anno* [1481–2] *appreciandorum in denariis . . .*'.
12. e.g. Aldington in 1451–2, *averagia* and enclosing works were sold for £4 12*s*. 4*d*. but gavelerth, gavelrip and wattle-making were delivered to the farmer, mowing, haymaking and hay-carrying were shared between the archbishop and the farmer, and the cutting and carrying of wood, enclosing round the woods, making malt and constructing the piggery were not demanded at all (S.C.6 1129/3).

works lasted longer than regular ones. But when we reflect on the small amount of really arduous service that was demanded on the archbishop's Kentish estates, the small size of the demesnes in relation to the extent of the tenant lands, the availability of labour in the thirteenth century to perform what tasks there were, even customary tasks, on behalf of those who owed them by reason of tenure; when we recall likewise the stubbornness of the Kentish tenants, and the way in which the farmers of the demesnes in fact got their work done by means of contractual servants and their own efforts, then it appears that the lord's exaction of services and his relaxation of them are not central events in an important economic development but a border warfare about lesser conveniences in a society where the chief care of both sides was personal freedom or its converse, seignorial rights and dignity. In the later Middle Ages the archbishop's tenants objected much more to the idea of servility than to the oppression of a taskmaster.

From services we pass to rents. In the south-east of England, rents were of far greater importance to the lord than the performance of work, even at the most intense period of demesne exploitation, and even on the estates of the Canterbury monks, whose demesnes played a bigger part in their economy than did those of the archbishop in his.[1]

Rents were of two main varieties, those rendered in kind, and those rendered in cash, and each is of an antiquity which forbids us to see its beginnings. It may be that food renders are the older of the two, though even of this one cannot be sure. An indication of what an early food render was like comes from a document called the *Consuetudines de Newenton* which lists the income of the church of Newington-by-Sittingbourne as it was known to a Canterbury scribe about the time of Domesday. To the church, he said, belong seven sulungs and seven denns in the Weald, a weir at *Baedinge*, twenty-eight weys of cheese from Milton, twenty-eight weys of cheese from Sheppey and *Binnen ea*, twenty-four pounds of pence as *gabulum* from the land of the seven sulungs, and 10*s*. a year from the church of St Sexburga in Sheppey. Newington church also possessed the church of Marden in the Weald, two houses in Rochester rendering 2*s*. a year, and three houses in Canterbury on the west part of Eastbridge at which, so the docu-

---

1. R. A. L. Smith, *Canterbury Cathedral Priory* (1943), ch. VIII.

ment appears to mean, were paid 30*d*. and six carts. The men of the Weald owed a summer gift called *sumerhus* or else 20*s*.[1] The archbishop had a claim to part of Newington, though the complex story cannot be followed out here. The same document refers to the archbishop's right in the church of St Martin of Dover, the prebends of which were divided up in Domesday. One of these, held by Stigand, was in Deal, and in the Middle Ages the archbishop certainly continued to hold the prebend of Deal. By the thirteenth century this was rendering, besides the profits of its demesne fields, £2 9*s*. 1*d*. in cash rents, together with cocks, hens, eggs and male hawks, and also a twenty-first part of the oblations in wax, of the tithe of fish taken at Dover, and of offerings on the feasts of St Margaret and Our Lady's Birthday.[2] The intermingling of money and produce is well illustrated from these examples, partly because physical objects or services tended to be turned into money equivalents, but partly because of the large and perhaps aboriginal place taken by money rents themselves. The *gabulum* from Newington's sulungs, it will be noted, comes to 1*d*. an acre if the sulung was of just over two hundred acres, as it was elsewhere in that vicinity.[3] Rents in kind were habitually called *consuetudines*, or occasionally, *redditus mobiles*. Probably this is the significance of the *constumes* in the *Domesday Monachorum* document which shows payments from the archbishop's manors.[4] But already they were passing into cash form. In the thirteenth-century custumal they are itemized with immense prolixity, but a better overall view of them can be got from the full year's account which survives almost intact from 1273-4.[5] Each manor owed large numbers of hens and eggs, originally the Christmas and Easter presents (*exennia*) owed to the monks but ultimately kept by the archbishop from his own manors.[6] Almost as common was the rent of plough-shares (*vomeres*). Other renders are found with more or less frequency upon different manors: plough-wheels, carts (*plaustra*

---

1. Lambeth MS. 1212, pp. 335-6. There are other copies of this document, one of which is in Canterbury Cathedral Register P, fo. 28. I am obliged to Dr W. G. Urry for this reference. See also A. Ballard, 'An Eleventh Century Inquisition of St Augustine's Canterbury' in *British Academy Records of Social and Economic History of England and Wales*, IV (1920), section 2; and some discussion by Professor David Douglas in *Dom. Mon.*, p. 14 and *n*.8.
2. L.R. 2068.   3. See above, p. 118.
4. *Dom. Mon.*, pp. 98-9; cf. R. Lennard, *Rural England 1086-1135* (1959), p. 119. See below, pp. 179, 199.
5. Addit. MS. 29794.   6. R. A. L. Smith, op. cit., p. 7 and references there.

or *carri*), iron, horseshoes, herrings, eels, cummin, pepper, oats, barley, salt, currycombs (from Wimbledon only), oysters (from Teynham, not far from Whitstable) and ploughtails (from Aldington). From the woodlands was paid an entirely separate set of rents, with its own historical development reflecting the ever greater part played by the tenants in their settlement.[1] Pannage for the right to pasture pigs is the oldest, together with *danger*, which was a fixed payment in 'damage' or compensation for the natural lack of oak or beech mast from which the woods suffered in many years, especially after bad summers, and which thus involved the lord in loss. Even medieval men confused *danger* with *lefgavel* or *lefsilver*, but this was a higher payment, made by tenants for leave to cultivate in the woodlands, and thus deliberately to destroy the pannage. If they paid this they did not have to pay *danger* as well. By degrees the archbishop was edged out of the deep woodlands by the flourishing life within them. The custom of building him 'summer houses' there was converted to payment, as we saw with Newington. Increasingly he concentrated upon his more accessible woodlands near his demesne manors, the products of which he could exploit and market. By the thirteenth century, not only his woodland rents and services but virtually all others were being paid in money, yet the superb archaism of the account rolls preserves the full description of the *consuetudines* year by year till the end of the medieval period.

The history of the money-rents is one of successive increments which can be dimly discerned amidst the general 'assessed' rents[2] of the later medieval accounts. The earliest identifiable rent was the *gafol* or *gabulum*, amounting on the archbishop's estates to 1*d.* an acre payable on tenant-lands at mid Lent. To this was generally added a rent called *mala*, at a variable but higher rate, and payable at the four principal terms of the year, Easter, Nativity of St John the Baptist (24 June), Michaelmas and Christmas.[3] If the later assessed rents are much higher than the gabulum, this is to be accounted for, first, by the imposition of the *mala*, which more than doubled it, and then by the addition of a whole crowd of rents for

1. For this subject, see 'Denns, Droving and Danger' by the present writer in *A.C.*, LXXVI (1961), pp. 75–87.
2. The term assessed rents has been preferred as a translation for *redditus assisae* to the less intelligible 'assized rents' or rents of assize.
3. Jolliffe, op. cit., p. 33; Neilson, *Customary Rents*, pp. 42–3. In East Anglia the 'gafol' of 1*d.* an acre, a *hundredal* due of royal origin, was called 'hidage'.

freshly cleared or settled land, often subsumed under the name
'new rents', and perhaps going as far as to double again the basic
gabulum plus *mala*. The main process was over by the mid thirteenth century. Some indication of these workings may be gained
from comparing *Domesday Monachorum* with thirteenth-century
accounts, and again with the rental of 1284–5. In *Domesday
Monachorum* there is a schedule of payments due from the archbishop's manors, and from each one is a sum described as
gabulum. If we take it that this represents a rent of 1*d.* an acre, and
reduce the sums to pence, the result will be a hypothetical number
of acres for each of the manors. If next the number of acres of
tenant-land on each of the manors is worked out, as it can be with
fair approximation from the rental, and compared with our
hypothetical Domesday acreages, they will be found to correspond
quite nearly. To take an example, Boughton-under-Blean in
1285 had 32½ yokes of older tenant land, the local yoke being
of forty acres, making a total of 1,300 acres. At 1*d.* the acre the
gabulum for this should be £5 8*s.* 4*d.*, and in *Domesday Monachorum* the Boughton *gabulum* is given separately as £5 15*s.* 4*d.*[1]
In the accounts of the thirteenth century, however, the assessed
rents of Boughton were not in the region of £5 but of £25,[2]
and payable not only at mid Lent but at the four principal terms
and at St Martin's. Luckily, the rental names the different rents
of which the total was made up. The original *gabulum* had risen
to £6 16*s.* 8¾*d.*, and to this had been added *mala* of £5 0*s.* 6½*d.*
In addition, the manor had acquired a further four yokes, some
cotlands and more recently enclosed lands called *Sidlands* from
which a higher, Michaelmas, rent was owing besides *gabulum*
and *mala*. There were also Michaelmas rents from developed
property (*haghae*), and some other assarts and pieces let out
by Archbishop Hubert Walter. Together these bring the total
up to about £25, and at this figure the assessed rents remained,
more or less, for the rest of the Middle Ages.[3] The same development can be seen at the neighbouring manor of Charing.[4] In
Domesday Monachorum the *gabulum* was £4 7*s.* 2*d.* together with
£2 16*s.* '*constumes*'. In 1273–4 the *consuetudines* amounted to

1. *Dom. Mon.*, p. 85.   2. Addit. MS. 29794, m. 8d.
3. For Boughton, see MS. E 24, fos. 41–6.
4. For Charing, *Dom. Mon.*, pp. 85, 98; Lambeth MS. 1212, p. 212, where the
gabulum under Archbishop Richard (1174–82) appears as £4 6*s.* 1½*d.*; Addit. MS.
29794, mm. 8, 8d.; MS. E 24, fos. 47–53.

£2 6s. 9d., and this inelastic form of revenue may well correspond with the earlier *constumes*. But the assessed rents were now £38 1s. 10½d. Analysis of the rental shows that again the *gabulum* itself had increased somewhat to £5 6s. 2¾d., no doubt because new land brought into cultivation owed the basic *gabulum* in addition to new rents. But the greatest single item was the *mala*, which in itself was over twice as much as the *gabulum*. The yoked lands now produced £20 16s. 3¼d. from their *gabulum*, *mala*, and smaller payments like swinegavel, woodgavel and summerhouse. An almost equal amount again, however, came from a variety of sources which may be summed up as new settlements and development: tenements of five acres each, cotlands, inlands and forlands, rents from the weald, from meadow and from 'places' in the market. The total is £39 11s. 3¾d., which is close to the assessed rents of the account rolls. This sum remains astonishingly stable, though not ossified, for the rest of the Middle Ages.

In this way may be seen the geology of the rents. At bottom is the stratum of the *gabulum*, itself thickening a little as time goes on. Above this is the large layer of the *mala*, the imposition of which seems once to have been resented.[1] On top again come various smaller items, like the money value of former customs and more realistic rents for assart and meadow, and together these form the backbone of the archbishop's fiscal resources throughout the Middle Ages. In some ways the newer items which appear in the account rolls under the heading of assessed rents or new rents have the greatest interest, for they tell something of the progress in land values. Even in the rental of 1285 the thirteenth-century increase in assart prices can be seen here and there: 'Old assart' in Sussex dated from the times of Archbishops Stephen, Richard and Edmund (1207–40) and was at 1d. an acre, the 'new assarts' of Archbishop Boniface's time (1245–70) were at 2d.[2] But in respect of mere bulk, the traditional rents remained the most important.

As with services, so with money payments, the burden which fell upon men, and against which they sometimes rebelled, was not the age-long exaction but the extraordinary demands of the later Middle Ages, coupled as often as not with some emphasis on their subjection. Up to the thirteenth century the king had habitually

1. cf. Jolliffe, op. cit., p. 14.   2. *S.R.S.*, vol. 57, pp. 31, 66, etc.

tallaged the men of the archbishopric during vacancies of the see, and when vacancies became shorter and of less interest to the king, this impost was transformed into the demand made by each new archbishop for a sum from every manor as a 'recognition' of him by his tenants.[1] In the earlier thirteenth century little is heard of the personal freedom of Kentish men or their rightful exemption from such tallages. In 1231 Henry III ordered his keepers to assess the tallage '*super villanos et eos qui per archiepiscopum possent talliari*', and the amount collected suggests that the ordinary gavelkinder paid.[2] But after Edward I's time tallages fell off. Kentish men were becoming more conscious of their 'rights', and they would not pay the 'recognitions'.

THE CONDITION OF MEN

Only about forty miles separated South Malling in east Sussex from the archbishop's Kentish manor of Aldington, but in making this journey over the Rother he passed from a countryside where bondage was known till the end of the Middle Ages to one in which royal judges had admitted in Edward I's day that personal freedom was the rule.[3] Is it true that Kentish men were free, and, if so, for how long had this been so, and what did such freedom mean? Work is still necessary before answering these questions properly, but some preliminary comments may be made here. The legal freedom of Kentishmen appears fairly well established by the thirteenth century. Since the Conquest they had often been socially and economically of a class with knights, and knights were soon to be thought rare in the county.[4] Archbishop Walter had not only been allowed to convert gavelkind lands into fee but also to hold the Grand Assize of gavelkind holdings on his estates.[5] Gavelkind tenure was, in fact, treated as free tenure. In the negative way, there is no clear evidence of personal bondage in

1. M. Howell, *Regalian Right in Medieval England* (1962), ch. v.
2. *C.P.R. 1227–31*, p. 574; P.R. 76, m. 5d. (£317 4s. 8d. was realized from the archbishop's lands aside from Middlesex, and this cannot all have been collected from the Sussex *villani*.) See also the tallages of 1168 on the *homines* of all the archbishop's manors, which raised over £200 (*P.R. 14 Hen. II*, pp. 153–6).
3. Jolliffe, op. cit., p. 31; *Eyre of Kent*, III, p. 155.
4. See above, pp. 103, 111.   5. Lambeth MS. 1212, pp. 48, 196; LCM, XI, p. 10.

Kent, except for one doubtful instance, whereas there are many instances of Sussex villeinage among the archbishopric records. The Kentish exception is the will of Sir William Septvans of Milton by Canterbury who in 1407 bequeathed to his *servi et nativi*, Adam Standarde, Thomas Hamonde, Robert Cherche and John Ryccheford, their full liberty, and desired them each to have a charter of manumission.[1] The wording is unambiguous, but it is quite possible that these men belonged to the Septvans lands in Sussex or Essex, and it would in any case be rash to build a theory of Kentish villeinage upon a single instance of this kind. On the other hand, there are signs in the custumals that servile conditions of manorial life existed before 1200 and survived later. Frequently the gavelkinders, and not merely the cotters and inlanders, had to seek permission before they might marry off their children outside the manor. At Reculver the licence cost 2*d*.[2] At Thanet the men had to bargain with the bailiff, though the custumal guaranteed them against a fine heavier than 5*s*.[3] At Teynham and Bexley a man might marry off his daughter within the manor but not with an outsider unless permission had been granted, and the amercement for those who had done this without leave was 3*s*. 6*d*.[4] At Otford and Wrotham the cotters had to do services which were uncertain and at the precept of the lord's agent,[5] and elsewhere the whole tenant population was in some respects subject to ancient customs which perhaps bear the stamp of unfreedom: at Petham and at Bexley there were compulsory scotales, and in Bexley again the custumal tells us that the archaic condition dues of *childwite* and *blodwite* were owed.[6] It is possible to explain away these matters by saying that they had once been imposed by ecclesiastical authority upon free native traditions, but there is as yet little evidence either of the tradition's nature or

1. This was noted by A. Savine, 'Bondmen Under the Tudors' (*TRHS* n.s. xvii (1903), p. 284), who quoted it from *A.C.*, xii, p. 285. For the names quoted correctly from the enregistered will at Maidstone I am indebted to Mother Mary de Sales. None of these names are in the Subsidy Roll of 1334–5 under Westgate Hundred, in which Milton lay.
2. ms. E 24, fo. 19.   3. L.R. 2068.
4. ms. E 24, fos. 40v., 91v.   5. ibid., fos. 73v., 83.
6. ibid., fo. 91v.; L.R. 2068; cf. Neilson, op. cit., pp. 86, 90. The scotale was a party to which all customary tenants had to come; at Petham the cotters had to carry brushwood, bear water and prepare the fire, having dinner in return, when there was a scotale; at Bexley, it says that when the archbishop makes a scotale, every man and wife shall give 2*d*. on the Sunday and 1*d*. on the Monday; if one of them is ill and cannot come, he shall send the money to the *curia*, and shall have ale. The archbishop was trying to abolish them in 1275 (see below, pp. 303-4).

the mode of imposition. When these disabilities found expression in the thirteenth-century custumal they were already old, and so far as we can tell were not asserted. Theoretical freedom is a sophisticated idea. It may be that the famous Kentish freedom was a thirteenth-century concept which arose from the practical power of Kentish landholders to handle their own estates, and that the condition rents just described were obsolete survivals.

But Sussex was in strong contrast to Kent. The rental of South Malling alludes time and again to 'neifs'. Bondmen were manumitted in west Sussex as in east. This is not to say that the quality of agrarian life, the lord's needs or the spirit of men were transformed the moment the Rother was crossed. There were Sussex *nativi* who throve better than the free-born, and sold their lands to free men,[1] while, on the contrary, a later medieval archbishop could, as we shall see, insist upon the services of his humbler Kentish tenants in a manner every bit as crushing as his handling of the Sussex unfree. It is simply that in Sussex the institution of villeinage had been allowed to develop, and governed the relationship of the lord with his men. A particular case will illustrate this. In 1359 Archbishop Islip summoned the brothers John and Robert atte Broke, sons of John atte Broke of the borgh of Framfield within the woodland of South Malling, and in his chamber at South Malling accused them of removing themselves from his lordship and power although they were his *servi* or *nativi*. At first they denied this, saying that they had been born in the archbishop's lordship, that the younger brother had the tenement of his father according to the custom of the country, and that they had lived by their labour from their youth up, but they agreed to abide by the result of an inquiry into their status. Six weeks later they were forced to admit the archbishop's case. They placed themselves in his grace for their rebellion, and swore their bondmen's fealty (*fidelitatem nativam*) on his cross, kissing it as they completed the formula.[2] Three days later their half-brother Nicholas took the same oath. All three had to appear at the next court at Uckfield to make a similar recogni-

1. Reynolds complained in 1314 of South Malling bondmen who sold their servile lands to free men, to the loss of his church (Reg. Reynolds, f. 111).
2. Reg. Islip, fos. 151v.–152, 174–5; *Lit. Cant.*, II, no. 880. For a manumission from Shripney in west Sussex as late as 1481, see *Registrum T. Bourgchier*, p. 38.

tion before the steward or bailiff. But nearly two years later the archbishop executed a deed of manumission in favour of Nicholas the half-brother and Nicholas's sons, Richard, John and William, with all their *sequela*. The youngest son, Walter, however, with his progeny, were to remain in servitude, 'and him we do not wish through this instrument to enjoy any liberty'. Nicholas had held two villein tenements, but now, according to the custom of the manor, had to leave them, with the principal chattels in them, to the next tenant. The manumission was followed by an interesting agreement in which Nicholas pledged himself to pay £100 'which I have received of my lord archbishop as a loan' at Mayfield any time after Michaelmas 1361, pledging also his goods and chattels. This was a usual form by which one party secured the contractual agreement of another to perform some action, and in this case the action was described next day, when the archbishop required Nicholas to hold himself ready to serve as life-warden of one of his manors, or in any other office suitable to his status. To this Nicholas swore in the vulgar tongue, and the obligation of £100 was remitted. The service the archbishop wanted of him, as warden of a manor, was an honourable one but at unimpressive pay, and probably it was not always easy to get good men to perform it, especially during those plague-stricken years.[1] The incident shows up the legal victory of Kentish landholders in the thirteenth century. Somehow, freedom had there been juridially born. In Sussex it had not, and the late medieval conflicts between the archbishop and his tenants, visible everywhere, were outside Kent concerned with status itself, not merely with obligations.

In reality, the changing distribution of riches are of crucial importance in understanding the changing condition of men. In the struggle for income old custom became a weapon in the lord's hands. A late medieval correspondent of the prior of Canterbury wrote to tell him that 'therebe bondmen longyng to the . . . manor [of Blakham in Sussex], and they be richemen'. Naming them, he added,

---

1. When George Guston in 1526 was appointed warden of Otford manor it was said that former archbishops had paid a fee of 2*d*. a day, but that now the manor had been remade with many buildings, promenades, towers and gardens so much labour was needed that none would undertake it for that sum. Accordingly the archbishop allowed 4*d*. a day. (Dean and Chapter of Canterbury MS. Reg. T, fo. 272.)

wherfor yf hit please your lordship to serch your tresory among your evidences of olde court rolles of the forseid maner, or if ye may fynde ony names of men *semblabill to the forseid names* . . . hit will avayle to the churche and yow 100 marke . . . [for] hit is seid *quicquid servus adquirit domino suo adquirit[ur].*[1]

The ancient maxim thus still had a flicker of power behind it, the more so as it was being used in a county where money had long spoken loud enough to make villeins the landlords of free men.[2] The point indeed was in the new wealth of the formerly obscure, and this was visible in every county. From the fifteenth century, abundant account rolls and wills show what must long have been a fact, the flourishing of private skills, trades and landed enterprise behind the façade of manorial routine. Not only in the clothmaking area of Cranbrook, not only among the yeomen who took over and made a good thing of his demesne arable and his marsh pastures, but also from within the continuing manorial society over which the archbishop exercised his lordship, many men were prospering and raising their families into positions of undramatic strength: in the chalk and lime business on the north Kent coast at Northfleet and elsewhere, in river transport, like the Scudders of Erith, in tile-making, brewing, and in building, where a competent man might achieve a contractor's position, like that of William Cornford, carpenter to Archbishop Warham, who could command and pay workmen with money from the household.[3] What created resentment was the startling contrast between the opportunities of self-help in a society that paid the unskilled workman at least 5*d.* a day,[4] and the demands of a lordship which offered no final relief from its personal vexations, nor saw the folly of treating disobedience as sacrilege. It is difficult to disentangle the crossed threads of fear and anger which become so often apparent after the mid fourteenth century, but the spirit of disobedience which was abroad may be distinguished readily from the ruffianism which gets into the judicial records of every age. It is not in the robberies that this spirit is manifest, nor even in the park-breaking and poaching

1. *Christ Church Letters*, ed. J. Brigstocke Sheppard (Camden New Series, XIX, 1877), no. lxxx.
2. See above, pp. 166, 171. 3. L.R. 1255.
4. e.g. in 1414–15 the repair of Maidstone mill employed nine cementers at 3*s.* 8*d.* each a week for several weeks, four apprentices at 4*d.* a day and twelve *servientes* cutting down trees at 5*d.* a day.

which long ago Winchelsey had chosen to regard as sacrilege,[1] nor in the hanging inflicted easily enough upon small-time thieves and *ignoti*,[2] while others were too powerful even to be distrained for their arrears of rent,[3] but in the deliberate acts of defiance, however crude or small, performed in combination with others, in the belief that rights of some sort, and not merely appetites, were involved. Such were the refusals of rents and services to which allusion has been made,[4] the persistent refusal here and there of the common fine, and of the 'recognition', servile tallage's unproductive heir.[5] When in 1538 some of the estates were being forcibly exchanged, Walter Hendley wrote to Cromwell that the king had sent him to Otford, Knole and Maidstone, where the archbishop had had courts, to attorn the tenants, and that they had done fealty 'with right good will: never were so many tenants seen at the courts'.[6] Thus at the breath of King Henry the disobedience vanished, but we have not to judge the tenants of the archbishop by this more terrible test, but rather to see the manner in which the disobedience had arisen and to judge, if anyone, the archbishop. To Polydore Vergil the sort of obstinacy that the archbishop met was something natural to the people of Kent—'*Cantiani populi, tam injuriam intoleranter patientes quam novarum rerum semper cupidi. . . .*'[7] But the foreigner can hardly have known why his clever remark was true. As long ago as the thirteenth century Kentishmen had been resisting the efforts of archbishops to take their valuable wardships from them or exact a fine for allowing them.[8] By the end of the century common opinion in the county was strong enough to win judicial recognition for the people's unique landholding privileges, and this in a county said to be seriously short of knights. The plagues of the fourteenth century brought suffering to these people, yet at the same time strengthened

1. *Reg. Winchelsey*, pp. 399–400; cf. Reg. Courtenay, fo. 45.
2. Register of Pecham, fo. 200v. (1283); cf. at Otford in 1462–3: '. . . *diversi ignoti qui capti fuerunt et suspensi ad sectam Laurencii Hencley*', the owner of the cattle, worth £3 6s. 8d., which they had stolen (Mins. Accts 1129/7).
3. 1296–7: 20s. rent detained by Henry de Shyneholt of Otford, '*pro quibus non est ausus amplius distringere*' (L.R. 831); 1465–6: £6 6s. rent in arrears at Willop, near Aldington, from Sir John Fog, for which the collector 'has in no manner dared to distrain' (L.R. 1194).
4. See above, p. 175.
5. Otford 1460–1 (L.R. 1243); Wrotham 1468–9 (Mins. Accts 1130/2); *Medieval Bexley*, p. 28 and *n.*; and above, p. 181.
6. *E.H.R.*, LXVII (1952), p. 33.
7. Cited by A. Réville, op. cit., p. lxxv. 8. See above, p. 145.

the position of those who survived against seignorial control. In turn, the difficulties experienced by the archbishop, and the fear which seems to have been experienced by many great lords, especially churchmen, in the late fourteenth and early fifteenth centuries in face of rebellion, heresy and plebeian improvement, made him, like other lords, very sensitive of his authority and quick to put down protests which in themselves were about trivial matters. It is against such a background that we must explain the incidents of manorial strife which are scattered through the later medieval records. At Otford in the terrible famine year 1315–16 wheat had risen steadily in price from 10s. a quarter on 1 November to 24s. at midsummer. The roll which tells us this tells also a few paragraphs farther on of sixteen men from surrounding villages who had been taken with stolen goods and led off to Maidstone jail.[1] Soon after this the plagues began, creating in the memory of many families, as doubtless the famine had done, a series of landmarks by which they could date events in after days.[2] Yet the consequences were hardly as grim for the survivors in the villages as for the lord himself. Archbishop Islip's register tells in 1352 of the ruin of Wrotham manor through the pestilence, and of the widespread decay of property for lack of money to maintain it.[3] Land fell vacant and the price of it fell.[4] Almost at once it became permanently difficult to get agricultural labour at a price the great estate organization could afford. The statute of labourers could not keep wages at the pre-plague level. In Essex in 1352 workmen of every sort were being indicted for asking double or more for their services and products.[5] In 1349–50 an attempt was made to withhold from the *famuli* at Bexley the allowance of corn which was part of their wage, presumably on account of the grain shortage, but the decision was soon reversed on the discovery that the men would not work if this were done.[6] At Teynham the same year higher stipends had to be paid 'on account of the dearth of *famuli*', and there was no hay and little corn from the mill *causa pestilencie*.[7] At Gillingham there were few people to pasture sheep

1. L.R. 832.
2. *IPM*, XIV, 344 (Chichester 1377), recalling the 'middle pestilence'.
3. Reg. Islip, fo. 60; cf. *Lit. Cant.*, II, no, 791.
4. e.g. Reg. Islip, fos. 37v., 49v., 212.
5. B. H. Putnam, *The Enforcement of the Statute of Labourers* (New York, 1908), pp. 401–6.
6. L.R. 240; cf. *Medieval Bexley*, p. 32.   7. L.R. 1222.

on the marsh, no miller, and none either to cut rushes or to buy them.[1] Even before the pestilence this area of north Kent had probably not been an easy labour market,[2] but the rewards given to *famuli* to work better appear more frequently still at the end of the fourteenth century,[3] and about this time demesne cultivation was abandoned by the archbishop fairly generally. Whether one looks at the Broke manumissions at South Malling or the wages commanded by daily 'hyressemen'[4] in the later Middle Ages, it is obvious enough that social changes were being worked by the price mechanism apart from the conscious will of individuals.

If these changes which were transforming society owed nothing to the foresight of men, they were none the less forming in men fresh attitudes towards the order they knew. When passions flared up at moments of general disturbance they betrayed, of course, local anger and fright, but also some intelligible purpose and the early shadows of the egalitarian idea. In 1381 at Thanet the rebels raised a cry that no tenant should do service or custom to the lordships there as they had done hitherto, nor allow distraints to be taken to enforce them.[5] Throughout the country held by the archbishop there was much of the usual resentment against men of means: the vicar of the well-to-do church of Wrotham was threatened;[6] the house of a rich man at North Cray near Bexley was pillaged;[7] the stocks of lime at the works belonging to the Makenades at Preston by Faversham were destroyed.[8] But William de Makenade, soon to be the archbishop's steward,[9] was representative not only of superior wealth but of the customary subjection of men. Everywhere the destruction of records commemorating such subjection was held by the rebels to be more important than makeshift economic levelling. At Thanet the books and rolls were flung out and burned and a local taxation demanded

1. ibid.
2. e.g. extra stipend given to carter and ploughmen at Maidstone in 1298-9 at the steward's direction (L.R. 658). For higher wages in the vicinity of London, see J. E. T. Rogers, *History of Agriculture and Prices*, iv (1882), ch. xvii.
3. e.g. Wrotham in 1393-4: '*et in rewardo facto omnibus famulis manerii ut melius se haberent in servicio domini*' (KAO U 55, M 64; cf. L.R. 1142 (1400-1)).
4. The schedules of memoranda about building and maintenance expenses which survive from archiepiscopal manors in the later fifteenth century give an idea of the volume of work available for *hyressemen* at 6*d*. or 7*d*. a day for the unskilled (e.g. L.R. 1249, bailiwick of Otford 1486-7).
5. W. E. Flaherty, 'The Great Rebellion in Kent, 1381', *A.C.*, iii (1860), pp. 71-2.
6. ibid., p. 90.   7. Réville, op. cit., p. lxxv.   8. Flaherty, op. cit., p. 90.
9. In 1397-9 (L.R. 668, and see below, pp. 269, 394).

to maintain proceedings against the lordships.[1] At Teynham the manor was entered and rentals and muniments burned.[2] The chronicler painted a vivid picture of the disturbance at Lambeth where rebels broke the barrels of wine and threw the dishes against each other in the kitchen, shouting 'a revell, a revell'![3] But the purposeful acts of that June day were the burning of custumals, rentals and memoranda 'through which the farms, rents, services and other profits rightfully belonging to the archbishopric can be levied'.[4] The rebellion collapsed and made no perceptible difference one way or the other to the process of emancipation, but its occurrence left evidence which proves the bitterness felt in a county where proudly copied manuscripts were proclaiming that the bodies of all its men were free. Events show the unimportance of mere juridical freedom. Islip's assertion of lordship over his Sussex villeins in 1359 could in the years after the revolt be paralleled in Kent itself, where Courtenay in 1390 summoned six customary tenants from Wingham for failing to perform their due service of driving cartloads of hay and litter to his palace at Canterbury. The service was not particularly arduous and could have been performed without hardship, and indeed it had been performed in a partial manner. What offended the archbishop was that the work had been done secretly (*sub latibulo*) on foot and not with carts, so that the men, ashamed of the obligation, were refusing to acknowledge it openly, and this, as his tribunal at Saltwood found, was in contempt of the archbishop. The sentence was that they should parade like penitents round Wingham church, each carrying on his shoulders a sack of hay and straw and walking with slow steps: *'lentis incessibus procederent humiliter et devote'*.[5] Nothing could give sharper point to the social meaning of obligation at that time and place.

After the reign of Richard II the tension between the archbishop and his tenants grew less, though it did not evaporate altogether. But the society of the country in which the archbishop's estates lay was not quiet or static in the fifteenth century, and however important the conflicts between lord and tenants, it would be

1. Flaherty, op. cit., pp. 71–2. 2. ibid., pp. 95–6.
3. *Polychronicon*, IX (R.S. 1886), pp. 1–2.
4. Réville, op. cit., Appendix II, Series A.
5. Reg. Courtenay, fo. 337v. See Frontispiece. The ecclesiastical proceedings for a manorial crime are interesting. Note also that the British Museum possesses a golden seal inscribed 'Jurisdiction of Saltwood', and possibly made *c.* 1385 when Courtenay improved Saltwood Castle (*A.C.*, XLI, pp. 1–11).

wrong to interpret social change simply in these terms. The complexity of events is illustrated by the Kentish rising of the 1450s, usually described as Cade's rebellion, but in fact a series of disturbances under the leadership of men like Parmenter, Wilkins, and Hasildene as well as Cade.[1] These were directed partly against the gangster-like extortion of money by royal and seignorial officials during the 1440s and partly against the government of the 'court party' itself and fear of what it would do. The rebels had serious grievances, but at the same time the situation got out of hand and led to incidents like the poaching raid of 1451 in which eighty-two deer were stolen from the Duke of Buckingham's park of Redleaf at Penshurst by about a hundred armed yeomen and labourers, wearing long beards, their faces blacked with charcoal, and hiding their identities under the general title of 'servants of the queen of the fairies', which had been a name used by a conspiracy leader of the year before. As a consequence of the disturbances the government sent commissions of oyer and terminer into Kent. These were of two kinds. One was to investigate the extortions which had been committed by officials, great and small, and was actually in response to the demand of the rebels: the government's promise of 1450 to investigate the wrongs was honoured, as that of 1381 was not. The other commissions were simply to indict rebels and repress malefactors, and were more effective than the private accusations. The mass of indictments recorded as a result of these commissions give a good idea of the people who had been expressing their discontents so forcibly. It is impossible to say that they were simply 'the poor', or 'tenants' as opposed to 'lords'. Those against whom extortion had been practised were, almost by definition, substantial people who had something worth extorting, and they were often in status no lower than those who were performing the oppression. But they were not in power. For example, one of those indicted was Robert Est, gentleman, one of the chronicler's 'gret extorsioners of Kent',[2] who was a keeper of the archbishop's jail at Maidstone and who, among his other misdeeds, maintained quarrels in the archbishop's court at Canterbury palace. Another of the villains was the John Alpheigh who has been met

1. For these paragraphs I am much indebted to Dr Roger Virgoe who has edited some of these indictments (P.R.O. K.B.9, Files 46, 47 and 48) for *Kent Records*, vol. XVIII.
2. *Three Fifteenth-Century Chronicles*, ed. James Gairdner (Camden New Series, XXVIII, 1880).

in these pages before,[1] one of the archbishop's bailiffs, but also under-sheriff to the notorious William Crowmer, sheriff of Kent, 1449–50. James Fiennes, lord Say, Crowmer's father-in-law, another leading 'extorsioner', had himself been steward of the lands to the archbishop.[2] Yet these men had been out for their own interest, not the archbishop's, and the victims themselves were also sometimes men who had places in the archbishop's organization, like William Wangford, serjeant-at-law, himself one of the royal commissioners, who had a lease of the archbishop's profitable chalk quarries at Northfleet,[3] or John Hockeridge, the park-keeper of Otford, or even Reynold Peckham, esquire of Wrotham, whose consent to an exchange of land had been demanded in 1448 with menaces of drawing and hanging.[4] As to the people indicted for treason and rebellion, one is struck by their variety of type. There were three or four gentlemen from London among their number, and the others described in three files of indictments belonged to almost the whole range of contemporary occupations: there were fifty labourers (the term included threshers and agricultural piece-workers), thirty-nine husbandmen and thirty-six yeomen. From the agricultural world there were also wheel-wrights, thatchers, reapers and a malt-miller. From the constructional trades there were carpenters, smiths, cementers, sawyers, masons and a tile-maker. From the clothing trades there were numerous weavers, especially from the Sevenoaks area, tailors, fullers, skinners, tanners and a glover. From the food and drink trades there were many butchers, some coopers, a baker, poulterer, fisherman, vintner and spicer; and of miscellaneous occupation there were shipmen, fletchers, parish clerks, a pardoner, a summoner, a chapman, a barber and a servant.

It is impossible to gauge with accuracy the economic condition of all these types. The existence of some poverty cannot be doubted: the old, infirm and unfortunate were always present. Archbishop Warham noted poverty in Kentish villages in 1525, though this was after the fall in real wages had begun about 1510.[5] Much more

---

1. See above, pp. 113, 175*n*.
2. *Lit. Cant.*, III, no. 1024; *HMCR*, IX, App., pp. 104, 114.
3. Rochester Will Book 5, fo. 387 (KAO); L.R. 1240, etc.
4. For the Peckhams, see above, pp. 154–6.
5. *Historical Journal* (1963), p. 17; E. H. Phelps-Brown and Sheila V. Hopkins, 'Seven Centuries of the Prices of Consumables Compared with Builders' Wage-Rates', *Economica*, n.s., vol. 23, no. 92.

certain in the fifteenth century is the diffusion of wealth and the private enterprise of hundreds of individuals. To select a few instances from the indictments, Thomas Hilles the cementer also possessed a close and some houses in Maidstone; John Burd of Chipstead was robbed of 6 oz. of saffron, 10 lb. of pepper, 10 lb. of ginger, 2 lb. of cloves, twenty gold and silver rings and £7 in cash which he had in his house; and even quite humble Englishmen had their ways of profiting from the French war, like Richard atte Welle and John Jardyn, whose families had probably lived for a long time on the archbishop's manor of Wingham.[1] They had got as prisoner of war a Picard called John Seynard and were going to get eight marks ransom for him. The negotiator was a certain John Carter who was a brewer of Sandwich and had crossed the Channel under royal safe-conduct to get the ransom. He was a man of multiform enterprise, for he abducted the prisoner for his own advantage, and thus found himself indicted, with the result that he is known to us. These are illustrations from criminal life and necessarily show the fruits of disorder. At the same time, it is evident that the real enemy of this world was not only an ancient lord like the archbishop, but disorder, insecurity and doubtful authority.

APPENDIX TO CHAPTER 4

The wills analysed on pp. 159–61 are as follows. They have been selected on no other principle than that the testators were connected in some way with the estates.

John Alpheigh, gent., Sevenoaks, etc. 1489. (PCC Milles, fos. 147v.–149.)

Richard Bamme, esq., Gillingham. 1452. (PCC Rous, fo. 133.)

John Beele, Sevenoaks., 1471. (PCC Wattys, fos. 64–5.)

Thomas Boone, Sevenoaks. 1486. (PCC Milles, fo. 8v.)

Thomas Brampston, Northfleet. 1511. (PCC 2 Fetiplace.)

Robert Cawode, Bexley, London, etc. 1465. (PCC Godyn, fos. 75v – 77v)

John Chown, Shipbourne 1514. (Ro. vii, fo. 156.)

John Clerk, senior, gent., Wrotham. 1480. (PCC Logge, fo. 15v.)

1. These names, are drawn from the King's Bench Indictments of 1451 (K.B.9 File 46 m. 7), (*Kent Records*, vol. xviii, p. 241).

John Clerk, husbandman, Bexley. 1527. (PCC 25 Porch.)

John Colyn, Wrotham. 1488. (PCC Milles, fo. 245.)

Thomas Cooke, Otford. 1465. (PCC Godyn, fo. 55.)

John Dyne, senior, Wrotham. 1463. (Ro. ii, fo. 268v.)

John Freman, Dartford. 1474. (Ro. iv, fos. 127–8.)

William Gens, Maidstone. 1479. (Ro. iii, fo. 225.)

John Goodwin, Wrotham. 1495. (PCC 29 & 34 Vox.)

George Guston, Otford. 1536. (PCC 12 Dyngeley.)

Thomas Hall, yeoman, Bexley. (PCC 20 Porch.)

William Hall, yeoman, Bexley. 1512. (Somerset House filed will.)

William Hampton, pouchmaker, Wrotham. 1492. (PCC Dogett, fo. 104.)

John Hastlyn, Erith. 1524. (Ro. vii, fo. 356 (i).)

George Howton, gent., archbishop's auditor, Maidstone. 1473. (PCC Wattys, fo. 207.)

Nicholas Hubert, Shoreham. 1496. (PCC 28 Vox.)

John Judde, gent., Tonbridge. 1492. (PCC 29 Dogett.)

John Kelom or Draper, gent., Lessness. 1466. (Ro. iv, fo. 221.)

William Kene, gent., archbishop's receiver, Woolwich. (PCC Godyn, fo. 163.)

John Ketyll, Southfleet. 1460. (Ro. ii, fo. 178.)

John Langton, widow and Silkwoman, Bexley. (PCC 18 Wattys.)

Robert Multon, gent., Otford. 1532. (PCC 20 Thower.)

John Mylle, gent., Sevenoaks. 1459. (PCC 21 Stokton.)

William Nicholas, Speldhurst. 1480. (Ro. iii, fo. 259.)

James Pekham, Wrotham. 1400. (Reg. Arundel, fo. 176v.)

James Pekham, esq., Wrotham. 1532. (PCC 23 Thower.)

Reynold Pekham, esq., Wrotham. (PCC 31 Bodfelde.)

Thomas Pekham, gent., Wrotham. 1515. (PCC 6 Holden.)

Richard Pette, Sevenoaks. 1513. (PCC 30 Fetiplace.)

Robert Qwikerell, Rochester. 1483. (Ro. iv, fo. 35.)

William Roger, yeoman, Otford. 1475. (PCC Wattys, fo. 172.)

Thomas Romnaye, Chelsfield. 1509. (Ro. vi, fo. 259v.)

Walter Sexten, Wrotham. 1491(?). (PCC 46 Milles.)

John Shelley, gent., Bexley. 1531. (PCC 5 Hogen.)

Thomas Sparrowe or Lamendby, Bexley. 1505. (PCC 24 Fetiplace.)

William Surrenden, clerk in Chancery, Boughton Malberbe, etc. 1469. (PCC Godyn, fo. 221.)

William Swetesyre, yeoman, North Cray. 1527. (PCC 23 Porch.)

Robert Tottisherst, gent., Sevenoaks. 1512. (PCC 8 Fetiplace.)

William Wangford, serjeant-at-law, Northfleet. 1498(?). (Ro. v, fo. 387.)

Thomas Wombwell, yeoman, Northfleet. 1483. (PCC Logge, fo. 82.)

CHAPTER 5

The archbishops' demesnes

THE PHASES OF THEIR MEDIEVAL HISTORY

'Demesne' implies lordship, but it is a word used in both broad and narrow senses.[1] As one of the greatest lords of medieval England, the archbishop held his whole temporality 'in demesne as of fee' of the king. More narrowly, the archbishop retained in demesne those properties which were neither enfeoffed to knights nor allocated to the monks of the cathedral. In the Domesday texts, the lands of the knights were certainly said to be 'manors of the archbishop', and the archbishop was also described as 'holding' the manors of the monks; but these were not the archbishop's demesnes, and he did not draw from them their full available revenue. On the other hand, those thirty or so manors which he kept under his direction to supply his income and provide him with lodgment, attendance and transport were indeed his own (*propria maneria*), and were held by him in demesne: '*ipse archiepiscopus tenet Wingeham in dominio*'. More precisely still, only a portion even of these manors was in the fullest sense in demesne, namely, the fields, woods and buildings exploited directly for him by his agents or servants, in distinction from the lands and villages of his tenants. It was of such a home farm that Domesday said '*in dominio sunt VIII carucae*'—'on its demesne are eight ploughs'—though to the arable and its ploughs must be

1. In medieval texts the word is *dominium* or *dominica*. 'Demesne' was used by the legal antiquaries of the seventeenth century.

194

added the woods, pastures, fisheries, ferries, mills and even churches which appear in descriptions of the demesnes from the time of Domesday through thirteenth-century rentals to the accounts and leases of the later Middle Ages.

After the turmoil of the Conquest, with its losses and recoveries, enfeoffments and rearrangements, the demesnes remained fairly stable for the rest of the Middle Ages. To protect the estates in their physical integrity was a duty laid upon the archbishops by religion and law, interpreted with a literalness that modern trustees or Church Commissioners would find excessive. Anselm would not bargain with William II about property for which he must answer exactly to God,[1] and even in 1523, when Archbishop Warham was about to lease out an unprofitable little Sussex manor-court, he felt bound to explain that his intention was to increase and not diminish the goods of his church.[2] The idea of freely improving a church estate by timely realizations and reinvestments was foreign to the age, and it is this dutiful petrifaction just as much as the obvious fact that church estates were not subject to family fortunes like lay ones that accounts for their stability. But it was possible to buy new lands or to exchange them under painstaking safeguards. Consequently, although the demesne map of 1500 is much the same as that of 1100, it is not completely so. Lambeth was finally acquired in 1197 by exchange with the monks of Rochester for Darenth.[3] Ranscombe in Sussex was acquired under Archbishop Edmund.[4] Waddon in Surrey was exchanged for Croydon church with Bermondsey Priory by Archbishop Courtenay in 1390.[5] Knole was bought in 1456 by Archbishop Bourgchier from Lord Say and Sele.[6] A group of valuable rectories in the archbishop's gift appear among the temporalities of the see in the early fifteenth century, appropriated by the archbishop to augment his own income: Cranbrook, Ford and Herne, Northfleet, and Thanet, all in Kent, Mayfield and Wadhurst in the Sussex weald. Other places unheard of in Domesday Book appear in the thirteenth century in the fuller light of documentary day; closer inspection shows

1. R. W. Southern, *St Anselm* (1963), ch. IV. But Anselm was willing to *lease out* an estate to raise money (ibid., p. 157).
2. Dean and Chapter of Canterbury MS. Reg. T, fo. 212v.
3. LCM, XI, 17; Lambeth MS. 1212, pp. 76, 135-7. For an account of the whole negotiation, see Dorothy Gardner, *The Story of Lambeth Palace* (1930), pp. 9-18.
4. Lambeth MS. 1212, p. 27 (between 1233 and 1240).
5. *Lit. Cant.*, III, no. 957; Reg. Courtenay, fo. 175.
6. *A.C.*, LXIII, p. 135.

Map 3. THE DEMESNE MANORS IN THE LATER MIDDLE AGES, GROUPED IN BAILIWICKS

Key

Demesne manors named in Domesday are underlined

Note

The organization of the demesne manors into administrative units called bailiwicks was fixed during the vacancy of the see after Archbishop Pecham's death, that is, between 8 December 1292 and 4 February 1295, when the temporalities were restored to Archbishop Winchelsey. The dotted lines on the map give a diagrammatic view of these groupings. They remained stable until the break-up of the medieval estates of the see under Archbishop Cranmer. For further discussion of the bailiwicks, see pp. 268, 272, 327

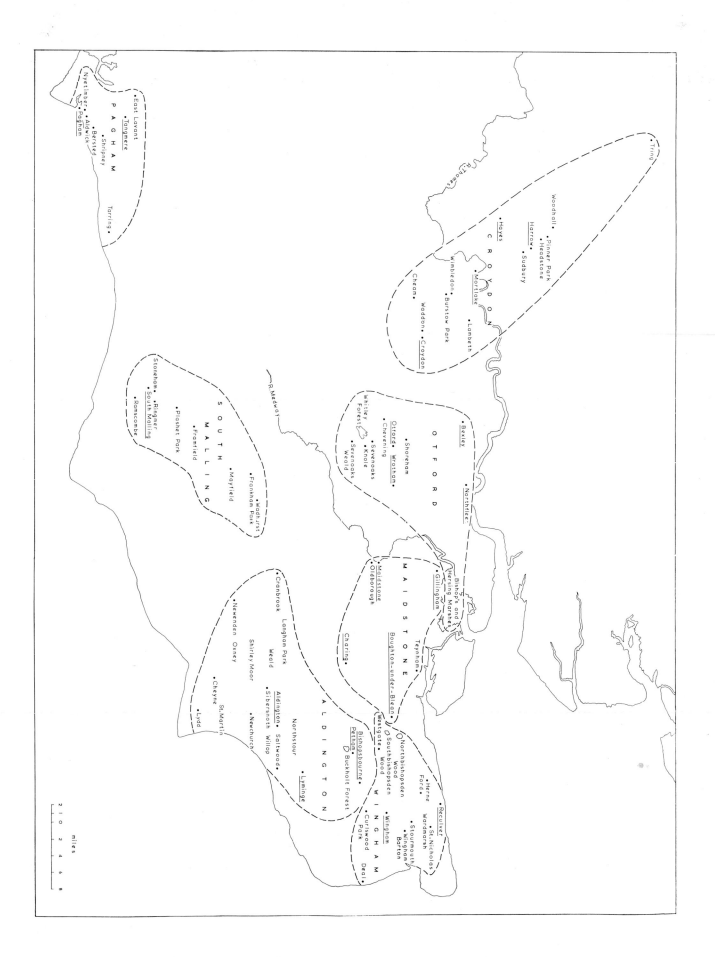

these to have lain within the Domesday manors, but now newly named, peopled, exploited and administered, like Sudbury and Woodhall in Harrow, Cheam in Croydon, or the bartons of Nyetimber, Aldwick, Bersted and Shripney in Pagham. In sum, the medieval demesnes formed a mass of property which changed only marginally over five hundred years and can be evaluated without too great a fear of making false comparisons over this long time.

Within this period there are three main phases. Up to about 1200 the demesnes were mostly leased out whole and entire to 'farmers' who were themselves men of substance and importance, but the evidence relating to the age is slight and sporadic. Between roughly 1200 and 1400 the demesnes, fields as well as rents of tenants, were exploited directly for the archbishop through the well-known manorial apparatus of bailiffs, reeves, serjeants and *famuli*, helped by the customary services of tenants. In the 1380s and 1390s the leasing of individual manors began again, uncertainly, at first, with occasional returns to a few years' direct farming, until by the 1440s all the demesne fields were again in lessees' hands. From this chonological sketch it will be clear that the reeve and bailiff manorialism, so often regarded as typical of the Middle Ages and as agriculture's best medieval manifestation, was hardly more than a substantial interlude in an age-long system of leasehold farming. But the truth of this must not disguise a further fact, that the late medieval phase of leasing was quite different from the early. Though it had bad moments it was not, as it has usually been painted, a terminal age of decline and gloom, but one of moderate prosperity for all concerned; for the numerous class of yeoman and gentry farmers, for the professional managers who toured and administered the properties, and for the archbishop, whose rent-roll held firm and began to expand as the fifteenth century passed into the sixteenth. The documentation increases from phase to phase and, though these things are necessarily subjective, the historian's interest quickens as the traditional demesnes are seen to become enlivened and possessed by new classes.

1086 TO *c.* 1200: THE DEMESNES LEASED

The archbishopric was not unique in leasing out its demesne manors in the twelfth century. The same method was being practised on many if not most of the great estates, ecclesiastical and lay, and in different parts of England at the time of Domesday and for much of the twelfth century.[1] By this method the manors which remained unenfeoffed for knight-service were none the less committed to an intermediary person who stood between the lord and the tenantry, and who in return for a certain rent acted as the effective exploiting lord, collecting the dues of the tenants and directing in ways now obscure the routines of production. He was the *firmarius*, farmer, or lessee. When Domesday says that a manor was worth so much, this value (*valet*) was often a round figure, expressed as a whole number of pounds, paid by the farmer. Among the archbishopric lands, for example, Westgate was 'worth' £40, Wingham £100, Bishopsbourne £30, and so on. Less often the sums were an odd number of pounds: Gillingham £23, or Aldington £101. More rarely still, manors were said in the Domesday survey to be worth a sum expressed in pounds, shillings, and pence: Boughton-under-Blean paid £13 16*s.* 3½*d.* and Northwood £50 14*s.* 2*d.* Further, in twelve instances Domesday says that despite this value an even greater one was actually paid over. 'In the time of King Edward Lyminge was valued at £24, afterwards £40 and now the same, *and yet it renders* £60.' Or, to take a more eloquent instance, Pagham in Sussex 'was worth £40 in the time of King Edward and afterwards, in the time of King William £60, yet it renders £80, but that is too heavy'. At South Malling the story is the same and the farmer himself is named: the price had fallen from £40 to £30 when the manor changed hands, but in 1086 it was valued at £70, yet 'Godfrey held it to farm for £90'. These sums represented the prices paid for the leases, and this is made yet clearer by the text of *Domesday Monachorum* (*c.* 1090), which in nine instances explicitly described the amounts paid as *firmae*. Another list printed with *Domesday Monachorum* but probably of a slightly later date[2] describes almost

---

1. Reginald Lennard, *Rural England 1086–1135* (1959), esp. ch. v.
2. *Dom. Mon.*, pp. 98–9.

all the main payments from the archbishop's manors as 'farms'. There are thus three historical texts available at close intervals from 1086, and they supplement each other to show the archbishop's demesne manors leased out at prices which were liable to fluctuate, usually in an upward direction.

The mechanics of the leasing is not quite as simple as these general remarks may suggest. In addition to the round sums due from the farmers there were other sums payable to the archbishop and occasionally to others from the demesne manors. These odd amounts of money were on occasion included in the *firma* as it is described in the Domesday survey, though the survey does not often announce it in so many words. But in the later of the two *Domesday Monachorum* texts the extra payments from the farmed manors are systematically noted. For example, 'Boughton and Teynham £73 and 10s. to the archbishop. *Gabulum* £14 9s. 0¾d. *Constumes* 64s.'[1] In almost every case the rents additional to the *firma* are *gabulum* and *constumes*, and it is not hard to see in the first of these the ancient basic rent of 1d. an acre rendered at mid Lent from the customary tenant-lands,[2] and in the second the money valuation of various renders in kind or small services which generally appear in the later account rolls as *consuetudines*.[3] For some reason the archbishop's clerks continued to record these renders separately even when the farmer was paying a lump sum for the manor, and *Domesday Monachorum* in the earlier list tells us as much: 'Boughton was valued TRE at £10 and from it the archbishop had £5 15s. 3d. *gabulum*. Now it is worth £20, but it renders £25 and the archbishop has his *gabulum* as before.'[4] The total lease price might thus change according to private arrangements between the archbishop and his farmer. The *gabulum* and *constumes* changed less (though change was possible) for they corresponded to the holdings of customary tenants within the manor. The two excerpts about Boughton which have been given here point to another possible variation, namely, the regrouping of the demesne manors in the hands of their farmers. In the one text of *Domesday Monachorum* Boughton and Teynham are separate, in the other they have evidently been placed together in the hands of the same farmer. They were adjoining manors. Likewise, Mortlake in Surrey and Hayes in Middlesex became grouped

1. *Dom. Mon.*, p. 98. 2. See above, p. 179.
3. See above, p. 180. 4. *Dom. Mon.*, pp. 84–5.

in a way which foreshadows the bailiwicks of the thirteenth century.

Much remains obscure in these early arrangements, such as the relationship of the Domesday texts to each other, and the circumstances under which the payments were fixed, supervision exercised and the detailed responsibilities of the farmers carried out. But in general it is clear enough that the archbishop retained a control over the disposition of his demesnes even though they were leased. There are indications that he received entry-fines of 20*s.*, 30*s.* or 40*s.* in addition to the farm, and that his reeve might benefit in the same way.[1] Sundridge rendered him a knight, in addition to an economic fee-farm rent.[2] The great manor of Pagham was doubtless still leased out in 1120–2 when Archbishop Ralph granted from it the annual render of thirty-six loads of beans as churchscot (*circescet*) to Lewes Priory, saying that this render he had retained in demesne.[3]

From the Domesday texts we step away into a darkness which is little enlightened by evidence until the thirteenth century. It is therefore impossible to know much about the way in which the farmers of the archbishopric demesnes made their living and treated the tenants, nor indeed to know often who they were. The annual rents they paid were very large in the money of the time, and doubtless they enjoyed in return the whole range of demesne equipment and amenities to which Domesday normally ascribed a total value: ploughs, pastures, meadows, fisheries and mills. What was the archbishop's was theirs for the long duration of their contracts. The most complete illustration is provided by the manor of Charing, which lies twelve miles south-west of Canterbury and possessed about five hundred acres of arable in the thirteenth century. In the last years of the eleventh century the archbishop took back some tenant land 'to his own plough' (*ad propriam carrucam*),[4] but the same Domesday text makes it clear that the manor was none the less farmed out, with its four

---

1. 20*s.* from Aldington, Wrotham, Northfleet, Bexley, West Malling, Mortlake, Hayes, Harrow; 30*s.* from South Malling; 40*s.* from Croydon (cf. R. Lennard, op. cit., p. 181). From Tangmere an ounce of gold and 20*s.* to the reeve (*Dom. Mon.*, pp. 98–9).
2. 'He who holds it renders £24 and a knight from the farm to the archbishop' (*Dom. Mon.*, p. 87).
3. *Ancient Charters prior to A.D. 1200*, i, ed. J. H. Round (*P.R.*, vol. x, 1888, pp. 16–7).
4. *Dom. Mon.*, p. 85.

and a half plough-teams, its twenty-six *villani* and twenty-seven bordars and their twenty-seven plough-teams, its twelve serfs and the mill which brought in 3*s*. 4*d*. a year, its twenty-five acres of meadow and its woodland sufficient to render twenty-six pigs as annual rent.[1] By a happy chance, a charter survives from 1174–82[2] to show that this scheme had continued at Charing over the years. There is no reason to think it untypical. It testified that Archbishop Richard had granted to Adam of Charing, son of Ivo, and to his son after Adam's death, the whole manor of Charing at farm for £32 of silver a year, on condition that if the archbishop wished to stay there, then Adam or his son would prepare for him the farm of two weeks and deduct its value from the sum of £32. In addition, Adam or his son was to render £4 6*s*. 1½*d*. to the archbishop's chamber as *gabulum* at mid Lent, and Adam was to hold the manor 'as freely as his father Ivo had done in the times of Archbishops Ralph, William and Theobald, and as he himself had done in the times of Theobald and Thomas [Becket]'. By this renewal of an ancient agreement the tenure of one of the main demesne manors by Adam's family is seen to stretch back to within a generation of Domesday, and into a future defined only by the lifetime of the heir, which might be expected to last well into the thirteenth century. Furthermore, the annual price of the lease tended after a time to diminish. The farms that were being extorted from the archbishopric manors in 1086 had brought the income up by about sixty per cent since William I's arrival,[3] but the ascending curve did not extend far into the twelfth century. In King Edward's day Charing had been valued at £34, and had been made to pay £60 in 1086; in the 1090s it was paying £40 together with a *gabulum* of £4 7*s*., and £2 16*s*. in the name of '*constumes*'. Yet in the last quarter of the twelfth century the farm was only £32, with almost the same *gabulum*. Possibly the lowness of the rent was a favour to Adam's family; possibly it was due to the general stagnation of income from which chief lords tended to suffer under the farming system and from which they strove to free themselves when prices began to move sharply upwards.

1. When in 1183 the archbishop was beginning to bring some of his manors back into demesne, the vacancy account notes that the mills had hitherto been included in the total farms of the manors (*P.R. 30 Hen. II*, p. 151).
2. Lambeth MS. 1212, p. 212.
3. cf. R. W. Southern, op. cit., p. 256, for a similar comment on the monastic manors.

In any case, it is dangerous to build too much theory upon a single charter.

Yet it is highly likely that the system under which the farmers paid cash and provisioned the archbishop for a week or two during the year if he gave them due notice was a general one. Preparations to receive the archbishop on such occasions were standardized and written into the thirteenth-century custumals,[1] and what happened at Charing was in the thirteenth century still happening at Wrotham in Kent and Tarring in Sussex. Wrotham had paid £25 in 1086 and £30 a little later, together with some other small renders. It was still paying about the same (£32) when Archbishop Pecham brought it back into demesne, and under the fee-farm terms the archbishops could exercise the right to come and take provisions. A detailed account shows Boniface of Savoy doing this on 6 and 7 October 1267. He was represented by a full and distinguished household, and the farmers themselves, men of considerable rank, sent their own representatives. Exactly valued quantities of wheat, wine, ale, beef, mutton, pork, poultry, eggs, salt fish and oats were handed over to the several officers of the archbishop's household, and the total of £10 5s. 9¼d. was deducted from the farm outstanding.[2] At Tarring, the farmer held the manor for £15 at the time of Domesday and £18 in *Domesday Monachorum*. In 1277 he was still doing so,[3] but if he gave forty days' notice the archbishop might come there once during the year and daily take a quarter of wheat for 18d., a quarter of oats for 8d., four gallons of the best ale for 1d. ('and if it be not the best let the cask be smashed and the ale spilt'), a fat ox carcass for 16d., a male pig of reasonable size and over a year old for 8d., a fat mutton carcass for 4d., two fat geese for 1d., a hundred eggs for 1d. and another hundred for nothing, and dishes, plates, salt-cellars, cups, skewers, firewood, coal, salt, earthenware pitchers, hay and litter for nothing. Again, the farmer's expenses were deducted from the annual rent.

Judging by what happened on other estates in the south of England, the twelfth-century farmers must have been men of substance and with money to invest. On the Ramsey Abbey estates

1. Canterbury MS. E 24, fos. 47v., 48v., 53; Lambeth MS. 1212, p. 25; see above, p. 167.
2. Lambeth MS. 1212, pp. 421–2; and see below, p. 254.
3. See above, pp. 100–3 and refs. there.

we find Simon the chamberlain and Adam son of Henry the archdeacon as farmers;[1] at Lifton in Devon, Coluin, steward to Queen
Edith; in Cambridgeshire, William the chamberlain and Otto the
goldsmith;[2] on the estates of St Paul's cathedral, Richard the
archdeacon gathered more than one manor into his hands, and
there were canons, a scribe and a goldsmith as farmers there at
the end of the twelfth century.[3] These were prosperous clerks,
administrators and capitalists rather than knights, counterparts
perhaps of the *maiores* or stewards of great church estates in
Germany and France, who even at that moment were enlarging
their rights and helping themselves to the insignia of knighthood.[4]
On the Canterbury estates the person of the twelfth-century
farmer is to be seen only at South Malling and Charing. At the
first, Godfrey of Malling was certainly a knight, owing the service
of three fees, though his ability to pay £90 a year for the lease of
South Malling makes him in a way more remarkable still. But at
Charing the farmer seems not to have been a knight. Neither
Adam nor Ivo appears in the archbishop's list of knights under
Henry II. Adam was a well-to-do man with widespread interests.
He helped to enclose the city of Canterbury in 1166-7.[5] One of his
name founded a leper hospital at Romney.[6] In 1188 he was the
archbishop's *dapifer* or steward.[7]

Below the farmers and responding to their orders were the
manorial tenantry, but of them at this time we know little. The
theory that the demesne fields were being sub-let to them in small
parcels during the second half of the twelfth century has little to
support it.[8] Customary tenants were certainly performing reaping
services on the South Malling demesnes about 1150-4 when
Archbishop Theobald granted tithes to the canons there.[9] During

1. A. Raftis, *The Estates of Ramsey Abbey* (Toronto, 1957), pp. 77-8.
2. R. Lennard, op. cit., p. 149, and the whole of ch. VI for many other instances.
3. *The Domesday of St Paul's*, ed. W. H. Hale (Camden Old Series, LXIX, 1858),
   pp. 122-39.
4. G. von Below, *Geschichte der deutchen Landwirtschaft* (1937), p. 66; H. Sée,
   Les Classes rurales (1901), pp. 330-7.
5. *P.R. 13 Hen. II*, pp. 196-202.
6. *HMCR*, VIII, Appendix, para. 341b.   7. *P.R. 34 Hen. II*, p. 202.
8. R. A. L. Smith, *Canterbury Cathedral Priory* (1943), p. 114, based his view of the
   'crumbling of the demesne into the hands of the tenants' on Gilbert Slater's
   essay in the *V.C.H., Kent*, iii, pp. 342-3. Slater did not give exact references to
   his sources in Canterbury Cathedral Library. However vigorous the tenantry,
   the dissolution of the demesnes on both the monastic and the archbishopric
   estates is open to question.
9. A. Saltman, *Theobald* (1956), No. 179.

Becket's exile the manors were still being farmed for a total sum which corresponds nearly with that obtained from the *Domesday Monachorum*, and money was being allowed by the Exchequer between 1169 and 1171 for oxen and oxherds on the manors in a way that suggests the necessary demesne stock was being kept up.[1] At present, it looks as though the twelfth century on the archbishopric estates was not a time of dramatic demesne dissolution but one in which the traditional farming system worked on the whole to the advantage of everybody. The archbishop received an assured income without undue fatigues of management. The manors remained in the church's chief lordship, visited in turn by the archbishop when he was in England, and kept in mind of their allegiance to him by these visits and by the direct payment of small ancient dues like the *gabulum*. The farmers exercised a more immediate lordship, put their money to profitable use, and bore a risk which must have become increasingly unreal as the pressure of population forced up the price of the food they produced. If the archbishops thought that they were the losers they could set about to terminate the leases and end the system, and this is what happened.

DEMESNE EXPLOITATION IN THE THIRTEENTH AND FOURTEENTH CENTURIES

Towards the end of the twelfth century, popes began to write with increasing frequency to churchmen ordering them to recover control of their demesnes. Earlier in the century, ecclesiastics had often been disturbed about enfeoffments of church lands and about permanent losses,[2] but the leasing of manors had appeared tolerable, and even Anselm had been willing to lease estates to raise money.[3] But it did not take an advanced knowledge of economics to see during the reign of Henry II that long traditional leases to farming families and middlemen would deprive the chief lord of more and more income as prices rose, and it is probable

1. *P.R. 17 Hen. II*, p. 142; *18 Hen. II*, p. 114.
2. e.g. Innocent II's letter to Ely in 1138 (E. Miller, *The Abbey and Bishopric of Ely* (1951), pp. 167–8), and Chapter 2 above.
3. R. W. Southern, op. cit., p. 157.

that the papal letters were informed by a sound knowledge of these movements, and may even have been asked for by the recipients as a convincing excuse for action which was bound to be unpopular among the lessees. In 1179 Alexander III told the monks to stop granting perpetual leases on their manors, and in 1187 Urban III did the same.[1] Innocent III wrote on 5 February 1199 to Archbishop Hubert Walter:

We order you to recall to the archiepiscopal table the possessions of the church of Canterbury which have been illicitly alienated, to the grave damage and loss of the church, since the times of Richard and Baldwin your predecessors, and to apply them without delay to their due employment.[2]

These losses cannot be measured but were certainly to be expected if things were not altered. In fact, alteration had already begun. When the see was in the king's hands between 1165 and 1172, the gross annual receipts averaged £1,560 a year from the manors which were all leased.[3] After Archbishop Richard's death in 1184 the pipe-roll shows a receipt of about £1,136 for a vacancy of some ten months, but manors worth £203 1s. 9d. and mills worth £39 18s. 7d. had already been brought into demesne.[4] By 1205, after Hubert Walter's death, the picture had entirely changed. Receipts were much higher than before, and they derived directly from the exploitation of the demesne manors. For the fifteen months of this vacancy they amounted to £3,438 3s. 10½d., and this is to omit tallages and extraordinary payments. This sum can be broken down into the assessed rents of tenants (£1,423 13s. 11¼d.), profits of courts (£300 15s. 10d.) and agricultural produce (£1,713 14s. 1d.).[5] The middlemen had been excluded and large sums made available through vigorous exploitation by the king's officers. The recall of manors to demesne had thus been begun by Archbishop Richard, and was substantially complete by the time of Hubert Walter's death in the summer of 1205. The accounts of the vacancies in 1228–9 and 1231–2 likewise show expenditure

1. R. A. L. Smith, op. cit., p. 114, citing W. Holtzmann, *Papsturkunden*, II, pp. 374, 444.
2. Lambeth MS. 1212, p. 241. King John also ordered Archbishop Hubert Walter to recall all his demesnes unjustly alienated (Lambeth MS. 1212, pp. 49, 201).
3. M. Howell, *Regalian Right in Medieval England* (1962), p. 214.
4. *P.R. 30 Hen. II*, p. 151.   5. *P.R. 8 John*, pp. 54–5.

on seed-corn, horses, and oxen, and payments to *famuli* and boon-workers on the demesnes.[1] This does not mean that flexibility was lost. Manors could still be let to farm at choice, and this was done with a good many of them in 1272 after the death of Archbishop Boniface, but the leases were on an annual basis and a close watch was kept on receipts and maintenance.[2] The high tide of demesne exploitation was reached under Archbishop Pecham (1279–92) who recalled the last of the long-term leases, ousting the Waleys from Tarring, buying out the fee-farmers of Wrotham and augmenting the demesnes in smaller ways.[3]

The intensive and profitable exploitation of demesnes on great church estates in the thirteenth century has attracted much attention from historians, but it has to be seen in due proportion. During the best demesne period the bishopric of Ely derived only forty per cent of its gross income from the profits of agriculture.[4] The archbishopric of Canterbury gained a slightly higher proportion than this,[5] but the period of high profits from cereal marketing was neither long nor unbroken, and depended upon areas of territory that formed only about one seventh of the lordship of Canterbury. Few of the demesnes were really large. At Wingham there were about 1,200 acres of demesne arable, including those of Wingham Barton, at Aldington and in the Sussex manors of South Malling and Pagham about 850, at Otford in Kent and at Harrow and Hayes in Middlesex about 600 acres each, but the other manors possessed only 200, 300 or 400 acres apiece. These are maximum figures from the thirteenth century and include fallow. It is unlikely that the demesne acreages had changed much between Domesday and the thirteenth century. Accounts show that on an average a plough could cope with about a hundred acres. If we look at those Domesday manors where the witnesses said there were as many demesne ploughs as were necessary—in other words, the fully-stocked ones—it may be observed in each case that the number of ploughs corresponds very roughly with the number of hundreds of demesne acres in the thirteenth-century rental. At

1. P.R. 73 m. 1; P.R. 76 m. 5d.
2. P.R. 119 m. 41d.; *C.P.R. 1266–72*, p. 605.
3. See above, p. 202; Lambeth MS. 1212, pp. 23–5, 119, 121–2. cf. Dorothy Sutcliffe, 'The Financial Condition of the See of Canterbury Under Archbishop Pecham', *Speculum*, X (1935).
4. Miller, op. cit., p. 82.
5. For a discussion of monetary values, see below, pp. 240–6.

Westgate there were four demesne ploughs in 1086 and 300 acres of demesne arable in 1285; at Reculver three ploughs and 332 acres; at Pagham seven ploughs and 857 acres. This is only an approximate test and leaves out of account not only the possibility of error in the rental but also the mechanical properties of the soils. But it suggests that demesne arables had remained on the whole static during the twelfth century, in contrast with the areas cultivated by the tenantry themselves.

In the thirteenth century, which is the earliest period for which such information exists, the demesne arables did not lie intermingled in strip formation with that of the tenants as in the so-called 'Midland system', but were situated in blocks, sometimes within larger fields, and cultivated in severalty even if not always separated off by permanent physical barriers from other men's crops.[1] All the demesne manors possessed some large or very large fields, but some of them also had more or less numerous small fields and pieces as well. East Kent was a land of large fields. Two of the Wingham demesne arables[2] were of over a hundred acres each, most of them between twenty and sixty acres, none of them less than seven acres, and they were all concentrated near the township of Wingham itself, not scattered over the vast manorial area. The same lay-out is visible in Thanet,[3] at Westgate by Canterbury,[4] and at Aldington.[5] But Aldington was a very scattered manor, and at one of its marshland members, Willop,[6] there were fifty-one parcels of demesne—arable, meadow and pasture intermixed—ranging between three and twelve acres each. In west and north-west Kent there were more small fields as well as the larger ones. Wrotham, for example, possessed arable in considerable blocks: fifty acres in East Field, thirty-two acres in Stony Furlong, but also many pieces of from three to thirty acres lying in 'shots'.[7] The largest demesne fields were at Wimbledon, where they stretched out east of the Common: 237 acres 'in the field to the north of Wimbledon', 160 acres in Middle Field, 148¾ acres in South Field, 51 acres 'in a field by the *curia*', and other great 'furlongs' at Mortlake.[8] Both Hayes and Harrow in Middlesex had three great demesne fields of nearly two hundred

1. See above, pp. 130–3.
2. MS. E 24, fo. 1.
3. L.R. 2068.
4. MS. E 24, fo. 22v.
5. ibid., fo. 54.
6. ibid., fo. 56.
7. ibid., fo. 75.
8. L.R. 2068.

acres each.[1] Only in Sussex were the demesnes said to lie in butts, lands or strips, of about one third to one acre each, within larger fields; but even here the wording suggests that the fields themselves were wholly demesne, without the intermixture of tenants' portions, for at Lavant the rental describes a portion of forty-eight and a half acres lying in forty-nine 'lands' but says that the fallow was in the same field.[2] The grain accounts also show that the demesnes were cropped and fallowed in blocks independently of tenants or others. In the course of time these demesne fields might be leased out, whole or piecemeal, or they might go out of tillage, partly or wholly, temporarily or for a longer time; but they generally retained their identity during the medieval period. The best detailed instance comes from Otford. The rental of 1285[3] noted, besides smaller pieces, 68 acres *in la Combe*, 26¾ acres *in Wycham*, 153¾ acres *in Northfeld* and 83¾ acres *in Estfeld*. In 1516 a description of the Otford demesnes[4] itemized various small fields and closes which cannot be identified in the earlier document, but the larger blocks had endured recognizably: 'in a field called the Combe *in one piece* 66½ acres 6½ dayworks', 'in Wykham 24 acres 3 roods 5 dayworks', 'in Northfield *in one piece* [two closes of eighteen and fourteen acres]', and 'in East field 62 acres 8 dayworks and 3 perches'. Here the identity of four major demesne fields can be traced through 250 years, though all were liable to diminution of the tilled area and to further enclosure into portions.

The demesnes of the archbishopric were mainly given over to the production of wheat, barley, oats, and the leguminous vegetables, vetches, beans and peas. The account of 1273–4 records the sowing, in round numbers, of 2,100 acres of oats on the estates, 2,000 of wheat, 1,600 of legumes, 1,200 of barley (mostly of the spring variety) and only 120 of rye.[5] The vacancy accounts of 1295 and 1334, on the other hand, show a preponderance of wheat and legume sowings.[6] More precise knowledge is to be had from those few manors where a series of serjeant's accounts survive to tell the acreages sown over a run of years and some-

1. ibid.
2. MS. E 24, fo. 109 (*S.R.S.*, vol. 57, p. 16): 'there are in *Eldewik* 48½ acres which contain, *preter terram friscam*, 49 *londes*. . . '. This may, however, mean that the field contained some uncultivated land.
3. MS. E 24, fo. 69v.
4. De Lisle and Dudley MSS. at the Public Record Office, Roll 478.
5. Addit. MS. 29794.
6. P.R. 141 m. 41d. (*Kent Records*, vol. xviii); Mins. Accts 1128/10.

times the exact fields upon which the sowings were made. From Bexley there are nine accounts dating between 1270 and 1350.[1] Here the principal cereals were sown in the following annual averages: wheat 54 acres, barley 42, oats 34½, legumes 17½. Rye was grown in only four years, on a dozen acres. The demesne fields were treated as entities, each of which might be fully cropped, partly cropped and partly fallow, or wholly fallow, but it was rare for a single field to be under a crop of one kind only. Table 5 (p. 210) is sufficiently similar to others which can be constructed for Maidstone,[2] Northfleet,[3] Otford[4] and Wrotham[5] to serve as a typical specimen. There are only two consecutive accounts, but these will illustrate in part a rotational course of husbandry. About a third of the arable was left fallow every year.

In general, the accounts show a predominance of wheat on the north Kentish manors, oats falling in the third place, and barley and legumes interchangeably occupying second and fourth places. The available sources for other parts of the estates show the east Kentish and west Sussex manors as wheat producers *par excellence*. Barley was universally grown, and oats too, but with an emphasis at Hayes and Harrow in Middlesex. Rye featured little, and what there was appeared mostly at Croydon. Of the legumes, vetches were ubiquitous, peas were frequently placed alongside vetches but in smaller acreages, and beans were grown in significant quantity only at Nyetimber and Shripney, near Pagham in west Sussex. The only long-term change in crop type that can be detected in the existing records is the displacement of winter barley by the spring variety.

Too few consecutive accounts survive to make a calculation of yields possible, but the densities of sowing are adequately known. In the mid thirteenth century, wheat was generally sown at a standard four bushels to the acre, but from the end of the century there was a tendency to reduce the amount. At Otford, for instance, the density fell steadily from three and a half bushels in 1296 to three throughout the fourteenth century, and then down to two and a half in the earlier fifteenth. There was a similar movement at

1. L.R. 234–240. Only five of these name exact fields.
2. L.R. 656–62.   3. L.R. 777–85.
4. L.R. 832–8, 841, 846, 846A, 850, 853, 857–8, 860, 863, 865, 868, 871. cf. 'Late-Continued Demesne Farming at Otford', *A.C.*, LXXIII (1959), by the present writer.
5. L.R. 1139, 1142, 1143A, 1145; KAO U55/M65, 67, 68.

Table 5. Bexley Demesne fields sown.[1]

	Berefield (48·5 acres)	La Reden' (28·5 acres)	Melleveld (20 acres)	Brocland (30·5 acres)	Seamarsh (75 acres)	Edmersland (14 acres)	Puttefield (c. 35 acres)
1279–80	47a. barley 2a. oats	8a. oats	10a. wheat	—	11·5a. peas 5·5a. vetches	—	28·5a. wheat
1283–4	20a. peas 7a. vetches	—	—	32a. oats	80a. wheat 10a. rye	6a. oats 8a. dredge[2]	34a. palm barley 2a. oats
1300–1	2a. oats 46a. barley 3a. dredge	7a. oats	24·5a wheat 6a. maslin[3]	18a. wheat 2a. maslin	6·5a. peas 8a. vetches	13a. oats	12a. barley
1301–2	9·5a. peas 10a. vetches	—	14a. barley 6a. oats	9a. barley 8a. dredge 10a. oats	64·5a. wheat 2·5a. rye 2a. oats	—	—
1349–50[4]	27a. palm barley[5] 11a. vetches	—	with Puttefield 35·5a. wheat	—	—	11·5a. oats	see Melleveld

1. The names and acreages of the fields given at the head of the columns are taken from the rental of 1283–5 (Dean and Chapter of Canterbury MS. E 24, fo. 88v.).
2. Dredge is a mixture of oats and barley sown together.
3. Maslin is generally a mixture of wheat and rye.
4. Also 14a. peas in unspecified field(s).
5. Account mentions weeding of lord's wheat in Berefield this year.

Wrotham and Northfleet. Winter barley, when used, was sown at four bushels to the acre, but spring barley's density varied from four and a half at Charing to five at Bishopsbourne and Maidstone and six at Gillingham, Lyminge, Saltwood and Boughton-under-Blean. Oats required between five and eight bushels to the acre, rye two or three, and legumes four. Everywhere the density of sowing tended to decrease in the fourteenth and early fifteenth centuries, so far as the records survive to tell, and there was an especially marked reduction in the immediately post-plague year 1349–50.[1]

Not all the corn stored up in the archbishop's barns and accounted for year by year on the dorse of the parchment rolls came from the harvest of his fields. A certain amount, especially of barley, was collected as toll from tenants who used the lord's mills. Some more was bought on the market. Some might be brought from another manor. What was not sown back on the fields was, according to its kind and quality, sent to the archbishop's household, sold on the local market, issued to the manorial workers, or fed to animals. This disposal of grain was naturally governed by its kind. Wheat was often sent to be made into bread in and for the lord's household. The more important of the lord's local servants also had their allowances in wheat. Most of the balance was sold, frequently on the local market (*in patria*) but sometimes further afield. After Archbishop Stratford's death in August 1348, over 1,000 quarters of wheat were threshed on the various manors by the king's order, carried to hired granges at the ports of Northfleet, Rochester, Sarre, Sandwich, Wittering

---

1. L.R. 240. A modern estimate of the amount of seed-grain required is: wheat 2¾ bushels per acre, barley 3, oats 4¾ (W. Beveridge, 'The Yield and Price of Corn in the Middle Ages', reprinted in *Essays in Economic History*, i, ed. E. M. Carus-Wilson (1954), p. 14, from the *Economic Journal* (Economic History Series, no. 2) May 1927).

Densities, however, depend upon soil-type. There is an important discussion of these matters by Ann Smith, 'Regional Differences in Crop Production in Medieval Kent', *A.C.*, LXXVIII (1963), pp. 147–60. Studying the Cathedral Priory manors between 1271 and 1379, she shows the relationship of dominant crops to local geology and notes an increasing use of legumes in the fourteenth century combined (with exceptions) with a decline in barley and oats production in favour of the more profitable wheat. Her analysis of sowing densities suggests the archbishopric figures for barley density were low and for oats density were high, though it must be remembered that the soil-type of the individual manor was relevant. Miss Smith also noted the curious standardization of wheat density at four bushels to the acre and ascribes it to wheat's special adaptability to a variety of soils. She prints figures for yields per bushel, which cannot safely be done for the archbishopric.

and Faversham, and shipped thence to victual Calais at 3d. a quarter comprehensive transport charge.[1] In bad years the wheat harvest could be supplemented by purchase, and some bought wheat was nearly always used for sowing, together with wheat from the manor itself. But seed from the latest yield (*novum granum*) was rarely sown back. With barley, a high and steady demesne production was augmented by the multure of the mills. Bexley mill, for instance, supplied sixty quarters a year. The purchase of barley on the market by the archbishop was rare. What was not required for seed corn was used partly for brewing and partly for issue to the hired and customary labourers of the manor. In a sense, barley was a common article of currency among the labouring population, and it features not unusually as rent and as legacies. The demesne yield of oats, however, was more often augmented by purchase, for this grain had to be sown rather more densely than the others, and much was wanted for feeding beasts. Less was sold. Rye does not feature much in the accounts, and the legumes were chiefly used for sowing on portions of the fallow and for feeding animals. Seed of all these kinds could be brought from other parts of the countryside, but only with wheat and oats was this done to much extent, and when it occurred it seems rather to have been with the intention of making good a manorial shortage than according to the scientific principles of changing seed. Of course, Walter of Henley had taught his readers that seed ought to be changed,[2] but the contemporary custumal obliged tenants to fetch seed from neighbouring manors or markets if seed were lacking locally, and when oats were bought at Bexley in 1279 the accountant carefully noted that this was because of a lack of sheaves this year.[3] Yet some care was taken about the quality of seed-corn. In 1302, to take one example, six Bexley women were paid for three weeks' work in selecting and preparing wheat from the sheaves for sowing.

The relatively small part played by customary labour in demesne production, except at harvest, was discussed in the previous chapter. The solid core of labour consisted of full-time servants of husbandry, paid an annual stipend (*stipendium*) in money, a weekly allowance of a bushel or half a bushel of corn, and some-

1. P.R. 196 m. 44.
2. *Walter of Henley's Husbandry*, ed. Elizabeth Lamond (1890), p. 18.
3. MS. E 24, fo. 91; L.R. 234.

times a weekly wage (*vadium*) as well during the periods of their service on the demesne. The designation and the payment of these people varied a good deal. The royal accounts kept during vacancies tended to call them all *servientes*: fourteen at Harrow and four at Hayes were paid 5*d*. a week in 1231–2, although they clearly included ploughmen, carters and others, while the reeve got 6*d*. a week,[1] for he was the local overseer and at that time accounted jointly with the bailiff. The bailiff himself, as a local manager, often with more than one manor under his charge, got 6*d*. a day.[2] In the records of the archbishopric the man in charge of demesne agriculture was usually (but not always) called the serjeant (*serviens*), and the best paid of the local staff were the ploughmen (*carucarii*), sometimes called oxherds.

During the thirteenth century, plough traction could be both by oxen and by horses. The Bexley custumal of 1285 said that the manor's two demesne ploughs used twelve oxen with eight horses or else sixteen oxen with four horses, and this did not include the harrowing animal, which was noted separately.[3] Not far away, at Otford, the serjeant in 1315 bought a number of plough horses at between 15*s*. and 17*s*. each and some plough oxen at 18*s*.[4] Archbishop Boniface, who died in 1270, laid down minimum scales of livestock for the manors as a whole, and in 1274 the estates were carrying 292 horses for plough and harrowing work and 405 draught oxen.[5] In 1279 the figures were 260 and 419.[6] Oxen were much more used in west Sussex: they far outnumbered the horses in the thirteenth century, and even in the sixteenth the archbishop and the *firmarii* there were using oxen for ploughing.[7]

The accounts betray little other sign of manorial specialization in livestock. Horses and cattle were naturally found everywhere. The supply and training of horses is an interesting subject which has not yet been studied. To some extent it must, of course, have been done locally, but by the early sixteenth century there are signs of local experts who may well have been dealers, like Robert Morley, esquire of Glynde, one of the archbishop's farmers, who

1. P.R. 76 m. 5d.   2. *Cal. of Liberate Rolls 1240–5*, p. 43.
3. MS. E 24, fo. 91v.   4. L.R. 832.
5. Addit. MS. 29794.   6. P.R. 124 m. 23d.
7. PCC 24 Holder (Miles Hodgson of Tarring, d. 1516); Reg. T fo. 150 (Bersted). Likewise at Stonham in 1397 there were eight-oxen teams (*C. Inq. Misc.*, VI, no. 365). A reference to modern ox-ploughing in Sussex (near Lewes) appeared in *The Times*, 29 May 1964.

bred and broke in riding horses.[1] The estates did not go in for specialized sheep or wool accounts, and it is in fact rather hard to get a clear view of the archbishop's wool marketing except in glimpses. In 1337 Archbishop Stratford made to Edward III a loan of forty-nine sacks, eight cloves of Kentish wool, valued abroad at £436 4s. 11d. As no export was allowed at the time, this may represent the bulk of the estates' yield.[2] The stock accounts of the thirteenth century show well enough the concentration of sheep on those manors to which were attached marshland pastures on the north coast of Kent: Gillingham, Boughton, Teynham, Northfleet, and also on the southerly coast near Wingham. Later on, the sheep-rearing activities of tenants and farmers in the Romney Marsh area is visible.[3] A striking impression of the demesne accounts is the very high mortality among sheep.[4]

The south-east of England was once a densely wooded area and was still during the Middle Ages only in the midst of progressive clearing. The woodlands deserve a prominent place in any account of the archbishopric, not so much because of intrinsic profitability, though this was at times appreciable, as because they played an important part in the development and quality of society. Some woodland became the settled home of rent-paying tenants, and some became the special preserve of landlords and rich men who made of them both parks and centres of timber production. It was largely a question of geography. The nearer to London, the greater was the commercial value of woodland, and the more marked the dominance of the rich. As late as 1724 Defoe drew a vivid and relevant sketch:

From this side of the country, all pleasant and gay, we go over Shooter's Hill, where the face of the world seems quite alter'd; for here we have but a chalky soil, and indifferently fruitful, far from rich; much overgrown with wood, especially coppice-wood, which is cut for faggots and bavins and sent up by water to London. Here they make those faggots which the wood-mongers call ostrey-wood, and here in particular those small light bavins which are used in taverns in London

---

1. PCC 23 Holder.
2. P.R.O. Exch. Accts Various (E 101) 457/30; K.R. Memoranda Roll (E 159) 115 m. 27. I owe this reference to the kindness of Dr Fryde.
3. See above, p. 139, and below, p. 236.
4. e.g. in 1273–4, 409 out of 545 sheep at Wingham Barton died before shearing, and this was not unique (Addit. MS. 29794).

to light their faggots, and are call'd in the taverns a brush, [though] the woodmen call them pimps; 'tis incredible what vast quantities of these are lay'd up at Woolwich, Erith and Dartford; but since the taverns in London are come to make coal fires in their upper rooms, that cheat of a trade declines; and tho' that article would seem to be trifling in itself, 'tis not trifling to observe what an alteration it makes in the value of those woods in Kent, and how many more of them than usual are yearly stubb'd up, and the land made fit for the plow.[1]

This too was the situation by the later fifteenth century, but the archbishop's woodlands had by then gone through a long evolution. Before the Norman Conquest the Canterbury manors had shared woodland rights for the pasturing of swine in the depth of the Weald and within the blocks of woodland which lay outside the Weald proper, vestiges of which still remain in Wrotham and Blean woods. These 'denns', where the boundaries can have been only vaguely delimited, lay often at great distances from the parent manors, and the journeying to and fro would have been reckoned in days not hours, especially when it was a matter of droving pigs.[2] In the course of time the denns became settled and slowly cleared by tenants and by others, who paid to the lord a variety of rents for the activities which they needed to pursue.[3] These remoter settlements were early sundered and effectively lost to demesne exploitation. Another destiny awaited the woodlands in the neighbourhood of the demesne manors. By the thirteenth century the archbishop was little interested in the forest rearing of pigs (except as a source of extra rents from his tenants, and from others, who paid double), for his own stock could be raised more usefully in the tiled piggeries in the manorial precincts. His woodland could be turned to parks where the pleasures of hunting could be had, entertainment given, and luxury food like venison, swans or herons preserved. Some of Bexley woods were imparked, to the annoyance of the tenants;[4] two deer parks were carved out of Wrotham woods; and so on. At the same time, woodland on

1. Defoe's *Tour of England*, ed. G. D. H. Cole (Everyman edition), I, pp. 100–1.
2. A difficult animal to drove. The custumal of 1283–5 notes arrangements for collecting stragglers (Canterbury MS. E 24, fo. 12v.). Thomas of Walsingham in 1379 illustrated the plague's devastation of the north by reporting that the Scots had been able to drive away herds of swine, a thing no one had ever tried to do before (T. Walsingham, *Historia Anglicana*, ed. H. T. Riley (*R.S.*, 1868), I, p. 410).
3. See above, pp. 137–40, and references there. A map of the archbishop's woods is opposite p. 216.
4. MS. E 24, fo. 91v.

Map 4. THE ARCHBISHOP'S WOODLANDS
IN KENT, *c.* 1285

Notes

1 The map shows places mentioned in the text
and is not a complete account of the archiepiscopal manors and woodlands

2 Hernhill and Graveney formed part of the
manor of Boughton-under-Blean, but have
been shown separately here as their customs
were separately described

3 Certain denns are not shown either because
they have not been identified or because they are
now lost. They are: *Betherinden* in *Sandhurst,
Bikynden, Bithelegh, Bordherst, Cheldynden,
Ealdingheth* or *Eldchecche, Edynden, Halling-
hurst* in *Smarden, Haythurst* in *Marden, Helden,
Henden* in *Woodchurch, Herdelmere, Lollesden,
Lymeryngden, Metekingham* or *Myddyllyngham*
(in the area of *Rolvenden*), *Mettelingham,
Plashead* in *Sandhurst, Presden, Rempendene*
in *Woodchurch, Ridgeway* in *Woodchurch,
Sibersnoth* in *Orlestone, Slepinden* in *Smarden,
Trindeherst* (probably either in *Biddenden* or
Yalding), *Wandigsuode, Westrynden*

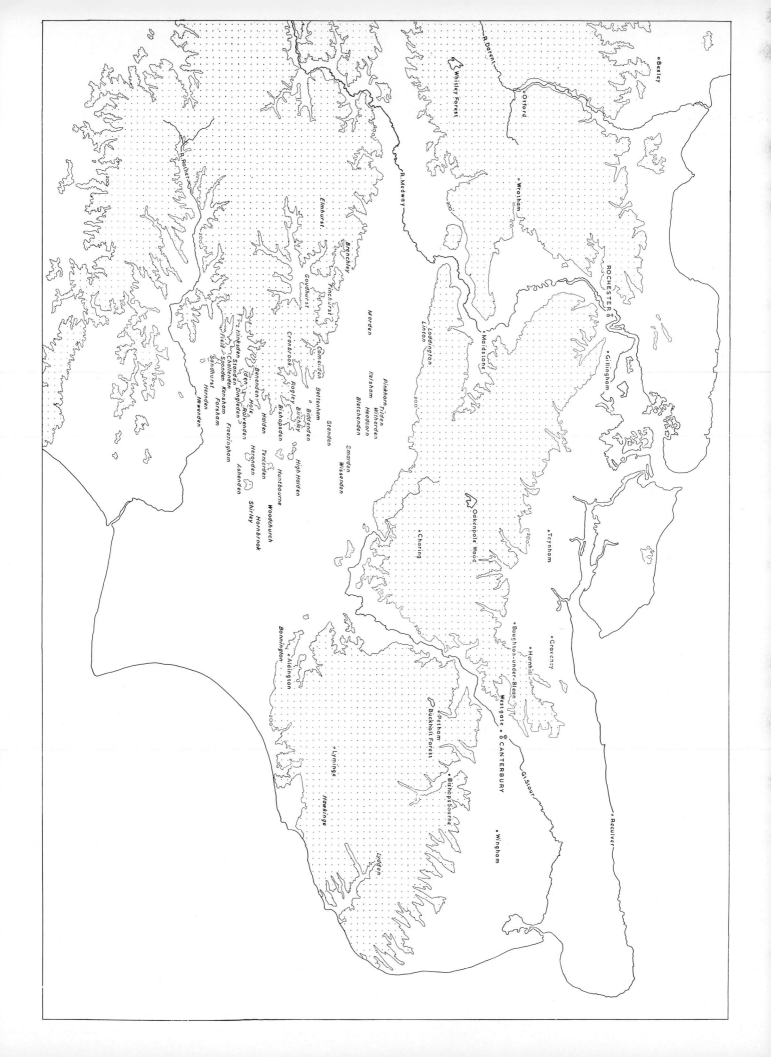

convenient lines of transport could be turned to the production of timber and brushwood for sale as well as for building operations on his own property. This was done at Buckholt Forest near Petham, Oakenpole Woods between Charing and Teynham, Whitley Forest near Otford, and above all at Bexley. Parks usually ran at a loss and their annual accounts often had to be squared by subventions from other manorial accountants, but the better-placed woods could make some profit on their own account, and they continued under the archbishop's direct exploitation even when the demesne manors themselves had been leased out. When the manor of Bexley was in demesne its woodlands were in the care of the bailiff, subject to the over-riding authority of the master of the archbishop's woods or some other member of the estate council. In 1300 trees for sale in West Wood were selected by the steward of the lands and sold 'by view of the bailiff and men of the neighbourhood'. But in the fifteenth century wood management was specialized under the woodward, sometimes also known as parker or forester; towards the end of the medieval period he could also be described as 'seller of wood' (*venditor bosci*). In the earlier fifteenth century between £10 and £20 were realized annually from the sale of timber and brushwood at Bexley, but in the later fifteenth and early sixteenth century the figure went up, so that a taking of £40 a year was not unusual. After 1522 the sale of wood was organized inter-manorially and the local Bexley accounts became barren formalities. But when Henry VIII made his valuation of church lands in 1535, wood sales from Bexley were reckoned to be worth £20 a year. The woods were carefully exploited and not pillaged. Enclosures were kept up to protect the young growth. Hedging, ditching, repair to gates and fences and other overheads absorbed thirty-eight per cent of the gross takings in the fifteenth-century woodwards' accounts. Until the end of the fifteenth century, most of the timbers, faggots and firewood were cut and sold in the woods by the archbishop's own workmen. The buyers were shipmen, coopers and, above all, brewers, some of them local but many from London. Regular consignments were conveyed overland from Bexley to Woolwich or Erith, just as they were in the eighteenth century, and there stored temporarily by factors like William Scudder. Thence they were sent by water to London or to Lambeth for the archbishop's London household. In 1471 the stout type of firewood called *talwode* in the accounts was taken from Bexley to Woolwich at 40*s*. a thousand, and from Woolwich to Lambeth by boat, nearly twice as far, at 20*s*. The smaller cut wood called *tosards* were conveyed at 13*s*. 4*d*. and 6*s*. 8*d*. respectively, and short faggots at 20*s*. and 10*s*. Wharfage at Woolwich was paid to Scudder at the rate of 10*d*. a thousand for *tosards*, and the other types *pro rata*. Transport added a lot to the basic prices. After about 1487 takings from sales rose on account of both increased turnover and higher prices. *Talwode*, which had sold at about 20*s*. the thousand for half a century, now sometimes fetched 50*s*., but the first figure was presumably for sales on the spot and the second included transport charges. There are not enough figures to do more than suggest a considerable rise in price. In the early sixteenth century the purchase of wood by the acre became more usual than selling by quantity and type in the north Kentish woodlands. There was still some individual selling of oaks, but generally the customers would view the wood and contract to buy, paying between 20*s*. and 45*s*. the acre, and themselves undertaking the labour and transport. These transactions are illustrated by a letter of 1510 from one of the archbishop's surveyors to the woodward at Bexley, instructing him about a deal with Sir Edward Poynings, then comptroller of the king's household:

To Thomas Deane, keper of Weste Woode.
Thomas Deane, I pray yow serue m. Controller of ij acr' of harde woode acordyng to his desyre, but see that ye brek not the woode, disfugering it, and also my lorde chargeth yow that ye kult none downe by the hyghwey, be cause it is in sight. And if his maistership be not content with the price of xls. [40*s*.] the acre, serue hym of v nobles [33*s*. 4*d*.] the acre, for I thynke ther be non acres to his plesor except the wode be fore rehersed at xls. the acre of harde wood; and ther fore serue hym to his plesor of a lower price; and this byl shalbe your discharge at Lambhith, the vijth. day of Marche. T. Wyks.[1]

THE DEMESNES FINALLY LEASED

During the fourteenth century there was a contraction in the amount of demesne land placed under cultivation. The contraction was not dramatic, but it was perceptible. Otford had at

1. L.R. 1254.

least 300 acres in yearly tilth (not counting fallow) up to 1316, but after mid century this was rarely more than 200, and from 1422 to 1444 it was consistently about 150.[1] Wrotham's cropped area was 184 acres in 1310 and about 150 acres between 1398 and 1402. Northfleet probably maintained 200 to 300 acres under annual crop up till the 1360s, but this dropped to 150 or 200 during the later part of the century. The accepted interpretation of the general English transition from direct exploitation to demesne leasing is that during the course of the fourteenth and early fifteenth century—at different times and speeds according to local conditions—the rising cost of labour and the difficulty of getting it, combined with a low demand for agricultural produce, made the great landlords' demesne organization uneconomic. To avoid loss they ceased to crop marginal land and then began to lease out their demesnes to men who would take them at a fixed annual rent and bear some of the costs of maintenance. In this way the large-scale risks of a great estate were broken up among numbers of smaller men and their families, who could use their wits to take on the best land on the best possible terms, and win the highest yields with the lowest overheads. No doubt such an explanation is in the main accurate, and the later medieval history of the Canterbury estates exemplifies it. The most serious doubt is whether the archbishopric really suffered the economic distress which such landlords are supposed to have done. Accounts which exist for the transitional period give no certain picture of such difficulties. This is partly because demesne accounts are hard to interpret when they do not form a continuous series. Receipts and costs fluctuated from year to year in a way that allows no clear tendency to be exhibited. Northfleet, for example, was exploited directly during most of the fourteenth century. There the liveries, or payments in money terms, which were actually made to the lord's household and which form the nearest approach to an annual 'profit', are seen to vary in the eight available years between £19 (in 1367) and £120 (in 1391), against an average of £58. Costs likewise varied between £21 in 1369 and £62 in 1367, though the average for the eight years was £39. Arrears were not very high: they were £68 in 1304 and had settled to about £34 in

---

1. For Otford, see *A.C.*, LXXIII (1959). Arable contraction is also apparent in the inquisitions of the archbishopric lands in 1397 after the forfeiture of Archbishop Arundel (*C. Inq. Misc.*, VI, 1392-9, nos. 246, 312-31, 363-6).

1369 and 1391. At Otford the archbishop was getting payments of £35 to £100 in each of the eight complete demesne accounts which also survive for that manor between c. 1300 and 1444, and his costs were inclining downwards in the last phase of direct exploitation. It seems wise to be cautious about the archbishop's motives for leasing. It is true that several comments occur in the account rolls of the late fourteenth and early fifteenth century about the expensive demands of the *famuli*.[1] But there is room for a positive as well as a negative explanation of the whole change. Once the age of high agricultural profits was over, demesne leasing was a safe and suitable policy, not just a last expedient for the near bankrupt. It had the merit of simplicity and flexibility. The lord could negotiate for a rent which was as certain as anything could be before the days of the gilt-edged funds, and the conditions were reviewable after an agreed period. His surveyors knew more about land and business than their twelfth-century forebears had done. On the other side, there were now more people with money to spend on suitable farm tenancies, and the termor was achieving a consequent respectability in the eyes of the law.[2] Except during the worst moments, the lord could exercise some choice in his farmers, and would-be farmers had an option on what land, and indeed what landlord, they would select. There seems nothing strange or wrong about a contractual economy in which both sides stood to gain something and neither was the powerless victim of adversity.

Three periods can be discerned in the later medieval history of the demesnes: the transition from direct exploitation to systematic leasing, which occupied the span from the 1380s to the 1440s; a phase of mid-century doldrums; and an age of recovery that began about 1480 and was being well maintained when Cranmer surrendered his church's inheritance to Henry VIII.

The chronology of the changeover cannot be dated with extreme precision, for it occurred more gradually than upon the Canterbury monastic estates, which turned over to leasing quickly in the 1390s. Archbishop Courtenay (1381–96) was responsible for leasing out

---

1. See above, p. 188. Also, in 1444 the corn liveries of the Otford *famuli* had to be converted to money at a rate favourable to them, and the serjeant had to receive an external subsidy *super husbondriam faciendam* (L.R. 871, 872).
2. cf. T. F. T. Plucknett, *A Concise History of the Common Law* (4th ed., 1948). pp. 539–43.

at least eighteen demesnes in Kent and Middlesex,[1] but there were liable to be sporadic returns to direct exploitation, as at Wrotham, until the 1420s.[2] A *valor* of the archbishopric from 1422 gives an overall view and proves that the great majority of the demesnes were leased out by that time.[3] A few widely spaced ones were still (or again) in demesne that year: Otford, which was not permanently leased till 1444, Wingham Barton, Northfleet, and possibly Teynham in Kent; Tarring, Stonham, and possibly Wadhurst in Sussex. This was less likely the result of any inability to lease than a device to keep the archbishop's itinerant household supplied at convenient points, but another way was found before long of dealing with this problem, as will be seen.[4] In general, the demesnes were mostly farmed out by 1400, and wholly by 1450, together with manorial stock, certain buildings, and customary services, but rarely rents of tenants.

The men who became demesne farmers round about the year 1400 were not insubstantial creatures who tried their luck for a season or two and sank without trace. Most of them, of course, were only local figures: Thomas Brounswayn farmed demesne land at Otford in 1403 where previously he had been the archbishop's serjeant; Roger Beresford, an early farmer of Wrotham, and his wife both had shop property there. But some of the names later became better known, or were already a little more eminent, or recur over a period long enough to suggest a hidden family strength. John Daundelyon, farmer of Bishopsbourne in the 1390s, was possibly the father of the armoured gentleman to be seen on the brass in St John's church, Margate. The Dorkingholes or Darknalls, farmers of Otford, are traceable from the early thirteenth century and by 1400 had acquired considerable property in the Sevenoaks area. Richard, who died *c.* 1408, built himself a brick house on the site of the present Rose and Crown at Dunton Green, and the family prospered.[5] The Shelleys of Bexley and the Deryngs of Aldington and Lympne became more important still. The lease of Wimbledon in 1422 by John Romney, prior of Merton, is a

1. *C. Inq. Misc.*, VI, nos. 246, 312–31, 363–6.
2. Wrotham was always unusual. It had been at fee-farm from Domesday till *c.* 1280 (Lambeth MS. 1212, p. 121); it was devastated by the plague (see above, p. 187); although leased on short term in the 1450s it failed to get a lessee (*conductor*) in the 1460s and 1470s and was placed under an *appruator*.
3. LCM, XI, p. 89.   4. See below, p. 230.
5. Lt-Col. C. S. Durtnall, O.B.E., was kind enough to lend me his typescript history of his family, which is full of valuable information.

reminder that the search for good leases in the early fifteenth century was not confined to simple countrymen.

Although the farmers left no accounts, their economy, even in the late fourteenth century, can be well understood in outline through a few seignorial accounts and, even more, through the inquisitions of 1397, after Archbishop Arundel's forfeiture. Local jurors assessed the value of everything belonging to each demesne. Comparison of their assessments with contemporary ministers' accounts establishes that they spoke accurately and without undue minimization. The length of terms for which the demesnes were leased was normally of the order of five to ten years, though sometimes smaller properties were let for longer, like Northfleet water-mill leased to John Darell, steward of the lands, for ninety-nine years. The farmers had to find anything from £5 to £80 a year and to bind themselves to return a stock of animals, corn and equipment worth from £20 to £80 at term. It is not possible to make an easy calculation of what they paid per acre because the properties they took were mixed and complex ones, consisting of arable, pastures of differing qualities, woodcutting rights, some services, and even, on a few occasions, rents of the tenantry. But it is possible to gain clear notions of what the various kinds of land were worth per acre, and also what the archbishopric farmers were getting, in the aggregate, for their money.

Arable was priced at anything from 2d. to 8s. the acre. These valuations were net of expenses. When above 1s. the acre, they refer to land under crop, hoed and weeded: below that figure the land is often described as 'of poor quality' or 'in poor condition'. Barley fields range between 8s. and 2s., wheat between 6s. 8d. and 2s. 6d., oats between 5s. 10d. and 1s. 6d., legumes between 4s. and 1s. 4d., rye occurs only at 2s. 6d. the acre. No fallow was priced above 1s. 2d. the acre. The highest values appear to have obtained at Saltwood and Teynham, but the evidence is not sufficient for a more detailed analysis. In the same way, meadow varied between 8s. 8d. at Cranbrook Rectory and 6d. the acre for poor quality at Croydon and in Sussex. Pasture might sink as low as ½d. an acre (Croydon) and rise as high as 1s. 4d. (Deal). All pasture above 10d. the acre was for cattle or horses, and all pasture below 4d. the acre was for sheep.

It will tell us something more about the farmers if we reckon what proportions of their annual rents were spent upon arable, pasture, and so on. There were fifteen demesnes in Kent and Middlesex which were being farmed in 1397 and for which detailed figures of valuation exist. These figures can be broken down as follows to show what percentages of the total value of their leased estates the farmers were getting from different kinds of property: rents of tenants, thirty-seven per cent; arable fields, twenty-six per cent; pasture of all sorts, fourteen per cent; services of tenants or their commuted equivalent, fourteen per cent; meadow, three per cent; wood, two per cent. The remaining four per cent is accounted for by occasional properties like mills and fisheries. The high proportion of farmed rents is surprising, but it must be remembered that in this analysis it includes perquisites of a few courts and, even more important, is accounted for by the high value of leased rents in only five manors (Wingham, Westgate of Canterbury, Lyminge, Petham, and Downbarton, all in east Kent). On the other hand, every single leased manor included a sizeable nucleus of arable, and it is clear enough that what the average Canterbury lessee was taking on in the late fourteenth century was a mixed agrarian holding. These figures represent money valuations. If we turn to regard the acreages we get a different and perhaps more concrete view of the same thing. The 'average' Canterbury farmer at this time, if such a notional being may be permitted a moment's existence, took on 184 acres of arable, inclusive of fallow, about 15 acres of meadow, and perhaps 220 acres of pasture for sheep, cattle or both. It goes without saying that these averages provide only an abstraction, relevant mainly to east Kent. In reality the leased demesne arables might be as small as 25 acres (Petham) or as large as 500 acres (Wingham). The figures for pasture and meadow are also very variable and those for woodland in which there were cutting rights are usually obscure. But they serve to demonstrate the scale of enterprises and their mixed character.

Nor is it to be supposed that what the farmers took from the archbishop was all that they possessed. The stock they borrowed from him was often of a substantial value—worth anything between £5 and £90—but it must at times have served only to augment what they already had at work upon their own lands, for they could become the archbishop's lessees only because they were already working agriculturalists disposing of a certain capital equipment on their own account.

In most instances, the farmers hired a few of the demesne buildings: some barns and perhaps a room for a servant of husbandry which were not reckoned in the valuations. Apart from the handful of exceptions, the collection of tenants' rents remained in the hands of the reeves, with whom the farmers maintained close relations. The reeves changed every year and the farmers rather less frequently, but they were local men and knew each other and had constantly to arrange business matters among themselves, like agreements about arrears or the handing over of stock. In 1397, to give a single illustration, John Brykhill took on the demesne at Northfleet at £16 per annum.[1] This comprised 167 acres under crops, 4½ acres of hay, 2 cart horses, 4 stots (work horses), 9 oxen, 145 sheep, 1 sow, 5 pigs and 5 piglets, 2 fully equipped ploughs, a new harrow and a couple of carts, worth some £45 in all. He got to work in making a new sheepfold on the marsh and was allowed his expenses in getting wood for it from Wrotham and Bexley. At the same time the reeve was collecting the assessed rents of the tenantry and the payments for such commuted services as the farmer did not or could not use. Brykhill's contract terminated in 1401, the stock was handed back, and the demesne for some reason again came under the archbishop's serjeant until it was leased in 1428 for £19 10s.[2] This stop-go pattern of leasing is characteristic of the early fifteenth century, but it resolved itself in the 1420s into a system of continuous leases broken only by bad years and local difficulties. As the century wore on the annual price of the leases sometimes fell and sometimes rose, but the changes were not very marked save on east Kent marsh properties like Willop and Cheyne, in Aldington, where the tendency was healthily upward.

It is interesting but not very conclusive to see what the farmers were paying in comparison with the assessed annual value of their farms. On nearly all the demesnes the lessee's rent was substantially greater than the property's locally reckoned annual value, and this is to be accounted for by the value of the lord's stock, of which the farmer had the use. At Downbarton, the annual value of the demesne was said to be £46 9s. 5d. and the farmer paid £66 13s. 4d. a year for it, but then he had nearly £150 worth of stock. At Petham where he received only £20 worth of stock he paid a rent of £25 a year for demesnes worth £21 11s. 7d. The length of term

1. L.R. 785–6. 2. L.R. 797.

for which the farmer took on the demesne cannot be shown on the evidence to have been significant in fixing the price. All that can be certainly said is that these leases were the result of local and individual bargains of the sort frequently referred to in fifteenth-century correspondence, and issuing in arrangements that could doubtless be shown to have a statistical significance if enough were collected, but which were not standardized or individually pre-dictable.

In the middle of the fifteenth century it became rather harder to make satisfactory leases. This experience was not confined to the south-east of England, and the Paston Letters provide several instances from Suffolk, Norfolk and Hertfordshire where farmers were in arrears and had to be pressed, corn was too cheap to sell, or leases could only be made at a reduced rent.[1] On the Canterbury lands, Otford and Shoreham had a bad year in 1437–8 when only twenty-three acres of the demesne could be let, piecemeal and on an annual basis, and the rest was turned over to the archbishop's sheep while the estate council made strenuous efforts on the spot to get tenants.[2] Northfleet was leased piecemeal in 1450–1 and again in 1467;[3] between these dates the price declined and did not begin to recover till 1491. The farmer of Northfleet Rectory was forgiven £26 13s. 4d. arrears in 1463 'by reason of a great detriment touching him with his farm in previous years'.[4] In east Kent, Lyminge had to be leased piecemeal in 1447, and at Petham in 1467 the farmer was unable to raise money to pay off arrears.[5] It would be wrong to make too much of this collection of cases. No serious general decline in revenue is visible. Most demesnes continued to find lessees who paid up, and the sluggish areas were to some extent compensated by good results in the marshland leasings at Willop, Cheyne Court and Shirley Moor. The picture is put in perspective by the full and continuous series of account rolls for the nine manors, two marshes, one forest and one park that comprised the bailiwick of Otford. The rolls cover eighty years, from c. 1450 to c. 1530, and yield the names of sixty-two people who at one time or another farmed an entire demesne and a further fifty-one who farmed portions only, mainly in the difficult years 1450–60 when men were unwilling to take

---

1. *The Paston Letters*, ed. James Gairdner, I, nos. 101, 135, 183, 284, 306.
2. L.R. 863.   3. Mins. Accts 1129/1.
4. ibid., 1129/7.   5. L.R. 1195.

up a whole demesne. The contracts were short, but family names recur, and the termination of a lease in favour of someone else meant not the failure of the farmer but perhaps a sub-let, a marriage settlement, an executor's arrangement, or any one of a dozen devices of domestic policy within a thriving, tightly knit family society. Figures of payments underline the soundness of the economy. Under direct exploitation Otford had yielded an average of £76 a year and had cost an average of £67 to maintain. Under the farming system much greater stability from year to year was possible, and the corresponding figures are £84 and £14.

Marked improvement came during the last twenty years of the fifteenth century. The arrears at the head of the accounts dwindle away as farmers and reeves paid in nearly all they should have done. There was a positive increase in revenue on the estates as a whole, not only from better collection, but from expanding rent-rolls on the manors nearest to London, particularly Maidstone, Croydon, Wimbledon and Harrow, where a growth in population was probably being felt, and from higher-yielding leases of the east Kent demesne properties like Wingham, Thanet and Deal, and the marshland tenancy of Cheyne. In this recovery a prominent part was played by the demesnes in the hands of farmers, who were contributing an overall forty per cent of the archbishop's landed revenue.[1]

An accurate idea of the demesne leasing system must be sought through the financial records and by comparing the main periods of demesne history with each other, and this will be attempted in the last section of this chapter. But it is also desirable to form an impression of demesne organization and the people involved in it at the end of the Middle Ages from a more personal viewpoint, and this can be done by studying a full collection of demesne leases made under Archbishop Warham (1503–32) and preserved in a register of Canterbury cathedral priory.[2] There are 156 leases of archbishopric demesnes for the period. The larger demesnes were leased out whole, though a few very big ones, like Wingham, were divided into two or three lots. The prices of the best arable and pasture demesnes, in east Kent and west Sussex, ranged from

1. For a more detailed discussion of the leasehold economy, see *Ec.H.R.*, 2nd series, vol. XVI, no. 3 (1964), pp. 427–38.
2. Dean and Chapter of Canterbury MS. Reg. T, calendared in *Kent Records*, vol. XVIII (1964). See also *Ec.H.R.*, 2nd series, vol. XVII, no. 3 (April 1965).

about £30 to £120 per annum. Nearer London demesnes were more often let for a price within the scale of £10 to £20. There were also a few rectories in the archbishop's own collation which had been appropriated in the fifteenth century to augment the temporalities. A lesser one like Wadhurst in the Weald fetched £11 13s. 4d. a year; valuable ones like Reculver and St Nicholas in Thanet fetched £40. In addition, there were some thirteen mills and thirty-four other, miscellaneous properties, such as portions of marsh and meadow, gardens, park rights and a ferry, a fishery and a brewery which were leased during these years, and though their annual rent rarely reached £10 individually, they were collectively of financial importance. The leases agreed between the archbishop and his farmers were embodied in sealed indentures. By 1500 the lease for term of years was an instrument with a long history behind it,[1] and some of the clauses of which it was constructed had more formality than reality behind them. Such were those designed to secure prompt payment of rent by threats to distrain or re-enter. It is doubtful if such clauses were often if ever invoked in the times and places before us, though farmers rarely made their payments religiously at the 'four usual terms' specified in the leases, and not seldom fell mildly into arrears. On the other hand, there were many clauses which had more immediate meaning. It might be serious for a receiver to be obstructed by being kept waiting for the money, or by not finding food and stabling ready for him on his tour: the lease of Slindon warned the farmer not to detain the receiver more than a day when he came for the rent, on pain of paying the extra expense,[2] and many leases arranged for the provisioning and free movement of the lord's officers. In fact, the leases, though formal in structure, give copious evidence of how the archbishop safeguarded through them his scheme of economic life.

The estate council exercised continual care to maintain and improve the property. Farmers had to pay for the results of their own negligence: the auditors compelled the farmer of Bishopsbourne to pay for a barn he had carelessly allowed to burn down.[3] Farmers were sometimes required to erect new buildings: a new, tiled house was demanded of Richard Lawdys, yeoman, lessee of

1. cf. Thomas Madox, *Formulare Anglicanum* (1702), pp. 130–53, for examples of the demise for term of years between 1196 and 1545.
2. Reg. T, fo. 52.   3. L.R. 1199.

six acres at Knole in 1524.[1] Even when the archbishop paid for work, the farmer might have to feed the men on the job.[2] In order to provide raw material for repairs, farmers were always assigned specified pieces of woodland, and in this way the archbishop at the same time protected himself against the unrestrained felling of his timber. Where timber was scarce, even a great farmer like William Knatchbull, lessee of Willop, was forbidden to cut anything locally except brushwood.[3] Wood was of increasing value, and the farmers had to enclose woodland to protect the young growth at Harrow, Wimbledon and Teynham,[4] and might not lay hands on oak, ash, elm, or 'right-beryng beche' at Lewes.[5] Even the husband of Archbishop Warham's niece might not touch the oak and beech in Wrotham parks.[6]

The archbishop continued to be interested in the maintenance of arable and pasture farming as well as in wood production. Most leases involving demesne arable required it to be kept in good and seasonable tilth, and some insisted upon particular operations. At Hayes in Middlesex a proportion of the arable had to be marled each year as well as manured with compost of wheat-straw.[7] Sixty derelict acres of Maidstone were to be brought back into good cultivation in 1516 in return for a very low rent.[8] At Wimbledon in 1518 the farmer might have free wood if he cleared and cultivated forty acres within four or five years.[9] At Bersted in Sussex the farmer had to allow pasture for eight oxen of the archbishop during the last year of his lease so that they might plough for wheat the following year.[10] At Tarring, also in Sussex, the farmer in 1514 was to make two new ponds in the pastures to water the herds, and to hand them over at term in good order.[11] Pasturage was to be improved at Wrotham by clearing,[12] and protected at Hampton and Burstow.[13] Further extension of productive land was envisaged at Cheyne Court in 1518, where the lease allowed the archbishop to inn more salt-marsh if he wished and either to retain it or let the farmer have it at a rent settled by arbitration.[14]

1. Reg. T, fo. 243v. 2. ibid., fo. 265v. (Gillingham, 1526).
3. ibid., fo. 152v. 4. ibid., fos. 121, 158, 298v.
5. ibid., fos. 221v., 299. 6. ibid., fo. 243.
7. ibid., fos. 76, 317. 8. ibid., fo. 132.
9. ibid., fo. 158. 10. ibid., fo. 150.
11. ibid., fo. 120v. 12. ibid., fo. 243.
13. ibid., fos. 266v., 357. 14. ibid., fo. 153.

To keep property in good heart continuous occupation was necessary, and the leases frequently sought this by requiring farmers to live on the manors they leased. The farmer of Boughton-under-Blean was to dwell there and not sub-let without leave;[1] so too the farmer of Wimbledon, who agreed to live there with his own household in 1518.[2] At Lyminge the farmer was to reside and keep hospitality.[3] In 1529 a father and son leased Woodhall in Middlesex, and the lease demanded that at least one of them should reside continuously with his family.[4] The same principle lay behind the archbishop's stipulation in making a joint lease of Lambeth Wick to three of his *familiares* that if one or two of them died, then he might join one or two others to the survivors.[5]

Farmers were asked to help in the estate's economy in other ways. One was to have new rentals made at regular intervals, with the names and surnames (*cognomina*) of tenants in order to facilitate the collection of rents.[6] Another was the provision of stabling for the archbishop's horses on a scale which makes it clear that his whole transport system depended in large measure upon the co-operation of his lessees. At Charing in Kent,[7] Wimbledon in Surrey,[8] and Headstone in Middlesex[9] stable accommodation was reserved out of the property leased off. Wimbledon supplies a good and typical example:

> The archbishops shall have their horses at livery to stand within the manor as often as they please with as many keepers as necessary, and these shall be at bed, meat, drink and laundry with the farmer, the archbishop paying 1s. 2d. a week for each of them. The farmer shall provide 30 loads of hay and 40 quarters of oats according to the measure used at Kingston market at 1s. 8d. the quarter, and shall provide the straw of wheat, rye and oats for litter at 1s. the load. . . .

In many of the manors arrangements were made for hay, litter and oats to be supplied by the lessee to the archbishop and his estate officers on their rounds, and free passage had to be allowed them by the farmer of Oxney ferry.[10]

1. ibid., fo. 130v.　　2. ibid., fo. 158.　　3. ibid., fo. 287v.
4. ibid., fo. 337.　　5. ibid., fo. 238.
6. ibid., fos. 162 (Stonham, Sussex); 174 (Harrow, Middlesex); 217 (Barton Wingham, Kent); 223v. (Charing); 253 (St Nicholas at Wade, Thanet); 321 (East Lavant, Sussex); 332v. (Northfleet).
7. ibid., fo. 223v.　　8. ibid., fo. 158.
9. ibid., fo. 121v.　　10. ibid., fo. 165v.

No less than the arable, mills had to be kept in repair and production. In a miller's lease it was frequently stipulated that the lord's surveyors should be allowed free access to inspect and order what repairs they thought fit and that no sub-letting should take place except to professional millers and on a yearly basis.[1]

The leasing policy ministered not only to the financial advantage of the archbishopric but to the supply of the household. During the fifteenth century the annual rents owed by the farmers had sometimes been paid partly in the form of meat and corn for the household in London and elsewhere. This itself was a more flexible development of the ancient system of food-farms described above.[2] By Warham's time it was unusual for this to be done at all, but farmers might occasionally discharge some of their debt by paying the archbishop's bill with a London grocer or draper. The tendency towards centralization is also seen in Warham's lease in 1518 to William Lowman of the city of London and his wife Joan of a fully equipped brewery and residence at Brittons near Sevenoaks. The lessees were required to pay a rent of £6 13s. 4d. and supply good and wholesome ale in reasonable quantities, carriage free, to the lord's household at Otford or Knole.[3]

During the last generation of the medieval system the interests of the *rentier* archbishop and the lessees of his demesne were fairly evenly balanced, and it is hard to say that one side was operating at the expense of the other. The farmers had the money to take the leases, to pay the wages of enough covenant servants to help them in house and field, and, as their wills indicate, to live well. Lease prices were steady, while the terms for which the demesnes were let tended to lengthen on all parts of the estates after about 1510: what was being leased for ten or fifteen years up to about 1500 was by the 1520s passing into the hands of farmers for twenty, thirty or forty years. This may be explained, at least in part, by the contemporary fall in the cost of labour.[4] At the same

1. ibid., fos. 164, 275v., 276v.; cf. fos. 323v., 327v., 268.
2. See above, pp. 167, 202.
3. Reg. T, fo. 309. Brittons had been bought along with other property in Knole by Archbishop Bourgchier. It was being farmed in 1466–7, but the brewery had probably not yet been set up there (L.R. 543).
4. E. H. Phelps-Brown and Sheila V. Hopkins, 'Seven Centuries of the Prices of Consumables Compared With Builders' Wage-Rates', *Economica*, new series, vol. 23, no. 92 (November 1956), reprinted in *Essays in Economic History*, ed. E. M. Carus-Wilson, vol. II (1962); cf. A. R. Bridbury, op. cit., p. 24. I cannot agree with Dr Bridbury (p. 92) that the farmers of the later Middle Ages had little use for hired labour.

time, leases tended more often to be varied or extinguished in mid term. The appearance of a new farmer before a lease's expiry was sometimes owing to the first farmer's death, and sometimes to a fresh arrangement with the consent of both parties. In no case was it the result of a farmer's financial failure. Those who ended their leases prematurely were frequently well-to-do people, and the transactions were clearly for their own advantage. On the other hand, the archbishop himself was not in a bad position. He was achieving the continuous occupation of whole demesnes without lessening the rents, and was able to impose conditions for their maintenance and improvement. True, the terms of the leases were being lengthened, which means he was giving more for the money he received. But it is more than probable that he was getting a greater return than the account rolls and leases themselves betray. These documents hardly ever refer to entry fines.[1] But it is important to know whether the lessees had to pay entry fines before enjoying their farms. Cranmer's secretary tells us that in the early 1530s some valuable farms were being made in Middlesex and Surrey without fines being charged, but he writes as if this were exceptional.[2] By this time, would-be farmers were almost certainly ready to offer considerations for their leases. A proceeding in Star Chamber shows how some time before 1518 the archbishop had been offered nearly £50 for the lease of Sudbury near Harrow, together with £3 6s. 8d. or an ox and a boar for every year that he would grant the farm.[3] The failure of the bribe is not to the point here, and the case itself is a precious illustration that men were keenly competing for leases, since a sum of this size could be offered for a lease of which the nominal yearly rent was only £22.

It is often asked who the later medieval farmers were. The feeling that they were a rather obscure class of people of limited interest may be ascribed partly to the well-known fact that they did not leave financial accounts and therefore cannot be thoroughly understood, partly to the fact that no serious attempts have in

1. The only entry-fine explicit in Register T was one of 40s. for a forty-year lease of ten acres in Maidstone (fo. 347v.).
2. *Narratives of the Days of the Reformation*, ed. J. G. Nichols (Camden Society, LXXVII, 1859), p. 264.
3. P.R.O. Star Chamber Proceedings 2/23/54. I owe this reference to the kindness of Dr Michael Kelly. For the effective lease, see Reg. T, fos. 157v. and 297, and L.R. 1362.

reality been made to study them, and partly to the vague perception that they were people of the most diverse sort and that analysis might be little more revealing than a modern list of ordinary shareholders in a public company. But it is neither difficult nor unrewarding to gain a general view of Archbishop Warham's farmers. About a third of them were described as gentlemen, about a half were yeoman or husbandmen, and a few were London merchants. These 'classes' cannot be correlated with the type of property they leased. The biggest and dearest leases were usually held by yeomen. But a gentleman also might take on a demesne farm: Hawte at Bishopsbourne, Shelley at Bexley, Morley at Ranscombe and Brent at Charing are cases in point. Furthermore, yeomen freely succeeded gentry and vice versa on the same estate. The only kind of lease directly connected with the social status of the lessee was that of a park with its pasture and hunting rights. Warham let these to men of high rank: Wrotham to Sir William Rede, his kinsman by marriage, Burstow to Sir John Gage, Hampton to Sir Richard Broke, Justice of the Common Bench, and, in 1530, to the Lord Chancellor, Sir Thomas More.

In general, the archbishop's choice of his lessees was dictated by two motives which might coincide on the same occasion but more often stood separate and distinct: the wish to patronize those who had some claim on him through kinship or familiar service, and the policy of placing a local demesne in the hands of someone who was suitable from the economic point of view.

Patronage is the obvious intention behind many agreements, and may have influenced others in ways now hidden. Let us take the Warham family. Hugh Warham, the archbishop's brother, had portions of the demesnes of Maidstone;[1] William Warham, son of Hugh, shared in this Maidstone demesne and in other land at Lambeth Wick;[2] William Warham, archdeacon of Canterbury, and possibly the archbishop's natural son, held leases at Wingham and Teynham;[3] John Warham, the archbishop's youngest brother, had some marsh in the Isle of Oxney,[4] the manor of Saltwood,[5] previously let to Sir Edward Poynings, and (jointly with his son

1. Reg. T, fos. 132, 234v., 365v.   2. ibid., fos. 365, 238, 315v.
3. ibid., fos. 172, 298v. Mr Michael Kelly has helped me by commenting on Archbishop Warham's kinsmen, some of whom received offices and favours not referred to in this chapter.
4. ibid., fo. 236v.   5. ibid., fo. 274.

George) two mills in Wingham.[1] Sir George Warham, son of the archbishop's brother Nicholas, took a lease of demesne at Otford.[2] Anthony St Leger, son-in-law of Hugh Warham, held the demesne of Slindon in Sussex,[3] and Sir William Rede, a landowner of Buckinghamshire and Oxfordshire, was granted a lease of the parks of Wrotham 'in consideration that [he] hath maried with dame Anne, one of the daughters of Nycholas Wareham, brother of the lord archebusshop, for the advauncement and preferment of the seid Sir William...'.[4] Favour was shown to the archbishop's servants as well as to his family. Master John Colman, registrar of the consistory court of Canterbury and a churchwarden of All Saints, Canterbury, was granted marshland in Oxney in 1502 and 1524,[5] some of it jointly with John Warham. Men whom a modern reader might regard as quite humble benefited in similar ways. A yeoman of the archbishop's slaughterhouse at Sevenoaks was granted a lease there, in the vicinity of Knole, where he already possessed some holdings and where other household servants of the archbishop were settled.[6] Another good instance is a joint lease of the demesnes of Lambeth Wick (or Wick Court) made in 1523 to three Lambeth servants. No will survives for William Bever, but Richard Barowe was a yeoman of the archbishop's stables there, a parishioner of St Mary's, Lambeth, and a man of means enough to dress himself in satin and velvet. His best friends were also in the archbishop's service, one in the stables at Lambeth, the other a park-keeper at Otford.[7] Thomas Kyrkeby, the third joint lessee, was also a yeoman of the archbishop's service and a Lambeth man who wore good clothes, employed his own servants, had a regular seat in the parish church, and was landlord of local house property.[8] His brother was a tailor in Fleet Street, but it will be obvious that a yeoman might be a local personage, however much others might boast of being 'gentlemen born'. It is also to be observed that none of these leases, save possibly those to Hugh Warham and Anthony St Leger, were made at less than market value. Men were glad to pay this.

1. ibid., fo. 372v. 2. ibid., fo. 254v.
3. ibid., fos. 144v., 307. 4. ibid., fo. 243.
5. ibid., fos. 424, 236v. See also B. L. Woodcock, *Medieval Ecclesiastical Courts in the Diocese of Canterbury* (1952), p. 120.
6. Reg. T, fo. 344. William Potkyn, then archbishop's registrar, had some property there.
7. ibid., fo. 144; PCC 24 Bodfelde. 8. PCC 3 Ayloffe.

Willing though he was to help his circle to the offices of profit and the leases available on his estates, the archbishop had in general to look for farmers whose tenure would turn out a reasonable business proposition. The marks of the good farmer were an ability to pay, a willingness to pay and a mind to be a good tenant; and what better ordinary guarantee of these qualities was there than that he should be a man of the locality whose family were familiar with the terrain and whose neighbours would think well of him? Requirements like these placed a certain premium upon long-established families, and the records often in fact testify to the continuity of farming families as local residents and participators in the local demesnes. A certain number of family names can be traced back in the locality over some two centuries. A Knatchbull (nickname for butcher)[1] occurs in the Lay Subsidy roll of 1334–5 in the Romney area. Becks, Everards, Homewoods and Tokes can be found in the same source in the regions where they were flourishing as demesne farmers a century and a half later.[2]

Where a full series of account rolls survives, as in the bailiwick of Otford, this continuity can be tested minutely. The Shelleys held Bexley for nearly a century. There was a complex sequence of lessees at Otford, but they were all members of a small group of substantial local families, and their names alternate with each other as though they never lost interest in the demesnes there. Wrotham was the same. Northfleet when Warham became archbishop was in the hands of Thomas Brimpston or Brampston, a speculator in house property whose family had been notable in Kent in the thirteenth century and of knightly status in the fifteenth. When he died in 1511 his widow married Richard Hunt, who had been farming Wrotham and who then farmed Northfleet until his own death in 1516. After that, Widow Hunt farmed on alone, but was joined by John Brimpston, son of her first marriage, for the last two years of her life, which ended in 1531. She died rich, the benefactress of numerous covenant servants and of her poorer neighbours.[3]

In other parts of the estates the continuity of lessee families cannot usually be scrutinized so closely, but their qualities of

1. P. H. Reaney, *A Dictionary of British Surnames* (1958), p. 192; *Kent Records*, xviii, p. 147.
2. *Kent Records*, xviii, indexes under these names.
3. PCC 13 Thower.

economic reliability are often shown precisely and vividly in the testaments and last wills left by their members. Four of these may be chosen as examples, each to illustrate a different area and a different economic role, though none can justly be called untypical. They are the Hodgsons, husbandmen of Tarring in Sussex, the Knatchbulls, yeomen of Romney Marsh, Robert Amadas, Goldsmith of London and lessee of meadowland at Lambeth, and the Blackhedes, millers of Tring.

In 1514 the 300 acres of demesne at Tarring near Worthing, with all the manorial buildings, were leased to Miles Hodgson, husbandman, for fifteen years at £18 per annum.[1] The Hodgsons had not previously taken on archbishopric land, but Miles was prepared to pay £2 a year more than his predecessors and was a man of some means, despite his official description. It is possible that the illness which killed him in 1516 was some epidemic, since not only were the testaments of himself, his wife, and his sister all made and proved at the same time,[2] but he himself became intestate through the immediate death of all his executors. His *ultima voluntas*, which ought to have been a disposition of his real estate, reads like the rambling dictation of a failing patient. None the less, the documents portray a solid agricultural family which had some sheep but concentrated on the raising of wheat and barley, ploughed with oxen, and possessed their own halled house, cottages, shops, and other fields in several neighbouring parishes. There was plenty of cash and much household furnishing. The women, who had an Austin friar as favourite confessor, left wheat, malt, sheep, and fat piglets for the poor. The unexpired portion of the lease itself passed to Edward Weston, Mistress Hodgson's executor, with whom the archbishop immediately made a fresh lease for twelve years, and another when this was almost expired, renewing for a further twenty years, but jointly with his son John.[3] John was still farming Tarring in 1553.[4] There is no special patronage here, only the provision of a successful continuator to the suitable but unfortunate Hodgsons.

The Knachbulls became Lords Brabourne in 1880, when they possessed over 4,000 acres in Kent. The family is, of course, a famous one that can be traced back through the seventeenth-century baronetcy and the earlier knighthood until its members

1. Reg. T, fo. 120v.   2. PCC 24 and 25 Holder.
3. Reg. T, fos. 148v., 293v.   4. L.R. 1376 m. 3.

appear upon our present canvas as the most substantial of all Warham's yeoman farmers, working hard in that very part of Kent where they still reside. At the end of the fifteenth century the inning of Romney Marsh was still continuing actively, under the larger local tenants who would do and maintain the work, share in the levies or 'scots' by which the dyking system was kept up, and make their profit out of sheep and grain. By about 1500 the Knatchbulls, already long resident in the area, had nearly 2,000 acres at Willop and Cheyne (in Ivychurch) on lease from the archbishop, though their own principal residence was already at Mersham, and they were allowed an option to lease more if they wished to reclaim it from marsh. They worked with covenant servants, and paid their own huge rents without delay. Their profits spilled over into education for their boys, whom they treated as equals with each other rather than favouring the elder or younger son, and they supplied the new printed missals for neighbouring parish churches.[1]

By the Thames at Lambeth during these years there was a large area of meadow-land, prized for its hay and split into parcels intersected by paths and ditches. Some belonged to the Duke of Norfolk, and some to the archbishop who in 1528 leased thirty-three several acres at 4s. 4d. each to Robert Amadas. Here is an instance of a small area of high-value land taken on by a rich citizen, for Amadas was a Goldsmith who lived in the parish of St Mary Woolnoth and held houses and real estate as far apart as Lombard Street and Dagenham. He mixed with the great too, and persuaded the Duke of Norfolk, Sir Thomas More, and Richard Rich, then 'gentlemen at the law', to act together as overseers of his will,[2] and as a lessee of the archbishop he provides an instructive contrast with the servants of Lambeth Palace and the countrymen far away to the south.

Finally, there was the family of Blackhede, joined to this scene by Thomas's lease of an insignificant water-mill in the Hertfordshire village of Tring, the archbishop's most northerly demesne.[3] Yet Thomas Blackhede was, like others of long-established and respectable local families, a man who could easily keep a mill

1. Reg. T, fos. 153, 284. For the testaments of both William and Richard Knatchbull, see PCC Maynwaryng (1522).
2. PCC 7 Hogen (1531). I am grateful to Mr T. F. Reddaway for pointing out that Amadas was Master of the Jewel House in 1524–5.
3. Reg. T, fo. 214; PCC 25 Maynwaryng.

going while attending to his other affairs. He wrote quite casually in his will of the 'newe mill lately taken of the lorde [archbishop] by indenture', and the phrase appears amidst a tale of lands bought and houses disposed of in Hertfordshire and Buckinghamshire. Probably a capable technician was put in to work the apparatus, to be numbered like the shepherd among the covenant servants whom Thomas kept and paid, for there is no sign that he himself was a miller. Not that this was quite the plebeian calling sketched by Chaucer or John Balle a century before.[1] Maidstone had a gentleman miller, and the next archbishop himself a miller for brother-in-law.[2] In any case, Thomas Blackhede was of at least the third generation to live there, raising sheep, corn, and cattle, buying property and leasing it, selling it and taking it on lease, so that like our other examples he typifies the late medieval lessees of a great estate, being at home in the countryside yet flexible in their ambitions, modest enough in the figures they cut, but diversified and well-grounded in the possessions they collected.

THE ARCHBISHOP'S RESIDENCES

To many archbishops much of the time the demesnes meant home, and it would offend against the humanity of historical study to leave this altogether out of account. Yet unlike his monks, the lord of Canterbury lived a life of movement and took his household with him as he went, treating one or more manors perhaps with special affection but itinerating constantly. The amount of this travel, and the reasons for it, differed at different periods. A primitive court moved in order to feed itself, and this is as true of an archbishop as of any king who passed from residence to residence consuming the supplies prepared for him. But economic necessity can scarcely have been a basic reason for this mode of life. Carrying-services were well developed, as we have seen,[3] and communities of religious men found no difficulties in their static existence. Bishops, of course, were pastors, and their duty to

1. *The Canterbury Tales*, ed. W. W. Skeat, Prologue, lines 545–65; Miller's Prologue, line 3182; Thomas Walsingham, *Historia Anglicana*, ed. H. T. Riley (R.S., 1864), II, p. 34.
2. Reg. T, fo. 323v.; Jasper Ridley, *Thomas Cranmer* (1962), p. 14.
3. See above, pp. 166-8.

confirm and consecrate and visit their jurisdictions was reason enough for regular travel. But even this is not the whole of the matter; the less so in the later medieval age when spiritual courts and coadjutor bishops performed so many functions on the archbishop's behalf. A Pecham might be dedicated to his office and his people, but it is realistic to admit that an archbishop traversed his great estate, despite the discomforts of doing so, for secular reasons. A medieval lord brought his power to bear by his presence more than anything. People felt they had to entertain him if he was in the vicinity, like the bishop of Chichester in 1228,[1] or to obey him, like the jurors in the Waleys case.[2] Sometimes the archbishop was frightened, or found it convenient to withdraw from trouble: Baldwin went to Wingham during his quarrel with his monks; Reynolds fled from London during the disturbances of 1326,[3] and so on. More simply, archbishops sometimes preferred some places to others. Dunstan and Becket liked Charing, Courtenay felt happier after 1381 in Saltwood Castle, Bourgchier rejoiced in Knole, Morton and Warham refreshed themselves at Aldington. Apart from individual preferences, it is in general true that the later the period the more residences there were for the archbishop on his manors, and the more important to him became those in or near London. Eleventh- and twelfth-century archbishops cared a great deal about Canterbury. The occupation of Saltwood and of the archbishop's house in the cathedral city was one of the issues between Becket and the de Brocs. But although Canterbury palace remained a principal residence, often repaired, sometimes enlarged, and the scene of splendid occasions, it became after the late-twelfth-century quarrels more clearly one centre among others, and its place was in many ways taken by Lambeth. The manor-house at Lambeth had in fact been used by the archbishops since the time of Anselm, who had held ordinations and a council there in 1100, long before the acquisition of the whole manor, and by Theobald's time it was recognized as the archbishop's town residence. The papal prohibition in the late twelfth century on establishing a college of archbishop's clerks there is well known, but the exchange of Darenth for Lambeth with the monks of Rochester was completed in 1196–7, and as

1. W. H. Blaauw, 'Letters to Ralph de Neville, Bishop of Chichester . . .', in *Sussex Archaeological Collections*, III (1880), p. 51.
2. See above, p. 103.   3. See above, p. 115.

the papal monitions passed into oblivion Stephen Langton became the tacit creator of this new provincial capital,[1] and thereafter no archbishop could be long absent from the banks of the Thames. Pecham and Winchelsey were indefatigable travellers, and regularly dated their letters from some seventeen places in Kent, seven in Sussex, three in Surrey and one in Middlesex. The passage of time saw the fall of some places and the rise of others. The fourteenth century dealt hardly with the archbishop's houses. Pestilence ruined Wrotham, from which materials were taken in 1352 to repair Maidstone.[2] Courtenay found many houses dilapidated and pulled some down, Lyminge among them. The inquisitions of 1397 have a long tale of ruin, the more credible for describing Headstone and Wimbledon as in good condition, but there was dilapidation at Wingham, Westgate, Gillingham, Bishopsbourne, Boughton, Teynham, and Northfleet, and the palace of Canterbury was said to contain fine furnishings, but stained, moth-eaten and in poor condition.[3] The fifteenth century, on the other hand, was an age of improvement. Receivers' accounts are full of details of repairs, and it was especially the places within easy access of London that gained favour: Otford, Gillingham, Lambeth, and, above all, Knole, acquired by Bourgchier in 1456,[4] enlarged and beautified by Morton, and much used by Warham. Convenience aside, this is only one more instance of that growing delight among the well-to-do in the escape from an unpleasant but necessary London into the meadows of the suburbs and Home Counties, celebrated by Chaucer himself for whom in Greenwich

> when comen is the May
> That in my bed ther daweth me no day,
> That I nam up and walkyng in the mede. . . .[5]

Royalty felt the same way, and Otford and Knole were in due course to excite the covetousness of Henry VIII.[6]

1. *Epistolae Cantuarienses, 1187–99*, ed. W. Stubbs (*R.S.*, 1902), p. 419; Dorothy Gardiner, *The Story of Lambeth Palace* (1930), chs. I and II. See also J. Cave-Brown, 'Medieval Life Among the Old Palaces of the Primacy' among his *Topographical Pamphlets* (n.d.) in the Institute of Historical Research.
2. *Lit. Cant.*, II, nos. 752, 791; Reg. Islip, fo. 60.
3. *C. Inq. Misc.*, VI, nos. 246, 313–14, 318, 320–1, 324–7, 329–30, 363.
4. *A.C.*, LXIII (1950), pp. 135–9.
5. Prologue to *The Legend of Good Women*, Text B, lines 45–9.
6. See below, Chapter 7.

HOW MUCH WAS IT WORTH ALTOGETHER?

The historian of a great medieval estate desires, like William I, to know about its value, but the inquiry is even more complicated than it was in 1086. Although it is not hard to produce reasoned valuations at various points in time, it is quite a different matter to justify the relationship between these figures and hence to argue about the estate's developing productivity. But the attempt ought to be made, if only to lay the evidence before the reader and offer him the chance of criticizing it.

Four main questions present themselves. What was the value of the archbishopric in relation to other major lordships of medieval England? How did its total value change during the course of the Middle Ages? What were the main constituents of its landed income, in proportion to one another? And what was the geographical distribution of this value? The first of these questions is too wide to be answered in the present study, save by remarking in general that the archbishop was throughout the period one of the richest men in the realm, but the other three questions may be attempted with the aid of contemporary valuations and the accounts of the receivers.

For the problem of the archbishopric's value over the whole of the Middle Ages only complete valuations are of any use. The local ministers' accounts are too fragmentary and only begin in the thirteenth century. The receivers' accounts, though of great interest, did not begin before the fifteenth century. But there are valuations of different kinds which appear at irregular intervals from 1086 to 1535. They are the Domesday texts, the accounts on the royal pipe-rolls during vacancies of the see, the Taxation of Pope Nicholas IV in 1291, two *valors* made by the archbishopric itself in the fifteenth century, and the *Valor Ecclesiasticus* of 1535.

In order to use these materials in conjunction, it is necessary to decide if they can all be made to yield the same kind of information, and it is a hypothesis of these pages that they will all yield a 'net annual value' of the years in question. The proviso, of course, is that corrections and allowances will have to be made before the series of figures can be regarded as comparable. By 'net annual value' is here meant the amount of money (or the

240

value of provisions) payable by the individual manors to the archbishop's household after the local costs of those manors had been
met. It is important to try, even if vainly, to be consistent about
costs. They are taken to mean all those items of strictly manorial
labour and equipment which appear in detail in the demesne
accounts of individual manors. They do not include expenses
paid at bailiwick or household level, such as the fees of estate
officers and centrally authorized building expenses. Arrears must
also be excluded. Although it was the practice of medieval
accountants to include outstanding arrears in the *valor* of a manor,
and thus to reckon what was still owing as part of the value, this
principle cannot be applied in the general valuations now under
consideration. Of all our general documents, only the two fifteenth-
century *valors* note arrears, and then separately, so the task of
preparing a table of clear profits is to that extent simplified. The
net annual value will therefore correspond simply with the sums
which in each manor ought to have been received from rents and
sales, less the manorial expenses. Profits from local courts have
been counted in, but not those of wardships and franchises which
constituted what was called 'the Liberty' and were separately
accounted for after the late thirteenth century. Tallages have also
been omitted. Those taken by the king in the twelfth and early
thirteenth century were proportionally very large; later they
turned into 'recognitions of the tenants at the coming of a new
archbishop' and became rather smaller, and were in any case
often unpaid. Their omission is to preserve the 'net annual value'
of the manors as the basis of long-term comparison.

Apart from these general points, each kind of valuation has its
own characteristics. That worked out from the Domesday survey
comes from adding together the sums described as actually
rendered in 1086 from each of the manors then in demesne, and
naturally includes a few manors later enfeoffed or otherwise
eliminated from the list of demesnes; but conversely it naturally
omits the manors and appropriated rectories later acquired, so
that a broad comparability is maintained. There are also certain
discrepancies between the Exchequer Domesday and the *Domesday
Monachorum*, for the latter consistently includes *gabulum* and
constumes in manorial values, while Domesday itself may often
not take account of them. But again the sums involved are
relatively small.

When we come to the twelfth- and thirteenth-century figures from the pipe-rolls, it is to be remembered that the farmers themselves in that age of leasing bore many manorial costs, so that the pipe-roll totals again represent a net annual value. In any case, expenses of the crown were separately stated on the rolls.[1] But the vacancies were, of course, for odd periods, and the receipts have therefore to be corrected to make them equivalent to the takings of precisely one year. This does not affect the series of whole years when Becket was in exile, but the totals for thirteenth-century vacancies have to be 'grossed up' in this way, which leaves them with a notional value. In the fourteenth century the vacancies of the see became shorter, and the total receipts arrived at by grossing up the receipts of a few months appear on that account too artificial to be useful, so they have been omitted. This leaves an unfortunate, but inevitable, gap in the series of valuations. An imponderable factor is the possibility that the estates were unusually heavily exploited when in royal hands, but nothing more can be done about this than bear it in mind, especially when considering the enormous receipts for 1206.

With the archbishopric account for 1273-4,[2] the net annual value is obtained by adding together the payments to the archbishop's treasurer and deducting manorial costs. The resulting figure for this year must certainly be regarded as below average, for it was a bad year, as the account itself complains, and Wrotham and South Malling were in any case absent from the list.

The *Taxation of Pope Nicholas*[3] was made in 1291 by ecclesiastical commissioners, who had to raise money for the pope. It was made at a time when most of the manors were in demesne, and therefore faced even the most honest of assessors with the problems of an estimated annual value when real profits fluctuated widely,[4] but furthermore it was required for an unpopular papal levy when

1. Figures from the enrolled accounts are printed up to 1295 by Miss Margaret Howell in her *Regalian Right in Medieval England* (1962), pp. 214–15, but they have here been re-worked from the rolls to include only manorial receipts and costs. An English abstract of the big account of 1292-5, together with some notes about the fourteenth-century enrolled accounts, is printed in *Kent Records*, vol. xviii. 2. Addit. ms. 29794.
3. Printed by the Record Commission, 1802. Archbishopric properties are on pp. 6, 13, 14b, 52, 139b, 140 and 206.
4. See W. E. Lunt, *The Valuation of Norwich* (1926), p. 129; 'The Taxation of Pope Nicholas IV', in *Ecclesiastical Studies* (1929) by Rose Graham. The Rev. T. Hogan, s.j., tells me that the *Taxation* for Canterbury Cathedral Priory was only about two thirds of Prior Henry of Eastry's careful valuation made for his own purposes.

the excuse for minimizing was especially strong. How much it minimized may perhaps be gauged by comparing its total (£2,140) with the net annual value for 1292–5, which has been averaged out from the vacancy account for those years at £2,616.[1]

The *valors* of 1422, 1446 and 1535 are more like each other than like the *Taxation* of 1291.[2] They were made at times when the demesnes were nearly all leased, and they report the net values of the individual manors for the years in question (*de clara firma* or *valet ultra onera et reprisas*). In the last of these, the *Valor Ecclesiasticus*, certain expenses are recorded from each bailiwick, but to deduct these would interfere more with the net annual value of the manors than would occur if they were ignored.

After this brief commentary on the sources which yield the figures, the valuations themselves may be given in tabular form in Table 6.

Table 6. The net annual value of the archbishopric lands for certain years

1066	£772	Domesday Book
1086	£1,246	Domesday Book
c. 1100	£1,483	*Dom. Mon.*, pp. 98–9
1165	£1,348	*P.R. 11 Hen. II*, p. 108
1166	£1,377	*P.R. 12 Hen. II*, p. 114
1167	£1,245	*P.R. 13 Hen. II*, p. 201
1168	£1,596	*P.R. 14 Hen. II*, p. 153
1169	£1,380	*P.R. 15 Hen. II*, p. 165
1170	£1,379	*P.R. 16 Hen. II*, p. 161
1172	£1,375	*P.R. 18 Hen. II*, p. 139
1184	£1,019	*P.R. 30 Hen. II*, p. 151
1206	£3,473	*P.R. 8 John*, p. 54
1212	£1,409	*P.R. 13 John*, 101; *14 John*, p. 40
1229	£1,507	P.R. 73, m. 1
1232	£1,788	P.R. 76, m. 5d.
1272	£1,644	P.R. 119, m. 21
1274	£1,724	Addit. MS. 29794
1279	£3,148	P.R. 124, m. 23d.
1291	£2,140	*TPN*
1292–5	£2,616	P.R. 141, m. 28d. Average for each year.
1422	£3,015	LCM, xi, no. 89
1446	£3,049	P.R.O. Rentals and Surveys, Roll 343
1535	£3,467	*Valor Ecclesiasticus*

1. P.R. 141 m. 28d.; *Kent Records*, XVIII.
2. LCM, XI, p. 89; P.R.O. Rentals and Surveys (S.C. 11), Roll 343; *Valor Ecclesiasticus* (Record Commission, 1810), pp. 1–7.

Despite the fewness of these figures, they illustrate the main phases in the history of the demesnes. After an initial increase of about sixty per cent during the reign of the Conqueror, the yield of the manors while they were leased in the twelfth century was static. During the thirteenth century, when they had been brought into demesne, high profits were possible during good years: profitability seems to have increased during the later part of the century, but it ought not to be regarded as dramatic or continuous. The yield maintained a general buoyancy during the last century of the Middle Ages, which was again a period of leasing, though the estate remained under the close supervision of a professional council. During the whole of this era the rise in prices must naturally be borne in mind, especially during the later twelfth and earlier thirteenth centuries, and again, in respect of manufactured goods, in the second half of the fourteenth century; but in the absence of reliable indices no more can be done than to suggest the stability of the archbishop's landed income throughout the whole span of the Middle Ages. Summary form can be given to the argument by tabulating the average valuations for each of the three phases:

1086 to c. 1200	£1,345
c. 1200 to 1295	£2,128
1422 to 1535	£3,178

A view from a different angle can be obtained by analysing the income's composition. This does not become possible until the more detailed accounts of the thirteenth century are available, but thereafter the proportion of revenue which derived from demesnes and from tenants can be worked out. The four most complete accounts from the era of direct exploitation show strong fluctuations, as might be expected. In 1206 agricultural production brought in forty-nine per cent of the gross revenue, in 1232 thirty-five per cent, in 1279 fifty-nine per cent and in 1292–5 sixty-three per cent. These figures strengthen the impression that King John concentrated on exploiting the tenants and Archbishop Pecham the demesnes, which by then were in any case benefiting from better prices. In the last phase of the Middle Ages receivers' accounts become available in sufficient numbers to show again the proportion of revenue contributed by the (now farmed) demesnes. From c. 1480 to 1525 this was forty per cent, or forty-two per cent if wood sales are added in. In general, therefore, the demesnes contributed some fifty-two per cent to the archbishop's income in the thirteenth century, and forty-two per cent at the end of the Middle Ages. The difference signalizes the high profits possible at times from thirteenth-century agriculture, but the fact should not be forced to point a gloomy contrast with the fifteenth and early sixteenth century.

Finally, there is the geography of the income. The different regions of the lordship had different amounts and types of wealth to contribute. From the beginning the fertile soil and rich pastures of east Kent pushed up the value of the manors situated there, especially those of Wingham and the neighbouring district of Thanet. When the regions were given administrative form in the late thirteenth century by being grouped into bailiwicks, it was the bailiwick of Wingham that headed the list in the order of wealth, followed not far behind by Aldington, the members of which were vastly scattered over weald and marsh.[1] In the fifteenth century the value of these east Kent regions was maintained and enhanced by profitable leases to rich yeoman. By contrast, the Sussex manors of South Malling and Pagham began as very valuable members of the archbishop's temporalities, but had lost their high position by the thirteenth century and never recovered it. Their production was not markedly increased nor the number of their tenants augmented. Of equal interest with agriculture is the concentration of rent-paying tenants. The course of the Middle Ages saw an apparent shift of this away from the remoter parts of Kent and Sussex towards London. The assessment of the manorial tenants to the tallage of 1168[2] provides a gauge of the relative taxability on the different manors. At the top again came the men of Wingham, assessed at £30 3s. 4d., followed by those of Reculver (£24 10s.), Teynham (£18 16s. 8d.), Aldington, Pagham, Northfleet, South Malling, Bishopsbourne, Gillingham and Otford (all over £10). Leaving aside the high returns to be expected from the very large manors of Wingham, Aldington, Pagham and South Malling, the list shows a concentration of taxable tenantry in the manors along the north Kent coast, which forms an interesting contrast with the later medieval increase of rent-rolls

1. See P.R. 141 (*Kent Records*, XVIII), and Addit. MS. 29794. Aldington was perhaps the most strikingly undervalued of the manors in the *Taxation of Pope Nicholas*.
2. *P.R. 14 Hen. II*, pp. 153–6.

in the Surrey and Middlesex manors nearer to London. By the fifteenth century, though Wingham and Aldington kept a pre-eminence in the hands of their yeoman, the bailiwick of Croydon, peopled with an increasing number of tenants, ran them very close. At the end of this survey an overall impression is left. It is of the tenantry's dynamism, not the lord's, in the exploitation of the soil since the Norman Conquest. Their superior vigour was glimpsed in the twelfth century. Even in the thirteenth they often contributed the major part of their lord's income. Their leaders ended in possession of the demesnes themselves.

CHAPTER 6

Management

THE PERSONAL POLICIES OF ARCHBISHOPS

None of Cranmer's predecessors had a Ralph Morice[1] to explain
with any precision their personal views about estate policy. There
are indeed only a few moments in the Middle Ages when the
attitude of the archbishop himself can be supposed or seen to
have affected the management of his temporalities, and these were
mostly when they were threatened from outside. It is hardly
doubtful that to Lanfranc personally was due the drive to secure
the property of his see which had been dispersed or commandeered in the revolutionary years of the Norman Conquest.
Anselm, as Eadmer said, recoiled from secular business like a
child from an unpleasant taste,[2] but those who find this revulsion
edifying may recall that it was not typical of fine minds or strong
and dutiful personalities, even among professed religious. Becket,
as we might expect, defended his own with pugnacity, striking the
occupiers of Canterbury lands and churches with censures and
refusing throughout his exile to compromise about their restitu-
tion,[3] but in quieter times Richard was said to care about

---

1. 'Anecdotes and Character of Archbishop Cranmer by Ralph Morice, his
   Secretary', in *Narratives of the Days of the Reformation*, ed. J. G. Nichols
   (Camden Old Series, LXXVII, 1860).
2. *Vita Sancti Anselmi*, ed. R. W. Southern (Nelson's Medieval Texts, 1962), pp. 80–1.
3. His greatest foes were the de Brocs, who occupied Saltwood and Canterbury
   Palace during the exile and farmed the estates of the see (*P.R.s 11 Henry II*

production,[1] and in a time of even greater prosperity Pecham, a Franciscan vowed to poverty, showed himself the greatest of all the administrators of his see. The new era of demesne prosperity that opened about 1200 called for a closer and more expert surveillance of the temporalities, and it is likely that the archbishops' interest in them became less general and political and more detailed and administrative even while they were setting up new organization for their exploitation. It is a pity that we do not know more about the work of Hubert Walter and Stephen Langton, but they certainly ordered the withdrawal of many demesnes from the rule of *firmarii* and appointed that great official Elias of Dereham, under whom a new and authoritative survey was made.[2] The ever more abundant records of the thirteenth century reveal Boniface of Savoy not only as an aristocratic archbishop more magnificent than even those of the fifteenth century but as an outstanding negotiator of agreements on behalf of his temporal as well as his spiritual lordship. The agreement with the Cathedral Priory about jurisdiction, with Rochester about knight-service, and with the earl of Gloucester about the service due from him, all date from 1258-9, and in laying down the exact establishment of stock to be left on the manors by every archbishop he showed that care for physical detail which, as with the Conqueror himself, is a mark of greatness.[3] In that age of civilized precision, the archbishops were in their own sphere as capable of competent innovation as the king. Though Pecham's work in recalling manors to demesne has been exaggerated, since this had mostly been done already, it would be false to underestimate the systematic improvement in management that occurred in his pontificate: the permanent grouping of the estates into seven administrative bailiwicks, the

1. Gerald of Wales quotes Pope Urban III's comment on the contrasting characters of Thomas, Richard and Baldwin: '*Dicebat enim quia Thomas de equitatu ad villam veniens statim aulam petebat, Ricardus grangiam et Baldewinus ecclesiam*' (*Opera, R.S.*, VIII (1891), p. 68).
2. See above, in Chapter 1, p. 11.
3. Lambeth MS. 1212, esp. pp. 138-78; see also above, p. 85, and below, pp. 292-6, for discussions of these agreements.

---

to *16 Henry II*; *Materials for the History of Thomas Becket*, ed. J. C. Robertson (*R.S.*, III, 1877), p. 126), but he excommunicated the occupiers in general terms as well as by name when that was known (*Materials*, V, p. 388; VI, pp. 601-2; VIII, p. 402), and constantly raised the question of the Canterbury lands in negotiations with the king (ibid., VII, Letters 610, 684, 690, 723). I am indebted to Miss Anne Heslin for these references.

elaborate inquiry of 1283–5 through which his stewards drew up a new survey of tenants and demesnes, the use of secular professionals to govern the manors, and his reorganization of financial methods.[1] His successor, Winchelsey, was just as active. The space given in his register to temporal concerns exceeds that of all other archbishops. It is true that most of the entries deal with the lordship in the jurisdictional sense rather than the economic, and in one way this is accidental, for the registers served as legal compendia rather than records of accounts. None the less, they probably reflect the conscious attitude of the archbishops accurately enough as the fourteenth century progressed, the plagues took their toll, and the amelioration of labouring conditions presented to the great lordships an ever more bewildering transformation of the social order. An age in which lesser landowners were enriched, the Commons in Parliament became critical and demanding and peasants and craftsmen downright rebellious, made great lords like the archbishops understandably sensitive about their jurisdiction quite apart from their financial position. It was only a mild sign of the times when Winchelsey and Islip were unable to prevent local settlers from felling the archbishop's woods and clearing his denns.[2] It was quite another thing when in 1381 the archbishop was murdered and Lambeth Palace sacked in an outburst of hatred for lordships. The reactions of the archbishops at the turn of the century reflected the economic and social changes. It is not that they lost their close administrative interest in the estates that provided their livelihood. On the contrary, the new leasing policy shows a care for detailed and constant supervision, a businesslike attitude from which masterful oppression was absent because it would not have worked. But Courtenay and Arundel were aristocrats and more detached from personal contact with their tenants and manorial communities than Pecham had been a century earlier. Courtenay's popularity with the Londoners does not alter the fact that he was a lord of the old school, viewing refractory tenants as sinners and punishing them in a humiliating way.[3] To him and his successors it was important to deal fairly with the new class of farmers and officials

1. D. Knowles, 'Some Aspects of the Career of Archbishop Pecham', in *E.H.R.*, LVII (1942), esp. pp. 183, 191–6.
2. cf. *A.C.*, LXXVI (1961), esp. pp. 85–6.
3. See above, p. 189.

that was in process of evolution on the estates—yeomen and gentlemen who shared a common characteristic of wealth and in whose hands the estate was productively run for their rentier lord. But the body of the tenantry were now at a greater remove from the lord himself, their services and sometimes even their rents farmed with the demesnes to the intermediate managerial class who were becoming a vested interest in the lordship. Fifteenth-century archbishops, then, were not economically or socially weakened figures, defensive and run-away rentiers. They had survived the threats of the late fourteenth century and found new ways to deal with new conditions. But they operated through a machinery that almost ran itself, and they concentrated on judicious patronage to keep it in tune. The business was centrally audited and ably run, but beside the professionals were the stewards and bailiffs, men of influence in the kingdom and appointed for handsome fees, and the wardens of manors, and foresters, and lessees of parks, occupying positions of benefit to themselves and with a degree of local authority. Chichele and Warham, bourgeois though they were, were no different from the aristocrats in promoting their own relations and clients, defending the spiritual power yet placing their kinsmen about them, just as was being done on a grander scale in Rome. There was little further scope for personal estate policy in a world where family enterprise throve better than the large exploiting lordship.

In one special way, of course, the lord of Canterbury was at a disadvantage in being a bishop. He could not get rid of parts of his estate that might have been better sold. The medieval doctrine of church property stated by Augustine, Julianus Pomarus and Aquinas was universally if implicitly accepted.[1] It belonged to God and was in stewardship, inalienable. Further, the archbishops were bound to have their greatest preoccupations elsewhere, in the affairs of kingdom, province and diocese. Nor were they elected like abbots out of a body of local men whose corporate landlordship from generation to generation was to them a matter of tradition, long knowledge and pride. An archbishop might come

---

1. Julianus, the African rhetor, became a refugee at Arles at the end of the fifth century. His *De vita contemplativa* (*Patrologia Latina*, 59, cols. 430 *et seq.*), Book II, influenced the Carolingian reformers who concerned themselves with ecclesiastical property and formed the basis of the classical medieval theory. See also Aquinas, *Summa Theologica*, IIa, IIae, Qu. clxxxv.

from anywhere, and he came suddenly and expected to make new appointments on his arrival. When he died, the process happened all over again. It is these facts that make the professional management of the estates more significant than the personal policies of archbishops.

THE HOUSEHOLD

The medieval household of the archbishops has attracted scholars who were mainly interested in intellectual life and ecclesiastical administration. This is not surprising, for in contrast with the brilliant Canterbury *familia* of the twelfth century there is little to be learned about the control of the lordship from those witness lists to charters that provide the staple evidence of the age. But it would be untrue to the nature of the church to neglect the centre from which all control stemmed. There is meaning, too, beyond the accident of record survival, in the early obscurity of the lay household and in the way this obscurity melts as time goes on and the men of letters and of prayer become of less account than the administrators. From the Conquest until about 1200 the archbishops lived chiefly on fixed revenues supplied by local *firmarii* and relied for provisions upon those same local managers whom they visited by turns. There was little need for anything elaborate in the way of central accounting, nor for expertise to intensify production and reduce overhead costs. The task was to maintain sufficient communication, to insist upon the due renders, and to supply an agreeable, well-run home for the lord. For two generations after the Conquest the household was 'familiar' not only in this sense but also because it was monastic in direction and character, and because the archbishop as abbot found it only natural to delegate important temporal business to one or more of his brethren. Gundulf, monk and later bishop of Rochester, lived with his friend Lanfranc at Canterbury from 1070 to 1077 and occupied himself with external business.[1] Anselm's household was generally looked after by the monk Baldwin, the archbishop's *provisor et dispensator*.[2] It would be satisfying to know how

1. R. A. L. Smith, 'The Place of Gundulf in the Anglo-Norman Church', in *Collected Papers* (1947), esp. p. 86.
2. R. W. Southern, *St Anselm and his Biographer* (1963), p. 96 *et seq.*; cf. pp. 194–7.

matters were arranged outside this little circle, and in particular what relation the nominal household officers bore to the daily work in their departments, but the evidence will not take us far. Several superior officers are named in *Domesday Monachorum*, and their endowments stated. Ralph the chamberlain had land worth £4 in Westgate, Canterbury;[1] Richard the constable had the 'manor' of Graveney in Boughton-under-Blean, valued at £6, as well as land worth £1 in Leaveland;[2] William *dispensator* had land worth £3 in Wrotham,[3] and Godfrey *dapifer* was settled with land worth £12 10s. in Lenham and £5 in Thanington;[4] Osbern *pincerna* held land for the service of half a knight's fee in Fleet near Sandwich.[5] These men were knights of the archbishop, and in some cases the descent of their fees can be traced for a long period.[6] High rank and dispersed possessions were, of course, quite compatible with a life of itinerant service with the archbishop, but these men can hardly have been functionaries whose hourly attention was required in the household. It was common medieval form to assign to men of rank a household office on great occasions, and the course of time saw a stratification of offices which might bear the same name but differed entirely in dignity. There was a world of difference between the earls of Gloucester, butlers at the archbishops' enthronements in the thirteenth century, and the men in charge of weekly drink consumption, and probably this stratification was already developed in the early twelfth century, so that the butlers endowed with the manor of Fleet may even then have been no more the real butlers than was Richard de Clare in the time of Archbishop Boniface.

A comprehensive gathering of household officers at work together is not found until 1150–3, when a charter of Archbishop Theobald was witnessed, in order, by the archbishop's cross-bearer, three of the archbishop's nephews and a clerk described as their master, the archbishop's chancellor, two monk-chaplains, a butler (*pincerna*), dispenser (*dispensarius*), chamberlain (*camerarius*), steward (*senescallus*), master cook (*magister cocus*), usher (*ostiarius*), porter (*portarius*) and marshal (*marescallus*).[7]

1. *Dom. Mon.*, p. 82. 2. ibid., pp. 85, 93.
3. ibid., p. 87. 4. ibid., pp. 81, 93.
5. ibid., p. 105, and *Kent Records*, xviii, pp. 32–3.
6. See Appendix A.
7. A. Saltman, *Theobald*, p. 482, where the text differs slightly from that printed by Sir Frank Stenton, *First Century of English Feudalism*, Appendix, doc. 16.

The first three of the lay officers are the same as those named in *Domesday Monachorum*. The constable is absent, and the steward, cook, usher, porter and marshal are additions at the end of the list, but their first appearance here does not necessarily signify that they were new positions. In fact, the effective household must have been much larger than the chance little groups the sources allow us to see. Customary arrangements for receiving the itinerant household at Boughton-under-Blean are described in the thirteenth-century custumal in language which suggests twelfth-century practice, and we are shown the tenants of this manor obliged to cater for the almoner, the 'chief clerk of the household' (*summus clericus de familia*), the usher, a knight, an unspecified number of messengers (*nuntii*), the cross-bearer, a monk, washerwomen, the purveyor (*emptor*), janitor, baker and the chief steward.[1] Although this too can only have been a partial enumeration of the retinue, it gives an idea of the humble, necessary servants who did not get into charters. At Nyetimber in Sussex the custumal says that the lord's (local) household was 'attorned' or summoned against his arrival, so there was even a sense in which his local tenants formed a temporary part of his entourage.[2]

By the thirteenth century the household had undoubtedly become more secular. Not that the monastic contact was wholly lost, even in the later Middle Ages. Indeed, it was obligatory. Pope Alexander III in 1174 told Archbishop Richard that since he was professed as a monk and wore the habit he ought to keep monks about him, and should in particular choose a suitable one to carry his seal.[3] Archbishop Edmund employed a monk as chaplain,[4] and as late as 1314 Archbishop Reynolds, being unable to carry out some corrections he had ordered on visitation, deputed 'the Canterbury monk whom, in accordance with an ancient custom he keeps about his person', to act for him.[5] But the tendency from the later twelfth century onwards was to use clerks not monks in the literate posts, and probably also to increase the number of secular employees. The next collective appearance of the household is at Wrotham on 6 and 7 October 1267.[6] At

1. Dean and Chapter of Canterbury MS. E 24, fo. 46 (2nd numeration).
2. ibid., fo. 92.
3. W. Holtzmann, *Papsturkunden in England*, II (1935), no. 137; also cited by C. R. Cheney, *English Bishops' Chanceries 1100–1250* (1950), p. 33.
4. C. H. Lawrence, *St Edmund of Abingdon* (1960), p. 21.
5. *Lit. Cant.*, I, no. 41.   6. Lambeth MS. 1212, p. 421

this time direct demesne exploitation was in full swing, but there were still a few farms in operation on manors from which, according to the old system, the household collected its fortnight's provisions. Wrotham was one of these, and a memorandum records the procedure:

It is to be known that there were personally present to take their farm master Stephen de Monte Luelli, then archdeacon of Canterbury, master Hugh de Mortimer, then Official of Canterbury, master Peter de Satiniaco, then Chancellor of the archbishop, master Peter Albus, then rector of Wrotham church, the lord William de Bocwelle, then prior of St Martin's, Dover, and chaplain of the archbishop, the lords Roger de Northwode and Gerard de Scescelle, knights, stewards of the archbishop, the lord Gerard de Seycelle [sic], treasurer of the archbishop at Canterbury, the lord Hugh de Gebennis, then treasurer of the household, Poncetus de Marento, then rector of Tangmere, Hugh Burgundio, then rector of Great Chart, Stephen de Iford, clerk of the accounts, Ralph de Hever, bailiff of Otford, and Maurice de Northwode, usher of the archbishop's Hall. . . .

After noting the agents who were present on behalf of the farmers, the account enumerates the household officers who received the supplies, namely, Jakemettus de Beleys, the *panetarius*, Ralph de Aucton, the butler (*butilarius*),[1] Lambert de Monneto, clerk and purveyor, Walter de Pageham, the marshal of horses, and an unnamed scullion (*scutilarius*). The whole document is of interest in showing the distinction between the household's superior officers composed of foreign clerks and English laymen and the less dignified functionaries who checked in the wheat, wine, carcasses and dishes.

In the later thirteenth century the household was becoming more firmly departmentalized. The impetus towards elaborate organization visible in every sphere of government affected the archbishop's estates in general and his household in particular. The testament of Archbishop Winchelsey reveals a large domestic hierarchy in 1313.[2] A group of *valleti* were bequeathed 40 to 60 marks each and included some knightly figures like William de

1. The 'honorary' butler at this time was probably the father of that Walter le Botiler for whose wardship in the half-fee of Fleet £40 was paid between 1270 and 1272 (P.R. 119, m. 41d.).
2. *Reg. Winchelsey*, pp. 1340–5.

Swantone, steward of the household, Alan of Twitham, John of Dene, a literate layman, John of Grofhurst, James of (Bishops)-bourne, 'our special valet', master Godard the cook and Richard the marshal. Another group who were left lesser sums included the tailor, the usher, a subordinate cook, a clerical almoner, and 'Ivo of the buttery', and lower still were the barber, scullion, janitor, pantler, baker and an anonymous number of 'men of office'. The structure of the household departments appears in the inventories of property left by fourteenth-century archbishops at their deaths. In 1313 the contents of Winchelsey's household, valued at nearly £1,000, were distributed among ten identifiable departments: wardrobe, chapel, chamber, almonry,[1] buttery, pantry, kitchen, stables, armoury and hall. A list of 1349 after Stratford's death contains the chapel, wardrobe and armoury combined, treasury, stables, kitchen, hall, pantry and buttery combined, and larder.[2] The difference of grouping depended upon the need to value the household's contents at a given moment, but both lists emphasize the financial value of the chapel and the books, silver vessels and vestments associated with it, and the jewels which it or the wardrobe contained. These departments formed a reservoir of liquid wealth which could be added to or drawn upon at need. The chapel also contained, of course, an outfit of expensive liturgical equipment suitable for the Primate of All England which the new archbishop would usually have to borrow until he had collected his own and which he might ultimately leave, at least in part, to his successor.[3] But it possessed also the double character of financial security and aesthetic treasure. An excellent illustration of this is the chapel of Archbishop Reynolds, which came at his death into the custody of John of the Chamber, was delivered by him to the keepers of the temporalities during the vacancy, and was passed in the end by them

---

1. The almonry does not appear subsequently as a department of the household though it had a separate building at Maidstone in 1297 (L.R. 687).
2. Dean and Chapter of Canterbury MS. Chartae Antiquae, A 37. The total value of the household contents on this occasion was about £3,000.
3. In 1315 Reynolds borrowed from his cathedral priory some chapel ornaments which Pecham had bequeathed to it, and others which Kilwardby and Winchelsey had left. They were restored to the sacrist. In due course the priory likewise lent ornaments to Meopham, delivered in two red, enamelled coffers, until he had received those which had belonged to his predecessor (J. W. Legge and W. H. St John Hope, *Inventories of Christ Church, Canterbury* (1902), pp. 2–3, 7–8). But the contents of the archbishops' chapels during their lives were different from each other. They were personal property, subject to personal disposal.

to Archbishop Meopham in 1328.[1] The objects were packed in nine chests lettered A to J (omitting I). The first three held vestments of which the most valuable were a white set worth £26 13s. 4d., a red set worth £13 6s. 8d., and a jewelled mitre worth £10. Chest D contained fourteen books, including a three-volume Bible worth £8 which he bequeathed to his cathedral,[2] some chronicles, a book of geometry, an ordinal, a quaternion on the life of Thomas the Martyr, and a painted roll of Genesis. Four chests were full of 'muniments, rolls, bulls and charters of the archiepiscopal liberties', and the last one held ornamental knives, a pastoral staff 'of little or no value' and a quaternion of sermons.

Household rolls themselves are more valuable than wills and inventories for displaying the economic structure. These rolls were vulnerable documents, more readily discarded after audit than ministers' accounts. Only three fragments survive from which the Canterbury system in the later Middle Ages can be pieced together. A roll for half of December 1341 and one for the whole of March 1343 disclose the household of Archbishop Stratford's time and possess an added rarity interest in that Stratford's register has disappeared and his pontificate is poorly documented.[3] The various departments of household made daily returns of their expenditure and these were added up weekly with notes of how much had been spent on the market and how much drawn from stock. The face of the rolls was used by the internal departments, the dorse by the wardrobe which saw to the bulk purchase of spices, the wages of messengers and other things exterior to the domestic departments themselves. It is striking how high a proportion of the archbishop's spendable income was consumed by the household, and by certain departments of it in particular, though the surprise may be mitigated if the modern householder reflects upon his own domestic budget. The net annual value of the lands, as was shown in the previous chapter, was in the region of £2,500. If the five weekly totals of expenditure given in these rolls of Archbishop Stratford are averaged, the result is £46 a week, which, applied

---

1. Mins. Accts 1128/7 and 8. I am grateful to Professor Francis Wormald for his help in identifying some of the objects in Reynolds's collection, though there is no space here for further details of them.
2. cf. *HMCR*, v, App. p. 460. Reynolds's will is Dean and Chapter of Canterbury MS. Chartae Antiquae, A 14.
3. Westminster Abbey Muniments, nos. 9222, 9223.

over a year, comes to £2,392. Small though the number of sample weeks is, the rolls emphasize credibly that the kitchen was the chief spending department, using nearly £14 a week. The *coquina* in fact occupied an ancient and central place in the domestic arrangements of the household. In Domesday, the 'little borough of Seasalter' had been assigned to finance the kitchen of the archbishop and the monks, then probably undifferentiated.[1] Nearly every manor-house appears in thirteenth-century accounts to have been provided with a kitchen as a permanent and separate building.[2] Stratford's rolls suggest in addition that the kitchen on the march, like other household departments, needed one cart with a complement of up to six horses. At this time and later, the archbishop's kitchen organized all the foodstuffs for human beings other than bread, drink, poultry and condiments. The clerk of the kitchen, however, had a more general oversight of the household provisioning and was not confined to the kitchen in its more limited sense. Next in financial importance came the stables (*marchalcia*), to which was assigned the feeding of all the horses, whether the mounts of members and guests, sumpter horses or draught beasts, and the shoeing of the horses of household. This transport office was equally ancient, and was housed on many of the manors by separate buildings, although the size of the retinue made some billeting on the local tenantry necessary.[3] Other branches of the household were more modest. The buttery dispensed ale and wine under the working butlers who were sometimes dispatched to distant manors for supplies. Their accounts are embellished in the margins with pen sketches of barrels calling attention to the number of gallons of wine consumed. The pantry controlled the baking and distribution of loaves, the poultery the supply of edible birds, tame or wild, and the feeding of domestic fowls, though here, as elsewhere in the household, there was a certain flexibility. In 1349–50, for instance, the reeve of Bexley sent pigs as well as hens and eggs to the household and was credited on tallies drawn against the poultery.[4] In the final accounting the wardrobe had to answer for these, and local ministers who

1. *D.B.*, I, p. 5; *Dom. Mon.*, p. 90.
2. See, for example, the accounts of repairs to kitchen buildings, often tiled, in 1273–4 at Lambeth, Croydon, Gillingham, Wingham, Aldington, Bishopsbourne (where there was a new, wooden one), Lyminge, Otford, Bexley, Northfleet and Charing (Addit. MS. 29794).
3. See above, p. 167. 4. L.R. 240.

delivered victuals of any sort to the household generally got a bill of wardrobe as acquittance.[1] To the hall fell the provision of heat and light in the form of charcoal and candles, together with arrangements for their carriage and distribution. The 'men of office' in charge of these domestic departments were of a status which in the fifteenth century would be called 'yeoman', and were endowed by the archbishop with suitable property. William Altremoz, Stratford's pantler, was given a cottage and three acres in Herne[2]; master John Cayly, one of Islip's cooks, was granted a wardship and marriage in 1356.[3] These are merely examples of how a great lord rewarded his own servants without simply relying upon wages, and they reinforce the well-known picture of such lordships as vested, stable and familiar interests. Finally, there was the wardrobe, which accounted separately, on the dorse of the household rolls. This was a major spending department in the earlier fourteenth century. Winchelsey's keeper of the wardrobe, Robert Crul, was receiving and spending between £3,000 and £4,000 a year in 1308 to 1310.[4] Some of this was from ecclesiastical sources, and a small proportion of it went to the Roman court. But most of it went on household expenses, either consumable, or durable, like silver plates and dishes. In the brief period covered by Stratford's rolls, the wardrobe's disbursements were irregular and depended much upon the special requirements of entertaining or communication with the world of affairs. It bought quantities of white sugar at nearly 1s. a pound, pepper, madder, rice, ginger, red wax for the archbishop's seal at 8d. a pound, cloth and canvas for 'napery' against Christmas and for the guests' beds and sheets, green silk of Lucca and other fine furnishings for the chamber. It also dispatched messengers. In the first half of December 1341 alone, it sent riders from Croydon to the bishop of London at Hadham in Hertfordshire, to Penshurst and Sutton, to the bishop of Chichester at Aldingbourne in Sussex, to London (twice), to Maidstone, to east Kent in order to invite men for Christmas, and to Norwich; also from Otford

---

1. L.R. 1140 (of 1356–7).
2. Reg. Islip, fo. 16v. A number of tenements on various manors left vacant by deaths from plague were granted to second-rank household officers by Islip, with their services commuted except for rents and suit of court. But the principle of such grants was ancient: Theobald c. 1153 gave land near Canterbury to William his cook and his heirs (Saltman, op. cit., no. 51), and a mill to William his baker (L. Delisle, *Receuil des actes de Henri II*, I (1916), no. CLXIV).
3. Reg. Islip, fo. 130v.   4. *Reg. Winchelsey*, pp. 1062–3.

to Hendon, and again to Hadham and to London. The wardrobe also bore the cost of transporting and cellaring pipes and casks of wine at Lambeth, of presenting 2*s*. to the boy-bishop of St Nicholas at Croydon on his feast, and of presents to clerics going to and from the court of Rome. Wardrobe expenses in March 1343 were lighter, and ranged from £7 6*s*. 8*d*. spent on saffron at 3*s*. 4*d*. the pound, to 10*s*. given to the son of Reginald the watchman when he went off to school at Maidstone, and 1*s*. to 'a certain fool [*cuidam fatuo*] who begged from the marshal of the archbishop's household at St Thomas's tomb in Canterbury Cathedral'. The overall impression of Stratford's household rolls is of a curious combination of luxury and discomfort: the routine fatigues of perpetual motion, and the privileged plenty of delicacies brought in great variety from all quarters to the tables in hall. Hospitality, too, accounted for a large part of the expense. The household fed not only its own numerous members but guests who arrived daily with their parties, and whose names or numbers were entered daily in the accounts. In Stratford's rolls, important guests were present on twenty-six out of forty days, and sometimes the parties were large as well as distinguished. On Sunday, 23 March 1343, to choose one instance, the archbishop entertained the earl of Huntingdon, the prior of Canterbury, the lord Bartholomew Burghersh, and 'many of the countryside'.

In the thirteenth and fourteenth centuries, the revenue from the manors was usually paid over by the local ministers to the archbishop's treasurer, known also as the treasurer of Canterbury palace or the treasurer at Canterbury. This important official should be distinguished from the treasurer of the archbishop's household who, like the steward of the household, might also from time to time receive modest in-payments from the manors. The archbishop's treasurer had his headquarters at Canterbury, whether or not in the store-house at St. Gregory's Priory,[1] but the remittances from manorial officers were not necessarily made to him there. For instance, in 1352 William Islip, treasurer of Canterbury, received money from the serjeant of Northfleet by the hands of various intermediaries at Otford, Maidstone and Lambeth, giving tallies of receipt on each occasion. But money was certainly kept at Canterbury and sent when needed to the

---

1. I. J. Churchill, *Canterbury Administration* (1933), I, pp. 546–7.

household in large sums, where it was passed through the wardrobe, and sometimes through the Chamber.[1] The treasurers of Canterbury were among the highest of the archbishop's managers and ranked with the stewards of the lands and of the Liberty, but an inspection of the list of office-holders makes it difficult to pin them down to a given type.[2] Up until the early fourteenth century, all appear to have been clerks, and often rectors of important churches in the archbishop's collation. Robert Crul, treasurer to Reynolds, had been keeper of Winchelsey's wardrobe and rector successively of Sundridge, Biddenden and Godmersham. John de Ringwood, Reynolds's next treasurer, was a knight, and William Vygerous, treasurer c. 1330, may have been a layman, for he became steward of the household in 1350. But there was no permanent recourse to lay treasurers, for the list contains William de Woghope, treasurer in 1331, a monk who examined ordinands in literacy, Guy de Mone, treasurer in 1386, who became bishop of St Davids in 1397, and Roger Heron, master of Maidstone College, who was treasurer in the early fifteenth century. After this payments were made to receivers rather than treasurers, and the office becomes obscure.

The archbishop's household is illuminated by a third roll, which is of a rather different character. It belongs to 1459 and covers the month of October.[3] But this time it is not a financial document, and not a single sum of money appears on it; it is a physical account of household consumption, department by department. In his daily entry, the accountant proceeded in a fixed order, writing in the left-hand margin the numbers of *familiares* and the names of guests present, and in the right-hand margin the amount of baking done and the number of beasts slaughtered for food. In the body of the account he enumerated the supplies consumed under the regular headings of Pantry, Buttery, Ale, Wardrobe, Kitchen, Poultery, Saucery, Scullery, Marshalcy and Oats. The scale and variety of provisions do not differ much from those of the century before, but more is now to be learned of the system of internal distribution. Every member of household had one loaf

---

1. Reg. Reynolds, fo. 283v.; L.R. 834; Churchill, op. cit., I, p. 549.
2. Appendix B, pp. 396–7. Pecham's commission (1279) to Thomas, rector of Chartham, as treasurer of Canterbury, is the first extant one, but its generality implies that the duties of the office were well known (*Reg. Pecham*, p. 3; cf. Reg. Reynolds, fo. 128v.).
3. L.R. 1973.

a day, and special issues of bread were made daily for breakfasts, to the kitchen, and as alms. The buttery dispensed red wine to the archbishop's chamber, to the kitchen, and to the senior members of the household for private consumption apart from meals. Much larger quantities of ale than of wine were distributed, for breakfasts, to kitchen and chamber, as alms, and again for drinking outside meal-times. There were two daily meals in hall, dinner (*prandium*) and supper (*cena*), and at each of these the people who sat down were divided into guests and *familiares*, and the latter classified into the gentry (*generosi*) and the others (*alii*).[1] During the month in question there was a daily average of twenty-two gentry and fifty-two 'others' to dinner, sixteen gentry and forty-six 'others' to supper. If the guests were of high rank they were named in the roll. Such were senior officials and clerics in the archbishop's service as well as lords and knights from outside, and they were usually described as coming with two, three or four in attendance. Only the numbers of other guests were noted. The daily average was four important and eighteen less important guests in hall, and they were to be found there on most days, even on Fridays and vigils when there was no supper.

During the last half-century of the medieval period the household accounting system appears to be different from what had gone before. Neither the treasurer of Canterbury nor the keeper of the wardrobe were any longer in evidence. Instead, money was paid over from the manors to the receivers, who in turn delivered it to officers of the household, namely, to the steward of the household, the treasurer of the household, the clerk of the kitchen and, from the time of Archbishop Morton (1486–1500), very often to the archbishop's cofferer. Although these domestic officials were not new ones, they give the impression of becoming more important in the latest medieval period, and a few words are due to each.

1. The bishop of Hereford in the thirteenth century divided his staff into the well-known categories of *armigeri*, *valletti*, *garciones* and *pagii* (*A Roll of Household Expenses of Richard de Swinfield, Bishop of Hereford*, ed. J. Webb (Camden Old Series, LIX, LXII), but the bishop of Bath and Wells in the fourteenth century made the interesting and broader social distinction between the *libera familia*, the *officiales*, and the *garciones* (*The Household Roll of Ralph of Shrewsbury, Bishop of Bath and Wells*, ed. A. H. Thompson, Somerset Record Society, *Collectanea*, I, vol. XXXIX). Canterbury also spoke of the *libera* or *specialis familia* in the thirteenth century (Dean and Chapter of Canterbury MS. E 24, fos. 12 and 46v., (2nd enumeration)).

The steward of the household had authorized out-payments in Stratford's time, but he was keeping accounts in fairly large sums with London merchants in the fifteenth century.[1] A paper draft of an account rendered by him survives from 1522–3.[2] In it, Warham's steward of the household took considerable amounts for the household's use from receivers as well as quantities of food-stuffs in bulk and some cash from farmers of the manors and others who gave the archbishop presents. He also took cash from the cofferer for expenses when the archbishop went hunting at Croydon and Otford, or rode to Salisbury for the feast of St Osmund's translation. His account notes wine and bulk supplies consumed from the household stock and the issue of food and robes made to *familiares*. He kept a 'book of diets' and had access to the archbishop's books of accounts with his creditors. John Peers was Warham's steward of household between 1504 and 1523, and he also served as receiver in Pagham and Croydon bailiwicks from 1516–7.[3] John was a scholar of Winchester and New College, an ecclesiastical lawyer ultimately beneficed by the archbishop as Dean of South Malling College, who died in 1536 leaving livestock to his executors, a 'great double chest covered with red hide' to Sir John Gage, and loaves to be distributed 'where great necessity demands and want prevails'.[4] The steward of the household might equally well be a layman, like Sir William Tyrrell under Bourgchier, Edward Ferrers under Warham or Richard Neville under Cranmer, but he was a man of high importance in Church and State.

The treasurer of the household had almost certainly kept a financial account since the beginning of his office, and Stratford's household rolls were very likely his. In the fifteenth and early sixteenth centuries, he often received provisions and, to a lesser extent, cash. He initiated entries in 'the book of the household', issued receipts by indented bill, and warranted expenditure under the signet of the archbishop. His account was regularly and separately audited at one of the manors.[5] But unlike the steward of the household, he seems no more important a figure under Warham than he had been in the early days.

1. L.R. 1343, 1363; Mins. Accts 1129/4, 8, 10.
2. P.R.O. Exch. Accts Various (E 101), 518/33.
3. L.R. 1363.
4. *Biog. Reg. Oxford*; PCC 2 Crumwell.
5. Mins. Accts 1130/1, 3, 4, 8 (1468–80).

A major responsibility for household expenditure fell upon the clerk of the kitchen. In the fifteenth century he occasionally received victuals or cash from outside, giving acquittance by signed warrant, and he authorized payments, as he did to the stable lads at Charing in 1457-8,[1] when the sum was said to be noted in the book of the household. But within the household itself he had supervision of what was consumed throughout the various departments. A note of 1529-31 shows that in money terms the clerk of the kitchen disposed of over twice as much income as the steward of the household,[2] and it is possible that the roll of 1459, already discussed, was a product of the clerk's office.

Finally, the archbishop's cofferer appears in the receivers' rolls quite frequently in the second half of the fifteenth century and more regularly from the 1490s, when the office was filled by master John Ryse, priest, cofferer to Morton. He took custody of very large sums from the receivers, kept a book which recorded standing debts to the archbishopric, gave receipts for cash and sometimes for provisions, but does not seem to have kept an account of his own.[3]

The general impression of the archbishop's household—and in default of continuous, detailed evidence it can be no more than this—is of a body whose structure mirrored economic change and whose personnel reflected the archbishop's natural choice: monastic under Anselm, more clearly divided in the later twelfth and thirteenth centuries into clerical and lay, but both halves becoming more professional as time went on, until in the fifteenth century the earlier pattern is reversed and the lay element became the socially dominant one, Lambeth a more natural focus than Canterbury, and influence in political or even polite society as a whole an apter qualification for the archbishop's household service than Kentish connexions or ecclesiastical interests. Perhaps, too, the household had become a less grave place by

---

1. L.R. 1243 (1460–1), L.R. 1349 (1473–4), Mins. Accts 1129/4 (1455–6).
2. *L. & P.*, v., no. 450 (29 September 1531). Here. the average of three years' household expenses in the steward's book were £921, and in the clerk of the kitchen's book, £1,920.
3. L.R. 98: payment of £26 13s. 4d. from the prior of Christ Church as his annual pension for having his Liberty, 'as in the book of master John Ryse'. A good pair of his indented bills receipting over £1,150 in 1489–90 are sewn to Mins. Accts Hen. VII, no. 331. Ryse was probably the bachelor of laws who helped to administer the vacant see of Exeter in 1503–4 (Churchill, op. cit., ii, p. 261).

that afternoon in Arundel's pontificate when Margery Kempe and her husband went into the hall at Lambeth to find clerks 'and other reckless men, both squires and yeomen', cursing and swearing.[1] Later still a worldly gaiety was prevailing when Morton's household put on *Fulgens and Lucrece* for its Christmas dramatics. Written by Henry Medwall, Morton's chaplain, this is the earliest known secular play in English.[2]

THE DEVELOPMENT OF LOCAL MANAGEMENT

Even in the Norman age, rent collection and the production of the countryside needed a management, but the details are lost to us. The reeve of Domesday Tangmere in Sussex got 20*s.* out of a manor worth £6 a year, but this is a unique and enigmatic allusion. If the way in which the leased estates were regulated during the twelfth century was anything like that at Tarring under the farmership of the Waleys family in the thirteenth century, then the lessees must have had a wide practical discretion in 'keeping the manor according to their tenures', though remaining subject to the archbishop's overriding control and to the 'ancient and approved custom of the archbishopric'.[3]

The movement into direct demesne exploitation called for innovation both in local management and in a central but mobile control. The first of these took a form quite usual on other estates of the time. Every large manor was accounted for jointly by a bailiff and a reeve.[4] The names of the reeves tell us they were local men. They collected rents and sometimes had responsible tasks in agricultural production like fetching stock from Essex to Kent, and they even carried money to London.[5] The reap-reeve, whom Mr Denholm-Young calls the real task-master, occurs in the accounts, but so do *clavigeri* of the manors and the bedels who were also sometimes in charge of customary work.[6] A bailiff,

1. *The Book of Margery Kempe* (World's Classics edition, 1954), p. 47.
2. R. W. Chambers, *Thomas More* (Bedford Historical Series, 1938), p. 61.
3. *C.P.R. 1272–81*, pp. 204–7; cf. Lambeth MS. 1212, p. 63 *et seq.*, and see above, p. 103.
4. The earliest surviving ministers' account is of 1236–7 (L.R. 1193); cf. N. Denholm-Young, *Seignorial Administration* (1937), ch. II.
5. Addit. MS. 29794 (1273–4).
6. See above, Chapter 4, p. 170, and references there given.

however, was put in charge of more than one manor. Lefward was *prepositus et collector* of Northfleet in 1236–7, and Robert of Blendon the same at Bexley, but William Bullok was *ballivus* of both, though the two places lay eight miles apart. The same picture is visible with great clarity in 1241 and again in 1273–4.[1] Bailiffs earning 6*d.* a day and robes, with clerks on half this pay, were set over groups of manors in a way that differed little from the formal bailiwick organization of Pecham's day, while the reeve or serjeant dwelt continuously on the manor and might hold court when the bailiff was absent. True, the reeve was not necessarily a lowly figure in thirteenth-century Kent, let alone later: Adam of Twydole, reeve of Gillingham in 1273–4, had more than fifty acres of his own and a son a priest.[2] But the bailiff was altogether grander. On many manors he had quarters set aside for him. The office was desirable: John Fareman, member of the notable Wrotham family, made himself bailiff there without licence in 1309.[3] By the thirteenth century the archbishop's bailiffs were taking an oath in French in which they promised to hold their courts and leets properly, to become thoroughly acquainted with the property and put it to profit, to survey repairs and the filling of vacant tenements, supervise the sale of wood, making a special note of prices, watch the numbers and the health of livestock, keeping written testimony of disease, levy debts for the lord, attend audit punctually and, not least, uphold the archbishop's tenants against outsiders.[4]

The later history of local management, after the changeover into demesne leasing, is in fact one of elaborate specialization and not of pruning. Naturally, the apparatus of direct agrarian exploitation was removed. The serjeants, ploughmen, carters and other servants of husbandry who are discussed above were no longer employed by the archbishop, who lived as a rentier. But the office of bailiff continued, its holders knightly or gentlemanly in status and concerned with court-keeping alone.[5] Reeves, woodwards, parkers and some bedels continued to have their own accounts alongside those of the farmers, answering for the business

1. *Cal. of Liberate Rolls 1240–5*, pp. 43, 239–40; Addit. MS. 29794.
2. For Adam, see 'Gavelkind and Knight's Fee in Medieval Kent' by the present writer in *E.H.R.*, LXXVII (1962), p. 510.
3. L.R. 1139. The bailiff's 'chamber' is alluded to at Bexley, Maidstone and Otford at least (L.R. 234, 657).
4. L.R. 2068: a fifteenth-century copy, but attached to a rental in a hand of *c.* 1300.
5. For the later medieval bailiff, see Chapter 7 below.

of rent collection and maintenance, and every manor-house had its warden who in certain cases combined this post with that of local forester. The reeve was not dealt with in the chapter on the demesnes, and his evolution is of special interest. Mr Denholm-Young found that the importance of this officer diminished in the fourteenth century and that he became indistinguishable from the bailiff.[1] On the Canterbury estates this did not happen. It remained an elective office on an annual rotation, and evidently an irksome one, but it was prone to come into the hands of people of high social rank. Most of the archbishopric estates lay in a countryside of desirable properties freely to be acquired for money, and it was entirely commonplace for modest socage tenements to be bought up by men or women of status, or corporations, who were thus rendered liable for election as reeve in the local court in respect of their holding. At Bexley, the Lord de Lovell was reeve in 1473-4, the well-to-do yeoman William Hall in 1504-5, the Prioress of Dartford in 1515-16, John Draper, gentleman, in 1524-5, Richard Walden, knight, in 1528-9. It might be argued that the reeveship of a gentleman or nobleman could hardly be more than a formality and that the work of actual collection must have been done by deputy, and it is admittedly hard to see these officers demanding rents in person from individuals. Yet account rolls carefully specify deputies when they were appointed, and in 1516 Sir Thomas Kempe, knight, bedel of Saltwood, had no deputy but delivered money to the receiver with his own hands.[2] In 1474-5 Cardinal Bourgchier's eldest brother, the earl of Essex himself, was amerced 13s. 4d. for failing to take up his office as reeve of Otford, and the fact that he was exonerated 'by special grace' suggests that others would not be.[3] Even when the reeve did appoint a deputy, that deputy might himself be a man of consequence, like Thomas Boleyn, later earl of Wiltshire, who acted for John Draper in 1524-5. No doubt there were perquisites to be made: even in the bad 1270s rent-collecting offices had sometimes been purchased.[4] But once in office, the reeve had fiscal obligations to the lord of Canterbury and might find himself required to convey cash, or see to the state of the manor. Normally the costs he incurred were

1. N. Denholm-Young, op. cit., p. 32.
2. L.R. 1207. Likewise, the prioress of Dartford at Bexley in 1515-16 (Mins. Accts Henry VIII, no. 1687).
3. Mins. Accts 1130/6.
4. *Rot. Hundr.*, I, p. 211 (bedelry of Teynham).

recoverable on production of his warrant, but the business and delays in getting reimbursed were liable to be tiresome. In 1482 the reeve of Sevenoaks wrote:

> To my lorde Cardinall. Moost humbly besecheth your noble grace youre oolde servaunte and trewe bedeman Robert Butvilan, that hit may please your said grace in consideracion of his long service to commaunde your Auditor to discharge him of the summe of £5 2s. 10d., or parte thereof, as may accorde with your moost noble pleasure, of whiche summe he is in arrerage by meane of being your Reve this yere at Sevenok for his londe at Wikeherst, wherunto he is but newly come, and never toke avauntage of the same. Moreover, at your commaundement your said servaunt belded your logge at Otforde to his charge of £5 and more money, whereof as yut he never hadde allowaunce. All whiche consideracions he besechethe you to call unto your graciouse remembraunce, with the povertie that he is nowe in. . . .[1]

The central control that could thus manage the estates and their local officers was a tough one, and to it we must now turn.

The chief representative of the archbishop on his estates, mobile but vested with centralized authority, was the steward of the lands. As on other estates, he was at least from the thirteenth century quite distinct from the steward of the household.[2] The first of whom we have any detailed knowledge was perhaps the greatest of all, Elias of Dereham, who died in 1245.[3] He did not always act alone, for it was not unusual in the thirteenth century to have more than one estate steward, but he earns special attention by reason of his multifarious public activities and long career in the service of both Hubert Walter and Stephen Langton. He was an architect, he served in the royal chancery, and he probably did much to set the see's temporal affairs to rights in 1213 after Langton's five years of exile. His detailed inquisition of the estates, possibly the first ever made, is a memorial of this activity, though the document itself has not survived.[4] Elias's sympathy for the opposition to King John reflects a sense of political independence the archbishop's household never lost in the Middle Ages, and it has an interesting counterpart in a future steward of

1. Mins. Accts 1130/10.   2. N. Denholm-Young, op. cit., p. 67.
3. For whom see K. Major, 'The Familia of Archbishop Stephen Langton', in *E.H.R.*, XLVIII (1933), and J. C. Russell, 'Elias of Dereham', in *Speculum*, II (1930).
4. See above, p. 11.

the estates, Henry, prior of St Radegund's, Kent, who served Archbishop Boniface in 1261, and whose appointment as treasurer of England in 1263 and 1264–5 was a distinctly baronial one.[1] These thirteenth-century stewards were not dedicated to single estates but, whether clerks or laymen, passed easily from one administration to another. Such were Robert of Bermondsey, the knight who was acting as steward of the archbishopric in 1215 after serving the same office for St Augustine's and Faversham abbeys,[2] or master Simon de St Lyz, probably steward for Archbishop Edmund in 1236–7, and a lively correspondent as steward for the bishopric of Chichester in the 1220s, when he advised his master to offer the archbishop entertainment on his arrival in Sussex, knowing he would not wish to accept it, and arguing that the bishop of Chichester would thereby get the credit for hospitality without having to pay for it.[3]

As with the household and with the manorial staffs so with the directing machinery of estate government a more clear-cut and permanent system becomes visible after the mid thirteenth century. It is hard to point to a precise moment when such development began. The manors were grouped under bailiffs in the 1230s, but no accounts present formal bailiwicks until the vacancy after Pecham's death (1292–3), when they appear in their full and final form as the bailiwicks of Wingham, Aldington, Maidstone, Otford, Pagham, South Malling and Croydon.[4] In the pipe-roll for that year the Liberty too appears for the first time as a separately accounting entity, but the appointment of stewards of the Liberty, distinct from manorial officers, antedates Pecham.[5] The lists of office-holders that can be compiled from the registers and rolls[6] show that members of this higher estate-management could at need supply each other's functions. Thomas of Chartham, treasurer

1. F. M. Powicke, *Stephen Langton* (1928), pp. 137–9; C. H. Lawrence, in *St Edmund of Abingdon* (1960), shows that Dereham continued to work for the archbishopric at least till 1240. For Prior Henry, see Appendix B and *Handbook of British Chronology* (2nd. ed.), p. 100.
2. K. Major, art. cit., p. 549.
3. *C.P.R. 1215–25*, p. 572; W. H. Blaauw, 'Letters to Ralph de Nevill, Bishop of Chichester 1222–44 and Chancellor to King Henry III', in *Sussex Archaeological Collections*, III (1850), pp. 35–76.
4. P.R. 141 m. 28d. See the map opposite p. 196.
5. Pecham appointed William Norman to defend the liberties of his church in 1279, but Norman had been steward of the liberties to Kilwardby in 1275 (*Reg. Pecham*, pp. 2–3; Lambeth MS. 1212, p. 412). For the Liberty, see Chapter 7.
6. Appendix B, p. 393 ff., below.

of Canterbury in 1279, for instance, was in 1301 a joint steward of the Liberty with the Sussex knight, Edmund de Passele, and both were asked to act as steward of the manors whilst Sir William Trussel was away acting as Justice of Chester in the service of the Prince of Wales, and there are numerous similar instances. But already a *cursus honorum* was appearing among the professional clerks of the estates, as in the promotion of Stephen de Iford, clerk in 1259–61 and clerk of the accounts in 1267, to the steward-ship of the lands in 1279. In this office he supervised the new rental and custumal of 1283–5, a worthy successor to that of Elias of Dereham.[1] The scope of the steward's work was not defined in detail in the earlier registers, for the letters of appointment were standardized and general. The steward's commission of 1349 speaks of his power to hold courts and punish crimes by the archbishop's tenants *in foro seculari*.[2] A more developed form occurs in 1397 when William Makenade was appointed as steward of the lands 'to survey, inquire and ordain concerning the state of all manors belonging to the archbishopric, to receive recognitions and entry-fines from tenants, to hold courts everywhere in the see's properties and do all that is necessary, appoint and remove bailiffs, sub-bailiffs, parkers, warreners, woodwards, reeves, reapers and other ministers however called, and do whatever he think useful to the archbishop and church of Canterbury'.[3] The breadth of the steward's duties can be illustrated from the account rolls, in which he is constantly traceable on his manorial rounds, riding and sojourning at local expense. It was no sinecure. If he needed expert advice, he sought it by letter,[4] but his own discretion was wide and his decisions authoritative. He could order extra pay for labourers,[5] or decide on the sale of timber.[6] Losses could be allowed if he thought fit, but an unsatisfactory minister might find himself arrested and cross-examined, like the serjeant of Maidstone in the famine year 1316–17 who was questioned about his high costs by steward and bailiff in the presence of the Master of Maidstone College and six townsmen, the archbishop's tenants,

---

1. Lambeth MS. 1212, pp. 83, 417–18, 421; Dean and Chapter of Canterbury MS. E 24, fo. 60; *Reg. Pecham*, p. 1. John de Rodswell, Reynolds's steward in 1314, was at Lambeth in a subordinate role in 1284 (L.R. 235).
2. Reg. Islip, fo. 9.   3. Reg. Arundel, I, fo. 4.
4. L.R. 657 (Maidstone, 1297).
5. L.R. 658 (Maidstone, 1298): '... *ex gratia senescalli* ...'; L.R. 781 (Northfleet, 1365), etc.
6. L.R. 238 (Bexley, 1301).

and told to find a fixed amount of wheat and oats the next year.[1] In 1292 three men of Bexley, including a former reeve, were heavily amerced by the steward *in transitu suo* for trespasses they had committed.[2] His competence was financial as well as judicial. William Makenade in 1399 heard the accounts of the steward of the Liberty and on another occasion heard accounts of local ministers with the aid of unnamed auditors and the receiver, whose office is here mentioned for the first time.[3]

Like the treasurer of Canterbury, the steward of the lands could be either a clerk or a layman, but the lay steward was much more usual and probably invariable after Guy Mone, treasurer 1386, steward 1390–2 and bishop of St Davids in 1397. In the fifteenth century the archbishop's stewards were often connected with the royal household, and a letter from Archbishop Stafford to the prior of Christ Church in 1443 openly explained the reciprocal advantages of this when it referred to Henry VI's wish that James Fenys be appointed and his own gladness at having a man 'standing about the king'.[4] The steward's annual fee of £40 in addition to his expenses made the post yet one more of the multitude available to men who followed the ascendant political stars.

The Yorkist kings saw that it was not much good to set lands at farm unless they were constantly surveyed for upkeep and rent adjustment.[5] Archbishops were aware of this as soon as they began systematic leasing at the turn of the fourteenth and fifteenth centuries. To the stewards and bailiffs, by now mainly jurisdictional and administrative officers, were added receivers and a specialized section of auditors. Further, the archbishop's council now regularly comprised common lawyers and influential knights.[6] It has been suggested that the development of efficient baronial councils like this worked to the detriment of ancient manorial courts and the local liberties enshrined in them by giving the lord's will a brisker and more authoritative expression. For the archbishopric,

1. L.R. 659 (Maidstone, 1317).   2. L.R. 236.
3. L.R. 668. The succession of specially appointed auditors does not appear till *c.* 1411. Makenade was accompanied in 1399 by the treasurer and by William Lyndwood, clerk in the archbishop's household. If this was the great Lyndwood it seems he began his career in the service of Roger Walden.
4. *HMCR*, IX, App., p. 104; *Lit. Cant.*, III, no. 1024.
5. B. P. Wolffe, 'The Management of English Royal Estates under the Yorkist Kings', in *E.H.R.*, LXXI (1956), p. 21.
6. A. E. Levett, 'Baronial Councils and their Relation to Manorial Courts', in *Mélanges d'histoire du moyen âge offerts à M. Ferdinand Lot* (1925), reprinted in *Studies In Manorial History*, ed. H. M. Cam *et al.* (Oxford, 1938).

this idea seems a wrongly formulated one. There was, after all, much room for oppression in the thirteenth century, however much the custumals may be supposed to testify to give-and-take between jurors and stewards, for the simple economic reason that the pressure of population made labour cheap and land dear, and resistance by poor to rich difficult. The fifteenth century, on the other hand, saw an often bitter resistance of simple people and dignified lords to each other's claims. The archbishops of the later days certainly relied upon efficient councillors and administrators for their living, but there is little sign that the tenantry, let alone the *firmarii*, were easy to oppress permanently.

The receivers come into view in 1399. During the 1390s payments were still being made by local ministers to the treasurer of Canterbury, but in that year a receiver was said to be hearing accounts at Maidstone,[1] and in 1400 the reeve of Wrotham, whose accounts happen to survive for this crucial period, began to deliver his cash to the receiver of the archbishop.[2] This seems late in the day by comparison with the thirteenth-century receivers whom Mr Denholm-Young showed at work upon baronial estates,[3] but the archbishop's receivers were different, in that they were neither local nor central officers but intermediate ones, charged to look after one or more bailiwicks, to ride round collecting money from all manorial ministers, and to pay it over to the archbishop's household wherever it might be. The receiver was not a treasurer under another name. He did not keep cash in his possession for long, but paid it over frequently during the year, getting in return for the sacks of money delivered by him to the steward or treasurer of the household, clerk of the kitchen, or archbishop's cofferer bills of acquittance, sometimes indented, sometimes signed, and sometimes sealed with the archbishop's signet. A proportion of the money he collected was disbursed by the receiver in accordance with written or verbal instructions from the household. In 1455–6, for example, the receiver of Otford settled household bills with John Upnore, Draper of London, Thomas Hill, Grocer of London, Thomas Markham of Hastings and Thomas Mayhew of London, Fishmongers.[4] Building expenses were often met with funds in the receivers' hands. Large sums for the rebuilding of Knole after Bourgchier's purchase in

1. L.R. 668.
2. ibid., 1142.
3. N. Denholm-Young, op. cit., p. 13.
4. Mins. Accts 1129/4.

1456 were paid over by the receiver of Otford from monies he had gathered in the district,[1] and contributions for the building of the Bell Harry tower of Canterbury Cathedral were made in 1496–7 by the receiver of Aldington and Wingham.[2] Most of the fees and pensions to high officials and important people were paid by receivers: the annual pension of £2, for instance, to Dr Thomas Wells, bishop of Sidon and prior of St Gregory's, Canterbury, who worked as a coadjutor bishop in the diocese of Canterbury and had a room in Knole; and also the present of about £50 to Erasmus of Rotterdam in 1524–5.[3] In 1471, 14s. was spent on the nursing and eventual funeral of three boys of the archbishop's chapel, and 8s. 2d. on shoes, socks and capes for the survivors at Knole.[4]

Fairly early in the fifteenth century it was possible for two or more bailiwicks to be grouped together under a receiver or receiver-general. This was a matter of temporary convenience and followed no clear system, but the tendency was to place adjacent bailiwicks together under a single receiver, such as Pagham and South Malling in Sussex, so that, even when they were grouped with Croydon, the receiver could make his rounds without detours into Kent. There was at one time a receiver-general in Kent to whom the receiver of a simple bailiwick like that of Otford would account, but the general receivership did not become a settled institution until the reign of Queen Elizabeth.

The late medieval receiver was an experienced and substantial man, but not necessarily a professional in the sense that he held his office for a long time and did nothing else. Some receivers were ecclesiastics, others were clerks of accounts and at different times surveyors or auditors, but as receivers they seem to have been replaced after acting for a few years. The receiver got a fee of between £2 and £6 a year, depending upon the size of his area, together with travelling expenses which came to nearly as much again. Nicholas Hulme, receiver-general in 1438–9, was probably the same man as the receiver-general of the same name who acted for the bishop of Durham in 1421–3.[5] Robert East, receiver

1. *A.C.*, LXIII (1950), pp. 135–9.   2. L.R. 1358, 1360.
3. L.R. 1362, 1364, 1366, 1366A.   4. Mins. Accts 1130/3.
5. R. L. Storey, *Thomas Langley and the Bishopric of Durham, 1406–37*, pp. 74, 78–9. Langley innovated with receiverships, and no doubt men like Hulme, who also served the countess of Salisbury as receiver-general, spread their experience far and wide. For other receivers, see Appendix B, pp. 399–400.

c. 1444–55, was one of the 'great extortioners of Kent' accused by Jack Cade's rebels.[1] Robert Tottisherst, receiver of Otford in 1481–2, was a married gentleman of Sevenoaks of early middle age with a good deal of town and country property in the district and friends in the archbishop's household.[2] John Mascall, Warham's receiver for Otford, Croydon and Maidstone, was also his valuer for probate, a gentleman who resided at Chart, farmed the archbishop's manor of Lambeth Wick, and seemingly practised as a money-lender.[3]

The short duration of receivers in office was probably because of its arduous nature. Receivers were always on the move and were responsible for the transport of large sums which they had to parcel up in canvas sacks supported on horseback by *bougez*, or yokes, guarded by parties of hired horsemen.[4] Their accounts were audited annually, either in the autumn or at Christmas time, and this process meant for each of them several days' stay at Sevenoaks, Canterbury, Slindon or Lambeth, depending upon the bailiwick concerned.[5]

The cream of the professionals was the auditor. The succession of office-holders can be traced from about 1412 in the account rolls, and their commissions, entered in the registers, like that to John Chapman in 1454, empowered them to hear and terminate accounts of receivers, farmers, reeves, bedels, collectors, stewards and bailiffs of liberties and all other officers and ministers. The office was during pleasure, and its emoluments were in the fifteenth century charged upon the rich manor of Wingham.[6] It is not, of course, to be supposed that auditors were unknown before this. They can from time to time be glimpsed acting with or without the steward. But the fifteenth century, as in so many other ways, saw a systematic specialization of function. The auditor travelled

1. *Kent Records*, xviii, pp. 221 and *n.*, 224, 227–8, 231, 233–5, 240.
2. PCC 8 Fetiplace.
3. PCC 5 Populwell; *Reg. Bourgchier*, p. 65*n.*
4. L.R. 1347; LCM, xiii (1), p. 14.
5. e.g. L.R. 1344, from which a timetable of accounting in 1437–8 can be worked out: 28 October for the accounts of Pagham, Nyetimber, Shripney, Bersted, Aldwick, Lavant, Tarring, Tangmere; 29 October for those of Slindon and to finish off Pagham and Lavant; 31 October for Ranscombe; 4 November for Ranscombe again, Mayfield and Framfield; 5 November for Stonham and Ringmer and again Framfield; 6 November finishing off Framfield; the manors of north Kent, Surrey and those north of the Thames were dealt with between 17 and 25 November inclusive, which meant some accounting was done on a Sunday.
6. *Reg. Bourgchier*, pp. 13–14.

about with a party of three or four, one of whom was his special clerk and another his valet. He got £15 a year, of which £5 was supposed to cover the purchase of parchment and paper, ink, green cloth and the counters needed for the account. His clerk got £5, and sometimes extra for engrossing the accounts.[1] Like the receivers and surveyors, the auditor was a member of the estate council, and might find himself engaged in non-fiscal administration, such as holding a manorial court for the election of reeves, 'surveying' manors, or carrying money himself if an audit had taken place at a distance from the archbishop who wanted the cash. Since he had to audit all the accounts of all the manors and of the household as well, the occupation was a busy though not necessarily a full-time one. The auditor was, for instance, at Sevenoaks for eighteen days at Christmas 1465 in order to audit the ministers' accounts of Otford bailiwick, the manor of Knole and its members, the receiver-general of Kent and the other receivers,[2] and he had to make 'evidence' of lands acquired by the archbishop and to audit separately the account of the treasurer of the household.[3] Warned by the bailiff of Sevenoaks the local accountants came streaming in.[4] For his comfort, special accommodation was provided for the auditor at Knole, where a room at the end of the hall was set aside and beds with straw mattresses and decent hangings made ready.[5] It is possible that auditors had organized training at a school like the one in Oxford,[6] but on the Canterbury estates we know only that they gained experience as clerks of accounts and got promoted when there was a vacancy. Some were men of wide experience. George Houton, or Hooton, was auditor to the archbishopric from 1460 to 1471, but he had been feodary for Oxfordshire and Berkshire in the service of the Duchy of Lancaster since 1450, controller of customs at Yarmouth in 1455, bailiff of the abbot of Cirencester, and Member of Parliament in 1449, 1450 and 1453. He was a lawyer, a gentleman of London and a parishioner of St Olave's, Silver Street, who with his wife was admitted into the

---

1. L.R. 1243. In 1467–8, 1s. 3½d. was spent on seven quaternions of paper and 6½d. on ink for making up the (draft) accounts of Otford bailiwick (Mins. Accts 1130/1).
2. Mins. Accts 1129/8.   3. ibid. 1130/8.
4. ibid. 1130/10.   4. ibid. 1130/1; L.R. 1348.
6. H. G. Richardson, 'Business Training in Medieval Oxford', *American Historical Review*, XLVI (1941).

confraternity of St Giles outside Cripplegate. He possessed lands in Wiltshire and Gloucestershire as well as Kent, and had some connexion with Worcestershire, for his brother was a merchant of the city of Worcester.[1] When he was archbishop's auditor his clerk was Humphrey Rotsey, who was already taking a major share of the work in 1471. Houton was probably ill: he made his will in the autumn of 1473 and died in 1474, and in 1473 Rotsey was given verbal instructions to act as auditor and was formally appointed soon afterwards.[2] It is interesting that Rotsey also had a connexion with Worcestershire. The account of 1474 allowed his expenses in riding thence from his house to Lambeth for the audit. He served the archbishopric as auditor for another ten years and was in 1482 made warden of the park and woods of Pinner by way of reward.[3] Like many good careers, his own probably began by a friendly recommendation from someone already on the ladder. It is a matter of luck to light upon the records of these men's lives, but they illustrate well enough not only the growth of professional society in the later Middle Ages but its inter-regional connexions.

The archbishop's estate council in the fifteenth and early sixteenth centuries receives constant incidental mention in the accounts but gives no sign of formal constitution. It was composed of the stewards of the lands and of the Liberty, the receivers and the auditor; there were also several 'surveyors' (*supervisores*) who received separate commissions 'to survey, inquire and give orders for the good estate of the archbishopric, take fealties, recognitions and entry-fines, hold courts, appoint and remove bailiffs and other officers, and do whatever is necessary',[4] and to act, in short, just like stewards. The rolls show them often on the scene, arranging leases and prescribing repairs to property. The two other main categories of estate councillors were the influential knights and the men of law. Edward IV's victory in 1461 depended in good measure upon the three 'Captains of Kent', Horne, Scott and Fogge, and the two last of these became treasurer and comptroller of the household respectively to the king and, as well as serving him in various local capacities, were retained for their counsel by

1. PCC 26 Wattys (fo. 207); R. Somerville, *History of the Duchy of Lancaster*, I (1953), pp. 411, 625.
2. Mins. Accts 1130/3, 4. 3. L.R. 1349; *Reg. Bourgchier*, pp. 45–6.
4. Appointment of William Makenade as surveyor, 1396, before he was made steward of the lands (Reg. Arundel, I, fo. 404).

10

Archbishop Bourgchier at £6 13s. 4d. a year each. Scott also was bailiff of Aldington at £9 2s. 6d.[1] As for lawyers, there was room for both the civil and the common varieties. In 1480 William Donynton *legisperitus* was retained *de concilio suo* by the archbishop at 26s. 8d. a year; so too were William Hede, attorney of the archbishop in the royal chancery, at 13s. 4d., William Holgrave, attorney-general, at £2 13s. 4d., and William Catesby (of later notoriety), serjeant-at-law, who was retained with the archbishop at 26s. 8d. and made bailiff of Pagham in 1484 when he was squire of the body to Richard III.[2] A number of superior posts were created more to provide patronage than to fulfil a needed function, and this was the sort of thing done increasingly everywhere during the later Middle Ages as dominant families which possessed political rather than economic initiative sought to accommodate their members and supporters within the framework of their estates and jurisdictions. Such was the office of Master Forester awarded to Humphrey Stafford in 1453 at £20 a year[3] and to Thomas Bourgchier the elder, knight, in 1479,[4] or the keepership of parks, warrens, chaces and woods within the whole archbishopric given for life in 1381 to Henry Castelayn, king's squire. Nominally charged to supervise hunting, he received an annual fee of £10, a robe of the suit of archbishop's esquires or 13s. 4d. in lieu from the manor of Bexley, free pasture for a number of his animals and a right to trees blown down by winds 'as long as it was not an excessive storm'. Castelayn's brass is still to be seen with a hunting horn engraved on it in the parish church of Bexley where he died in 1407. He left money for a new window in the church and all his bees to provide a candle each before the images of St Katherine, St Margaret and the Blessed Virgin in the chancel.[5] A successor in the post, Edward Neville, Cranmer's master of game, was executed for the doubtless expert remark that Henry VIII was worse than a beast, and his office was given to Thomas Cromwell.[6]

1. L.R. 1351.
2. ibid. 1350; *Reg. Bourgchier*, p. 65.
3. L.R. 1240–1.
4. ibid. 1351.
5. Reg. Arundel i, fo. 237; *C.P.R. 1381–5*, p. 12; for a photograph of the brass, see *Medieval Bexley*, Plate ii.
6. Jasper Ridley, *Thomas Cranmer* (1962), p. 173.

CHAPTER 7

The Liberty

THE DEFINING OF THE LIBERTY

In 1678 Roger North was appointed Temporal Steward of the see of Canterbury by Archbishop Sancroft. The post was one for a common lawyer with ecclesiastical sympathies, and North was a happy choice, able, versatile and charming, unlike his predecessor Dolben, brother of the archbishop of York, Recorder of London, and an 'arrant, peevish old snarler'. Directly to our use, North explained his new office in his *Autobiography* and thus outlined with some exactness the form into which after so many centuries the archbishop's Liberty had set.[1]

This office [he wrote] hath three patents. First, Judge of the Palace Court of Canterbury. This court is like to the court of the King's household called the Marshalsea, and hath jurisdiction in all personal actions of any value arising within the Liberty, that is, in any of the towns whereof the church of Canterbury had the seignioralty, which is a large circuit in the county of Kent. For although there were no demesnes, yet the services and other incidents of dominion in old time were considerable. This court hath a prison and a bailiff or goaler, who executes all processes and is *minister curiae*, as the sheriff in the county at large under the courts of Westminster. The court is constantly [held] by a deputy, who paid me £30 p.a., not by articles, which would have made the office void by the statute, but by private understanding between us. Second, the Office of Keeper of the Liberties in the county of Kent, that is coroner and admiral within the Liberty, and to collect

1. *The Autobiography of Roger North*, ed. A. Jessopp (1887), esp. pp. 110–13.

277

the green wax profits upon the totted schedules out of the Exchequer, and to act as minister in all the business of the Liberty. . . . And the sheriffs were commonly so just as to send their [mandates to the bailiff], according to right, and then the bailiff of the court executed the process. . . . And once a year he sued out the escheats [*recte* estreats?] from the Exchequer, and accounted to me for the levies, one half whereof were the archbishop's and the other half my own, and usually amounted to £25, £30 or £40 p.a. This office was of great profit before the Court of Wards was taken away, for all wardships and liveries within the Liberty belonged to the archbishop, and the steward of the Liberty had the benefit of them in half. The third patent was the stewardship of the manors and keeper of the liberties in the county of Surrey. This carried a salary of £4 p.a. for the two courts of the manors of Croydon and Lambeth. But the Liberty profits came to nothing, being not worth the charge of totting in the Exchequer, and therefore in those manors, though the right was the same as in Kent, save only the Palace Court, the Liberty was not executed. But once a year I kept the two courts, which yielded me about £18 or £20, so that in the whole this office was worth to me about £60 p.a., sometimes more, and often less. . . .

This was the terminus of an age-long development. The Liberty had become a lawyer's perquisite nourished by minor actions and casual profits in south-eastern townships, a small matter to a man whose income was about £4,000 a year, but a recognizable vestige of what it had been for five hundred years. The difficulty is to understand the origins and nature of what later became a fiscal habit. It is partly a documentary difficulty, for the formal charters of the eleventh and twelfth centuries that gave public expression to the archbishop's special rights used obscure formulas, and the administrative records of the same period are very slight. But it is also a difficulty of substance, since 'liberty' and 'jurisdiction', proprietary rights though they were, connoted to medieval men more than a set of causes that could be listed and valued, and touched in fact upon their possessor's very dignity. It was a common sight to see liberties asserted by struggles the cost of which was out of all proportion to their financial value. On a wider stage this almost mystical sense of 'liberty' lent significance to 'the rights and unharmed liberties of the Church in England',[1] but on

1. '. . . *quod Anglicana ecclesia libera sit, et habeat jura sua integra, et libertates suas illaesas* . . .'—Magna Carta, 1215, para. 1, W. Stubbs, *Select Charters* (9th ed.), p. 292.

the smaller scale, when John granted to the archbishop that he might recover all his domains unjustly alienated, acting 'in his court by the oath of free and legal men of the neighbourhood *according to the custom and liberty of his court*', he was using the same language.[1] The 'Liberty' might, of course, act as a quite specific protector. The archbishop was not bound to contribute to the defence of the city of Canterbury, and this was reckoned a liberty belonging to him and his church.[2] Or it might even be a limitation. Homicides could not be judged in the archbishop's court, according to his liberty.[3] But the word was protean. The archbishop's Liberty was geographical, for it extended over particular areas such as his hundreds and his *borghs*, or territorial tithings. It was also personal, in touching his men and tenants, either by subjecting them in certain cases to his jurisdiction even when they dwelt in another's lordship or by freeing them from tolls when they travelled afar. In the singular the Liberty freed the archbishop and his communities from some kinds of direct royal administration and justice, but the plural was needed to enumerate the liberties exercised in courts or profitably realized by stewards, bailiffs and bedels. The pipe-roll of 1272 spoke of the 'liberty of the Great Court of Canterbury and the liberties of all the manors of the archbishopric'.[4]

Needless to say, the distinction between the theoretical Liberty and its practical application in the courts and departments of government is quite artificial, but it is a useful one with which to introduce the two main forms of historical evidence for the archbishop's secular jurisdiction. In the first place, there are numbers of writs or charters by which kings really or supposedly made over rights to the archbishops and, allied with these, agreements composed after more or less prolonged dispute between archbishops and neighbouring holders of liberties under which the ambiguities which had arisen were regulated. All these grants and agreements were embodied in formal instruments intended to have perpetual force and were entered, naturally enough, in the archbishopric's book of precedents under the sections entitled 'Charters of Kings'

1. Lambeth MS. 1212, pp. 49, 201.
2. ibid., p. 95; cf. *Rot. Hundr.*, I, p. 203.
3. ibid., p. 151: '*Si autem aliquis pro morte hominis, suspicione latrocinii vel quocunque alio malefacto pro quo secundum libertatem . . . archiepiscopi . . . iudicium dampnationis in curia sua subire non possit . . . .*'
4. P.R. 119 m. 41d.

and 'Compositions'.[1] As they were put into practice, these liberties generated practical records, both in the form of local court-rolls and accounts of ministers of the Liberty, and of memoranda of claims made by officials of the Liberty at the Exchequer, asking the king's officials there to approve in detail year by year what the king through his Chancery had granted with solemn generality. Without the practical records the formal ones have little meaning, and the attempt will be made to explain the one kind in the light of the other. But at different periods of the Middle Ages different kinds of evidence are prominent: in the eleventh and twelfth centuries there are the general grants of privilege, but no court-rolls and only slight traces of administrative relations with the Exchequer; in the thirteenth century the privileges become more precise and defined and it is likewise the age of detailed compositions with other franchise holders, though the administrative records on the pipe-rolls and in the ministers' accounts leave much to be desired. Not until the late fourteenth century do court-rolls survive in any number, and by then it is also possible to see more clearly the work of the steward of the Liberty at the Exchequer. By then, too, the constitutional pattern is set, the charters merely record changes of detail, and the machine had taken charge.

ARCHBISHOP AND KING

Although a detailed discussion of the pre-Conquest archbishopric is beyond the scope of this book, it is impossible to write of its jurisdiction without reference to the earlier privileges bestowed by kings. We may begin with Cnut, that great benefactor of churches, whose authentic writ, delivered between 1017 and 1020, confirmed the position of dignity and powers of protection over his men that it was felt the archbishop had enjoyed in the past and ought always, under royal confirmation, to hold:

> . . . I inform you that the archbishop spoke to me about the freedom of Christ Church,—that it now has less *mund* than it once had. Then I gave him permission to draw up a new charter of freedom [*freols*] in my name. Then he told me that he had charters of freedom in plenty if only they were good for anything. Then I myself took the charters of

1. Lambeth MS. 1212, pp. 14 *et seq.*, 131 *et seq.*

freedom and laid them on Christ's own altar, with the cognisance of
the archbishop and of Earl Thurkill and of many good men who were
with me—in the same terms as King Aethelbehrt freed it, and all my
predecessors: that no man, be he ecclesiastic or be he layman, shall
ever be so presumptuous as to diminish any of the things that stand
in that charter of freedom. . . .[1]

That the archbishop and his church should have enjoyed liberties
going back to King Aethelbehrt, the founder of the see, is quite
probable. The writ's own reference to earlier charters of freedom
has a ring of truth. But they were subject not only to the hazards
of decay or fire but to a kind of wasting in confidence unless they
were confirmed from time to time in solemn form. Throughout the
twelfth century archbishops obtained from every king these verifi-
cations of estates and liberties they had received from previous
kings. Though bilingual, the Anglo-Saxon terms that could not be
latinized and scarcely corresponded with the 'social facts' of the
time[2] were carefully repeated and the documents kept in the
archbishop's treasury, to be copied, registered and re-confirmed as
late as the fifteenth century. Some of them, like Cnut's writ just
quoted, were quite general grants of 'freedom', acting almost as
covering letters to more specific grants embodied in separate
documents. Their object was not to particularize but to reassert
tradition at any moment when it might fall into question, whether
at the accession of a new king or of a new archbishop, and to gloss
over doubts that might have been created by the loss of documents
or even their lack of intelligibility. The series of general confirmations was continued through the twelfth century.[3]

The earliest recitation of the liberties themselves appears in
another writ of Cnut sent in 1020 to the bishops, earls and reeves
in every shire in which the archbishop and community of Christ
Church had lands:

I inform you that I have granted him that he be entitled to his *sake*
and *soke*, and to *grithbreach* and *hamsocn* and *foresteall* and *infan-*

1. In what follows the debt to Miss F. E. Harmer's *Anglo-Saxon Writs* (1952),
   esp. pp. 166–90 and 446–54, will be obvious; her translations of the writs of
   Cnut and Edward the Confessor have been used.
2. P. Vinogradoff, *English Society in the Eleventh Century* (1908), p. 3.
3. By Henry II (Lambeth MS. 1212, p. 28); the young Henry (LCM xi, p. 6);
   Richard I (LCM xi, pp. 5 and 8; Lambeth MS. 1212, pp. 32, 33); John (Lambeth
   MS. 1212, p. 55; *Rot. Chart.*, pp. 24, 68).

gentheof and *flymenafyrmth* over his own men within borough and
without, and over Christ Church, and over as many thegns as I have
granted him to have. And I forbid anyone to take anything therefrom
except himself and his officers. . . .[1]

This grant was renewed in almost identical terms by every king up
to John, and included in comprehensive confirmations during the
fourteenth and fifteenth centuries.[2]

It was once thought that the Old English phrases of these
charters had conveyed a full criminal jurisdiction which was
drastically reduced by the reforms of Henry II, after which serious
crimes could only be judged by the royal justices while the franchise
holders came simply to receive the profits of this judicial activity.
More recent study has shown convincingly that these Anglo-
Saxon words referred only to the right to deal with lesser matters.[3]
It is true that they were thought of as royally bestowed rights, but
they were not the greatest ones. *Sake* and *soke* signified actual
jurisdiction as well as its profits, but in cases of fighting and
wounding and probably petty theft. *Toll* and *team*, though distinct
in original meaning, form in the writs the minor franchise of
imposing tolls on the sale and transit of merchandise and the
mulcts of warranty procedures held in markets as a safeguard
against traffic in stolen goods;[4] like the other terms they were
archaic in the twelfth century, but their descendants might be
recognized in the frequent grants of markets and their concomitant
jurisdictions. *Grithbryce* by the early twelfth century, and probably
by the time of Domesday Book, meant a breach of the peace
within the jurisdiction of some subordinate of the king, like the
sheriff: in the later court-rolls of the archbishopric the offences of
disorderly countrymen were said to be 'against the peace', though

---

1. Harmer, op. cit., pp. 183–4.
2. The writs of Edward the Confessor though spurious are thought by Miss Harmer
   to be founded on fact (op. cit., nos. 31, 33, 34 and cf. 35); for William I and II,
   Regesta, nos. 38, 336; for Henry I, *Regesta*, II, nos. 1055, 1388; for Stephen,
   Lambeth MS. 1212, p. 24, where those forbidden to interfere are specified as
   'neither French nor English'; for Henry II, LCM xi, p. 2, where *heimfare* is used
   instead of *hamsocn*, and LCM xi, p. 3, and cf. Earle's *Land Charters*, p. 346;
   for Richard I, Lambeth MS. 1212, pp. 30, 33; for John, *Rot. Chart.*, p. 24, where
   the spellings also sometimes differ; for later confirmations, *C.Ch.R.*, IV, pp.
   345–8 (1335) and *C.P.R. 1429–36*, p. 415 *et seq.* (1434).
3. N. Hurnard, 'The Anglo-Norman Franchises', *E.H.R.*, LXIV (1949), pp. 289–323,
   433–60.
4. cf. J. Goebel Jr, *Felony and Misdemeanor* (Commonwealth Fund, New York,
   1937), pp. 369–70.

not 'against the king's peace'. *Foresteall* was an unpremeditated assault or obstruction, and *hamsocn* the forcible entering of a house, though not the offence committed once the house was entered. These last three crimes were aggravations, exceeding what could be understood under *sake* and *soke*, but not the really grave offences of murder and robbery, for which the penalty was capital. *Infangentheof*, it is true, entailed the death penalty and forfeiture of the culprit's personal property, but since it meant the right to punish the thief caught in the very act upon the lord's territory there was a strong presumption of guilt and little need for a complicated judicial procedure. *Flymenafyrmth* was the right to punish those who harboured outlaws, but by the twelfth century had become transformed into the right to seize and sell the personal effects of convicts. The need to interpret a whole vocabulary of ancient rights is shown by the manufacture of hand-lists, not always very accurate, at least one of which was kept in the Exchequer.[1] The medieval archbishop, in fact, was not one of those rare lords of liberties who possessed the high franchises of judging felonies. Cases which his stewards and bailiffs themselves might determine were matters for his hundred courts.[2] Until the Conqueror's time the bishops had been involved in serious pleas in the shire courts where they had sat with the earls, and this itself may account for the archbishop's lack of a superior temporal jurisdiction, for he had not needed the special grant of what in a sense he already had. On the other hand, after William I had separated the spiritual and temporal jurisdictions the archbishops were allowed special privileges when their own men were up for judgment before the royal judges, and these may have been intended as compensation for the prelate's loss of position as a secular justice.

The charters of the archbishopric include a series in which another distinct list of privileges was granted. The first in the collection is from Henry II:

. . . I have granted all the possessions and liberties that my great grandfather King William and my grandfather King Henry granted

1. *Red Book of the Exchequer*, III, pp. 1032–9.
2. At Taunton, to cite a parallel instance which shows the level at which such cases were judged, tenants had to pay fines and wites in regard to *hamsocn* and *foresteall*, breach of the peace, etc., in the manorial hundred (Vinogradoff, op. cit., p. 106).

and confirmed to the same church. Also I give them . . . these liberties:
geld and Danegeld, hidage, money for *murdrum*, work on bridges,
castles, parks, enclosures, aid for the army, war[d]penny, blodwite and
childwite throughout the demesnes and villein lands of the archbishop
and monks. And I wish them to be free of shires, hundreds and lests
of hundreds. . . .[1]

Charters in this form were not uncommon in and even before the
time of Henry II, though their significance is vague and was
diversely interpreted at the time.[2] It is clear, however, that the
privileges were fiscal ones and very like the hundred-court revenues
possessed by the abbot of Bury St Edmunds, some of which go
back to pre-hundredal times. Charters were soon to become more
explicit, but the old forms were not altogether discarded and were
used in the growing sheaf of evidences with which the archbishop
buttressed his claims to the revenues of his men. The *murdrum* fines,
chattels and amercements that were being exacted and allowed
from Henry II's time onwards were explicitly acknowledged in 1275
'through the liberty of the archbishop's charters and by writ of the
king in which it is contained that the liberties and acquittances
should be allowed him as they used to be in the times of Kings
Richard and John in whose annual rolls it is found that liberties
and the amercements of men of the vills and hundreds were
allowed the archbishop in various counties . . .'.[3]

From the late twelfth century royal grants of franchise took
more precise forms, though it is not easy to track down their first
occurrences. Return of writs, for instance, was already being
confirmed to the archbishop in 1235.[4] In the inquisition of 1275
the jurors of hundred after hundred acknowledged that the
archbishop had the profits of return of writs, the assizes of bread
and ale, wreck of the sea, pleas of forbidden distress, gallows
and pillory, but they usually said he had these from of old and
they knew not by what warrant.[5] They were allowed by the
justices, and they appear in the great confirming charters of the

1. LCM xi, p. 4; Lambeth MS. 1212, p. 26.
2. N. Denholm-Young, *Seignorial Administration* (1937), pp. 89–93; R. H. C.
   Davis (ed.), *The Kalendar of Abbot Sampson* (Camden Third Series, LXXXIV, 1954),
   Introduction, I, p. iii. See also the enumeration of the common fiscal immunities
   in F. Pollock and F. W. Maitland, *History of English Law to the time of Edward I*
   (2nd ed.), I, pp. 574–5.
3. Lambeth MS. 1212, p. 415.   4. *C.Cl.R. 1234–7*, pp. 117, 149.
5. *Rot. Hundr.*, I, pp. 200–36.

fourteenth and fifteenth centuries. In that one granted to Archbishop Stratford in 1335,[1] all the archaic privileges were rehearsed, and their obsolescence admitted by providing that the archbishop should not be impeded in his enjoyment of them by reason of non-user in the past; the charter then went on to confirm to him the return of writs and amercements of all pleas of the Crown throughout his lands, the chattels of felons and fugitives, fines for trespasses by his men and for their licences to agree, and all other pecuniary penalties and profits of justice which derived from his men. The list was lengthened in 1399 by awarding the archbishop forfeitures from writs of attaint and *praemunire*.[2] In 1448 a new charter granted the archbishop the custody of his tenants who were idiots, with all their possessions, and confirmed his jurisdiction over pleas of debt, covenant, detention of charters and chattels, trespasses and conventions, personal and real actions and assizes of fresh force held in his own courts at Canterbury and South Malling.[3] In 1463 former liberties were confirmed in yet more elaborate language by Edward IV, who in the preamble expressed himself grateful to his cousin, Archbishop Bourgchier, for 'coming with the king into his realm and there assisting him'.[4]

Even a brief account of the archbishopric's liberties would be seriously incomplete without a reference to the Canterbury mint, though the subject is technical enough to need separate treatment. By the twelfth century the mint and exchange at Canterbury was a royal institution in which the archbishop had rights and a share of the profits. It was situated in the High Street, on the site of the modern Crown Inn. The officials, some of whom were appointed by the archbishop, enjoyed certain privileges like exemption from taxes and jury service just as the royal officials did, but they all had to be approved by the Exchequer.[5] Charters from the time of Richard I at latest confirm the archbishop's right to have three dies there, and he seems to have received three eighths of the profits and borne three eighths of the expenses.[6] It is impossible at present to calculate the annual worth of the mint and exchange to the archbishop. In 1300 Winchelsey's letters patent acknowledged

1. *C.Ch.R.*, IV, pp. 345–8. 2. ibid., V, pp. 384–6.
3. *C.P.R. 1446–52*, p. 171. 4. *C.Ch.R.*, VI, pp. 192–4.
5. *Medieval Government at Work 1326–37*, III, pp. 35–66; Lambeth MS. 1212, pp. 416, 420–1; *Reg. Winchelsey*, p. 473.
6. *C.Ch.R.*, V, p. 126; VI, p. 195; Lambeth MS. 1212, pp. 34–5, 44, 45.

receipt of £249 15*s.* 8*d.* from the mint and exchange, and a few months later he required the keeper of the mint, John Cendal, to pay £100 on his behalf to Lapinus Roger, merchant of Florence and an attorney of the archbishop, who had married a Canterbury girl and settled in Westgate.[1] Again in 1314 the archbishop's treasurer acknowledged £5 received from William de Trent, keeper of the king's exchange at Canterbury, as the archbishop's portion of the issues.[2] The revenue he enjoyed from this source doubtless fluctuated considerably, but the exchange was a useful financial instrument to him and represented a service as well as an investment.

Whatever judicial activity these charters granted or prescription allowed, it was in practice carried out on two levels. In the towns and villages the courts were kept, suitors came, tithings were viewed, bread weighed, verdicts given, amercements levied, small disputes composed, land transactions registered, and pillories, tumbrils and gallows put to their uses. But on a higher level, the steward and bailiffs of the Liberty had to maintain relations with the royal Exchequer. The Chancery might in a sense authorize the liberties, since they were formalized through charters and patents, but the Exchequer had to regulate them by auditing the accounts of those who claimed the revenues flowing from them. From all those parts of the counties where no franchise like the archbishop's Liberty operated, the sheriffs reaped the profits sown by the royal justices in their passage, and brought their harvest to Westminster. But from the liberties the sheriff was excluded. The royal justices entered, of course, to hear the graver matters, though it would be a mistake to think of them as different kinds of being from the archbishop's own officials. The same men might even have experience in both worlds, like Roger Northwood, consecutively steward of the lands and Baron of the Exchequer, or William Trussel, another steward and sometime royal justice. When the amercements had been pronounced or the convicts hanged, it fell to the archbishop's own servants to collect the monies or the chattels and account for them in due course at the Exchequer, so that the records of both parties should agree, and king and archbishop each have what was owing to him. Accordingly, an organization grew up under the archbishop's steward of the Liberty, one of whose

1. *Reg. Winchelsey,* pp. 391–2, 398; *Kent Records,* xviii, p. 197.
2. Reg. Reynolds, fo. 283v.

highest functions from the thirteenth century onwards was to visit the Exchequer periodically and 'petition for allowances', or claim the archbishop's judicial profits. Doubtless these matters were usually concluded in the Upper Exchequer in the agreeable atmosphere of professional converse. But the very needs of the case warranted a sort of administrative tension. It was a question of business and, more gravely, of royal law, and the archbishop had to struggle at times, not so much for privileges from a king who was probably a political friend or even an affectionate kinsman, as for interpretations of privilege that the king's acute ministers sought to narrow in his interest. Justices were liable to exclaim with disgust at franchisal claims.[1] Henry III had to order sheriffs to permit the archbishop his return of writs. Edward I told his Barons of the Exchequer in 1275 and again in 1276 to continue to the archbishop his former liberties and acquittances, which they had grudged. Edward II did the same, specifying the amercements of all men of the archbishopric in all royal courts and the chattels of all felons and fugitives, upbraiding his Exchequer for obstructing these rights, and writing in the same sense to the steward and marshal of his household. Letters like this were eagerly copied into the archbishop's book of precedents.[2] A new situation would bring a new battle. After the Statute of Labourers (1351), the archbishop thought to use the ancient charters granting him the money penalties imposed upon his men to claim at the Exchequer the penalties imposed by the new Justices of Labourers upon his own tenants who had infringed the statute by demanding higher wages. He was refused by the Barons of the Exchequer, and when the king told them to make the allowances or tell him their reasons why they would not, they preferred the latter course, explaining with a logic of which an Inspector of Taxes would be proud that the statute had decreed that the penalties, including the 'excess' wages, were to be levied for the use of the king. The argument lasted through 1356–7, and in the end the decision went in favour of the lords of franchises, on condition they contributed to the justices' salaries. Even then the Exchequer ministers arranged the last advantage for themselves by insisting that every delinquent must be

1. See below, pp. 291–2.
2. Lambeth MS. 1212, pp. 291, 330–1, 412, 422, 424. The practice of recording the types of claim (rather than the sums of money) allowed at the Exchequer was continued by the archbishops' registrars. See *Reg. Winchelsey*, pp. 282–3, 989–91; Reg. Islip, fos. 89–95, 98 ff.

correctly named and his penalty certified by the justices to have been inflicted after the opening of the parliament in which the allowances had been defined, and indeed, to have been the penalty only, and not the 'excess' wages, since these were still to come to the crown.[1]

The routine by which the archbishop sought from the Exchequer to keep the profits of his Liberty has to be pieced together from the technical details in the manuscripts.[2] Every year the steward of the Liberty, or an attorney on his behalf, came up to the Exchequer to account. He brought with him, or had previously brought, any money which might be owing to the king from his bailiwick, such as the farm for particular hundred courts or amercements before royal justices that had been collected from those who did not happen to be the archbishop's tenants, and when these sums had been paid into the Receipt and tallies received in acknowledgement, he was ready to do business with the 'foreign apposer'. Amercements levied by the royal justices on the archbishop's own tenants, and other judicial profits to which the archbishop was entitled, would have been already collected locally and paid into the archbishop's treasury. In 1314, for example, Archbishop Reynolds acknowledged the receipt of £40 in silver from fines and amercements levied in Kent before Justice Stanton and various other summonses of the Exchequer which had been paid over to him by the steward of the Liberty.[3] In the presence of the foreign apposer, it was the steward's task to request that these sums be allowed. He also, as will be explained in the next section, had to request the allowances on behalf of the bishop of Rochester and the prior of Canterbury Cathedral. Royal charters upon which these rights were based were enrolled by the Lord Treasurer's Remembrancer among his *recorda*, and these documents were at the disposal of the apposer. So too were the details of the actual sums. Sent into the Exchequer by the justices who had imposed them, they appeared in the office of the Lord Treasurer's Remembrancer as 'parcels of the pipe', and were forwarded by him to the foreign

1. B. H. Putnam, *The Enforcement of the Statute of Labourers* (New York, 1908), pp. 141–5.
2. In the following paragraphs use has been made of Mins. Accts 1128/16, 17, 18; L.R. 95–9. See also M. S. Giuseppi, *Guide to the Public Records*, I, p. 131; H. M. Cam, 'Shire Officials', in *English Government at Work, 1326–1337*, III; and Miss M. H. Mills's introduction to 'The Pipe Roll for 1295, Surrey Membrane', *Surrey Record Society*, no. xxv (1924).
3. Reg. Reynolds, fo. 283.

apposer to give him the necessary information before the steward or bailiff of the Liberty appeared. The business between the steward and the foreign apposer was largely of a routine character. Doubts and difficulties were often referred to the Barons of the Exchequer for decision. In 1436, for instance, the steward, John Tattersal, appeared by two attornies, Robert Est and Andrew Kebbyll, to claim a series of allowances for fines and amercements levied on the archbishop's tenants in Croydon and Cheam by the Justices of the Peace sitting at Guildford and Leatherhead.[1] The steward also asked the apposer for discharge from certain sums that he could not levy because the king's debtors were dead and had left no property in the archbishop's Liberty. These requests were referred to the barons, who allowed some and postponed their answer on others.

Naturally, the archbishop's steward did his best to make friends at the Exchequer, and the rolls of the Liberty show him handing out presents to officials of all grades: in 1273 a present of cheese to the barons;[2] and in the fifteenth century breakfasts for the barons and sums of half a mark and downwards to the foreign apposer and others who helped in allowing his claims. Such were the remembrancers and their clerks, 'for their benevolence and friendship and attendance in their offices', the clerk of the foreign estreats, the clerks of the pipe 'for scrutinizing the petitions of the Liberty', and even the doorman 'for his favour in opening the gates during the sitting of the court'.

In the thirteenth century the profits of the Liberty had been enrolled on the general account roll of the archbishopric, but subsequently the steward of the Liberty came to have his own annual roll in which he answered to the archbishops separately. This may have happened before 1292 when the royal vacancy accounts mark for the first time 'The Liberty' as an entity distinct from the manorial bailiwicks, but none survives from a time earlier than the fifteenth century. The five that still exist, however, permit a clear view of the Liberty's nature and profitability in the course of the fifteenth century, for they are well spaced out between 1419 and 1491. The largest sources of his revenue were the fines and amercements levied before the justices in the counties where the archbishop had lands, and the wardships and reliefs of feudal

---

1. L.T.R. Memoranda Roll (E 368), no. 210, mm. 22 and 23 from end.
2. Addit. MS. 29794, m. 7.

tenants, though these naturally fluctuate and appear also to have suffered diminution during the fifteenth century, probably because the archbishop granted them out. The Steward of the Liberty also accounted for certain escheats and farms of liberties, for perquisites of the Liberty's courts at Canterbury Palace and Otford over which he nominally presided, the chattels of convicted felons and fugitives, fines for breaches of market law before the steward acting as clerk of the market and, when there were any, deodands, wrecks, treasure-trove and 'great fish' caught round the archbishop's coasts. These last were rare, but the chattels of the condemned are described in profusion and variety and ranged from wretched livestock disposed of by sale[1] to rich vestments allocated to the archbishop's own chapel. Like any other accountant, the steward had to meet certain expenses, of which the most consistently high were the fees of himself and other officers of the Liberty. There were also alms for the prisoners in Maidstone jail at the traditional $\frac{1}{2}d$. a day, the costs of moving prisoners under escort, of executions on Penenden Heath, and of supplying ducking-stools and stocks in the villages. He had to bear the expenses of Justices of Jail Delivery, pay Justices of the Peace at the rate of 4s. a day each, give presents to their staffs and pay the coroner a 10s. fee when he viewed the body of a murdered man. The steward of the Liberty bore too the serious responsibility of maintaining properties held in the archbishop's custody during the minority of their heir. The balance was paid over to the archbishop's treasurer.

With his annual fee of forty marks, the steward of the Liberty was of the same dignity as the steward of the lands. The commission of 1350 required him to answer for the liberties in all courts, to claim and petition for allowances, to receive and return royal writs, hold courts, punish or arrest rebels, and allowed him to appoint substitutes in his place.[2] During the thirteenth century stewards of the Liberty were occasionally clerics, but it was commoner in the Middle Ages to draw them from the ranks of laymen with legal and administrative experience, as reference to the list of office-holders will show. Often they had served estate administrations in other capacities. Elias de Waddesworth, who in

1. e.g. from the account of the reeve of Northfleet in 1455: 'from the goods of a felon, name unknown . . . nil because they are being valued and are not yet exposed for sale but remain in the custody of William Kene, steward of the Liberty, who will account for them' (L.R. 1241).
2. Reg. Islip, fo. 9.

1333 deputized for the archbishop's steward in Kent, had in 1329 acted for the bishop of Salisbury in Dorset and the bishop of Winchester in Hampshire and Somerset.[1] John Basket, Archbishop Stafford's first steward of the Liberty, had been the royal escheator in charge of the see's temporalities in Sussex and Surrey after Chichele's death. From the names that have been collected, it looks as though the fifteenth-century stewards of the Liberty tended to come from higher social strata than before, and men like John Chichele, John Alpheigh and Sir Thomas Bourgchier seem more prominent figures than their earlier counterparts. At the same time, it remained a post in which expert work was required, and it was perfectly possible for its holder to be no more than a moderate property-holder living a life of hard work, divided between professional travelling and the quiet advancement of his family, like William Kene of Woolwich, who died in 1467, leaving lands in Kent, Somerset and Dorset, with five sons, four daughters and a stepson to share his effects.[2] It was the post of bailiff that attracted the more eminent men at the end of the Middle Ages. Though nominally inferior to the stewardship, and feed at 4*d*. or 6*d*. a day, it was probably a sinecure. The patents of appointment permitted the office-holder to act by deputy in the holding of local courts, and this was undoubtedly done by the duke of Norfolk, bailiff of Pagham in 1517,[3] and Thomas Boleyn, Viscount Rochford, made bailiff of Otford for life in 1527 at the instance of Henry VIII, his future son-in-law.[4]

AGREEMENTS BETWEEN
THE ARCHBISHOP AND OTHER HOLDERS
OF LIBERTIES

The value of a jurisdictional Liberty depended not only upon the nature of the privileges it allowed but upon the number of people who lived within its ambit, and whose money and service were available for its lord. Justice Stanton saw this point clearly enough when in 1313 a man of the Cinque Ports tried in court to claim his privileges even in respect of lands he had acquired outside the Cinque Ports. 'Supposing one of the Liberty were so rich,' he cried,

1. *English Government at Work, 1326-37*, III, p. 146.
2. PCC Godyn, fo. 163.
3. L.R. 1363.   4. Addit. ch. 23786.

'that he could buy all the county, do you mean to tell me that he could tack it on to his own land within the Liberty, and so there should be none to serve the King? No, no. . . .'[1] Men of the thirteenth century, so adept at juridical compromises, not unnaturally found it important, therefore, to define the geographical areas within which private jurisdictions were valid, and the relationships between them, as well as the quality of the jurisdictions themselves. For the archbishopric this meant certain peripheral agreements, like the arrangement of hunting rights with the Waleys of Glynde and with the fitzAlan lords of Arundel,[2] but principally the general compositions with his own cathedral priory, with the bishop of Rochester, and with the earls of Gloucester in their lowy of Tonbridge. Discussion of these will throw light on the working of a medieval liberty itself.

The power and influence of Archbishop Boniface of Savoy gave his monks at Canterbury some grounds to fear for their own privileges, but in 1259 a mutual agreement was ratified before Hugh de Bigod, justicier of England. In order to understand it, a sketch of the regional judicial structure is needed. In the first place, the archbishopric and the priory each had local courts within its own manors and, enjoying some kind of eminence, certain principal courts of the Liberty, under their stewards—the priory's at Canterbury, the archbishop's also at Canterbury and, it seems, at South Malling in Sussex and possibly at Otford as well. Now some of these manorial courts, both of the archbishop and of the prior, were also hundred courts in which jurisdiction was exercised over trespasses and civil pleas too small to require the attention of the king's justices but more allied with public order than mere problems of manorial custom: such pre-eminently were the view of frankpledge, the assizes of bread and ale, and pleas of debt and trespass between individuals. But this hundredal jurisdiction was not necessarily co-extensive with the manors. By the middle of the thirteenth century, Kent was interlaced by a network of hundredal boundaries, but the manorial properties of the archbishop and others were scattered between them. It is true that the archbishop might possess complete jurisdiction over a hundred, but then there would be tenants and properties of others within its

---

1. *Eyre of Kent*, I, p. 19.
2. See above, pp. 101–3, and also Lambeth MS. 1212, pp. 69, 165, and *C.Ch.R.*, II, p. 188.

bounds. Conversely, the archbishop had some tenants who dwelt in hundreds that were not his. It might well happen, therefore, that the archbishop or the prior would find cases coming before their courts that touched tenants of the other (or of neither), and this was liable to lead to dispute, since each lord of a liberty desired to compel the maximum number of suitors to come to his own courts and to pay there the fines and penalties that might be inflicted. It is to be emphasized that jurisdiction concerned both areas *and* men, and there were many 'floating' suitors who lived on lands held of other lords. Indeed, a man might have many lands and more than one residence and be liable for suit to the courts of both archbishop and prior among others. The agreement of 1259 was to regulate this situation. That it did so satisfactorily is evident from the later medieval confirmations, like those of 1403 and 1434, which did little to alter it.[1]

In 1259 it was agreed that the prior and convent of Canterbury should have the return of writs concerning their own tenants. That is to say, when any writ dealing with some judicial or administrative matter touching a priory tenant was issued from the royal chancery or other department of government, it was sent to the sheriff in the first instance, but could not be served or executed by him, since the privilege of doing this lay with the bailiffs of the prior and convent. Such writs had to pass through the hands of the *archbishop's* bailiffs on their way to those of the prior and convent, and after the action had been taken, the priory's officers had to report what they had done to the *archbishop's* officers, who 'returned the writ', or reported back, to the crown. In this way, the priory was placed in a kind of juridical dependence upon the archbishopric in respect of all those matters in which the crown was directly interested, just as happened at the same time in respect of feudal service, discussed in a previous chapter. It was a general rule in the country that if the bailiffs of a liberty failed to act properly on any royal writ, then the sheriff might after due warning enter and execute the action. But if the priory's bailiffs neglected their work, it was the archbishop's officers who were empowered to serve the summonses, execute the distraints, and so forth, though they were enjoined not to make trouble by deliberately looking for such opportunities and to allow three weeks before remedying any

---

1. *C.P.R. 1429-36*, pp. 415-24; Lambeth MS. 1212, p. 168 *et seq.* cf. also Provisions of Westminster, 1259, para. 4 (W. Stubbs, *Select Charters*, 9th ed, p. 391).

complaint about the priory's default. When fines deriving from royal franchise (as opposed to amercements in local courts) had to be collected, then the priory bailiffs were to pay them over to the archbishop's bailiffs either in coin or Exchequer tallies. The archbishop's officers would then negotiate for them to be allowed at the Exchequer at the same time that they petitioned for the allowances on behalf of the archbishop himself. The profits were presumably handed to the priory afterwards. There was also to be appeal from the prior's principal court at Canterbury to the archbishop's court there. If any tenant of the priory found himself charged with a grave crime and taken before the county court to be kept in prison till the royal justices arrived, he had to pass at least formally through the hands of the archbishop's bailiff, though he would remain in the custody of the priory. Even in counties where the archbishop had no tenants, like Devonshire or Oxfordshire, the priory's custody of their prisoners was in theory to be authorized by the archbishop's special mandate. All this did not mean that the priory lost its financial profits of justice. Amercements of their tenants continued to belong to them. If a man were tenant of both prior and archbishop and got into trouble, he was to be imprisoned in whichever fee he happened to be residing in at the material time, and if he were executed, his chattels were divided between archbishop and prior according to the fee in which they were found. Likewise, the priory retained its rights to have pillories, tumbrils and gallows in its own manors. But there were provisions which recalled that the archbishop, the prior's titular abbot, was his superior: any personal process against the prior was to be answered by him in the archbishop's court, though he might not be mulcted in more than half a mark for any one trespass; amercements incurred by the prior himself before the king's justices were to belong to the archbishop, just as though the prior were like any other of the archbishop's men; and if the prior and convent encouraged their men to withdraw their suit from the archbishop's courts where it was due, the amercements imposed were to belong to the archbishop. This last clause refers to the special arrangement in the archbishop's hundreds of Calehill and Toltingtrough, to which men of the priory manors of Westwell, Little Chart and Meopham were to continue suit and the making of presentments of offenders, though the routine amercements imposed on the priory's tenants as a consequence were to belong to the priory.

For all these privileges, such as they were, the priory was to pay to the archbishop's treasurer the sum of forty marks a year, secured on the manor of Godmersham. This pension, or *census*, 'for having their Liberty' was still being duly paid in the sixteenth century.[1]

The composition between Archbishop Boniface and the bishop of Rochester followed the same pattern.[2] It was admitted that the bishop had the liberty of returning royal writs directed to his own tenants, but these too had to pass to and fro through the hands of the archbishop's bailiffs. The bishop kept his own principal court, just as the prior of Canterbury did, equivalent to that of the shire, in which cases begun by writ or *querela* could be heard and from which he took the emoluments, and only the 'apparent neglect or malice' of his bailiffs would allow the archbishop's officers to enter. Similarly, the bishop had the chattels of felons and fugitives among his tenants. But again, the archbishop stood in some respects between the bishop of Rochester and the king. If the bishop were amerced personally in a secular court the money went to the archbishop. Fines which had to be claimed at the Exchequer were claimed through the archbishop and delivered to the bishop of Rochester through the hands of the archbishop's officers. Pleas of unjust judgment against the court of the bishop of Rochester were to be terminated on the day of the shire court but outside the shire court itself and before the archbishop's steward, who was to associate with himself free and suitable men according to his choice. In pleas of the crown, prisoners and condemned men were handled under the surveillance of the archbishop's bailiffs, as in the Canterbury agreement. The whole arrangement was secured on the mutual security of the manors of Hayes and Northwood in Middlesex, but, in addition, the lord Abel, brother of the bishop of Rochester, was required to pledge his manor of Fordham that the bishop would keep the agreement. This arrangement was still working in the fifteenth century.[3]

The thirteenth-century earl of Gloucester was a greater neighbour than the bishop of Rochester or even the prior of Canterbury,

---

1. The payment appears in the royal vacancy accounts of the thirteenth and fourteenth centuries and the archbishop's receivers' rolls of the fifteenth, and a receipt acknowledging the payment in 1514 is preserved as Canterbury Cathedral Chartae Antiquae A 19a.
2. Lambeth MS. 1212, p. 143 *et seq*. Heard at Westminster before Richard of Cornwall and other magnates.
3. L.R. 96.

and the franchisal agreement between him and the archbishop reflects his eminence.[1] He was lord of the lowy of Tonbridge, a geographical enclave surrounding Tonbridge Castle and carefully perambulated and delimited at the time,[2] and he successfully claimed the right to have royal justices sent there for special session to hear all pleas that arose within the lowy's bounds. None the less, the earl held certain manors of the archbishop, and both earl and archbishop were lords of some tenants who resided within the other's territory, and the composition had to regulate this situation. In general, the earl agreed that he would recognize his sub-tenure of Tonbridge and Hadlow by sending his attorney to the first autumn court held by each new archbishop at Canterbury and at Otford. In return, the archbishop acknowledged that the earl had the usual return of writs and fines and amercements of his own tenants within his lowy, without any interference of the archbishop's officers unless the king sent a special written precept. The earl was also agreed to possess within his manors the liberties of *infangentheof*, view of frankpledge and emends of the assizes of bread and ale. But although the archbishop might not correct the negligence of the earl's bailiffs as easily as in the other cases, the same elaborate handing up and down of writs *gradatim* through the archbishop's bailiffs was to be employed. As to the archbishop's tenants within the lowy, they were to come to the archbishop's hundred courts, and any summonses or distraints on them were to be made by someone who resided in the lowy but held of the archbishop and was to be named archbishop's bedel for the occasion. Profits from their wrongdoings remained to the archbishop, and their arrest for felony was to be conducted through the archbishop's bailiffs, who were to keep them in Maidstone prison against the arrival of the royal justices. As a mark of face-saving the earl's bailiffs were to take formal delivery of such prisoners. The reverse procedure applied to the earl's men in the archbishop's territory, but in this case the archbishop's bailiff might decide they could not be accommodated in Maidstone prison, and if this happened the earl's bailiffs were to send them through the sheriff of Kent to the royal jail.

1. The composition embraced also the question of the earl's feudal service and his claim to be high steward and butler at the enthronement feast. See pp. 85-7 above, and references there.
2. Dumbreck, art. cit., p. 85, *n*. 4, above.

THE ARCHBISHOP'S OWN COURTS AND LOCAL RIGHTS

These thirteenth-century compositions belong to a stage when the courts of king, shire, hundred and manor were well developed and the interaction between them clearly regulated. This is more than can be said of the late eleventh century. Until the Conqueror removed ecclesiastical pleas from the hundred courts in about 1072, it seems that the archbishop or his representative sat in the shire court with the earl and dealt with serious pleas. Such cases naturally produced a revenue: *wites* or amercements from those convicted of crimes that could be paid for, the property of those executed for crimes that were capital. According to Domesday, there was some sort of arrangement between king and archbishop for dividing such profits. Half the goods of the condemned went to the king, and similarly half the penalty money for adultery wherever committed throughout Kent. A cognate text says that when adultery was punished, the king had what the man paid and the archbishop the money from the woman, except in the territory of the church of Canterbury, where the king had neither.[1]

With lesser crimes, there is no reason to think that the archbishop did not get the full revenues from convicts among his own men, in accordance with the terms of the writs already discussed. In one of the accounts of the trial on Penenden Heath[2] these lesser 'liberties and customs' of the church were rehearsed, and the text went on to add that within the lands of the church of Canterbury the king had three customs only: the 'emend' paid when a man of the archbishop dug up a royal road leading from city to city, when anyone cut down a tree so that it obstructed the royal road, and when anyone drew blood from or killed another on the royal road or 'did anything else that by no means is allowed to be done', provided that he was taken in the act. Otherwise the king could demand nothing, presumably because the culprit would have vanished into the archbishop's territory and would have to be sought and dealt with there. The same text substantiates the Domesday statement that the archbishop drew profit from the

---

1. *D.B.*, I, 1b; *Dom. Mon.*, p. 98. Evidently the birth of an illegitimate child was the normal occasion of this penalty, the 'childwite'.
2. *Studies Presented to F. M. Powicke*, pp. 23–4.

penalties for adultery and serious crime 'in all the lands of the king and the earl [of Kent]', but with the variation that he received either the whole or half 'the penalty called childwite' at all times, and the penalty for shedding blood during Lent.

The medieval archbishop did not deal with major crimes in his own courts, but he had some claim to take a special part in the trial of his own men before the royal judges. In 1195 tenants of both archbishop and prior when accused of crimes underwent the ordeal by water in the archbishop's ditch outside Westgate, Canterbury, in the presence of the itinerant justices.[1] Bracton in the thirteenth century said that a tenant of the archbishop accused of a plea of the crown should be tried in the king's court, but that at the moment before judgment was given the proceedings could, at the request of the archbishop's bailiffs, be transferred to the archbishop's court, judgment given there in the presence of two or three royal justices, and the man either freed or condemned. In 1277 it was the opinion of the county that judgments had been given in the archbishop's court in this manner when trial was by ordeal of fire or water, but that in felonies the accused went straight from the verdict of the hundred to the royal justices. The jurors thought that the archbishop had had custody of these prisoners by writ of the king and leave of the sheriff but not by any decision of the county or the itinerant justices. Anyhow, Bracton records that the archbishop was allowed this special privilege of participating in judgments on his men, and in 1304 there was certainly a case in which a murder was committed within the *curia* of Canterbury cathedral priory and the culprit was handed over by the steward of the priory's Liberty to be sentenced by the justices in eyre meeting within the archbishop's palace at Canterbury.[2] Whether felonious tenants of the archbishop in the country at large continued to hear their sentences from the lips of royal judges but in the presence of the archbishop's steward is possible but doubtful. They were regularly tried before the justices at Maidstone or Rochester or Canterbury.[3] The Eyre of 1313-14 sat in the great hall of the archbishop's palace at Canterbury.[4] At both Canterbury and Maidstone the archbishop's local ministers had to meet the expenses of the royal justices of jail

1. R. A. L. Smith, op. cit., citing Gervase of Canterbury, *Opera* (*R.S.*), I, pp. 530-1.
2. Smith, op. cit., p. 87.
3. L.R. 656, 657, 658, 659.
4. *Eyre of Kent*, II, pp. xv, 30.

delivery and construct the benches for them to sit on and the bar before which prisoners were brought.[1] On the civil side there is some evidence that the archbishop enjoyed a privileged position, since on 4 May 1201 John granted to Hubert Walter that he might hold Grand Assizes for gavelkind lands in his own court if he asked for some royal justice to be present. The resulting amercements were to belong to the archbishop if the suitors were his tenants, and to the king if they were not.[2]

After the Conquest, the shire courts were in no sense the archbishop's, though like other people he made use of them, some of his tenants were suitors there, and his influence was doubtless a strong one. Lanfranc's great claim against Odo of Bayeux and others was made before the shire court on Penenden Heath. An exchange of property in Pagham and Chichester between Archbishop Hubert Walter and Roger of Crimsham was sworn to both in the archbishop's court and in the full shire court of Sussex before the sheriff of Sussex and the archbishop's bailiff and steward and others.[3] A dispute between the archbishop and St Augustine's Abbey, Canterbury, about the possession of marsh and meadowland in Shirley was settled in detail in the shire court of Kent in 1240 by royal writ.[4] Men of free condition went regularly from the archbishop's estates to the shire, not only as heads of tithings, or *borghsalders*,[5] but also, apparently, men who at Wingham were called 'shiremen', as tenants of particular pieces of land called 'shirelands', and who numbered among their customary services the presentment of accidental deaths and other matters touching the king's crown.[6]

But the archbishop acquired, kept and even enlarged a 'public' jurisdiction in his hundred courts. Some slight evidence suggests that certain principal courts of the archbishop had a wider jurisdiction than his ordinary hundred courts. The composition of 1259 with the cathedral priory refers to the archbishop's principal courts at Canterbury and South Malling, and implies that they, like the prior's principal court, were the equivalent of shire courts; and

1. L.R. 661 (1319), 96 (1427–8).
2. LCM, XI, 10; Lambeth MS. 1212, p. 47. Such a case, however, was heard before the Justices in Eyre in 1313 (*Eyre of Kent*, II, p. 83).
3. Lambeth MS. 1212, p. 216.
4. ibid., p. 135.
5. Dean and Chapter of Canterbury MS. E 24, fo. 27.
6. ibid., fos. 7, 7v.

the royal charter of 1448 also alludes to these two main courts of the archbishopric's secular jurisdiction.[1] But there is little to show that their business was much different from that exercised in any of the archbishop's twice-yearly hundredal courts. Rolls of the Canterbury Palace court survive only from 1400, but they are the same in kind as for other hundred courts. No court-rolls have been found from South Malling, but a composition of 1266 between Archbishop Boniface and the abbot of Robertsbridge arranged that future abbots should make suit to the court of South Malling 'wherever it be held within the ambit of the manor of South Malling'.[2] This court was similar to that of Otford, another large and ancient manor which broke up into smaller manors. Sessions of its courts came to be held in the surrounding hamlets of Shoreham, Sevenoaks, Sevenoaks Weald, Crayford, Swanley, West Preston and Cliffe as well as at Otford Palace under the steward. The relative importance of the various courts was largely a matter of geographical convenience.

Although the royal charters conferred or confirmed what was later called hundredal jurisdiction, it is no good expecting to isolate the original grant of particular hundreds. In Kent especially, the numerous small hundreds were late in forming and unstable in their boundaries as the older lathe structure dissolved, new land was settled and local lords competed for rights. Where his tenants were, there the archbishop claimed and won recognition for his prescriptive rights. Miss Cam's dictum, 'some hundreds were born private', was above all true of the archbishopric.

In *Domesday Monachorum* of *c.* 1100, the manors of the archbishopric were usually described according to the hundred in which they lay. Bishopsbourne, for example, was said to be in the hundred of Barham (later called Kinghamford), Petham in that of Petham (later amalgamated into the hundred of Bridge and Petham),[3] and so on. Some were hundreds in themselves: *Stursaete* (later Westgate, Canterbury) was also the hundred of *Stursaete*,[4] and under Maidstone it was said 'this manor has a hundred in itself'.[5] In the extracts from the pipe-rolls of the later twelfth century made by the officers of the archbishop, he is frequently

---

1. *C.P.R. 1446-52*, p. 171. In the fifteenth century the steward at Canterbury Palace kept a record of amercements in a paper volume (L.R. 98).
2. Lambeth MS. 1212, p. 89.   3. *Dom. Mon.*, p. 83.
4. *Dom. Mon.*, pp. 81-2.   5. ibid., p. 86.

found receiving judicial profits from these hundreds,[1] and if one follows their history forward to the Hundred Rolls inquiry of 1274–5 it can be seen that most of the same hundreds then belonged in whole (or occasionally in part) to the archbishop himself.[2] But it would be wrong to suppose the archbishop's list of private hundreds was something fixed by the twelfth century. Some of those which on Domesday evidence might be supposed to be his were later not so, while many others, in which he had little or no demesne property, fell to his lot. If in 1100 there were eighteen hundreds that contained the archbishop's Kentish manors, by 1220 ten of these at least were contributing judicial profits to the archbishopric, but so were twenty others. From the inquiries of 1274–5 it is apparent that the archbishop then held eleven whole hundreds and parts of nineteen others in Kent as well as two whole hundreds in Sussex. The areas of his hundredal jurisdiction were in fact shifting and fragmented, and accrued to him in different ways, sometimes by clear purchase or grant but at other times by local prescription or unrecorded usurpation. Bexley in Domesday was explicitly placed in the hundred of *Aelmestrou* or *Helmestrei*, later called Ruxley. But in the custumal of 1285 it was said, 'there is no hundred here, and neither do the men go to any hundred',[3] though the proceedings of its court, known through later rolls, were obviously like those of any other manorial hundred. The Hundred Rolls reinforce this impression of local change and jurisdictional competition.[4]

Hundred courts were often farmed out as pieces of real estate, like the hundred of Bridge and the half-hundred of Eastry, leased out by Henry of Malmains for £32, though the jurors said the old price had been £10. Arrangements like this were the work of private speculators. There was a constant tendency too for lords to compel their tenants to stop away from other people's courts and attend their own, and this not only reduced the value of the hundred courts thus deserted but helped towards the obliteration of the ancient Kentish lathes. The jurors of 1275 noted, for instance, that in recent years the hundred of Bewsborough had

1. Lambeth MS. 1212, pp. 412–15: '*De amerciamentis hominum archiepiscopi ad ipsum archiepiscopatum pertinentibus.*'
2. H. M. Cam, *The Hundred and the Hundred Rolls* (1930), Appendix IV.
3. Dean and Chapter of Canterbury MS. E 24, fo. 91v. For Bexley business, see p. 306 below.
4. *Rot. Hundr.*, I, pp. 200–36; II (1), p. 211.

been separated from the lathe of St Augustine, Wingham from the lathe of Haddling (another name for St Augustine's lathe), Felborough and Tenterden hundreds also from their lathes. Changes like this in jurisdictional geography were more rapid when the central government was distracted and local figures powerful. But hundreds were also sometimes transferred by formal transactions. One good example was Archbishop Pecham's re-acquisition in 1284 of his Domesday manor of Wrotham 'with its hundred, liberties and customs' from the fee-farmers.[1] Under these farmers the men of that manor [explained an inquiry of 1273] had been used to make execution of judgments of thieves convicted in that manor and hundred before any justices, buying ropes and cords and hanging such thieves and homicides, and answering if any escaped, and having under colour of this liberty and heavy farm all the goods and chattels of condemned thieves and fugitives, and year, day and waste of the land of such men, and all amercements of all men of the manor and hundred before all justices. . . .[2]

Another leading example of acquisition was the transfer to the archbishop of the Seven Hundreds of the Weald. These were Blackbourne, Selbrittenden, Rolvenden, Cranbrook, Barclay, Tenterden and Barnfield. Once they had formed a great area of 'denns', connected with the royal hundred of Milton by Sittingbourne. Gradually the woodland was cleared and settled by the men of different lords, the archbishop among them. As an administrative unit, it had a chequered history. In the early thirteenth century, it was for a time farmed for £5 to Willikin of the Weald by the sheriff of Kent,[3] but ultimately the archbishop got a royal lease of it for £2, somewhat to the indignation of the men of Kent, who considered that Archbishop Boniface had forced the issue and was making a handsome profit.[4]

Changes like this explain why successive lists of the archbishop's hundreds differ from each other. The latest of the series was copied about 1350 into the Register of Archbishop Islip,[5] evidently from an earlier roll. Although incomplete, it is of great interest, for it made a systematic effort to show the structure of the archbishop's Liberty in Kent. It was headed 'Roll of hundreds and borghs and

1. Lambeth MS. 1212, p. 121.
2. C.Cl.R. 1272–9, p. 23.
3. Rot. Hundr., p. 214.
4. ibid., p. 217.
5. Reg. Islip, fos. 96–9.

appurtenances of hundreds and borghs in the county of Kent which are of the Liberty of the archbishop of Canterbury'. The information is arranged under lathes. Within each of these are shown the hundreds which composed it in which the archbishop possessed rights. In turn, every hundred is dissected into its territorial borghs, and even these are seen sometimes to be shared in respect of jurisdiction by the archbishop and others. Not only, therefore, might a hundred be described as a half or a third or a sixth the archbishop's, but so too a borgh, especially in the wealden regions, where particular houses might be assigned to the Liberty. In this way, the scattered nature of the Liberty is strikingly illustrated, with its hundreds, borghs and houses dispersed in a haphazard fashion. It suggests that a large part was played in the successful running of a private jurisdiction by the local knowledge and forceful characters of its officials, who knocked on doors and made sure the inhabitants were aware of the courts in which their attendance was expected.

The work of the archbishop's local courts becomes fairly clear after the late thirteenth century, but is obscure before then. They were held by the bailiffs, who swore an oath on taking office, the first specific clause of which was that they would 'loyally hold the leets and courts in my bailiwick at the due times and usual places and make them profitable to the lord according to right and reason and the custom of the manor'.[1] On 7 October 1275 Archbishop Kilwardby issued from Otford a set of instructions to his stewards and bailiffs which ordered them to stop fining suitors for formal mistakes in the pleadings, and to expunge from their records any references to this bad old custom of *beupleyder*.[2] General strictures against 'miskenning' had already been made in the Provisions of Westminster of 1259, and now Kilwardby went on to explain and justify its prohibition in terms more pastoral than legal: '. . . for we desire and order you who are judges to hold simple courts and instruct those who do not know how to plead in the telling of the truth; and for us it is enough to inquire and learn the truth of what you have to judge, no matter in what words . . .'. Nor, he added, were his judges to take any present from either party or organize unjust exactions like scotales, even for the benefit of the

1. L.R. 2068. In the thirteenth century the oath seems to have been taken in French.
2. Lambeth MS. 1212, p. 423; cf. Provisions of Westminster, para. 5 (W. Stubbs, *Select Charters* (9th ed.), pp. 391–2).

archbishopric, 'for these are inventions of the devil'; and they were to keep about them a copy of these instructions and to carry them out.

Such watchfulness was not superfluous. The civil and criminal pleas heard in the archbishop's courts, though small matters by comparison with what went on before the king's justices, affected the tenants frequently and seriously in their daily lives. Land deals were ratified or notified by twelfth-century archbishops in their hundred courts,[1] and even those *minora placita* like the assizes of bread or ale, sometimes thought of as no more than the modern purchase of a trader's licence, seem vital enough when chance records illustrate their practical impact. In 1280 a dispute flared up in Southwark, a rowdy quarter where the archbishop had an area of jurisdiction.[2] His bailiff, one Alan Panyt, complained that he had been arrested and put into the stocks for a whole night by the king's bailiff, who had also been in the habit of snatching and breaking his wand of office as he went about the town. Alan further said that although the archbishop had the jurisdiction there over the assize of bread, the king's bailiff had none the less stopped a woman who was carrying some bread she had just bought, and taken it off to weigh it. The baker who sold it was a tenant of the archbishop, and as a result the royal bailiff was excommunicated and the quarrel brought before the king in parliament, where each side told its story at some length. A jury was empanelled and found that there had in fact been a complaint by a spicer and his wife against the archbishop's bailiff. This official had then been arrested by the king's bailiff and clapped into the stocks, even though he had at once found pledges for himself and should have been set free. The royal bailiff was therefore committed to jail. On the other hand, the jury agreed that the king's bailiff had (justifiably) seized the bread in the shop and not from the woman purchaser, and that the archbishop's bailiff had never in the past gone round carrying a wand of office except on court days or when he was

1. A. Saltman, *Theobald*, nos. 34, 35 and 51 for the hundreds of Westgate and Teynham; Lambeth MS. 1212, p. 206, for a ratification by Archbishop Richard before the hundred of Pagham. Some of Lanfranc's claims to recover lands were to be determined in the hundreds, see p. 37 above.
2. *Rotuli Parliamentorum hactenus inediti*, ed. H. G. Richardson and G. O. Sayles (Camden Third Series, LI, 1935), pp. 8–11. The assize of bread was not invariably a mere excuse for taxation. In the early fifteenth century, for example, it was said to produce nothing at Groombridge Fair near Otford 'because the bread weighed enough' (L.R. 839, 844).

issuing summonses to court. The disturbance was settled in the light of these findings, and no more was heard, but it illuminates for a moment the passions as well as the formalities of these small-town franchises: the sharp practice, the self-importance, the quick rivalries. Later in the Middle Ages the Liberty of Southwark was usually leased to some 'valet of the archbishop's chamber' in return for a rent. This gentleman levied the fines and amercements on his own account but had to answer to the steward of the Liberty for the king's debts.[1]

Survival of rolls from the archbishop's own local courts begins from the late thirteenth century, sparsely and unevenly but in quantity enough to portray their character. As in other liberties, the private hundreds, known variously as the 'great' courts or the 'lawdays' as well as the 'hundreds', were held twice-yearly, in October and April, and the ordinary or 'small' courts nominally every three weeks, though in practice somewhat less often. View of frankpledge, in theory a regalian right, usually took place in the hundred, but it was quite possible when convenience dictated to organize views in the remoter localities where the archbishop had tenants. Thus some of the tenants of Sevenoaks Weald had their view with their *halimote* at Shipbourne and others a *halimote* at Penshurst, while the hundred of Somerden itself was taken at Chiddingstone. In most places the manorial court and the hundred had the same venue and were distinguishable only by the rather greater number of suitors at the latter and the larger amount of money collected. On a view day the one court simply succeeded the other and their proceedings could be noted, albeit separately, on the same roll.

To the casual eye, the range of business may look both narrow and unvarying. These country courts of the Middle Ages served a function now taken up in part by the post-office counter as well as by the police court, but to the modern scene one has to add in imagination a sense of chronic minor subjection, actualized in the need to walk or ride to the meeting-place month after month and lend one's presence to a series of tedious and even costly formalities. Yet each court had an individual character, now visible

1. Reg. Witleseye, fo. 66v. (1347, to Ralph de Marcheford); Reg. Courtenay, fo. 66v. (1386, to John Haukyn); Reg. Arundel, ii, fo. 126v. (1410, to John James); Reg. Stafford, fo. 51v. (1452, to Henry fitzJohn).

only dimly, but shaped by the problems of its particular locality. To provide a few examples is all that can be done to describe the diversity within the sameness.

An 'estreat roll', or list of fines and amercements extracted from the tale of court proceedings, is tacked on to the reeve of Bexley's account of 1292, and shows how the year's 'profits and perquisites' were made up.[1] Here in descending order of financial importance are the items:

Heriots after death of tenants	£2	14s.	0d.
Breaches of the assizes of bread or ale	£1	8s.	0d.
Illegal cutting of wood, hedges or other men's corn		8s.	6d.
Various defaults and trespasses, such as absence from court		7s.	4d.
Failure to prosecute actions		6s.	6d.
Reliefs on succession to holdings		6s.	5d.
The 'common fine'[2] from the two borghs		6s.	3d.
Payment for having an inquiry made		2s.	0d.
Entry fine		1s.	0d.
For unlawful removal of a building on the land of delinquent's brother		1s.	0d.
For drawing blood		1s.	0d.
Failure to produce pledges			6d.
For contempt of court			6d.
Unauthorized making of a right of way			6d.
Non-payment of a relief			6d.
Non-payment of a rent			3d.

Not far away was the large manor of Otford, where the three-weekly court in the later fourteenth century might deal with about a hundred items of business. That held on 14 December 1388, to take a random example,[3] heard one stage or another of thirty-three pleas of debt, fourteen of trespass, thirteen queries about changes in land-holdings, received eight fealties and reliefs after new acquisitions of land, dealt with six pleas of covenant, three of detinue, recorded two re-apportionments of gavelkind yokelands

1. L.R. 236 m. 2.
2. Maitland thought the common fine might be a relic of the lord's tallage on his unfree tenants (*Select Pleas in Manorial Courts* (Selden Society), I, p. 23n.). But in the archbishop's courts, where it was regularly claimed from the borghs, it was alternatively called the fine for concealment (*de concelamento*), and may have been the general fine for all murders which the hundreds were said at the Eyre of Kent in 1313 to pay in lieu of the former 100s. for each murder (*Eyre of Kent*, I, p. 81; cf. p. 57). 3. L.R. 804 m. 1.

for the purpose of fixing rents and services, and took one heriot, and one amercement for default of court. But the progress of business was abysmally slow. It began with the essoins—legitimate excuses for absence vouched for by someone present. Every suit had at least three stages, of which no two ever seemed to occur on the same day: the initiation of the plea, when the plaintiff's case was written down in outline, the appointment of a jury to inquire into the truth of the matter, and the return of that jury's verdict. Between these stages innumerable delays were normal, since plaintiffs often failed to proceed with prosecutions, defendants could not be got to court, and jurors were individually elusive or collectively tardy. Against this incomprehension of urgency, distraint was a weak weapon.[1] A court at Otford must have lasted all day and seen perhaps half a dozen verdicts. The procedure was a curious mixture of old and new, amateur and professional work, with the emphasis on the ancient, the formal and the unchanging. It is true that the recurrence of the same men acting as pledges suggests professionals at work, or that an unauthorized alienation into mortmain would bring a quick reference to the archbishop's council,[2] and that the courts witnessed the new and flexible techniques of the enfeoffment to use.[3] But in general the business was conducted by the familiar body of more or less rustic suitors, meeting in the ancient places, like 'the open space by the gate of Penshurst churchyard' for the Penshurst *halimote*.[4] The gentry who owed suit by reason of their local land purchases tended to stay away and pay the fines for relaxation of suit. The same old group of elected 'affeerers' continued to assess the traditional penalties, and tenants sued for debts or trespasses might defend themselves with three or six oath-helpers.[5] In the business of the hundred

1. The ancient franchise of 'withernam' possessed in his hundreds by the archbishop gave remedy against over-harsh distraint, but from the thirteenth century royal justice itself was quite quick to protect men against distraints that really hurt. A bailiff of the archbishop, who kept two ploughbeasts for a week when he might have distrained by something else, was in 1313 committed to jail till he had paid a fine of 40s. (*Eyre of Kent*, I, p. 132).
2. P.R.O. Delisle and Dudley MSS., Roll 459 (Bexley, 25 October 1526: a tileworks acquired by the prioress of Dartford).
3. ibid. (28 April 1514). The tenants declared that William Hall (a yeoman) had during his life enfeoffed John Shelley, esquire, both of Bexley, with all his lands in the lordship.   4. *IPM*, IX, 183.
5. e.g. John Bocher of Sevenoaks, sued for 30s. by Sir Thomas Colpeper in the court of Otford in 1389, wagered his law and had a day '*ad faciendum legem se septima manu*' (L.R. 804 m. 3); but there are more examples *tertia* or *quarta manu* (e.g. m. 5).

courts, the subject-matter was somewhat more extensive, but the persons involved little different. The borghs came represented by their elected *decennarius*, or 'borghsalder', and twelve men, who paid the common fine, presented offences and reported events that touched the archbishop's liberties, like the wreck of wherries on the north Kent coast or the washing up of porpoises or other 'great fish'.

Away to the west, the archbishop's Sussex courts were going through the same motions, save that the flavour of unfreedom was here stronger and more en uring. At Tangmere, in the 1430s,[1] men were fined for dwelling outside the lordship without licence and for failing to repair their houses, and entry fines at 5s. for half a virgate, or even three acres, were a much more prominent feature than in Kent, where succession in gavelkind was by 'fine certain' in something like ½d. an acre.[2]

The courts of the manor of Wimbledon present a different picture again.[3] During the later Middle Ages, if not before, both views and little courts were held, among other places, at Putney, and proceedings were dominated by the problems of the common. Arable farming had clearly been suffering in favour of pasture, and the impulse towards enclosure was becoming strong. The Dean of St Paul's and Sir Henry Wyatt were among those who overburdened the common with their sheep, and the court was worried about the excess number of cattle, mangy horses and unrung pigs roaming about. There were many attempts in the area, organized in court, to improve enclosures. In 1481 woodland and waste land in Wimbledon, 'which anciently were arable and now for many years have been overgrown and choked with brambles, thorn and furze', were granted out in inheritance to five tenants in severalty. Other enclosures were being made either with or without authority at Hampton, Putney, Mortlake and Sheen. Some individualists went too far. In 1512 and 1513, Walter Crumwell, alias Smyth, said to be Thomas Cromwell's father, was in trouble for sub-letting common land and for 'fraudulently erasing evidences and terriers of the land in divers particulars, to the disturbance and disinheritance of the lord and his tenants'.

The archbishop's local courts concerned themselves with changes

1. L.R. 995–1000. 2. cf. L.R. 233 (Bexley, 1496).
3. *Extracts From the Court Rolls of the Manor of Wimbledon from 1461 to 1864* (privately printed 1866: available in Wimbledon Public Library), esp. pp. 24–82.

in land-tenure among the tenants, but as was explained on an earlier page this was largely a formality running parallel with the busy, continuous exchange of private deeds.[1] To the men and women of the communities, the courts must have appeared most prominently as places where penalties were prepared or executed, in the loss of money, liberty or life itself. These deserve a moment's reflection.

It is extremely hard to be certain how severely the amercements bore upon individuals, and no generalization is safe over the whole period and social spectrum, however strongly it may be argued that twelfth-century amercements were arbitrary and ruthless.[2] There is some evidence that the archbishop's local courts measured their penalties to the delinquent's capacity to pay. Beside the traditional twopences, sixpences and shillings, Sir Henry Wyatt's amercement in £10, with the threat of £20 next time, for his trespass in putting too many sheep on Putney Heath seems very severe.

Imprisonment for a defined term as a punishment in itself was not used. The idea of 'serving time' is only practicable when the public authority can apply funds to ensure that convicts in large numbers over a long period neither die nor escape. In general, medieval men and women were only imprisoned as a temporary and secondary measure: to hold them before trial or execution, to compel them to answer or plead or pay debts, or, in the case of convicted clerks, to stay in custody indefinitely or until they could win their release through compurgation. When somebody was arrested on the manors he was kept locally until he could be passed on. In the custumal of 1283–5, the tasks of jailer were laid upon particular manorial holdings. At Hernhill, Graveney and the Isle of Grain, all in north Kent, it was said

. . . if anyone is arrested for robbery or for committing another delict against the lord archbishop, [the cotters] ought to keep him imprisoned in the archbishop's *curia* at their own expense, or to lead him to jail if they get the order.[3]

At Westgate, Canterbury,

. . . when any outsider is arrested for some ill-doing, or felony, the following shall guard the prisoner by night: the heirs of Stacy of

1. See above, pp. 151–3.
2. A. L. Poole, *Obligations of Society in the XII and XIII Centuries* (1946), ch. v.
3. Dean and Chapter of Canterbury MS. E 24, fos. 33v., 44, 46v.

Hackington in Little Mill, the heirs of Henry of Langham in Samuels Mill, the heirs of Richard of Hackington and William Diford in Shepfotes Mill. And the miller of Westgate Mill shall guard them by day. In this way the eight shall answer for the peril of the night and the other for the peril of the day. And the lord shall find iron and fetters for the prisoner. And at the next hundred court they shall be discharged of the duty of custody, and if the man is re-imprisoned for any reason he shall remain on the lord archbishop's charge.[1]

Similar instances of local custody in mills or manorial buildings are not hard to find,[2] and they explain the situation graphically. It was most important to prevent escapes, and if they occurred the negligent were heavily amerced. This fear of escape rather than deliberate inhumanity was the reason for the fetters.

When a suspect had been arrested and presented at the next hundred for felony, he was, if the verdict went against him, led to a proper jail to await the royal justices. It belonged to the archbishop's Liberty to possess his own prisons, and of these most is known about the one at Maidstone.[3] Here, in the early fourteenth century, men and women from all parts of the archbishop's estate were kept under the charge of the jailer. They were allowed $\frac{1}{2}d$. a day each as alms for their keep, and year by year the account of the reeve of Maidstone was charged with these sums, and with the expenses of the justices who came and delivered the jail about twice a year. The costs amounted to about £20 per annum. At any one time between thirty and forty prisoners were lodged in Maidstone jail. Most of these were men, and perhaps a third of them were convicted clerks. The average stay in jail for all types of prisoner was on a very approximate reckoning about six months. From time to time clerks purged themselves and were set free. During the autumn and sometimes upon other occasions during the year, the justices of jail delivery heard the cases against the lay prisoners. The results are not recorded in the reeve's accounts, but that of 1297 noted that many 'went quit'. Sometimes prisoners had to be sent elsewhere. The movement was authorized by the bailiff of Maidstone, not the jailer. On these occasions, carts were hired and

1. ibid., fo. 23v.
2. At Otford, whence some Sussex men escaped from the archbishop's prison (*C.Cl.R. 1227–31*, p. 260); archbishop's prison at Uckfield (ibid. *1259–61*, p. 163); prisoners guarded in 1236–7 at Meopham and brought to the county court and then to jail at Otford (L.R. 1193).
3. See esp. L.R. 657–65.

escorts engaged, some mounted and others to ride on the carts. When prisoners were taken to the royal justices at Rochester, they were lodged in a building hired for the purpose by the archbishop, and in 1314 the purchase of an iron bar for the women's room was noted in the account. Maidstone jail itself appears to have been grim. Repairs were carried out with stone and ironwork. Chains, rivets and keys were bought. In the terrible famine year of 1317, numbers of prisoners rose, and no fewer than seventy-one died there. The cost of 1s. 11d. for burying them suggests a mass grave. Sixteen more died in 1318. In 1336 four men were hired for seven days to clear out the *camera secreta* (probably the privy) with wooden forks and scoops by the light of candles, and were paid the high rate of 6d. a day each with a bonus of 4d. between them. After this the jail costs disappear from the reeve of Maidstone's accounts, but reappear in the fifteenth century on those of the steward of the Liberty.

Judicial hanging was common but comes to the historian's notice chiefly when the value of a felon's chattels are entered in the accounts. A curious insouciance often leaves the dead man unnamed: 'a certain robber', 'certain unknown malefactors'. Since the archbishop had the liberty of gallows concomitant with his right to the convict's goods, it was his men who performed the executions, sometimes his ploughmen acting according to the custom of the manor, at other times hired men. The steward of the Liberty in the fifteenth century was paying 11s. 8d. a year to a hangman (*patibulator*) and his mate by contract for executions carried out at Penenden.[1] Though the judgments were the king's, there is the sense communicated in the extract above, referring to robberies and delicts against the archbishop, that the felonious offences were against the lord of the Liberty more directly than against the lord of the realm, or the community, or private people. But occasionally too there is a glimpse of local unwillingness to destroy a compatriot who was felt not to have been locally condemned, as in 1274 when a man from the hundred of Teynham was arrested and appealed in the hundred for robbery, and adjudged to death, and the men of the hundred claimed to do judgment on him as it belonged to the Liberty of the church of Canterbury; but when he had been delivered over to them they

1. L.R. 96.

were unwilling to execute him unless he were appealed of the same fact elsewhere in the hundred also.[1] Despite the frequent occurrence of capital punishment, and the common modern view that 'medieval' is a synonym for 'barbarous', it is difficult to think that the people of these communities were quite as heedless of human life as those of modern collectivist or frontier societies. It was, after all, a form of awe that gave the custom of deodand its meaning: that the animal or object instrumental in an accidental death must be given to God in the way of pious uses. This is consonant with seignorial arrogance and even a life of violence but not with mere brutishness. The custom slipped into a seignorial profit, but almost undue trouble was taken to collect it, as when in 1298 the steward of the Liberty claimed at the Exchequer the value of a certain tree that had killed one of the archbishop's men.[2] A sense of the *mens rea*, too, protected the lunatic from the consequences of his disordered actions, as when Stephen le Pope of Bexley was charged in 1313 with the death of Joan Shepey, his maidservant.[3]

He comes and, asked how he pleads, disputes the death and all, and pleads not guilty and for good and ill places himself upon the country. And the jury of the hundred of Ruxley say in their oath that Stephen killed Joan, but that he was at that time raving mad, namely, on the . . . night of which he killed her [22 June]. And, asked how long the said Stephen had been mad before he killed Joan, they say that on [that day] madness seized him, and he remained mad for three weeks afterwards. And on that Friday, after he became mad, he was in his garden and there made images of wood and stones and worshipped them as gods, and that same night before midnight he killed Joan. . . . Therefore let him remain in custody.

THE MONEY VALUE OF THE LIBERTY

To a seventeenth-century steward, the value of the Liberty was chiefly to himself, and we may reckon that in the later Middle Ages also a handsome proportion of the net revenue was eaten up in the fees of stewards, bailiffs and lesser officials. It is impossible,

1. *Rot. Hundr.*, I, p. 210.   2. *Reg. Winchelsey*, p. 282.
3. Cited by W. H. Mandy in *Woolwich and District Antiquarian Society, Annual Reports and Transactions*, XXIII (1920–5), pp. 25–37.

however, to evaluate the Liberty in money terms that are anything like comprehensive or accurate. The most that can be done is to produce certain figures that offer an impression of the Steward's scale of activity, and of the financial importance of the archbishop's local courts.

The difficulty lies in the form of the records. As far back as one can see, the archbishop got money from his Liberty in two main ways. The first was from all those incidents that, though directly collected, had to be accounted for through the royal Exchequer: amercements of his men before royal justices, chattels of felons and fugitives, and so forth. The second was the immediate levying of 'pleas and perquisites' from his own courts in manor and hundred. Until the later thirteenth century, all these revenues were noted together on the general pipe-rolls of the see, but since only two (incomplete) examples of these are extant it is useless to expect firm figures from this source. There are also entries on the royal pipe-rolls during vacancies in the archbishopric to show receipts from pleas and perquisites of courts and other sources which may be included within 'the Liberty', but these accounts are for irregular periods and are too incomplete to be valuable in a statistical sense. After the late thirteenth century, the issues of local courts were noted on the manorial account rolls and treated as manorial revenues, and here there are fortunately quite enough figures to give a clear idea of the courts' fiscal importance. The steward of the Liberty's own accounts survive in only a few instances and are all from the fifteenth century, and these, while extremely interesting in themselves, can in general only demonstrate that the Liberty's revenue was fluctuating and modest. In addition to these cautionary remarks, it must be borne in mind that the sums from court perquisites and from allowances claimed at the Exchequer were gross ones, from which some kind of deduction would have to be made before the archbishop's own profit from them could be decided.

We may turn first to the more uncertain of the franchisal profits —the allowances made to the archbishop at the Exchequer. Considering the eagerness with which the archbishops' clerks minuted their claims, it is surprising how little attention they paid to the actual sums involved. In the twelfth century the chief subject-matter of claims consisted of the proceeds of the *murdrum* fine in the various hundreds and the chattels of those who fled from justice. For all such claims as they were noted out of the pipe-rolls, the following sums allowed emerge:[1] 1174–5, £1 17s. 11d.; 1175–6, 3s.; 1176–7(?), £7 15s. 4d.; 1190–1, 5s.; 1195–6, £6 13s. 8d.; 1196–7, £17 3s. 4d.; 1197–8, £11 10s. 2d.; 1200–1, £35 19s. 2d.; 1202–3, £5; 1219–20, £26 11s. 4d.; and then from 1220–1, which includes the Eyre of Benedict, bishop of Rochester, the more impressive sum of £203 13s. 4d. In general, it would seem that the archbishop took much trouble to stand up for his franchisal profits, partly because it was a question of dignity with a more than economic significance, partly because if the principle were upheld there would be worthwhile windfalls in some years, and partly because their fiscal importance was in any case tending to increase as population grew and judicial business became more active.

At the other end of the Middle Ages, the accounts of the steward of the Liberty present a small series of allowances that are just as uneven in their incidence. It will be clearest to present a digest of these accounts in tabular form, as in Table 7.[2] The short lesson of this table is that the fiscal importance of the Liberty was both varying and relatively small. Wardships were in reality a feudal revenue and were by no means all accounted for by the steward, and they may properly be discounted in the present context, though they were often of considerable value, as Roger North himself recalled of the days 'before the Court of Wards was taken away'. The value of wardships forms an independent subject of great interest that has not been much studied for the medieval period. Otherwise, the main profitability of the archbishop's Liberty was in one way or another from the amercements and fines imposed upon men and women before the king's courts; the chattels of felons and fugitives may with consistency be added under this head. A moderate income continued also to be derived from the sums paid according to the thirteenth-century compositions by the prior of Canterbury and the bishop of Rochester and a few lesser but similar 'farms' in return for the right to exercise local franchises. After all expenses had been met, the archbishop in the fifteenth century might expect to receive something like £40 or £50 a year through the steward of his Liberty.

Income from the manorial and hundred courts was rather more constant. Naturally, the courts of some localities were more pro-

1. Lambeth MS. 1212, pp. 412–15. 2. L.R. 95–9.

Table 7. Receipts and disbursements of the Steward of the Liberty's receipts

RECEIPTS

	Year ending													
	1419			1427			1479			1489			1491		
	£	s.	d.	£	s.	d.	£	s.	d.	£	s.	d.	£	s.	d.
Wardships and feudal reliefs[1]	122	14	4¾	11	13	4		nil		11	13	4	11	4	2½
Farms of land in archbishop's hand by escheat	0	11	2	26	0	8	0	9	6	0	9	6	0	10	6
Fines and amercements in various counties	176	9	7	85	13	9	9	10	4	9	7	6	23	6	2
Ditto, before steward and marshal of the king's household	2	8	0		—			—			—			—	
Annual farms for the franchises of the prior of Canterbury, bishop of Rochester, etc.[2]	33	6	8	4	6	8	32	17	8	32	18	8	35	0	10
Perquisites of courts directly under the steward (Canterbury, Otford and Northfleet)	7	11	4	11	5	10	7	16	9	8	10	9	6	19	10
Chattels of felons and fugitives; and waifs and strays	9	17	7	9	14	4	25	10	9	28	8	1	8	11	4½
Wreck of the sea		—			—			—		3	15	0		—	
Deodands and goods of suicides		—		0	0	0½		—			—		0	6	0

1. Not comprehensive figures. Some wardships were granted out and escaped the steward's account.
2. The prior paid his forty marks direct to the archbishop in 1428.

DISBURSEMENTS

	Year ending													
	1419			1427			1479			1489			1491		
	£	s.	d.	£	s.	d.	£	s.	d.	£	s.	d.	£	s.	d.
Fees and expenses of the officials of the Liberty	29	6	8	34	7	2	32	10	5	29	11	5	29	12	6
Alms for prisoners in Maidstone jail	7	4	6	3	7	10½	1	10	5	1	10	5	3	1	0½
Other costs of prisons and prisoners	0	6	8	1	3	4½	7	8	8	0	18	4	0	11	9
Costs of instruments of punishment in various places		—		3	13	1	0	10	6		—			—	
Expenses of Justices delivering Maidstone jail	8	6	4	8	9	10½	2	13	4		—			—	
Wages of Justices of the Peace	2	3	4	11	12	0		—			—			—	
Gratuities and expenses at the Exchequer		—		2	0	0	1	10	0	1	11	4	1	11	4
Outside payments[1]	23	6	8	0	3	0	0	18	0		—			—	
Payments to the archbishop	65	6	8		—		38	18	0	40	3	4	27	19	2

1. e.g. repairs to properties in feudal custody; cost of parchment and ink for accounts.

ductive than those of others. That of Aldington averaged nearly £11 a year, and that of Northfleet £5 or £6, as against the £2, more or less, that issued from less populous manors. Long series of accounts exist for the bailiwicks of Aldington and Otford, and from these it is possible to calculate the average annual value of the courts held within the constituent manors. These figures can be compared with their counterparts in the *Valor Ecclesiasticus* of 1535. If this is done, it appears that the average perquisites of manorial courts during the fifteenth and early sixteenth centuries were always higher than those recorded in 1535. The amount by which the *Valor Ecclesiasticus* figures fell below those from the ministers' accounts varies from manor to manor, but on an average the *Valor* court revenues were thirty per cent lower than those of the previous century. It is not necessary to throw doubts upon the honesty of the *Valor*. The survey was made with close reference to local accountants. For instance, in the account of the reeve of Sevenoaks in 1536–7, a debt against a farmer was marked 'Memo that he has a discharge of this rent and it is not charged in the *valor* made for the lord king'.[1] The *Valor Ecclesiasticus* may have been made rather conservatively, but it showed a return of court revenues lower than the average of the past century because court profits were in fact tending to decline after about 1500. This is borne out in numbers of places, of which Northfleet and Bexley are examples. Sometimes the decline starts only a few years before 1535. The reason is most likely an increased reluctance on the part of suitors to attend.

In the *Valor Ecclesiasticus* the sum of manorial pleas and perquisites is £143 19s. 6¼d. By extrapolation it is possible to estimate the revenue from the manorial courts in the fifteenth century as approximately £200 a year. This form of revenue amounted, then, to about four per cent of the see's gross income in 1535, and about six per cent during the fifteenth century. The proportion is not impressive when set against the dignified apparatus of 'the Liberty', but it is well to recall an earlier observation, that the Liberty meant more than money, and that in any case it supported stewards and bailiffs whose dignity and wealth were enhanced by their office and who served the archbishopric with their influence and expertise, though not perhaps giving it as much as, on balance, they took from it.

1. P.R.O. Mins. Accts Hen. VIII, no. 1698.

CHAPTER 8

Cranmer and the end of the medieval temporalities

The year which saw the suppression of the lesser religious houses marked also the end of the Canterbury estates as the Middle Ages had known them. The revolution was rapid though not instantaneous. Between 1536 and 1546 the larger number of the manors that had for centuries supported the archbishopric were granted or exchanged away and in their place other lands and revenues were made over to Cranmer, so that the composition of the temporalities was entirely changed and their total value undoubtedly lessened.

It is easier to follow in detail what happened than to see exactly why Cranmer was forced into this course of action. Needless to say, the age was not the first in which particular church estates had been envied and seized, nor the first in which theoretical attacks upon ecclesiastical endowments had been launched. Wulfred, Dunstan, Lanfranc, Walter and Arundel had in their times and ways defended the lordship against a variety of secularizers thrown up by changing circumstances. But in the 1530s the assault was more formidable than ever before because the king, for all his personal friendship with the archbishop, was not on the side of those who defended church property or thought it rightly inalienable. He, and those who formed policy with him, were determined upon a fundamental scheme of secularization, and beside the dissolution of the monasteries a certain free handling of episcopal lands appeared a small enough thing. The threat to bishops' temporalities was indeed more drastic than the eventuality. In the early 1530s foreign ambassadors were reporting major plans for disendowment. In 1531 the Venetian ambassador thought that Henry was going to annex all ecclesiastical revenues to the crown.[1] In January 1533 Chapuys told Charles V that Cranmer would renounce all the temporalities of his see to the king as a good way to force the others to do the same,[2] and two months later heard from the king's own lips that he intended to repair the damage done by John in making England tributary to the pope, and that his very coronation oath bound him to 'reunite to the crown the goods which the churchmen held of it' and which his predecessors had not been able to alienate.[3] By November 1534 a coherent plan had been thought up to create stipendiary bishoprics.[4] The document in which this is embodied looked forward to an act of parliament to provide that 'the archbishop of Canterbury for maintenance of his estate shall have 2,000 marks yearly and not above, and that all the residue of the possessions appertaining to the archbishopric may be made sure to the king's highness and his heirs for the defence of his realm and maintenance of his royal estate'. Other clauses assigned 1,000 marks a year to the archbishop of York and to bishoprics which already possessed an income of that amount, and outlined schemes for the royal acquisition of the first-fruits of all benefices, of all the property of small religious houses and some of that of large ones, of collegiate churches and of archdeaconries, together with certain compulsory contributions from the clergy. The paper also provided that all the franchises and liberties belonging to ecclesiastical bodies should revert to the crown, with the exception of 'courts baron and leets'.

No bill for such a destruction of the bishoprics appears to have been introduced. As everyone knows, much of the programme was fulfilled, but the radical policy of stipendiary bishoprics was dropped. Had Edward VI lived longer, or Northumberland not fallen, the tale might have been different: annexations of property in the dioceses of London, Winchester, Durham and Gloucester might have led on to a general liquidation of bishopric

1. *Venetian Calendar*, IV, p. 694.
2. *L. & P.*, VI, p. 89; cf. ibid., p. 180.
3. ibid., p. 235.
4. Brit. Mus. Cottonian MS. Cleopatra E IV, fos. 207–8 (new foliation); cf. F. C. Dietz, *English Government Finance 1485–1558* (1921), pp. 112–14, 200–2.

endowments. But the process was reversed by Mary and stabilized under Elizabeth, so that Archbishop Parker was able to remain lord of rent-rolls and feudal casualties.

The attack upon the lordship of Canterbury owed less to any theory of church property than to cupidity. Henry VIII liked to possess what pleased him personally, and it is hardly to be expected that a fancy which would not be denied an Anne Boleyn or a Katherine Howard would fail to arrange the acquisition of Otford and Knole. Nor was an eye for desirable landed property unique to the king in that age of rising land values and gracious domestic building, when every gentleman felt the lure of the country life. In their efforts to enrich themselves at the expense of anciently endowed churches, the powerful men of early Tudor England were in a way re-enacting the depredations of the Norman adventurers, and it would be rash to assert that their motives were widely different, however much more subtle the methods that cloaked them. This time an eye-witness is available to explain what happened in circumstantial detail. Ralph Morice was for much of his life secretary to Cranmer and had been occupied in all sorts of literary business on his master's behalf.[1] He had taken part in estate administration too, for during Henry VIII's later years, and until after Elizabeth's accession, he was warden of the archbishop's manor of Bekesbourne and was at one time warden of woodlands at Tring in Hertfordshire. After early struggles to support his wife and children, 'yearly growing unto a more number', he acquired his own lands at Bekesbourne, and died there some time after 1570. He also had an elder brother, William Morice, who was a gentleman usher at court, able to hear what people said to the king and to pass on information. Ralph Morice was therefore in a good position to know how the exchanges of lands took place. When he wrote his anecdotes of Cranmer at Archbishop Parker's request, he was defending the memory of his late master against accusations that Cranmer had squandered the lands and revenues of his see, and pointed out that

. . . yf he hadd nott well behavid hymself towards his prince and the worlde, his successours shold not [have] byn cumbered with any pece

1. *Narratives of the Days of the Reformation*, ed. J. G. Nichols (Camden Old Series, no. lxxvii, 1860). See also 'Archbishop Cranmer and the Canterbury Temporalities', *E.H.R.*, LXVII (1952), pp. 19–36, by the present author, who is grateful to the Editor for permission to make use here of that article.

of temporall revenewe, either in landes, wooddes, or other revenewes. . . .
For as towching his exchanges, men ought to consider with whome he
had to do, specially with suche a prince as wolde not be brydeled, nor
be aginste-said in any of his requeste, oneles men wolde danger
altogethers.

But it was not simply a matter of the king's covetousness. Morice
had a bad opinion of what he called 'our new officers', surveyors,
auditors and receivers, 'brought upp and practized in subverting
of monasteriall possessions', and eager by working on the king to
do the same with the possessions of the secular clergy. It was they
who suggested, as a means to this end, that Cranmer did not keep
hospitality according to his station but used his revenues for his
private and family purposes; and it was they who were behind
the proposals to disendow the bishoprics. Morice has a story that
Sir Thomas Seymour, brother of the future duke of Somerset and
gentleman of the privy chamber, spread rumours at court that
Cranmer was acting in this way. He was contradicted by William
Morice, but none the less went and told the king that Cranmer
kept a poor house and spent his money on lands for his wife and
children. The sequel was possibly a little joke between Henry VIII,
Cranmer and the Morices at Seymour's expense, for one morning
about a month later the king told Seymour to go at once to
Lambeth and require the archbishop to come and see him at two
o'clock that afternoon. Seymour was shown into the hall at
Lambeth by the porter and found the tables set for an elaborate
and hospitable dinner. Ralph Morice described Seymour's
apparently guilty conscience at the lies told to the king and his
attempt to pass the message quickly to Cranmer and slip away
without being seen to have observed all the preparations. But he
was button-holed by the steward of the household, Richard
Neville, and found himself unable to refuse the cordial invitation
to dinner. He got away as soon as he could, on the excuse that he
had to report to the king, and on his return to court told Henry
that the archbishop would come. 'Had he dined?' asked the king.
'No,' answered Seymour, 'I found him at dinner.' 'Well,' said the
king, 'what chere made he you?' If these words were really
uttered, it is hard to believe the king was not suppressing laughter.
The narrative says that Seymour fell on his knees and confessed
that the stories about Cranmer were false and that he kept the

finest household in the kingdom after that of the king himself. The moral is hammered home with such insistence that the incident is in fact worthy of some suspicion. 'Ah,' quoth the king, 'have you espied your awne faulte nowe? . . . I knowe your purposes well enoughe; you have hadd emonge you the commodities of the abbeis, whiche you have consumed some with superfluous apparell, some at dice and cardes and other ungratious rule, and nowe you wolde have the bishopp landes and revenewes to abuse likewise.' Not that Morice shed tears for the monasteries: on the contrary, he was of a reforming temper and obviously disapproved of the idle rich. His details are sometimes inaccurate. But the main drift of his case seems credible. He tells how the courtiers and speculators pestered Cranmer for offices and the reversion of leases, and it has already been shown in this book how this had been happening for some time before Cranmer became archbishop. Under Warham the length of the demesne leases had tended to increase markedly. At the beginning of the sixteenth century they were often for ten, fifteen or even twenty years, but by about 1530 they were not infrequently for forty or even fifty years. Morice claimed that Cranmer was subjected to great pressure to grant ninety-nine-year leases and in order to resist without a show of incivility privately asked the chapter at Canterbury not to give their necessary confirmation to any lease of more than twenty-one years. This may have been devious but is not particularly discreditable. Nor was it very effective, and the manoeuvre appears to have been the occasion for the exchanges, for it was at this point that the speculators began to get the king to make exchanges of lands with the archbishop. By this means the 'goodly farms' they wanted would no longer be subject to approval by the chapter of Canterbury, and they could quickly obtain the reversion of leases and even sell them again for considerable sums and for very long periods. The next stage was for Cranmer, on legal advice, to lengthen the terms of the leases he granted, so that his demesnes would seem less attractive to men on the make. He was, after all, discovering that the lands he was receiving in exchange were themselves already leased out to farmers and were coming to him 'with yeres enough apon thair backes'. Consequently, the archbishop now made some lettings for long periods. True, this was hardly ideal for the see's interests, but the leases could at any rate be made to men of whom the archbishop approved, like his household steward, Richard Neville, member of a family that had served the archbishopric for a long time. These devices were only partly successful. Many of the best lands were lost in exchange, and it is impossible to say that the archbishop was protected against a class of property speculators by another class of faithful servants. Men's interests were very diversified and their motives mixed. For instance, Sir James Hales, the lawyer who advised Cranmer, was himself a beneficiary of the exchanges. A basic trouble was that Cranmer was ignorant of estate management, and in debt, and very dependent upon Cromwell and the king. His letters of the years 1533 to 1537 show him oppressed by his creditors. He wrote to the prior of Christ Church, Canterbury, asking with some circumlocution for a loan 'for the contentation of such as I am indebted and dangered unto, which . . . hath grieved me more of late than any worldly thing hath done a great season'.[1] On several occasions his demesne farmers, who were bound by agreement to return either the manorial stock or its equivalent in money at term, were actually asked for cash, a procedure hitherto unknown.[2] Cranmer even spoke of his distress in letters to Cromwell. In 1537 a large debt to the king was still unpaid, and this, he wrote, 'of all other things lieth most near unto my stomach'.[3] Cromwell was not much impressed. His memoranda for 1534 and 1535 contain notes of Cranmer's obligations and, ominously, jottings about various woods and temporalities belonging to the archbishop.[4] On 11 September 1535 John Gostwick, treasurer of First Fruits, wrote to Cromwell, 'as to your marvel that I have not received from the archbishop of Canterbury . . . the money due to the king, I cannot see how I shall get it till next term. . . . On my return I shall quicken the archbishop and other debtors with sharp letters, as you command, to pay up instantly.'[5]

Cranmer's inexperience in secular administration and weakness in the face of Cromwell are illustrated in a letter written at a time when the large-scale exchanges of the Canterbury lands were

1. *Cranmer's Letters*, ed. J. E. Cox (Parker Society, 1846), II, p. 260.
2. e.g. in 1533 the farmer of Aldington, William Harte, delivered £13 6s. 8d. to Thomas Cranmer now archbishop at his consecration, being the value of his stock, as in a warrant of the archbishop's auditor dated 20 November 1533 (L.R. 1210).
3. *Cranmer's Letters*, II, pp. 276, 338, 348.
4. *L. & P.*, VII, pp. 923, 1125.
5. ibid., IX, pp. 341, 451; cf. X, p. 1257.

already beginning. On 31 August 1537 the archbishop addressed Cromwell:[1]

My very special good lord . . . I commend me unto you. Likewise thanking you . . . for your good mind towards me concerning my debts to the King's highness. . . . And as concerning such lands of mine as the King's highness is minded to have by exchange at Maidstone and Otford, forsomuch as I am the man that hath small experience in such causes, and have no mistrust at all in my prince on that behalf, I wholly commit unto you to do therein for me as by you shall be thought expedient, not doubting but that you foresee as much for my commodity as you would that I should do for you in such a like matter. . . .

Compassion for poor Cranmer at this letter is the keener if one believes him unprotected by the gift of irony. Aside from this, the exchanges were by this time well begun. The first Canterbury properties to go, in 1536, were the manors of Wimbledon and Mortlake with the advowsons of their churches, quickly followed by Burstow in Wimbledon, which were secured to Thomas Cromwell himself.[2] This was home ground to the king's secretary, a Putney boy. The transaction is a reminder that however much men welcomed good property wherever it was to be had, they are often found in this age of new acquisition bidding for the lands they had known in their early years. Cranmer himself later received property in Whatton and Aslockton in Nottinghamshire, the country of his childhood. Perhaps the old bonds of locality were felt more strongly amidst the rapid change. The point was well put in 1536 by Lord Delawarr, an old-fashioned peer who cared much for rural Sussex and not at all for politics, when he wrote to Cromwell begging that the monastery of Boxgrave, of which he was founder, might be spared, as many of his ancestors and his wife's mother lay there. If the king would not forbear to suppress it, he might translate it into a college; otherwise, he begs that he might have the farm, and Cromwell would be well recompensed for his pains.[3]

During the next year the archbishop let Henry VIII have the

1. *Cranmer's Letters*, II, p. 348; cf. *L. & P.*, XII (2), p. 600.
2. Stats. 27 Hen. VIII, c. 34; 28 Hen. VIII, c. 50; *L. & P.*, x, p. 1087; R. B. Merriman, *Life and Letters of Thomas Cromwell* (1902), pp. 1–9.
3. Quoted from *L. & P.*, x, p. 216, by David Mathew, *The Celtic Peoples and Renaissance Europe* (1933), pp. 7, 8 and *n*.

manors that had composed the bailiwick of Otford, that is to say, the large manor of Otford itself with its members of Shoreham, Sevenoaks, Sevenoaks Weald, Chevening, and Knole with its adjacent properties of Panthurst and Brittons which had formed an entity for nearly a century; also Wrotham, Northfleet and the Medway pastures of Bishop's Marsh and Hersing Marsh.

I was by when Otteford and Knolle was given hym [recalled Morice]. My lord, mynding to have reteynid Knoll unto hymself, saied that it was to small a house for his majestie. 'Marye (saied the king), I had rather have it than this house (meanyng Otteforde), for it standith of a better soile. This house standith lowe, and is rewmatike, like unto Croydon, where I colde never be withoute sycknes. And as for Knoll [it] standeth on a sounde, perfaite, holsome grounde. And if I should make myne abode here, as I do suerlie mynde to do nowe and than, I myself will lye at Knolle, and moste of my house shall ly at Otteforde'. And so by this meanes bothe those houses were delivered upp into the kingis handes. . . .[1]

At the same time the king took Maidstone with the archbishop's jail there, and a collection of churches and chantries which constituted a valuable investment: Northfleet rectory and vicarage, the 'Arundel' chantries in Canterbury Cathedral and Maidstone, the nomination of a chantry priest in Sevenoaks parish church, Maidstone College, St John's Hospital, Sevenoaks, and the advowsons of Shoreham with its dependent chapel of Otford, and of Sevenoaks.[2]

The year 1538 saw the sale to the king of East Cheam in Surrey, and in 1540 he gained the largest of all the archbishopric manors, Aldington and its members as well as Saltwood, Cheyne Court and Lyminge, Hythe bailiwick and the rectory of Cranbrook, all in Kent, and the park and seventy acres of woodland in Croydon, Surrey.[3] In 1542 it was the turn of Sussex. Cranmer then granted the king Slindon, Tangmere, East Lavant, Aldwick, North Bersted and Shripney, with Slindon Park and the advowson of All

1. *Narratives*, p. 266.
2. P.R.O. Deeds of Purchase and Exchange A 21, E 7; LCM, xiii (1), no. 20. The receiver of Otford had been used to pay the two chaplains of the Arundel chantries a stipend of £10 a year each, £6 13s. 4d. to the Master of Maidstone College, and £1 to the perpetual vicar of Sevenoaks for tithe of herbage from the park (L.R. 1355, 1357, etc.).
3. Deeds of Purchase and Exchange A 28; LCM, xii, no. 13; E. Hasted, *History . . . of Kent* (2nd ed., 1797), ix, p. 227.

Saints in the Pallant of Chichester.[1] This block of property was more or less equivalent to the medieval bailiwick of Pagham. In 1545 large parts of the bailiwicks of South Malling and Croydon went the same way: Mayfield with its rectory and park, Frankham Park and Wadhurst rectory, and the manors of Harrow, Woodhall, Hayes, Headstone and Sudbury, with Pinner Park, all in Middlesex, and Tring in Hertfordshire. The same year Charing manor and rectory in Kent were granted to the king, and so too the archbishop's properties in the Isle of Grain.[2]

To judge from Morice's complaints, it might be thought that all this wealth quickly found its way into the hands of courtiers and speculators. In fact, much of it remained for a considerable time with the crown. Wimbledon, it is true, went at once to Cromwell, but when he was destroyed it passed to Queen Katherine Parr for life. Mary I returned it to Cardinal Pole, and only after this did it leave ecclesiastical hands for good, when Elizabeth gave it to Christopher Hatton, who in turn sold it to Sir Thomas Cecil.[3] Otford, Shoreham and their members became part of the 'Honour of Otford' under a high steward, and remained with the crown until the death of Charles I.[4] Bexley continued in crown hands till James I granted it to his jeweller, Sir John Spilman.[5] Northfleet was granted by Queen Elizabeth to James Guildford, but before long it returned to the crown and stayed there till 1648.[6] Henry VIII had a particular affection for Knole, and he kept and enlarged its area by further purchases, but under Edward VI it was distributed to Dudley and others. For a brief moment it returned to Cardinal Pole, but Elizabeth made it over to Henry Carey lord Hunsdon, and under James I it came to the Sackvilles.[7] In east Kent the crown was also the gainer for a long time, though this might not have been so if John Dudley had not come to grief. Aldington acquired more park land and stayed in royal hands (except for two years in Dudley's possession) till the time of Charles I.[8] The bailiwick of Wingham was the most substantially unimpaired of all. Though

1. Deeds of Purchase and Exchange C 50; LCM, XII, no. 12.
2. Deeds of Purchase and Exchange D 78; Statutes of the Realm 37 Hen. VIII, c. 16.
3. O. Manning and W. Bray, *History and Antiquities of the County of Surrey*, III (1814), p. 268.
4. E. Hasted, op. cit., III, pp. 3, 23.   5. ibid., II, p. 165.
6. ibid., III, p. 307.   7. ibid., III, p. 66 *et seq.*
8. ibid., VIII, p. 319. An outline plan of the manor made in the first year of Elizabeth's reign is among the Rentals and Surveys in the Public Record Office (S.C. 12/30/31).

certain mansions and hamlets were granted or sold to individuals, like Walmestone to Walter Hendley, Henry VIII's attorney-general, the bulk of these properties, the nearest of all to Canterbury and among the most ancient of the see's possessions, remained to the archbishops throughout the sixteenth century.[1]

It was the exchanged manors of the second rank that were alienated by the crown more easily. Edward VI granted Wrotham to Sir John Mason, from whom it passed to Robert Byng, who himself lived there till his death in 1596.[2] Maidstone went under Edward VI to Sir Thomas Wyatt of Allington Castle, and after his execution to Sir John Astley, son of the master of the Queen's jewels, who lived there till he died in 1639.[3] Lyminge was acquired by Sir Anthony Aucher, himself master of the Queen's jewels, in whose family it continued till the mid seventeenth century.[4] In east Sussex a substantial quantity of land, including Mayfield, was bought in 1545–6 by Sir Edward North, Chancellor of the Augmentations, and passed thence by sale to Sir Thomas Gresham, who occasionally lived there in magnificence.[5] Much of South Malling bailiwick was assured to Sir John Gage in 1543, when he was already steward of the archbishop's Liberty.[6] In west Sussex, Elizabeth sold Slindon to Anthony Kempe, esquire, Tangmere to Sir Richard Baker and Richard Sackville, esquire, and East Lavant also to Sir Richard Baker.[7]

This is by no means a complete account of the fate which overtook those lands subtracted from the lordship of Canterbury by Henry VIII, but it is an outline illustration of the main events. Rich men and the crown's servants benefited considerably, especially under Edward VI, and they would have done so more permanently and on a greater scale if Dudley had been successful in perverting the succession and sustaining his ambitions. Under Mary there was a chance that the archbishopric might have recovered some considerable part of its ancient property, but

1. Hasted, op. cit., IX, p. 227 *et seq.* A detailed survey of the Wingham manors, still part of the archbishop's possessions, was made in 1624–5 (P.R.O., S.C. 12/20/22).
2. Hasted, op. cit., V, pp. 11–12.
3. ibid., IV, p. 288.
4. ibid., VIII, p. 84.
5. *L. & P.*, XXI (1), 149 (6); T. W. Horsfield, *History, Antiquities and Topography of the County of Sussex*, I (1835), p. 417.
6. *L. & P.*, XVIII (1), 66 (29, 37). There is a collection of Gage MSS., including material relating to the former bailiwick of South Malling, in Barbican House, Lewes.
7. Horsfield, op. cit., II (1835), pp. 67, 69.

Elizabeth acceded, retained or took back important properties, and disposed of several second-grade ones to secular luminaries.

What did the archbishopric get in return for these amputations? Cranmer's transactions were exchanges, not in theory forced sales or confiscations, and the gaps in the rent-roll left by the medieval manors were filled by other assets, especially by appropriated rectories and tithes, taken from dissolved religious houses. The story of the exchanges is extremely complex, for the archbishop's new property was of variegated character and was sometimes made over to him only temporarily until other compensation was substituted. It is necessary to abbreviate. In general, the medieval bailiwicks had by the end of Henry VIII's life been decimated. Those of Aldington, Maidstone, Otford, Pagham and South Malling had disappeared. The bailiwicks of Wingham and Croydon remained, for the archbishop had not, as we have seen, been required to relinquish all the rich possessions round his cathedral city, nor that chief manor of Croydon which the king had found too near the river for his liking. But though the name of the bailiwick endured, some of the best manors once subsumed under Croydon had gone, and in their place the archbishop received former monastic endowments, especially those of Malling Abbey. After 1540 the bailiwick of Wingham, too, was somewhat altered, for it was consolidated with the remnants of the bailiwick of Aldington, and to these were added lands previously in the possession of the east Kentish religious houses of Langdon, Dover, Bilsington, Bradsole, St Sepulchre's in Canterbury and Horton. At first this jumble of properties were accounted for piecemeal by the farmers to whom they were leased, but from 1543 onwards they were committed to a special receiver, Christopher Nevinson, Cranmer's commissary, a kinsman by marriage, and an ardent reformer and image-breaker, whose family long held monastic lands in east Kent. About 1553 Nevinson became receiver-general for the new large bailiwick of Wingham and West Langdon. In mid Kent, the remnants of Maidstone bailiwick were placed with newly acquired lands in the same area to form the bailiwick of Boughton. In east Sussex, the lands left to the see of Canterbury made up in the same way the bailiwick of Ringmer. After a short period of administrative experiment a new structure emerged in 1561. From then until 1597 a new series of account rolls exists in which the Canterbury estates were no longer divided into bailiwicks but were grouped together under a single receiver-general.[1]

The breach with Rome, the dissolution of the monasteries and the compulsory exchanges of lands may not unreasonably be thought of as a revolution in the structure of the possessioner church, yet it is curious to find how little disruption there was in the exploitation of the countryside by the well-to-do families which had for long been supplying the farmers of local demesnes and officials of the estates. Holders of leases were not disturbed when the Canterbury lands were exchanged away. For example, the archbishop parted with his property in and about Maidstone, but Walter Herenden, gentleman, still held the lease of Padsole mill there when he died in 1556, and bequeathed the remainder of it, though he then held of Christopher Roper.[2] The Hawtes were another family that knew how to maintain continuity. Sir William, farmer of Bishopsbourne, died in 1538, leaving instructions for the sowing of barley and oats on the demesnes, and his successors lost nothing by the upheavals. They were not irreligious people, nor extreme. A Henry Hawte had left the Charterhouse in 1535,[3] but William left 40s. to widow Jane Villars 'towards the good kepyng of her brother Christopher, late Observante frere'.[4] Sir William was well in with the Culpepers, and with Peter Hayman, the archbishop's receiver in Kent, whom he had bribed to help get himself made sheriff, and Hawte's house and garden in 1538 were full of tiles and lead from St Sepulchre's nunnery, which he had bought. Like so many others, these gentry had a lasting quality. There are many other instances: Robert Morley continued as farmer of South Malling, and John Weston of Tarring.[5] Simon Gason, gentleman, and descendant of John Gason, farmer of Wingham Barton under Archbishop Warham, was farming Lydd rectory in 1560.[6] William Bever had been a co-farmer of Lambeth under Warham, and in 1560 John Bever was to be found as bedel there.[7]

As for the archbishop's new temporalities, they continued to be managed by men who had a stake in the properties themselves, but they appear even more than in Warham's time to have been men of superior social rank, gentry, esquires or knights. In the

1. L.R. 1401–26. 2. PCC 1 Wrasteley.
3. Ex inf. Mr G. A. J. Hodgett. 4. PCC 14 Crumwelle.
5. L.R. 1376. 6. L.R. 1401. 7. ibid.

1540s, Edward Cartwright, gentleman, was receiver-general in Croydon bailiwick and also farmer of the archbishopric property deriving from Malling Abbey. For this he rendered no less than £130 a year. He was succeeded in both the post and the farm by Hugh Cartwright, esquire, who remained untroubled throughout the short pontificate of Cardinal Pole.[1] Likewise, Richard Neville, archbishop's bailiff and collector for the lands late of Langdon and Bradsole Abbeys, and receiver-general of Ringmer bailiwick, himself farmed some of the archbishopric's new property, formerly of St Gregory's Priory, Canterbury.[2] Many of those who acquired archbishopric possessions after the exchanges recur as farmers of the former monastic demesnes given to the archbishopric in compensation. Such was Anthony Aucher, whom we have met as purchaser of Lyminge and who farmed the demesnes of Langdon and the rectory of Westwell. He became a knight, and was succeeded in due course by Mark Aucher.[3] Sir James Hales was farmer of lands of St Sepulchre's and of Boughton, and Thomas Hales, gentleman, was named receiver-general in the bailiwick of Wingham and West Langdon when Cranmer was attainted.[4] The list could be extended, but already it shows the firm hold acquired by families of substance upon property where the ecclesiastical overlords came and went. The tale may end with a last glance at the Knatchbulls, already encountered as large-scale farmers of pasture and arable in south-east Kent in the early years of the sixteenth century. When Aldington fell to the crown in 1540, Willop, a profitable member of the manor, was passed at once under an eighty-year lease to master John Knatchbull.[5] The manor of Cheyne Court went in 1553 to Sir Thomas Cheyny, treasurer of the king's household, but the now very valuable demesne lands came to be separated from the manorial site and were bought of Queen Elizabeth by Richard Knatchbull.[6] Such were the new men, not merely courtiers and speculators but workers and investors, riding the storms and awaiting the acknowledgement that is given in time to consolidated worth.

1. L.R. 1369, 1372.
2. L.R. 1370; LCM, XIII (1), 18, 22.
3. L.R. 1370, 1376, 1377.
4. L.R. 1376.
5. Hasted, op. cit., VIII, p. 298.
6. ibid., pp. 402–3.

APPENDIX A

Knights' fees held of the Archbishop of Canterbury

The order of this list is alphabetical, with cross-references where necessary. Places are in Kent, and held of the archbishop, unless otherwise noted. The attempt has not been made to trace manorial descents in detail, but rather to show the location and feudal values of the knightly lands as they appear in the principal sources. Other notes are added where they throw light on the history of a fee.

Enfeoffments by the bishop of Rochester are in a special case (see pp. 83-5 above). They are shown on the map but not included here, and nor is the Meinill fee in Yorkshire. Fees have not been included, except possibly by mistake, which were in the archbishop's hands for short periods only, through some special grant, and did not form part of the church of Canterbury's permanent endowment.

Certain recurring dates in the appendix refer to documents which provide the main landmarks in the history of the fees. These are as follows:

1086   Domesday Book. Lands specially described in the Kentish Domesday as *Terrae Militum* have been noted as such. TRE of course signifies the time of King Edward the Confessor, who died on 5 January 1066.

c. 1090 *Domesday Monachorum*, ed. David Douglas (Royal Historical Society (1944), pp. 81–95). This text has been used to amplify or qualify information given under 1086, but not to repeat it.

1093–6 The list of *Milites archiepiscopi*, printed by Professor Douglas, op. cit., p. 105.

1171   The list of *Milicia totius archiepiscopatus* edited and dated by Mr H. M. Colvin in *Kent Records*, vol. xviii, from Glynde MS. 954.

1210–12 The list of knights holding of the archbishopric printed in *The Red Book of the Exchequer*, ed. Hubert Hall (*R.S.*, 1896), pp. 469–73.

1253-4   The fees of knights within the lathes and hundreds of Kent (only), contained in Brit. Mus. Cottonian MS. Galba E iv, fos. 37-44v., and in Public Record Office, Treasury of Receipt Miscellaneous Books, vol. 70, and printed from the latter by James Greenstreet in *A.C.*, vol. XII (1878), pp. 197-237.

1346   List of fees contributing that year to the aid for knighting the king's eldest son, printed in *Feudal Aids*, vol. III.

*

ADISHAM (including Eythorne)

1086   Manor belonged to monks' table; 3 of its 17 sulungs were held by 2 knights of the archbishop. On their demesne(s) 4 ploughs, and 18 *villani* with 5 bordars who had 1 plough. The knights' portion worth £11, though it rendered £13.

c. 1090 Robert son of Wazo held 2 sulungs, that is, Eythorne, worth £7, though he who holds it renders £8; 1 sulung at Barham, worth £4, held by Roger.

1093-6   Robert son of Wazo answered for 6 fees; Roger *pincerna* (probably Roger D'Ivry, see *Dom. Mon.*, p. 56) for 1; Wulnoth of Bereham for $\frac{1}{4}$.

1171   Some portion of the lands held for the service of 3 knights by Thomas son of Thomas son of Bernard was in Eythorne.

NOTE: Robert son of Wazo's fief held for his 6 knights seems to have included Eythorne, Sibton and Sundribge, and also Appledore and Brook which were subsequently transferred back to the monks and the service reduced to three knights. (See Colvin, op. cit., pp. 15-16.)

One knight owed by Lamdert of Barham, though he acknowledged only $\frac{1}{2}$.

1210-12 2 fees in Eythorne, Sibton, Eastleigh in Lyminge and Sundridge held by Ralph son of Bernard. This was probably the son of Thomas, above under *c*. 1171. For the future of these fees, see under SIBTON and SUNDRIDGE. $\frac{1}{2}$ fee held by Warin de Barham.

1253-4 $\frac{1}{2}$ fee in Kingston (near Barham) held by Henry son of Gilbert of Barham; $\frac{1}{20}$ fee in *Burne* and *Dutinton* held by Henry de Burne.

NOTE: This is Bishopsbourne, near Barham, a demesne manor of the archbishop, which occurs as *Bourne archiepiscopi*, at least by 1330 (*IPM*, VII, no. 292); *Dutinton* is Doddington in Teynham (Dean and Chapter of Canterbury MS. E 24, fo. 39).

1279   ½ fee, unnamed, held by Henry de Barham. $\frac{1}{20}$ fee in vill of Bishopsbourne held by Henry de Burne (*Reg. Pecham*, p. 5).

1346   ½ fee in Barham held by Henry de Barham. The family presumably stemming from the Roger of *c.* 1090 is said by Hasted to have continued in Barham until the reign of James I (*History of Kent*, III, p. 755).

ALDINGTON. See under STOWTING

ALLINGTON

1210–12 ½ fee held by Avelina de Longo Campo (Longchamp) (*F. of F.*, CXIII, p. 3).

1253–4 ½ fee held by Robert de Lungechampe.

1324   Manor of Allington held by Joan, da. of Stephen de Penecestre, deceased, of Roger de Kyrkeby, by service of 1 fee, and by him of the archbishop (*IPM*, VI, no. 564).

1340   Castle and manor of Allington held by Avice, late wife of Stephen de Cobham, for life, of the heir of Roger de Kyrkeby, a minor in the wardship of the archbishop, for service of ½ fee (*IPM*, VIII, no. 272).

1346   ½ fee held by John de Cobham, kt, son of Stephen de Cobham, kt, and formerly by Margery de Pencestre (Penshurst), of John de Roos as of the manor of Horton Kirby, and he of the archbishop.

NOTE: This was evidently not one of the archbishop's own enfeoffments. The circumstances of his tenure of the Horton Kirby fief have not yet been clarified.

ASH. See under WINGHAM

BARHAM. See under ADISHAM

BENSHAM. See under CROYDON

BENSTED, in Hunton

1171   Some portion of the lands for 3 knights held by Daniel de Crevequer were probably in Bensted. This was part of Hunton in East Farleigh (q.v.), which had belonged to the church of Canterbury in Domesday. Bensted in Domesday was held of Odo by Adelold the chamberlain; so also were Deane in Wingham (or Dean in Westmill), and Leeds, Kent, both held in the twelfth century by the Crevequers, the former of the archbishop. For other fees held by Crevequer of the archbishop, see under CHEVENING, TILMANSTONE and Deane in WINGHAM.

But it is just possible that the place meant here in the 1171 list is Denstead in Chartham (q.v.). Yet Bensted was certainly held of the archbishop by 1316 (see under LENHAM, where other knightly land held in Hunton of the archbishop will be found).

BERTONE (Barton Court, near Canterbury?)
1210–12 ¼ fee held by John de Bertone.

BERWICK-IN-LYMPNE

1086   *Terra Militum*. ½ sulung held as one manor by William of Adisham. Land for 3 ploughs. On the demesne 2 ploughs; 9 *villani* with 9 bordars have 1½ ploughs; 18 acres of meadow; woodland to render 20 swine. TRE worth 60s., afterwards 20s., now £7, yet it pays £11.

c. 1090   A manor of the monks, held of the archbishop by William of Adisham. Formerly held by Godric the Dean. Valued at £11.

1093–6   William de Eadesham answered for 1 fee.

1171   1 knight owed for Westenhanger by William de Auberville.

       NOTE: In the Glynde MS. this entry corresponds with that for William of Adisham in the 1093–6 list. Berwick and Westenhanger adjoin, and both were later held by the Auberville family.

1210–12 1 fee held by Hugh de Auberville. This was a son-in-law of William of Eynsford (IV).

1253–4   1 fee held by Nicholas de Crioil. See also under EYNSFORD.

1346   1 fee held by John de Crioil, kt; ¼ fee held by John de Crioil, kt, and formerly by Benjamin de Sturton and John de Sturton.

       NOTE: Sturton, like Westenhanger, is in Stanford. This extra ¼ fee is of unexplained origin.

BERWICK (?), Oxfordshire
1242–3   ⅕ fee held of the archbishop's fee by Hugh de Berewik (*Book of Fees*, I, pp. 829, 841).

BISHOPSBOURNE. See under ADISHAM

BOUGHTON (Malherbe)
1086   *Terra Militum*. ½ sulung, belonging to the 6 sulungs of Hollingbourne, held by Ralph son of Thorold. Land for 1½ ploughs. On the demesne 1 plough; 3 *villani* with 2 bordars have

1 plough; a church, 2 acres of meadow, woodland to render 16 swine. TRE worth 40*s*., and afterwards the same.

c. 1090   A manor of the monks, forming ½ sulung of the 6 sulungs of Hollingbourne, but held of the archbishop by Ralph son of Thorold, and formerly by Ratel. Worth 40*s*.

1171   ½ knight owed for Boughton and the marsh enfeoffed by St Thomas (MS. mutilated).

NOTE: The implication is that Archbishop Becket extended the original enfeoffment, adding marshland which had been drained.

1210–12   ½ fee, unnamed but presumably here, held by Robert Malherbe.

1255   ½ carucate in Boughton Malherbe acquired by Fulk de Payforere (see also under TEYNHAM) from Robert de Gatton, 'doing for a scutage of 40*s*. when it shall happen ⅕ part of a knight's fee', and proportionately, for all service (*F. of F.*, pp. 270–1).

BRASTED

1086   *Terra Militum.* 1½ sulungs held by Haimo the sheriff. Land for 10 ploughs. On the demesne 2 ploughs; 24 *villani* with 16 bordars have 12 ploughs; a church, 15 serfs, 2 mills worth 24*s*., woodland to render 80 swine; 9*s*. 6*d*. from herbage. TRE worth £10, when received the same, now £17. Formerly held of the archbishop by Abbot Alnos (Wlnod Cild).

1171   Some portion of the lands held by the earl of Gloucester of the archbishop for 3 knights was in Brasted.

1259   The archbishop claimed from the earl of Gloucester, as part-heir of Haimo the sheriff, suit of court at Otford from Brasted and service of 4 fees from Filston (in Shoreham: see under OTFORD), HORSMONDEN (q.v. below), Milton (in WESTGATE, q.v.) and Pett in Charing (see under LITTLE CHART); knight-service was tacitly abandoned, but the earl's service as Chief Butler at the archbishop's enthronement feasts was recognized in respect of Brasted (Lambeth MS. 1212, p. 148). The tenure of the manor of Brasted on these terms is referred to in *IPM* during the fourteenth century (*IPM*, IV, no. 435; V, no. 538; IX, nos. 57, 63; XIII, nos. 210).

1396   After controversy between Archbishop Courtenay and the cathedral priory, agreement was reached, and confirmed by Richard II's letters patent in 1396, that the prior and convent should keep one third of the revenue from the wardship of the earl of Stafford since the death of Courtenay and the other two thirds until the king decided to whom it should go.

The castle of Tonbridge was to be delivered at once to the archbishop until the majority of the heir (Reg. Arundel, fos. 8v., 9).

1401 Homage and fealty were done on 23 January at Lambeth by Edward, earl of Stafford (d. 21 July 1403), for the castle and lordship of Tonbridge and other lands and lordships held of the archbishop (ibid., fo. 374). In November 1403 the archbishop issued a letter from Tonbridge Castle where presumably he was staying during the time when it was in his hand by reason of the minority of the new earl of Stafford (ibid., fo. 387).

BUCKLAND, in Woodnesborough

1086 *Terra Militum.* 1 yoke held by Osbern son of Letard. On the demesne 1 plough. The yoke is worth 10*s.*

c. 1090 Placed in the list of monastic manors.

For later references to Buckland, see under MAIDSTONE.

BURLEIGH, in Charing

1284 2 yokes, 12½ acres in *Bernefeud* (Barnfield, in Charing, next to Burleigh), of land anciently yoked, together with certain *forlands* there, and a garden of free land, held by the lord John of Ruxley for 41*s.* 10*d.* p.a. payable to the *curia* of Charing, and three-weekly suit of court to Canterbury and the hundred of Calehill (Dean and Chapter of Canterbury MS. E 24, fo. 47).

1310 ½ fee in Burleigh and *Hole,* parish of Charing, held by Thomas of Rokesle (Ruxley), and formerly by John de Bernefeud (*Reg. Pecham,* p. 22).

NOTE: Thomas and William Bernefeld, probably brothers holding in gavelkind, were exchanging about forty acres in Charing and Boughton in 1203 (*F. of F.,* p. 32). The entries above suggest another conversion of gavelkind land to knight's fee.

BURSTOW. See WIMBLEDON

BUXTED, Sussex. See SOUTH MALLING

CANTERBURY. See WESTGATE

CHARING. See under BURLEIGH and NEWLAND; and for Pett in Charing, see under LITTLE CHART

CHEVENING. See also under OTFORD

1171   Some portion of the land held for 3 knights by Daniel de Crevequer was in Chevening.

1210–12   1 fee held by Robert de Crevequer, and probably 1 fee held by Adam de Cheveninges.

1279 $\frac{1}{4}$ fee in Chipstead, parish of Chevening, held by John de Scepstede (*Reg. Pecham*, p. 12).

1281   Confirmation by Queen Eleanor to Archbishop Pecham of $2\frac{1}{4}+\frac{1}{8}$ fees which Robert de Crevequer and his predecessors held of the archbishops and which he sold the queen, and which John de la Haye, Henry Huse, Roger of Tilmanstone, Adam of Chevening and William de Crevequer hold in the vills of Tilmanstone, *Suthden*, Chevening and Foots Cray (Lambeth MS. 1212, p. 70).

     NOTE: In the reign of Edward I most of the Crevequer estate passed to Queen Eleanor when she acquired Leeds Castle, but in 1281 she relinquished her rights in the above lands, subinfeudated to the men named, to the archbishop. There was an Adam of Chevening, kt, who was said to be sixty in 1300 (*IPM*, III, no. 619).

1346 $\frac{1}{2}$ fee held by the heir(s) of William of Chevening, and formerly by Adam of Chevening;
$\frac{1}{10}$ fee in Chipstead held by the heir(s) of John of Chipstead, and formerly by John of Chipstead.

CLIFFE, near Rochester

1086   A demesne manor assigned to the monks' clothing.

1171 $\frac{1}{4}$ knight owed by William of St Alban.

c. 1200   In the time of Archbishop Hubert Walter, Hawise de Gornaco, widow of Roger de Cleva (Cliffe), granted to the archbishop and to Ralph, son of Ralph de Cleva, the service of all knights who held of her dowry; the grantees to acquit her of scutage (Lambeth MS. 1212, p. 99).

1253–4 $\frac{1}{2}$ fee held by Matthew Sibby, Peter de Schirlonde and John Salamon.

COCKING, Sussex

1279 $3\frac{1}{10}$ fees held by Adam de Bavante, kt (*Reg. Pecham*, p. 12).

     NOTE: Pecham's Register gives this as Bocking in Suffolk, where the cathedral priory possessed a demesne manor. But Adam d. about 1293 holding the manor of Cocking in Sussex (extent given, *IPM*, III, no. 75). This and the next entry clinch the identification.

1314 $3\frac{1}{10}$ fees in Cocking, Linchmere, Minsted and Selham, Sussex, held by the archbishop of Henry de Percy, deceased (*IPM*, v, no. 536).

1326   After discussing the homage of Roger Bavent, and the manors of Petworth and Cocking, with the archbishop's bailiff of Wingham, Prior Henry of Eastry considered that this functionary could give the archbishop the fullest information about these questions (*Lit. Cant.*, I, no. 178).

COGGESHALL, Essex

1086   3 virgates in Little Coggeshall held in demesne by the monks of Christ Church. Possibly the Norman tenant was Withard who owed the service of $\frac{1}{2}$ knight in 1093–6.

1171 $\frac{1}{2}$ knight owed by Wiard Puintel in Essex (place not specified).

1210–12 $\frac{1}{2}$ fee held by Osbert Wischard.

1290   Homage of Ralph Faber of Coggeshall for the lands of John Pointel in Little Coggeshall (*Reg. Pecham*, p. 18).

COOLING. See under MAIDSTONE

COSSINGTON. See under MAIDSTONE

COURTHOPE, in Wadhurst, Sussex. See also SOUTH MALLING

1171   Some portion of the lands held for 4 knights by the Count of Eu was in C . . . [MS. illegible].

NOTE: The identification of this with Courthope (or Crowhurst) is suggested for the following reason: in Domesday (*V. C. H. Sussex*, I (1905), p. 398*n*.) a sub-tenant of the Count of Eu in Crowhurst was an ancestor of the Scotneys of Crowhurst. Sir Peter Scotney was a knight of the archbishop, and in 1285 was holding in Courthope (see below). Further, since the Count of Eu in 1093–6 owed the archbishop the service of 4 knights, and held Ulcombe for 2 and Stowting for 1, this manor may have been held even at this time (1093–6) for 1.

1285 $\frac{1}{2}$ fee held by the lord of *Curtehope* by the free service of his arms (MS. E 24, fo. 141v., printed in *S.R.S.*, vol. 57, p. 117); further information about this is in ibid., fo. 146 or p. 118: 80 acres of land at Courthope and a mill, held by Sir Peter de Scotney, who owed suit of court only, saving to the lord wardship and marriage when they fell due. For the Waleys' hunting claims, which involved Crowhurst, see ibid., p. 119, and above, pp. 103-4.

CRAYFORD (*Earde, Earhethea, Herhée, Herde*)[1]

1086   Still a demesne manor of the archbishop, assessed at 4 sulungs. Land for 8 ploughs. On the demesne 2 ploughs; 27 *villani* with 2 bordars have 8 ploughs; a church; 3 mills worth 50*s*. 6*d*.; 5 serfs; 10 acres of meadow; wood to render 40 swine. TRE and when received worth £12, TRW £16, but it renders £21.

1093-6   Hugh de Port answered for 2 fees to the archbishop. That this was in respect of Crayford appears from the entries below.

1108   In the possession of Henry de Port (*Textus Roffensis*, ed. T. Hearne (1720,) p. 195).

1171   2 knights owed for Crayford by Adam de Port. (Adam was son of John, who d. 1167.)

1210-12   2 fees in *Herde* held by Adam de Port.

1253   1 fee held by Robert de sancto Johanne.

    NOTE: This man had some interests in Slindon, Sussex, another of the archbishop's manors. That he was probably the grandson of Adam de Port is suggested by the next entry (Lambeth MS. 1212, p. 87).

1284-5   In archbishopric rental, under Bexley, which was the demesne manor nearest to Crayford, and in the paragraph headed '*Milicia*', occurs the entry: '*Willelmus de sancto Johanne filius Ade de Porte debet de hered*[*itate*] *2 milites*' (MS. E 24, fo. 91). This portion of the text was probably copied from an early thirteenth-century roll, and it is most likely that the Robert of St John who held in 1253 was the son of William and the grandson of Adam de Port.

1302   Manor of *Earde*, including 40 acres of *Brokelese* and 2 acres of brushwood, held by service of 2 fees and three-weekly suit at archbishop's court at Otford by John de sancto Johanne, deceased, whose heir is his son, John, aged twenty-eight (*IPM*, IV, no. 96).

1349   Manor, as above, held by John de sancto Johanne of Basing (Southampton), deceased, whose heir was Hugh, his son, aged nineteen. For further details of this family's transactions with the manor see *IPM*, VII, nos. 229, 244; IX, nos. 37, 52; *C.Cl.R. 1327-30*, p. 462.

1349   Manor of Crayford held by Henry Burghersh, deceased. He had married Isabel, younger daughter of Hugh of St John (*IPM*, IX, no. 241).

    1. For the name, see *F. of F.*, p. 210, *n*.1

1506   Manor of Newebery, otherwise called Crayford, with advowson, and 500 acres of land, 100 acres of pasture, 40 acres of meadow, 20 acres of wood and £14 annual rent in Crayford, worth £25, held of archbishop by knight-service by Thomas Kyngeston, esquire, deceased, who had enfeoffed them to use (*IPM Hen. VII*, III, no. 133).

CROYDON, Surrey

1086   Demesne manor of the archbishop, of which 7 hides were held by Restold and 1 by Ralph. From these they had £7 8s. for *gabulum*. TRE and afterwards the whole manor (80 hides TRE) was worth £12, now (TRW 16¼ hides) £27 to the archbishop and £10 10s. to his homagers.

>   NOTE: This entry is exceptional in saying to whom the value of the portion not in the lord's possession was due, but it is not clear if the portions of Restold and Ralph were enfeoffed or farmed.

1093–6 Wulsi de Croindene answered for 1 fee.

1210–12 ½ fee in *Bonchesham* (Bensham in Croydon) held by Robert de Valognes, for which he answers to the king for 1 hide of land.

1285   ½ fee held by the Preceptor of the New Temple, and $\frac{1}{20}$ fee in Croydon by Walter of Bensham, who owed suit and scutage for $\frac{1}{20}$ fee when it fell due. 'After his death his riding horse with saddle, reins, spurs, sword and arms, if there are any (*si fuerint*) shall be delivered to the lord archbishop, and relief shall be paid for the holding by the heir (Dean and Chapter of Canterbury MS. R.E. 86, fo. 152).

>   NOTE: A Walter of Bensham occurs in a Surrey plea in 1200 (*C.Cl.R.*, I, p. 223), and another as witness to Croydon charters *temp.* Archbishop Pecham (Lambeth MS. 1212, p. 120).

1296   Homage due to archbishop from the bishop of London for *Benchesham* (*Reg. Winchelsey*, pp. 74–5, 984).

1338   Manor of Bensham held for life by Stephen de Gravesend, bishop of London, deceased, of the archbishop as of his manor of Croydon, by service of 21s. and suit of court at Croydon, with reversion to Hugh de Nevill (*IPM*, VIII, no. 176).

1359   Manor of Crowham (in Croydon) held of the archbishop for 1 fee (*IPM*, X, no. 507).

DANE (in Boughton Aluph?)

1253–4 ¼ fee in *Dene*, Wye Hundred, held by John de Plesetis and Agnes Heuse.

12

DEANE, in Wingham. See under WINGHAM

DENSTEAD, in Chartham

1086–7   Denstead, with Whiteacre, Wadden Hall and Little London in Petham, were granted as 1 fee by Lanfranc to Nigel and Robert (*Cart. of St Gregory's, Priory* p. 2).

1210–12 ¼ fee in *Denestede* held by Thomas of Denestede.

1279   ½ fee in Wadden Hall (see under PETHAM) and in Denstead, parish of Chartham, held by William de Hawte (*Reg. Pecham,* p. 14).

1346   ⅙ fee in *Denestede* held by John de Poldre.

DETLING. See under MAIDSTONE

DEVENDEN. See under ROLVENDEN

DODDINGTON. See under TEYNHAM

EAST FARLEIGH (Hunton)

1086   ½ sulung held *in feuo* of the archbishop by Godfrey, who has there 2 ploughs; and 7 *villani* with 10 bordars have 3 ploughs; 4 serfs; 1 mill worth 20*d.*; 4 acres of meadow; wood to render 30 swine. Godfrey's portion worth £9.

c. 1090 The ½ sulung worth £9 held by Godfrey *dapifer* was called *Huntindune* (Hunton), and belonged to the 6 sulungs of East Farleigh, a manor allocated to the monks' clothing. For his ½ sulung Godfrey is here said to render *farm*.

> NOTE: This must have been Godfrey of Malling, since the successor here (*c.* 1171) was Ralph of Lenham who also held Lenham, where his Domesday predecessor was certainly Godfrey of Malling. Godfrey was a great farmer as well as a tenant by knight-service, for he held South Malling at farm for £90 as well as part of it (Glynde) in feudal tenure (see p. 100 above). The farm for Hunton was probably the £6 due to the monks referred to under 1257 (in the entry for Lenham). Lenham, too, though *terra militum*, was farmed by him from the monks.

(Further entries on Hunton will be found under LENHAM.)

EASTLEIGH, in Lyminge. See also under LYMINGE and SIBTON

1210–12 2 fees in Eythorne (see ADISHAM), Sibton and Eastleigh (*Lega*) held by Ralph fitzBernard.

1347   Manor of Eastleigh in Lyminge (*Leghe*) held for ¼ fee by Margaret, deceased, late wife of Robert de Kendale and former wife of John de Leghe, of the earl of Northampton at the manor of Tonge, and he of the archbishop (*IPM*, IX, no. 16).

EAST PECKHAM

1086   ½ sulung held by a man of the archbishop, and TRE it gelded with the 6 sulungs of the manor but did not belong to it as the land was free. Also, 2 sulungs 1 yoke held by Richard of Tonbridge, who had 27 *villani* having 7 ploughs; wood to render 10 swine. Worth £4.

c. 1090   ½ sulung of this manor (which belonged and belongs to the monks' food) is called *Stotingeberga* (Stockenbury, and possibly identifiable in the modern Stocking Lane) and was held TRE by Edric of King Edward, and gave scot voluntarily. 2 sulungs 1 yoke held by Richard of Tonbridge, and are worth £4, but never paid geld since he had them.

1210–12   1 fee in *Pecham* (East Peckham?) held by Roger de Lege.

EDBURTON, Sussex. See under TARRING

ELMSTED, near STOWTING (q.v.)

1171   ¼ knight owed for Elmsted by an unnamed tenant.

1210–12   ¼ fee in Elmsted held by Hamo of Elmsted.

1253–4   ⅙ fee in Elmsted, hundred of Stowting, held by Thomas de Marinis (Mares).

1279   ½ fee in Elmsted held by Thomas de Marinis.

NOTE: A later Thomas de Marinis, who d. 1298, held knightly and gavelkind lands of the king in Otterpool and Blackmanstone and certain rents of the archbishop in Aldington, etc. (*IPM*, III, no. 470; cf. no. 556).

1498   The manor of Elmsted, worth £3, was held of the archbishop by William Haute, kt, deceased, service unknown; he also held in Petham and Bishopsbourne, both demesne manors of the archbishopric (*IPM Hen. VII*, II, no. 145).

EVEGATE, in Smeeth

1086   1½ yokes held in chief by Hugh de Montfort, who had 1 *villanus* with 1 plough; 8 acres of meadow. TRE worth 20*s.*, afterwards 10*s.*, TRW 20*s.*

NOTE: This probably belonged to that part of the Constable's Honour which was grouped round SALTWOOD (q.v.).

The Honour passed to the Crown in 1163 (J. H. Round, *The Commune of London*, p. 281). For the descent of this manor, see N. H. MacMichael in *A.C.*, LXXIV (1961), pp. 1–47.

1171   ⅓ fee, tenant unnamed, held of the archbishop.

1210–12 ⅓ fee held by Henry de Grelley.

1244   ⅓ fee held by Geoffrey de Heveresleg (Eversley) (*Book of Fees*, II, p. 1153).

> NOTE: In 1246 Geoffrey de Eversley d. seised of 98 acres of land, sixteen acres of meadow, a pasture and 13s. 8d. assessed rents, mills, etc., in Smeeth of the inheritance of Alice, his late wife, the marriage of whose heir was worth 10 marks (*IPM*, I, no. 59).

1279   ⅓ fee held by Henry de Grelley; fealty sworn in the *curia* of Aldington (Reg. Pecham, fo. 5).

1310   ⅓ fee held for the manor of Evegate by Edmund de Passele (*Reg. Pecham*, p. 21).

1346   ⅓ fee.

1478–9 The manor of Evegate was in the archbishop's custody during the minority of William, son and heir of John Passhley (d. 1468), but farmed to Richard Nanseglos (second husband of Alice, the heir's mother) and John Hert (L.R. 97).

EYNSFORD

1086   *Terra Militum*. 6 sulungs held by Ralph son of Unspac. On the demesne 5 ploughs; 29 *villani* with 9 bordars have 15 ploughs; 2 churches and 9 serfs and 2 mills worth 43s.; 29 acres of meadow; woodland to render 20 swine. TRE worth £16, now £20. Of the manor Richard of Tonbridge held in his lowy as much woodland as would render 20 swine, 1 mill worth 5s. and 1 fishery.

1086–7 Eynsford described by Lanfranc as 'a vill we have given to the other William' (*Cart. of St Gregory's Priory*, p. 2).

c. 1090 6 sulungs held by Ralph son of Hospac, worth £20.

1171   Land held for 7½ knights (though he recognized the obligation only for 4¾) by William of Eynsford in the manor of Eynsford, in Ightham, *Toppesfield* (Essex) and RUCKINGE (q.v.).

> NOTE: Glynde MS. 954 says *Topesfeld* was in Essex. This was part of the Honour of Boulogne, and it is not clear how it came to belong to the manor of Eynsford. But it is just possible that the return of 1171 recorded in the Glynde MS. was in error and that the place was Tovil (*Topevelde*) which was in Maidstone, not far from Eynsford, and which belonged to the

archbishop's demesne manor of Maidstone (Dean and Chapter of Canterbury MS. E 24, fo. 27v.).

1210–12   4¾ fees held by William of Eynsford.
¼ fee held by William de Beseville.

1253–4   The manor of Eynsford, with his barony, held by William of Eynsford.

1261   A detailed inquisition, with pedigree, found that the barony, possessing members in Ightham, Toppesfield and Ruckinge, had passed to Crioil and Herengod and was held for 4¾ fees although archbishops used to claim 6¾ fees [sic] (Lambeth MS. 1212, p. 417).

1289   ⅛ barony of Eynsford, held in Warehorne, besides other land there, of Nicholas de Crioil by Richard de Bedford, deceased (*IPM*, II, no. 718).

1291   ½ fee of this barony in Foots Cray (q.v.) (*IPM*, II, no. 824).

1302   Nicholas de Crioil, deceased, held ½ manor of Ightham (full extent given) of the manor of Eynsford by service of ¼ fee; also the manor of Westenhanger (see BERWICK-IN-LYMPNE) of Sir William de Leybourne for service of 1 fee; and ½ town and castle of Eynsford (full extent given) including various lands in fields, and rents for tenements from heirs of master Ralph of Farningham and parceners, held of archbishop by service of ½ fee and rendering 20s. p.a. at archbishop's manor of Otford and doing three-weekly suit there (*IPM*, IV, no. 162).

1309   Barony of Eynsford held in equal portions by William Inge and Nicholas Cryel for the service of 4¾ fees (*Reg. Pecham*, p. 21).

1322   Manor of Ightham and ½ manor of Eynsford (extents given) held by William Inge, deceased, of the archbishop by service of ½ and ¼ fee respectively. Half of Ightham had been acquired by William and his wife from Nicholas Crioil (*IPM*, VI, no. 328).

1347   ¼ fee at Pedham in Eynsford held by Margaret, deceased, widow of John Kendale, of John Crioil, kt, at the manor of Eynsford, and he of the archbishop (*IPM*, IX, no. 16).

1501   Manor of Eynsford, worth £6, with the manor and advowson of Ightham, worth £10, held of the archbishop, service unknown, by Elizabeth, deceased, sometime wife of William Chaworth, kt, and later wife of John Dunham, esquire (*IPM Hen. VII*, II, no. 612).

EYTHORNE. See ADISHAM

FARNINGHAM. See also HORTON

1086   *Terra Militum.* 1 sulung held by Ansgot. On the demesne 2 ploughs, and 13 *villani* with 5 bordars have 3½ ploughs; 60 acres of meadow; woodland to render 20 swine, and the same amount of woodland in the lowy of Tonbridge. TRE worth £7, now £11, from which the monks of Canterbury have £4 for their clothing.

c. 1090   A manor allocated to the monks' clothing, which Ansgod held of the archbishop, but it rendered farm to the monks.

    NOTE: Farm was paid to the monks from land held in fee at East Farleigh, Graveney and Swarling, but it is uncertain whether Ansgot held in fee or as a lessee only.

1171   1 knight owed by William de Cheriton.

    NOTE: For other interests of William of Cheriton, in Farningham and Newington-by-Hythe, *F. of F.*, pp. cxxxi, 23.

1253–4   1 fee held by Waleran de Cerytone. (The estate came to be known as Cheriton or Charton.)

1279   ⅛ fee in Farningham and Rolvenden (q.v.) held by Ralph of Kensham (*Reg. Pecham*, p. 10).

1287   ½ fee held by William of Chelsfield (ibid., p. 17).

1346   ¾ fee held by Ralph of Farningham, kt, son of John of Farningham, and formerly by John of Ifield, of the manor of Horton Kirby (*Kyrkeby*), of the archbishop.

FILSTON, in Shoreham. See under OTFORD

FINGLESHAM

1086   *Terra Militum.* ½ sulung held by William Folet, who had there 6 *villani* with 1½ ploughs. (For its value see under STATENBOROUGH.)

c. 1090   Listed under the manors of the monks, and described as held TRE of the archbishop by Liuenot; TRW by William Folet as ½ sulung, worth 20*s.*

FLEET. See under WINGHAM

FOOTS CRAY

1210–12 1 fee held by Robert de Crevequer, but subinfeudated to William of Eynsford.

1281   Part of an estate formerly held by Robert de Crevequer of the archbishop, then sold by Robert to Queen Eleanor, and in 1281 confirmed by the queen to Archbishop Pecham. The Foots

Cray part of the estate was probably held by John de la Haye and/or Henry Huse as sub-tenant(s) (Lambeth MS. 1212, p. 70). See also under TILMANSTONE.

1291 The manor of Foots Cray held for ½ fee by Gregory of Ruxley, who died this year, of Nicholas de Crioil (parcener of the Eynsford inheritance in 1261, see Lambeth MS. 1212, p. 417) and Ralph of Sandwich, doing 2 suits of court every 3 weeks at the court of Eynsford (*IPM*, II, no. 824).

FREEZINGHAM. See ROLVENDEN

GILLINGHAM
1086 Land for 1 plough of this manor held by a Frenchman who has there 2 bordars. His portion is worth 40s.
c. 1090 What Anschetil de Ros and Robert Brutin hold is worth 40s.
1093–6 ½ knight owed to archbishop by Robert Brutin.
1171 Land called *Brutini* (clearly in Gillingham) held for ½ knight.

NOTE: In 1170–1 Robert Brutin had paid 50s. relief on ½ fee (*P.R. 17 Henry II*, p. 142). Richard Brutin of Gillingham gave tithes to Rochester Priory when his brother became a monk there (*Textus Roffensis*, p. 181). Ralph Brutin was a knight of Rochester in the time of Henry I. In 1285 there was a yoke of gavelkind land called *Jugum Brutini* in Gillingham, now probably to be identified with Britton Street.

1210–12 ½ fee held by Robert of Gillingham.

NOTE: In 1202 Robert of Gillingham and his wife Margaret had subinfeudated 40 acres in Gillingham (*F. of F.*, p. 29).

1253–4 ½ fee in Chatham Hundred, unnamed, but clearly in Gillingham, held by Hugh of Gillingham.
1273–4 Ministers' account of the land of Adam son of Hugh of Gillingham in the custody of the archbishop during the minority of the heirs (Addit. MS. 29794, m. 2d.).

NOTE: For this enfeoffment, see F. R. H. Du Boulay, 'Gavelkind and Knight's Fee in Medieval Kent', *E.H.R.*, vol. LXXVII (1962), pp. 505–10.

1346 ½ fee held by Thomas of Gillingham and his parceners, and formerly by Hugh of Gillingham.

GLYNDE. See under SOUTH MALLING

GODINTON, in Chart, or **GODDINGTON** in Chelsfield
1086–7 Godinton enfeoffed by Lanfranc to Robert (*Cart. of St Gregory's Priory*, p. 2).

1093–6   1 knight owed by Robert son of Godbert. (This knight occupies the place in the list corresponding to that of Simon of Godint' in the list of 1171 below.)

1171   1 knight owed for unnamed land by Simon de Godint', though he recognized the service of only ½ knight.

NOTE: The editor of St Gregory's Cartulary identifies Lanfranc's enfeoffment, above, as Godinton in Chart, with good reason since the clause in the charter describes together the grant to Robert and Richard of the *villulae* of Godinton and Leaveland, which are fairly near one another, whereas Chelsfield is much farther away. On the other hand, it seems that the same family had possessions in both places (*PNK*, p. 16), and after the death of Simon of Goddington the settlement of his knightly lands shows he held in Goddington (Chelsfield) and St Mary Cray, which is also near Chelsfield (*F. of F.*, p. 7, *s.a.* 1197). In another fine of the same period Simon may be the same as Simon of Chelsfield, who held in Farningham and Horton (ibid., p. 10; cf. *A.C* XXIII). If this family is connected with Chelsfield, it is also possible that an ancestor was Arnulf of Chelsfield who in a charter of 1143 refers to his demesne land called *Godricesdune* (*Textus Roffensis*, p. 236).

1210–12   ½ fee in *Godintone* held by Stephen of Yaldham; ½ fee, possibly in Goddington, held by Robert de Geddinges. (One reading of *Godintone* in the *Red Book of the Exchequer*, under Stephen of Yaldham, is *Goddinges*.)

1279   ½ fee in Codington [*sic*] held by William de Hastings (*Reg. Pecham*, p. 16).

GOLDSTONE. See under WINGHAM

GOSS HALL. See under WINGHAM

GRAVENEY

1086   *Terra Militum.* 1 sulung held by Richard. On the demesne is 1 plough, and 8 *villani* with 10 bordars have 2 ploughs There are 5 serfs; 10 acres of meadow, and 4 salt-pans worth 4*s.* TRE and afterwards worth £5, now £6. From these the monks of Canterbury have 20*s.*

c. 1090   A manor called Graveney, assessed TRE and now at 1 sulung, and belonging to Boughton (under Blean), held in fee by Richard the constable (p. 85). Also described (p. 95) as a manor of 1 sulung assigned to the monks' clothing, held *in fee* of the archbishop by Richard the constable, yet rendering farm to the monks.

NOTE: Richard held Leaveland as well as Graveney, but as these manors descended separately (q.v.) it is likely that he died without male heir, but with two daughters who may well have married Bainard and Wimund of Leaveland respectively (cf. Sir Charles Clay, 'The Keepership of the Old Palace at Westminster', *E.H.R.*, LIX (1944), p. 3 *n*.1).

1171   2 knights owed for Graveney, of the honour of Baynard, by Walter son of Robert.

NOTE: 'Bainiard' in 1093–6 owed the archbishop the service of two knights. He was the predecessor of the fitzWalter lords of Dunmow in Essex, and the lord of Baynard's Castle in London (*Dom. Mon.*, p. 61). Walter, above, who d. in 1198, was the son of Robert fitzRichard, to whom the lands of William Bainiard were granted by Henry I after his rebellion in 1110 (I. J. Sanders, *English Baronies*, p. 129).

1210–12 2 fees held by Richard de Gravenel.

1228   Heirs of Hamo of Graveney in royal disposal *sede vacante* (*C.Cl.R. 1227–31*, p. 75).

1272   Death of John Gravenel, whose heir was his son Richard, aged 14. Richard had held Graveney manor of the archbishop, but its custody was in the king's hands *sede vacante* (extent given). Out of the services he was bound to pay 20*s*. p.a. at mid Lent to the monks of Christ Church. He also had held 20 acres of the abbot of Faversham and 13 acres in small parcels of other lords in barony (*IPM*, I, no. 802).

1279   ½ fee in *Granham* (Graveney?) held by Richard de Granham (Reg. Pecham, fo. 2v.: homage done at Charing).

1346   1 fee held by Roger of Northwood, kt, through Joan his wife, who was the wife of Thomas of Faversham; formerly held by Richard of Graveney.

HADLEIGH, Suffolk

1242–3 ½ fee, held by Richard de Ros of William of Eynsford, and William of the archbishop (*Book of Fees*, I, p. 920).

HALSTEAD, near Rochester

1171   ½ knight for Halstead owed by Robert de Maleville.

1210–12 ½ fee in Halstead and Preston held by Philip de Maleville, of which ¼ fee in Preston was subinfeudated to Roger de Luddesdene.

1279   1 fee held by John de Maleville (*Reg. Pecham*, p. 15).

NOTE: John de Maleville had succeeded his father William at the age of sixteen in 1272 in the ½ fee held in Halstead and

Cuddenham; the chief lord at that time was the king by reason of the vacancy of the see. There were also one yoke of gavelkind land in *Godingeston*, held by various services which were paid *for him* by the tenants to Otford court, and further parcels of gavelkind land and meadow specified, all pertaining to Halstead manor; also ½ fee and ¼ fee at Crofton in Orpington held of the lady Lora de Hortone, and ¼ fee in Little Orpington held of Sir John de Rokesle (*IPM*, I, no. 805).

HARROW, Middlesex

1086   1 hide held by a priest, and 6 hides by 3 knights, *et sub eis manent 7 homines*. . . .

1171   ¼ knight owed for Harrow by the heir of Walter of Herteffeld, now in the hands of the archbishop.

1210–12 ½ fee held by Walter de Hertfelde.

1279   1 fee in Harrow and Hayes (see below) held by William de Broke (*Reg. Pecham*, p. 16).

1488–9 Lands in Harrow producing £6 13s. 4d. p.a. in the archbishop's custody during the minority of the heir of Thomas Boys, but farmed to William Nix, LL.D., and Richard Nix, LL.D. (L.R. 98).

HAYES, Middlesex

1086   6½ hides held by 3 knights.

1171   1 knight owed for Hayes, Southall and *Tochint'* (unidentified), with ⅙ part of a knight that Ralph of Tochinton owes.

1210–12 1 fee in Southall held by William de Suhalle.
       ¼ fee held by Godfrey of Tokinton. (It is an inference that this ¼ fee was in Hayes, since Godfrey immediately follows William in the list.)

1242–3 1 fee in Hayes held by Alice de Suhaul', who resisted the scutage this year (*Book of Fees*, II, p. 897).

1279   1 fee in Harrow and Hayes (as above, under HARROW).
       ½ fee in Hayes held by John de Pilardestone (*Reg. Pecham*, p. 16).

HEVER. See under OTFORD

HORSMONDEN

1171   Some portion of his lands held for the service of three knights by the earl of Gloucester was in Horsmonden.

1210–12 1 fee held by Philip de Albeyni (Daubeney).

1259 Service of 4 fees for Filston (in Shoreham, see OTFORD,) Horsmonden, Milton (in Canterbury, see WESTGATE) and Pett (see under LITTLE CHART) claimed by the archbishop of the earl of Gloucester, but by composition the earl was to hold them in future for the service of Chief Butler at the archbishop's enthronement feast (Lambeth MS. 1212, p. 148 *et seq.*).

1348 ½ fee held by John Baud of Hugh d'Audley, earl of Gloucester, deceased, of the archbishop (*IPM*, IX, no. 65).

HOTHFIELD, near Chart

1171 ¼ knight owed for *Hedfeld* by John of Dover.

NOTE: John of Dover, lord of Chilham, succeeded to his estates in 1171 or 1172, and died *c.* 1194. His grandson Fulbert III of Dover (who died before 1212) left a widow Isabel who married Baldwin Wake III, lord of Bourne, Lincolnshire (d. 1213) (I. J. Sanders, *English Baronies* (1960), pp. 107, 111). This ¼ fee evidently formed her dower.

1210–12 ¼ fee in *Hatfeld* held by Baldwin Wake.

1253–4 ¼ fee in *Hathfeld*, Boughton Hundred (*recte* Chart and Longbridge), held in serjeanty by William of Wilton, through his wife, Rose.

NOTE: Rose was the daughter of Fulbert II of Dover, and sister of Fulbert III who d.*s.p.*, as above. She married William of Wilton as her second husband before 1253. William, a royal justice, probably d. 1264 (Sanders, op. cit., p. 111). In 1257 William and Rose granted the manor of Hothfield and certain denn rents, less the advowson and manorial wood, as a life-lease to Alfred de Dene in return for Alfred's surrender of two carucates in Sibertswold which he had held on life-lease from Rose (*F. of F.*, p. 287).

1279 ½ fee in Hothfield held by Alexander de Balliol (*Reg. Pecham*, p. 9).

NOTE: Rose, above, was the mother of Richard II of Chilham, d.*s.p.*, and of Isabel, the heiress, whose second husband was Alexander of Balliol, of Cavers, co. Roxburghe. After his death in 1310–11, the lordship of Chilham reverted to Bartholomew Badlesmere, who was executed in 1322 (Sanders, loc. cit.).

1328 Hothfield held of the archbishop by the serjeanty of attending upon him with water to wash his hands on the day of his enthronement at Canterbury, by the late Bartholomew de Badlesmere, who had the ewer and basin, and was also archbishop's chamberlain for the night, and had the archbishop's couch for his fee (*IPM*, VII, no. 104).

1338   As above, held by Giles de Badlesmere, kt, deceased, whose heirs are his four sisters: Elizabeth, wife of Sir William de Bohun, earl of Northampton, twenty-eight years old; Maud, wife of Sir John de Veer, earl of Oxford, thirty; Margery, wife of Sir William de Ros, thirty-four; Margaret, wife of Sir John Typetot, twenty-one (*IPM*, nos. 136, 185).

1343   Manor of Hothfield held by William de Roos of Hamelak (Helmsley, Yorks.) of the inheritance of Margery his wife, of the archbishop, by the service of ½ fee (*IPM*, VIII, no. 474).

1363   Manor of Hothfield held for ½ fee and by service of being archbishop's chamberlain, and doing three-weekly suit to his court at the palace of Canterbury, by Margery, late wife of William de Roos of Helmsley (*IPM*, XI, no. 528).

1418–19   Manor of Hothfield in archbishop's hands by reason of the minority of lord de Roos, but issues of the custody (£20) granted to Robert Marchall, Thomas Danyell and William Tulmond from 31 March 1415 to the full age of the heir, reserving only the fishery (L.R. 95).

1427–8   £8 farm of ⅔ manor of Hothfield assigned by the archbishop's special grace during the minority of Thomas, brother and heir of William de Roos, to the same Thomas who is now of full age; the assignment being apart from the dower to Margery, the widow (ibid. 96).

1488–9   Relief of 50s. from lord de Roos on ½ fee in Hothfield in arrears (ibid. 98).

HUNTON. See EAST FARLEIGH and LENHAM

ICKHAM. See RUCKINGE

IFIELD, near Gravesend

1093–6   William de Ifelde answered for ½ fee.

1171   ½ knight owed by Walter of Ifield.

1210–12   ½ fee held by Walter de Eure (*Hever, in Ifield*).

    NOTE: A William of Hever married Joan of Auberville who in 1229–30 sold (some of?) her dowry in Ifield for 11 marks and £3 annuity to Stephen of Cossington (*F. of F.*, p. 107). In 1236 William of Cossington, kt, transferred to James of Hever ½ fee in Ifield for 10 marks, with ⅓ as life-interest reserved to Joan, widow of William of Hever (ibid., p. 125). James of Hever had brothers Ralph and Robert alive in 1245 (ibid., pp. 183–4); he also sold six acres in Thanington to Warrisius de Valognes (ibid., p. 201).

1306   Ifield held of archbishopric for ¼ fee, and consisted of a capital messuage, 297 acres of arable, 5 acres 1 rood of salt meadow, 6 acres 1 rood of several pasture, 19 acres 1 rood of wood, and a windmill. From this were due yearly 7 marks to the heirs of William of Ifield of Stone, and 72s. 1½d. at the archbishop's manor of Northfleet, from Thomas of Ifield, deceased, whose heir is Richard, his son, aged seventeen on 28 May 1306. Thomas also held 64 acres in gavelkind at Northfleet, to which the heirs are Richard and his brothers Thomas (sixteen) and John (thirteen) (*IPM*, IV, no. 389).

IGHTHAM. See under EYNSFORD

ISFIELD, Sussex. See under SOUTH MALLING

KENSHAM. See under ROLVENDEN

KNELL. See under WINGHAM

LAGNESS. See under PAGHAM

LANGPORT, near Lydd
1086   *Terra Militum.* 1½ sulungs held by Robert of Romney. Land for 6 ploughs. On the demesne 2 ploughs; 29 *villani* with 9 bordars have 9 ploughs; 7 salt-pans worth 8s. 9d. To this manor belong 21 burgesses who are in Romney, and from whom the archbishop receives the fines for these three forfeitures: *latrocinium, pacem fractam* and *foristellum*; but the king has all the service due from them, and they themselves have all dues and other fines, in return for service on the sea, and they are in the king's hands. TRE and afterwards worth £10, now £16.
c. 1090   A monastic manor, which Earl Godwin had once held, and which the archbishop had claimed from the bishop of Bayeux. Robert of Romney has the three forfeitures. It adds that '*adhuc pertinet ibi 1 iugum terre*' 'included in the £16 value'.
1093–6   Lambert of Romney owed the service of 3 knights.
1171   1½ knights owed for Langport by William de Jarpunville; also 1½ knights, location not given, by Peter de Langeport.

        NOTE: William de Jarpunville had married Aubrée, successor and presumably daughter of David of Romney (drowned in Romney Marsh *c*. 1167) (J. H. Round, *The King's Serjeants*, (1911), pp. 303–9). The original estate had evidently been split into two.

1210–12 1½ fees held by Aubréc (Albreda) de Jarpunville.
       1½ fees held by Jocelin of Spain.

> NOTE: In 1227 Alice de Jarpunville granted 40 acres in Langport to Thomas son of Godfrey and his wife Mabel and their heirs for ½ mark p.a. payable at Michaelmas at Lydd church, and a payment of 20 marks (*F. of F.*, p. 101).

1253–4 1 fee held by Mabel de Peumhelle.

1338 Manor of Langport, with rents in Old and New Romney, held for life by grant of Giles de Badlesmere, kt, by John le fitz-Bernard, of the archbishop, by service of 13*s*. 4*d*. (*IPM*, VIII, no. 142).

1486 Manor of Langport, worth £8, held of the archbishop as of the manor of Aldington, by John Wrytell, esquire, service unknown. Similarly the manor of Old Romney (*IPM Hen. VII*, I, no. 109).

1508 Manor of Langport, worth £4, and Old Romney, worth £8, held by John Wretyll, deceased, son and heir of above (*IPM Hen. VII*, III, no. 430).

LAVANT, Sussex

1086 3 hides held of the archbishop by Ralph, who has 1 *villanus* with 3 bordars and 1 plough. Worth £3.

1093–6 Ralph de Ferno and William Pollex who together owed the service of 1 knight were probably the tenants here.

1171 1 knight owed for manor of *Lauinton* (West Lavant) by William de Falaise and Ralph son of Ralph.

1210–12 ½ fee held by William de Falesia.
       ½ fee held by John de Lovintone.

1242–3 ½ fee in West Lavant held by William de Faleyse and William de Lovinton (*Book of Fees*, I, p. 692).

1281 ½ fee in West Lavant held by Alice, widow of Peter de la Falayse (*Reg. Pecham*, p. 17, fealty in 1281, homage in 1289).

1285 ½ fee in Lavant held by Alice de la Falaise. She owes suit of court, and her tenants shall come to two lawdays every year; ½ fee similarly held by John de Mildebi (MS. E 24, fo. 109, printed in *S.R.S.*, vol. 57, p. 16).

1292 ½ fee in West Lavant. Fealty of John de Stokes (*Reg. Pecham*, p. 19); homage postponed *quia timetur de placito dicte terre* (ibid.).

LEAVELAND

1086 *Terra Militum.* 1 sulung held by Richard a man of the archbishop. On the demesne 1 plough; 2 *villani* with 1 bordar have 1 plough; woodland to render 5 swine. TRE worth 30*s.*, afterwards the same, now 20*s.*

1086-7 Leaveland and *Godintune* (see under GODINTON) enfeoffed to Richard and Robert (*Cart. of St Gregory's Priory*, p. 2).

***c.* 1090** A monastic manor, but held in fee of the archbishop by Richard the constable. TRE assessed at 1 sulung, and now the same. Worth 20*s.*

1093-6 Wimund de Liueland answered for 1 fee.

> NOTE: For the suggestion that Wimund may have been the son-in-law of Richard the constable, see under GRAVENEY.

1171 Land for 1 knight at Leaveland held by Nathaniel of Leaveland, though he acknowledged the service only of ½.

> NOTE: Nathaniel in 1198 established his claim to be keeper of the Palace of Westminster (Sir Charles Clay, art. cit. under GRAVENEY).

1210-12 ½ fee held by Robert of Leaveland.

> NOTE: In 1228 the king granted the wardens of the archbishopric custody of the daughter and heiress of Richard of Leaveland who had held of the king in chief (*C.Cl.R. 1227-31*, p. 85).

1253-4 1 fee held by Ralph of Grendon.

1279 ½ fee held by Ralph of Leaveland (*Reg. Pecham*, p. 12).

> NOTE: This was probably the same as Ralph de Grendon or Grandone of Leaveland who d. 1280 holding from the king the serjeanty of keeping the Fleet prison and from the archbishop the manor of Leaveland for service of ½ fee and doing suit at his court at Canterbury (*IPM*, II, no. 356).

1360 Manor of Leaveland held by Robert de Northwode, kt, deceased, for ½ fee and annual suit at archbishop's court of Westgate, Canterbury (*IPM*, X, no. 623); assigned as dower to Alice the widow in the presence of Thomas, the son and heir (ibid., no. 624). Thomas was dead by the next year. He held no other lands in the county, and left as heirs his two sisters, Joan and Agnes (ibid., XI, no. 147).

LENHAM (and Hunton)

1086 *Terra Militum.* 2 sulungs held by Godfrey *dapifer.* On the demesne 2 ploughs; 15 *villani* with 2 bordars have 4 ploughs;

4 serfs; 6 acres of meadow; 1 mill worth 7s.; woodland to render 10 swine. Worth £8, yet it pays £12 10s.

c. 1090   Listed as a monastic manor, but held in fee of the archbishop by Godfrey de Mellinges. TRE and TRW 2 sulungs. Worth £8 but pays £12 10s. *de firma.*

NOTE: Godfrey also held Hunton in EAST FARLEIGH (q.v.).

1171   Land for 2 knights held in Lenham and Hunton (in East Farleigh) by Ralph of Lenham.

1210–12   2 fees in Lenham and Hunton held by Roger of Lenham.

1257   Nicholas of Lenham agreed in future to pay the annual rent of £6 due from the manor of Hunton to Canterbury Cathedral Priory on 24 June to the Treasury at Canterbury, and was forgiven any arrears (*F. of F.*, pp. 228–9).

NOTE: Other similar agreements date from this time, see p. 82 above. Nicholas of Lenham, like his predecessor Godfrey of Malling, held land in South Malling (Lamberhurst) at farm, though he sub-let in 1259 to the abbot of Robertsbridge (Lambeth MS. 1212, p. 83).

1316   John of Lenham, deceased, sometimes called 'the elder', held the manor of Hunton with rents in East Lenham and the third presentation to Rolvenden church, jointly with Margaret his wife, by the service of a rose yearly, of the gift of John of Lenham the younger, who holds the same of the archbishop by the service of ¼ fee. In the same way he held the manor of Bensted in Hunton (q.v.) for ¼ fee, and the manor of Lewis Heath (in Horsmonden) for ¼ fee (*IPM*, VI, no. 40).

1334   Manors of Bensted (q.v.) and Hunton recently held jointly by John de Lenham and Margaret his wife, the latter of the archbishop for ¼ fee and suit at the archbishop's great court at Canterbury once a year; a rent-charge of £10 due to the prior and convent of Canterbury. Heir is Eleanor, wife of John Giffard and daughter of John of Lenham, son and heir of John and Margaret aforesaid (*IPM*, VII, no. 599; *C.Cl.R. 1333–7*, p. 421).

1346   ½ fee in East Lenham held by Simon de Hadelo, and formerly by Roger de Hadelo.

1348   Manor of Hunton, except a tenement called Bensted which is parcel of that manor, held of the archbishop by service of 1 fee and three-weekly suit at the archbishop's court by John Giffard of *Bures* (Bowers Giffard, Essex), deceased. Bensted is held of Isabella, Queen of England, of her manor of Leeds, by service of ¼ fee and three-weekly suit at her court (*IPM*, IX, no. 111).

1367   ⅓ manor of Hunton held by Juliana, countess of Huntingdon, deceased, in dower, of the archbishopric by knight-service, amount not known (*IPM*, XII, no. 146).

LITTLE CHART

1086   ½ sulung of the 2½ hides [*sic*] there were held of the archbishop by William. On the demesne 1 plough with 4 serfs; 10 acres of meadow; wood to render 20 swine; worth 40*s*.

c. 1090   A manor allocated to the monks' food. The ½ sulung held by William son of Hermenfrid of the archbishop in fee was *Pette* (Pett Place, near Charing). He renders 25*d*. to the altar of Holy Trinity for all customs.

1171   Some portion of his lands for 3 knights was held by the earl of Gloucester in *Pettes*. See under BRASTED, and references there.

1210–12   ½ fee and ¼ fee in *Pettes* held by Robert de Wicforde and William de Pettes.

1346   ¼ fee in Pette held by Geoffrey ate Pette, of *Welles*.

LOSSENHAM, in Newenden and Sandhurst

1171   Some portion of his lands for 3 knights was held there by Richard le Waleys (see also under SOUTH MALLING).

    NOTE: Newenden in Domesday is neither enfeoffed nor farmed, but appears in the early sixteenth century as a fee-farm for £5 p.a. (L.R. 1207).

1303   1 fee held by Bartholomew of St Leger, saving the right of Richard le Waleys *et cujuslibet alterius*. He pledged his relief, at £15, for this and the 2 fees in Ulcombe (q.v.) (*Reg. Pecham*, p. 19).

    1½ fees in Camton [*sic*] and Lossenham, parish of Newenden, as well as 1½ fees in Glynde and Buxted, held by Godfrey le Waleys, brother and heir of Richard le Waleys. Relief of £15 (ibid.). (See also under SOUTH MALLING.)

LULLINGSTONE

1171   1 knight owed for Lullingstone and Yaldham (see also under WROTHAM) by William Malet, and also ½ for Stonepit (see under TEYNHAM).

    NOTE: William Malet was the successor of Geoffrey de Ros who in 1086 held Lullingstone and two other manors of Odo. King Stephen granted Archbishop William all that Geoffrey de Ros had held of him in chief (Lambeth MS. 1212, p. 197).

1210–12   1 fee held by William Malet, who also held $\frac{1}{2}$ fee in Yaldham. Stonepit was now in the hands of Robert Malet, another member of the family.

1308   1 fee held by Nicholas Poyntz (*Reg. Pecham*, p. 20; cf. *IPM*, II, no. 193; V, no. 45).

1346   1 fee formerly held by Hugh de Poyntz, now by Roger de Chaundos.

1360   Homage and fealty done by John de Poyns, kt, for his lands in Lullingstone (Reg. Islip, fo. 60).

1380   On 20 March the archbishop's steward was ordered to deliver to Robert Poyns, son and heir of John Poyns, who had reached his majority, the lands in Lullingstone for which he had done homage and fealty to the archbishop (Reg. Sudbury, fo. 74v).

LYDD. See under LANGPORT

LYMINGE. See also under EASTLEIGH, SIBTON and SANDHURST

1086 $2\frac{1}{2}$ sulungs and $\frac{1}{2}$ yoke of this manor held by three men of the archbishop; on the demesne(s) $5\frac{1}{2}$ ploughs and 1 serf; 2 mills worth 7s. 6d.; 40 acres of meadow; wood to render 11 swine; 2 churches. All this worth £11.

c. 1090   2 sulungs of this manor held by Robert fitzWazo (*filius Watsonis*); $\frac{1}{2}$ sulung by Robert of Hardres; $\frac{1}{2}$ yoke by Osbert Pasforera. 1 yoke, called *Sturtune*, of a separate sulung called *Aelmesland* in Romney Marsh (belonging to the alms of the monks) held by William Folet, and the other three yokes of it (called Orgarswick, *Cassetuisle* and *Eadrunesland*) held by the aforesaid Robert.

> NOTE: In both Domesday (I, p. 5) and *Domesday Monachorum* (p. 92) Robert fitzWazo is said to hold *Aelmesland* (*Asmeslant*) as 1 sulung from the prior of Christ Church *at farm*, paying to the sacrist at Canterbury, and of this William Folet had 1 yoke, worth 10s. p.a. to him. It is also remarkable that if *Cassetuisle*, one of the constituent yokes of the sulung in question, is the modern Castweazel (and it is hard to believe it is not), then it was some twenty miles away from Lyminge, and not in the Marsh.

1093–6   Osbern Pasforir owed the service of $\frac{1}{4}$ knight, possibly for his $\frac{1}{2}$ yoke here.

1171   Some portion of his lands for 3 knights were held by Thomas son of Thomas fitzBernard in *Sibetun* (Sibton (q.v.) in Lyminge).

MAIDSTONE. See also under IFIELD

1086 4 sulungs of this manor held by 3 knights. On the demesne
3½ ploughs; 32 *villani* with 4 bordars have 6 ploughs and 10
serfs; 1 mill worth 5*s*.; 13 acres of meadow; 2½ fisheries
rendering 180 eels; 2 saltpans; wood to render 23 swine. The
land of the knights is worth £15 10*s*.

c. 1090 1 sulung worth 50*s*. held by Ralph; 2 sulungs worth £10 held
by William the brother of Bishop Gundulf; 1 sulung worth 60*s*.
held by Anscetil de Ros.

1093–6 William de Detlinge (Gundulf's brother) answered for ½ fee;
Anscetil de Ros answered for 1½ fees.

1171 1 knight owed by William of Detting (*Denlung*) in Detling;
some land in fee held in Shofford, Maidstone, by William son
of Haimo.

NOTE: This was Vitalis's grandson who also held land in
Stourmouth, etc. (see under WHITSTABLE). His father was called
Haimo son of Viel (=Vitalis) of Shofford in a twelfth-century
charter (W. G. Urry, *Annales de Normandie* (May 1958), p. 132).
In Archbishop Langton's time ¾ fee was held in Shofford by
William of Shofford, kt (Lambeth MS. 1212, p. 214).

Land for 1 knight in Cooling and ½ knight in Cossington held
by William de Ros, though he acknowledged only 1 knight.

NOTE: Odo had held two manors in Cooling and a large
manor at Hoo near by, of which Anscetil de Ros had held
three sulungs. These may represent the fee in Cooling held by
his successor, William de Ros, in 1171. The archbishop
evidently had some claim here. King Stephen had granted to
Archbishop William all that Geoffrey de Ros had held of him
in chief (Lambeth MS. 1212, p. 197). In 1202 King John granted
the archbishop the whole fee of William de Ros over which
there had been contention between former kings and archbishops (Lambeth MS. 1212, pp. 47, 197–8; LCM, XI,
p. 16).

1210–12 ½ fee in Detling held by William of Detling; two ½ fees, each
held in both Cooling and Cossington, one by William de
Culinges, the other by Stephen de Cusintone, and both of
William de Ros; another ½ fee in Cossington held by William
de Ros directly: all these of the archbishop. $\frac{1}{20}$ fee in Buckland
held by Alan de Boclonde.

NOTE: That this is Little Buckland in Maidstone would
appear from the entry under 1279, below.

1253–4 ¾ fee in Shofford (*Saford*) held by William de Saford.

NOTE: This was probably the descendant of Vitalis. In 1253–4 there was a fee in Stourmouth (see under WHITSTABLE), where Vitalis's family also held, said to be held by the tenants of land formerly of William of Shofford. See also note under 1171, above.

$\frac{1}{2}$ fee in Shofford held by the daughter of Alan the clerk, who holds it of Simon of Cray, who holds it of the archbishop. Detling, held freely in fee-farm, by William of Detling.

1279 $\frac{1}{20}$ fee in Buckland, parish of Maidstone, held by Walter de la Bockland (*Reg. Pecham*, p. 13);

1 fee in Detling held for £13 p.a. by William of Detling (*Reg. Pecham*, pp. 11–12).

1291 $\frac{1}{2}$ fee, unnamed, held by William de Detelinge, which William his father held (*Reg. Pecham*, p. 18).

1346 $\frac{1}{2}$ fee held by John of Detling and Thomas of Buckwell, and formerly by William of Detling.

$\frac{1}{4}$ fee in Shofford held by the lord Bartholomew de Bughersshe, and formerly by Ralph of Ditton.

1355   Manor of Shofford held of archbishop for $\frac{1}{4}$ fee, of the prior of Leeds for 5s. p.a., and of Robert Vyntner for 2s. 10d., and of Thomas Colpeper for 8d. p.a., by Bartholomew de Burgherssh, deceased (*IPM*, X, no. 253).

1361   Half the manor of Detling held of the archbishop *in gavelkind* by Thomas Bakwell, deceased, and his first wife, Katherine, by service of 14s. p.a. and three-weekly suit to his court at Canterbury (*IPM*, XI, no. 29).

MAKINBROOK. See under WHITSTABLE

MALLING. See under SOUTH MALLING

MAYTHAM. See under ROLVENDEN

MILTON, in Canterbury. See under WESTGATE

MOULTON, Suffolk
1210–12 2 fees held by the heir(s) of Adam Kokefelde.

NEWCHURCH, near Bilsington
1253–4 $\frac{1}{4}$ fee held by Richard Organistre.

NEWINGTON, Bucks. See under RISBOROUGH

NEWINGTON, by Sittingbourne. See under SHEPPEY

ORPINGTON

1086   *Terra Militum.* 3 yokes held by Malger. TRE assessed as 3
yokes separately from Orpington, but TRW as 2 yokes inside
and 1 yoke outside Orpington. On the demesne 1 plough; 4
villani with 1 bordar and 4 serfs have ½ plough; 3 acres of
meadow; woodland to render 10 swine. TRE worth 40s., when
received 20s., now 50s.

c. 1090   A manor assigned to the monks' clothing. 3 yokes held of it
from the archbishop by Malger had been held TRE by a
certain free man. They were claimed by the archbishop from
Odo, and did not pay scot with the manor. Valued at 50s. Of
the same sulungs Dirman has ½ sulung at Keston.

1093–6   Malger owed the service of ¼ knight.
Dirman owed the service of ⅓ knight.

1171   ¼ knight owed from Little Orpington (no name of tenant).

1210–12   ¼ fee held by Philip de Maleville of Robert of Ruxley, and by
him of the archbishop.

NOTE: Philip de Maleville was also the archbishop's tenant
in HALSTEAD (q.v.), not far away.

1251   Robert de Maleville transferred quarter of ½ fee in Orpington
to Philip de Maleville (*F. of F.*, p. 236).

NOTE: In 1270 Adam, Philip's son, was acquiring land in
Orpington and Cudham (*F. of F.*, p. 361).

1279   ¼ fee in Little Orpington held by William de Maleville,
deceased, of John de Rokesle, kt (*IPM*, I, no. 805).

OTFORD

1086   1½ sulungs held by 3 'thegns'. On the demesne 3 ploughs, and
16 *villani* with 11 bordars have 4 ploughs; 5 serfs; 2 mills worth
24s.; 28 acres of meadow; wood to render 30 swine. The land
of the thegns now worth £12.

c. 1090   Haimo holds land worth 70s.; Robert the interpreter and
Gosfrid de Ros hold land worth £8 10s.

NOTE: The earl of Gloucester as lord of Tonbridge held in
his lowy a portion of Otford among other places.

1171   Some portion of his land for three knights held by the earl of
Gloucester in Filston (in Shorebam, part of Otford). See also
LITTLE CHART (Pett Place), BRASTED, HORSMONDEN and WESTGATE
(Milton).

NOTE: For the earls' inheritance from Haimo, see above, p. 86.

Land for ½ knight held in Dunton (Green) in Otford by an unnamed tenant.

1210–12 1 fee held by the countess of Clare.
½ fee in Dunton (*Donintone*) held by Ralph Morin.
⅛ fee in Shoreham held by Ralph de Planaz.
There were also 7 fees described as held of the manor of Otford by the bishop of Rochester, but these were not carved out of the Canterbury lands. See above, p. 84.

1247 Bartholomew of Wateringbury (*Oteringebyr'*) was holding 1 fee in Filston of William of Shofford; he was successfully sued for its service, and in turn successfully sued Haimo of Filston in 1248 for service which included 40*s.* scutage when it shall happen (*F. of F.*, pp. 195, 198). In 1271 Haimo of Filston received a life-grant of the manor of Filston from Hamo son of Hamo and his wife Alice (*F. of F.*, p. 389).

1274 Reliefs paid this year in the Otford bailiff's account after the deaths of the following tenants by knight-service: Matilda, widow of Geoffrey Percy, £33 6*s.* 8*d.*; Nicholas Poynt, £5; Ralph of Hever, 12*s.* 6*d.* and £1 for the mill (Addit. MS. 29794, m. 7).

NOTE: Nicholas Poynt or Poynz d. 1273 holding land in military tenure of the king in other counties as well as Kent (*IPM*, II, no. 18). He held gavelkind lands in Otford also (Dean and Chapter of Canterbury MS. E 24, fo. 69v.); also a fee in LULLINGSTONE (q.v.).

1279 1 fee in Dunton, parish of Chevening, held by Osbert de Longchamp (*Reg. Pecham*, p. 12).

NOTE: Dunton Manor had been leased in 1245 for twenty-six years by William de Longchamp to John of Gisors for £140 (*F. of F.*, p. 186).

Homage in Otford recorded, but not the fee, of master John Planace (*Reg. Pecham*, p. 15).

NOTE: John de Planaz d. 1293 holding a 'messuage, dovecote, 42 acres of arable, 8¼ acres of meadow, 70 acres of pasture, 16 acres of underwood and a water-mill in Shoreham of the archbishop for ⅛ fee in Shoreham'; also numerous other small parcels there of other tenants for nominal rents. No other lands (*IPM*, III, p. 118).

¼ fee in vill of Otford held by John de Bockele (*Reg. Pecham*, p. 9).

1346   1 fee in Filston held by Reginald de Cobham, kt, by grant of the king, but formerly held by John son of John of Filston.
$\frac{1}{4}$ fee at Dunton held by William Moraunt, and formerly by the heirs of Osbert Longchamp (*de Longo Campo*).
$\frac{1}{4}$ fee at Denhull (lost, in Sevenoaks) held by master Henry de Grofherst, and formerly by Richard de Esshwy.

1348 $\frac{1}{4}$ fee in Filston, Penshurst and Chiddingstone held by John de Cepham of Hugh d'Audley (earl of Gloucester), deceased; and 1 fee in Filston held by John of Filston and John de Cepham of Hugh d'Audley; both of the archbishop (*IPM*, IX, no. 63).

1361   Manor of Hever held by John de Cobham of Randall, deceased, by service of $\frac{1}{2}$ fee, of archbishop as of his manor of Otford (*IPM*, XI, no. 240).

OVERLAND. See under WINGHAM

OXNEY. See under WITTERSHAM

PAGHAM, Sussex. See also TANGMERE

1086   1 hide held of the archbishop by Oismelin, who has there 2 bordars.

1093–6   Osmelinus owed the service of $\frac{1}{4}$ knight.

1171   Land for $\frac{1}{4}$ knight in Pagham held by Elias of Lagness.

NOTE: Elias of Lagness was living in 1178–9 (*P.R. 25 Hen. II,* p. 37); see also Lindsay Fleming, *History of Pagham* (privately printed, 1949), I, pp. 151–6.

1202   Mundham in Pagham, formerly disputed between Archbishop Becket and John Marshal (*Materials for the History of Thomas Becket,* ed. J. C. Robertson, Rolls Series 1877, III, p. 50), to be held now by William Marshal of the archbishop for service of $\frac{1}{2}$ fee and 100*s*. p.a., with wardship of the heirs to the fee to the archbishop (Lambeth MS. 1212, pp. 48, 195; Lindsay Fleming, op. cit., I, pp. XLVI, 17–20).

NOTE: Walter of Pagham was the archbishop's marshal of horses in 1267 (Lambeth MS. 1212, pp. 421–2).

1210–12 $\frac{1}{4}$ fee held by Hamo of Lagness.
$\frac{1}{10}$ fee (unnamed) held by Richard de Paggeham.

1242–3 $\frac{1}{4}$ fee in Lagness held by Thomas of Lagness (*Book of Fees*, I, p. 692).

1285 $\frac{1}{4}$ fee held by William of Lagness who owes homage and suit of court; $\frac{1}{2}$ fee in Mundham and Bowley held by the Earl Marshal: he ought to come to court if any judgment remains in respite upon a king's writ for default of peers, and owes 100s. p.a. in quarterly instalments.

PETHAM

1086 1½ sulungs and 1 yoke held by Godfrey and Nigel, who have there 4 ploughs, and 4 *villani* with 8 bordars have 3 ploughs. Worth in all £9, from which the monks have 8s. p.a.

1086–7 Whiteacre and Wadden Hall, Little London and Denstead granted as 1 fee to Nigel and Robert (*Cart. of St Gregory's Priory*, p. 2).

c. 1090 ½ sulung at Swarling belonging to the monks' clothing held by Godfrey *dapifer*; Godfrey dapifer renders farm to the monks (*Dom. Mon.*, p. 95); 1 sulung 1 yoke, valued at 40s., held by Nigel.

1093–6 Niel de Huatacra (Whiteacre, in Waltham near Petham) answered for ½ fee. Robert de Hardes (Hardres) was probably the holder of Wadden Hall, though in *Dom. Mon.* he held lands of the archbishop in Westgate and Lyminge.

1171 Land for 1 knight in Swarling held by William son of Nigel, and by Godfrey of Fawkham.

Land for ½ knight held in Whitacre (no tenant named).

NOTE: Godfrey of Fawkham was also a knight of the bishop of Rochester (*Textus Roffensis*, p. 223).

½ knight owed by Roger of Wadden Hall.

NOTE: This and the ½ fee in Whiteacre were probably the two halves of the enfeoffment made in 1086–7 to Nigel and Robert. A Maurice of Wadden Hall occurs in 1176 (*Facsimiles of Royal and other Charters in the British Museum*, ed. Warner and Ellis (1903), no. 57).

1210–12 1 fee in Swarling held by John de Valognes.

½ fee in Whiteacre (*Watekene*) held by William Gallarde.

1 fee in Wadden Hall held by Thomas de Wodenhale.

NOTE: Thomas and John of Wodenhale were brothers, and sold marshland on the Kent–Sussex border to Archbishop Langton for £20 (Lambeth MS. 1212, p. 93).

1253–4 1 fee in Swarling held by Warrisius de Valognes.

NOTE: In 1254 Warrisius made a settlement with Canterbury cathedral priory by which he was forgiven some twelve years' arrears of the 8s. annual farm with which he was charged upon certain lands called *Underdune* in Swarling, provided it was henceforth paid regularly at Easter (*F. of F.*, p. 255).

½ fee in Whiteacre held by Furmentinus de Whetacre.
½ fee in Wadden Hall held by John de Wodenhale.

NOTE: In 1272 Thomas of Wadenhale paid 50s. relief for ½ fee in Wadden Hall (P.R. 119, m. 41d.).

1279   1 fee (in Swarling?) held by Warrisius de Valognes, kt (*Reg. Pecham*, p. 2).
½ fee in Wadden Hall and in Denstead, parish of Chartham, held by William de Hawte (ibid., p. 14).

1292   1 fee in Swarling and ¼ and ⅛ fee in Stourmouth (q.v.) held by Warrisius de Valognes (ibid., p. 18).

NOTE: Warrisius de Valognes evidently enfeoffed both his sons, Warrisius and Henry, with property in knightly tenure. It was Henry who kept many armed followers at Swarling in 1324, to the terror of local people (*Lit. Cant.*, I, p. lxviii and nos. 99, 129).

1346   ½ and ⅙ (?) fee in Swarling held by Geoffrey de Say, and formerly by Warrisius de Valognes.
$\frac{9}{40}$ fee in Whiteacre held by the heirs of Nigel of Whiteacre, and formerly by Furmentinus of Whiteacre.
$\frac{1}{10}$ of the same held by the prior of St Gregory's, Canterbury.
$\frac{9}{80}$ of the same held by the heirs of Sarre of Whiteacre, and formerly by the prior of St Gregory's, Canterbury.
$\frac{9}{80}$ of the same held by the heirs of William of Cranbrook, Alice his sister and their tenants.
¼ fee in Wadden Hall held by Henry de Hawte, and formerly by William de Hawte.
$\frac{1}{12}$ fee, unnamed, held in Petham Hundred by Thomas de Poldre.

NOTE: John de Poldre held ⅛ fee in DENSTEAD (q.v.) in 1346. Tenure in Denstead was connected with tenure in Petham, as will be observed above, under 1086 and 1279.

1370   Manor of Wadden Hall held for ½ fee and 3-weekly suit to the archbishop's Palace of Canterbury by Henry de Haute, deceased, who also held 2 fees elsewhere of the king, and 10 acres in socage of the archbishop in Aldington (*IPM*, XIII, no. 33; cf. *C.Cl.R. 1369-74*, p. 165). During the minority of Nicholas, kinsman and heir of the deceased, custody was granted by Archbishop Whittlesey to Benedicta, widow of Thomas Uvedale (Reg. Whittlesey, fo. 35v., *s.d.* 6 November 1370).

1498   Manor of Wadden Hall, worth £13 6s. 8d. p.a., held of the archbishop by William Haute, kt, deceased, service unknown;

he had also held Bishopsbourne and Elmsted of the archbishop (*IPM Hen. VII*, II, no. 145).

PETT PLACE, near Charing. See under LITTLE CHART

PLUCKLEY

1086   Still a demesne manor of the archbishop, assessed at 1 sulung; land for 12 ploughs; in demesne 2½ ploughs; 16 *villani* and 7 bordars have 11 ploughs; 8 serfs; 12½ acres of meadow; wood to render 140 swine. TRE worth £12, when received £8, now £15 yet it renders £20 (*Dom. Mon.* adds *de firma*).

1086–7   Pluckley enfeoffed to 'William' (*Cart. of St Gregory's Priory*, p. 2).

NOTE: This was doubtless William Folet, who also held of the archbishop in Finglesham, Tilmanstone and STATENBOROUGH (q.v.), and Sandtun near Lympne.

c. 1090   In *Dom. Mon.*, however, Pluckley is still described in the same terms as in the Exchequer Domesday of 1086, possibly through a scribe's error.

1093–6   William Folet owed 2 fees.

1171   Land for 2 knights in Pluckley held by William Folet.

1210–12   2 fees held by Stephen Folet.

1253–4   1¾ fees (Malmains in Pluckley?), Calehill Hundred, held by Henry Malmeyns and John of Selling.

1279   1 fee in Pluckley held by John Malmeyn (*Reg. Pecham*, p. 8).

1287   1 fee in the vill of Pluckley held by John de Sellynge (ibid., p. 17).

1303   ⅞ fee in Pluckley held by John Malemayne, son and heir of John Malemayns, kt (ibid., p. 19).

PRESTON, EAST, in Aylesford

1171   1 fee of the Honour of Talbot held for Preston by Walter de Mayenne.

NOTE: The Honour of Talbot meant the lands of Geoffrey I Talbot, lord of Swanscombe (d. 1129–30) and his son Geoffrey II (d. 1140). The latter left two daughters, one of whom married Walter de Mayenne.

1210–12   2 fees held by the countess of Arundel, of which John of Dammartin holds 1. (This is not certainly Preston in Aylesford.) ¼ fee (unnamed but occurring in the list between Tottington in Aylesford and Boughton Malherbe) held by Ralph de Prestone.

NOTE: In 1219 Emma of Luddesdown alleged that her brother had given her ¼ fee in East Preston by charter, but that Reginald of Luddesdown, the brother's son, had impleaded his aunt in the court of Warin de Munchesny, so that she had to put herself on the Grand Assize (*F. of F.*, p. cxxix). The sequel is unknown. But see also under HALSTEAD.

1253–4 1 fee in Preston, Larkfield Hundred, held by John de Marisco.

NOTE: In 1093–6, a Richard de Mares (=de Marisco) had owed the archbishop the service of one knight, and in 1086 had held of Odo at Ospringe.

1279 1 fee held by William de Munchesny (*Reg. Pecham*, p. 4).

NOTE: Henry III gave his half-brother, William de Valence, custody of the land and the heir of Warin de Munchesny who was a tenant-in-chief, whereupon William took possession of the knight's fee in Preston. King's council decided in 1258 that the archbishop should suffer no prejudice through this (*Reg. Winchelsey*, p. 881; *C.Cl.R. 1256–9*, p. 276).

1491 Manor of East Preston, worth 66s. 8d., held of the archbishop by the service of 1 fee by Joan Brent, deceased, formerly wife of John Gaynesford, esquire, amongst other properties which she had enfeoffed before her death (*IPM Hen. VII*, I, no. 781).

RATLING. See under WINGHAM

RICHBOROUGH. See under WINGHAM

RISBOROUGH, Bucks

1171 Land for 1 fee held in the manor of Risborough by Walter de Pend' and his *socii*.

NOTE: Comparison with the list of 1093–6 suggests that the Norman tenants were Ulf and Herebert. The estate is the hamlet of Owlswick in Monks' Risborough (*V.C.H. Buckinghamshire*, II, p. 257).

1210–12 1 fee in Newington and Risborough held by Thomas de Berewike with Henry de Lawike and Humfrey de Reda.

1242–3 ¾ fee (in Bucks.) held by Baldwin de Wulneswyk and Bartholomew de la Ponde (*Book of Fees*, II, p. 897).

1274 Relief of 25s. (i.e. for ½ fee) paid by Bartholomew de Ponte of Risborough (Addit. MS. 29794, m. 1d.).

1289 ½ fee in Risborough held by John son of Henry Baudewyn of Risborough (*Reg. Pecham*, p. 17).

ROLVENDEN

1237 $\frac{1}{4}$ yoke in Freezingham bought by William of Kensham (*F. of F.*, p. 146).

1253-4 $\frac{1}{20}$ fee in Maytham, parish of Rolvenden, held by William of Kensham; $\frac{1}{20}$ fee in Devenden, same parish, similarly held.

1279 $\frac{1}{8}$ fee in Kensham, parish of Rolvenden, and in Farningham (q.v.) held by Ralph of Kensham (*Reg. Pecham*, p. 10).

1284 $\frac{1}{2}$ virgate in Kensham and $\frac{1}{2}$ yoke in Freezingham, both in Rolvenden, held by the heirs of Ralph of Kensham for rent (7s. 6d. ancient rent and 2s. 8d. increment) and suit of court only. This tenement (which probably included all the places here mentioned under Rolvenden) had been made free by Archbishop Edmund (1233-40) by his charter as $\frac{1}{20}$ fee (MS. E 24, fo. 59v.; also R. Furley, *History of the Weald of Kent*, vol. II, Part I, pp. 202-4).

RUCKINGE. See also under EYNSFORD

1086   Ickham was listed among the monks' manors, and of this William, the man of the archbishop, held only what was worth £7.

c. 1090   1 sulung at Ruckinge out of the 4 which composed the manor of Ickham, assigned to their food, was held by William of Adisham, the man of the archbishop, and was worth £7.

1093-6   William of Eadesham answered for 1 fee.

1171   Some portion of the lands for $7\frac{1}{2}$ knights (of which he recognized the obligation for only $4\frac{3}{4}$) was held by William of Eynsford in Ruckinge.

1148-51 Archbishop Theobald confirmed the grant of Ruckinge to Christ Church made by William of Eynsford *senex*, whose wife was Hadewisa, and confirmed by his own son and grandson of the same name. Theobald, however, retained the service of 1 knight which that land owed (A. Saltman, *Theobald*, no. 42).

1261   Member of the barony of Eynsford (q.v.) (Lambeth MS. 1212, p. 417).

SALTWOOD

1086   *Terra Militum*. TRE assessed at 7 sulungs, now at 3, and held by Hugh de Montfort of the archbishop. Land for 15 ploughs. On the demesne 2 ploughs; 33 *villani* with 12 bordars have $9\frac{1}{2}$ ploughs. A church, 2 serfs, 9 mills worth 20s., 33 acres of meadow, woodland to render 80 swine. To the manor belong 225 burgesses in the borough of Hythe. Borough and manor together were worth £16 TRE, when received £8, now £29 6s. 4d.

c. 1090   Listed under the manors of the monks, and held as 1 manor from the archbishop by Hugh de Montfort; formerly by Earl Godwin. Formerly assessed at 7 sulungs, now at 5, but pays scot only for 3. From the 225 burgesses in Hythe, Hugh only has the three forfeitures. Valued at £28 6*s.* 4*d.*

1093–6   Hugh de Montfort (III) (son of Hugh (II) of 1086) answered for 4 fees.

1171   4 fees in Saltwood, 2 in the hands of the king and 2 of the fee of Robert de Montfort.

NOTE: On the death of Hugh de Montfort III his estates passed to his son Robert, who was banished in 1107, and then to Henry of Essex, one of the king's constables. Archbishop Theobald evidently recovered partial control of Saltwood, for between 1154 and 1161 he granted lands there to Robert de Montfort, a member of the family which had held the manor of his predecessors (*P.R. 15 Henry II*, p. 111). In 1163 Henry of Essex suffered forfeiture at the suit of Robert de Montfort, but his lands were taken into the king's hands (*P.R. 9 Henry II*, p. 70; cf. *8 Henry II*, p. 54, and *14 Henry II*, p. 154). Archbishop Becket demanded the restoration of Saltwood, and this became one of the issues between him and Henry II. At the pacification of 1170, Henry II ordered his son, the young king Henry, to call before him '*de antiquioribus et legalioribus militibus de honore de Saltwde, et eorum sacramento [facere] recognosci quid ibi habeatur de feudo archiepiscopi Cantuariae*' (Gervase of Canterbury, *Opera Historica*, ed. W. Stubbs (*R.S.*, 1879), I, p. 221; *Materials for the History of Thomas Becket*, ed. J. C. Robertson (*R.S.*), vii, Ep. 690). During the archbishop's exile Saltwood, like Canterbury Palace, had been in the hands of the keeper of the archbishopric, Ranulf de Broc, and his nephew (*P.R. 13 Henry II*, p. 201, etc.; *Materials for the History of Thomas Becket*, III, p. 126), and it was at Saltwood Castle that the knights mustered before approaching Canterbury to murder the archbishop. By 1171 two of the four fees were still in the king's hands, and in 1175 he demolished the castle. In the thirteenth century Saltwood appears to have become a demesne manor of the archbishopric (Addit. MS. 29794, m. 6d.; P.R. 124, m. 23d., etc.).

1197   Richard I returned to Archbishop Walter and his church Saltwood which Henry of Essex had held in fee of the archbishop and forfeited for felony, and which Henry II and the present king had long held thereafter (Lambeth MS. 1212, p. 34). In 1197, however, the then Hugh de Montfort had evidently been holding it and had let it out to farm, for he now quit-claimed the archbishop of it, provided that the fee-farmer, Ingram de Praers (*Pratellis*), might continue to hold it thus, at 100s. p.a., of the archbishop (ibid., p. 76). Richard's concession was confirmed by John in 1199 (*Rot. Chart.*, p. 23).

1210–12 2 fees held by Ingram de Praers.

NOTE: This appears to be an instance of a local fee-farmer and estate-builder becoming a direct knightly tenant of the archbishop. In 1225 Archbishop Langton sued him for the ser-vice of two fees and 100s. annual rent in respect of one carucate of land at Saltwood. It was difficult to get a jury together, and no result is known, but the de Praers family was not disseised (*Curia Regis Rolls*, XII, nos. 1466, 2455). In 1228 the king granted Ingram, son of Ingram de Praers, whose homage he had taken for lands which the father held in chief of the arch-bishopric and which the son had inherited, the corn in the fields this autumn, the see being vacant (*C.Cl.R. 1227–31*, p. 76). In 1236 Ingram is glimpsed buying and selling property in the neighbourhood (*F. of F.*, pp. 129, 142).

1253–4 $\frac{1}{2}$ fee in Thorn (in Saltwood) held by the heir(s) of Ingram de Praers.

$\frac{1}{40}$ fee in *Blakewose* (Blackhouse Hill Shaw, in Saltwood) held by John Edwy.

NOTE: In 1285 a William Eadwy was holding freely in Salt-wood for suit to the archbishop's court at Canterbury (Dean and Chapter of Canterbury MS. E 24, fo. 62v.).

1308 1 fee in Brockhill, otherwise known as Thorn, parish of Salt-wood, held by Ralph Bluet (*Reg. Pecham*, pp. 20–1).

1346 1 fee, of the Honour of Perche.

$\frac{1}{3}$ fee at Thorn, of the same Honour.

$\frac{1}{80}$ fee at *Blakewose* held by Nicholas ate Morehalle and formerly by William Edewy.

$\frac{2}{3}$ fee in Thorn and Saltwood held by Thomas de Brokhull and formerly by William de Brokhull.

SANDHURST

1349 1 messuage and 100 acres in *Betryngdenne* held by John son of John of Betryngdenne for the service of $\frac{1}{8}$ fee (*C.Cl.R. 1349–54*, p. 122).

NOTE: Betherinden was a denn of Lyminge (Dean and Chapter of Canterbury MS. E 24, fo. 64v.). It is locally understood to be the same as Old Place, Sandhurst (*ex. inf.* Mr F. C. Clark, of Sandhurst).

SARRE. See under WHITSTABLE

SHEPPEY (belonging to TEYNHAM (q.v.))

1086   *Terra Militum.* ½ sulung held by Godfrey *dapifer.* On the demesne 1 plough with 2 bordars and 4 serfs. TRE and afterwards worth 30*s.*, now £4, yet it pays £5.

c. 1090 ½ sulung of Teynham in Sheppey held by Godfrey de Melling. Worth £4 yet renders £5. TRE Osuuard held it of the archbishop.

1171   Land for 1 knight held by Richard de Luci in *Neutun'* (Newington by Sittingbourne) and Sheppey.

     NOTE: Richard de Luci was the justiciar and d. 1179. His land here mentioned cannot with complete confidence be identified with the Domesday ½ sulung described above. Richard de Luci was granted land worth 60*s.* in Teynham during Becket's exile (*P.R. 13 Henry II*, p. 201). But de Luci's fee is probably to be equated with that held in 1093–6 by Ralph Guiz or Goz, who held lands in Newington (*Regesta*, II, no. 1142). Luci was also granted lands in Newington by Henry II (*Black Book of St Augustine*, ed. G. J. Turner and H. E. Salter, pp. 283–4).

1223   William Briwer enfeoffed Geoffrey de Luci in a carucate in Newington for the service of ½ fee, in return for property in Cornwall (*F. of F.*, p. 79; cf. pp. cxix, cxxx).

1279   ¾ fee held by Thomas de Thymeford (*Reg. Pecham*, p. 16).

SHOREHAM. See under OTFORD

SIBTON, in Lyminge. See also under LYMINGE

1210–12 2 fees in Eythorne (q.v.), Sibton and Eastleigh in Lyminge (*Lega*) (q.v.) held by Ralph fitzBernard.

     NOTE: The fitzBernards, lords in Sibton, possessed their court there in 1250 (*F. of F.*, p. 231).

1279   3 fees in Sibton, parish of Lyminge, and in New Romney (q.v.) held by Ralph fitzBernard (*Reg. Pecham*, p. 14).

1306   Manor of Sibton (extent given) together with advowson of church of Old Romney held for 1 fee and three-weekly suit at archbishop's court; also 11 acres arable in the same manor in gavelkind held of archbishop by service of 2*s.* p.a. and three-weekly suit at his court at Lyminge, by Ralph fitzBernard, deceased, whose heir is Thomas son of John fitzBernard, aged over 18 (*IPM*, IV, no. 387).

NOTE: The tenure of the manor of Sibton in the fourteenth century is also noted severally as for ¼ fee (*IPM*, VII, no. 606), two fees and three-weekly suit at the archbishop's palace of Canterbury (*IPM*, X, nos. 519, 523), and merely 3*s*. p.a. payable at Lyminge with three-weekly suit there (*IPM*, VIII, no. 185; XIII, no. 212).

SLINDON, Sussex

NOTE: Henry I gave the archbishop two fees in Slindon, service being demanded from the earl of Arundel, but in 1210–12 the archbishop claimed to hold nothing from this, and there is no sign of knightly land in the 1285 rental of Slindon (*S.R.S.*, vol. 57, pp. 1–10).

SNARGATE

1253–4 ¼ fee held by Gervase Alard.

1368 Manor held by Agnes Alard, deceased, of the archbishop by service of ½ fee (*IPM*, XII, no. 209).

SOUTH MALLING, Sussex

1086 5 hides held by Bainiard. On the demesne 2 ploughs, and 14 *villani* with 2 bordars have 2 ploughs; 35 acres of meadow; from pasturage 3 swine. Worth £8.

2 hides held by (William?) son of Boselin (de Dives?). On the demesne 1 plough, and 11 *villani* with 2 bordars have 3 ploughs; 2 mills worth 10*s*.; from pasturage 2 swine; from woodland 20 swine. Worth £3.

1 hide (probably Glynde) held by Godfrey (of Malling). On the demesne 2 ploughs; 2 *villani* with 3 bordars; a mill yielding 5*s*.; woodland yielding 1 swine. Worth 50*s*.

⅔ of ½ hide held by Walter. On the demesne 2 ploughs; 1 *villanus* and 1 bordar have 1 plough; 3 acres of meadow; woodland yielding 3 swine, and pasturage yielding 1 swine. Worth 40*s*.

1 virgate at Alchorne (in Buxted and Rotherfield) held by William de Cahainges.

1093–6 In the list of knights, Godfrey of Malling owed the service of 3 knights, and also held South Malling at farm for £90 p.a. He also held in LENHAM and Hunton in EAST FARLEIGH (q.v.).

1171 Some portion of his lands for 3 knights was held by Richard le

Waleys in Buxted and Glynde. (See also under THANINGTON and LOSSENHAM.)

NOTE: Buxted was part of the manor of Glynde (*S.R.S.*, vol. 57, p. xxvii).

¼ knight in the tenure of Malling owed by William, of Ringmer (?—MS. obscure).

1210 Godfrey Waleys sued Ralph de Arderne for the manors of Glynde, Tarring and Patching in Sussex, and Thanington and Newenden in Kent. His mother Denise, probably the descendant and heiress of Godfrey of Malling, had, after the death of Richard Waleys, her first husband, married Ralph de Arderne. Though she had no issue by her second husband, nevertheless Ralph received these lands from Archbishop Walter. Godfrey Waleys won the suit, but at high cost, and he granted Ralph a life-interest in Patching (*Curia Regis Rolls*, VI, pp. 11–12; *F. of F.*, p. 56; *P.R. 11 John*, p. 37).

NOTE: A Godfrey, son of William of Malling held the farm of Patching in 1155 (A. Saltman, *Theobald*, pp. 535–6). This may have been the father or the brother of Denise.

1210–12 1 fee in Glynde held by Robert son of Walter.
1½ fees in Glynde held by Godfrey Waleys.
¼ fee in *Grenestede* (East Grinstead) held by William de Kahainges.

NOTE: The identification of East Grinstead is from R. G. Robert, *Place-Names of Sussex* (1914), p. 74. The tenure of de Cahainges of South Malling will be noted above, in the Domesday entry. The classification into East and West Grinstead, however, does not appear until the Hundred Rolls of 1274.

1279 ½ fee in *Grenestede* held by Roger de Leukenore (*Reg. Pecham*, p. 12). Homage done by Richard le Waleys, but his fee is not mentioned (ibid.).
1 fee in Isfield held by Roger le Ware (Warre) (ibid.).

NOTE: In the time of Stephen Langton, custody of land at *Ysefeld* had been granted to Ralph of Wydington during the minority of the heir (Lambeth MS. 1212, p. 93).

1285 3 fees (probably) held by Richard Waleys in the *tenura* of Malling at Glynde (Dean and Chapter of Canterbury MSS. E 24, fo. 141, printed in *S.R.S.*, vol. 57, p. 117).
1 fee held by the lord of Isfield, by the free service of his arms (ibid.).

NOTE: The custumal says, under Isfield, that Sir John de la Ware holds about six hundred acres of land, etc., and owes the archbishop suit only therefor, and holds a view of frankpledge for his tenants at his court, but by what warrant it is not known (ibid., p. 83).

$\frac{1}{2}$ fee held by the lord of Courthope (q.v.) by the free service of his arms (ibid.).

1303   1 fee in Glynde and $\frac{1}{2}$ fee in Buxted held by Geoffrey le Waleys, brother and heir of Richard (see also under LOSSENHAM) *Reg. Pecham*, p. 19).

1305 $\frac{1}{4}$ fee held by the lord of *Horstede* by the free service of his arms (*S.R.S.*, vol. 57, p. 117).

1320   Manor of Isfield held by Roger la Ware, deceased, for life by demise of John la Ware, his son, as appears by a fine levied in the king's court, of the archbishop of Canterbury by service of 1 fee (*IPM*, VI, no. 249).

1323 $\frac{1}{12}$ fee in Worth by Buxted (a messuage, a carucate of land, 8 acres of wood and 7s. 6d. rent) held of the archbishop by Richard of Pevensey and Ela his wife and heirs (*IPM*, VI, no. 499).

1349   Manor of Buxted held for life of Joan, widow of Roger de Maryns, now deceased, of the gift of Roger, of the inheritance of Henry de Haute, who survives, of Sir John de Waleys, kt, by the service of $\frac{1}{4}$ fee to the archbishop; the see now void (*IPM*, IX, no. 140).

1349 $\frac{2}{3}$ manor of Isfield held for life by Margaret, late wife of John la Warre, by gift of Sir John la Warr, his father, who held the manor of the archbishopric for 1 fee (*IPM*, IX, no. 237).

1359   Manor of Buxted held jointly by Geoffrey de Say, deceased, Maud, his wife, and William their son, who survives, by gift of Richard de Chuderlegh, parson of the church of Marnhill (Dorset) and John Cramphorn, to be held of John de Waleys, kt, by service of $\frac{1}{2}$ fee and 33s. 8$\frac{3}{4}$d. p.a. to the archbishop at his manor of South Malling (*IPM*, X, no. 517).

1370   Manor of Isfield held jointly by Roger de la Ware, kt, deceased, and Elizabeth, his wife, by feoffment of Thomas de Wyke and John his son, etc., as in a fine in the king's court, for 1 fee (*IPM*, XIII, no. 57).

1375   Buxted held by William de Say, kt, deceased, of Sir John Waleys, kt, for $\frac{1}{2}$ fee and rent of 32s. 8$\frac{3}{4}$d. p.a., as above (*IPM*, XIV, no. 207).

1418–19 Manor of Glynde, to which belongs the manor of Patching and the mill called Millynke, in custody of the archbishop since

4 October 1418 by reason of the death of John Waleys and the minority of his son John: the manor of Glynde is valued at £24 p.a., Patching at £11 and the mill at £6 13s. 4d. (L.R. 95).

1489   Manor of Isfield, worth £24 and held by service of 1 fee as of the archbishop's manor of South Malling by Mary Grene, widow, deceased, with reversion to Nicholas Gryfyn. (Her son was a knight.) (*IPM Hen. VII*, I, no. 522.)

1491–2   Isfield in archbishop's custody by reason of minority of the heir, John Gryffin (L.R. 99).

STATENBOROUGH

1086   *Terra Militum.* ½ sulung held by William Folet, who has there 12 *villani* with 1½ ploughs. These estates (probably meaning this and Finglesham (q.v.)) were TRE worth £2, and when the archbishop received them 10s., and now 30s.

c. 1090   Allocated to the list of monastic manors. Held for ½ sulung by William Folet, and TRE by Godwin from Archbishop Aediz (Eadsige); worth 30s.

NOTE: William Folet also held in TILMANSTONE and LYMINGE (q.v.) of the archbishop. He was a man of Hugh de Montfort, but also owed the archbishop the service of 2 knights in 1093–6 (*Dom. Mon.*, 48, 105).

STISTED, Essex

1171   ¼ knight owed from Stisted, but the tenant not named.

NOTE: In 1086 this was a demesne manor of the monks. Under Anselm it was held at farm by one Ansfrid, whose son John forcibly occupied it during the vacancy of the see between 1136 and 1139. After John's death Theobald restored it to the monks, who granted it in farm to Matilda de St Sidon (A. Saltman, *Theobald*, pp. 271–2). Stisted was held from the monks of Canterbury by William de Elinton, who rendered them £10. He was father of Avelina who in 1185 was in the king's gift. Stisted then, in the king's hands, was in the custody of the sheriff of Essex, who received in the first year £3 16s. and in the second year £1 13s 4d ; the stock consisted of 10 oxen and 5 horses, 'and if there were there 16 oxen and 4 horses, 6 cows, 1 bull, 4 sows, 1 boar and 60 sheep, the vill would be worth £6 besides the £10 farm to the monks' (*Rotuli de dominabus*, (*P.R.* 35, 1915), pp. 71–2).

STONEPIT. See under TEYNHAM

STOURMOUTH. See under WHITSTABLE

STOWTING, in Aldington

1086   Held as a manor by the Count of Eu, and assessed TRE at $1\frac{1}{2}$ sulungs, TRW at 1. Land for 8 ploughs. On the demesne 2 ploughs; 27 *villani* with 13 bordars have 7 ploughs; a mill worth 25*d*.; a church, and 20 acres of meadow; wood to render 10 swine; 8 serfs. TRE worth £8, afterwards the same, TRW £10.

c. 1090   Stowting held as a manor by William of Arques, formerly by Aelfhere.

1171   Some portion of the lands held for 4 knights by the Count of Eu was in Stowting.

1210–12   1 fee in Stowting held by Stephen Harringod.

NOTE: In Domesday, Herengod held in WINGHAM (q.v.) and appeared in the 1093–6 list of knights. By the thirteenth century men of this name were living at Wingham as gavelkinders, but the knightly members of the family are found elsewhere. Stephen was one of the sons-in-law of the William of Eynsford who died in 1231. He held his fee in Stowting of the countess of Eu (d. 1246) who held it of the archbishop (*Book of Fees*, II, p. 1153, *s.a.* 1244; cf. *F. of F.*, p. cxxvii). Stephen d. 1256–7, leaving his son William, aged forty, as his heir. He had held Stowting Hundred of the king by service of 20*s*. p.a. and providing 6 men and a constable to guard the passage of the sea if necessary, on account of the king's enemies, at Sandgate. He had also held the manor of Stowting as one fee of the lord of Elham, and the advowson; also land at Stanford and Sturton of other lords (*IPM*, I, no. 389).

1253–4 $\frac{1}{4}$ fee in Stowting held by Haimo de Chagworth.
$\frac{1}{6}$ fee in Stowting held by the prior of Horton.

NOTE: During the fourteenth century the descent of the manor of Stowting with the hamlet of Stanford can be traced, often with full extents. It was held of the archbishop by service of one fee and three-weekly suit at his court at Canterbury. The hundred of Stowting, and the fair, however, were held of the king in fee-farm, and 20*s*. were payable annually to the sheriff of Kent (*IPM*, IV, nos. 91, 376; V, no. 207; VII, no. 3; XI, no. 9; XIV, nos. 183, 184).

1489   Manor of Stowting, worth £22, held for 1 fee by Thomas, bishop of London, deceased (*IPM Hen. VII*, I, no. 380).

SUNDRIDGE

1086   A fee-farm of $1\frac{1}{2}$ sulungs, probably held by Robert fitzWazo. On the demesne 3 ploughs; and 27 *villani* with 9 bordars have

8 ploughs; 8 serfs, and 3½ mills worth 13*s. 6d.*; 8 acres of meadow; wood to render 60 swine; a church. TRE worth £12, when received £16, now £18, but it renders £23 and one knight (*miles*) in the service of the archbishop.

c. 1090   A manor held TRE unjustly by Godwin, and Lanfranc justly won it at law by the king's concession against the bishop of Bayeux. Worth £18, yet he who holds it renders £24 and a knight (*eques*) as the farm of the archbishop.

1171   Some portion of his lands for 3 knights held by Thomas son of Thomas fitzBernard in Sundridge.

1210–12   Sundridge, Eythorne, Sibton and Eastleigh in Lyminge (q.v.) held for 2 fees by Ralph fitzBernard (who was probably the son of Thomas, above).

1255   ⅓ manor of Sundridge granted by Henry of Aperfield, kt, and his wife Lettice, to Henry of Aperfield (possibly his son), reserving a life-rent to the grantors (*F. of F.*, pp. 264–5).

> NOTE: In 1258 a Henry of Aperfield augmented his Sundridge holding by 60 acres (*F. of F.*, p. 298).

1279   1 fee in Sundridge held for £22 12*s.* p.a. and suit at archbishop's court by Henry of Aperfield (*Reg. Pecham*, p. 11).

> NOTE: Henry of Aperfield occurs as a knightly witness in 1261 and (with his son, Henry, also a knight) *c.* 1284 (Lambeth MS. 1212, pp. 417, 121, 123).

1346   1 fee held by Ralph of Farningham, kt, and formerly by Henry of Aperfield.

1349   Manor of Sundridge held by John son of Ralph of Farningham, deceased, as of the archbishop's manor of Otford, for 1 fee, rendering £22 and 1 mark as fee-farm (*IPM*, IX, no. 401).

1471   Manor of Sundridge had been in hands of Thomas Cobham at his death, and Henry VII claimed that Cobham's daughter, Alice, wife of Edward Brough, kt, had since had issues from it without having received livery of the manor (*IPM Hen. VII*, II, no. 920).

1486   Manor of Sundridge held by Ralph Bothe, deceased, of Edmund (Audley), bishop of Rochester, as of the palace of Rochester in right of his church of Rochester, by knight-service, three-weekly suit to the palace and 4*d.* rent to the sheriff's tourn there (*IPM Hen. VII*, I, no. 65).

SWANTON, in Mereworth

1369   A toft and 100 acres held by the courtesy of England by Lionel, duke of Clarence, deceased, in right of Elizabeth his wife, deceased, of the archbishop of Canterbury, by knight-service (*IPM*, XII, no. 331).

SWANTON, near Bilsington
1253–4   ⅙ fee held by James of Wilmington.

SWARLING. See PETHAM

TANGMERE, Sussex
1086   Held of the archbishop by 'clerks'. TRE 10 hides, TRW 6 hides. Land for (blank). On the demesne 2 ploughs, and 15 *villani* with 15 bordars have 4 ploughs; a church. TRE worth £6, afterwards £5, now £6 of which the reeve of the manor has £1. To this manor belong 4 haws in Chichester which render 22*d*.
1171   Land for 1 knight, in the archbishop's hands.

NOTE: Although noted as a demesne manor in Domesday, William of Pagham, who answered for one fee in the list of 1093–6, occurs in the list in the place which corresponds to this entry in the Glynde MS. list. Further, a John of Pagham gave Tangmere church to Monks' Horton Priory in 1154–8. Doubtless, therefore, Tangmere was enfeoffed by 1093–6, even though in 1171 it was again in the archbishop's hands. In 1218 Richard of Pagham sued the archbishop for nine hides on a writ of *mort d'ancestor* (*V.C.H. Sussex*, IV, p. 237; *Curia Regis Rolls*, VIII, pp. 40, 295; IX, p. 236). In 1221 a settlement appears to have been reached when Richard of Pagham gave Archbishop Stephen nine hides at Tangmere and received back one hide (sixty acres, boundaries given) for the service of ⅑ fee (Lambeth MS. 1212, p. 216).

1284   2 hides in Tangmere held for ¼ fee by William of Pagham, who had to maintain the fence of the park as far as his land extended alongside; and if on the king's writ some judgment in court was held in respite for default of peers, then he had to come to the court (MS. E 24, fo. 106v., printed in *S.R.S.*, 57, p. 11). An example of such a case where peers from the archbishop's knights were required is in *Curia Regis Rolls*, XII, pp. 1466, 2455.

TARRING, Sussex
1086   4 hides held by William de Braose. On the demesne 1 plough, and 4 *villani* with 5 bordars have 1½ ploughs; 5 acres of

meadow; 10*d.* from woodland; 20*s.* and 2 swine from pannage. Worth 70*s.*

1093–6 William de Brausa owed the service of 1 knight.

1171 1 knight owed for Edburton, Sussex, by William de Braose.

NOTE: Edburton was about three miles from William de Braose's castle of Bramber, and is about eight miles from West Tarring.

1210–12 ¼ fee in Tarring held by Godfrey de Waleys.
1 fee in Edburton, held by William de Braose.

NOTE: In 1210 William de Braose fled to France, his lands were seized by the king, and his son murdered at Corfe.

1285 ¼ fee held by John le Fry, who owes suit and as heriot his horse with harness (MS. E 24, fo. 111; printed in *S.R.S.*, 57, p. 23).
1 fee held by the lord of Edburton by the free service of his arms (ibid., p. 117).

1418–19 Archbishop received 10*s.* as issues of a garden in Tarring held in feudal custody during the minority of the lord de Hungerford (L.R. 95).

TEYNHAM. See also under SHEPPEY

1171 ½ knight owed for Doddington (in Teynham) by Hugh of Doddington.

NOTE: Doddington was farmed for 60*s.* in *Dom. Mon.* This and the other enfeoffments in the Teynham area were probably subsequent to the Norman period.

½ knight owed for *Stanpett* (Stonepit, lost, in Teynham. See Dean and Chapter of Canterbury MS. E 24, fo. 40v.) by William Malet, who also held in military tenure in WROTHAM (q.v.).

1210–12 ½ fee in Doddington held by William de Dodintone.
¼ fee in Stonepit held by Robert Malet.

1253–4 ½ fee, unnamed, in Teynham Hundred, held by Simon of Doddington.
$\frac{1}{40}$ fee, unnamed, but probably in Sharstead (in Doddington) held by John de Scharstede.
$\frac{1}{20}$ fee in Bishopsbourne (see under ADISHAM) and Doddington held by Henry de Burne.

NOTE: Small quantities of land in Sharstead and in Doddington seem to have been made free, i.e. converted from gavelkind to military tenure, by Archbishop Boniface (1245–70). See under 1284, below. There is some confusion also between the

377

lands held by the Peyforers in gavelkind and in knight's fee in thirteenth-century Sharstead (*F. of F.*, pp. 339–40; *IPM*, II, no. 230).

1279 $\frac{1}{2}$ fee in Doddington held by William of Doddington (*Reg. Pecham*, p. 13).

     NOTE: This was the manor later known as Downe Court (E. Hasted, *History of Kent*, II, p. 694).

     $\frac{1}{40}$ fee in Sharstead, parish of Doddington, held by John de Schaftestede (*Reg. Pecham*, p. 13).

1284 $\frac{1}{2}$ fee held by William of Doddington.
     $\frac{1}{2}$ fee at Stonepit in Teynham Hundred held by Salomon de Roffa, and formerly by William Malet. It used to render 2*s.* 6*d.*, but this is now taken away.
     1 yoke made free by Archbishop Boniface held by John de Burne, kt.
     $5\frac{3}{4}$ acres of free land in Sharstead and $1\frac{1}{4}$ virgate in Brithmerston, freed by Archbishop Boniface, held by John of Sharstead (Dean and Chapter of Canterbury MS. E 24, fo. 40v.).

1311 $\frac{1}{20}$ fee in Bishopsbourne (see under ADISHAM) and Doddington held by Henry de Bourne (*Reg. Pecham*, p. 22).

1335   44 acres of arable and 2 acres of wood in Sharstead held of the archbishop for $\frac{1}{4}$ fee by Robert of Sharstead, rendering 12*s.* p.a. and doing three-weekly suit at his court at Canterbury. He also held a small amount jointly with his wife, and other land there in gavelkind (*IPM*, VII, no. 617).

1375 $\frac{1}{40}$ fee in Sharstead held by Robert de Notyngham, deceased. It comprised a messuage and adjoining garden of 2 acres, where the tenant dwelt, 58 acres of land adjoining the garden, 45 acres of wood in Peddynge (lost, in Doddington); and it paid 10*s.* 1*d.* p.a. to the manor of Teynham and did three-weekly suit to the archbishop's court at the Palace of Canterbury (*IPM*, XIV, no. 44).

THANET. See under WHITSTABLE

THANINGTON. See under WESTGATE

TILMANSTONE

1086   *Terra Militum.* 1 sulung held by William. On the demesne 2 ploughs and 5 bordars Formerly worth 20*s.*, now 30*s.*

c. 1090   Allocated to the list of monastic manors, but held as a manor of the archbishop for 1 sulung by William Folet. Worth 30*s.*

1171   Some portion of his lands for 3 knights held by Daniel de Crevequer was in Tilmanstone.

     NOTE: A Fulk Folet was one of Daniel de Crevequer's own military tenants in Kent in 1166 (*Red Book of the Exchequer*, p. 190).

1210–12   1¾ fees held by Robert de Crevequer; possibly also the ¼ fee in Stourmouth held by Gilbert of Tilmanstone (see under WHITSTABLE).

     NOTE: In the reign of Edward I most of the Crevequer estate passed to Queen Eleanor when she acquired Leeds Castle. But she relinquished her right to Archbishop Pecham in 2⅜ fees which Robert de Crevequer and his predecessors had held of the archbishops. These included Tilmanstone, subinfeudated to Roger of Tilmanstone (Lambeth MS. 1212, p. 70).

1308   ½ fee held by John de Sandhurst, brother and heir of John de Sandhurst, in Tilmanstone (*Reg. Pecham*, p. 20).

1346   1 fee held by Katherine, widow of John of Sandhurst, and Henry Wardenne, formerly by John of Sandhurst and William of Tyldenne.

1349   A messuage, 26 acres of arable, 8 acres of pasture and 23*s*. rent in Tilmanstone held by Margery, deceased, widow of William de Tydyngden, by the service of a third of ½ fee (*IPM*, IX, no. 307; cf. *IPM*, XI, no. 475).

TONBRIDGE. See under BRASTED

TOPPESFIELD. See under EYNSFORD

ULCOMBE

1086   *Terra Militum*. 2 sulungs held by the Count of Eu. TRE assessed at 2½ sulungs. Land for 9 ploughs. On the demesne 2 ploughs; 23 *villani* with 8 bordars have 7 ploughs; a church; a mill worth 4*s*.; 8 acres of meadow, and woodland to render 80 swine. TRE worth £10, when received £8, now £11. It was held by Alfer of the archbishop.

c. 1090   Held by the Count of Eu as 2 sulungs. Worth £11.

1093–6   Count of Eu answered for 4 fees, who in 1086 also held Stowting (q.v.) and whose successor in 1171 also held Stowting.

1171   4 knights owed by the Count of Eu for Ulcombe, Stowting and Courthope in Sussex (q.v.).

1210–12   2 fees held by Ralph of St Leger.

1244   2 fees, held by John of St Leger (*Book of Fees*, II, p. 1153).

1253–4   2 fees held by Richard of St Leger.

1303   2 fees held by Bartholomew of St Leger (see also LOSSENHAM) (*Reg. Pecham*, p. 19).

1346   1 fee held by Ralph of St Leger.

WADDEN HALL, in Waltham. See under PETHAM

WALMESTONE. See under WINGHAM

WAREHORNE. See also under EYNSFORD
1210–12 ¼ fee held by Anfridus de Dene.

WESTENHANGER. See under BERWICK-IN-LYMPNE

WESTGATE of Canterbury (*Stursaete*)

1086   Of this demesne, 5 men of the archbishop had 1 sulung 6 yokes, and they had there 5½ ploughs on (their) demesne(s), and 8 *villani* with 26 bordars who had 2 ploughs; 3 mills; 34 acres of meadow; wood to render 10 swine. Altogether it was worth £9. Also of this manor Haimo the Sheriff held ½ sulung of the archbishop and had there 2 ploughs with 5 bordars and 1 serf, and 2 mills worth 15s. His portion was worth £5. In the vill of St Martin which belonged to the archbishop and was attached to Westgate, Ralph held ½ sulung of the archbishop and there had 2 ploughs on his demesne, and 5 *villani* with 3 bordars who had 2½ ploughs. The ½ sulung of St Martin and another ½ sulung were worth TRE and TRW £4: the vill of St Martin itself was assessed at 1½ sulungs and was worth £7.

1086–7   Thanington granted to Godfrey (*Cart. of St Gregory's Priory*, p. 2).

c. 1090   Godfrey *dapifer* had 1 sulung of the whole manor's 7: it was called Thanington and was worth £5. Vitalis had 1 yoke of the archbishop, worth 20s. Haimo likewise held ½ sulung which Alric Bigge held TRE from the former archbishop, worth £5. Robert of Hardres held 1 yoke of the manor, worth 30s. Of the archbishop's sulung which belonged to the 7 and was at St Martin, Ralph the chamberlain had ½ sulung in fee, worth £4. Aethelard held 3 yokes in Nackington, rendering TRE and TRW to the altar of Holy Trinity 12s., and worth 40s. Albold held 1 yoke called Wick of the manor, which was of the land of the monks of Holy Trinity and was worth 30s.

1093–6   In the list of knights, Godfrey of Thanington answered for 3 fees; he is doubtless to be distinguished from Godfrey of Malling who held at Hunton, Lenham, and also owed the service of 3 knights.

       Albold owed the service of ¼ knight.

1171 Some portion of his lands held for the service of 3 knights by Richard le Waleys was in Thanington. (See also under SOUTH MALLING and LOSSENHAM.)

¼ knight owed in Westgate (Wick?) by Payn son of Ivo of Wich.

Some portion of his lands held for the service of 3 knights by the earl of Gloucester was in Milton in Westgate (cf. Lambeth MS. 1212, p. 149).

1210–12 1 fee in Thanington held by Godfrey Waleys.

¼ fee in Wick held by Payn de Wike.

½ fee in Milton held by Robert de Sevanz.

1253–4 1 fee in Milton, Westgate Hundred, held by the heirs of Robert de Septvans of the earl of Gloucester of the archbishop (cf. also *IPM*, I, no. 155);

¼ fee in Wick held by John le Taylor.

1306 ½ fee in Hackington held by Henry de Aketon (*Reg. Pecham*, p. 20).

NOTE: A William de Acton received a mill in Westgate from John de Valognes in 1227 (*F. of F.*, pp. 84–5). He may have been another whose holding was converted in the thirteenth century to military tenure.

1346 1 fee in Thanington held by William de Septvans, kt, and formerly by Robert Septvans and John de Valognes.

¼ fee in Wick, held by the heirs of John Tauncre, Stephen de Wyke and Richard Bett, formerly by the heirs of John le Tayllour;

⅛ fee in *Wymundesse, Ealde*, Romney, Ivychurch and the vill of St Martin, held by Robert Furneaux, John ate Wode and Thomas Tutewys, and formerly by Nicholas de Bere and the heirs of Robert ate Wode.

WHITEACRE. See under PETHAM

WHITSTABLE (*Nortone* or *Northuuode*)

1086 3 sulungs 1 yoke 12 acres held by Vitalis, who has 5 ploughs, 29 bordars, 5 serfs; 7 salt-pans worth 25s. 4d.; a church; 1 small denn of wood. The portion is worth £14 6s. 6d.

c. 1090 1 sulung 1 yoke of the manor, 1½ sulungs in Thanet. 12 acres and ½ sulung in Makinbrooke (in Herne), held by Vitalis of Canterbury. And *Ezilamerth* (Stourmouth) and all this land valued at £14 6s. 6d.

1093–6 In the list of knights, Vitalis owed the service of 3 fees.

NOTE: In the time of Henry I, Haimo son of Vitalis gave to

381

Rochester the church of his demesne at Stourmouth (*Textus Roffensis*, pp. 167–8).

1171   Some portion of his lands for $4\frac{3}{4}$ knights held by William son of Haimo in Stourmouth, Sarre, Makinbrooke. (See also under MAIDSTONE (Shofford) and WINGHAM (Walmestone).)

NOTE: William son of Haimo was the grandson of Vitalis (W. Urry, *The Normans in Canterbury*, Annales de Normandie no. 2 (1958), pp. 131–2), and was dead by this year when his son owed a relief of £12 15s. to succeed him and his widow Sybil rendered account of 40 marks to have her dowry in Stourmouth (*P.R. 19 Henry II*, pp. 87, 90).

1210–12 $\frac{1}{2}$ fee, unnamed, held by Haimo of Makinbrook.
$\frac{1}{4}$ fee in Stourmouth held by Hugh de Lale (*or* la Leg).
$\frac{1}{2}$ fee in Stourmouth held by Hugh de Sanforde.
$\frac{1}{8}$ fee in Stourmouth held by Alan de Sturremue (Stourmouth).
$\frac{1}{4}$ fee in Stourmouth held by Gilbert de Tilmanstone.
$\frac{1}{4}$ fee in Stourmouth held by Walter de Valognes.
$\frac{1}{2}$ fee in Sarre held by Bertram de Crioil.
$\frac{1}{2}$ fee in Sarre held by Thomas de Lenei.

1253–4   1 fee in Stourmouth held by the tenants of land formerly of William de Shofford (possibly the descendant of Vitalis (see under MAIDSTONE)).
$\frac{1}{8}$ fee in Stourmouth held by the heirs of Thomas of Stourmouth.
$\frac{1}{2}$ fee, unnamed, held by Haimo of Makinbrook.

1279 $\frac{3}{8}$ fee in Stourmouth held by Roger of Tilmanstone, kt (*Reg. Pecham*, p. 13); $\frac{1}{8}$ fee in Stourmouth held by Nicholas Sifrewaster (ibid., p. 16, but crossed out).

1287 $\frac{1}{8}$ fee in Stourmouth (20 acres) held by Thomas de Morton (ibid., p. 17).

1291 $\frac{1}{4}$ fee in Stourmouth and $\frac{1}{4}$ fee in Dene, Wingham (q.v.) held by Henry Huse, which Henry his father held (ibid., p. 18; *IPM*, II, no. 779).

1292 $\frac{3}{8}$ fee in Stourmouth and 1 fee in Swarling (q.v.) held by Warrisius de Valognes (*Reg. Pecham*, p. 18).
$\frac{1}{2}$ fee, unnamed, held by Haimo of Makinbrook (ibid.).

1303 $\frac{1}{4}$ fee in Stourmouth held by Rose of Tilmanstone, heiress of Roger of Tilmanstone, kt (ibid., p. 20).

1346   1 fee in the vill of St Nicholas (Thanet) and in Sarre held by John de Crioil, formerly by Margery de Crioil, the heirs of Hugh de Lene, the heirs of Ralph le Kene and the heirs of Walter Thorold.

1427–8   £11 13s. 4d. due to archbishop from issues of lands at Sarre in Thanet, held by Agnes Wykes in chief of the archbishop but in his custody by reason of the minority of John, her son and heir She also had held a marsh in Chislet in gavelkind of the abbot of St Augustine's (L.R. 96).

>   NOTE: In 1431 Archbishop Chichele still had custody of the manor of Sarre with its appurtenances in the village of St Nicholas in Thanet, held by the service of 1 fee, during the minority of the heir of John Wykes (*Feudal Aids*, III, p. 64).

1488–9   Relief of 50s. paid by Robert White for ½ fee in Sarre after the death of John White, his father (L.R. 98).

WICK. See under WESTGATE

WIMBLEDON, Surrey

1093–6   In the list of knights Peter de Buresto owed the service of ¼ fee.

1171   ¾ knight in Wimbledon owed by Alan of Wimbledon.
   ½ knight in *Heding'* also owed by Alan of Wimbledon.
   ¼ knight in Wimbledon owed by Ralph son of Silvester.
   (blank) in Burstow (in Wimbledon) owed by Peter of Burstow.

>   NOTE: References in *V.C.H. Surrey*, III, pp. 176–7, suggest the following succession for the latter fee: Peter of Burstow; Haimo; Stephen son of Haimo; Roger of Burstow; Peter of Burstow (occurs 1171); John of Burstow (occurs 1210–12).

1210–12   ¾ fee held by Robert of Wimbledon.
   ¼ fee *warda quam tenuit m. Benedictus de Scaccario.*
   ½ fee held by John of Burstow.

1242–3   ⅓ fee held by Robert of Wimbledon of the archbishop (*Book of Fees*, I, p. 633). But ½ fee is noted in ibid., II, p. 897, where he is said to have resisted paying the scutage this year.

1343   A capital messuage and 120 acres of arable called 'la Logge' in Burstow (extent given) held jointly by Roger Saleman or Salaman, deceased, and Alice his wife, of John de Burstowe by service of 36s. p.a. and three-weekly suit at John's court; also 6 acres of land held as above directly of the archbishop by service of 12d. p.a. (*IPM*, VIII, no. 455).

1418–19   Steward of the archbishop's liberty charged to answer for £12 12s. 10¼d. as issues of the manor of Burstow, formerly held by John Seyntcler son of Philip, and in the archbishop's custody by reason of the minority of Thomas the heir, from 2 November to 29 September, at £13 6s. 8d. (L.R. 95).

1499   The manor of Burstow, worth 8 marks, held of the archbishop as of his manor of Wimbledon by fealty and £6 p.a. rent; 15 acres of this manor, called 'Horscroftes', held of the duke of Buckingham, service unknown; by William Gauge, esquire, deceased (*IPM Hen. VII*, ii, no. 209; cf. no. 212).

WINGHAM

1086   1 sulung in Fleet held by William of Arques. On the demesne 1 plough, 4 *villani* and 1 knight (*miles*) with 1 plough; a fishery with a saltpan worth 30*d*. The whole worth 40*s*.

        5 men of the archbishop hold 5½ sulungs and 3 yokes. On their demesne(s) 8 ploughs, 22 bordars and 8 serfs. Altogether worth £21.

1086–7   Goss Hall and Goldstone in Wingham had been enfeoffed by this time by Lanfranc to Arnold, and some of Fleet to Osbern (*Cart. of St Gregory's Priory*, p. 2).

c. 1090   1 sulung held by William of Arques in fee, worth £6; 1 sulung held by Vitalis, worth 45*s*.; 3 sulungs worth £12 held by Wibert and Arnold; 1 sulung less 10 acres held by Herengod, worth 40*s*.; 1½ sulungs held by Godfrey *archibalistarius*, worth £5.

The complexity of the fees in Wingham makes it advisable to describe them from this point according to the hamlets in which they were held.

Fleet

1093–6   Nigel de Monville answered for 1 knight.

1093–6   Osbern *pincerna* owed the service of ½ knight, clearly for land in Fleet.

1171   1 knight in Fleet owed by William de Auereng (Avranches).

NOTE: Nigel de Monville had married Emma, da. and heiress of William of Arques, tenant of Folkestone from Odo and of Fleet from the archbishop. On Nigel's death his lands passed to his da. Matilda, who married Rualon d'Avranches, father of William d'Avranches (Colvin, op. cit., p. 27; I. J. Sanders, *English Baronies*, p. 45; cf. *F. of F.*, pp. cxxvi, 5, 90).

½ knight owed for Fleet by Hugh *pincerna*.

NOTE: This was the successor of Osbern *pincerna*. Robert *pincerna Theobaldi archiepiscopi* was one of the knights excommunicated by Becket in 1169 (*Materials*, vi, p. 602), and witnessed charters for Theobald (A. Saltman, *Theobald*, pp. 263, 273–4, 388–9, 482). The place was later called 'Butler's Fleet' (cf. E. Hasted, *History of Kent*, iii, p. 685, and below under year 1488–9).

1210–12 1 fee in Fleet held by Elias de Beauchamp with Robert de Vere.
$\frac{1}{2}$ fee in Fleet held by Thomas *pincerna*.

1253–4 1 fee in Fleet held by William of Avranches.

NOTE: In 1264 the manor of Fleet was held by Hugh de Vere, earl of Oxford, then just dead, of the heir of Folkstone, and by him of the archbishop (*IPM*, I, no. 586, and Sanders, op. cit., pp. 45–6).

$\frac{1}{2}$ fee in Fleet held by the heir(s) of Walter le Boteler.

NOTE: During the vacancy of 1270–2 John of Estwode paid £40 for having the wardship and marriage of Walter le Botiller who held of the archbishop in chief (P.R. 119, m. 41d.).

1331 The manor of Fleet is noted as descending in the family of the earl of Oxford during the fourteenth century in *IPM*, VII, no. 379; x, no. 638; XII, no. 81; XIII, no. 125; but a feudal value is noted only in 1346.

1346 1 fee in Fleet held by the earl of Oxford and Nicholas of Sandwich, formerly by Thomas of Sandwich.
$\frac{1}{2}$ fee in Fleet held by heir(s) of Robert le Boteler.

1418–19 Archbishop received £29 6s. 8d. issues from Fleet manor held of him in military service by Richard de Vere, earl of Oxford, deceased, and now in custody for John his son and heir, the rest having been assigned to the executors for dower (L.R. 95).

1427–8 As above, but the manor leased to John Broke of Snaxton.

1488–9 Relief of 50s. paid for land and marsh in Fleet, otherwise called *Butlersflete*, coming to William Berton by reason of the death of lady Katherine Septvans who held of the archbishop by the service of $\frac{1}{2}$ fee (L.R. 98).

Knell and Goss Hall (including Goldstone)

1093–6 Wibert and Arnold answered for 1 fee each, probably in Knell.

1171 $\frac{3}{4}$ and $\frac{1}{20}$ knight owed by S(tephen?) de Ulmis.

NOTE: This is Knell in Wingham, near Ash. S— was probably the successor of Wibert and Arnold of the Domesday texts, for Arnold's lands were, like Knell, in Ash; he and Wibert each owed the service of 1 knight. Stephen may have been a family name: there is a Walter son of Stephen of Knell in 1262–3 (*F. of F.*, 341). The present fractions are hard to explain, but in 1210–12 and 1253–4 the holdings in Knell and Goss Hall add up to two fees. The lords of Goss Hall are for some reason omitted from the return of 1171, but in collating it with the list of 1093–6 the names of Wibert and S(tephen) of Knell correspond.

1210–12 ½ fee in Knell held by William de Ulmis.
  1½ fees in Goss Hall held by Robert de Gosehale.

1253–4 2 fees (unnamed but clearly in Knell) held by Walter de Gosehall and the heir(s) *de Ulmis*.

1346 ¼ fee in Knell in Ash held by Anne, widow of William de Lyeghe.
  1½ fees in Goss Hall and Goldstone (*Golstanston*) held by the widow of John of Goss Hall.

1354 ½ manor of Goldstone (*Goldstanton*) in Ash by Wingham held by William de Clinton, late earl of Huntingdon, of the archbishop. He also held gavelkind lands of the archbishop and others in the vicinity (*IPM*, x, no. 193).

1449 John Clinton, esquire, accused of disseising Roger Cliderowe, esquire, of his manor of Knell (*Kent Records*, XVIII, p. 223).

1486 Manor of Goldstone, worth £15, held as to ¾ of the archbishop in right of his church for 1½ fees, and as to ¼ of John, earl of Oxford, as of the manor of Fleet, service unknown, by John Nores, esquire (*IPM Hen. VII*, I, no. 127).

1508 Manor of Goldstone, worth £25, held for service of 1 fee of archbishop of Edmund Nores, gent., deceased (*IPM Hen. VII*, III, no. 514).

Overland

1093–6 Herengod answered for 1 fee, probably in Overland.

1171 1 knight in Overland owed by Peter of Bendeng.

  NOTE: This was probably the successor to Herengod, and Overland seems to have been sold by the Bendengs, a substantial Kentish family, to Robert de Valognes.

1210–12 1 fee in Overland held by Robert de Valognes.

1253–4 1 fee in Overland held by the heir(s) of Bertram de Crioil.

  NOTE: In 1264 Bertram succeeded his father John de Crioil in the tenure of ½ fee at Overland of the archbishop (*IPM*, I, p. 593).

1279 1½ fees (unnamed but probably in Overland) held by Bertram de Crioil (*Reg. Pecham*, p. 2).

1310 Manor of Overland (extent given) held jointly by William de Leyburne and Juliana his wife of the gift of Fulk Peyforer, of the archbishop, by service of 10*s.* p.a. and suit of hundred court of Wingham. Heir of William, now deceased, is Juliana, daughter of Thomas de Leyburne, aged over six (*IPM*, v, no. 220).

  No further reference found to Overland or knight-service therefrom.

NOTE: Juliana, heiress of the Leybourne family, married the earl of Huntingdom and survived him (see under LENHAM).

Ratling

1093–6 Godfrey *(archi)balistarius* answered for 1 fee, probably in Ratling.

1171 1 knight owed from Ratling by Alan of Ratling.

NOTE: His succession to Godfrey is made probable by his position in the list.

1210–12 1 fee in Ratling held by Thomas de Retlinge.

1253–4 1 fee, unnamed, held by the heir(s) of Ratling (*Rething*).

1279 ½ fee in Ratling, parish of Nonington, held by Ralph Perot.
½ fee in Ratling held by Richard de Dovere (*Reg. Pecham*, p. 8).

1309 ½ fee in Ratling held by John de Retlynges (*Reg. Pecham*, p. 21).

1346 1 fee in Ratling held by the heirs of Sarah of Ratling and Margery her sister.

1502 James Isaak, deceased, had held Ratling, but had enfeoffed it, ¼ to his own use and ¾ as jointure for his daughter-in-law, Benedicta, daughter of John Guldeford, kt. The ¾ was said to be worth £6 and rendered 12*d*. p.a. to the archbishop in his manor of Wingham; the ¼, lately John Hall's, was worth 43*s*. 4*d*. and also rendered 12*d*. Both parts held by knight-service (*IPM Hen. VII*, II, no. 642).

Ash

1093–6 Reiner owed the service of ½ knight, and probably held in Ash.

1171 ½ knight owed for Ash by Richard Musard, according to his place in the list probably the successor of Reiner.

1210–12 ½ fee in *Heth'* (Ash in Wingham, cf. *PNK*, p. 527) held by Richard Danesi (de Aneseye).

1253–4 ½ fee in *Hethe* (Ash), hundred of Wingham, held by the tenants of the land of Richard Musard.

NOTE: In 1236 William Musard had sold ½ fee in Ash to Richard le Chamberleng for 43 marks (*F. of F.*, p. 130).

1427–8 Issues worth £9 6*s*. 8*d*. from lands late of Thomas Guston in Ash by Wingham were due to archbishop during the minority of John, the son and heir, but not rendered because John was now of full age (L.R. 96).

Deane

1093–6 Robert Liuegit owed ½ knight and may have held in Deane.

1171 Some portion of his lands for 3 knights held by Daniel de

Crevequer were in *Dene* (this was probably Deane in South Wingham).

½ knight owed by the sons of William de Denum (Deane), though they acknowledge only ⅛.

NOTE: These were probably the successors of Robert Liuegit, and perhaps the same as Thomas de Dene and his brother Harlewin, who in 1196 gave Thomas de Godwinestone (for whom see below, under 'Other fees in Wingham') 1½ sulungs in East Ratling in return for 18 acres 1 virgate in a field called *Uikham*, and 6 marks (*F. of F.*, p. 3).

1210–12 ¼ fee in Deane held by Robert de Crevequer.
⅛ fee in Deane held by Bertram de Crioil.
⅛ fee in Deane held by Brian de Dene.

1253–4 ⅛ fee in Deane held by Richard de Dene.

1279 ⅛ fee in Deane, parish of Wingham, held by Richard de Dene (*Reg. Pecham*, p. 8).

1291 ¼ fee in Deane, parish of Wingham (and ¼ fee in Stourmouth (q.v.)), held by Henry Huse, which Henry his father had held there (*Reg. Pecham*, p. 18).

1332 Henry Husee, deceased, had given lands in Deane, Chilston and Stourmouth, held of the archbishop by various services, in frank marriage *c.* 1314 to Henry his son and Maud, the son's wife, on the day of their marriage, to hold to them and the heirs of their bodies with reversion to the right heirs of Henry the father (*IPM*, VII, no. 468).

1346 ¼ fee in Deane (said here to be in the hundred of Wye), held by Henry Huse.
⅛ fee in Deane held by heirs of Alan of Dene.

1349 Henry Huse, kt, deceased, had held Deane manor for ⅛ fee (also Stourmouth for ⅛, and Chilston in Boughton Malherbe for $\frac{1}{7}$) (*IPM*, IX, no. 222; *C.Cl.R. 1349–54*, p. 129).

NOTE: In 1361 the manor of *Dene* is said to have been held by Thomas d'Aldon, kt, of the archbishop for 10*s*. p.a. to him and 8*s*. p.a. to the abbot of St Augustine's (*IPM*, XI, no. 9).

Walmestone

1171 Some portion of his lands for 4¾ knights held by William son of Haimo were in Walmestone (see also under WHITSTABLE).

NOTE: This corresponds with the sulung held by Vitalis (Viel): William son of Haimo was the grandson of Vitalis. He died in 1173 and left a son, also called Haimo.

1210–12 ½ fee in Walmestone held by Simon de Vielmestone.

1253–4 1 fee in Walmestone held by the heir of Robert de Septvans.

> NOTE: Robert II had died in 1249, when Robert III was about forty. He had held ⅓ barony of Aldington from the king through his grandmother Emma, as well as one fee in Milton (Canterbury) from the earl of Gloucester (see under WESTGATE), two unspecified fees in Essex from William de Shofford (for whom, probably a descendant of Vitalis, see under MAIDSTONE), and ½ fee [*sic*] from the archbishop in Walmestone (*IPM*, I, no. 158; Sanders, op. cit., p. 1). Robert III d. in 1253 and the heir, also called Robert and here referred to, came of age *c.* 1271 and d. 1306 (*IPM*, I, no. 265).

1346 1 fee in Walmestone held by William de Septvans, and formerly by Robert de Septvans.

Other fees in Wingham

1253–4 ¼ fee, unnamed, in Wingham Hundred, held by John of Goodnestone.

¼ fee in Wingham held by Alan of Twitham.

⅛ fee in Wingham held by Thomas of Ackholt.

1272 25*s.* relief paid by Thomas of Godwineston for ¼ fee there (Goodnestone in Wingham) (P.R. 119, m. 41d.).

1279 ¼ fee in Goodnestone held by Thomas de Guodwinestone (*Reg. Pecham*, p. 8).

> NOTE: In the archbishopric rental of 1284–5 Thomas of Goodnestone appears as tenant of 310½ acres of the tenement of Ralph, and 62 acres of the tenement of Gilbert Thurston of Geremund. For these 372½ acres he ought with Richard de Woghope to perform the customs of a full 'Shireland', the other customs being commuted. Thomas also held 418¾ acres in the vill of Goodnestone for which he ought to do the customs of a 'Shireland' in respect of the king's crown (Dean and Chapter of Canterbury MS. E 24, fo. 8v.).

¼ fee in Twitham held by Alan of Twitham, kt (*Reg. Pecham*, p. 7).

> NOTE: In the 1284–5 rental Alan appears as holding 300 acres in Twitham freely for rent, ancient customs and a small sum for services and customs relaxed, '*et quantum ad presentamenta casuum infortuitorum et coronam domini regis* [*tangentium*?], *faciet sicut alii Shirmanni*' (MS. E 24, fo. 7).

1346 ¼ fee in Goodnestone held by the heir(s) of Thomas of Goodnestone.

¼ fee in Twitham held by the heirs of Theobald of Twitham, and formerly by Alan of Twitham.

⅛ fee in Ackholt (in Nonington) held by the heirs of Thomas of Acholt.

1351 Manor of Twitham held as of the manor of Wingham by Alan de Twitham, now deceased, by homage, fealty and the service of 60s. and three-weekly suit at the archbishop's great court at the palace of Canterbury. Alan had granted the manor in 1350 to Robert Cheyne, kt, and Robert Borbache, clk, for two years, to pay his debts. The heir is Alan, son of Theobald of Twitham (*IPM*, IX, no. 628).

1364 11 acres in Wingham held by service of ¼ fee and three-weekly suit at court of Canterbury by Mariota, late wife of Henry Seneschal. She d. in 1347, and the land came into the possession of Richard Seneschal who was leasing it from the sheriff of Kent (*IPM*, XI, no. 602).

WITTERSHAM and OXNEY

1171 ½ knight owed for Wittersham and Oxney by the heirs of Robert le Palstre.

NOTE: Palstre Court, in Wittersham, belonged to the estate of Odo from whom it was held by Osbern Pasforir. Its former ownership by the church of Canterbury is recorded (see above, p. 38). Pasforir also held of the archbishop in LYMINGE (q.v.) by the service of ¼ knight.

1210–12 ½ fee held by Geoffrey de Oxenel.

NOTE: In 1268 Thomas de Palstre and Joan his wife acquired fifteen librates of land in Wittersham from Matthew de Knelle (*F. of F.*, p. 350).

1310 ½ fee in Wittersham held by Edmund de Passele (*Reg. Pecham*, p. 21).

1346 ½ fee in Wittersham held by Thomas de Passele and William de Wittersham, formerly by James de Palstre and Richard de Wittersham.

1478–9 The manors of Palstre, Crombury(?), Hadlow and Boughton Monchelsy in the custody of the archbishop by reason of the minority of Katherine, daughter and heiress of Robert Watton, who held them in military tenure of the archbishop. They are now farmed to William Harlakynden and Alice his wife (L.R. 97).

1491 200 acres in Wittersham worth £8 held by service of ½ fee by Katherine Pekham, deceased, who also held the manor of

Palstre worth £8 of the king in chief by service of $\frac{1}{2}$ fee and the manor of Boughton Monchelsey worth £7 of the duchess of York, service unknown, and the manor of *Crokouvery* [*sic*] worth 8 marks of Jasper, duke of Bedford, in right of the lady Katherine his wife, service unknown (*IPM Hen. VII*, I, no. 737).

WOOTTON, in Kinghamford Hundred

1171   1 knight owed by Alan of Wootton, though he acknowledged only $\frac{1}{2}$.

     NOTE: Giddinge (*Gedinges*) in the parish of Wootton belonged to the Canterbury monastic manor of Eastry. Lanfranc granted Wootton in fee to a certain Ralph (*Cart. of St Gregory's Priory*, p. 2), and a knight called Ralph of Eastry occupied a place in the 1093–6 list which almost corresponds with that of Alan of Wootton in the list of 1171. Each owed the service of 1 knight. Probably, therefore, Alan was the successor of Ralph.

1210–12 $\frac{1}{2}$ fee in Wootton held by John de Gestlinges.

1253–4 $\frac{1}{2}$ fee in Wootton held by John and William de Gestling.

1279 $\frac{1}{2}$ fee in Wootton held by John de Frethenseye (*Reg. Pecham*, p. 8).

1346 $\frac{1}{2}$ fee in Wootton held by John de Ore and the heirs of Richard of Wootton, formerly of the aforesaid John and Richard.

WROTHAM[1]

1086   1 sulung held by William *dispensator*. On the demesne 1 plough, and 2 *villani* have $\frac{1}{2}$ plough. 1 sulung held by Goisfridus. On the demesne 1 plough, and 6 *villani* with 1 bordar have 2 ploughs.

     $1\frac{1}{2}$ yokes [*sic*] held by Farman who has 3 ploughs and 6 *villani* with 12 cotters having 2 ploughs. 10 serfs there. Land of the knights (*militum*) worth £11.

c. 1090   1 sulung worth £3 held by William *dispensator*; 1 sulung worth £3 held by Gosfridus de Ros; $1\frac{1}{2}$ sulungs worth £5 held by Fareman.

1093–6   Gosfridus de Ros answered for 1 fee; William de Wroteham for $\frac{1}{2}$.

1171   1 knight owed for Lullingstone (q.v.) and Yaldham (in Wrotham) by William de Malet.

     NOTE: William de Malet corresponds in the list to Geoffrey

---

1. The enfeoffments at Wrotham should not be confused with the demesne manor, which was set at fee-farm to knightly tenants of the archbishopric, but brought back into demesne by Archbishop Pecham.

de Ros in the earlier list, who was probably his predecessor and may well have held his sulung at Yaldham.

½ knight owed for Yaldham (*Aldeh'*) by William son of Payn.

NOTE: His Norman predecessor was probably the William who appears in the texts as *dispensator* and in the list of 1093–6 as William of Wrotham.

1210–12 ½ fee in Stansted (in Wrotham) held by Walter de Perepunt.

NOTE: In 1284 the 'lady of Ightham' was said to hold the manor of Stansted in Wrotham 'freely', and it is probable that scutage was rendered in respect of this (Dean and Chapter of Canterbury MSS. E 24, fo. 79v.). But in 1302 and 1322 Stansted manor is recorded as held of the archbishop in gavelkind (*IPM*, IV, no. 91; VI, no. 328).

½ fee in Yaldham held by William Malet (who also held 1 fee in LULLINGSTONE (q.v.)).

½ fee held by Achard of Yaldham.

½ fee held by Stephen of Yaldham.

NOTE: ½ fee in Yaldham was said in 1275 to have been held by Thomas of Yaldham and his ancestors of Hugh Poynz and his ancestors in chief of the manor of Lullingstone since the time of King Richard, Thomas holding no land of the king in chief (*IPM*, II, no. 193).

¼ fee in *Siburne* (Shipbourne in Wrotham) held by Robert of Siburne.

NOTE: For transactions with Shipbourne in 1196 and 1221, see *F. of F.*, pp. 1, 73.

1253–4 ½ fee, unnamed and said to be in Milton Hundred, held at farm by Robert of Raleghe from the heirs of William Malet.

1418–19 The archbishop received £5 6s. 8d. issues of Wrotham, in feudal custody for Thomas, brother and heir of John Seyntcler, kt (L.R. 95).

APPENDIX B

Lists of some office-holders in the archbishop's temporal administration to *c.* 1540

These lists are not, of course, complete, and the years given are those in which a man is found acting, unless 'ap.' signifies his appointment.

STEWARDS OF THE LANDS

1197 perhaps to 1240	m. Elias of Dereham	K. Major, *E.H.R.*, XLVIII, pp. 542–545; C. H. Lawrence, *St Edmund of Abingdon*, pp. 141–2
c. 1215	Robert of Bermondsey, kt	Major, art. cit., p. 548.
c. 1220–*c.* 1231	Robert of Ruxley, kt	ibid., pp. 545–7.
1227	Robert de Muscegros, kt	ibid., p. 547
1258–74	Roger Northwood, kt	Lambeth MS. 1212, pp. 71, 83, 116, 158–9, 421, 424; Addit. MS. 29794 m. 1. Baron of the Exchequer 1278–9 (P.R. 124, m. 23d.); d. 1258 (*IPM*, II, no. 582); cf. *C.Ch.R.*, II, pp. 164–5
1261	Henry, prior of St Radegunds	Lambeth MS. 1212, pp. 97, 417–18. Addit. ch. 2343.
c. 1268	m. Peter de Soleriis	Canterbury Cathedral MS. E 24, fo. 11v.
1273–4	Ralph of Sandwich, Roger of Northwood and Adam of Illegh [Monks Eleigh, Suffolk]	Addit. MS. 29794, m. 1. Ralph Sandwich, kt, was keeper of the king's wardrobe, Jan. to Aug. 1265 (*Handbook of Brit. Chronology*, p. 77).
ap. 1279	Stephen of Iford	*Reg. Pecham*, p. 1; Lambeth MS. 1212, pp. 417–18, 421; MS E. 24, fo. 60. cf. clerk in 1259 (Lambeth MS. 1212, p. 83) and 1271 (*C.Ch.R.*, II, pp. 164–5).
ap. 1279	Abbot of St Radegunds	*Reg. Pecham*, p. 3.
ap. 1279	m. Henry Lovell	*Reg. Pecham*, p. 11; Lambeth MS. 1212, pp. 71, 97, 178.
1279–80, 1313–14	Robert de Cliderou, clerk	MS. E 24, fo. 69; L.R. 234; Reg. Reynolds, fo. 6v.

393

1298–1301	William Trussell, kt	*Reg. Winchelsey*, pp. 291, 356, 401, 681; L.R. 657. Edmund Passele and Thomas of Chartham (see under Treasurers) acted for him in 1301.
ap. 1301 to before 1306	William de Melesope, kt	*Reg. Winchelsey*, p. 428; *S.R.S.*, vol. 57, p. 135.
1313	Richard of Ruxley, kt	*Reg. Winchelsey*, p. 1342.
1314, 1316	m. John de Redeswelle *or* Rodeswelle	Reg. Reynolds, fos. 14v., 196v., 284v.; LCM, v, fo. 52; clerk in archbishop's service 1284 (L.R. 235); later steward of the Liberty when with Braydston (q.v.) he sat on a commission of oyer and terminer to punish those who entered archbishop's parks and woods in king's hands during vacancy (*C.P.R. 1327–30*, 295).
1336	J. de Hampton	*Lit. Cant.*, ii, no. 604.
ap. 1349, 1351–2	John de la Lee	Reg. Islip, fo. 9; L.R. 779.
1354–6	Walter Waleys, canon of Salisbury	Reg. Islip, fos. 109v., 110.
1356–7	John de Bray *or* Wray	L.R. 1140.
1364–5	Thomas de Wolton	L.R. 781. See also under Treasurers.
ap. 1367	Stephen de Valognes	*Reg. Langham*, pp. 116, 172.
ap. 1368–9	John de Woodhull, rector of Risborough	Reg. Witlesey, fo. 2v.; see also *Biog. Reg. Oxford.*
ap. 1382	William de Topclyve	Reg. Courtenay, fos. 10v., 51v. Formerly archbishop's valet, bailiff of courts of Aldington, Maidstone and Wingham (Reg. Islip, fo. 173; Reg. Witlesey, fo. 2v.) and steward of the Liberty (Reg. Islip, fo. 199v.). Widow Elizabeth pensioned, and chantry in Maidstone (L.R. 670).
1390–2	Guy de Mone	L.R. 784, 836, 946. See also under Treasurers. Receiver of king's chamber 1391–8, keeper of privy seal 1396–7, treasurer 1398, bishop of St Davids 1397–1407 (*Handbook of Brit. Chronology*, pp. 92, 102).
1393–4	John Wotton	KAO U55/M64. Surveyor in 1390–1392 under Mone and possibly still surveyor rather than steward.
ap. 1397–9	William Makenade	Reg. Arundel, i, fos. 4, 242 (will); L.R. 668.
1400–1	John Clement	L.R. 668.
1400–12	Gregory Ballard, esquire	Reg. Arundel, ii, fo. 113v. *Reg. Chichele*, ii, pp. 114–15 (will), 638; L.R. 670, 671, 838, 839, 844, 849. See also under Treasurers.

1416	William Chichele	*Reg. Chichele*, IV, p. 36 and index.
1423–37	John Darell	L.R. 674, 675, 677, 858, 860; KAO U55/M69; *Reg. Chichele*, IV, pp. 156, 161.
ap. 1443	James Fyneux *or* Fenys, esquire of the king's body	Reg. Stafford, fo. 7v.; *Lit. Cant.*, III, no. 1024; *HMCR*, IX, App., pp. 104, 114.
1453–6	John Audley, esquire	L.R. 1240, 1241; Mins. Accts 1129/4.
ap. 1484	Robert Brackenbury, kt	*Reg. Bourgchier*, pp. 64–5. Constable of the Tower of London, 1483. (*C.P.R. 1476–85*), p. 364, etc.
ap. 1537–53	Thomas Cheyney, kt	L.R. 1376.

STEWARDS OF THE LIBERTY

ap. 1279	William Norman	*Reg. Pecham*, p. 1; but had acted previously (Lambeth MS. 1212, p. 412).
ap. 1279	Henry of Leeds	*Reg. Pecham*, pp. 4, 8; Lambeth MS. 1212, p. 71.
1295–6	m. John de Bestane, canon of Hereford, and Alexander de Insula	*Reg. Winchelsey*, p. 62; *Surrey Record Society*, no. XXI (1925), pp. 20, 26.
before 1301	Thomas of Chartham and Edmund de Passele	*Reg. Winchelsey*, p. 414; Lindsay Fleming, *Hist. of Pagham* (1949), pp. 93–105.
1304	Henry de Bruton	Appointed archbishop's attorney to protect liberties, and possibly not steward of the Liberty proper (*Reg. Winchelsey*, p. 486).
1305	Henry de Hales	*Reg. Winchelsey*, p. 500.
1310–12	Thomas le Gegg'	*Reg. Winchelsey*, pp. 989–91. Simon Poyntel was bailiff of liberties in Essex, Suffolk and Herts in 1312 (ibid., p. 989).
ap. 1313–14 and temp. archbishop Islip	Thomas de Birston	Reg. Reynolds, fos. 6v., 8v., 283; Reg. Islip, fos. 89–95; also bailiff of Maidstone in 1314.
1317	William Merry	Reg. Reynolds, fo. 89; also bailiff of Croydon in 1313 (ibid., fo. 6).
1323–4, and ap. 1326	John de Braydston (Bredestone, Breideston)	Reg. Reynolds, fo. 196v.; Lambeth MS. 1212, p. 291; L.R. 778. Also appointed steward of the Liberty to the cathedral priory 1334 but dismissed 1335 for inefficiency (*Lit. Cant.*, II, nos. 553, 566–7). See also under Redeswelle, steward of the lands.
1327–33	William of Reculver	*HMCR*, IX, p. 74; L.R. 662.

c. 1333, 1339	H. de Bradeweye	*HMCR*, IX, p. 82; P.R. 14 Edw. III, Item Kancie.
1341–2	Reginald le Dyke	P.R.s 15 and 16 Edw. III, Item Kancie; Chanc. Misc. 8714, no. 25.
ap. 1350, 1360	Robert Vyntier, of Maidstone	Reg. Islip, fos. 9, 16v., 60.
ap. 1361	Roger Diggs	Reg. Islip, fo. 169v.
1362	William of Aperfield	Reg. Islip, fo. 192.
ap. 1363	William de Topclyve	Reg. Islip, fos. 199v., 17ɔ. Previously archbishop's valet and bailiff in various courts, later steward of the lands (q.v.). Reg. Witlesey, fo. 2v.; Reg. Courtenay, fos. 10v., 51v.
1366	William de Nesfield	Steward of liberties in Yorks. (*Reg. Langham*, 132).
1396–9, 1402–3	John Colpeper	L.R. 838, 668; possibly the John son of Godfrey who had been bailiff of Otford and South Malling (Reg. Courtenay, fo. 23v.). Also had been steward of Liberty to the priory (*HMCR*, IX, p. 110).
1409–19	Peter Hall	Reg. Arundel, ii, fo. 113v.; L.R. 95; Mins. Accts 1128/17, 19. Called bailiff of the Liberty in 1410–11 (L.R. 846A).
1426–7	John Chichele	L.R. 96; also appointed steward of the Liberty to the priory in 1428 (*Reg. Chichele*, IV, p. 294).
1427–8	Roger Rye, 'late steward of the Liberty'	L.R. 96; bailiff of Wingham in 1414 (*Reg. Chichele*, IV, p. 5).
1436–9	John Tattersal	L.R. 678; L.T.R. Mem. Roll (E368), no. 210, m. 23 from end.
1442	probably Richard Broun	P.R.O. Ancient Indictments K.B. 9/46, m. 6.
1449	John Basket	*Kent Records*, XVIII, pp. 233, 234; 1443–4 royal escheator in Sussex and Surrey (Mins. Accts 1128/21).
1451–67	William Kene	Mins. Accts 1129/7; Will, PCC 20 Godyn, proved 1467.
1472–3	possibly John Alphey	Called steward of the lord's courts, but possibly only in Otford (Mins. Accts 1130/4). Will, PCC 18 Milles.
1478–91	Thomas Bourgchier, kt	L.R. 97, 98, 99; Canterbury Cathedral Reg. S, fo. 229v.

TREASURERS OF THE ARCHBISHOP, TREASURERS OF CANTERBURY,

OR

TREASURERS OF CANTERBURY PALACE

1236–7	possibly Walter of Ferriby and Robert of Bath	L.R. 1193
1258	Peter of Cambiaco	Lambeth MS. 1212, p. 96.

1267	Gerard de Seycelle	Lambeth MS. 1212, p. 421. Also here called steward of the archbishop, perhaps in error. Seyssel was a notable Savoyard name.
1273–5	Thomas of Lynsted	Lambeth MS. 1212, p. 412; Addit. MS. 29794.
1279	Thomas of Chartham, canon of South Malling	*Reg. Pecham*, p. 3; *Reg. Winchelsey*, p. 1288; cf. L.R. 657. See also Stewards of the Liberty.
1281–3	Roger Burt	Churchill, op. cit., p. 547 and *n.*
1291–2	Peter of Guildford	L.R. 234. Treasurer of archbishop's wardrobe in 1288 (Churchill, op. cit., I, p. 547).
1296–8	William of Lynsted	L.R. 657, 658, 831.
1300–1	m. William	*Reg. Winchelsey*, p. 426.
1303–4	the lord G.	L.R. 777.
1309–10	Richard Franceys	L.R. 1139.
1313–19	Robert Crul	Reg. Reynolds, fos. 8, 283v.; L.R. 656, 659, 660, 661, 832, 1139; MS. E 24, fo. 69; keeper of archbishop's wardrobe 1304–10 (*Reg. Winchelsey*, pp. 1062–3).
1313–14, ap. 1321–5	John de Ryngwode, rector of Saltwood	Reg. Reynolds, fo. 128v., cf. fo. 4; L.R. 656, 833; KAO U 270/M304; cf. Lambeth MS. 1212, p. 127.
c. 1330	William Vygerous	L.R. 663. See also under Stewards of the Household.
1331	William de Woghope, monk	*HMCR*, IX, p. 80.
1331	Thomas de Bonhope	L.R. 664. It is possible these last two were the same.
1335–6	Richard de Longedone	L.R. 665.
1349–52	William de Islip	*Reg. Islip*, fos. 37v., 128v. Also cross-bearer in 1356; L.R. 779. Bailiff of Croydon in 1368 (Reg. Witlesey, fo. 2v.).
possibly before 1351, 1353, 1355–6, 1363–5	Thomas de Wolton, rector of Westwell and of Eynsford	L.R. 779, 780, 781, 834; *Lit. Cant.*, II, no. 793; wardrober 1349–50 (L.R. 240). See also under Stewards of the Lands and of the Household.
1366–7	John Walkelyn	L.R. 782
1368–9	John Suldern	L.R. 783.
to May 1383	William Lyndon	KAO U55/M63.
from May 1381	William Lye	KAO U55/M63.
1386	Guy de Mone	Reg. Courtenay, fo. 168. See also under Stewards of the Lands.
1390–5	Richard Lentwardyn	L.R. 139, 784, 836, 946; KAO U55/M64. Possibly the canon of Wingham alive in 1417 (*Reg. Chichele*, II, pp. 131–3).
1397–9	John Waldenn	L.R. 668, 785–6; KAO U270/M305. The treasurership changed on 20 June (L.R. 788).

1398–1401	Gregory Ballard	L.R. 668, 788, 790–1. See also under Stewards of the Lands.
1402–11	Thomas Burton	L.R. 241, 593, 668, 670, 671, 793, 839. Also Master of Eastbridge Hospital, Canterbury.
1414–15, 1418–19, 1428, 1430–1	Roger Heron	L.R. 95, 613, 675, 853; KAO U270/M306, U55/M69; also Master of Maidstone College (*Reg. Chichele*, II and IV, indexes). d. by 1442 (L.R. 679).
1543–4	John Cumberforthbe, gentleman	L.R. 1370.

AUDITORS

ap. 1359	John le Bray, William de Tratyngton and William de Colbroke	Reg. Islip, fo. 152v., cf. fo. 181v.
1411–12	John Burton	L.R. 849
1423–4	William Urswick	L.R. 674.
1430–9, 1442–3	William Balle	L.R. 675–8. Receiver of Otford 1428–9 (KAO U55/M69).
ap. 1444	William Stevenes and William Balle	Reg. Stafford, fo. 17v.
ap. 1454–6	John Chapman	*Reg. Bourgchier*, p. 13.
1460–71	George Houton (Hooton)	L.R. 1243, 1347; Mins. Accts 1129/7, 9, 1130/1. R. Somerville, *Duchy of Lancaster*, I, pp. 411, 625.
ap. 1473–82	Humphrey Rotsey	Mins. Accts 1130/3, 4; L.R. 1349 *Reg. Bourgchier*, pp. 45–6.
1493–4	John Prynce	L.R. 1354.
1500–1	Robert Cliff and Robert Mortimer	L.R. 1202.
1514–23	John Noote	L.R. 1364.

CLERKS OF THE AUDITOR, OR OF THE ACCOUNTS

1267	Stephen of Iford	Lambeth MS. 1212, p. 421. See also under Stewards of the Lands.
1359	William de Topclyve	Reg. Islip, fo. 152. See also under Stewards of the Lands, and of the Liberty.
1414	John Brynkele	L.R. 850.
1423–4	William Balle	KAO U270/M307. Receiver 1429–1430 (L.R. 859). See also Auditors.
1436–9	James Hope	L.R. 678.
1442–3	John Uffington	KAO U55/M70.
1460–1	William Welwyk	L.R. 1243.
1462–3	Richard Basshe	Valet of the auditor (Mins. Accts 1129/7).
1462–72	Humphrey Rotsey	L.R. 1347; Mins. Accts 1129/8. See also Auditors.

RECEIVERS

Where possible, the bailiwick in which the receiver acted is placed in brackets after his name, but the information is necessarily incomplete and he may have acted elsewhere as well.

1398–9	John Clement	Possibly a receiver; travelled about estates with money to pay in. L.R. 668.
1400–1	Robert Savage	(Otford) L.R. 1142. Possibly canon of South Malling coll.
ap. 1416	Roger Herne (Heron)	Receiver-general. *Reg. Chichele*, IV, p. 36.
1421–2, 1423–4	Nicholas Capron	(Otford; Aldington) KAO U55/M69, U270/M307; L.R. 674. Also canon of Lichfield, etc. *Reg. Chichele*, IV, index.
1423–8	Adam Pekeman (*or* Pykeman)	(Otford) L.R. 482, 483, 854, 854A. With Richard Pekeman was granted wardenship of Croydon manor, park and woods for life in 1441, *Reg. Chichele*, I, p. 318.
1423–30	John Ely	(Aldington) L.R. 598, 674; KAO U270/M307.
1429–33	Thomas Astell	(Otford) L.R. 484, 485; KAO U55/M69. Clerk of archbishop's kitchen (L.R. 860) and a kinsman of Archbishop Chichele (*Biog. Reg. Oxford, s.n.*).
1427–30	William Balle	(Otford) KAO U55/M69; L.R. 859. Clerk of accounts 1423–4 (KAO U270/M307); auditor 1436–1437, 1442–3 (KAO U55/M69–70).
1432–8	Thomas Baxter	(Otford) L.R. 487, 861; KAO U55/M69.
1436–7	William Palmere	(Maidstone) L.R. 677.
1437–9	Nicholas Hulme	(Otford) L.R. 488, 863, 864. Acted also for bishop of Durham and countess of Salisbury (R. L. Storey, *Thomas Langley* (1961), pp. 74, 79, etc.).
1437–9	Simon Morley	(Aldington; Otford) Mins. Accts 1129/3; L.R. 678; KAO U55/M69.
ap. 1440 to 1442	Thomas Taupener	Receiver-general (South Malling, Otford, Croydon and Pagham). *Reg. Chichele*, I, p. 318; KAO U55/M70; L.R. 489, 866.
1442–4	William Cleve	(Aldington; Otford) L.R. 615, 871. Possibly the canon lawyer and rector of Harbledown, etc. (*Biog. Reg. Oxford*).

1444–50 and 1454–6	Robert East	(Otford) L.R. 680; cf. *Kent Records*, xviii, index.
1449–50, 1460–1	John Grymesdyche	(Otford) Mins. Accts 1129/1; L.R. 1243, etc.
1451–2, 1465–6	John Bedale	(Aldington) Mins. Accts 1129/3; L.R. 1194, 1347, etc. Possibly the canon lawyer and vicar of Herne, etc. (*Biog. Reg. Oxford*).
1453–9	William Green	Receiver-general in Kent. L.R. 1240.
1455–6	Alexander Wood	Receiver-general in Pagham, South Malling and Croydon. LCM xiii (1), no. 14.
1464–81	Thomas Nysell	(Otford) Mins. Accts 1129/8, L.R. 1245, etc.
1481–5	Robert Tottisherst, gentleman	(Otford) Mins. Accts 1130/10, etc.
1489–90	Roger Shelley, gentleman	Receiver-general in Kent. Mins. Accts Hen. VII, 331.
1493–1500	m. Ralph Haines	(Otford) L.R. 1250, etc.
1504–16	John Millett	(Otford) L.R. 1251, etc. Possibly the canon lawyer practising in court of archdeacon of Canterbury (*Biog. Reg. Oxford*).
1516–30	John Mascall, gentleman	(Otford; Maidstone; Croydon) L.R. 1257, etc., 1366A, etc. Valuer to Archbishop Warham (see references in text).
1497–8	John Colman	(Aldington; Wingham) L.R. 1360.
1490–7	Roger Lewkenor	(Pagham; South Malling; Croydon) L.R. 1352, etc.
1516–17	John Peers	(Pagham and Croydon) L.R. 1363. Dean of South Malling college, etc. (*Biog. Reg. Oxford*, under Piers).
1532–4	John Milles	(Otford) Mins. Accts Hen. VIII 1696, etc.
1536–42	Edward Cartwright, gentleman	Receiver-general in Otford and Croydon. L.R. 1369, etc.

STEWARDS OF THE HOUSEHOLD (AFTER 1200)

1209	Alexander *senescallus*	
temp. Elias of Dereham	William de Bec	
1230	John de Wanton *or* Walton	*C.Ch.R. 1227–31*, p. 398.
1258, 1267	Gerard de Seycelle	Lambeth MS. 1212, pp. 97, 225, 421, 422–3; Major, art. cit. Also archdeacon of Canterbury.
1279–80	John of Windsor	L.R. 234.
before 1313	William de Swanton	*Reg. Winchelsey*, ii, index.
1316	Richard de Kanefeld	Reg. Reynolds, fo. 284v.

c. 1331	John de Dene	HMCR, IX, p. 81.
1350	William Vygerous	Reg. Islip, fo. 16v.
1350	Robert Flemyng	Reg. Islip, fo. 37v.
1359	Thomas de Wolton, rector of Westwell	Reg. Islip, fo. 151v.
1398–9	Thomas Wysbech	L.R. 668.
1421–30, 1436–7	John Birkhed	L.R. 859; KAO U55/M69. Biog. Reg. Oxford.
1453–5	John Hay	L.R. 1240. Previously receiver-general in Sussex and Surrey (LCM, XIII (1), no. 14); keeper of the temporalities 1454.
1457–9	William Porter	
1460–2	John Clerk	HMCR, v, p. 523. Previously bailiff of Aldington (Canterbury Cathedral Reg. S, fo. 205).
1464–8	William Tyrrell, kt	L.R. 1347, 1348; receiver of Kent 1469 (Mins. Accts 1129/8).
1486–7	William Cole	
1504, 1523	John Peers	Also receiver of Pagham and Croydon in 1516–17 (L.R. 1363). PCC 2 Crumwell.
1508–9	Edward Ferrers (later kt)	
1522–31	m. Richard Parkhurst	
1528–9	m. Thomas Hunt	
1532–4, 1535–6	William Sowode and Henry Stokheth	L.R. 1367. Henry Stokheth was comptroller in 1535–6.
1536–7	m. Asshe	
1536–7	Richard Neville, gentleman	L.R. 1368
1541–2, 1547	Richard Markeham, gentleman	L.R. 1369, 1374 (1).

TREASURERS OF THE HOUSEHOLD

1267	Hugh de Gebennis [Genève]	Lambeth MS. 1212, p. 421. A Savoyard. Called clerk in 1268 (C.Ch.R., II, p. 165).
1310	John Mansel, rector of Croydon, canon of Lincoln	Reg. Winchelsey, pp. 1080–1 (where he is also called receiver). Le Neve, Fasti: Lincoln (1962), p. 77. Treasurer of archbishop's wardrobe 1298–9 (L.R. 239).
1315–16	Henry de Halis and William	L.R. 832.
1324–5	William de Drax	Reg. Reynolds, fo. 285v.; L.R. 832–834; archbishop's clerk 1283–4 (KAO U270/M304).
1349–50	Thomas de Waleton	Called 'wardrober' (L.R. 240). See also Wolton, under Treasurers. Received money from wardrober (L.R. 834).
1467–71, 1473–4	Richard Shodwell	L.R. 1278–81; Mins. Accts 1130/1.

401

1477–82	m. Thomas Wilkinson, rector of Wimbledon, Harrow and Orpington, dean of Pagham	L.R. 1348–9 (also receiver of Pagham); Will in PCC 25 Fetiplace, *Biog. Reg. Oxford*
1484–5	Thomas Garthe	L.R. 1200.
1532–4	John Goderyce [Goodrich], esquire	L.R. 1367.

INDEX

403

407